ABHANDLUNGEN

DER AKADEMIE DER WISSENSCHAFTEN IN GÖTTINGEN

ABHANDLUNGEN
DER AKADEMIE DER WISSENSCHAFTEN
IN GÖTTINGEN

PHILOLOGISCH-HISTORISCHE KLASSE
DRITTE FOLGE
Nr. 108

GÖTTINGEN · VANDENHOECK & RUPRECHT · 1978

Buddhism in Ceylon and Studies on Religious Syncretism in Buddhist Countries

(Symposien zur Buddhismusforschung, I)

Report on a Symposium in Göttingen

edited

by Heinz Bechert

With 26 Plates

GÖTTINGEN · VANDENHOECK & RUPRECHT · 1978

Vorgelegt von Herrn H. Bechert in der Sitzung vom 4. Juni 1976

CIP-Kurztitelaufnahme der Deutschen Bibliothek

Buddhism in Ceylon and studies on religious syncretism in Buddhist countries : report on a symposium in Göttingen / ed. by Heinz Bechert. — Göttingen : Vandenhoeck und Ruprecht, 1978.
(Symposien zur Buddhismusforschung ; 1) (Abhandlungen der Akademie der Wissenschaften in Göttingen, Philologisch-Historische Klasse : Folge 3 ; Nr. 108)

ISBN 3-525-82387-8

NE: Bechert, Heinz [Hrsg.]

Gedruckt mit Hilfe von Forschungsmitteln des Landes Niedersachsen

Gesamtherstellung: Hubert & Co., Göttingen

TO THE MEMORY
OF ERICH FRAUWALLNER

Contents

Editor's Preface

This volume originated from a symposium which was held under the sponsorship of the Akademie der Wissenschaften (Academy of Sciences) in Göttingen on July 12th–14th, 1974. It was organized by the Kommission für buddhistische Studien (Comittee for Buddhist Studies) of the Academy, and the Academy received a grant from the Deutsche Forschungsgemeinschaft for the symposium. The participants of the symposium were Prof. Dr. Jacob Ensink (Groningen), Prof. Dr. Richard F. Gombrich (Oxford), Prof. Dr. Herbert Härtel (Berlin), Prof. Dr. Robert Heinemann (Genève), Prof. Dr. Oskar von Hinüber (Mainz), Prof. Dr. Siegfried Lienhard (Stockholm), Mr. K. R. Norman (Cambridge), Dr. Peter Schalk (Göteborg), Mr. Christopher H. B. Reynolds (London), Prof. Dr. Emanuel Sarkisyanz (Heidelberg), Prof. Dr. Bardwell L. Smith (Northfield, Minn.), Dr. Hermann Bode (Göttingen), Dr. Heinz Braun (Göttingen), Dr. Gustav Roth (Göttingen), Dr. Hans Ruelius (Göttingen), Prof. Dr. Georg von Simson (Göttingen), and the editor of the present volume. Dr. Klaus Hausherr (Heidelberg), Prof. Dr. Trevor Ling (Manchester), Rev. Dr. Aloysius R. Pieris, s. j. (Colombo) and Dr. (Mrs.) Valentina Stache-Rosen (Bangalore) contributed to the symposium, but were not able to attend the meetings in person. Dr. Amit Das Gupta who has contributed to the preparation of the paper summarized below, pp. 214–216, during his stay in Göttingen, was prevented from attending by obligations abroad.

The Akademie der Wissenschaften in Göttingen has a long tradition in the field of Buddhist studies. The work of Hermann Oldenberg, like that of Heinrich Lüders, Emil Sieg, Ernst Waldschmidt and others, is connected in many ways with the activities of the Academy. The Committee for Buddhist Studies which was formed in 1972 with the idea of intensifying Buddhist studies in continuation of this tradition decided to select "Buddhism in Ceylon (Sri Lanka)" as the topic of the first major conference organized by the Committee. Buddhism in Sri Lanka not only holds a key position in the history of Theravāda Buddhism, but also in the history of Buddhist studies, because it was from this island that European scholars got access to the Pāli scriptures and their traditional interpretation. The study of these texts resulted in a revolution in Buddhist studies, when Thomas Williams Rhys Davids, Hermann Oldenberg and others succeeded in discovering the historicity of the Buddha and consequently in establishing a reliable history of early Buddhism. The essential contribution made by Sinhalese scholars towards this development by their cooperation with the European scholars during the pioneer period deserves to be stressed here.

For a number of reasons it was, unfortunately, not possible to bring together the scholars working in this field from all parts of the world. From USA, Prof. Bardwell Smith who was in Europe at the time of the conference, could be welcomed as a participant. Two scholars from overseas—Dr. Valentina Stache-Rosen (Bangalore, India), and Rev. Dr. Aloysius Pieris, s. j. (Colombo, Sri Lanka)—kindly agreed to submit papers though they could not personally attend. All other contributors are scholars working in European academical institutions.

The editor is fully aware that it may be considered difficult to discuss Buddhism in Ceylon without the participation of our colleagues from Sri Lanka. At the given moment, however, delaying the conference or its limitation were the only alternatives, and we preferred the second one. However, to make a virtue of necessity, we think that a discussion of the situation of Western scholarship on the topic of our symposium could be considered a very useful step in the process of orientation and in the progress of research in this field. It should serve as a basis for a world-wide exchange of opinions and inspire our friends and colleagues in Sri Lanka to take the lead in convening a greater international conference on Buddhist studies as a next step. This would be a worthy continuation of the great role Sri Lanka has taken so far in the modernization of Buddhist thought. So far it has been mainly with the Encyclopaedia of Buddhism begun by the late Prof. Dr. G. P. Malalasekera that Sri Lanka has taken the initiative for a great project of international cooperation in Buddhist scholarship. Thus, the members of the Committee and the participants of this symposium hope that our attempt to formulate some problems and results of Buddhist studies in a very limited sphere, may bring about new initiatives on a much broader basis in countries where Buddhistic studies have direct relevance to the tradition of national culture.

We have divided the program of the symposium into three sessions, viz. "Buddhist Literature in Ceylon", "Buddhism and Society in Sri Lanka", and "A Comparative View of Religious Syncretism in Buddhist Countries". In the third session, we transgressed the limits of our main topic, viz. Buddhism in Ceylon, by including a comparative study of religious syncretism in several Buddhist countries including Sri Lanka. The problem of the relation of Buddhism and non-Buddhist elements in the religion of the Sinhalese has been formulated and systematically studied by anthropologists, sociologists and students of religious science since the beginning of the last decade, but so far no study of this phenomenon has been carried out in a comparative way. We hope that our attempt in this direction will not only provide a better understanding of the religion of Sri Lanka, but also of the phenomenon of religious syncretism in the Buddhist world in general. It may also serve as a reminder to historians of religion that the methodology for the study of these phenomena deserves to be further developed. It is because of this section that the present volume was renamed "Buddhism in Ceylon, and Studies on

Religious Syncretism in Buddhist Countries", and the new title seems justified, because this part has grown into a rather comprehensive documentation of religious syncretism in the Buddhist world which readers would not expect to find in the volume if the original title of the symposium had been retained.

Most of the papers were circulated amongst the participants before the meeting so that it was possible to deliver summaries only during the conference and to devote most of the time to a well-prepared discussion. The main points of the proceedings are summarized in the introduction of the present volume. For this report, I could rely on the "Minutes of the Conference" which were circulated after the symposium so that corrections suggested by the participants could be taken notice of. In some instances it was, however, necessary to supplement this information by referring back to the original notes made by Dr. H. Braun and by the editor during the symposium to supplement the information incorporated in the Minutes. Many suggestions made during the meeting were accepted by the authors and incorporated into the final version of their contributions so that there was no point in recording them in the introduction. I have mentioned, however, some points in the introduction where opinions remained different, but without claiming to be exhaustive. In general, a discussion of these points in the introduction seemed sufficient, and I have taken the liberty of formulating my own views in some cases. In one particular instance, the views of two participants remained different on a basic methodological issue so that I invited both sides to state their views, viz. Dr. H. Ruelius's study on Netrapratiṣṭhāpana (below, pp. 304–334) and Prof. R. F. Gombrich's comments on this subject (below, pp. 335–338). Some contributions submitted to the symposium will be published elsewhere, but summaries are included in this volume as far as we could obtain them.

For the transliteration of the Sinhala language, we have followed the system used in the Dictionary of the Sinhalese Language. The transliteration of other South Asian languages generally follows the tables published by the Library of Congress. The Burmese transcription used in the contribution by Prof. E. Sarkisyanz is based on that used by W. S. Cornyn, whereas in other parts of the volume the transliteration of the Burma Research Society is followed. It was not possible to achieve uniformity on all points of abbreviation, citation, bibliographical references etc., so that separate lists of abbreviations and bibliographical references are added at the end of the contributions, wherever necessary.

The editor would like to express his gratitude to the Akademie der Wissenschaften and to the Deutsche Forschungsgemeinschaft, the institutions which enabled him to organize the symposium. His thanks are also due to the participants and contributors who cooperated before, during and after the conference so that the publication could take place without too much delay. I should also mention those who have assisted me in the practical organization of the symposium. We are grateful to the Academy which has today agreed in its plenary session to accept the volume for the series of the Abhandlungen. Prof. Richard F. Gombrich has kindly provided a financial contribution which has made it possible to include the colour plates illustrating his study of a Sinhalese cloth painting of the Vessantarajātaka. Mr. K. R. Norman was kind enough to read over the draft of the introduction, and Prof. R. F. Gombrich kindly read through my paper on the popular religion of the Sinhalese, and they made a number of observations and useful comments for which I would like to express my sincere gratitude. Thanks to Dr. Heinz Braun are due for his taking care of the final proof-reading of the book during my absence from Göttingen.

The volume is dedicated to the memory of Professor Erich Frauwallner, one of the founding members of the Comittee of Buddhist Studies of the Akademie der Wissenschaften, who was expected as a participant in the symposium. It was during the conference that we received the sad news that the great scholar had died on July 5th, 1974.

Göttingen, June 4th, 1976 Heinz Bechert

Introduction: Report on the Symposium

By HEINZ BECHERT

As explained in the preface, the Symposium was divided into three sessions, dealing with Buddhist literature in Ceylon, Buddhism and Society in Sri Lanka and a comparative view of religious syncretism in Buddhist countries with special regard to Ceylon.

First Session: Buddhist Literature in Ceylon

The first contribution to the Symposium was submitted by Mr. K. R. Norman (Cambridge) and dealt with "The Role of Pāli in Early Sinhalese Buddhism" (see below, pp. 28–47). The explanations of the language of the Canon were, of course, the occasion of a number of comments. It seems to the editor of the present volume that it is essential to search for the particular conditions under which non-Pāli forms were retained, a method which was, e. g., applied by Hermann Berger (Zwei Probleme der mittelindischen Lautlehre, München 1955). This principle was also applied in the editor's explanation of nom. sg. forms ending in *-e* found in the language of the heretics and in uneducated speech as Proto-Sinhalese Prakrit forms which crept into the language of the Pāli Tipiṭaka in the period after the introduction of the texts in Ceylon but before their being written down (see H. Bechert, Über Singhalesisches im Pālikanon, in: Wiener Zeitschrift für die Kunde Süd- und Ostasiens 1, 1957, pp. 71–75), while other forms which were correctly explained as Māgadhisms by Heinrich Lüders (Beobachtungen über die Sprache des buddhistischen Urkanons, ed. Ernst Waldschmidt, Berlin 1954, §§ 12–21) were retained as a consequence of misunderstandings of the grammatical construction when the text was rendered into Pāli. Mr. Norman who referred to this point in his paper with the remark that the explanation of these forms as Proto-Sinhalese forms cannot be accepted "in view of the existence of other Māgadhisms which cannot be explained from Sinhalese Prakrit" (see below, p. 32), has informed the editor that he agrees with him insofar as he considers that the forms of the nom. sg. ending in *-e* in the speech of the heretics (in the Sāmaññaphalasutta, Dīghanikāya I 53ff., and Sandakasutta, Majjhimanikāya I 515ff.) are probably not Māgadhisms, but rejects the editor's explanation that these forms were borrowed into Pāli from Proto-Sinhalese. In his opinion, these anomalous forms were taken over "from a mainland, probably North-Western Prakrit" (see K. R. Norman, Pāli and the Language of the Heretics, in: Acta Orientalia 37,

1976, pp. 113–122). The editor's argument that a Proto-Sinhalese explanation is further supported by the occurrence of the oblique pl. in *-uno* was not accepted by Mr. Norman, because the oblique pl. in *-un* is attested only from the 8th century onwards in dated inscriptional sources and never as *-uno* (see D. J. Wijayaratne, History of the Sinhalese Noun, Colombo 1956, pp. 134–136; cf. Norman, loc. cit., p. 121, n. 39). However, in the editor's opinion, the considerable differences between the spoken and written language in all known stages of the development of the Sinhala language with the archaic features being retained in the written language, and what Helmer Smith describes as "la scriptio defectiva du proto-singalais épigraphique" which obscures many details of Proto-Sinhalese (Helmer Smith, Wilhelm Geiger et le vocabulaire du singalais classique, in: Journal Asiatique 1950, p. 184), justify doubts whether this argument completely rules out the explanation of these forms as Proto-Sinhalese, and I would like to remind readers of the fact that the occurrence of *u* in *-uno* is in full agreement with the rule that "the umlaut is confined to originally heavy syllables" which was first observed by Helmer Smith (see Wilhelm Geiger, A Grammar of the Sinhalese Language, Colombo 1938, § 12, and Smith, loc. cit., p. 190f.) which seems to reflect an early development in the spoken language. If both possibilities—that of an introduction from a mainland, probably North-Western dialect, and that from Proto-Sinhalese—are left open, a final answer may be derived from a detailed study of the earliest history of the tradition of the Pāli scriptures which could not be attempted at this symposium.

The possibility of early Sinhalese influences on linguistic peculiarities found in Pāli works also remains controversial for other forms ending in *-e* (for skt. *-aḥ*) in late canonical and early commentarial texts. The nom. sg. in *-e* was, of course, not restricted to Māgadhī alone, but could be traced in other mainland dialects as well. Mr. Norman drew our attention to such forms in the Kathāvatthu which in his opinion was originally composed in Māgadhī, and Mr. Reynolds stressed that about half a dozen such forms can be found in commentaries. The present editor prefers to follow the explanation of many, though not necessarily all, of these forms in the Kathāvatthu and in the commentaries as Proto-Sinhalese traces which was proposed by Helmer Smith (see Smith, loc. cit., p. 184, and Critical Pāli Dictionary, s. v. ²*avitakka*). Mr. Norman, however, proposes a different explanation (see below, p. 34f.).

An exhaustive treatment of the problems relating to the language of the Pāli Canon was considered outside the scope of the topics to be discussed at this symposium. The Committee for Buddhist Studies of the Academy has since organized a conference on the language of the most ancient Buddhist tradition in July, 1976 which has continued the discussion of these problems in a broader context. The results of this conference will be published in the "Abhandlungen der Akademie der Wissenschaften in Göttingen".

In the context of the present symposium, it is most important that the statement found in Mr. Norman's contribution "that the language of the canon when introduced (into Ceylon) was not appreciably different from that in which it was written down" (below, p. 32), notwithstanding the possibility of minor changes, can be accepted as a basis for further research. The language of the scriptures was called *Māgadhī* for the first time in the commentarial literature.

The question of the sources of Dīpavaṃsa and Mahāvaṃsa (see below, pp. 35–37) remains another controversial issue. The present editor's views are formulated in an earlier publication of the Akademie der Wissenschaften in Göttingen (H. Bechert, Zum Ursprung der Geschichtsschreibung im indischen Kulturbereich, in: NAWG 1969, pp. 52ff.) which is based on the analysis of the sources as first suggested by Erich Frauwallner (see: Die ceylonesischen Chroniken und die erste buddhistische Mission nach Hinterindien, in: Actes du IVe Congrès International des Sciences Anthropologiques et Ethnologiques, Vienne 1952, T. 2: Ethnologica, 1, Wien 1955, pp. 192–197) and, with a detailed argumentation, in Frauwallner's unpublished study on the chronicles ("Über die Glaubwürdigkeit der ceylonesischen Chroniken") which will be edited by Ernst Steinkellner in the first volume of Frauwallner's posthumous papers to be published by the Österreichische Akademie der Wissenschaften in Wien. The sources of the chronicles were also analyzed in detail in a recent dissertation by Frank Perera (The Early Buddhist Historiography of Ceylon, doctoral thesis, Göttingen 1974, not yet printed). Classical Sinhalese literature in prose is interspersed with Pāli and Sanskrit verse, but practically nowhere with Sinhalese verse, whereas Sinhalese verse literature has no prose passages. There is no evidence of a late origin of this convention, and, in view of the other arguments proposed by Hermann Oldenberg, Wilhelm Geiger, G. P. Malalasekera, E. W. Adikaram, Erich Frauwallner and others, the editor prefers to retain the view that the source material of the chronicles consisted of Sinhalese prose and original Pāli verses. He therefore considers the Dīpavaṃsa with its duplicate versions of several episodes as an excerpt from the *ākhyāna* and memorial verses of at least two, and probably three, versions of this source which were rightly described by Frauwallner as the monastic chronicles of the centres of the rival sects of early Ceylonese Theravāda.

The problem of the language of early Mahāyāna in Ceylon which is also dealt with in Mr. Norman's contribution (pp. 40–41) is of crucial importance for the understanding of the religious history of the island. I can refer here to the existence of at least one clearly Mahāyānistic text in Pāli which was incorporated into one of the latest parts of the canonical literature, viz. the text named Buddhāpadāna which forms the first part of the Apadāna book of the Pāli scriptures (see H. Bechert, Buddha-Feld und Verdienstübertragung: Mahāyāna-Ideen im Theravāda-Buddhismus Ceylons, in: Académie Royale de Belgique, Bulletin de la

Classe des Lettres et des Sciences Morales et Politiques, 5e śerie, t. 62, 1976, pp. 27–51). It may be termed a work of the Mahāyāna-Sthaviras of Ceylon and was composed in the 1st or in the beginning of the 2nd century A. D., and, therefore, can be identified as the earliest available source of information on particular views held by Mahāyāna Buddhists in Ceylon. The first explicit reference to a particular Mahāyāna work brought from India to Ceylon (Mahāvaṃsa 41.37–40) refers to the Dhammadhātu which was introduced into the island during the reign of king Silākāla (522–535). In all probability this work which was believed by S. Paranavitana to be nothing other than the Saddharmapuṇḍarīka (see University of Ceylon History of Ceylon, ed. H. C. Ray, vol. 1, part 1, Colombo 1959, p. 380) was a Sanskrit text. The earliest Mahāyāna inscription of Ceylon in Sanskrit is the Kuccavēli Rock Inscription which was dated between the 5th and the 8th century A. D. by Paranavitana (Epigraphia Zeylanica III, pp. 158–161). For the later period, the use of Sanskrit by Mahāyāna Buddhists in Ceylon is, however, well documented (see H. Bechert, Mahāyāna Literature in Sri Lanka: The Early Phase, in: The Prajñāpāramitā Literature and Related Systems, Berkeley Buddhist Studies Series, vol. 1, in the press).

The second contribution—"On the Tradition of Pāli Texts in India, Ceylon and Burma" by Prof. Oskar von Hinüber (see below, pp. 48–57)—was the background to a discussion on the application of editorial principles in the correction of obvious errors of the tradition, if these errors are unanimously accepted in the Pāli tradition itself. It is not always possible to follow the same principles as in Sanskrit philology, and it seems that it is virtually impossible to formulate principles which can be applied in all cases. In a general debate on the use of the word *pāli* as the name of the language, Mr. Reynolds remarked that this use was not started by Western Pāli scholars as believed by many authors, but was already accepted in 18th century Ceylon. In the Saṅgharājasādhucariyāva of Ayittāliyäddē Lēkama, which is dated śaka 1701 (1779 A. D.) we find several instances where the word *pāli* clearly means the name of a language. It seems probable that there are still earlier examples.

The author of the third contribution, Dr. (Mrs.) Valentina Stache-Rosen, could not personally attend the symposium. Her contribution deals with the Upālipariprcchāsūtra which is known from a Chinese translation only. Dr. Stache-Rosen has prepared a translation of this text with an introduction and critical remarks, from which the complete introduction and a specimen of the translation with parallel passages from the Parivāra (and from the Suttavibhanga) as well as a comparative table of the contents of the Upālipariprcchāsūtra and the Parivāra were distributed to the participants. Dr. Stache-Rosen intends to publish the complete study as a separate volume, because it is too voluminous to be included in this volume. She therefore provided a summary for the present volume; see below, pp. 58–60. For the determination of the place of this Upālipariprcchā which must not be confused with other works of the same name in Buddhist literature, the interpretation of one particular passage remains of crucial importance. It is the passage from the Mahāvaṃsa-ṭīkā (ed. G. P. Malalasekera, pp. 175f.) quoted in the paper (cf. below, summary, p. 60, note 10). This passage was mistranslated by George Turnour (1837) and the resulting erroneous information was uncritically reproduced by later authors until recently, e. g. by H. G. A. van Zeyst in the Encyclopaedia of Buddhism (vol. I, p. 28). It was unanimously agreed that the passage *Vinayapiṭakato Khandakaparivāraṃ atthantarapāṭhantarakaraṇavasena bhedaṃ katvā* means "after they had made a split on the ground of changing the meaning and the text of the Khandaka and Parivāra from the Vinayapiṭaka" (cf. also H. Bechert, Zur Geschichte der buddhistischen Sekten in Indien und Ceylon, in: La Nouvelle Clio VII–IX, 1955–57, pp. 331–334). Prof. von Hinüber remarked that this translation was in line with the rules of Pāli syntax. Therefore, there could be no doubt that the canon of the Abhayagirivāsins contained a version of the Parivāra different from that of the Mahāvihāra school. Mr. Norman referred to his contribution for a critique of the view proposed by earlier scholars that the Parivāra was the work of a Sinhalese thera (see below, p. 34). In his opinion the Parivāra as a whole was a work of Indian origin. Prof. von Hinüber added that it was almost certain that the Upālipariprcchā was a canonical text, particularly in view of the fact that it does not contain any material worth mentioning which is not found in the corresponding canonical work of the Mahāvihāra school i. e. the Parivāra. The identification of the Upālipariprcchā, the original Pāli name of which probably was Upālipariрucchā, as the text which replaced the Parivāra of the Mahāvihāra school in the Vinaya of the Abhayagirivāsins, was unanimously accepted by the participants of the symposium. This is of the utmost value for our knowledge of the history of early Buddhist sects in Ceylon.

Dr. Aloysius Pieris, the author of the fourth contribution (published below, pp. 61–77), was also prevented from personally attending the symposium. It was suggested in the discussion that a minor emendation of the text dealt with in para. 44–46 (see below, pp. 75–77) was to be preferred to the rejection of the whole of verse 4 as an interpolation, if such a minor emendation was possible. Prof. Gombrich proposed reading *āyācite* as a locative absolute instead of the reading *āyacito* found in the available texts. This emendation was considered to be easily acceptable by Pāli philologists, but it was also clear that its acceptance would invalidate Dr. Pieris' argumentation as far as it was based on his rejection of verse 4. It was then decided not to go into more detail in the absence of the author, but to inform him of this suggestion. His comment on this information is found below, p. 76, note 68, and it is left to readers to arrive at their own conclusions.

Prof. Richard F. Gombrich then introduced "A Sinhalese Cloth Painting of the Vessantara Jātaka" (see below, pp. 78–88). The publication of these paintings is of the highest importance not only for the history of Sinhalese art, but also for the understanding of the traditions of Sinhalese Buddhism. The Vessantara Jātaka is also the subject of one of the very few illuminated Sinhalese palm leaf manuscripts known so far (see H. Bechert, Eine illuminierte Handschrift des Vessantarajātaka, in: Folia rara Wolfgang Voigt LXV. diem natalem celebranti ab amicis . . . dedicata, Wiesbaden 1976, pp. 11–15).

The last contribution to the first session was "Mañjuśrībhāṣita-Citrakarmaśāstra: A Mahayanistic Śilpaśāstra from Sri Lanka" by Dr. Hans Ruelius; see below, pp. 89–99. The editor of this volume would like to express his gratitude to the Director of the National Archives of Sri Lanka, Mr. A. Dewaraja, who had given him access to the manuscript and permission to have excerpts transliterated into modern Sinhalese script by Pandit K. D. Wickramaratne and who had provided him with the microfilm which he made available to Dr. Ruelius for the studies resulting in this paper. Prof. Smith referred to Chinese and Japanese traditions of a similar character (cf. Takaaki Sawa, Art in Japanese Esoteric Buddhism, 1972; Minoru Ooka, Temples of Nara and Their Art, 1973).

Second Session: Buddhism and Society

The second session was opened with the contribution on "Kingship, the Sangha, and the Process of Legitimation in Ancient Ceylon (Anurādhapura Period)" by Prof. B. L. Smith (see below pp. 100–126). In the discussion the following main points were raised: Ceylon, being part of the sphere of Indian culture, has adapted didactic verses from Indian *nīti* literature. It was asked how far the particular way of representation of history in the chronicles can also be described as a type of didactical or *nīti* literature. The way of transformation of Indian ideas in a Ceylonese context must be studied when the question of the motivation behind the authors of the chronicles is raised.

The following paper was "Fragen zum Problem des chronologischen Verhältnisses des buddhistischen Modernismus in Ceylon und Birma" by Prof. Emanuel Sarkisyanz (below, pp. 127–133). From the discussion, Prof. Gombrich's remark may be repeated here that Ceylon Buddhists consider Burmese Buddhism slightly superior to their own. There were many forest hermitages in Burma. In this field, influence could have taken place. Pilgrims are, however, generally not aware of the development of ideology. Prof. Sarkisyanz remarked that the leftists in Ceylon and Burma hardly knew of each other. The idea of "wordly nibbāna" was first developed in Burma. It seems that Pridi's Buddhist socialism formulated in Siam in 1932 was not known in Burma when the leftist movement was started with Burmese Buddhists. The present editor outlined the example of the mobility of a rather small Buddhist élite in the Theravāda countries and mentioned the importance of Ceylon and centres connected with Ceylonese tradition, e. g. the Lankārāma in Phnom Penh, in this connection. Pāli was used for cultural exchange between traditional Buddhists of Ceylon and Burma in the 19th century, serving as a common language for educated bhikkhus in all Theravāda countries, notwithstanding the considerable differences in the pronounciation of Pāli. The so-called "international pronunciation" of Pāli is the Ceylonese one.

For the third contribution, "Religion and Social Position in British Ceylon" (below, pp. 134–145) by Mr. C. H. B. Reynolds, its author provided the following summary:

"The upper social classes of Ceylon remained substantially Christian until after 1920. However, owing to the Victorian-Sinhalese attitude to trade, prosperous traders tended to remain Buddhist. The increased Buddhist self-consciousness that arose in the second half of the 19th century was led by prosperous men of this kind, who had acquired a western education. Their evident success in arousing popular enthusiasm eventually persuaded many of the upper classes also to adopt a similar outlook. Missionaries (though in most cases sincere men) presented to the Buddhist population an image distorted by an essential connection with material advancement, and an unscientific fundamentalism. While the missionaries failed for some time to realize the effect of these factors, their Buddhist counterparts also showed features of which the missionaries felt themselves rightly critical, of which the Buddhist apologists probably also failed to recognize the effect. There was thus mutual incomprehension. As a result, Christian missions made progress among the Sinhalese only in certain limited social fields. Any successful Buddhist mission to the West would have to avoid similar errors."

In the discussion of the contribution, the author's views were corroborated by several remarks, particularly on Roman Catholic entrepreneurs in Ceylon, on the friendly reception of early missionaries by the Buddhists, and on the integration of the Roman Catholics as part of the Sinhalese nation.

A summary of the contribution "Population Growth in Ceylon, Buddhist and Non-Buddhist, 1911–1946: Causes and Implications", by Prof. Trevor Ling was then presented by the chairman of this session, Mr. Reynolds. It was very much regretted that Prof. Ling could not personally participate in the symposium.

Third Session: A Comparative View of Religious Syncretism in Buddhist Countries

Introductory Remarks

The problem of religious syncretism in the Buddhist world is by no means a new one. It is as old as the study of Nepalese Buddhism, Tibetan Buddhism and other forms of so-called "Northern Buddhism".[1])

[1]) Problems of the relation of Buddhism and non-Buddhist elements in the tradition of Indian Mahāyāna and Tibetan Buddhism are dealt with by David Seyfort Ruegg, Sur les rapports entre le bouddhisme et le "substrat religieux" indien et tibétain, in: Journal asiatique 252 (1964), pp. 77–95.

Scholars working on Theravāda Buddhism and its history have, however, tended to emphasize the philosophical and scriptural aspects of Theravāda as an élitist religious movement. The existence of other forms of religious beliefs and activities side-by-side with the orthodox tradition was observed by many Buddhologists, but it was hardly reflected in their presentations of Buddhism as a religion. There are very few references to the problem of the existence of non-Buddhist cults in the religious life of Theravāda Buddhists in most of the well-known surveys of Buddhism. In this respect, there is not much difference between Richard Pischel's "Leben und Lehre des Buddha" published in 1905 and recent surveys of Buddhism e.g. those by Edward Conze. There are a few exceptions to this general statement, e. g. Heinrich Hackmann, Der südliche Buddhismus und der Lamaismus, Halle 1905, pp. 28–30 and 46–49. But here, the way of dealing with the problem is connected with a rather one-sided and negative attitude to what is observed. Hackmann strongly criticizes the fact that the countries of Southern Buddhism are considered to represent the original form of Buddhism by most scholars. He claims that, in the religiosity of these countries, Buddhism and Animism are mixed together, so that Buddhism in Theravāda countries in a way is a degraded form of Buddhism as compared with what it should be.

It is one of the merits of recent anthropological studies that they have taken up the question again and shown by a critical observation of the interpretations given by the Theravāda Buddhists themselves and by the application of the *lokottara* : *laukika* dichotomy that both sides were equally wrong. We all know, however, that in this respect we are still far from having reached the stage where views are generally accepted, and that recent studies, e. g. those by Melford E. Spiro on the religion of Burma, have again put question-marks against many theories and findings.

Therefore, we considered it useful to deal with the aspects of religious syncretism in the religion of the Sinhalese not in an isolated way, but in a comparative context. During the symposium, contributions on syncretistic forms of and elements in Buddhism in Nepal, Java and Bali, Japan and Bengal were presented and discussed. It is unfortunate that, for practical reasons, we could not include here a paper on the cult of the Nats in Burma which might have been useful for a comparison with the popular religion of Ceylon, but I expect that already the study of these four different cases of so-called religious syncretism in the Buddhist world as compared to the religion of the Sinhalese will bring us an important step nearer to an understanding of these phenomena.

A major problem for the discussion of these questions is created by the lack of a generally accepted terminology for the description of the various forms of "syncretistic" phenomena i. e. the different forms in which religious traditions have influenced each other. Such differences of terminology remain visible in the contributions to the symposium, but—in view of the limited time available for the proceedings—improvement of the typology of those forms of religious syncretism, in a wider sense of the word, which can be observed in the history of Indian religions seemed more important than a discussion of questions of terminology. The editor of the present volume suggested a differentiation of several such types, and he also proposed to term one particular type "syncretism" ("Religionsmischung") in a narrower sense of the word:

"Der erste Typ besteht in der Übernahme von einzelnen Elementen — religiösen Vorstellungen im weitesten Sinne — aus einer Religion in eine andere Religion, wobei die übernehmende Religion nicht tiefgreifend beeinflußt wird; die übernommenen Elemente behalten dabei deutlich marginalen Charakter und werden oft auch umgedeutet. Ein Beispiel dafür ist die Übernahme des Kṛṣṇa-Mythos in die Mythologie der Jainas. Dabei haben sich die Jainas den kṛṣṇaitischen Legendenkreis der Purāṇas weitgehend angeeignet, ohne daß die Jaina-Lehre in irgendeinem wesentlichen Punkt verändert worden wäre. In einem solchen Fall kann man natürlich nicht von eigentlicher Religionsmischung sprechen, da die wesentlichen Merkmale der übernehmenden Religion nicht berührt werden."

"Auf der anderen Seite bietet die indische Tradition auch mehrere Beispiele für Religionssynkretismus im engeren Sinn oder eigentliche Religionsmischung. Ergebnis von Religionsmischung in diesem Sinne sind Religionsformen, in denen Elemente aus verschiedenen religiösen Traditionen miteinander vergleichbare Gewichtigkeit erlangt haben, d.h. es handelt sich dabei nicht mehr nur um die Einbeziehung einzelner Elemente anderer Herkunft in eine im ganzen stabile Tradition. Die Verschiedenheit der Herkunft der Elemente bleibt sichtbar, insbesondere im Bereich der sog. „Großen Tradition"; auch ist es noch nicht zu einer neuen Synthese gekommen, wie wir sie als eine andere Form des Ergebnisses von Religionsbeeinflussungen bestimmen werden. Ganz eindeutige Beispiele für diese Form der Religionsmischung sind der hinduistisch-buddhistische Synkretismus in Nepal und der Synkretismus in Bali und Java. Ähnliche Erscheinungen lassen sich in der Geschichte des indischen Tantrismus beobachten, wo wir ja, z.B. in Bengalen, häufig nicht genau bestimmen können, ob ein bestimmtes Tantra nun der buddhistischen oder der hinduistischen Tradition zuzuordnen ist. Bei genauerem Zusehen ergibt sich dann, daß eben diese Fragestellung des entweder/oder falsch ist und wir sowohl bestimmte hinduistische als auch bestimmte spätbuddhistische Traditionen vor uns haben."

"Eine Sonderform dieser Religionsmischung findet sich in dem Stufensystem des religiösen Gesamtsystems der sich zum Theravāda-Buddhismus bekennenden Völker. Aufgrund der strikten Abgrenzung der dem Buddhismus zukommenden Funktionen existieren hier in einem mehr oder weniger geordneten Nebeneinander mit dem Buddhismus andere Religionsformen, deren nicht-buddhistische Herkunft deutlich sichtbar bleibt, die aber doch in eine bestimmte Beziehung zum Buddhismus gesetzt werden; dies ist der Fall, den wir hier am Beispiel Ceylon zu erörtern haben."

"Die indische Religionsentwicklung bietet uns jedoch neben diesem Synkretismus im engeren Sinne noch einen ganz anderen Typ der Bewältigung einer Beeinflussung, nämlich ihre volle Integration. Hier erfolgt die Auseinandersetzung mit fremden Ideen in der Form, daß man sie in die überlieferte Religion einfügt und als Teil ihres Inhalts in Anspruch nimmt. Dabei ist man natürlich darauf bedacht, die Spuren ihrer Herkunft möglichst weitgehend zu verwischen. Diese Erscheinung läßt sich bei der Bewältigung westlicher Einflüsse in der neueren indischen Religionsgeschichte, besonders im Neo-Hinduismus, gut beobachten. Wir finden sie aber auch in der älteren indischen Tradition, so z.B. bei der Übernahme der *bhakti*-Lehre durch die Buddhisten, bei der Entwicklung des buddhistischen Tantrismus unter weitgehender Einbeziehung von Traditionen aus der hinduistisch-brahmanischen Überlieferung, aber auch bei der Aufnahme zentraler Lehren des Mahāyāna-Buddhismus in die hinduistische Philosophie. In all diesen Fällen wird nun versucht, die fremde Herkunft dessen, was man als wesentlichen Bestandteil der eigenen Tradition in Anspruch nimmt, zu verschleiern. Hinweise darauf werden nicht gerne gehört. So verrät sich Śaṅkara durch seine unsachlichen Ausfälle gegen die Buddhisten, und es gibt wohl kaum eine größere Beschimpfung für einen Advaita-Vedāntin, als ihn „Krypto-Buddhisten" zu nennen, was die Gegner Śaṅkaras bekanntlich sehr gerne taten."

"Die indische Tradition kennt nun aber noch eine Sonderform dieser Integration. Hier wird das übernommene Element ebenfalls vollständig integriert, der fremde Ursprung aber nur teilweise verschleiert, indem nämlich behauptet wird, die anderen hätten zunächst von einem selbst entlehnt."

"Mit der Ausbreitung indischer Zivilisation bei Völkern niedrigerer Kulturstufe vollzog sich eine weitere Art von Religionsbeeinflussung, die vermutlich, aufs ganze gesehen, die verbreitetste Form einer Verschmelzung von Elementen verschiedener religiöser Traditionen im indischen Kulturraum sein dürfte, uns aber naturgemäß in der Literatur der Hochreligion nur selten direkt faßbar wird. Indirekt freilich begegnen wir ihr in der Mythologie dauernd. Es handelt sich dabei um die „Hinduisierung" der Kulte nicht-hinduistischer Völker durch ihre Aufnahme ins Hindu-Pantheon, durch die Identifikation lokaler Götter mit bekannten Hindu-Gottheiten oder ihre Einordnung ins Gefolge übergeordneter Gottheiten. So wurden nicht-hinduistische Kulte hinduisiert und lokale schon teilweise hinduisierte Kulte in die großen Hindu-Konfessionen integriert. Hier handelt es sich aber nicht um eine Verbindung gleichberechtigter Traditionen, sondern um die Einbeziehung von Überlieferungen unterlegener Kulturen in die überlegene Tradition des Hinduismus."

"Eine besondere Variante dieser Entwicklung findet sich im buddhistischen Bereich, nämlich die Einbeziehung solcher Kulte in die sog. Volksreligion als Teil des religiösen Gesamtsystems der sich zum Theravāda bekennenden Völker im vorhin angedeuteten Sinne. Dabei werden die integrierten Kulte einerseits mit den dem Buddhismus zugeordneten volksreligiösen Kulten in Verbindung gebracht, andererseits aber auch in die direkte Beziehung zu volkstümlichen, also nicht-dogmatischen buddhistischen Vorstellungen gesetzt. Lassen Sie mich ein Beispiel aus Ceylon anführen: Hier werden die lokalen Götter dem wichtigsten Gott der Götterwelt der alten buddhistischen Texte, also dem Śakra, dem alten Indra, in einem speziellen singhalesischen Pantheon untergeordnet, gleichzeitig aber erhalten sie direkte Schutzgottfunktionen für die buddhistische Religion, Saman z.B. als Schutzgott für die aus einer vorbuddhistischen Kultstätte in einen Buddha-Fußabdruck umgewandelte Fußspur am Samanaḷa, am heutigen Adam's Peak. Auch einzelne westliche Einflüsse können so integriert werden, z.B. durch die Einbeziehung von Makkama, d.h. dem arabischen Mekka, in die Reihe der Fußabdrücke des Buddha (vgl. H. Bechert, Mythologie der singhalesischen Volksreligion, in: Wörterbuch der Mythologie, I, Abt., 15. Lieferung, Stuttgart 1976, s.v. Götter, Saman und Makkama)."

"Das gerade Gegenteil dieser Entwicklung ist ebenfalls im buddhistischen Bereich — und zwar nur dort, nicht aber im hinduistischen Bereich — zu beobachten. Ich meine hier die Schaffung eines eigenen Systems einer neuen Hochreligion aus den lokalen Kulten durch die Übernahme wesentlicher Elemente der vordringenden Hochreligion im Gegensatz zu ihr, ja im Abwehrkampf gegen deren Vordringen. Das geschieht durch Anpassung der eigenen Überlieferung an die Formen und, so weit als möglich, auch an die Inhalte der überlegenen Tradition, die dann fast spiegelbildlich in der religiösen Theorie und Praxis wiederholt wird. Das Paradebeispiel hierfür ist die tibetische Bon-Religion in der Form des ‚systematisierten Bon', das sich schließlich so weit dem Buddhismus angepaßt hat, daß es dem Betrachter fast als eine buddhistische Sekte erscheinen muß."

"Schließlich ist noch die vollkommene Synthese mehr oder weniger gleichberechtigter Traditionen zu erwähnen. Sie läßt sich deutlich vom vorhin beschriebenen

Synkretismus im engeren Sinne abheben. Hier werden die Elemente verschiedener Herkunft nämlich bewußt zu einer neuen Einheit verschmolzen, die den Anspruch erhebt, erst das volle Verständnis der Teilwahrheiten zu ermöglichen. Die erzielte Synthese tritt nun gegenüber den integrierten Traditionen mit einem absoluten und meist kompromißlosen Wahrheitsanspruch auf. Das bekannteste indische Beispiel dafür ist die Religion der Sikhs, in der islamischer Monotheismus und hinduistische Tradition zu einer neuartigen Synthese verbunden werden, wobei behauptet wird, die beiden überlieferten Religionen seien in dem letztlich relevanten Teil ihrer Aussagen, sozusagen in ihrem letzten Wahrheitsgehalt, identisch."

"Selbstverständlich lassen sich nun zahlreiche Zwischen- und Mischformen der aufgezeichneten Typen beobachten und wir werden manche dieser Zwischenformen bei der Besprechung unseres Gegenstandes zu erörtern haben."

Syncretistic Forms of Buddhism in Nepal, in Java and Bali, in Japan and in Bengal

The phenomenon of religious syncretism in the Buddhist world, but outside the sphere of Theravāda, was dealt with in the contributions "Religionssynkretismus in Nepal" by Prof. Siegfried Lienhard (see below, pp. 146–177), "Śiva-Buddhism in Java and Bali" by Prof. Jacob Ensink (see below, pp. 178–198) and "Buddhistisch-schintoistischer Synkretismus in Struktur und Praxis des Tempels Rinnōji in Nikkō, Japan" by Prof. Robert K. Heinemann (see below, pp. 199–213). In the first of these studies, which also served as a background to the later discussions of the problem of syncretism in other Buddhist countries, different types of syncretistic phenomena in the wider sense of the term ("Übertragung religiösen Guts von einer Religion in die andere", "religiöser Parallelismus", "Identifikation", see below, p. 151), were observed and described. The religion of Bali which forms the subject of the second of these studies was universally agreed to provide the clearest possible case of full-scale syncretism. Here again, different terminologies ("blending", "syncretism", "parallelism", "coalition") have been employed by the various scholars working in the field (cf. below, p. 182). The structure and development of the Javanese-Balinese religion and its particular use of Indian traditions can be understood only if the social order and the indigenous concepts of Java and Bali are fully taken into consideration. The situation is still more complicated in the case of Buddhist-Shinto syncretism in Japan where political decisions too come into the picture. In the discussions, parallel phenomena (e. g. Caodaism) were mentioned and a comparative evaluation of the different forms described in the contributions was attempted, but it may suffice here to refer readers to the final form of the papers as found in this volume.

The problem of religious syncretism in the sphere of Theravāda Buddhism was taken up by the paper "Religious Syncretism among the Buddhist Baruas and Chakmas in Bengal" by Dr. Gustav Roth and the editor. For a summary of this paper see below, pp. 214–216; a detailed study of Buddhism of the Baruas and of the Chakmas and their literature will be published elsewhere in the forseeable future.[2]) The editor would like to add here that the religion of another Buddhist community of Bangla Desh, viz. the Magh who now prefer to be named Marma, was described as syncretistic by Claude Lévi-Strauss, Le syncrétisme religieux d'un village mog du territoire de Chittagong, in: Revue de l'Histoire des Religions 141 (1952), pp. 203–237. Syncretism in the religion of the Marmas can be described as a form of co-existence of local cults and Buddhism which is similar to that observed in Burma. In the case of the Bauddharañjikā we find, on the other hand, syncretistic features in a particular literary work which do not necessarily find their counterpart in religious practice, because we know that the reform movement of the Barua and Chakma Buddhists strictly followed the lines of Theravāda orthodoxy. Prof. Lienhard pointed out that besides the obvious Śaiva influences Vaiṣṇava elements can also be observed in the terminology used in the Bauddharañjikā. An important methodical issue was raised by the question whether one could classify the particular form of the acceptance of Hindu elements in a Buddhist work as syncretism if it could not be related to the religious practice of the period. It seems more appropriate to describe it as a form of eclecticism with a view to encouraging non-Buddhists to read the text. The reference to Hindu deities seems to have served this purpose. The majority of the participants preferred not to use the term "religious syncretism" in this case which represents an example of the first of the above-described types of syncretistic phenomena in the wider sense of the word, where the essential features of the main tradition are not deeply affected by the admixture of elements from a different tradition (see above p. 21).

Sinhalese Buddhism and "Popular Religion"

The first paper dealing with Sinhala popular religion was "Zur Charakterisierung der singhalesischen Volksreligion", submitted by the editor, of which an English version is found in this volume under the title "On the Popular Religion of the Sinhalese" (below, pp. 217–233). Prof. Gombrich, in his comments, remarked that it is rather doubtful whether we should use the term "Volksreligion" (popular religion) here. "Folk religion" is a residual category and it would have the implication of indigenous origin. There are, however, many foreign elements in this "folk religion", e. g. Malayali elements in "devil dancing". However, a more suitable term has yet to be invented, so that there remains a practical necessity for using this term. Prof. Gombrich, however, preferred to use as much as possible the categories which are provided by the cultural tradition under review itself. With reference to the use of the term "syncretism", he proposed to call the religion of the Sinhalese not

[2]) See also Heinz Bechert, Zur Geschichte des Theravāda-Buddhismus in Ostbengalen, in: Beiträge zur Indienforschung, Ernst Waldschmidt zum 80. Geburtstag gewidmet, Berlin 1977, pp. 45–66.

"syncretistic", but "accretive" (see also Richard Gombrich, Precept and Practice, Oxford 1971, p. 49), because there are "accretions" to Buddhism, whereas the editor still prefers to term it a particular type of syncretism. For the problem of a correct description of the religion of India in the period of the introduction of Buddhism in Ceylon, the study by Allan Dahlquist (Megasthenes and Indian Religion, Stockholm 1962) and the controversy caused by it should be taken into consideration (for a critical review of this book, see Georg Buddruss, in: Gnomon 37, 1965, pp. 718–723).

Dr. Klaus Housherr, the author of "Kataragama: Das Heiligtum im Dschungel Südost-Ceylons—aus geographischer Sicht" (below, pp. 234–280) could not personally participate in the symposium. He provided the following English summary of his contribution:

"On the banks of the Menik Ganga, surrounded by the jungles covering the lowlands of SE-Ceylon lies one of the holiest places of this tropical island: Kataragama. This place, centre of the veneration of a god known in India and Ceylon by many names, e.g. Kataragama, Skanda, Murukam, actually consists of three holy areas. The most important one is the settlement: Kataragama itself. Temples, however, are also found in Sella Kataragama situated on an island in the Menik Ganga, a few miles to the north, and on the top of the Wedahitikanda, one of the hills in a short mountain range south of Kataragama. Apart from the stupa, no other religious structure breaks through the vegetative cover of the surroundings."

"The function of Kataragama as a place of worship can be traced back more than 2000 years; its beginnings, however, are lost in pre-Buddhist times, thus pointing to a cult which originally was not connected with Hinduism, Buddhism, or Islam. The followers of these religions, at least in Ceylon, see and have in Kataragama a place of worship and they have integrated the God Kataragama and/or the holiness of the place into their structure of religious belief to various degrees. Even a few Christians can be found here among the pilgrims every year."

"As far as evidence is available, Kataragama has never lost its significance as a holy place. It received, however, a great impuls in its development after the British annexation of the island in 1815, especially in connection with the rise of the tea industry. Since the cultivation of the tea requires a labour-intensive attention to the crop during the whole year, numerous Tamils from South India where the God Kataragama is also worshipped came to the island. The pilgrimage of these coolies from the highlands of the interior to the rather near holy place in the lowlands, especially during the main festival lasting a fortnight in the hot and dry months of July/August, endangered the smooth labour rhythm on the tea plantations, the economy in general and, last but not least, also affected the population of the whole island: Diseases threatened to spread regularly (cholera), or manpower was lost temporarily by other illnesses (malaria) contracted during the fulfilment of a religious obligation. Thus, the British colonial administration was forced to bring in regulations which aimed at a strict medical and hygienic supervision of Kataragama and its pilgrims."

"Subsequently, other factors influenced the development of Kataragama. Donations of pious Hindu devotees of the God Kataragama enabled the building of resthouses, thus the physical appearance of the place was changed; a permanent road connection to Tissamaharama was started; cheap transportation increased the number of pilgrims; businessmen settled down, changing the drowsy holy place which bustled only at times of religious festivals. Politics—so it seems—is the latest factor to enter the scene by using pilgrimages as 'political soothers'. Kataragama also became a more or less 'administrated' sacred place: The picturesque mixture of the holy and the profane, of temples, resthouses and shops standing side by side in Kataragama has been segregated by administrative measures into a purely holy and a purely worldly sector."

"Since the Second World War the isolation of Kataragama has been steadily reduced. As soon as the festivals are over, Kataragama does not drop back into the isolation of the jungles for the rest of the year anymore. Nowadays it is integrated into the economy and the infrastructure of the island, and it might even turn out to be a pattern for the development of the hitherto only sparsely populated areas of SE-Ceylon."

From the discussion of this contribution, Prof. Gombrich's remark that the participation of the Sinhalese in fire-walking started only after 1945 may be recorded here. Dr. Schalk drew our attention to a recent publication on Skanda from a Hindu point of view with three chapters on Kataragama: Ratna Navaratnam, Karttikeya, The Divine Child, Bombay 1973 (Bhavan's Book University, 182).

Prof. Richard F. Gombrich's study of the Kosala-bimba-vaṇṇanā (see below, pp. 281–303) was the occasion for several comments on the question whether Buddha images could have existed in Ceylon as early as the time of king Duṭṭhagāmaṇī (161–131 B. C. according to the chronology of Paranavitana) who is said in the Mahāvaṃsa (30.72–73) to have put a Buddha image inside the Mahācetiya. Prof. Gombrich stated that there is little reason to doubt the historicity of this relation (see below, p. 282), but this statement was contradicted by Prof. Härtel as well as by the editor. I still believe that the record in the passage in question, which forms part of the so-called "Duṭṭhagāmaṇī epic", cannot be quoted as a historical source for the existence of Buddha images during that period in Ceylon, but rather reflects the situation at the time of its author Mahānāma. The Duṭṭhagāmaṇī epic was described by Wilhelm Geiger as a part of the Mahāvaṃsa where many mythological elements and folk-traditions had been incorporated and which, therefore, could not be ranked equal with other parts of the chronicle as a historical source (see W. Geiger, The Dīpavaṃsa and Mahāvaṃsa and their Historical Development in Ceylon, Colombo 1908, pp. 19–22). Prof. Gombrich did not accept this argument, and his answer can be found below, p. 282. A number of other remarks on the text made during the symposium are also referred to in the final form of his contribution contained in this volume.

Dr. Hans Ruelius' study of the "Netrapratiṣṭhāpana — eine singhalesische Zeremonie zur Weihe von Kultbildern" (below, pp. 304–334) gave rise to a lengthy review of the categories used in this paper as well as of the methodology of the description and analysis of the consecration ceremony. Prof. Gombrich who had earlier published a study on this subject (Richard Gombrich, The Consecration of a Buddhist Image, in: Journal of Asian Studies 26, 1966/67, pp. 23–26) did not approve of the methods proposed by Dr. Ruelius. Dr. Schalk also remarked that the *netrapratiṣṭhāpana* ritual was not a "rite de passage" in the established sense of the word, because it was not a communal rite. Finally it was agreed in the conference that Prof. Gombrich should explain his view in an additional contribution which would be published along with Dr. Ruelius' paper in the volume, because the members of the conference were of the opinion that both sides should have the opportunity to state their case in this fundamental question. This additional contribution "The Buddha's Eye, the Evil Eye, and Dr. Ruelius" by Richard F. Gombrich is found below, pp. 335–338.

Dr. Peter Schalk spoke on "Der Paritta-Dienst in Śrī Laṃkā" and a summary of his study is found below, pp. 339–341. The results of his study are published in his thesis (Der Paritta-Dienst in Ceylon, Lund 1972). The *paritta* belongs to the Great Tradition, and it is part of the common heritage of all Theravāda countries. It has to be differentiated according to its various functions which are in some instances similar to those of rites of the so-called popular religion, and the particular importance of the *paritta* in the context of the study of religious syncretism lies in its intermediate position between canonical Buddhism and popular religion.[3])

---

[3]) See also below, pp. 221 f. It seems to me that Dr. Schalk has missed the point in his reference (see below, p. 341) to a remark which I made in 1968 (Heinz Bechert, Einige Fragen der Religionssoziologie und Struktur des südasiatischen Buddhismus, in: Internationales Jahrbuch für Religionssoziologie 4, 1968, p. 275). This remark on "eine Umorientierung des an sich auf das ‚überweltliche' Ziel des Nirvana ausgerichteten Sangha" refers to the participation of bhikkhus in the cult of the gods only, not to the *paritta* which I have described as part of the "official religion" (see Einige Fragen der Religionssoziologie . . ., p. 274). The *paritta* may also be described as belonging to the sphere of "popular Buddhism" (see below, pp. 221f.), but not as part of the cults of the gods, though it served, to a certain degree, the same functions as the popular religion.

I. BUDDHIST LITERATURE IN CEYLON

The role of Pāli in early Sinhalese Buddhism

By K. R. NORMAN

Introduction

In this paper I intend to examine, and if possible to define, the role of Pāli in early Sinhalese Buddhism. As a corollary of this, I shall at the same time try to define what was not the role of Pāli, i. e. the part played by other languages in Ceylon in the period under scrutiny. To do this I have examined all the references I can find in the early literature which refer to languages used in Ceylon: I cannot claim to have found any references not already noted by others. I have also examined the deductions made by others from these references, and I have commented on the viability or otherwise of their views. To a large extent this paper has proved to be destructive rather than constructive, in that I have tended to show that many inferences which have been drawn are untenable, or at least unprovable, but I have been unable in many cases to make better suggestions in their place. If, however, I have succeeded in removing misapprehensions then perhaps I have not been entirely negative in my approach to the problem.

I should start by defining terms. As is well known, the word *pāḷi* is not used in early Buddhist writings as the name of a language. There it is used in opposition to *aṭṭhakathā*, e. g., *piṭakattayapāḷiṃ ca tassa aṭṭhakathaṃ pi ca* (Mhvs 33.100) "the text of the three piṭakas and the cty thereon." I shall, however, use the word in the accepted European sense of the language of the Theravāda canon and the cties on that canon written by Buddhaghosa, Dhammapāla, etc. In fact, an alternative title to this paper might well be: why did Buddhaghosa write in Pāli?

By 'early Sinhalese Buddhism' I mean the Buddhism practised in Ceylon before and up to the fifth century A. D., i. e. up to the time of Buddhaghosa, or, to be more exact, up to the probable time of the composition of the cties ascribed to him. This, however, is not a hard and fast limit, and I shall have occasion to refer to Dhammapāla and to texts composed as late as the ninth or tenth centuries and even later where they seem to give any information which could be construed as having a bearing upon the earlier times I am dealing with.

The Coming of the Indo-Aryans to Ceylon

Tradition has it that Vijaya and his followers arrived in Ceylon on the day that the Buddha died (Mhvs 6.47). Vijaya came from N. India, from the kingdom of Lāḷa (Mhvs 6.36). Although the Mhvs (6.5) implies that Lāḷa lay between Vaṅga (Bengal) and Magadha, it is identified by some with Ptolemy's Λαρίκη = modern Gujarat (DPPN s. v.), and this would agree with the statement that on the way to Ceylon Vijaya landed at Suppāraka, i. e. modern Sopāra (Mhvs 6.46), or Bharukacchu, i. e. modern Broach (Dpvs 9.26). Vijaya is said to have had a purohita called Upatissa (Mhvs 7.44), and from this Adikaram deduced (p. 44) that Vijaya was accompanied by brahmans, and the religion of his court was brahmanical. The sacred language would therefore have been Skt, and if Vijaya and his followers were Indo-Aryans their language would have been some form of Pkt as spoken in the fifth century B. C. When Vijaya arrived in Ceylon the country was inhabited by yakkhas, and if this statement has any ethnological significance it can only mean that the island was inhabited by non-Aryans. From the fifth century onwards, then, Ceylon was inhabited by both Indo-Aryans and non-Indo-Aryans.

All this is surmise. There is not, to my knowledge, any direct evidence available about the language usage in Ceylon prior to the third century B. C. Tradition tells us that at the time of Aśoka Mahinda took Buddhism to Ceylon (Dpvs 12.9; Mhvs 13.21). The story as related in Dpvs, Sp, and Mhvs tells that Tissa met Mahinda, exchanged greetings with him and had a discussion. All three sources agree that the first sermon which Mahinda preached to the king was the *Cūḷahatthipadūpamasuttanta* (= M I 175–84), although Sp and Mhvs make some additions to the list given in the Dpvs of the sermons which were preached thereafter. Adikaram comments (p. 52) that "from the facility with which Mahinda and the people of Ceylon understood one another, we may incidentally observe how closely allied the languages of N. India and Ceylon must have been." It is, however, noteworthy that despite the ease of communication just referred to, Mhvs 14.65 states that Mahinda preached the true doctrine in two places in the speech of the island (*dvīsu ṭhānesu dhammaṃ bhāsitvā dīpabhāsāya*), implying that in the other places he did not 'translate'.[1]) Dpvs and Sp make no mention of this 'translation' process, and although there are instances of Mhvs including authentic historical material which was either unknown to, or consciously omitted by, earlier chroniclers, it is possible that the need for 'translation' was deduced by the author of Mhvs from the statement repeated at the begining of Buddhaghosa's cties, that they were based upon the cties which were brought to Ceylon by Mahinda and put into Sinhalese for the benefit of the islanders (*Sīhaḷadīpaṃ pana ābhatā 'tha vasinā Mahā-*

---

[1]) I use 'translate' to mean the change from one dialect of Middle Indo-Aryan to another, however closely related.

Mahindena ṭhapitā Sīhaḷabhāsāya dīpavāsīnam atthāya (Ps I 1). The author of Mhvs may well have thought that if Mahinda needed to 'translate' the ctíes then he must have 'translated' the canonical sermons too. The fact that the 'translation' process is said to have happened in only two places suggests, however, that the statement is based upon tradition. If it is true, we may deduce that in some places Mahinda preached the suttas in their canonical form, in Pāli, whereas in two places he added an exegesis, in Sinhalese Pkt.

Adikaram supports his belief that no 'translation' was required by the statement (p. 52) that a comparison of the earliest inscriptions of Ceylon and those of N. India in the corresponding age also leads to the inference that the languages were closely allied. Rahula says much the same thing (p. 60): "if we compare the language of Aśoka's inscriptions and the inscriptions of Ceylon in the third century B.C. we can see that the two languages are almost similar." These two writers are referring to the earliest authentic evidence which we have for the knowledge of the language of Ceylon, or of at least a portion of the population, for we may suppose that there was still a non-Indo-Aryan element. The earliest inscriptions which are datable refer to King Uttiya (c. 207-197 B.C.),[2]) although it is impossible to prove that they were inscribed in his reign, only that they could not predate him. They are probably, then, some 50 years later than Mahinda's arrival, but nevertheless the language is not likely to have developed much in 50 years, and we can probably assume that the language of the Sinhalese whom Mahinda met did not differ greatly from that of the earliest inscriptions. Karunaratne thought (pp. 82–3) that the language of these early inscriptions might well reflect, for some time at least, the language of the Buddhist missionaries, and not the original Sinhalese. It is true that, as all the early inscriptions are donative, commemorating gifts to the saṅgha or to individual bhikkhus, the possibility of influence by the language of the Buddhist missionaries upon the local vernacular cannot be denied.

The language of the inscriptions

The language of the early inscriptions in Ceylon has the following distinctive features:

a) the nom. sg. of *-a* stems is in *-e*
b) the only sibilant is *śa*
c) historic *ja* is everywhere replaced by *jha*
d) the distribution of *ra* and *la* follows the pattern of Skt
e) the gen. sg. of *-a* stems is in *-aśa* or *-aha*
f) there is sporadic loss of aspiration, e. g. *tera* (for *thera*), *saga* (*sa(ṃ)gha*), *koṭa* (*koṭha*), *gapati* (**ghapati* <*gahapati*), *baḍa* (*baḍha*)
g) *jhita* occurs for *dhita*.

[2]) Here and subsequently I follow the dates for Sinhalese kings given by W. Geiger 1950, pp. xxxvi–xxxviii.

It could be suggested that the first two characteristics showed the influence of Māgadhī,[3]) on the assumption that the missionaries spoke Māgadhī or included Māgadhī-speakers among their number, or even brought texts in Māgadhī with them, but it is clear that the other characteristics of Sinhalese Pkt do not support this suggestion. An examination of the Aśokan inscriptions shows that the Sinhalese inscriptions are written in a Pkt which does not agree with any of the extant Aśokan dialects, but which seems to have deviated much more from the norm of Skt than any of them. If this dialect was influenced by that of any of the missionaries, then they must have spoken a Pkt which differs from any other known to us. It seems more likely that Sinhalese Pkt developed in the way it did because it was introduced long before Mahinda, perhaps in the fifth century B.C., and thereafter had little contact with the Pkts of N. India. The script too of the Sinhalese inscriptions supports the idea of a pre-Mahinda introduction to Ceylon, for its form does not coincide with that of any known Aśokan site; e.g., the sign for initial *i-* is ·|· not :·, and Karunaratne (p. 70) suggested that the Brāhmī script was introduced into both India and Ceylon from a common source, and not into Ceylon from India. Later developments in the use of the script are, however, probably due to the influence of the missionaries. The distinctive *i-* sign disappears and is replaced by the standard Mauryan form. The aksaras *ja* and *sa* appear in the inscriptions and for some time exist side by side with *jha* and *śa*, and then, by the second century A.D., oust them. Such changes are likely to be merely of orthography, not of pronunciation. There has been no lack of attempts to decide where the Sinhalese dialect might have originated. The word *kabojha* (= Skt *Kamboja*) occurs in some early inscriptions, and this led Paranavitana to suggest that, not only were there people from Kamboja in Ceylon at that time, but that the original Sinhalese came from the North-West (p. 93). Geiger (1938, p. 2), on the strength of the preservation of the old initial *v* and other features, concluded that Vijaya spoke a Western dialect. Geiger and Paranavitana both accepted the fact that other features show an influx of speakers of an Eastern dialect at a later date.

The language of the Canon

As mentioned above, the chronicles name the suttas which formed Mahinda's first sermons in Ceylon. Whether the whole canon was introduced at one time we have no way of telling, but an inscription of the second century B.C.[4]) includes a reference to a *majhimabaṇaka*, which implies that some, at least, of the nikāyas were known by that date. We have no information about the language in which the canon was introduced, nor about the language in which it was transmitted in Ceylon.

[3]) Nom. sg. in *-e* is also found in the North-Western Pkt (Brough, p. 115).
[4]) Quoted by Karunaratne, p. 113.

We do, however, learn from the chronicles that in the reign of Vaṭṭagāmiṇī (29–17 B.C.) the canon and the commentaries were committed to writing (Dpvs 20.21; Mhvs 33.100). We may assume that after the canon had been written down no further changes took place in it, at least as far as the language was concerned. Since it is in Pāli now, we may draw the conclusion that it was written down in Pāli. This was either the language in which the canon had been introduced into Ceylon, or the form of the canonical language which had evolved between the time of introduction and the date of writing down. If there had been any development between the third and first centuries B. C., one would have expected it to have been in the direction of the Sinhalese Pkt. It is clear from the brief summary of the characteristics of this given above that Sinhalese Pkt had no great influence upon Pāli, and we may therefore conclude that very little change took place. What influence has been suggested can probably be explained in other ways. The nom. sg. in *-e* which is found in Pāli, and usually explained as a Māgadhism, has been regarded as arising in some contexts from the Sinhalese Pkt nom. sg. which is also in *-e*.[5]) In view of the existence of other Māgadhisms which cannot be explained from Sinhalese Pkt, e.g. the frequent verbal forms in *pali-* < *pari-*, I see no reason to accept this explanation. The very occasional appearance of *-ddh-* in Pāli where we should have expected *-jjh-* (v. CPD s.v. *addhăbhavati*) has also been put down to the influence of Sinhalese Pkt (cf. Sinhalese *d* < *j*), but as the earliest attested example of this change (*made* < *majjha* in an inscription of the fourth century A. D.)[6]) shows the loss of the aspirate, the aspirated *-ddh-* forms in Pāli must have come from some other source. The fact that comparable developments of groups of dental consonants in place of the expected palatals can be found in Indian Pkts, (e. g. AMg *dosinā* "moonlight" < *jyotsnā* < **dyotsnā*) where the influence of Sinhalese Pkt can be discounted, would suggest that these forms were already present in Pāli before its introduction into Ceylon.

It seems very likely, therefore, that the language of the canon when introduced was not appreciably different from that in which it was written down, i. e. Pāli. There is no direct evidence as to the home of the dialect in which the canon is written, nor where the canon was composed (which need not be the same place), nor from where the canon (as opposed to the missionaries who preached it)[7]) reached Ceylon. The view that the

---

[5]) CPD (Vol. I, s.v. *avitakka*) seems to refer only to the occurrence of *-e* in the cties, but H. Bechert, Über Singhalesisches im Pālikanon, in: WZKSO I (1957), pp. 71–5, states that the examples of *-e* occurring in the accounts of the heretics' doctrines are also from Sinhalese. I have examined this question at greater length in "Pāli and the language of the heretics", in: Acta Orientalia Vol. 37 (1976), pp. 117–126.

[6]) See W. Geiger, 1938, § 46.

[7]) E. Frauwallner (The earliest Vinaya and the beginnings of Buddhist literature, Rome, 1956, p. 23) concludes that the missionaries who went out from the

home of Pāli must be in the west of India, because of all the Aśokan dialects it is closest to that of Girnar, dates from the time when it was believed that the Aśokan inscriptions gave an accurate representation of the dialect distribution in India in the third century B.C. Now that we can see that the Aśokan pattern, with some exceptions, represents the scribes' own dialects, or their ideas of what the local dialects ought to be, rather than the actual state of affairs,[8]) such arguments are not conclusive. In fact, the view that Pāli came from Kaliṅga is just as likely. Although the Aśokan inscriptions from Kaliṅga show typically Eastern features, it is probable that the scribes were merely copying their exemplars with a minimum of change, for Khāravela's inscription at Hāthigumphā in the next century is more likely to give an accurate picture of the Pkt used for administrative purposes, at least, in Kaliṅga, and in that inscription the Eastern features are lacking. Each *-r-* does not become *-l-*, and nom. sg. is in *-o* not *-e*.

One thing is certain. The Pāli canon is not in the language of Aśoka's own capital; for the basic features of Māgadhī (*śa* for all three sibilants, *la* for *ra*, and nom. sg. in *-e*) are either lacking completely, or merely sporadic. The fact that the Pāli canon lacks these features makes it difficult to understand why the Sinhalese tradition tells us that the language of the canon was Māgadhī, and that Māgadhī was also the language of the Buddha. Although we find this tradition attested for the first time in Buddhaghosa's cties, we may presume that he found the idea of Māgadhī as the *mūla-bhāsā* in the Sinhalese cties he was translating. The information must have been brought from North India by the first missionaries, since the Jains have a similar view of AMg. We have no knowledge of the dialect distribution of India at the beginning of the fifth century B.C., but if we assume that the pattern of dialect differentiation was similar to that of the third century, except that the dialects were at an earlier stage of development, then it is likely that in the areas where the Buddha preached the inhabitants spoke a number of (slightly) different dialects, including Old Māgadhī. The Buddha probably varied his own dialect to suit his audience. Over the years a canonical collection was built up and subjected to one or more redactions which included a certain amount of 'translation' aimed at removing the Māgadhisms and other anomalous features. The traces of these features which still remain result from errors in the redaction process.

There is no certain evidence for any substantial Sinhalese additions to the canon after its arrival in Ceylon. The fact that the Parivāra refers

---

same centre took with them the same Vinaya, that current in the region of Vidiśā. I do not see that this proves that the canon was in the language of Vidiśā.

[8]) The indigenous population at Yerraguḍi were presumably then, as now, speakers of a Dravidian language. The dialect of the fragments from Sopārā, with its nom. sg. in *-e* and its mechanical conversion of every *-l-* > *-r-*, is not likely to have corresponded to any dialect spoken at that time in India.

several times to Ceylon and includes a list of elders of whom the last can be dated to the first century A. D. (Vin V 3 49), has prompted the suggestion that it was probably the work of a Sinhalese thera. Jayawickrama, however, considers these passages to be interpolations (p. 107). Buddhaghosa makes no reference either to Ceylon or the later theras in the list, but merely states (Sp 1304) that the verses beginning *Upāli Dāsako ca* were added by *porāṇakehi mahā-therehi*. The author of Pj II (p. 477) notes that the Sinhalese cty did not comment upon Sn 677–78 and he therefore excludes them from the number of verses in the original sutta.[9]) Adikaram (p. 12) takes this as pointing with more or less certainty to an addition made to the canon in Ceylon. The verses could equally well, however, have belonged to a different recension from that being used by the *Mahā-aṭṭhakathā*, and been either unknown to the author of the Sinhalese cty or ignored as being less authentic. It is clear that different recensions of some texts did find their way to Ceylon. Buddhaghosa and the other commentators frequently record the existence of variant readings, and it is questionable whether these would all have been in one and the same version of the canon.

The language of the commentaries

There is no evidence about the language of the cties which Mahinda is said to have brought with him to Ceylon. They could have been in the same language as the canonical texts, or have been in the language of the missionaries, in so far as they may have spoken a different Pkt. We have no evidence earlier than Buddhaghosa's statement (Ps I 1 etc.) that Mahinda did bring cties with him, but we have no reason to doubt that cties were brought from India either by Mahinda or other missionaries coming after him. The cties seem to have contained much information about India, and particularly N. India, which could only have been brought from there. Professor Brough has pointed out (p. 226) that the Pāli cties sometimes employ a form of words in their explanations which is closer to the versions found in Skt or Gāndhārī than the Pāli version which is being commented upon, and this can only be explained by assuming that the Pāli cty and the Skt and Gāndhārī versions must go back to a common source, which must have been in N. India. Similarly, the occasional explanation of one word by a cognate form from another dialect, e.g. *vissa* (Dh 266) explained by *visama* (DhA III 393), both of which are < *veśman* but are misunderstood by the cty, must antedate the introduction of the canon into Ceylon. So too must explanations which depend upon non-Pāli and non-Sinhalese Pkt forms, e.g. the explanation of *coḷa* (Thag 170) by *cora* must depend upon a source which, like Māgadhī, confused *l* (*ḷ*) and *r*.

---

[9]) *avasāne gāthādvayaṃ eva pana Mahā-aṭṭhakathāyaṃ vinicchitapāṭhe n' atthi, tenāvocumha "vīsatigāthāsū" ti*. This seems to be the only statement of this kind in the cty.

CPD (s.v. *avitakka*) refers to forms in *-e* in two cty passages (Mp I 71, II 273) and claims that these are from the ⟨*Sīhaḷa-*⟩*Aṭṭhakathā* (Proto-Sinhalese being an *-e* dialect). These two passages are virtually identical, and it seems unlikely that of all the hundreds of Sinhalese Pkt forms in *-e* which must have been in the Sinhalese cties Buddhaghosa not only forgot to 'translate' into Pali the first time he gave the explanation, but also repeated his error the second time. We may therefore deduce that Buddhaghosa deliberately quoted the passage with the *-e* forms (attributing it to the *Aṭṭhakathā* the second time), perhaps because it was invested with such authority in the Sinhalese cty (by its ascription to an early missionary thera?) that he felt obliged to quote it verbatim.

Childers (p. X) was of the opinion that the cties brought by Mahinda were in Pāli. If Childers was right, we have to assume a progression Pāli > Sinhalese Pkt > Pāli. While this is not impossible, it does raise the question of why the Pāli of the canon was sacrosanct, while the Pāli of the cty could be translated. It would seem more likely that the cties already represented a heterogeneous mass of material, in various dialects, and probably including comments on readings which differed from those in the canon as established in Ceylon. This would help to explain how Buddhaghosa came to have variant readings in his cty, as mentioned above.

The fact that the cty material was already of a disparate nature would have led to an attempt to impose homogeneity upon it and also to make it more intelligible to the Sinhalese bhikkhus by translating it into the vernacular. Because it was in the vernacular it would have been easy for additions to be made to it. That there was a continuing commentarial tradition in Ceylon itself is shown by the fact that Buddhaghosa quotes (from the Sinhalese cties he was using) the names of individual Sinhalese theras whose views he is accepting or rejecting.

Occasionally Buddhaghosa and later commentators quote verses which they ascribe to individual theras (e. g. Sp 538), or simply to the *aṭṭhakathās* (e. g. Sp 240 437, Paṭis-A 331). Since these verses are in Pāli when they are quoted, it has been assumed that they were in Pāli in the Sinhalese cties which Buddhaghosa and the others had before them. The statement is therefore made that the cties were in the Sinhalese language with Pāli verses, and Adikaram goes so far as to state (p. 16) that there was possibly in Ceylon an anthology of Pāli verse composed (by Sinhalese theras) after the model of the canonical Theragāthā. This question will be discussed in the next section in connection with the problem of the source material for the chronicles.

Sources for Dpvs und Mhvs

At the beginning of Mhvs it is stated that the work is intended as a replacement for the work which was produced by the *porāṇas* (Mhvs 1.2). Although Geiger (1950, p. xi) and others have thought that this is a reference to the Dpvs, the MhvsṬ (p. 42) makes it clear that the author of Mhvs was in fact referring to a history in the Sinhalese language, and Malalasekera accepts that this source material was a *Sīhaḷa aṭṭhakathā* of the same type as those just referred to (MhvsṬ pp. lvii–lviii). Oldenberg (p. 4) surmised that this *aṭṭhakathā* was in prose in the main, with verses interspersed. The MhvsṬ quotes a number of verses, which it ascribes to the *porāṇas*, which appear in virtually the same form in Dpvs (although MhvsṬ never quotes Dpvs by name). Since these verses are in Pāli when they are ascribed to the *porāṇas*, Oldenberg assumed that they were composed in Pāli, and concluded that it was highly probable that all the verses (in the cty) were composed in Pāli. He made the same deduction about Sp (p. 5) since he noted that Buddhaghosa also quoted verses which he ascribed to the *porāṇas* which were virtually identical with verses which occur in Dpvs. Buddhaghosa also quotes from the Dpvs by name, and Jayawickrama (p. xxxiv) has suggested that the reason for these two different practices is that the author of Dpvs and Buddhaghosa made use of the same material. Where Buddhaghosa saw that the author of Dpvs was quoting from the cty he ascribed the quotation to the *porāṇas*; where Dpvs was not quoting a verse from the cty, e.g. when versifying a prose passage, Buddhaghosa attributes that verse to Dpvs.

Although Oldenberg was careful to say nothing more than that the existence of Pāli verses in the Sinhalese cties was highly probable, no-one since his time, I think, has failed to accept his suggestion as a fact, and Geiger (1908, p. 45), Malalasekera (MhvsṬ pp. lviff.), Adikaram (p. 14), and Jayawickrama (p. xxiv n. 1) all speak of *aṭṭhakathās* in Sinhalese with verses in Pāli. There are usually slight differences between the verses as they appear in Dpvs and their form as they are quoted by Buddhaghosa and MhvsṬ, and these differences are variously explained. Geiger (1908 p. 43) thought that Buddhaghosa must have known a version of Dpvs which differed somewhat from the extant version. There are also differences between Buddhaghosa and Mhvs, and Jayawickrama (p. xxxiv) has explained these as being due to the fact that although both used the same sources, one wrote in prose and the other in verse, and the exigencies of the latter form led to differences in spelling, etc.

These writers do not seem to have considered the illogicality of their statements. They accept that the Sinhalese prose was 'translated' into Pāli verse by the authors of Dpvs and Mhvs, but refuse to accept the obvious possibility of Sinhalese verse being 'translated' into Pāli verse. This, however, is the most likely explanation of such discrepancies as that between Buddhaghosa and Dpvs, and MhvsṬ and Dpvs, e.g. Dpvs 19.9 reads *Sumanadevī ca*, while the same verse in MhvsṬ 528,15 (where it is ascribed to the *porāṇas*) has *Sumanadeviyā*, a variation which clearly shows a different way of interpreting *-deviya* written without vowel length in a (non-Sinhalese) dialect which had *ya* < both *ca* and *ya*.

The fact that 'translation' from verse in one language to verse in another language presented no difficulty can easily be seen by comparing parallel versions of the same verse in the Pāli Dhammapada, the Gāndhārī Dharmapada, and the Skt Udānavarga.

The existence of Dravidian commentaries

Among the cties used by Buddhaghosa was the *Andhaka-aṭṭhakathā*. Mrs. Rhys Davids (p. xxviii) says that this cty was handed down at Kāñcipura. Adikaram stated (p. 12) that it was very likely written in the Andhaka language. Probability then becomes certainty, and Adikaram states (p. 14) "the references relate to . . . the Sinhalese and some of the Dravidian cties", and (p. 16) "Buddhaghosa drew his material not only from Sinhalese and Dravidian but also from . . . Pāli." Comparable statements are made (p. 9) about Dhammapāla: "Dhammapāla . . . very probably was a Dravidian by birth. It is also likely that he made use of Dravidian cties."

There was in all probability some connection between the Andhaka cty and either the Andhaka country or the Andhaka sect, and it is very likely that the sect was so called because it came from the country. Probably the Andhaka cty came from the Andhaka country originally, for Buddhaghosa quotes it (Sp 747,23) as referring to conditions in the Andha country. It must, however, like the other cties, have had a core of material which came from N. India, for Buddhaghosa quotes the *Andhaka-aṭṭhakathā* when he is talking about the *Magadha-nāḷī* (Sp 702,23–27) but quotes the *Mahā-aṭṭhakathā* for the *Damiḷa-nāḷī* in the same passage. The fact that the Andhaka cty is usually quoted only to be refuted (e.g. Sp 697,17) tends to support the view that the basis, at least, of the Andhaka cty belonged to that sect.

About the language of the cty nothing can be said definitely, but it would seem clear that by Buddhaghosa's time the cty was no longer available in S. India. The statement that no cty was available in India (Mhvs 37.227) was not likely to have been included in the Sinhalese cties upon which the Mhvs was based while there were S. Indians such as Dhammapāla available to refute it, if it were false. It is in any case clear from Buddhaghosa's statement (Sp 646,11), that the view of the thera Mahāsumma was regarded as authorative in the *Andhaka-aṭṭhakathā*, that the cty must have been introduced to Ceylon long before Buddhaghosa's time, for Mahāsumma is datable to the first century A. D. Since, however, Buddhaghosa stated plainly that he translated *Sinhalese* cties into Māgadhī, we can be fairly certain that if the Andhaka cty was originally composed in a Dravidian language, it had already been translated into Sinhalese by Buddhaghosa's time.

The language of the Abhayagirivāsins

Tradition says (Mhvs 33.81) that the Abhayagirivihāra was founded by Vaṭṭagāmiṇī (29–17 B.C.). Shortly afterwards the first schism between the Abhayagirivihāra and the Mahāvihāra occurred (Mhvs 33.97). The schism is probably confirmed by Hsüan-tsang's statement (Beal II. 247): "when 200 years had elapsed, through discussion, the one school was divided into two." We learn from Buddhaghosa (Sp 582–3) that in the reign of Bhātiya (38–66 A.D.) a dispute arose between the two vihāras about a vinaya rule. The king appointed a minister, a brahman, named Dīghakārāyaṇa, described as *paṇḍito bhāsantarakusalo*, to solve the dispute. Adikaram (p. 88) makes much of the reference to linguistic competence, and assumes that the difference between the two schools was linguistic, rather than doctrinal. He suggests that because the Abhayagiri school was later greatly influenced by Mahāyānism, in which the canonical texts were preserved not in Pāli but in Skt, it was perhaps already using Skt versions of the canon. He claims that the choice of a brahman minister, who must have been well versed in Skt, lends support to the same hypothesis. I find it hard to believe that Skt versions of the canon were available in Ceylon in the first half of the first century A. D., or that, if they were, the Abhayagirivāsins would have completely abandoned Pāli in the short time since their secession from the Mahāvihāra. In any case, the statement "Hīnayāna texts in Pāli, Mahāyāna texts in Skt" is a facile overstatement which quite overlooks the problem of the development of Buddhist Hybrid Skt, and the Pkt upon which it was based. I would rather suggest that the reference to the brahman being *bhāsantarakusalo* explains his ability to read the vinaya in Pāli and also the *aṭṭhakathās* in Sinhalese Pkt, upon whose differing interpretations the argument was probably based.

Nothing is known for certain about the texts of the Abhayagirivihāra. The fact that the Saddhammopāyana was written by Abhayagiri Kavicakravarti Ānanda (DPPN, s.v. *Saddhammopāyana*) suggests that it was a product of the Abhayagirivihāra, but since this text probably dates from the thirteenth century it is of no value for the period under discussion. Malalasekera (DPPN, s.v. *Abhayagiri*) records the suggestions that the *Jātakaṭṭhakathā* and the *Sahassavatthuppakaraṇa* were the work of Abhayagiri monks, but the former work is linked by tradition with the Mahiṃsāsaka sect (see below), and Malalasekera had already rejected the latter suggestion (PLC 129). Bapat and Bagchi (see Bareau, p. 242) both thought that the *Vimuttimagga*, known to them only in a Chinese translation, probably belonged to the school of the Abhayagirivāsins. Bareau examined the contents of this work and concluded that it was a Theravāda text. Since, however, it is not listed among the Theravāda texts, seems to have used a recension of the canon which differed slightly from that of the Mahāvihāra, and is mentioned by Dhammapāla in the Paramatthamañjūsā as a heretical work, Bareau concluded (p. 242) that it was not composed by a monk of the Mahāvihāra, but by one either from Abhayagiri or Jetavana, probably the former.

If we could be certain about the authenticity of the Pāli version of the *Vimuttimagga* published in 1963, then we should definitely know that the Abhayagirivāsins were still using Pāli, but we cannot be.[10] In any case, it is possible that they employed both languages, for Hsüan-tsang stated (Beal II, 247) that the Abhayagiri school studied both the Mahāyāna and the Hīnayāna. It has, however, been pointed out that this state of affairs is in conflict with the evidence. Fa-hsien wrote of both the Mahāvihāra and the Abhayagirivihāra (Legge, pp. 106–7), but said nothing about the Mahāyāna leanings of the latter; I-ching said that all Buddhists in Ceylon belonged to the Āryasthavira-nikāya (Takakusu, p. 10). This, however, is not conclusive, for Hsüan-tsang stated that the Sinhalese principally followed the dhamma of the Sthavira school of the Mahāyāna sect (Beal II, 247). It seems clear that the nomenclature employed by the Chinese pilgrims does not accord entirely with modern usage.[11]

One piece of evidence which Adikaram quotes (pp. 94–95) to support the view that Skt was employed in Ceylon, at least at the beginning of the fifth century A.D., is based upon a statement made by Fa-hsien. Adikaram states that Fa-hsien took with him from Ceylon copies of certain works, all written in Skt. This view is based upon Legge's translation (p. 111). Legge uses the same translation in connection with Fa-hsien's work in Pāṭaliputra (p. 99). Beal, however, translates the latter passage "Skt" (I, lxx), adding "Fan" in brackets, while he translates the former "in the original language" (I, lxxi), adding "Fan" in a foot-note. These translations are incorrect. Fan is derived from a phonetic rendering of *brahma*, probably through the corresponding Gāndhārī *bramma*.[12] It means, then, "Indian (language)", and without further evidence there is no way of saying whether the language was Skt, Pkt, or Pāli. Professor Brough informs me[13] that in the Chinese version of the *Saṃyuktābhidharmahṛdayaśāstra*, which is one of the texts collected by Fa-hsien, the name is a transliteration of *-abhidhamma-*, not *-abhidharma-*, showing that the name, and therefore probably the whole text, was in Pkt or a prakritised form of Skt.

---

[10] In his review of this text (Journal of the Vidyalankara University of Ceylon, pp. 172–90) P. V. Bapat suggests that this is a modern production, based upon his book Vimuttimagga and Visuddhimagga: A Comparative Study (1937).

[11] H. Bechert ("Notes on the formation of Buddhist sects and the origins of Mahāyāna", in: German Scholars on India: contributions to Indian Studies, Varanasi 1973, Volume I, p. 13) explains that the Mahāyāna-Sthaviravādin are those sections of the Sthaviravāda community who had accepted Mahāyāna doctrines although they still belonged to the Sthaviravāda school as far as bhikṣu ordination and vinaya-karma was concerned.

[12] See H. W. Bailey, "Gāndhārī", in: BSOAS Vol. XI, pp. 788–9.

[13] In a letter of 5 March 1974.

The language of the Vetulyakas

Connected with the question of the language used by the Abhayagirivāsins is the whole question of the Vetulyakas. We read in Mhvs 36.41 that King Vohārika-tissa (263–85 A. D.) suppressed the Vetulya-doctrine. Adikaram (p. 90) quotes the *Nikāyasaṅgraha* (p. 11) as stating that it was the Abhayagirivāsins who followed this doctrine, and as giving the information that the Vaitulya-piṭaka was produced in the time of Aśoka by heretical brahmans called Vaitulyas who had assumed the guise of monks to destroy the sāsana. Rahula (p. 89) states that the reference to the brahmans suggests that the Vaitulya-piṭaka was composed in Skt, and "we know that Mahāyāna sutras are all in Skt." Rahula goes on to quote Asaṅga's statement in the *Abhidharmasamuccaya* that the terms *Vaipulya*, *Vaidalya*, and *Vaitulya* denote the same thing, and *Vaipulya* is defined as *Bodhisattva-piṭaka*. He adds that Kern and Paranavitana thought that there is hardly any reason to question the identification of Vaitulyavādins with the Mahāyānists. "Hardly any reason" does, however, imply some doubt, and in fact our knowledge of the Vaitulyavādins is so limited that there is every reason for being cautious. All we know about their views is a few doctrines in the *Kathāvatthu*, which are attributed to the Vetulyakas, not in the *Kathāvatthu* itself, but by Buddhaghosa in his cty on that text, written at least 650 years later. Even if he is correct in his identification there is no guarantee that the same views were held by the Vaitulyakas in Ceylon in the fourth century A. D. Bareau has examined the *Kathāvatthu* passages (pp. 254–6) and concluded that the Vaitulyakas had eclectic views, including tantric as well as Mahīśāsaka, Dharmaguptaka, and Lokottaravādin beliefs, e.g. their docetic view of the Buddha closely resembles that of the *Mahāvastu*. He suggests that their views are to be regarded as pre-Mahāyānist and that they may have been the sect who occasioned Hsüang-tsang's designation of Mahāyāna-Sthavira. Another reason put forward by Rahula (p. 88) for assuming that the Vetulyakas were Mahāyānist is the fact that Buddhaghosa calls them *mahāsuññatāvādins* (KvuA 167). The Burmese edition, however, reads *mahāpuññavādins* in this passage; this reading seems preferable in the context and is accepted by Bareau (p. 254). Moreover, the Ṭīkā on Spk makes no reference to *suññatā* in its explanation of what was included in the Vetulla-piṭaka (Be II 171).

We are, however, concerned not so much with the Vetulyakas' views as with the language in which they expressed them. In this respect the fact that the sect was variously called is of great importance. It has been pointed out that the only explanation for the variations of the sect's name lies in a Pkt origin.[14] *Vaitulya* and *Vaipulya* must be back-formations from Pkt *ve(y)ulla* and *vevulla*, which are presumably merely variants of the same word with *-y-/-v-* glide consonant alternation. There

[14]) See. H. W. Bailey, Buddhist Sanskrit, in: JRAS 1955, p. 20.

is no way of telling which, if either, of the forms with *-t-* or *-p-* is historically correct. The word *vaipulya* does not seem to be used in Skt in the specific sense of "Mahāyāna", but rather "extended" as the name of a particular class of text, e.g. the *Saddharmapuṇḍarīka-sūtra* calls itself a *Mahā-vaipulya-sūtra.* The fact that the sect was called by a Pkt name very strongly suggests that its texts were originally in Pkt. It is interesting to note that at the time of the introduction of the *Saddharmapuṇḍarīka* into Khotan its name was still in a Pkt form, for its name occurs in Khotanese as *Mahāvittūlyasuttrīnai ramnä,* with Pkt *-i-* instead of vṛddhi *-ai-*.[15])

The confusion of names in the stock list of heretical texts found in several places in the cties ascribed to Buddhaghosa, viz. *vetulla-piṭakaṃ* (Spk II 202), *vedalla-* (Sv 566, Mp III 160), *vedaḷha-* (Sp 742) indicates that the sources which Buddhaghosa followed were similarly dependent upon Pkt sources. Another point which must be considered in connection with the presence of the Vetulyakas in Ceylon is the fact that although Mhvs 36.41 calls the heretics *Vetullavādins,* in the earlier account of this same matter in Dpvs (22.43–45) they are called *Vitaṇḍa-vādas.* In Skt *vitaṇḍa* does not seem to be used of any particular sect, and in Pāli it is used rather in the sense of "sophist, arguer", e.g. in *Atthasālinī* 3 the *vitaṇḍa-vāda* objects to the *Kathāvatthu* being ascribed to the Buddha because tradition tells that it was composed 218 years after the Buddha's death. The *Maṇidīpa,* however, a late sub-cty on *Atthasālinī* quoted by Pe Maung Tin (p. 5 note 3), states that the *Vitaṇḍa-vādins* were sectarians of Abhayagiri and Jetavana. Perhaps the most cogent reason for thinking that the Vetullapiṭaka was not in Skt is simply that when Buddhaghosa condemns it as being *abuddhavacanaṃ* (Spk II 202) he does not give what would have been the most obvious proof, namely that it was not in the Buddha's own language, i.e. Māgadhī.

Buddhaghosa and Sanskrit

We must consider the question of whether Buddhaghosa knew Skt. If the tradition is correct in stating that he was a brahman (Mhvs 37.215), then he must have done so. The palpable errors in some of the etymologies he proposes and his mistake in the statement about the origin of the castes from the different parts of Brahma's body have led Kosambi to state (p. xii–xiii) that he was not a brahman. These objections have no force once it is realised that Buddhaghosa was giving, not his own ideas, but the material in the Sinhalese *aṭṭhakathās.* Evidence is not lacking in Buddhaghosa's cties for a knowledge of Skt, although there is of course no way of proving conclusively that this was not also taken over from the Sinhalese material. Adikaram suggests (p. 4)

[15]) Information received from H. W. Bailey in a letter of 5 December 1973.

that some of the Sinhalese teachers were conversant with Skt, although there is no direct evidence for this.

Assuming that he did not borrow from his predecessors, we can say that Buddhaghosa had some acquaintance with Skt literature. He refers to the *Rāmāyaṇa*[16]) (once by the name *Sītāharaṇa*, which is also found in the *Mahāvyutpatti*)[17]) and the *Mahābhārata*,[18]) and knows of the author Masurakkha and the fact that he wrote a *nītisattha*.[19]) He also knows more about the Vedas than one would expect a non-brahman to know, e.g. that the Veda was translated into Skt[20]) (showing knowledge of the distinction between Vedic and Classical Skt), and also into the Andhaka and Damiḷa languages.[21]) In Sp 170 and elsewhere he quotes a verse listing the usages of *āmeṇḍita* (re-iteration) which seems to be a quotation from an (unknown) Skt grammarian. We find what seems to be a reminiscence of Pāṇini in Vism 491,[22]) and in Pj II 43 (which may not be by Buddhaghosa) a discussion about the ending *-āmase* which he relates to the Skt ending *-āmasi*, although he quotes the view of the *aṭṭhakathācariyas* that *se* is a particle and the meaning is (*car*)*ema se*. In another text attributed to Buddhaghosa, i. e. Pj I, we find a number of references to Skt grammarians,[23]) but since the number of such references is unparalleled in other cties by, or attributed to, Buddhaghosa this probably supports the view put forward by Adikaram (p. 8) that the two Pj cties were not by the same man, and Pj I, at least, was not by Buddhaghosa.

Why did Buddhaghosa write in Pāli?

We know from Mhvs 37.225 that Buddhaghosa wrote a cty on Dhs, called *Atthasālinī*, while he was still in India. This raises the interesting, but unanswerable question, of what language Dhs and the cty were in, for we have no direct evidence for the existence of a canon in Pāli in N. India in the fifth century A. D. Tradition also tells us that there were no cties available in India at that time, and so the thera Revata suggested to Buddhaghosa that he went to Ceylon and translated the Sīhaḷa cties into Māgadhī (Mhvs 37.230). There is no reason to doubt that the reason

---

[16]) For *Rāmāyaṇa* see Sv I 84, Ps III 95; for *Sītāharaṇa* see VbhA 490.

[17]) See J. W. de Jong, An old Tibetan version of the Rāmāyaṇa, in: T'oung Pao 58 (1972), p. 191.

[18]) Called *Bhārata* in Sv I 84, Ps III 95, and *Bhārata-yuddha* in Sv I 76, VbhA 409.

[19]) *khatta-vijjā ti, Aṅgeyya-Māsurakkhādi nīti-satthaṃ* (Sv I 93).

[20]) See K. R. Norman, Middle Indo-Aryan Studies VIII, in: Journal of the Oriental Institute (Baroda), 1971, pp. 329–31.

[21]) *yathā hi desabhāsākusalo tiṇṇaṃ vedānaṃ atthasaṃvaṇṇako ācariyo, ye Damiḷabhāsāya vutte atthaṃ jānanti, tesaṃ Damiḷabhāsāya ācikkhati, ye Andhabhāsādisu aññatarāya, tesaṃ tāya bhāsāya* (Ps I 137–8).

[22]) See Harināth De, A reminiscence of Pāṇini V. 2. 93, in: JPTS 1906–7, pp. 172–3.

[23]) See Ñāṇamoli, Minor Readings and Illustrator, London (PTS) 1960, Index of Proper Names, s.vv. Pāṇini (p. 310) and Sanskrit (p. 311).

for his visit to Ceylon was because the cty tradition there was better than in India. Doubtless the story in Mhvs is based upon a statement made by Buddhaghosa himself and added to the stock of material which formed the basis for the later portion of Mhvs, although whether his statement was a half-truth or the whole truth is debatable.

We learn from Mp V 98 that Buddhaghosa had been to Kāñcipura before arriving in Ceylon, and presumably the cty tradition was no better there than in N. India. If the Atthasālinī really was written in India it must have been rewritten to some extent in Ceylon, for we find a statement at the beginning of that text that the Sinhalese cties had been translated into Māgadhī, and it also includes some references to Sp and Vism, although Sp (150) also quotes from Atthasālinī, and VbhA (43, 479) refers to it as the cty which should be consulted for certain explanations.[24])

Buddhaghosa's own reason for writing in Pāli is given in Sp 2: "Because that cty has been composed in the language of the island of Ceylon, and the monks outside the island cannot understand the meaning of it, I shall now begin this cty in conformity with the style of the canonical texts (i. e. in Pāli)." A similar remark is made at DhA I 1, although DhA is probably not by Buddhaghosa. The claim is sometimes made that the translation into Pāli was made inevitable by the threat which was posed by the spread of Skt in Ceylon,[25]) but I have given reasons for thinking that Skt was not as widely used in Ceylon in the fifth century A. D. as others have suggested.

I see no reason for ignoring the truth of Buddhaghosa's own statement. From what we know of Sinhalese Pkt in the fifth century A. D. it would probably be unintelligible to non-Sinhalese speakers. In fact Sīhaḷa is given as an example (Pj II 397) of a *milakkha-bhāsā* (non-Indo-Aryan language), and Jayawickrama's statement (p. xx) that Buddhaghosa pays tribute to the Sinhalese language, calling it 'a delightful language' is based upon a mis-translation.[26]) If the cties were unintelligible in Sinhalese, then Pāli was the obvious language to use, since anyone who could read the Pāli canon would also be able to read the cties. Buddhaghosa's statement, however, raises a question. Where outside the island did the monks live to whom the newly translated cties would be intelligible? We may assume that some of them, at least, lived in S. India, e.g. at Kāñcipura where in due course Dhammapāla was to be born. Additional evidence for the use of Pāli in S. India comes perhaps from the statement at the beginning of JA (I 1) that the author of the cty

---

[24]) *seso tesaṃ tesaṃ khandhānaṃ kusalādivibhāgo heṭṭhā Dhammasaṅgahaṭṭhakathāyaṃ vutto yeva* (VbhA 43); *cetaso līnattaniddeso heṭṭhā Dhammasaṅgahaṭṭhakathāyaṃ vuttattho yeva* (VbhA 479).

[25]) See Ñāṇamoli, Minor Readings and Illustrator, p. 285 n. 40.

[26]) *apanetvāna tato 'haṃ Sīhaḷabhāsaṃ manoramaṃ bhāsaṃ tantinayānucchavikaṃ āropento vigatadosaṃ* (Sv I 1). The sense demands that we take *manoramaṃ bhāsaṃ* as the object of *āropento,* not of *apanetvāna.* DAṬ I 20 makes this clear: *manoramaṃ bhāsan ti, Magadhabhāsaṃ.*

(reputedly, but probably not, Buddhaghosa) wrote it at the request of Buddhadeva of the Mahiṃsāsaka sect. The only other evidence we have for the existence of this sect in Ceylon at this time is the statement by Fa-hsien (Legge, p. 111) that he obtained in Ceylon a copy of the *Vinaya-piṭaka* of the Mahīśāsakāḥ school.[27]) The statement by the author of JA implies that the Mahiṃsāsakas in Ceylon possesssed the Jātaka (presumably in Pāli) and wanted a Pāli cty upon it. The Mahīśāsakas were strong in S. India, and if the followers of that sect in Ceylon made use of Pāli, perhaps those in S. India did too. It is reported that there was a Sinhalese Saṅghārāma at the Bodhi-maṇḍapa (Malalasekera, PLC p. 87), and it is possible that they used Pāli too.

Buddhaghosa and Pāli

Buddhaghosa's works are regarded by some as the turning point between the ancient and modern epoch of Pāli literature in Ceylon. Oldenberg (p. 7) thought that the Dpvs betrayed the characteristics of an age in which the Sinhalese first tried to write in Pāli. Once Buddhaghosa had shown the way, the author of the Mhvs was able to master Pāli grammar and style with a perfect ease. It is true that Dpvs is, for the most part, written in Pāli of a poor quality, and it is tempting to think that the much higher standard of Pāli in Mhvs is due to the appearance of Buddhaghosa's cties in the intervening period. To come to this conclusion, however, is to ignore the style in which Buddhaghosa wrote. His style is what we might call "later Pāli", showing an avoidance of archaic forms and the development of secondary forms, e.g. present participles in *-anta-* instead of the more historic forms found in earlier Pāli. To evolve such a style by himself would have demanded a modern view of the development of Pāli, i.e. an ability to distinguish between chronological layers, and to select only the later ones. It is clear that Buddhaghosa could not have done this, but must have been following a tradition. Although I have earlier cast doubt upon some of the accepted ideas about the usage of Pāli in Ceylon there can be no doubt that in Buddhaghosa's time there must have been a living tradition of writing in Pāli and he was merely one of a series of writers who made use of the style employed by his predecessors. We do not know who his predecessors were, but we know some of the books they wrote.

The *Milindapañha* is generally dated to the first century A. D.,[28]) and there is some evidence that it was composed in N. India, probably in a N. Indian Pkt. Somewhere, either in India or Ceylon, the task of

[27]) It is, however, very plausibly suggested by H. Bechert (W. Geiger, Culture of Ceylon in Mediaeval Times, Wiesbaden 1960, p. 208 n. 1) that, since there is no other mention of Mahāsaṅghikas in Ceylon, *Mahāsaṃghikabhikkhūnaṃ* in Mhvs 50. 68 should probably be read as *Mahiṃsāsakabhikkhūnaṃ*, thus giving evidence for the existence of the sect in Ceylon in the ninth century.

[28]) See. M. Winternitz, p. 175.

translating it into Pāli must have been accomplished. Similarly, an Indian origin has been deduced for the *Nettipakaraṇa*, and its date of origin may well have been about the first century A. D.[29]) Unless it was composed in Pāli (which would give evidence for the use of Pāli in N. India at that time), it too must have been translated from some Indian dialect. Since the *Peṭakopadesa* is said to be older than the *Nettipakaraṇa*,[30]) the same must apply to that text too. Mention has already been made of the *Vimuttimagga*, whose composition also, in all probability, predates Buddhaghosa. It is clear from the existence of these major works that it cannot be correct to regard the Dpvs as the first attempt to write Pāli. It would seem more likely that the poor quality of that composition was simply due to lack of ability on the part of the author.

After Buddhaghosa

The *Buddhaghosuppatti* (p. 7) states that the cties given by Mahinda and the additions thereto were burned in a great bonfire when Buddhaghosa had finished his cties. Although this has been recognised as being merely an exaggerated way of saying that the Sinhalese cties fell into disuse, there is evidence to show that the earlier cties were not, in fact, completely superseded. It is clear that the cties which Buddhaghosa used to write the historical introduction to Sp were not destroyed, for they were available to the author of Mhvs and even to the writer of MhvsṬ some centuries later.[31]) The same applies to the cties on canonical texts. MhvsṬ refers to the *Sīhaḷa-aṭṭhakathā* on the *Majjhima-nikāya* and includes information not given in *Papañcasūdanī* (MhvsṬ 193, 305). The Ṭīkā on *Sāratthappakāsinī* includes a reading for M I 255,16 (quoted at Spk I 13,29) which is not only not given by Buddhaghosa,[32]) but which shows by its form *ahunā* (< *adhunā*) = *idān' eva* that it was taken from a dialect other than Sinhalese and Pāli, probably a N. Indian Pkt, and perhaps even from a cty brought over by Mahinda. Nevertheless, at some unknown date the Sinhalese *aṭṭhakathās* must have fallen completely into disuse, and they seem now to be irretrievably lost. Only the Pāli cties which were based upon them are now extant.

References

1. Texts

(All references, except Dpvs, are to PTS editions)

DAṬ	Dīghanikāyaṭṭhakathāṭīkā
Dh(A)	Dhammapada (Aṭṭhakathā)

---

[29]) See M. Winternitz, p. 183.

[30]) See Ñāṇamoli, The Piṭaka-disclosure, London (PTS) 1964, p. XII.

[31]) Malalasekera (MhvsṬ p. cix) dates the text to the eighth or ninth century.

[32]) Both PTS editions read *ahu tañ ñeva aññatarassa*. Spk-pṭ (Be 1961) 41, 25 reads *ahunā idān' eva*. (Information received from L. S. Cousins in a letter of 25 December 1973).

Dhs	Dhammasaṅgaṇi
Dpvs	Dīpavaṃsa
JA	Jātaka-aṭṭhakathā
KvuA	Kathāvatthu-aṭṭhakathā
M	Majjhimanikāya
Mhvs	Mahāvaṃsa
MhvsṬ	Mahāvaṃsa-aṭṭhakathā (= *Malalasekera* 1935)
Mp	Manorathapūraṇī
Paṭis-A	Paṭisambhidāmagga-aṭṭhakathā
Pj	Paramatthajotikā
Ps	Papañcasūdanī
Sn	Suttanipāta
Sp	Samantapāsādikā
Spk(pṭ)	Sāratthappakāsinī(purāṇaṭikā)
Sv	Sumaṅgalavilāsinī
Thag	Theragāthā
VbhA	Vibhaṅga-aṭṭhakathā
Vin	Vinaya
Vism	Visuddhimagga

2. Books

(The titles quoted here are referred to by name of the author and year of publication only).

Adikaram, E. W.: Early History of Buddhism in Ceylon. 2nd impr., Colombo 1953.

Bareau, A.: Les sectes bouddhiques du petit véhicule. Saigon 1955.

Beal, S.: Buddhist records of the Western world. London 1884.

Brough, J.: The Gāndhārī Dharmapada. London 1962.

Childers, R. C.: Dictionary of the Pali language. London 1875.

Geiger, W.: The Dīpavaṃsa and Mahāvaṃsa. Colombo 1908.

— Grammar of the Sinhalese Language. Colombo 1938.

— The Mahāvaṃsa (translated into English). 2nd ed., Colombo 1950.

Gray, J.: Buddhaghosuppatti. London 1892.

Jayawickrama, N. J.: Inception of Discipline. London 1962.

Karunaratne, W. S.: Unpublished Brāhmī inscriptions of Ceylon (unpublished dissertation approved for the Ph. D. degree). Cambridge n.d.

Kosambi, D.: Visuddhimagga. Cambridge, Mass. 1950.

Legge, J.: Record of Buddhistic kingdoms. Repr., New York 1965.

Malalasekera, G. P.: Pāli literature of Ceylon. London 1928.

— Vaṃsatthappakāsinī. 2 vols., London 1935.

— Dictionary of Pāli Proper Names. Repr., London 1960.

Maung Tin, Pe: The Expositor. 2 vols., London 1920–21.

Oldenberg, H.: Dīpavaṃsa. London 1879.

Paranavitana, S.: University of Ceylon History of Ceylon. Vol. I, pt. i, Colombo 1959.

Rahula, W.: History of Buddhism in Ceylon. Colombo 1956.

Rhys Davids, C. A. F.: Buddhist Manual of Psychological Ethics. 3rd ed., London 1974.

Takakusu, J.: A record of the Buddhist religion. Repr., Delhi 1966.

Winternitz, M.: History of Indian Literature, Vol. II, Buddhist literature and Jain literature. Calcutta 1933.

3. General abbreviations

AMg	Ardha-Māgadhī
Be	Burmese edition
BPE	Mrs. C. A. F. Rhys Davids 1974
BSOAS	Bulletin of the School of Oriental and African Studies
CPD	Critical Pāli Dictionary
cty/cties	commentary/commentaries
DPPN	Malalasekera 1960
JPTS	Journal of the Pali Text Society
JRAS	Journal of the Royal Asiatic Society
Pkt	Prakrit
PLC	Malalasekera 1928
PTS	Pali Text Society
Skt	Sanskrit
WZKSO	Wiener Zeitschrift für die Kunde Süd- und Ostasiens

On the Tradition of Pāli Texts in India, Ceylon and Burma

By OSKAR VON HINÜBER

vicitranayaṃ hi Bhagavato pāvacanaṃ
Aggavaṃsa, Saddanīti 627. 16

The foundation of any philological investigation into a written text is the wording of that text as handed down by tradition. This selfevident statement means that we have to ascertain whether the wording of the text, as we have it today, reflects what has been written down by the author himself, or, if not, how much time intervenes between the autograph and our manuscripts. While editors, for example, or any literature written within the last few centuries in Europe are mostly lucky enough to possess early prints, perhaps contemporaneous to the author,[1]) sometimes even his autograph, this happy coincidence does not mark the situation an editor of older literature, say in Greek or Latin,[2]) is in. On the contrary, editors of texts belonging to the European or to the Indian antiquity have before themselves copies mostly separated by centuries, if not by more than a millennium, from the autograph.

The big gap between the first redaction of our Pāli-canon and the basis of the texts as we have them today, becomes evident at once, if we bear in mind that there is no manuscript older than about 400 years,[3]) with the only exception, as far as I know, of a tenth century Vinaya-fragment in Pāli found in Nepal.[4])

Thus the editors of this kind of text have to content themselves with the reconstruction of the archetypus of all our manuscripts, which might be quite far away in time from the autograph, or as we should rather put it in most cases when dealing with Indian texts, from the text as formulated by a teacher. The first task of an editor, therefore, should be to find out where and when his archetypus was written.

Now, as far as the canonical Pāli[5]) texts are concerned, we are in a very similar position to an editor of Homer, i.e. we do not know either

---

[1]) On the special problems of editing recent texts: Texte und Varianten, Probleme ihrer Edition und Interpretation, hg. v. G. Martens und H. Zeller, München 1971.

[2]) On editing these texts: P. Maas, Textkritik, Leipzig[3] 1957.

[3]) H. Smith, Saddanīti, La grammaire palie d'Aggavaṃsa, Lund 1928, Avant-propos, p. V.

[4]) Cf. P. V. Bapat, A Pāli manuscript in an Indian Script, in: Annals of the Bhandarkar Oriental Research Institute 33, 1952, pp. 197–210.

[5]) On editing Indian texts cf. W. Kirfel, Textüberlieferung und Textkritik in der indischen Philologie, in: Litterae Orientales 45, Leipzig 1931, pp. 1–11 and S. M. Katre, Introduction to Indian textual criticism, [2]Poona 1954.

the author or the exact time, from which the text tradition started. Many a Pāli text continued to grow over the centuries. Thus, just as an editor handling Homer cannot go back beyond the redaction of Aristarch and Zenodot in Alexandria, we cannot go back beyond the council held at the Aluvihāra (Ālokavihāra) under Vaṭṭagāmaṇī Abhaya (29–17 B. C.), where the Pāli canon was written down for the first time in Ceylon. This is the very starting point of our tradition handed down to us by the monks of the Mahāvihāra. About recensions of the Pāli canon different from the Mahāvihāra tradition and deviating from its wording, such as the one handed down by the monks of the Abhayagirivihāra, we scarcely have any knowledge at all.[6])

Although as a rule we cannot go back beyond the Aluvihāra council text, we may come much nearer to the original wording of the *gāthās* in the canon by applying the methods developed and used very successfully by S. Lévi, H. Lüders and others.[7]) The mechanisms of the translation from the eastern Language, as Lüders calls it,[8]) pave the way for reconstructing quite a lot of the original wording of the *gāthās*. The question, which has to be answered by an editor is: how are those eastern forms to be dealt with in editions, say of the Jātakagāthās?

This question can be answered by quoting an example. In the eastern dialect at the time when the *gāthās* were put together, there were surviving a very few reduplicated aorists of the root *pat*: *apaptat*. As forms like *ajjhapattā* < *adhyapaptat* or *udapattā* < *udapaptat* were non-existent in the western dialect, they were consequently misunderstood as past participles. Thus the ending *-ā* had to be adjusted to *-o*, where there is a masculine subject, but it survived, if the subject was of feminine gender.

As we find an absolutive *ajjhapattvā* in the Buddhavaṃsa already, we can date the misunderstanding to a fairly early time. That *ajjhapatta*

---

[6]) Cf. H. Bechert, Zur Geschichte der buddhistischen Sekten in Indien und Ceylon, in: La Nouvelle Clio 7–9, 1955–1957, pp. 311–360, especially pp. 351ff. On the Parivāra of the Abhayagirivāsins cf. below, pp. 58–60 in the present volume.

[7]) H. Lüders, Beobachtungen über die Sprache des buddhistischen Urkanons, hg. v. E. Waldschmidt. Berlin 1954 (Abh. d. Deutschen Akad. d. Wiss. zu Berlin, Kl. f. Sprachen, Lit. u. Kunst. Jg. 1952 Nr. 10).

[8]) Lüders originally called this language Old Ardhamāgadhī: Bruchstücke buddhistischer Dramen, Berlin 1911, p. 41 and "Epigraphische Beiträge III" (1913), in: Philologica Indica, Göttingen 1940, p. 288. Still later he says: "Dieser Dialekt (i.e. des Urkanons) stimmt im wesentlichen mit der Māgadhī der Aśoka-Inschriften überein" (1927) quoted in Beobachtungen zur Sprache des buddhistischen Urkanons, p. 8. I am not sure whether Lüders changed his opinion on the name of the language, or whether this "Māgadhī of the Aśoka inscriptions" is to be understood as "Old Ardhamāgadhī". In the last book published during his life-time, Lüders dropped any definite name of this language and simply states "... daß die Texte des Pali-Kanons aus einem in der Volkssprache des östlichen Indiens abgefaßten Kanon übersetzt sind", Bhārhut und die buddhistische Literatur (Abhandlungen für die Kunde des Morgenlandes XXVI. 3), Leipzig 1941 (repr. Nendeln 1966), p. 173.

as a past participle became part of the Pāli language is further corroborated by the Dhammapadaṭṭhakathā, where this word is used. Thus this is a good example for separating the different strata of the Pāli language: The eastern dialects had the correct aorist, misunderstood by the speakers of the western dialect, but, as it seems, not used as a past participle by them. Once Pāli was a dead language, as at the time of the commentaries, an author could draw upon the material found in the canon and so *ajjhapatta* was used by the author of Dhammapadaṭṭhakathā.[9])

As the absolutive *ajjhapatvā* in the Buddhavaṃsa shows, there can be hardly any doubt that at the time of the fixing of the Pāli canon in the Aluvihāra, the past participle *ajjhapatta* was felt to be part of the Pāli language. Thus it rightly finds its place in our edition; to print the pre-first century B. C. form in this particular case, viz. *ajjhapattā*, would mean mixing up two entirely different strata of our tradition. As it is impossible to reconstruct the Jātaka-gāthās as a whole in the original wording of the eastern dialect, the traces of this dialect should, when found, be put into a commentary on the edition, but should not be incorporated into the text itself.

The writing down of the canon in the Aluvihāra is the starting point of a tradition in Ceylon, where a number of texts were handed down from the first century B.C. in direct line to the present day. The most important stages, at which our texts underwent certain changes, are the different redactions of the canon, when commentaries were written. The first stage is the translation of the Sīhala-Aṭṭhakathā into Pāli by Buddhaghosa, Dhammapāla and others in the 5th/6th centuries. Very little is known about the development of the text tradition between the Aluvihāra council and the rewriting of the commentaries. It was the time of the coming into existence of the recension of the Abhayagirivāsins, only slightly different from the Mahāvihāra recension.[10])

The importance of the Aṭṭhakathā is twofold. First, if the wording of the *mūla*-text is quoted as a *pratīka*, it was generally fixed once for all. Secondly, the commentators sometimes kept alive variant readings, which otherwise would have been superseded by the tradition. The age of these various readings is difficult to ascertain. They may have their origin in Ceylon or even go back much farther into the past, that is to

---

[9]) On *ajjhapatta, udapatta* see my article: Reste des reduplizierten Aorists im Pāli, in: Münchner Studien zur Sprachwissenschaft 32, 1974, pp. 65–72. — Perhaps the aorists *apattha* Jātaka 5.391.21 and *pāpattha* Jātaka 5.255.20 are to be understood as reduplicated aorists: *apaptat, prāpaptat,* too, rebuilt on the model of *alattha,* cf. W. Geiger, Pāli, § 159 III; *mā laddhā* is, by the way, no aorist, as claimed by Geiger, but an absolutive. The verseis to be read: *patim aladdhā* Jātaka 3.138.21 instead of *patiṃ mā laddhā*; the manuscripts have *patimāladdhā,* the commentary paraphrases the verse: *patiṃ alabhitvā.*

[10]) On the development of Buddhism in Ceylon, up to the 5th century: E. W. Adikaram, Early History of Buddhism in Ceylon, Colombo 1946.

the time, when the texts were handed down in India. This may be illustrated by the vacillation of the tradition between *uppacca* and *upecca*.

The following verse occurs four times in the canon, in the Saṃyuttanikāya (SN), Therīgāthā (Thī), Udāna (Ud), and Petavatthu (Pv) with slight variants. It is furthermore quoted in Peṭakopadesa (Peṭ), Nettippakaraṇa (Nett), and Dhammapadaṭṭhakathā (Dhp-a):

> *sace va pāpakaṃ kammaṃ karissasi karosi vā*
> *na te dukkhā pamuty atthi uppaccā pi palāyato* SN 1.209.5f.

> "If evil thou now doest or wilt do, thou'lt not escape from pain and misery, though thou spring up and run in headlong flight." (C. A. F. Rhys Davids)

The controversial word is *uppacca* 'having flown up', which is treated differently by the commentaries. The Saṃyuttanikāya-commentary, the Sāratthappakāsinī (Spk) is clear: *uppaccāpīti uppatitvā* Spk 1.307.22. No variant is quoted; *uppatitvā ti ākāse uppatitvā* Spk-ṭ Be 1956 further supports this reading. The verse together with its context is quoted in the Dhammapadaṭṭhakathā from Saṃyuttanikāya:[11])

> *sace va pāpakaṃ kammaṃ karissasi karosi vā*
> *na te dukkhā pamokkh' atthi uppaccāpi*[12]) *palāyato* Dhp-a 4.21.16f.

This verse is paraphrased as: *evaṃ pāpakaṃ kammaṃ katvā sakuṇassa viya uppatitvā palāyato pi te mokkho natthi* Dhp-a 4.22.1f. Thus there does not seem to be any problem: a simple *gāthā* commented upon correctly by the Aṭṭhakathā. Although the edition of the Saṃyuttanikāya Be agrees with Ee, there is a very strange variant from the one Burmese manuscript used by L. Feer while editing the Saṃyuttanikāya:[13]) *upecca* instead of *uppacca*. The reading *upecca* is the only one in the Therīgāthā, a text which is based on the Burmese tradition only[14]):

> *sace ca pāpakaṃ kammaṃ karissasi karosi vā*
> *na te dukkhā pamuty atthi upeccāpi*[15]) *palāyato* Thī 247c–248b

---

[11]) Dhp-a quotes SN rather frequently: E. W. Burlingame, Buddhist Legends, Vol. I (Harvard Oriental Series 28), Cambridge/Mass. 1921 (repr. London 1969), pp. 45f.

[12]) Ee has *pamokkhanti* with v.r. °*ttha* in the Cambodian manuscript. Later editions (Be 1956, Ce 1956) have *pamuty* in accordance with the wording of the canonical texts. Comparing Peṭ 44. 21, however, *pamokkhanti* seems to be a corruption of *pamokkh'atthi*, which should be adopted in the light of the prose paraphrase *mokkho natthi*, too. The editor of Be 1903 reads *uppatitvā* instead of *uppaccāpi* in the verse following the wording of the prose. — *pamuty* < *pamutti* as *ratyā* Th 517 for *rattiyā*, *mutyapekkho* Sn 344 for *mutti-apekkho* or *khatyā* for *khattiyā* Ja 6. 397. 1.

[13]) For SN we have a genuine Sinhalese tradition, independent from the Burmese tradition: Preface to SN I (Ee), pp. XIIIf. and below.

[14]) R. Pischel, Introduction to Ee, p. 120.

[15]) The reading *upacca* in the manuscripts P (burm.) and S (singh.) are simple mistakes for *upecca*, as only one -*p*- is written.

Thī-a confirms *upecca*: *nirayādīsu catūsu apāyesu manussesu ca tassa phalabhūtaṃ dukkhaṃ ito etto vā palāyante mayi nānubandhissatīti adhippāyena upecca sañcicca palāyato pi te tato pāpato mutti mokkho atthi ... uppaccāti*[16]) *vā pāṭho uppatitvā ti attho* and gives at the same time the variant *uppacca*, the reading which should have been the original one.[17])

Corresponding to the Therīgāthā we find in the Petavatthu:

> *sace taṃ pāpakaṃ kammaṃ karissatha karotha vā*
> *na vo dukkhā pamutt' atthi uppaccāpi palāyataṃ*[18]) Pv 236 (B^e 244)

B^e (1956) has the readings *upecca* in *ka*, which may represent the text of the 5th council under Mindon in Burma[19]) 1868–71, that is, an old Burmese tradition. In Pv-a, on the other hand, in B^e (1956) *uppacca* is the only reading attested for the *pratīka*: *uppaccā pi palāyatan ti uppatitvā ākāsena gacchantānam pi mokkho natthi yevāti attho, upeccāti pi pāṭho* (E^e: *pāli*). *ito vā etto vā palāyante tumhe anubandhissatīti adhippāyena upecca sañcicca palāyantānam pi tumhākaṃ tato mokkho natthi*. The situation as to the readings, is in the Petavatthu thus exactly opposite to the Therīgāthā. Yet both of them do accept *upecca* and *uppacca* as alternative readings, whereas the Udāna tradition is restricted to *upecca*:

> *sace va pāpakaṃ kammaṃ karissatha karotha vā*
> *na vo dukkhā pamuty*[20]) *atthi upeccāpi palāyataṃ* Ud 51.17f.

While the manuscript A (burm.) in E^e reads *upacca*[21]) B (sgh.) *upadhāya* and D (sgh.) *upaddava*, the text given in E^e is in accordance with the Udāna commentary: *ito vā etto vā palāyante amhe nānubandhissatīti adhippāyena upecca sañcicca*[22]) *palāyantānam pi tumhākaṃ tato mutti mokkho natthi* Ud-a 295.14ff.

In the post-canonical Pāli literature this verse is quoted twice:

> *sace hi pāpakaṃ kammaṃ karosi vā karissasi*
> *na te dukkhā pamokkh' atthi upeccā pi palāyato* Peṭ 44.20f.

The readings in E^e are *upeccāpi* in B_2, *upaccāpi* in B_1, B_3, S and B^e 1956 has *upaccāpi* s.v. l. And:

> *sace va pāpakaṃ kammaṃ karissatha karotha vā*
> *na vo dukkhā pamuty atthi upeccāpi palāyataṃ* Nett 131.19f.

---

[16]) E^e w.r. *upaccāti vā pāṭho upanetvā*.

[17]) Cf. K. R. Norman, The Elders verses II: Therīgāthā, London 1971 on this *gāthā*.

[18]) V.r.: Pv-a (B^e 1956): ka: *te* instead of *vo*. E^e has *upacchāpi palāyitaṃ* following the corrupt Sinhalese tradition, while the Burmese manuscripts have *uppaccāpi*, once *upeccāpi*, and *palāyataṃ*.

[19]) Cf. W. B. Bollée, Some less known Burmese Pāli texts, in: Pratidānam, Festschrift F. B. J. Kuiper, Den Haag 1968, p. 496.

[20]) E^e *mutty*, cf. ct.

[21]) This is the reading of *ka* in B^e 1956.

[22]) B^e 1956 *upecca apecca* with v.l. *sañcicca* in *sī*, *syā*.

with Nettivibhāvinī (15th century): *evaṃ sati upeccāpi sañcicca palāyataṃ* ... In both quotations nothing points to an old variant *uppacca*.

When examining this material, it seems evident that there were two traditions of the wording of the verse. In the Saṃyuttanikāya text *uppacca* is the only reading accepted, the only sign of *upecca* found is in the Burmese manuscript in E^e, which almost certainly is influenced by the parallels, which have *upecca*.

In the Khuddakanikāya texts (Thī, Ud, Pv) the tradition is anything but uniform. Although the wording of Dhammapāla's explanations in the different parts of his Paramatthadīpanī is almost identical, there is a certain fluctuation as to the readings *uppacca* or *upecca*. These differences, which Dhammapāla did not suppress, most likely reflect the Sīhala-Aṭṭhakathā at Dhammapāla's disposal, for it would have been very easy to reconcile the conflicting readings by simply accepting the one or the other. We should be thankful to Dhammapāla that he showed so much respect for the tradition as handed down to him.

Thus the variants may be looked upon as readings older than the Paramatthadīpanī; but how much older? In ascertaining the date the quotations in the Peṭakopadesa and the Nettippakaraṇa may prove to be helpful. If the general view, that the Peṭakopadesa, being older than Nettippakaraṇa, was written about the first century B. C.[23]), is correct, the variant *upecca* may be a very old one, going back even beyond the text of the Aluvihāra council.

Before we can take this age for granted, we must have a closer look at the tradition of the Peṭakopadesa and the Nettippakaraṇa. For both texts there is no genuine Sinhalese tradition; both texts were reintroduced to Ceylon from Burma, as pointed out by E. Hardy and Ñāṇamoli.[24])

The dependence of a tradition on a Burmese archetypus can be inferred by miswriting typical only of the Burmese script. If, for example, in Peṭ 170.8 the more corrupt family of manuscripts represented by S, B_1 has instead of the correct *anugacchati*: S *antigacchati* but B_1 *antaṃgacchati*, this misreading, *i* instead of *anusvāra*, is possible only in Burmese script. The only manuscript in Sinhalese characters used for E^e of the Peṭakopadesa thus clearly is a copy of a Burmese manuscript.

Further, as Ñāṇamoli found out, a leaf of the Sumangalavilāsinī (Sv) intruded into a manuscript of Peṭ (Peṭ 239.8–240.19 = Sv 971.27–973.4), which was placed by mistake into the archetypus of all our Peṭakopadesa-manuscripts and consequently copied unnoticed even by all modern editors of this text. This leaf of the Sumangalavilāsinī in the Peṭakopadesa has two readings in common with the Burmese tradition of the Sumangalavilāsinī: Peṭ 239.14 *aṭṭakā* against *aṭṭhakā*

[23]) Ñāṇamoli, The Guide, London 1962, p. XXVIII, and The Piṭaka-Disclosure, London 1964, p. XI; cf. E. Lamotte, Le traité de la grande vertu de sagesse, Louvain 1949, I, p. 109 n. 2.

[24]) Nett (E^e), Introduction, p. XXXVIII; Piṭaka-Disclosure, p. XIII.

Sv 972.1, and Peṭ 240.12 °*paṭa*° against Sv 972.32 °*paddha*°. The third Burmese reading Sv 972.24 °*vatthehi* against manuscript B °*vaṭṭehi* is not found in the Peṭakopadesa by a mistake of the copist. Thus manuscript B in E[e] and the leaf of Sumangalavilāsinī in the Peṭakopadesa follow an identical tradition.

If the Peṭakopadesa-archetypus stems from Burma, it cannot be older than the Aṭṭhakathā.[25]) This means that it can reflect in adopting *upecca* instead of *uppacca* a rather recent view of the Burmese tradition, which seems to be prone to adopting *upecca*. This variant, however, seems to be very old in spite of the relatively recent date of the starting point of our Peṭ-tradition. For if we compare a text of Northern Buddhism, we read in Mahāvastu (Mv)

atha teṣāṃ chavimānsaṃ rudhiraṃ copajāyate
te ca bhītvā utpatitvāna alenā lenasaṃjñinā Mv III 456.4

'Then their skin and flesh and blood begin to grow once more. In their terror they run away, thinking there was shelter where there was none.' (J. J. Jones)

with a close parallel in Mv I 11.15, where all manuscripts have a form of *upeti*: BNAL: *upetitvāna* and CM *upentitvāna* (rather: *upettitvāna*?). As one *-p-* only is written, this can hardly be just a copist's error. The vacillation between *upetyā* and *utpatyā* thus proves to be common to both the northern and the southern traditions.

With the reading *upecca*, and *pamokkha*, which is close to the Udānavarga (Uv)

sa cet pāpāni karmāṇi kariṣyasi karoṣi vā
na te duḥkhāt pramokṣo'sti hy utplutyāpi pralāyataḥ Uv 9.4,

the Peṭakopadesa seems to bridge the gap between the northern and the southern texts. The Peṭakopadesa was most probably written in India at a fairly early date, perhaps even in North India.[26]) If we accept this position of the Peṭakopadesa, we may conclude that this text having *upecca* was the starting point of this reading for the Pāli tradition, which was accepted by the Khuddakabhāṇakas[27]) only. This assumption could account for the lack of any trace of *upecca* in the Saṃyuttanikāya-tradition. With a very old uncertainty common to many schools of Buddhism about the text, we should expect to find this reflected in

---

[25]) On the age of the Nettippakaraṇa (Nett) archetypus see below.

[26]) Ñāṇamoli, The Guide, p. XXVIII; Bechert, in: La Nouvelle Clio 7–9, p. 352.

[27]) Sometimes the textus receptus by the *bhāṇakas* of different parts of the canon is not identical in parallel passages. K. R. Norman draws my attention to the frequent variations in the wording of the two versions of Vangīsa's verses: Th 1209–1279 and SN 1. 185–196 in the Vangīsatherasaṃyutta. — On the *bhāṇakas* cf. H. Lüders, Bhārhut und die buddhistische Literatur, Leipzig 1941 (AKM), pp. 175f. and E. W. Adikaram, Early history, pp. 24ff.

all texts, not only in a part of them. The northern tradition rejecting *utpatya*, as the substitute *utplutya*[28]) in the Udānavarga attests, thus penetrated into the Southern tradition by means of a once very much used Piṭaka-handbook, i. e. the Peṭakopadesa.

As long as no more examples of this kind can be found, all these conclusions are highly conjectural. Nevertheless they can show the way the texts were handed down, and where variants might have sprung up from. It is even more difficult to find out why *utpatya*, which makes good sense in our verse, is partly shunned by the tradition[29]), and secondly why *upecca* is explained by *sañcicca* "on purpose". For *upecca* is, though not too frequent, well attested in the canon: *so sugatim upecca modati* Dīghanikāya 3.166.24 with v. l. *sugatisu pecca* in the Burmese tradition; *tuvaṃ . . . upecca vandiṃ* Vimānavatthu (Vv) 289 with Vv-a 127.25 *upeccā ti upagantvā*; *dibbaṃ sā labhate upecca ṭhānam* Vv 317 (quoted Jātaka 2.255.22) with Vv-a 146.21f. *upeccā ti upagantvā cetetvā vā. edisaṃ labbheyyan ti pakappetvā ti attho*; and several times in the Apadāna. There is no hint at a meaning differing from 'having reached' for *upecca* in canonical Pāli. This meaning, however, is not appropriate for the verse *upeccā pi palāyato*. Thus the explanation of *upecca* as *sañcicca* seems to be an ad hoc invention of the commentaries, which nevertheless kept alive a variant, which might have arisen between the introduction of the Peṭakopadesa to Ceylon and the writing down of the Aṭṭhakathā.

But the commentaries not only hand down old variants. They may even create new readings themselves, as in: *iminā pūtikāyena bhindanena pabhangunā aṭṭiyāmi* SN 1.131.11f. 'This body vile, this brittle, crumbling thing, doth touch me only with distress' (C. A. F. Rhys Davids) with Spk 1.191.30 *bhindanenā ti bhijjanasabhāvena*. The strange wordformation of *bhindana* and the fact that it is handed down by the Burmese manuscripts only, the Sinhalese having *bhindarena*, suggests that the latter may be the correct form. This is further corroborated by the parallel in Gāndhārī Dharmapada (G-Dhp) 157 *imiṇa pudikaeṇa vidvareṇa*[. It was Lüders, who, discussing the controversial *vidvareṇa*, draw the attention to the reading *bhindara*. Although the correspondence of *v*- in Gāndhārī-Prakrit to *bh*- in Pāli is difficult, there is by no means "a host of irregularities, that the suggestion (i. e. the one of Lüders quoted above) can safely be forgotten", as Brough puts it in his com-

---

[28]) As K. R. Norman suggests, *utplutya* substituted for *uppacca* might be due to a labialized **uppucca*. This would be a striking parallel to a verse discussed by L. Alsdorf, Die Āryā-Strophen des Pāli-Kanons, Wiesbaden 1968, pp. 54f.: Pāli *pannabhāra* against Mahāvastu *pūrṇabhāra* and Lalitavistara *prajñākāra*, where the once very similar *akṣaras ka* and *bha* have been mixed up, point to an underlying **paṇṇabhāra*. — These problems are discussed in detail by K. R. Norman, The labialisation of vowels in Middle Indo-Aryan, in: Studien zur Indologie und Iranistik II, 1977, pp. 41-58, esp. 51ff.

[29]) This may be due to some misunderstanding, as even Geiger, Pāli, § 86 wrongly analyses *uppaccāpi* as "*uppaccā* (statt *-ttiyā*)".

mentary on Gāndhārī Dharmapada 157[30]). For just as we have in the Uṇādisūtras *chitvara* 'scoundrel' against *chidvara* in the dictionaries (Kośa), or *chatvara* 'hut' against *chadvara*[31]) there is *vidvara* against *bhitvara* in the Saddharmapuṇḍarīka, for which see F. Edgerton, Buddhist Hybrid Sanskrit Dictionary (BHSD) s. v. *bhi(t)tvara*. Thus we should expect Pāli **bhiddara*, which might have become *bhindara* under the influence of *bhindati*. The later form *bhindana* most probably owes its existence to the explanation of the commentary by *bhijjana* with a possible formal analogy to *bandhana*. Thus the very rare *bhindara*[32]), which is replaced by *ātura* Therīgāthā 140 and Udānavarga 1.37, shows at the same time that the tradition of text and commentary may be independent from each other, and that we have a genuine Sinhalese tradition for the Saṃyuttanikāya.

If we consider the Pāli version of the Aluvihāra as the first stage of the text tradition and the Aṭṭhakathā, i. e. roughly the 5th/6th centuries as the second, a third stage is the time of the subcommentaries, the Ṭīkā, mostly written during the reign of Parakkamabāhu I. (1153–1186), or even later and Aggavaṃsa's Saddanīti, which strongly influence the text tradition.

That the Ṭīkās and their interpretation influenced the wording of the texts can be shown by an example from the Nettivibhāvinī of Saddhammapāla, who is said to have lived in Burma in the 15th century. It is in the Nettivibhāvinī that we find for the first time the absolutive *uppajja* misunderstood as an adjective. As I have discussed the grammatical problems involved elsewhere[33]), I should like to discuss this word now as a key word for the understanding of the text tradition.

As the Sāratthamañjūsā, the 12th century Ṭīkā on the Manorathapūraṇī, still has the absolutive *upapajja*, we may infer from this fact that between ca. 1150 and 1450 opinion on this word changed, and the wrong idea of taking it as a noun came into being. Thus Nettiṭīkā (Nettivibhāvinī) commenting on Nettippakaraṇa 37.14 says: *upapajje phalaṃ vedeti*, where *upapajja* clearly is a noun. This interpretation consequently leads to an alteration in the text of Nettippakaraṇa 37.15 into *diṭṭhe vā dhamme upapajje vā apare vā pariyāye*. This wrong wording, reflecting a recent change in the interpretation, is firmly rooted in the text of the Nettippakaraṇa as we have it. As the Nettivibhāvinī was written in Burma, and as we know that our archetypus of the Nettippakaraṇa is Burmese too, we may conclude that it must be younger than the Nettiṭīkā (Nettivibhāvinī), for otherwise we might expect more distinct survivals

30) J. Brough, The Gāndhārī Dharmapada, London 1962 (London Oriental Series, Vol. 7).

31) Quoted from J. Wackernagel, Altindische Grammatik II. 2, Göttingen 1954, p. 907 § 726b.

32) *bhidura*, too, is attested only once in *bhiduro kāyo* Thī 35, ct. *bhiduro*: *bhijjanabhāvo*.

33) Indo-Iranian Journal 13, 1971, pp. 241–249: Die ‚dreifache' Wirkung des Karma.

of *upapajja* in the text of the Nettippakaraṇa. Of course this conclusion needs support—or contradiction—from further observations. It shows, however, that in Pāli too we can get hints as to the date of our manuscript tradition from wrong readings.[34])

Further, the new reading *upapajje* in the Nettippakaraṇa was not without consequences for the text of the canon itself. As the wording of Nettippakaraṇa 37.17ff. is akin to Majjhimanikāya 3.214.13–16 and Anguttaranikāya 1.134.21–23, the new *upapajje* started to intrude into the text of these passages and into similar passages such as Anguttaranikāya 5.292.2–5 and Anguttaranikāya 3.415.17–20. In Anguttaranikāya 3.415.17–20 E^e has:

> *tividhāhaṃ bhikkhave kammānaṃ vipākaṃ vadāmi: diṭṭhe va dhamme upapajje vā apare vā pariyāye.*

But *tividhaṃ* is found in our Sinhalese manuscripts only, while the Burmese tradition has *imaṃ*, which is the original reading as I think I have been able to prove; for a threefold result of the *kamma* is alien to the canon. Once this is established, we have a very recent manipulation of the wording of a canonical text in Ceylon. If the Nettippakaraṇa is the starting point of *upapajje*, the reading *tividhaṃ* should be younger or at least not older than the reintroduction of the Nettippakaraṇa into Ceylon, a date which may be as late as the 18th century, when many texts were brought back from Burma along with the revival of Buddhism in Ceylon.[35]) Thus we can see how the very wording of the canon could be influenced by the scholastic views of the commentators living only a few centuries ago.

The four examples for the demonstration of the history of our text tradition—*ajjhapatta*, *upecca*, *bhindara* and *upapajja*—are meant to illustrate the different stages of our text tradition: the Aluvihāra council, the Aṭṭhakathā and the Ṭīkās. At the state which our knowledge of textcritical problems of Pāli is in, the conclusions drawn are certainly not final and perhaps need revision. Nor have we discussed here all the problems or possibilities of alteration of our texts.[36]) Thus this article is meant to be a stimulus to collect further examples of this kind and a first step towards a history of the Pāli text tradition.

Abbreviations used: -ṭ: Ṭīkā; -a: Aṭṭhakathā; v.r.: variant reading; w.r.: wrong reading; ct.: commentary; B^e and E^e means Burmese or English edition respectively.

[34]) On this method of dating texts cf. J. J. Meyer, Textchronologie aus Schreibfehlern in Indien, in: Zeitschrift für Indologie und Iranistik 10, 1935–1936, pp. 257–276.

[35]) Cf. M. H. Bode, The Pali Literature of Burma, London 1909 (repr. 1966), p. 78. On Pāli-studies in Burma cf. V. D. Mazo, Iz istorii izučenija jazyka Pāli v Birme, in: Problemy istorii jazykov i kul'tury narodov Indii, Sbornik statej pamjati V. S. Vorobeva-Desjatovskogo, Moskau 1974, pp. 159–172.

[36]) Cf. e.g. H. Bechert, Über Singhalesisches im Pālikanon, in: Wiener Zeitschrift für die Kunde Süd- und Ostasiens 1, 1957, pp. 71–75, whose results are disputed, however, with very convincing arguments by K. R. Norman, Pāli and the language of the heretics, in: Acta Orientalia 37, 1976, pp. 117–126.

Das Upālipariprcchāsūtra
Ein Text zur buddhistischen Ordensdisziplin

Von VALENTINA STACHE-ROSEN

(Zusammenfassung)

Der chinesische Text T 1466 Yu-po-li wen fu, „Fragen des Upāli an den Buddha", ist ein Vinaya-Text, in dem der Inhalt des gesamten Suttavibhaṅga zusammengefaßt ist. In der Einleitung zu diesem Text stellt Upāli fünf Fragen an den Buddha über die Eigenschaften, die ein Mönch haben muß, um unabhängig zu sein. Auf diese Einleitung folgt der eigentliche Text, in dem keine weiteren Fragen gestellt werden. Die Vorschriften des Pātimokkha und ihr Kommentar in Kurzform sowie die Klausel über die Schuldfreiheit (*anāpatti*) bilden den Inhalt des Textes.

Ein Vergleich dieses Textes mit dem Pāli-Kanon ergibt, daß — von geringen Ausnahmen abgesehen — jeder Abschnitt des Upālipariprcchāsūtras eine wörtliche Parallele im Pāli hat, allerdings nicht als zusammenhängender Text.

Drei von den fünf Fragen, die Upāli an den Buddha stellt, finden sich in dem Kapitel Upālipañcaka des Parivāra, wo im ganzen 157 Fragen mit Antworten in Fünfergruppen gestellt werden[1]). Zwei der Fragen Upālis haben keine Entsprechung im Pāli. Die Kurzfassung des Vibhaṅga findet sich ebenfalls im Parivāra, S. 33–46 der PTS-Ausgabe. Die Klauseln über die Schuldfreiheit, die am Ende jeder Rahmenerzählung zu den Pātimokkha-Vorschriften angeführt werden, entsprechen denen des Upālipariprcchāsūtra. Der gesamte chinesische Text des Upālipariprcchāsūtra hat also im Pāli-Kanon eine Parallele, wenn auch nicht an der gleichen Stelle und in der gleichen Reihenfolge.

Pārājika 1–4, Saṃghādisesa 1–11, Nissaggiya Pācittiya 1–22 und Pāṭidesaniya 1–4 werden in beiden Texten in gleicher Reihenfolge aufgezählt. Saṃghādisesa 12 und 13 sind miteinander vertauscht. Nissaggiya Pācittiya 23–30 zeigen Unterschiede in der Reihenfolge. Beide Texte haben zwar 92 Vergehen unter den Pācittiyas, diese werden aber verschieden aufgezählt. In Pācittiya 89 und 90 des chinesischen Textes heißt es, es sei ein Vergehen, wenn ein Mönch die beiden Obergewänder bzw. das Untergewand über das erlaubte Maß hinaus herstellt. Nach Pāli Pācittiya 90 und 91 dagegen dürfen ein Gewand für die Regenzeit bzw. ein Gewand zum Bedecken von Wunden eine bestimmte Größe nicht überschreiten.

---

[1]) Vinayapitakaṃ, Vol. V, ed. H. Oldenberg, reprint London 1964 (PTS), pp. 180–206.

Die größten Abweichungen finden sich unter den Sekhiya dhammas. Im Pāli Suttavibhaṅga gibt es 75 dieser Vergehen, im Upāliparipṛcchā-sūtra nur 72. Neun davon haben keine Entsprechung im Pāli, und auch die Reihenfolge weist Unterschiede auf.

Die beiden unbestimmten Fälle (*aniyata*) und die sieben Vorschriften zur Ordnung von Rechtsangelegenheiten (*adhikaraṇasamatha*) werden weder im Upāliparipṛcchāsūtra noch in der Parallele im Parivāra behandelt.

Der Übersetzer bezeichnet die Sprache des Originals als Fan, die Sprache der Brahmanen, was sowohl für Sanskrit als auch für andere indische Sprachen gebraucht wurde [2]). Die Wiedergabe der meisten termini technici und gewisse Abweichungen in der Übersetzung, die sich durch Hörfehler erklären lassen, lassen darauf schließen, daß dem Übersetzer kein Sanskrittext vorlag [3]).

Über die Herkunft des Upāliparipṛcchāsūtra ist nichts sicheres überliefert. In der Taisho-Ausgabe des chinesischen Tripiṭaka wird angegeben, die Fragen seien von Guṇavarman während der Yüan-chia-Periode der Sung-Dynastie übersetzt worden (424–454) [4]). Guṇavarman, der aus Kaschmir stammte, hielt sich einige Zeit in Ceylon und Java auf, ehe er von Kaiser Wen der Sung-Dynastie nach China gerufen wurde [5]). Sieben der zwölf Biographien Guṇavarmans nennen die Übersetzungen, die ihm zugeschrieben werden, doch das Upāliparipṛcchāsūtra ist nicht darunter. T 2154 Kai Yüan Che Chiao Lu führt ein Upāliparipṛcchāsūtra unter den Werken unbekannter Übersetzer der späteren Han-Zeit auf [6]), und T 2034 Li Tai San Pao Chi erwähnt zwei Übertragungen unbekannter Übersetzer, eine aus der späteren Han-Zeit, die andere aus der östlichen Chin-Dynastie [7]). A. H i r a k a w a hat sich mit der Terminologie des Sūtras befaßt und kam zu dem Ergebnis, daß der Text etwa zu der gleichen Zeit wie der Vinaya der Sarvāstivādins, also im 5. Jh., übersetzt worden sein müsse [8]).

Auch über die Frage, welcher Schule das Upāliparipṛcchāsūtra angehörte, ist nichts überliefert. Die weitgehende Übereinstimmung zwi-

---

[2]) Die „Drei Ausgaben der Sung, Yüan und Ming Dynastien" sowie die alte Sung Ausgabe von 1104–1148 haben statt Fan Hu, die Sprache der Barbaren.

[3]) Die Wiedergabe einiger Termini, z.B. Seng-chia-p'o-shih-shah läßt darauf schließen, daß der Übersetzer Sanskrit Saṃghāvaśeṣa und nicht Pāli Saṃghā-disesa im Sinn hatte. P. V. Bapat ist der Meinung, die Sanskritfassung bestimmter Begriffe habe sich eingebürgert und sei deshalb auch für die Wiedergabe von Pāli-Worten benutzt worden. Siehe P. V. Bapat, Shan-Chien-P'i-p'o-sha, A Chinese version by Saṃghabhadra of Samantapāsādika (Bhandarkar Oriental Series No. 10), Poona 1970, p. 356, note 15.

[4]) Nach der alten Sung-Ausgabe stammt das Werk von einem unbekannten Übersetzer.

[5]) Die Biographien Guṇavarmans sind besprochen in V. Stache-Rosen, Guṇavarman, A Comparative Analysis of the Biographies found in the Chinese Tripitaka, in: Bulletin of Tibetology (Gangtok, Sikkim), Vol. X, No. 1 (March 1973).

[6]) Vol. 55, p. 483 c 11.

[7]) Vol. 49, p. 54 c 24 und p. 74 b 9.

[8]) A. H i r a k a w a, Ritsuzō no kenkyū, Tokyo, pp. 243–45.

schen diesem Sūtra und dem Pāli-Kanon legt den Schluß nahe, daß der Text aus dem Bereich der Theravādins stammt. Die abweichende Anordnung der einzelnen Vergehen läßt aber darauf schließen, daß das Sūtra nicht zu den Schriften des Mahāvihāra gehörte.

W. Pachow hat die Prātimokṣas aller Schulen miteinander verglichen[9]). Ohne zu erkennen, daß das Upāliparipṛcchāsūtra eine wörtliche Entsprechung im Pāli-Kanon habe, kam er zu dem Ergebnis, daß dieses Sūtra und der Pātimokkha der Theravādins einander sehr nahe stünden. Er ist der Ansicht, das Upāliparipṛcchāsūtra sei der ältere der beiden Texte.

Im Mahāvaṃsa-Kommentar heißt es, die Spaltung zwischen den Anhängern des Mahāvihāra und denen des Abhayagirivihāra sei im ersten Jahrhundert n. Chr. aufgrund einer Änderung von Sinn und Wortlaut von Khandaka und Parivāra vom Vinayapiṭaka entstanden[10]). Man kann annehmen, das Upāliparipṛcchāsūtra sei ein kanonischer Text der Abhayagirivāsins, der dem Parivāra des Mahāvihāra entsprach. Die Möglichkeit, daß der Text aus einem Ort in Indien stammt, an dem die Sthaviravādins inschriftlich belegt sind, ist jedoch nicht vollkommen ausgeschlossen.

---

[9]) W. Pachow, A Comparative Study of the Prātimokṣa, Santiniketan 1955.

[10]) *Tesaṃ Abhayagirivāsino Laṅkādīpamhi sāsanassa patiṭṭhānā sattarasavassamattādhikesu dvisu vassasatesu atikkantesu Vaṭṭagāmaniraňňo kāle Bhagavato āhaccabhāsita Vinayapiṭakato Khandakaparivāraṃ atthantarapāṭhantarakaraṇavasena bhedaṃ katvā Theravādato nikkhamma Dhammarucikavādā nāma hutvā tena Vaṭṭagāminā Abhayagirivihāramhi kārāpite tattha te vasiṃsu.* Zitiert bei H. Bechert, Zur Geschichte der buddhistischen Sekten in Indien und Ceylon, in: La Nouvelle Clio, tome VII–IX (1955–57), Nos. 7–10, p. 332.

The Colophon to the Paramatthamañjusā and the Discussion on the Date of Ācariya Dhammapāla

By ALOYSIUS PIERIS s. j.

I. The state of the question

[1] In the Pāli school, Ācariya Dhammapāla is reputed to be the most prolific compiler of commentaries after Buddhaghosa. He is accredited with the authorship[1]) of at least twelve volumes[2]) of exegetical literature comprising seven commentaries or *aṭṭhakathā* which go under the general title of Paramatthadīpanī (abbreviation: Pd) and five sub-commentaries technically known as *ṭīkā*.

[2] The Pd consists of a series of *aṭṭhakathā* on seven scriptural texts belonging to the Khuddaka Nikāya; these scriptural texts are the Udāna, the Itivuttaka, the Vimānavatthu, the Petavatthu, the Theragāthā, the Therīgāthā and the Cariyāpiṭaka[3]).

[3] The remaining five works attributed to Dhammapāla are explanatory treatises on non-scriptural writings and are, therefore, to be regarded as *ṭīkā* or sub-commentaries. Among these, however, the exegetical treatise on the Nettippakaraṇa (a manual of hermeneutics ascribed to Kaccāyana) is called an *aṭṭhakathā* in the title itself.[4]) We are informed

---

[1]) The use of the word "authorship" is not inappropriate here. It is true that Buddhaghosa, as Dr. W. Rahula maintains in History of Buddhism in Ceylon, Colombo 1956, pp. xxiv–xxv, was more of an "editor-translator" than an author. Ācariya Dhammapāla, on the contrary, merits being called the "author" of the works ascribed to him because of the originality and individuality he displays in them.

[2]) The Gandhavaṁsa (ed. J. Minajeff, in: Journal of the Pāli Text Society 1886, pp. 54–80) [abbreviated: Gv] is not a reliable source to decide on the number of books ascribable to Dhammapāla. On p. 69, it groups them into fourteen items comprising not only those which we have split into twelve works and regard as definitely written by Dhammapāla (cf. notes 3, 4, 7 & 8 below) but also five others which certainly cannot have come from him, namely, an *anuṭīkā* on Ānanda's Mūlaṭīkā and a *ṭīkā* each on Aṃguttaraṭṭhakathā, Niruttippakaraṇṭṭhakathā, Jātakaṭṭhakathā and Buddhavaṃsaṭṭhakathā. On p. 60, the Gv again speaks of fourteen items but lists only thirteen, omitting, perhaps accidentally, the Therīgāthaṭṭhakathā; further, a *ṭīkā* on the Nettippakaraṇaṭṭhakathā is mentioned in place of the *ṭīkā* on the Niruttippakaraṇaṭṭhakathā occurring in the previous list.

[3]) These commentaries are abbreviated in the following way: UdA = Udānaṭṭhakathā; ItvA = Itivuttakaṭṭhakathā; VvA = Vimānavatthu-aṭṭhakathā; PvA = Petavatthu-aṭṭhakathā; ThagA = Theragāthaṭṭhakathā; ThīgA = Therīgāthā-aṭṭhakathā; CpA = Cariyāpiṭakaṭṭhakathā. All references are to the PTS editions of these texts.

[4]) Nettippakaraṇaṭṭhakathā, abbreviated: NettiA. See the selection of excerpts appended to the PTS edition of the Nettippakaraṇa (ed. E. Hardy, London 1902).

that in the Anurādhapura period, all non-canonical writings were indiscriminately referred to as *aṭṭhakathā* while the term *ṭīkā* with its specific connotation given above began too ccur only in the Polonnaruva period, i.e., about the 10th or the 11th century A.D., when the process of Sanskritization set in.[5]) Perhaps, the term *aṭṭhakathā* as applied to the Netti A could be justified also on another count. Circa 5th century A.D., or even before, the Nettippakaraṇa seems to have enjoyed a quasi-canonical status especially in the Burmese tradition and, together with the Milindapañha, Peṭakopadesa and Suttasaṃgaha, it used to be included among the books of the Khuddaka Nikāya.[6]) It is quite understandable, therefore, that Dhammapāla's commentary on it should have passed for an *aṭṭhakathā* almost on a par with the Pd and with the other commentaries written on the books of the Khuddaka Nikāya. Thus in categorizing it as a *ṭīkā*, here, we have adhered to a more precise, though less ancient, terminology.

[4] The other four *ṭīkā* are all sub-commentaries on the writings of Buddhaghosa. Three of them are known as Līnatthapakāsinī and are sub-commentaries on Buddhaghosa's Sumaṃgalavilāsinī (Dīgha commentary), Papañcasudanī (Majjhima commentary) and Sāratthappakāsinī (Saṃyutta commentary).[7]) Last but not least is the Paramatthamañjusā, Dhammapāla's monumental exegesis on the Visuddhimagga.[8])

[5] Like many of their kind, these exegetical writings, too, make no clear reference to the date of compilation. The colophons do give some information about the author; but this information is of a geographical rather than of a chronological nature. We are told where he lived but not when he lived there. Now, as the uniqueness of Dhammapāla's contribution to Pāli Scholasticism[9]) begins to draw the attention of scholars, the speculation about his date also tends to heighten. And so we see many theories put forward, some placing him in the 5th century, others in the 6th or early 7th century A.D. Recently, however, these theories have been revised on the basis of new data deduced from a verse in the colophon to the Pm.

---

[5]) W. Rahula, op.cit., p. XXVIII. See also our comment in para. 33.

[6]) E. Lamotte, Khuddakanikāya and Kṣudrakapiṭaka, in: East and West VII, No. 4 (January 1957), pp. 345.

[7]) Abbreviations: DAṬ = Dīghanikāyaṭṭhakathā-ṭīkā (ed. Lily de Silva, 3 volumes, London, PTS, 1970; MAṬ = Majjhimanikāyaṭṭhakathā-ṭīkā; SAṬ = Saṃyuttanikāyaṭṭhakathā-ṭīkā.

[8]) Paramatthamañjusā or Visuddhimagga-ṭīkā [abbreviation: Pm], of which a critical edition is being prepared by me.

[9]) A modest attempt at demonstrating this is made in my doctoral dissertation "Some Salient Aspects of Consciousness and Reality in Pāli Scholasticism as Reflected in the Commentaries of Ācariya Dhammapāla" [shorter title: Consciousness and Reality in Ācariya Dhammapāla] presented to and accepted by the University of Sri Lanka, Vidyodaya Campus in October 1972. The present article is a sub-section of its introductory chapter.

[6] What we propose to do in this paper is not only to assemble but also evaluate all the available data on which the discussion on the date of Dhammapāla is to be based, and, further, to sound a note of caution with respect to the last mentioned document.

II. The starting point of the discussion

[7] The discussion has to start with the assumption that Dhammapāla came after Buddhaghosa. This follows neatly from the fact that four of his *ṭīkā* are written on Buddhaghosa's works (cf. para. 4). Moreover, the Pd contains clear references to the writings of Buddhaghosa.[10]) The conjecture that our commentator would have lived before Buddhaghosa[11]) was made at a time when these facts were not known. Even the theory that Dhammapāla flourished in the 5th century,[12]) more or less contemporaneously with Buddhaghosa, should be tested against the fact that the extensive literature compiled by Buddhaghosa should have taken a considerable amount of time to be copied script by script and circulated among the confraternities before they could be so well absorbed into the Scholastic tradition as to have merited *verbatim* repetitions in the commentaries of Dhammapāla[13]) and also to have needed sub-commentaries for further elucidation. A good stretch of time must have elapsed between the two exegetes.

[8] Besides, it should be borne in mind that during Buddhaghosa's time, the canonicity of the Khuddaka Nikāya was still in dispute.[14]) Even the most archaic poetical works included in it [on some of which Dhammapāla wrote his commentaries] were regarded, in certain circles,

---

[10]) E.g., the Sāratthappakāsinī is mentioned by name and quoted twice in ThagA III 190–191; and the Visuddhimagga in UdA 24, 236, 268, 283; etc.

[11]) E.g., Mrs. Rhys Davids thought that Dhammapāla lived "either before or just after Buddhaghosa" (Psalms of the Sisters, London, PTS 1913, p. XVI).

[12]) E. Hardy, Netti A, pp. XII, XV–XVII and Mrs. Rhys Davids, loco supra cit.; see also The Guide, translation of Netti-ppakaraṇaṃ, London, PTS 1962, p. X, where Ñāṇamoli appears to be moving away from the position taken earlier in The Path of Purification (Colombo 1956), p. XXVII.

[13]) E.g., ItvA II 9–10 is a faithful reproduction of MA (i.e. the Majjhima commentary) I 275–278; similarly, MA I 137 is repeated in ItvA I 82; etc. We admit, however, that such repetitions could also be explained away by postulating a common source.

[14]) E. Lamotte, loc.cit., p. 345. We are inclined to think that the so called Saṃyukta-sañcaya-piṭaka, a sort of a "miscellaneous collection" of (scriptural?) texts which Fâ-Hien picked up during his visit to Sri Lanka in the beginning of the 5th century A.D. (Cf. Fâ-Hien, A Record of Buddhistic Kingdoms, transl. James Legge, Oxford 1886, reprint New York 1965, p. 111) was probably a recension of the Khuddaka Nikāya brought from India where, as Lamotte observes (loc.cit., p. 344), it was customary for Buddhist schools to gather the minor canonical texts into a "fourth Piṭaka quite distinct from the traditional Tripiṭaka." This, too, may indicate the undefined status of the Khuddaka during Buddhaghosa's time.

as mere utterances of great disciples rather than *Buddha-vacana* or the *ipsissima verba* of the Master himself.[15] Significantly, the commentaries that are unanimously agreed upon among scholars as coming from the pen of Buddhaghosa[16] are precisely those written on the first four Nikāyas which, unlike the Khuddaka, were universally acclaimed as *Buddha-vacana.* Hence it may not be altogether unreasonable to suppose that the commentaries on the books of the fifth Nikāya would have appeared when its canonicity was no more called in question.[17]

[9] Finally, there is a peculiar feature in Dhammapāla's style which compels us to place him about a century after Buddhaghosa. We notice often that, when analysing controverted issues, he displays a marked degree of proficiency in the science of logic; he is an adept at formulating arguments and counter-arguments, sometimes even syllogistically.[18] Now, in the history of Buddhism, the period of formal logic—if we may call it so— is said to have commenced in or around the 6th century.[19] The date of Dhammapāla, we therefore presume, could not have been much earlier than that.

---

[15] Lamotte, ibid., p. 346.

[16] Cf. L. R. Gunesekere, Buddhist Commentarial Literature, Kandy, Buddhist Publication Society 1967, pp. 16–17 and the chart annexed. See especially, A. P. Buddhadatta, Who Was Buddhaghosa? in: Corrections of Geiger's Mahāvaṃsa etc., Ambalangoda 1957, pp. 154 & 157.

[17] Since parts of some Khuddaka texts were originally found scattered in the rest of the Tripiṭaka before they were gradually assembled into a fifth Nikāya (Lamotte, loc.cit., pp. 346–347), the Sinhala and other commentaries that grew around them must have been in use in the 5th century; but there is no compelling reason to say that the existing Pāli commentaries on the Khuddaka texts were compiled in that era when, according to contemporary sources (DA II 566, AA III 159, Dīpavaṃsa V, 37), the greater part of the texts were rejected by some. If the commentaries on the Dhammapada and the Niddesa are believed to have been composed during this time, it is because the texts themselves claim to have been compiled under King Sirinivāsa and because Sirinivāsa is interpreted, perhaps rightly, as an epithet of Mahānāma who ruled from 409 to 431 (University of Ceylon History of Ceylon, Vol. I, 1959, pp. 291 & 391). But these claims made in the texts have not been tested by internal criticism of the texts themselves. Similarly, the tradition that attributes the commentary on the Buddhavaṃsa to a senior contemporary of Buddhaghosa is accepted without such a test. As a matter of fact, in the case of the Jātakaṭṭhakathā which was perhaps the first Khuddaka commentary to have been compiled (L. R. Gunesekere, op.cit., p. 17) and in the case of the Khuddakapāṭha commentary, the former belief that they were written by Buddhaghosa has been questioned (Cf. E. W. Adikaram, Early History of Buddhism in Ceylon, Colombo 1946, reprint 1953, pp. 6–7). It seems to us that a careful review of the Pāli commentaries on the Khuddaka texts may make us question the view that any of them was composed by Buddhaghosa or during Buddhaghosa's time.

[18] E.g., UdA 390; Pm (Sinhala Edition of M. Dhammananda, 3 parts, 1928, 1930, 1949) 537–539; regarding counter-arguments, see Pm 449–450, 534; etc.

[19] Cf. F. Th. Stcherbatsky, Buddhist Logic, Vol. I, reprint, New York 1962, pp. 3, 11–13.

III. A conspectus of current theories

[10] Apart from the basic assumption that Dhammapāla must have flourished (about a century?) after Buddhaghosa, very little can be asserted with precision and certitude about the exact period of his literary activity. Perhaps, one factor that complicates the issue and confuses the discussion is that history knows more than one writer going by the name of Dhammapāla.[20]) In fact, it would not be an over-simplification to say that the current debate on the date of Dhammapāla revolves round just these two questions:—

Question I: Were the five *ṭīkā* compiled by the same Dhammapāla who wrote the seven *aṭṭhakathā*? Or, were there two writers?

Question II: Was the Pāli exegete [be he the author of the *aṭṭhakathā* only, or of the *ṭīkā* also] the same as the famous Dharmapāla of Nālanda referred to as a native of Kāñcipura by Hiuen Tsiang?

[11] The first question had been raised already in 1936 by Mrs C. A. F. Rhys Davids herself.[21]) The theory of double authorship with regard to Question I and single authorship with regard to Question II has been proposed by Ven. Dr. H. Saddhatissa who places the author of the *ṭīkā* in the 10th century and the author of the *aṭṭhakathā* somewhere "before the seventh century", identifying the latter with the Dharmapāla of Nālanda (cf. paras 30–31). Dr. (Mrs.) Lily de Silva, however, sees no valid reason why the Yogācārin Dharmapāla from Nālanda who lived in the late 6th century could not have been the author of both the *ṭīkā* and the *aṭṭhakathā* (cf. paras 32–36). Ven. A. P. Buddhadatta who defended this same theory of single authorship (cf. paras 19–22) was, later, compelled to modify it on the basis of the colophon to the Pm; the modified theory (cf. paras 26–29) puts Ācariya Dhammapāla, author of both the *ṭīkā* and the *aṭṭhakathā*, in the 10th century so that he could not have been, as was held previously, the Yogācārin who flourished in Nālanda four centuries earlier. Naturally, Saddhatissa and de Silva also interpret the colophon in support of their respective positions. Finally, there is Dr. S. Paranavitana who has ascribed the Pd, the Pm and the Netti A to three entirely different commentators (cf. para. 16).

IV. Ācariya Dhammapāla as known from the Pāli sources

[12] The primary source of information on Dhammapāla is the usual reference to authorship made in the prose ending of the colophons to his works. In the Netti A, in the Pm and in all the seven works of the

20) Gv 66–67.
21) ItvA II, p. VI.

Pd, the colophons end with the assertion that the compiler was "Ācariya Dhammapāla residing in the monastery of [at?] Badaratittha."[22])

[13] We must insist, here, that this source does not give any clear indication as to whether Badaratittha was the name of a town or the name of a monastery; nor is it specified in which town Badaratittha was located in case it was the name of a monastery. Regrettably, this is not borne in mind by those who are engaged in the current discussion.

[14] It is true that the verse-section of the colophon to the Netti A testifies that its author lived in a monastery associated with the name of King Asoka [who might have been its builder, or at least its benefactor], and situated in Nāgapaṭṭana, a town "in the land where the Noble Dhamma descended,"[23]) i.e., in India. Note, however, that the name Badaratittha does not occur here at all; it re-appears in the stereotype prose formula coming at the end of the verse-section, a formula which is common to all other works ascribed to Dhammapāla (cf. para. 12). But, then, in this prose formula there is absolutely no mention of Nāgapaṭṭana. Hence Buddhadatta's conclusion that Badaratittha was a monastery in Negapatan (present name for Nāgapaṭṭana)[24]) is too hasty while Dr. E. W. Adikaram has taken a more cautious stand in saying that Netti A would have been written "at a time when Dhammapāla [of Badaratittha] was residing at Nāgapaṭṭana in the vihāra built by King Asoka."[25])

[15] The Sāsanavaṃsa, too, is ambiguous on this matter. It makes explicit mention of Badaratittha and not of Negapatan. Here again, Buddhadatta has too easily inferred that the allusion is to Nāgapaṭṭana,[26]) while all that the Sāsanavaṃsa says is this:

> The Elder Ācariya Dhammapāla should be regarded as belonging to the Siṃhala Island because he used to reside in Padaratittha in the Tamil country in the neighbourhood of the Siṃhala Island.[27])

Judging from the context, we would hold that the word *Padaratitthamhi* (variant for *Badaratitthamhi*) lends itself to be interpreted as referring to a town rather than a monastery.

---

[22]) UdA 436; ItvA II 194; VvA 355; PvA 287; ThagA III 210; ThīgA 301; CpA 336; NettiA 249; Pm (Burmese Edition Vol. II, Rangoon, 1913) 443.

[23]) NettiA 249:
Saddhammāvatarațțhāne paṭṭane Nāgasavhaye
Dhammāsoka-mahārāja-vihāre vasatā mayā.

[24]) A. P. Buddhadatta, The Second Great Commentator, Ācariya Dhammapāla, in: University of Ceylon Review III, No. 2, (November 1945), p. 49.

[25]) E. W. Adikaram, op.cit., p. 9.

[26]) Loc.cit., p. 50.

[27]) Sāsanavaṁsa [abbreviation: Sv], PTS edition, p. 33:
Ācariya-Dhammapālatthero Sīhaladīpassa
samīpe Damiḷaraṭṭhe Padaratitthamhi nivāsittā
Sīhaladīpe yeva saṁgahetvā vattabbo.

[16] In fact Paranavitana has taken Badaratittha to be the ancient name for modern Kaḍalur, a South Indian coastal town north of Negapatan and south of Conjeevaram (Kāñcipura). Consistent with this, is his other belief that the author of the Netti A who lived in Negapatan is not to be confused with Ācariya Dhammapāla, the author of the Pd who resided in Kaḍalur. Paranavitana seems to have ignored, or even rejected as spurious, the prose ending of the colophon to the Netti A. The colophon to the Pm has met with the same treatment, since he attributes this work to a third author.[28])

[17] It is our opinion that as long as the doubt about Badaratittha and Negapatan is not cleared up, one would do well to look for other reasons to prove that it was our commentator who compiled the Nett A (cf. para. 35), and that, consequently, the prose ending of its colophon is not a later addition.

V. Bodhisattva Dharmapāla as known from Northern sources

[18] While the association of Badaratittha with Negapatan is understandable though not explainable, it is altogether difficult to comprehend why Dr. Saddhatissa has quoted the colophon to the Netti A in support of his statement that "Dhammapāla, the commentator was definitely a native of Kāñcipura and wrote while dwelling in the Badaratittha Vihāra situated in Negapatan in South India."[29]) Besides assuming, here, that Badaratittha was not a town but a monastery in Negapatan, Saddhatissa has also taken for granted that our author was "definitely" the Yogācārin Dharmapāla whose name Hiuen Tsiang is said to have recorded in his diary after his visit to Kāñcipura about the year 640 A.D.[30]) Dr. G. P. Malalasekera has gone a step further, locating Badaratittha "a little south of Madras",[31]) which is where Kāñcipura is. Referring to Dhammapāla, Malalasekera states that "His works show that he was a native of Kāñcipura,"[32]) though the Pāli sources nowhere associate Dhammapāla with Kāñcipura!

[19] This tendency to identify our author with the Yogācārin Dharmapāla who was born in Kāñcipura and wrote in Nālanda dates back to the early PTS editors,[33]) though even among them it found resistance.[34])

---

[28]) History of Ceylon, Vol. I, p. 391.

[29]) Upāsakajanālaṁkāra, A Critical Edition and Study by H. Saddhātissa, London, PTS 1965, p. 30 [abbreviation: UJ].

[30]) Ibid., p. 29.

[31]) The Pali Literature of Ceylon, reprint, Colombo 1958, p. 113. See also Ñāṇamoli, The Path of Purification, p. XXX and Adikaram, op.cit., p. 9.

[32]) Dictionary of Pāli Proper Names, s.v. Dhammapāla, No. 8.

[33]) E.g., Paul Steinthal, Udāna, p. VII, n. 1; C. A. F. Rhys Davids, Psalms of the Sisters, p. XVI; T.W. Rhys Davids and J. E. Carpenter, DA I, p. VII; etc.

[34]) E.g., E. Hardy, PvA, p. VII.

But no one ever tried to establish the thesis until A. P. Buddhadatta Thera gathered pieces of evidence from the Pāli sources and from northern records, fitted them together, as one does in a jigsaw puzzle, and reconstructed the figure of a Dhammapāla who was a Pāli exegete in his youth and a Mahāyānist scholar later.[35])

[20] Among the northern sources consulted by him, the principal ones were the Chinese pilgrim Hiuen Tsiang's diary and his pupil Hwi Li's "The Life of Hiuen Tsiang." They give some bio-bibliographical information about a certain Bodhisattva Dharmapāla. All that Buddhadatta gathered from these and other sources can be compressed into the following set of statements:

1. Bodhisattva Dharmapāla was born in Kāñcipura.
2. He was admitted into the Order in a mountain convent many hundred *li* away from Kāñcipura.
3. A reputed polemicist, he had once, in a saṃghārāma near Kāñci, defended the Buddhist doctrine and had converted his opponent in a debate which, by the King's order, was to decide the fate of Buddhism in that country.
4. A connoisseur of other systems of philosophy, he is said to have written several tens of books among which were the following: Śabda-vidyā-saṃyukta-śāstra and commentaries on Śata-śāstra-vaipulyam, Vidyā-mātra-siddhi and Nyāya-dvāra-tarka-śāstra.
5. Virtuous and talented, he was one of the celebrities that studied at Nālanda where, later, as head of the University, he was succeeded by his own pupil, the reputed Śīlabadra who, when Hiuen Tsiang visited Nālanda in 640 A.D., was about seventy years old.
6. Dharmakīrti, who flourished during the latter half of the seventh century, was also a pupil of Dharmapāla.[36])

[21] This Dharmapāla was, evidently, a follower of the Yogācāra school. And, to have been the teacher of Dharmakīrti and of Śīlabadra (who was 70 years old in 640 A.D.), he should have been active during the latter half of the 6th century.[37])

VI. Ācariya Dhammapāla and Bodhisattva Dharmapāla

[22] In fairness to Buddhadatta, we should state here that he does not claim to have produced any positive evidence to prove that Bodhisattva Dharmapāla was, in actual fact, the same writer whom the southern

[35]) The Second Great Commentator, Ācariya Dhammapāla, in: University of Ceylon Review III, No. 2 (November 1945), pp. 49sq.

[36]) As for this statement, Buddhadatta (loc. cit., p. 52) refers the reader to Ryukan Kimura, Origin of Mahāyāna Buddhism, Poona 1939, p. 189.

[37]) This same date is assigned to Dharmapāli in a recent study, Bhāvaviveka, Sthiramati and Dharmapāla by Yuichi Kajiyama in: WZKSO XII–XIII, 1968–1969, pp. 193–203.

sources refer to as Ācariya Dhammapāla. Rather, assuming them to be one and the same person, he proceeds to answer a couple of objections that could be raised against such an assumption. The first difficulty arises from the fact that these two names are associated with two opposing schools of thought, the Yogācāra and the Theravāda, respectively. Buddhadatta resolves it by postulating a conversion on the part of Dhammapāla from one school to the other. In support of this hypothesis, he cites the classical example of Vasubandhu's conversion from Sarvāstivāda to Vijñānavāda. The second difficulty which is a chronological one arising from the alleged conversion of Dhammapāla from Theravāda to Mahāyāna is resolved in the following manner. Since in all but two commentaries, Dhammapāla is referred to as *ācariya* (teacher) rather than as *thera* (Elder), it can be argued that he would have finished most of his Pāli works when he was yet a young *bhikkhu*. With this explanation, Buddhadatta allots sufficient time to Dhammapāla's later Mahāyānist career in Nālanda.

[23] On the other hand, one cannot ignore the fact that the northern accounts (para. 20) and the references in the southern sources (paras 12–15) seem to run parallel with no common meeting point. That is to say, there is nothing in the Pāli sources which is even hinted at in the northern records, and *vice versa*. For instance, Hiuen Tsiang makes absolutely no mention of Badaratittha when speaking of Bodhisattva Dharmapāla. It is equally difficult to justify his total silence regarding Dhammapāla's alleged conversion from one school to another and also regarding his literary achievements prior to that "conversion". Such a silence appears strange when contrasted with Hiuen Tsiang's many references to Bodhisattva Dharmapāla's birth and youth. So important an event as a conversion in the life of such a celebrity, if it had really taken place, could not have escaped the Chinese pilgrim's attention. After all, does not Paramārtha's biography of Vasubandhu record not only the latter's but also his brother Asaṃga's conversion? Would it not be reasonable to conclude that the Chinese biographer of Bodhisattva Dharmapāla knew nothing of Ācariya Dhammapāla?

[24] At the same time, we readily concede that the Pāli exegete easily comes up to the stature assigned in the Chinese records to his northern namesake. The consummate ease with which he handles abstruse texts, his mastery of the science of logic, his flare for controversy and the inimitable precision with which he disjoins overlapping concepts[38]) reveal an intellectual acumen which can compare with that of the other Dharmapāla. His acquaintance with Jainism and various philosophical tenets contained in Sanskrit sources[39]) constitute another point of similarity. Yet all these cannot, *per se*, even cumulatively, prove that the

---

[38]) This is amply illustrated in my Consciousness and Reality in Ācariya Dhammapāla (see note 9 above).

[39]) Lily de Silva, DAṬ, p. L of the introduction.

two men are in fact one. At most, such points of convergence might have a confirmative value after the theory has been proved *ex aliunde.*

[25] Our conclusion then can be summarized as follows: the theory that identifies the Pāli commentator with Dharmapāla of Nālanda is substantially lacking in positive evidence. We should, nevertheless, hasten to add the following qualification: the arguments which we have advanced against the theory (cf. paras 23–24) are equally negative.

VII. The colophon to the Paramatthamañjusā

[26] It was in coming across the colophon to the Pm that Buddhadatta thought he had found the first ever positive evidence against the hypothesis just discussed (cf. paras 22–25). The curious bit of information which caused this change in the dating of Dhammapāla's works is deposited in verse 4 of the colophon where it is said that the sub-commentary was written "at the request of the Elder Dāṭhanāga residing in the Siddhagāma Pariveṇa."[40])

[27] The Cūlavaṃsa seems to furnish us with ample information regarding the person and the location alluded to in this verse.[41]) Sitthagāma or Siddhagāma[42]) was a village which, by order of King Sena IV, was transformed into a *Pariveṇa*, i.e., a secluded area for monks to reside in. Now, at Siddhagāma, there is said to have been an Elder called Dhammamitta (a name to be noted for later reference in para. 31) who was invited by Sena's successor, Mahinda IV, to write a commentary on the Abhidhamma. It is also reported that at this time there was a forest-dwelling monk called Dāṭhanāga who, at the King's invitation, used to recite the Abhidhamma. It may be inferred that Ābhidhārmika studies were a special field of interest in the Siddhagāma Pariveṇa.

[28] If it is true, then, that Dhammapāla wrote the Pm at the request of Dāṭhanāga Thera of the Siddhagāma Pariveṇa, as the colophon says, it follows that this *ṭīkā* was compiled somewhere in the latter half of the 10th century; for King Sena IV, who built the Pariveṇa, reigned from 953 to 956 A.D. and Mahinda IV, who made use of Dāṭhanāga for the recitation of the Abhidhamma there, reigned from 956 to 972 A.D.

[29] Thus a passing reference to "Dāṭhanāga" and "Siddhagāma" in verse 4 of the colophon to the *Pm* compelled Buddhadatta to conclude that its author lived in the 10th century A.D. and, therefore, was not to

---

[40]) Pm (Burmese Edition), Part II, p. 442. The full text is quoted below in para. 43.

[41]) Cūlavaṃsa 54.6, 35–36.

[42]) The Burmese Mss. tend to use *tha* where Sinhala Mss. would use *dha.* Cf. D. Kosambi, Visuddhimagga, Cambridge, Mass., 1950 (Harvard Oriental Series, 41), p. X.

be confused with Dharmapāla of Nālanda who lived four centuries earlier.[43])

VIII. Ācariya Dhammapāla and Culla Dhammapāla

[30] Dr. H. Saddhatissa goes a step further.[44]) He fully endorses the theory which, on the basis of the colophon just referred to, places the author of the Pm and the other *ṭīkā* in the 10th century. But he would not agree that the compiler of these *ṭīkā* was the same commentator who wrote the Pd. For, the period of the *aṭṭhakathā* and that of the *ṭīkā* were separated by the intervening period of the *ganṭhipada* literature. Further, the Sāsanavaṃsa gives a double list of works attributed to Dhammapāla, separating the *ṭikā* from the *aṭṭhakathā*. Saddhatissa interprets this double series as confirmative of the theory of double authorship and rejects the single list given in the Gandhavaṃsa.

[31] The author of the Pd, he maintains, was Dharmapāla from Nālanda who lived "before the seventh century", i.e., in the period of the *aṭṭhakathā*, while *ṭīkā* were compiled by Culla Dhammapāla, the senior pupil of Ānanda Vanaratana and the probable author of the Saccasaṃkhepa. Now, if Ānanda Vanaratana's sub-commentary on the Atthasālinī was called "Mūlaṭīkā" because it was the first ever *ṭīkā* as the Sāsanavaṃsa has it,[45]) and if according to its colophon it was written at the request of Dhammamitta Thera[46]) who could very well be the Elder associated with Siddhagāma in the 10th century (cf. para. 27), and, finally, if the senior pupil of the author of the Mūlaṭīkā was also known as Dhammapāla, or more precisely, Culla Dhammapāla,[47]) then, indeed, Saddhatissa's stand sounds plausible.

[32] However, the basic pre-supposition behind this reasoning calls for closer examination. The key argument is that the *ganṭhipada* literature evolved during the period subsequent to the commentaries and prior to the *ṭīkā* (cf. para. 30). This is not as convincing as it seems at first sight. Dr. Lily de Silva has pointed out that the *ganṭhipadas* were primarily an aid to the understanding of the Vinaya and that the *ganṭhi-*

---

[43]) The amended version of the article, The Second Great Commentator, Ācariya Dhammapāla appeared in: Corrections of Geiger's Mahavaṃsa etc., Ambalangoda 1957, pp. 189–197. Earlier, in his Sinhala treatise on the Indian Masters, Bhāratīya Bauddhācaryayō, Colombo 1949, p. 67, Buddhadatta did make a passing reference to this colophon without, however, making any comment on its historical implications.

[44]) UJ, pp. 28–30.

[45]) Sv 33: Abhidhammaṭīkaṁ pana Ānandatthero akāsi. Sā ca sabbāsaṁ ṭīkānaṁ ādibhūtattā, Mūlaṭīkā ti pākaṭā.

[46]) Abhidhamma Mūla Ṭīkā, ed. Dehigaspē Paññasāra and Polonnaruve Vimaladhamma, Colombo 1938 (Vidyodaya Ṭīkā Publication, II), p. 147:
Dhammamitto ti nāmena sakkaccaṁ abhiyācito
Ānando iti nāmena kato gantho subuddhinā ti.

[47]) See The Pāli Literature of Ceylon, pp. 112, 203.

padas on the Visuddhimagga, the Abhidhamma and the Paṭisambhidāmagga represent sporadic attempts at imitating the Vinaya-gaṇṭhipada and met with no success presumably because the *ṭīkā* were already in existence as explanatory aids to these books and in particular to the Sutta commentaries.[48]) Further, she assures us that no *gaṇṭhipadas* are mentioned in the DAṬ; this work, and consequently the other *ṭīkā* by the same author, seem, therefore, to have been compiled "at a time before *gaṇṭhipadas* assumed definite shape during the course of their evolution"[49]) and not as late as in the 10th century[50]) for, in the Polonnaruva period the *ṭīkā* authors "openly acclaim their indebtedness to these *gaṇṭhipadas.*"[51])

[33] By the same argument, the Pm, which also does not make mention of, or admit dependence on the *gaṇṭhipadas*[52]) and even the Mūlaṭīkā compiled by Ānanda Vanaratana,[53]) should have appeared long before the 10th century. Therefore, the generally accepted opinion that the *ṭīkā* literature began in the Polonnaruva period together with Sanskritization (cf. para. 3) needs to be qualified as follows: the *ṭīkā* were in existence already in Sanskrit Buddhist circles[54]) and what the Saddhammasaṃgaha reports as having taken place under the patronage of Parakramabāhu I was not an official inauguration of *ṭīkā* literature but only a public undertaking on the King's part to persuade the Sangha to acknowledge and foster a *ṭīkā* tradition that was already in vogue.[55])

[34] It is not, therefore, improbable that the Pm, the DAṬ and the Pd belong to the same period. Tradition has always assigned both the *ṭīkā* and the Pd to Ācariya Dhammapāla of Badaratittha;[56]) and there is no valid reason to doubt it. The separation of the *ṭīkā* from the *aṭṭhakathā* in the Sāsanavaṃsa catalogue of works ascribed to Dhammapāla need not necessarily imply a chronological difference in the compilation of the two sets, as Saddhatissa has suggested (cf. para. 30); it is only natural and logical to classify commentaries and sub-commentaries as two different types of literature as we ourselves have done in paras 1–3.

IX. The theory of single authorship

[35] It is significant that Saddhatissa has not appealed to any internal evidence in favour of the theory of double authorship. No instance of discrepancy in thought or discontinuity in style between the

---

[48]) DAṬ, p. VIII.
[49]) Ibid., p. XXXVII.
[50]) Ibid., p. XLVI.
[51]) Ibid., p. XXXVI. Here, a reference is made to Sāratthadīpanī, p. 2.
[52]) DAṬ, p. XXXIV.
[53]) Ibid., p. XXXV.
[54]) Ibid., p. XXX.
[55]) Cf. Malalasekera's comment in The Pāli Literature in Ceylon, pp. 193–194. Also, see UJ, p. 28.
[56]) Cf. DAṬ, pp. LI–LIII.

Pd and the five *ṭīkā* has been cited so far. On the other hand Dr. de Silva finds many a parallelism between the DAṬ (which has no colophon indicating the author's name) and the other works ascribed to Dhammapāla.[57]) The present writer, too, can testify to a striking continuity in style between the Pd and the Pm. Internal coherence in the manner and the matter expressed in the *aṭṭhakathā* and the *ṭīkā* is the ultimate test which can decide whether they came from the same pen or not.

[36] As for the suggestion that Culla Dhammapāla, the author of Saccasaṃkhepa would have written the Pm and the other *ṭīkā* in the 10th century (cf. para. 31), we would do well to test it against the following observations made by Dr. de Silva:—the DAṬ bears no resemblance to the Saccasaṃkhepa; the Gandhavaṃsa refers to the writer as an Indian Thera; the term *culla* (the lesser) applied to an author of so many important works needs to be explained; the grammatical terminology used in the DAṬ is the same as Buddhaghosa's rather than Kaccāyana's which was in vogue in the 10th century.[58])

[37] To these we would like to add an important observation of ours. Culla Dhammapāla, we are informed, was the pupil of Ānanda who wrote the Mūlaṭīkā. But the combined evidence gained from the Mūlaṭīkā and the Abhidhammatthavikāsinī tends to suggest that the relationship between Dhammapāla, the commentator and Ānanda was that of rival teachers rather than of pupil and teacher. For, quite frequently does Sumaṃgala, the author of the Abhidhammatthavikāsinī, speak of Dhammapāla, as having taken a position contrary to that of Ānanda.[59]) That this Ānanda was none other than the author of the Mūlaṭīkā can, of course, be deduced from a comparative study of references made by Sumaṃgala in his two books, the Abhidhammatthavikāsinī and the Abhidhammattha-saṃgaha-vibhavinī-ṭīkā.[60]) We may safely presume that, at least in certain matters, the Atthasālinī tradition commented upon in the Mūlaṭīkā by Ānanda differs somewhat from the

---

[57]) Ibid., pp. XLII, LI.

[58]) Ibid., pp. XLV–XLVI.

[59]) Abhidammatthavikāsinī ed. A. P. Buddhadatta, Ambalangoda 1961, pp. 298–299, 301–302, 304–305. See also note 60 below.

[60]) In his Sinhala biography of the Theravāda Masters, Theravādī Bauddhācaryayō Colombo 1948, pp. 69–70, A. P. Buddhadatta argues it out as follows. There is a passage in the Abhidammattha-saṃgaha-vibhāvinī-ṭīkā (Vidyodaya Edition, p. 118) where its author Sumaṃgala makes a reference to a position taken by "The teacher Ānanda and others" (Ānandācariyādayo) and says that the explanation of this position is to be read "in its summary form in the Mūlaṭīkā etc. and in detail in the Abhidhammatthavikāsinī." Now, in addition to this association of Ānanda with the Mūlaṭīkā and the reference to the Abhidhammatthavikāsinī, there is also a recurrence of the phrase *Ānandācariyo pana* on pp. 81 and 151 and *Dhammapāla* on pp. 86–87 and 100. From this it is inferable that the Ānandācariya whom Sumaṃgala mentions in connection with Dhammapāla in his other *ṭīkā*, i.e., the Abhidhammatthavikāsinī, is none other than Ānanda Vanaratana, the author of the Mūlaṭīkā.

Buddhaghosa tradition reflected in the writings of Dhammapāla.[61]) There is a classical instance where Ānanda is reported to have advocated the (Sautrāntika?) theory that denied the stage of duration (*ṭhiti*) to a unit of existence (*dhamma*) while Dhammapāla together with a certain Jotipāla is said to have maintained the (Sarvāstivāda?) position which admitted duration in a *dhamma*.[62]) It is also worth noting that in all such references to Dhammapāla, the title *thera* is added while Ānanda is always designated as *ācariya*. The former would have been a junior contemporary rather than a pupil of the latter.

[38] It is relevant to note that while alluding to these minor controversies within the Pāli school, Sumaṃgala would often couple the names of Dhammapāla and Jotipāla; they appear to have taken a common stand not always consonant with the views of Ānanda.[63]) If we exclude the Elder Jotipāla who is said to have requested Buddhaghosa to write the Majjhima and the Saṃyutta commentaries, there is only one more whom we can think of: the polemicist Jotipāla, the mighty defender of the Mahāvihāra tradition, who came from India towards the end of the 6th century during the reign of Aggabodhi I.[64])

X. The conclusion

[39] The data so far discussed and evaluated by us converge towards the proposition that the Pāli exegete traditionally known as Ācariya Dhammapāla wrote both the Pd and the five *ṭīkā* while residing in the South Indian town of Badaratittha towards the latter half of the 6th (or in the early 7th) century. Once it is granted that the Mūlaṭīkā was compiled long before the 10th century (cf. para. 33), we see no reason to doubt that its author, Ānanda Vanaratana, being himself an Indian Master[65]) was an associate and contemporary of Dhammapāla as is so clearly attested by Sumaṃgala (cf. para. 37). His other associate, Jotipāla, seems also to have been an Indian monk who lived towards the end of the 6th century (cf. para. 38). Their mutual acquaintance insinuated in the Pāli sources is best explained by postulating that all the three of them lived in South India in the 6th century rather than in Sri Lanka in the 10th century.

[40] Now, there is only one piece of evidence that seems to militate against this thesis: the statement in the colophon to the Pm that the request to write this *ṭīkā* came from Dāṭhanāga of Siddhagāma. Accord-

---

[61]) It is fairly evident that the Atthasālinī has a style and a doctrinal emphasis which could not have come from Buddhaghosa (cf. D. Kosambi, op.cit., p. XIV). H. V. Guenther has amply demonstrated this in the course of his treatise, Philosophy and Psychology in the Abhidharma, Lucknow 1957).

[62]) Abhidhammatthavikāsinī, p. 305.

[63]) Ibid., pp. 89, 216, 256, 297, 299, 302, 305 & 397.

[64]) Cūlavaṁsa, chapter XLII, verses 35–37.

[65]) UJ, p. 31.

ing to the obvious interpretation it lends itself to, the author of the Pm ought to be placed in the 10th century (cf. para. 29). This has led both Buddhadatta and Saddhatissa to hold positions that fail to explain all the other data—internal and external—which emerge from the Pāli sources. To us it is clear that it is the colophon to the *Pm* that needs to be explained with reference to these other data rather than the other way about.

[41] In fact, an explanation of this kind has been offered by Dr. Lily de Silva who favours the theory that identifies Dhammapāla the Pāli exegete with the famous 6th century scholar hailing from Kāñcipura. Siddhagāma, she contends, need not be the one mentioned in the Cūlavaṃsa (cf. para. 27); it could very well have been a locality in South India itself. She has compiled a list of places the names of which begin with the word *Siddha-*; near Madras alone (and, therefore, near Kāñcipura) there were sites bearing names such as Siddhakovil, Siddhamalai, Siddhavadi etc.[66]) Interpreted thus, the verse 4 of the colophon to the Pm does not contradict the position we have arrived at in the course of our discussion (cf. para. 39).

[42] Whilst accepting this interpretation as reasonable, we would offer one more reason why the verse 4 of this colophon should not be allowed to play a decisive role in the current discussion on the date of Dhammapāla, unless it is subjected to a critical examination. The reason is that this verse does not fit syntactically into the rest of the colophon.

[43] We reproduce here the first six verses of the colophon so that the fourth verse may be seen in its literary context. These six verses deal with the authorship of the Pm while the remainder which we omit here are mere benedictory stanzas.

1. Suvisuddha-samācāro visuddha-naya-maṇḍitaṁ
   Visuddhimaggaṁ lokassa yad-accanta-visuddhiyā
2. Abhāsi karuṇā-vega-samussāhita-mānaso
   Mahesi vipulodita-visuddhi-mati-pāṭavo
3. Tassa atthaṁ pakāsetuṁ katā, maggaṁ purātanaṁ
   Nissāya yā samāraddhā attha-saṁvaṇṇanā mayā
4. Āyācito Siddhagāma-pariveṇa-vāsinā
   Therena Dāṭhanāgena suddhācārena dhimatā
5. Sā esā paramatthānaṁ tattha tattha yathārahaṁ
   Nidhānato paramatthamañjusā nāma nāmato
6. Sampattā pariniṭṭhānaṁ anākūla-vinicchayā
   Aṭṭhāsītippamāṇayā pāḷiyā bhāṇavārato.[67])

[44] Note that in verse 4, the past participle *āyācito* (being requested) has no noun in the nominative singular to qualify . . . except *Mahesi*

---

[66]) DAṬ, p. XLVI–XLVII.

[67]) Pm (Burmese Edition) part II, p. 442.

in verse 2. Hence the meaning that results from the text as it stands is that the author of the Visuddhimagga was requested by Dāṭhanāga to compose the sub-commentary!

[45] According to the context, of course, the word *āyācito* should refer to Dhammapāla who speaks here in the first person: *mayā* (by me). It is obvious that the nominative *āyācito* cannot agree with the instrumental *mayā*. Whoever dismisses it as a copyist's error is obliged to suggest what the original "correct" form would have been. We cannot conceive of any alternative reading for *āyācito* such as would not offend the grammar or disturb the meter or deviate from the conventional Pāli idiom.[68]) Add to this the fact that in none of the Sinhala and Cambodian manuscripts and the Thai and Burmese editions which we have consulted did we find such a variant for *āyācito*. It is probable, therefore, that *āyācito* belonged to the original formulation of verse 4. In which case, the doubt that remains is whether verse 4 belongs to the colophon at all. What intensifies this doubt is the fact that the text of the colophon flows neatly and naturally when verse 4 is removed altogether as is shown in the following translation:—

3. Whatever commentary (*yā atthasaṁvaṇṇanā*) was begun by me (*mayā*) following the method of the Ancients and [was] composed for elucidating its (Visuddhimagga's) meaning,

---

[68]) There can be only three possible alternatives: a) *āyācitena* agreeing with *mayā*; b) *āyācitā* agreeing with *atthasaṁvaṇṇanā*; c) *āyācito yo* meaning "[by me] who was requested". Though grammatically correct, the first (a) is cumbersome both metrically and idiomatically. For, besides adding an extra syllable, it makes the phrase awkward since another substantive in the instrumental case (Dāṭhanāgena) governed and not qualified by it, follows immediately after. The second (b) is grammatically and metrically passable; but, idiomatically, it is an unusual construction. The third (c) is a form which we come across frequently in Pāli literature, as for instance in Dhammapāla's Prologue to the NettiA, verse 8: *Mahākaccāyano . . . tena yā bhāsitā Netti . . .* etc. This third form, therefore, is both grammatically and idiomatically correct, but metrically wrong, as an extra syllable is added to the line. [Note: When this paper was discussed at the "Symposium on Buddhism in Ceylon" in Göttingen, Dr. R. Gombrich is reported to have suggested *āyācite* (locative absolute) as a possible reading. The suggestion is valuable and is worth pursuing. However, it should be noted that even if such a construction were to be accepted as coming within the conventional idiom, the fact remains that it fails to appear in any of the available manuscripts. — Editorial note: In a letter dated July 15, 1976 Fr. Pieris makes the following remark which he authorized me to include here as additional information: "For the moment, the only emendation I would introduce would be a mere reference to the manuscript I consulted last week in the London Museum Library. There, the questionable verse in the colophon reads as follows: *āyācitena Siddhāgāmama-parivenāni-vāsinā therena adhatāṃgena suddhācārena dhimatā* etc. I had mentioned, that all the manuscripts I had upto then consulted have *āyācito*. This is the first time I meet *āyācitena* which is grammatically correct though syntactically clumsy and metrically wrong. Besides, note also the extra syllables *ma, na, ni-* etc. found in this verse; see also the variants *Adhatāṅgena* for *Dāṭhanāgena* (and other uncommon variants in the other verses too). Moreover, this text is of 1867 while the Cambodian manuscript of 1784 which I have has the reading quoted in my article."]

[4. (I) was requested by Dāṭhanāga of Siddhagāma Pariveṇa, faring pure and wise]

5. That very [commentary] (*sā esā*) which is named "The Container of the Ultimate Truths" (*Paramatthamañjusā*) because ultimate truths are arranged [there] each in its place,

6. [and] which is within easy understanding, has reached completion in [the form of] a text of about eighty eight *bhāṇavāras*.

[46] Thus, our difficulty regarding verse 4 can be summed up as follows: it has no grammatical nexus with the rest of the colophon; when it is removed, the reading is more natural; and, neither the traditional idiomatic usage of the Pāli language nor the available manuscripts and editions of the Pm present us with a variant reading that would redeem the authenticity of the verse. Now, Dhammapāla's association with "Dāṭhanāga of Siddhagāma" is nowhere mentioned in the Pāli sources apart from this instance, though it is true that a verse in the Prologue of the *Pm* does record Dāṭhanāga's request without making any reference to Siddhagāma.[69]) Hence it may be regarded as too rash to reject verse 4 straight away as an interpolation.[70]) Our contention, therefore, is simply this: that the current discussion on the date of Dhammapāla should not be allowed to pivot round "Dāṭhanāga of Siddhagāma" unless and until the authenticity of the fourth verse of the colophon to the *Pm* is thoroughly vindicated.

[69]) Pm (Sinhala Edition), p. 1 (verse 5):
Sampanna-sīlācārena dhimatā sucivuttinā
Ajjhesito Dāṭhanāgattherena thira-cetasā.

[70]) Nor is the possibility of interpolation ruled out altogether. Woodward has drawn our attention to scribes tampering with the very body of a commentarial text (cf. ThagA I, p. VII); the colophons, being mere appendices, are even more exposed to such interferences.

A Sinhalese Cloth Painting of the Vessantara Jātaka

By RICHARD F. GOMBRICH

In his monumental work on the arts and crafts of the Kandyan period, Ananda Coomaraswamy writes[1]) that he knows of no surviving paintings on cloth (*petikaḍa*). Nor am I aware that such a painting has ever been published, though several are known to exist. It may therefore be of interest to publish a very large and fine cloth painting of the Vessantara Jātaka. The main aim of this paper is to identify the scenes depicted, and to argue that the painting can confidently be dated to the middle of the eighteenth century, probably even to the 1750s. By way of introduction we shall also introduce some other interesting antiquities which are found in the same temple.

Coomaraswamy[2]) quotes literary and epigraphic evidence for the practice of painting sacred pictures on cloth: the Cūḷavaṃsa (LXXIII, 77) mentions it in the reign of Parākrama Bāhu I (1153–86); and a *sannasa* quoted by Lawrie[3]) ascribes the commissioning of such a painting to King Śrī Sanghabō Senasammata Vikrama Bāhu of Senkaḍagala. This king is not mentioned in the Cūḷavaṃsa or in the standard modern regnal lists of Sinhalese kings; but H. W. Codrington has shown that he ruled in Kandy from c. 1473 to 1510 or 1511, while kings Parākrama Bāhu VIII and IX ruled in the Low Country.[4]) No other historical records of cloth paintings are known to me.

It was Dr. Siri Gunasinghe who drew my attention to the existence of cloth paintings at Arattana Raja Maha Vihāra, and I much regret that he has not been able to publish them himself. I visited the *vihāra* in December 1969 and in June 1974. It stands just off the Rikillagaskaḍa road from Kandy to Nuwara Eliya, about half a mile before one reaches the more famous *potgul vihāra* at Hanguranketa. In a small building near the *vihāragedara* (image-house), a *poyagē* (chapter house) which also serves as a storeroom, are kept three paintings on cloth. The largest and finest of these depicts the Vessantara Jātaka, in nine tiers. The incumbent very kindly allowed me to photograph it, which I did with the assistance of Mr. Y. P. Jayatissa, Mr. R. M. U. Dharmavardhana and Mr. P. A. G. Jayaratna; some of the photographs are in fact by Mr. Jayatissa.

---

[1]) Ananda K. Coomaraswamy, Mediaeval Sinhalese Art, Broad Campden, Glos. 1908, p. 64.

[2]) Ibid., pp. 72–3.

[3]) A. Lawrie, Gazetteer of the Central Provinces of Ceylon, Colombo 1896, p. 910.

[4]) Epigraphia Zeylanica, IV, London 1943, p. 8. I owe this reference to Mr. U. A. Gunasekara.

The temple is already described by Lawrie[5]) as ancient. He calls it simply 'Arattana or Medapitiye Vihare'; the incumbent told me that it is called Devram Vehera (= Pali: Jetavana Vihāra). Its claim to be a Raja Maha Vihāra is securely based on two *sannas* (royal edicts) dating from Kandyan times and recorded by Lawrie. The first, issued by King Senevirat (Pali: Senāratana) (1604–35), is dated 1613; the second, issued by King Kīrti Śrī Rājasiṃha (1747–82), is dated 1758. Both *sannas* restore to the temple land which had previously belonged to it but had somehow become alienated to royal use.

None of the antiquities at the temple are dated. Worthy of note, apart from the cloth paintings, are two pairs of upright stone slabs on which are carved in high relief grotesque figures, doubtless guardians, which were described to me as *Bhairava*; they are wearing Kandyan costume, and look as if they date from the Kandyan period. The paintings in the *vihāragedara*,[6]) on the other hand, can hardly antedate the middle of the last century, nor is the building itself, a simple oblong structure, necessarily older.

The three cloth paintings are all much in the same style, but while the first and third look to me to be by the same artist, the second one, with the short Vessantara narrative, is clearly by another hand. I shall describe them in ascending order of size.

The height of the first, measured from mid-roller, is 92″, the breadth 55″ (minus the border 51½″). On top are the 16 "great places" (*mahāsthāna*), the places of pilgrimage in Ceylon which the Buddha is supposed to have visited,[7]) arranged in two rows of eight. Below this is a row of four seated Buddhas, each being adored by saints in profile. (Fig. 1). The sets of figures are identical. Sets of four Buddhas are not usual in Kandyan iconography. Probably all four are representations of Gotama Buddha; but if they are seen in conjunction with the pictures below them, it is also possible that they represent the four other Buddhas of our eon: Kakucchanda, Koṇāgamana, Kassapa, and the future Buddha Metteyya. However, I know of no other Kandyan representation of Metteyya as already Enlightened.

Below the Buddhas, occupying the bulk of the picture space, is a seated Buddha enthroned under the Bo tree, attended by a host of divinities; the scene depicted is the Enlightenment. This picture is very similar to the main scene shown on fig. 4 (see below). At the bottom, shown in just one tier, is the Dahaṃsoṅḍa Jātaka, half of it lost by being stitched onto the roller.

The second painting, which is in the worst condition of the three, is 110½″ high, measured from mid-roller, and 54″ across. Minus the borders,

---

[5]) Op. cit., p. 577, s.v. Medapitiya.

[6]) They include a Vessantara cycle. Sections of this cycle, and of many others, illustrate a book by Margaret Cone and myself, The Perfect Generosity of Prince Vessantara, Oxford 1977.

[7]) For details see my Precept and Practice, Oxford 1971, pp. 109–10.

the measurements are 105″ high and $49^1/_2$″ across. The top half (50″) is occupied by a painting of the future Buddha Metteyya sitting in his palace (*vimāna*) in the Tusita heaven (fig. 2). Below this is a seated Buddha attended by gods. The bottom part is the best preserved. There are two tiers of narrative painting, of which the upper shows the Sāma Jātaka, the lower the Vessantara Jātaka (fig. 3).

The largest painting is $120^1/_2$″ high, measured from mid-roller, and $80^1/_4$″ wide; minus the borders it is 117″ × $75^1/_2$″. It is divided into two almost equal halves. The upper half (fig. 4) is in two parts: in the centre is a Buddha seated under the Bo tree, iconographically very like indeed to the one on the first painting, but bigger and richer in detail (figs. 5 and 6). On both sides of this, badly damaged, are Jātaka stories, arranged in separate series, the sequence running from top to bottom. The lower half of the painting shows the Vessantara Jātaka in 9 tiers. The total height of the painting is $55^1/_2$″, and the height of the individual panels varies between just under 7″ and just over 5″. The story runs zig-zag downwards, beginning at the top left-hand corner.

The only painting to bear any inscription is the Dahaṃsoňḍa Jātaka panel at the bottom of the first *petikaḍa*. Here the title has been given, but the crude way in which it is done suggests a later hand. Though captions are common in Sinhalese narrative art, these paintings lack them, and any attempt at dating must rest on iconography and style. We shall focus our attention on the Vessantara Jātaka of the largest *petikaḍa*, much the longest and finest of the narrative paintings.

So few Kandyan paintings have been published (outside Ceylonese magazines and newspapers) that some extremely general remarks about style are perhaps necessary. Our Vessantara *petikaḍa* shows all the salient characteristics of Kandyan painting: a conventionally restricted palette, with shapes clearly outlined against a red background; a strongly linear style, the colour not covering the outlines; a two-dimensional effect, without perspective or shading; slim, elongated human figures, generally shown making lively gestures; rather rigid conventions in the depiction of costumes, deities, trees and buildings; a tendency to fill up the picture space (though this feature becomes more marked in some later styles), inserting decorative flowers where large gaps would otherwise occur; and an uninterrupted "comic strip" mode of narrative presentation, with the same figures constantly repeated as one scene flows into the next. The story sequence from top to bottom in a zig-zag is also a common feature of Sinhalese narrative painting (e. g. Hanguranketa *potgul vihāra*). Our painting also has certain distinctive stylistic features: (1) all the human heads, without any exception, are shown in three-quarters profile—though treatment of the bodies is quite varied; (2) the human figures are even slenderer than usual; (3) the quality of the drawing is exceptionally fine. This last characteristic has of course some relation to the unusual medium and the fact that the adult human

Fig. 1

Fig. 2

Fig. 3

Fig. 4

Fig. 5

Fig. 6

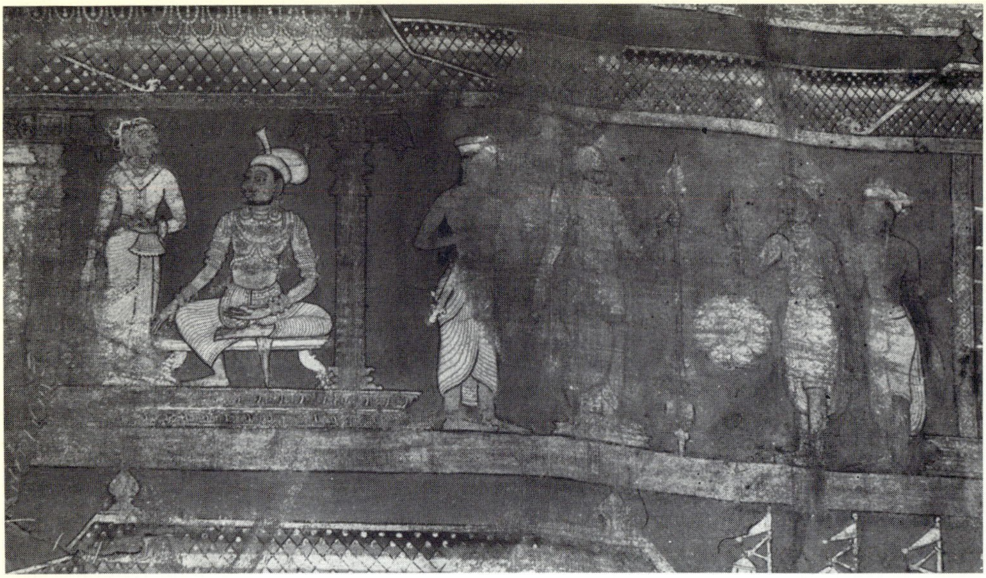

Fig. 7

Figures 7 and 8 overlap.

Fig. 8

Fig. 9

Fig. 10

Fig. 11

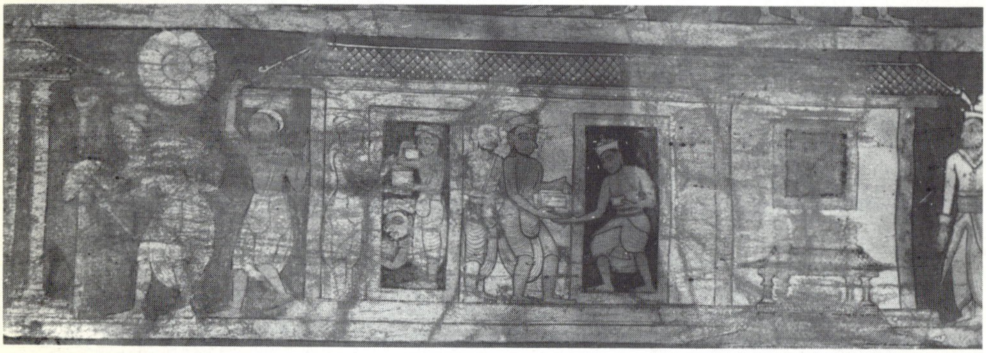
Fig. 16

Fig. 17

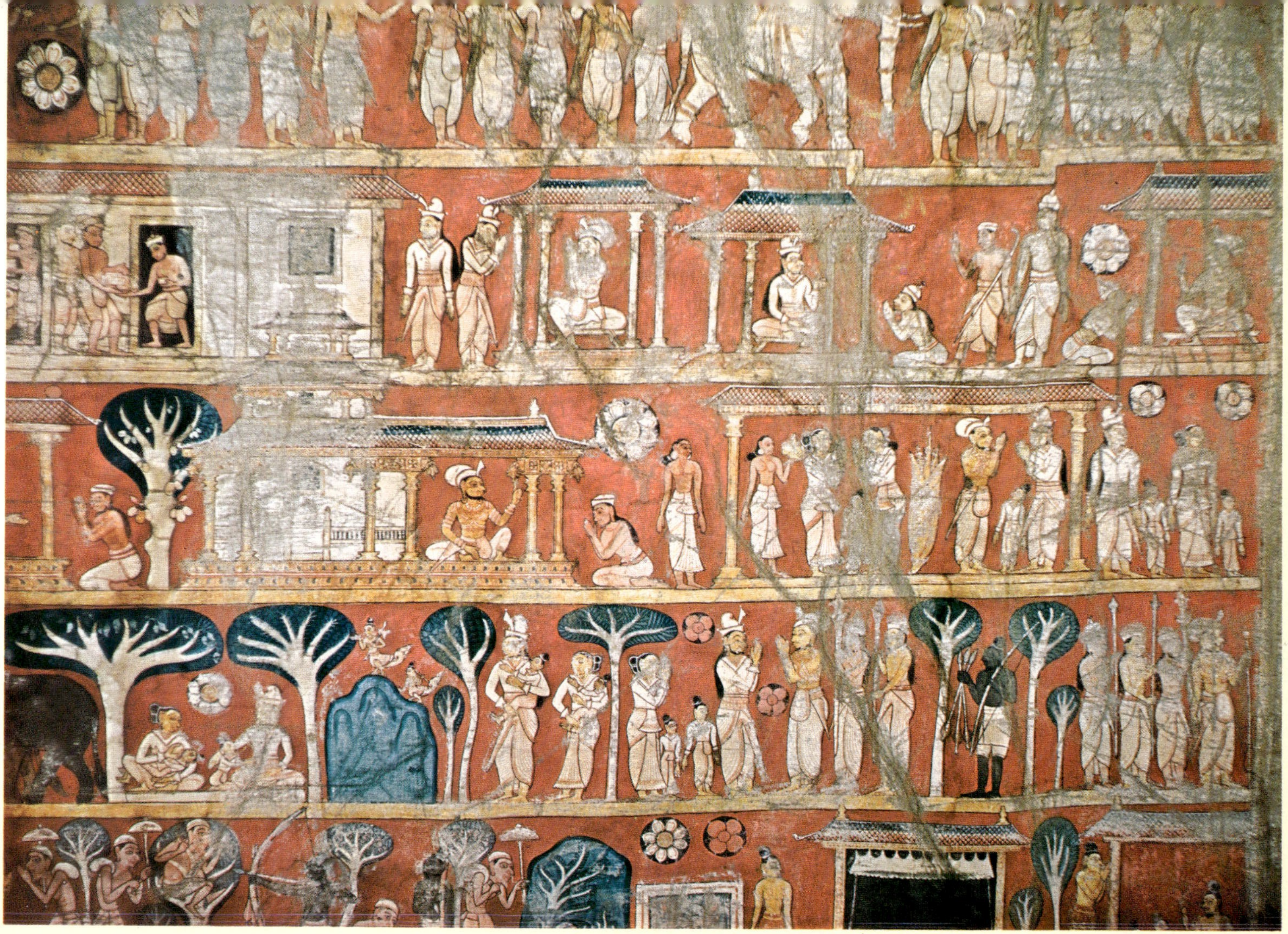

Fig. 12

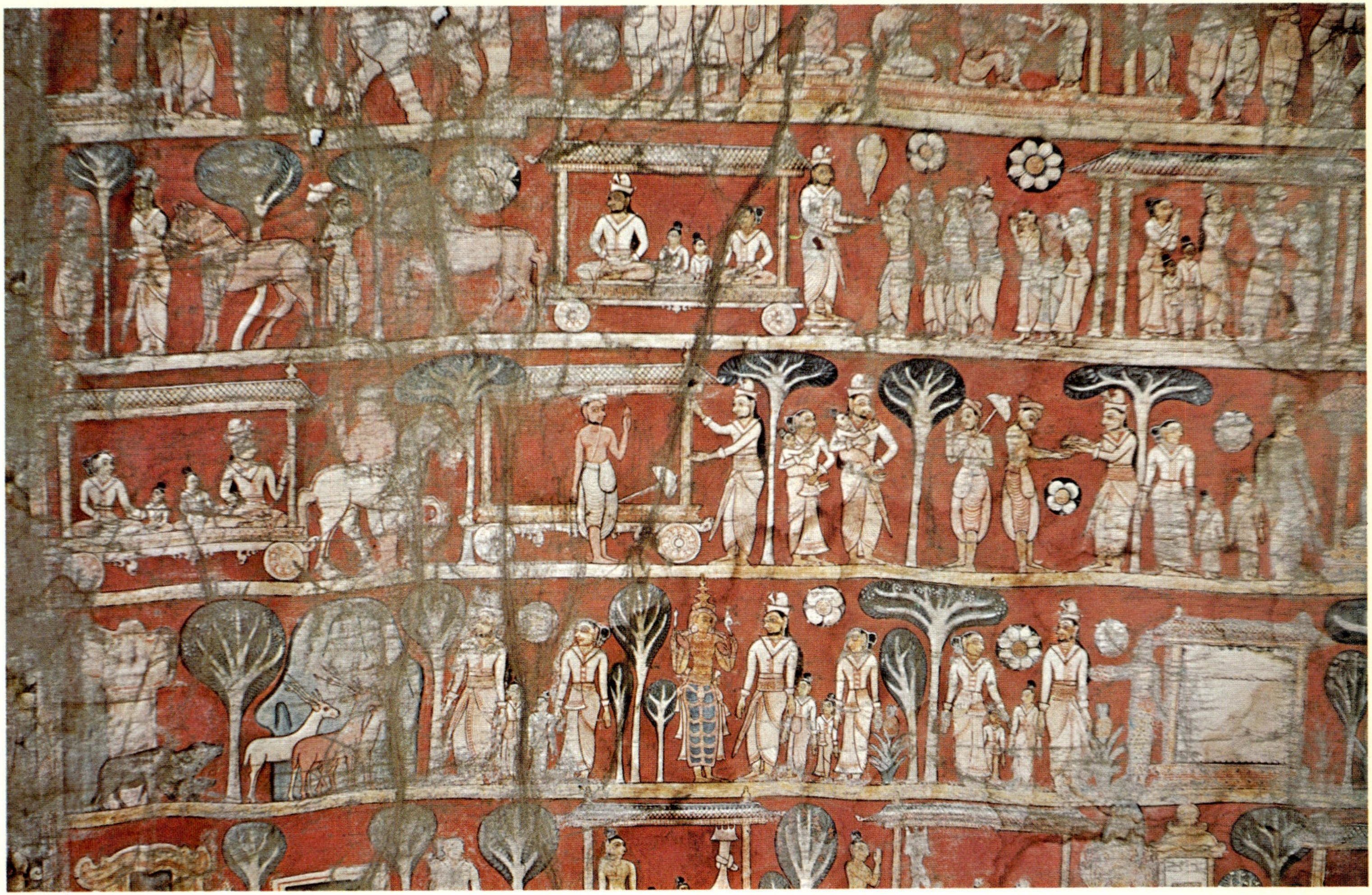

Fig. 13

Fig. 14

Fig. 15

Fig. 18

Figures 18 and 19 overlap.

Fig. 19

Fig. 20

Fig. 21 Figures 20 and 21 overlap.

Fig. 22

Fig. 23

Figures 23, 24 and 25 overlap.

Fig. 24

Fig. 25

Fig. 26

Fig. 27 Figures 26 and 27 overlap.

figures are only about three to four inches tall; but the animal drawing, for example, is remarkable.

When it comes to the iconography of the Vessantara Jātaka, published material is even scantier, though this was the most popular narrative theme in Kandyan art. Luckily we do have available for comparison the fine, albeit brief, Vessantara cycle painted on the shrine wall of Mädavala Raja Maha Vihāra. Not only have these paintings been published (in black and white reproduction);[8]) they are among the most accurately dated of Kandyan paintings, for we can deduce from a *sannasa* dated 1755 that they had been completed very shortly before that date.

The Vessantara Jātaka is also depicted at Degaldoruva, in a cycle which in both extent and quality rivals our own. Unhappily it is (like most Kandyan paintings) in a precarious physical condition, and already much damaged. (However, the temple is one of the very few which have had the benefits of expert cleaning in the recent past.) The names of three of the painters at Degaldoruva are known, and the paintings of which the Vessantara cycle is one were "completed in 1771, or at any rate before 1786, when the *sannasa* was granted."[9])

Mädavala and Degaldoruva are the two cycles to which our Vessantara painting bears the closest historical affinity. However, I know of four other *petikaḍa* (besides the second one at Arattana) which have Vessantara paintings. Two are in the National Museum of Sri Lanka in Colombo, and I am grateful to the Director for sending me photographs of them. On one of them the Vessantara Jātaka is depicted in five tiers, on the other in two. Both versions are, like ours, at the bottom of much larger paintings. The two differ in style from each other, but still more from the Arattana paintings; they are both much more crudely drawn and more crowded, the longer version in particular displaying a *horror vacui* untypical of the best Kandyan work. Both are so badly faded as to give but a very poor impression of the original colouring; only the red remains. Much the same can be said of the version in the Archaeological Museum in Kandy, which is also in five tiers, though smaller than the five-tier Colombo version. Again, the Vessantara cycle is at the bottom of a larger painting, under a sedent Buddha. This version too is comparatively crudely drawn, with ill-proportioned figures filling most of the picture space. It, too, is badly faded—so badly that the bottom tier is almost obliterated—and retains no colour but the dark red of the background. These three *petikaḍa* are all in the general Kandyan style, though of rather inferior artistry. The fourth is quite different. It probably dates from the turn of this century, and is kept in Agrabodhi Vihāra, Dehipāgoḍa, Uḍunuvara, Kandy District; it has been illustrated in my book (see note 6).

---

[8]) G. E. Godakumbura, Medawala Vihara Frescoes, Colombo, no date, plates 1–3.

[9]) Coomaraswamy, op.cit., p. 168.

The cloth painting closest in style to those at Arattana among those I have seen is in the museum of the Archaeological Department of the University of Sri Lanka, Peradeniya campus. It has no narrative cycle, and shows only a sedent Buddha surrounded by worshipping deities, who are mostly in full profile. However, the stylistic similarity of this painting to our main subject is less striking than is that of Mädavala (see below).

The Vessantara Jātaka is the last (no. 547) and longest of the Pali Jātaka stories.[10]) The old verse epic which forms the core of the text begins at the point when Vessantara gives away a magic rain-bringing white elephant to brahmin emissaries from another kingdom. The pages which precede this core are a kind of prologue in heaven, virtually irrelevant to the main story, and a brief account of Vessantara's early life, which serves to demonstrate his propensity for generosity and to introduce the dramatis personae. It is thus not surprising to find that it is this early part of the story which shows the greatest iconographic fluctuation; indeed, there seems to be no consensus about which episodes (if any) to show before the giving of the elephant, except that an alms-house, visualized much like a Sinhalese *kaḍē* (roadside stall) is a common theme. The top two tiers of our cycle deal with this beginning to the story, and they appear to be iconographically unique. Alas, they are also badly worn, which makes identification of the scenes all the harder. This necessitates a detailed description.

The very first scene, top left (fig. 7), shows a man (Vessantara's father, King Sañjaya?) seated at ease in a royal building, with a woman (Vessantara's mother, Queen Phusatī?) standing beside him. Both wear upper garments, which denote high status. To their right are two armed men facing away from the building (guards?); one of them appears to be on a pedestal. Facing them are two men with their right hands raised with index fingers pointing upwards; they are probably suppliants/beggars. Behind them is an alms-house (fig. 8) in which a low-status woman is feeding a man, and beyond this again a man is giving a box to another man, while a second seems to be holding such a box, which he has presumably just been given, and a third is waiting. This whole sequence may just illustrate the atmosphere of royal munificence into which Vessantara was born.

Next we find a (or the) royal couple again seated indoors; the queen is holding a rope with a tassle—a fanning device? The king is receiving the salutations of a man standing on the threshold. The next bit, badly worn, shows some figures in a carriage. A remarkable feature of all the carriages in this *petikaḍa* is that they look like buildings on wheels; moreover, all of them, except the one which the story specifically mentions as being horse-drawn, are propelled by a man punting from behind (see the bottom tier). I can only suggest that this scene represents Phusatī

[10]) The Pāli text is Jātaka, ed. Fausbøll, vol. VI, London 1896 (reprinted 1964), pp. 479–596.

touring the city, because it says in the text that she was on such a tour when she gave birth to Vessantara. In that case the previous scene would presumably be of Sañjaya and Phusatī ordering the charioteer to get ready for the trip. However, the next scene has me in perplexity. We are indoors again. In the centre sit two small children, apparently facing each other and holding hands. On the left are two bare-breasted ladies; the one on the far left is holding a breast—clearly they are wet-nurses—while the other is saluting the noble lady on the right, over the heads of the children. I would like this to be the infant Vessantara, but cannot convincingly explain the two children; this is a single scene, so the repetition of a figure within it is unlikely. The only possibility I can suggest is that the child on the left, next to the nurses, is a representative of the sixty-thousand noble children who are said to be brought up with Vessantara. The rest of the line is filled up with a huge palace, the upper storey of which breaks out of the frame into the picture above. Its poor preservation makes one unsure, but it seems to be empty of figures.

The second tier, like the bottom one, seems to show a set of scenes converging towards a centre; the dominant theme seems to be the marriage of Vessantara to Princess Maddī. The zig-zag pattern is followed to the extent that the right has some chronological priority over the left. On the far right, again badly worn and also torn, is an indoor scene (fig. 9) in which the king seems to have a child, presumably Vessantara, on his lap. Then we find a couple standing on a dais under a decorated arch, receiving the homage of two kneeling men and one standing. This I take to be the wedding of Vessantara and Maddī, although he is not holding her hand, which is the usual way of depicting weddings. Behind the men is a structure topped by a lot of pennants which leads us, moving left, to a grand decorated gateway. Left of this we find the couple seated indoors, she smelling a lotus while he holds the tasselled rope. I interpret this as the newly married couple. Left of this, she is shown arriving in a carriage drawn by attendants bearing fly-whisks (symbols of royalty); behind her advance a white horse, a red horse, and a grey elephant, all beautifully drawn in profile, and attendants on foot. The background to this procession is more of the pennant-topped structure. I take all this to be the arrival of Maddī for the wedding. Next left is another indoor scene (fig. 10) with Vessantara, Maddī, and two children of unequal size, who are therefore their son and daughter, Jāli and Kaṇhājinā. Left of this stand two men on pedestals, both of whom could be Vessantara; they are greeting the musicians who fill up the left end of the tier. These musicians are probably left over from the wedding procession, though they might just be playing for Vessantara and his family. They are playing the three common types of Kandyan drum (*bera*, *hēvisi* and *ṭämmäṭṭama*) and a small gong.

I have described these top two tiers in such detail because they are unique, and because their identification is uncertain. I shall now identify the rest of the scenes. Tier 3 is devoted to the gift of the white elephant, who is shown three times: he enters left, is given away centre (fig. 11), and led off on the right. The donor is Vessantara, the recipients a group of four brahmins, signalized by their umbrellas, who seem to be accompanied by a servant. Between the hailing scene and the giving scene is a building, an alms-house in which a woman is feeding three men.

Much of the rest of the cycle can be seen on the plates. Fig. 12 covers the right side (nearly half) of tiers 4–6; fig. 13 covers the same amount on the left side; fig. 14 covers the left side of tiers 7–9; fig. 15 the centre portion.

Tier 4 starts on the right, and is full of incident. I shall devote one sentence to each scene. Sañjaya despatches his steward to tell Vessantara of his banishment to Crooked Mountain. The steward breaks the news to Vessantara. Vessantara goes to see the king. He then gives away all his property (know as "the gift of the seven hundreds"), an episode which is always illustrated by depicting the people carrying off chests and boxes (fig. 16). Vessantara takes his family to say good-bye to his parents. He makes a farewell speech to the citizens (shown as four men and three women). He and his family then leave in a horse-drawn carriage, but are hailed by a brahmin (not by four brahmins, as in the text). He gives the horses (there seem to be two) to the brahmins.

At this point the text has it that the horses are miraculously replaced by gods in the guise of red deer. Our artist, more logically, has white horses reappear. So we begin tier 5 with the family again in a horse-drawn carriage—but again hailed by a brahmin, who is asking for the carriage. Vessantara gives him the carriage—at which point the phantom horses sensibly disappear. Vessantara and Maddī now walk along carrying their children. The next little scene is interesting, because it appears to be apocryphal. Yet another brahmin hails them, and Vessantara proceeds to give him—we cannot see what; presumably it can only be some valuable ornament taken off his own person. There is no such incident in the Pali text, but episodes of giving are multiplied in most of the later versions of the story. We cannot tell whether the painter drew on another text, or added something here on his own account.

Vessantara and his family now walk on—all four on foot—and come to the resting house (what is now called an *ambalama* in Ceylon) outside the city of the Cetas. They sit in it, and Maddī suckles her daughter; a Ceta respectfully addresses them (fig. 17). This Ceta then goes and reports their arrival to his king, who is sitting in a palace which like the one in the top tier breaks out of the frame of the tier and intrudes into the picture above. The king and (we assume) the queen of the Cetas come and visit Vessantara and his family and try to persuade them to stay; what we are shown is the woman talking to Maddī, by whom stands Kaṇhājinā, and the man talking to Vessantara, by whom stands Jāli. All four adults are standing making the gesture of respect (*añjali*), so presumably this is the moment of leave-taking. The four exiles then again proceed on foot.

But they have not left the Cetas behind yet, for at the right end of tier 6 we see their guard of honour. There is then another farewell at the edge of the forest: Vessantara and family are saluting the Ceta king, behind whom stand two armed guards and the swarthy forester whom they appoint to guard the approach to Vessantara's retreat. He has a bow and arrows, and is coloured black/dark grey. Vessantara and Maddī then carry the children on again. Most of the scenes at this stage in the story are divided by trees. Between the next trees is a mountain on which perch two creatures which are human above the waist and birds below—*kinnaras*. Between the next two trees the family are again resting seated; Vessantara has his arm round Jāli's shoulder and Maddī gives suck to Kaṇhājinā. Then come two dark grey elephants, beautifully drawn.

The next two scenes are again a puzzle. We are shown a small building with the entrance covered by a white cloth; comparison with what follows suggests that this is a hermitage shown unoccupied—there is an identical building behind Vessantara as he gives the children in tier 8. To the left of this stands a damaged male figure, who faces the exiles and has his arm stuck straight out in front of him, an unparallelled gesture. Then, beyond the next trees, the exiles are again walking on and encounter a unique figure, a god: his body is golden; he has a high gold hat and a blue lower garment, and in his hands he holds in hieratic manner two ritual implements, one of which is a conch. Though the conch is better known as an appurtenance of Viṣṇu, in Sinhalese iconography it can also belong to Sakka. The only two named gods who appear in the Vessantara story are Sakka and the gods' artificer, Vissakamma, who builds a hermitage for Vessantara at Sakka's bidding.

It seems that there has been a confusion between the progress of Vessantara's family to the Crooked Mountain and that of the wicked brahmin Jūjaka, who soon afterwards follows the same route. According to the text, before Jūjaka reaches Vessantara's hermitage he comes to the hermitage of an ascetic called Accuta, who points the way out to him (at great length). That the encounter with Accuta has been transferred from Jūjaka to Vessantara becomes more plausible when we find just up the road, at the Potgul Vihāra in Hanguranketa, a Vessantara mural (dated 1870) in which Vessantara and family at this point in the story meet a man who clearly is indicating the way. A displaced Accuta however still leaves the problem of the god with a conch. Vessantara does not appear to be interacting with him, so perhaps he cannot see him; maybe it is Sakka about to tell Vissakamma to make the hermitage.

After this encounter—or non-encounter—Vessantara and family are shown again walking through the forest, and there are charming drawings of deer and boar.

At the beginning of tier 7 stands an ornate doorway. A little further on in the same tier this signals a break in the story, but here it seems to have no such function; it is just a decoration. Then we see the square lotus pond, which the text says the family have to pass before reaching their destination. Now Maddī is shown twice with the children, first walking along with her hand on Jāli's shoulder and Kaṇhājinā on her hip, then in a building with both children standing beside her. Vessantara is omitted, because the text explains that there were two huts, in one of which Vessantara lived alone; during the day Maddī would leave the children while she went out to gather food, but at night she took them to her hut. In the next scene they are visiting and saluting Vessantara, who is seated in his hut, and as the children are inside it we may deduce that he is just about to begin (or to end) a stint of baby-sitting. Beyond the hut there is a damaged figure hovering in mid-air, presumably a divinity; this could be Vissakamma just after making the two huts, though in Sinhalese iconography he normally has ten arms.[11])

As in the text, the scene now shifts. The break is marked by an ornamental doorway. Enter Jūjaka, the old brahmin who provides the occasion for Vessantara's crucial act of generosity, the gift of his children. Jūjaka is first shown at home, being beaten by his young wife Amitatāpanā, who demands servants. Jūjaka, with his brahmin umbrella and a sack of provisions over his shoulder, then bids his wife farewell and sets off. When he gets to the forest which is being guarded by the Ceta, he climbs up a tree fleeing the Ceta's wrath. However, he tells the Ceta a plausible story: he is bringing Vessantara the news that his sentence of exile has been repealed. At this the Ceta relents and feeds him. He goes on, and when he reaches the Crooked Mountain it is early morning, so he hides behind a rock to wait till Maddī goes out foraging (fig. 18). The square lotus pond is shown again, with Maddī beside it. That night Maddī has a terrible dream of foreboding; its contents are not depicted, but she is shown (fig. 19) lying asleep with her two children; the hut's interior is black to show that it is still night. Then Maddī leaves the children with Vessantara, as usual, and says good-bye.

In tier 8 Maddī is foraging in the wood (fig. 20). Next to her is a maze, the conventional depiction of Crooked Mountain. The maze separates her from Vessantara's hut, which is empty (the entrance covered by a white curtain). Beyond the hut stands Vessantara, giving the children to Jūjaka (fig. 21). Jūjaka then ties their hands together and leads them off. He spends the night up a tree, binding the children to its foot; a deity disguised as Maddī comes and tends them. In the text this incident comes slightly later (see below). The next day Jūjaka drives them on, beating them. It is notable that the artist does not show the popular scene in which deities disguised as wild beasts keep Maddī away while Vessantara is giving the children, to prevent her from disturbing this supreme act of self-sacrifice. Instead we now find her fainting dead away at Vessantara's feet; he revives her by sprinkling her with water. Her bottom half is here shown only once, the upper half in its two consecutive poses appearing twice at right angles. The next scene, an important one in the

---

11) Coomaraswamy, op.cit., p. 79 and plate XXI.

story but often omitted in art, shows Vessantara giving away Maddī to Sakka disguised as a brahmin. (Sakka gives her back again immediately, but one group suffices for the whole scene.) It is at this point that the text places the incident when Jūjaka spends the night up a tree. The scene at the (left) end of tier 8 now conflates all that happens when Jūjaka reaches King Sañjaya's court. Sañjaya takes his grandson on his knee. (The text has Queen Phusatī do likewise to Kaṇhājinā, but here the grandmother is left out.) Sañjaya redeems Jāli by paying his weight in gold. Jūjaka uses the proceeds to eat so much that he drops dead. The deity who has guided Jūjaka and the children to the palace hovers over this scene of gluttony.

The beginning of the bottom tier disposes of Jūjaka: he is shown lying on his funeral pyre, surmounted by his knapsack and umbrella. The rest of the tier completes the happy ending. The white elephant comes back—this is not explicit in the text, but is a common embellishment to the story. King Sañjaya is then shown giving orders for a military procession to bring Vessantara home in style. Sañjaya and Phusatī then set out in a punted vehicle. They converge on a great ornamental doorway which marks the end of the story. From the other side, in a similar vehicle, come Vessantara and Maddī, reunited with their children, preceded by the white elephant and followed by musicians (fig. 22).

The only eighteenth-century Vessantara cycle of comparable length is that at Degaldoruva. There is of course generic similarity in style, and in such details as costumes and buildings, but the iconography of the story is strikingly dissimilar. The figures are not nearly so elongated—in fact they are almost squat—and they are shown sometimes in full profile, sometimes in three-quarters profile. They are somewhat more elaborately clothed; in particular, Maddī is covered above the waist. The buildings are much the same, and the vehicles are much like the buildings, but there is no punting (there are in fact no triumphal processions shown). The selection of scenes depicted varies a good deal from our cycle; for example, the giving of Maddī, and then everything in our bottom tier, are omitted. Though it is not in good condition, we reproduce here for comparison the final scenes of the Degaldoruva cycle: the last days of Jūjaka (figs. 23–25). Note that in the scene in which he spends the night up a tree there seem to be two deities, disguised as Vessantara and Maddī respectively.

Much of the closest parallel known to me is the short cycle at Mädavala. Here some of the similarities are really striking. The scenes shown at Mädavala, reading left to right, are: (1) Maddī out foraging; (2) Maddī and the children listening respectfully to Vessantara, who is in his hut; (3) Vessantara giving Jūjaka the children. (Fig. 26:) (4) Jūjaka leading them off; (5) Jūjaka up the tree; (6) Jūjaka leading the children on again; (7) Jūjaka being accosted by Sañjaya's steward. (Fig. 27:) (8) Jūjaka feeds, waited on by a maidservant, while a deity watches, and Jāli is being balanced against gold; (9) a steward kneels before King Sañjaya and Queen Phusatī. In the story sequence (2) precedes (1) and (9) precedes (8).

Mädavala scenes (7) and (9) have no parallel in our *petikaḍa*, and (2) is differently treated (near the end of tier 7). But much of our tier 8 is almost exactly the same as Mädavala, going the other way (i.e. right to left, not left to right). The most striking difference between the two depictions is that in the *petikaḍa* all the figures are in three-quarters profile, while at Mädavala they are in full profile. Were it not for this, one would suspect that the two were by the same artist. The costumes are identical, and so are the excessively small children (except for their colour). The figure of Maddī out foraging is almost the same, and so is the maze. The sequence Mädavala scenes 3–4–5 is almost identical with ours, except that Mädavala has no deity at the foot of the tree. A crucial point of resemblance is that scene (6) is not specifically mentioned at this point in the text (though it is not illogically placed); yet it is common to both cycles. Similarly, in scene (8) we again find a feature shared with the *petikaḍa* but not specifically mentioned in the text: the maidservant who is waiting on Jūjaka. The similarities are so close that they can hardly be explained as derived from a common model; besides, there were no pattern books for these paintings. One of the artists must have copied directly from the other. Moreover, as Mädavala is dated 1755, we can feel confident that our *petikaḍa* was done at a similar date. Maybe it is historically connected with the *sannasa* of 1758.

In conclusion let us compare our version with that at the bottom of the second *petikaḍa*, the first half of which is illustrated on fig. 3. Iconographically this is even closer to Mädavala than to our main cycle, but the drawing differs a good deal from both and is not so skilful. The scenes shown correspond to those at Mädavala as listed above, omitting numbers (2) and (7). (These two Mädavala scenes are also not in our main *petikaḍa*.) In scene (1) Maddī is shown without a maze, but with one of the wild beasts who is barring her way. In scene (5) there is a deity at the foot of the tree (as in our *petikaḍa*), though she is very small. In scene (8) there is no maidservant, and in scene (9) no Queen Phusatī or grandchildren—the artist may have run out of space. Jūjaka is too big for the top of his tree. This artist is more concerned than the others to fill up his picture space; he puts clouds in stretches of empty sky, and in the small spaces remaining puts stars, not flowers. The hermitage is shown in quite a different way, a cave seen in profile. (It is also a cave at Degaldoruva, but viewed frontally.) This artist has arranged his scenes in much the same way as the Mädavala painter, and is obviously working in exactly the same tradition, but his personal style is further from Mädavala than is that of our main *petikaḍa* painter.

Mañjuśrībhāṣita-Citrakarmaśāstra: A Mahayanistic Śilpaśāstra from Sri Lanka

By HANS RUELIUS

Amongst the palm leaf manuscripts kept in the National Archives of Sri Lanka in Colombo there is one manuscript attracting particular interest of scholars since some time. This manuscript, named Mañjuśrībhāṣita-Citrakarmaśāstra (MC)[1], is supposed to be one of the earliest palm leaf manuscripts preserved in Sri Lanka. According to Professor Bechert, Göttingen, it has to be dated into the 14th century A. D.[1a] The work is, as already indicated by its name, a Mahayanistic Śilpaśāstra. Therefore this manuscript is a very interesting document of Mahayanism in Sri Lanka.

Description of the manuscript

The manuscript contains sixty leaves. Though the end of the text is missing the manuscript, as such, seems to be complete. Perhaps, the manuscript from which it had been copied was already incomplete. On the obverse of the last leaf the text stops without a colophon. Instead of a colophon the scribe adds the formulas *siddhir astu—ārogyam astu—subham astu.* On the reverse of the last leaf we find three lines forming the beginning of a Sinhalese translation (*sannaya*) of a Pāli text.

The pagination, excluding the first leaf, runs from *ka* to *ghe.* The first leaf, instead of a number, bears the words *svasti siddham* on the left margin of the obverse. The number of lines varies from six to eight.

The script

Our manuscript shows quite a peculiar style of writing which seems to be considerably old, at least, earlier than the Kandyan period. A few examples are given next page:

---

[1]) No. 4/47/1(3/18). I recently had the opportunity to read this manuscript from a microfilm prepared by the National Archives of Sri Lanka, and to use a transcript of excerpts from the manuscript by Pandit K. D. Wickramaratne, both made for Prof. H. Bechert during his visits to Sri Lanka in 1973 and 1974.

[1a]) By personal communiticaon.

1. = *kri*, = *ṣu*, = *la* (or *ḷa*?), = *na*
2. = *khā*, = *ṭā*, = *thā*, = *cā*, = *mā*, = *vā*, = *dhā*.
3. The virāma is always = *m*, = *t*, etc.
4. = *pra*, = *tra* etc.
5. = *gu*, = *tu*, etc., = *pu*, = *pū*, etc.
6. = *la*, = *ṇa*,
7. = *dā*, = *kyā*.

Most of these letters can be characterized as cursive forms. Some of them, as the types of *na*, *ṇa*, *la* and *kri* given above, are occuring side by side with the usual modern types. The up-strokes of *ja*, *ṇa*, *ra*, etc. as well as the down-strokes of *kra*, *tra*, *pra*, etc. are unusually long and sometimes reaching beyond two or more lines. If we want to date the manuscript by means of palaeographical characteristics it needs, of course, a much closer examination of the script than it can be undertaken in this paper.

The contents of the text

A list of contents is given on the first page of the manuscript:

Bhagavān uvāca:

sthānam ālayabhedaṃ ca bhūmigrahaṇalakṣaṇam |
tattadgarbbhavidhānaṃ ca caturtthāgāralakṣaṇam ‖
ekasthānavidhānaṃ ca tasya dignirṇṇayan tathā |
caityasthānavidhānaṃ ca mānakarmmeṣṭikādīnām ‖
chattrabhedavidhānaṃ ca vṛkṣagrahaṇalakṣaṇam |
mānoddeśavidhānaṃ ca garbbhāgāravidhikriyā ‖
śūlalakṣaṇam eva ca caityapūjāvidhānakam |
rajjukarmmāṣṭabandhaṃ ca mṛttikālakṣaṇan tathā ‖
kaṭaśarkkaravidhānaṃ ca pramāṇalakṣaṇan tathā |
sarvvajñalakṣaṇam bodhisatvasyāpi ca lakṣaṇam ‖
bhrūṇādilakṣaṇaṃ caiva pañcabuddhādilakṣaṇam |
indrādilakṣaṇaṃ caiva varṇṇabhedavidhānakam ‖
gajāśvasiṃhamānaṃ ca akṣisthāpanam iṣyate |
. . . . [vā]stuśāstramārggān mayoktādikramam āgataḥ ‖ [2])

If we compare this list with the colophons of chapters, we can see that only a short passage from the end of the text is missing in our manuscript.

[2]) Scribal errors are corrected without notes.

The last chapter, named *gajāśvasiṃhamāna* in the above list begins on page 111 (*ghṛ* R 4) of the manuscript.[3])

The following colophons of chapters are given in the manuscript:

1.	ki R 1	sthānālayabheda
2.	[kṛ R 6	bhūmigrahaṇalakṣaṇa][4])
3.	khe V 2	caityalakṣaṇa
4.	kho R 7	vṛkṣasaṃgrahavidhāna
5.	khau R 7	vṛkṣasaṃcchedanavidhāna[5])
6.	ga V 1	garbhāgāravidhāna
7.	gi V 2	śūlalakṣaṇa
8.	gu R 5	ratnanyāsavidhāna
9.	gu V 2	aṣṭabandhavidhāna
10.	gu V 7	rajjukarmavidhāna
11.	gū V 1	mṛttikālakṣaṇa
12.	gṛ R 1	kaṭaśarkaravidhāna[6])
13.	ge V 2	pramāṇalakṣaṇa
14.	go R 3	lambamānavidhāna
15.	ghi V 2	pañca[buddhe]ndrā[di]lakṣaṇa[7])
16.	ghī R 4	varṇalakṣaṇavidhāna
17.	ghṛ R 4	akṣimokṣaṇa

In the colophon of chapter 1 the work is called *vāstuvidyāśāstra* (*iti Mañjuśrībhāṣite vāstuvidyāśāstre* ....) and in the colophon of chapter 3 simply *vāstuśāstra*. All other colophons read *iti Mañjuśrībhāṣite citrakarmmaśāstre* ..... I prefer the name *Mañjuśrībhāṣita-citrakarmaśāstra* in this paper because the text is generally known under this title.

Chapter 1 (*sthānālayabheda*) deals with the classification of buildings and the proper sites for them. As a Śilpaśāstra exclusively written for Buddhists, our text is, of course, confined to buildings belonging to Buddhist monasteries. It starts with an enumeration of the various kinds of parks for monks and nuns (1 R 7):

ārāmaṃ caiva vikrāntir dvividhaṃ vāstukalpanam |
hastyārāmavidhānaṃ ca hastivikrāntam eva ca ‖
siṃhārāmavidhānaṃ ca siṃhavikrāntakan tathā |
.... [vi]krāntam parikalpayet ‖
padmārāmavidhim padmavikrāntam paripaṭṭhyate |
bhikṣuṇyārāmavidhin tadvikrāntam iti kathyate ‖
śītalagulmavinyāsan tadvikrānta .... |

---

[3]) The text, in the following, is quoted by the number of the leaf (e.g. *ka*, etc.), side of the leaf (e.g. R[ecto] or V[erso]), and number of the line.

[4]) The colophon of the chapter is missing. I suggested this title from the above list. The manuscript reads instead of a colophon: *namo buddhāya*.

[5]) The MS reads: *vṛkṣasaredavidhānan* ...

[6]) The MS reads: *kaṭi*°

[7]) The MS reads: *pañca indralakṣaṇan* ...

. . . . vinyāsapadam anyan na kārayet ‖
. . . . ānte ca samudrānte . . . .
. . . . nte grāme vanānte rāṣṭrasaṃgame |
hastyārāmam prayuñjīyād anyatra na vidhīyate ‖
rājadhānīpurodyāne girau vā girisaṃgame |
gaṃgāre 'drisamīpe vā siṃhārāmam prakīrttitam ‖ [8])

Chapter 2 (*bhūmigrahaṇalakṣaṇa*) explains the rules for the exploration of the site, i. e. testing of the soil (*bhūmiparīkṣā*), establishing of the gnomon to ascertain the four cardinal points for the orientation of the buildings (*śaṅkusthāpana*) and the calculation of the auspicious time for these undertakings. The laying-out of the ground-plan is descibed in detail. The ground-plan is divided into twentyfive quarters each of which is reigned by a deity (*vāstupuruṣa-maṇḍala*). A list of the deities is given together with their iconographical descriptions (*dhyāna*). These iconographical verses possibly have to be recited during a consecration-ritual performed after the laying-out of the *vāstupuruṣa-maṇḍala*. [9]) Example (*kī* V 2ff.):

Marutaḥ	Mukhya	Soma	Aditi	Īśa
Soṣa	Rudra	Pṛthivī-dhara	Āpavatsa	Jayanta
Varuṇa	Mitra	Brahmā	Aryaman	Āditya
Sugrīva	Indra	Vivasvān	Savitṛ	Bhṛśa
Pitaraḥ	Bhṛṅga	Yama	Vitatha	Agni

Vāstupuruṣa-maṇḍala according to the Mañjuśrībhāṣita-Citrakarmaśāstra

[8]) The gaps in the text are due to the darkend edges of the manuscript, which appear black on the photographs. It may be possible to read these passages from the original.

[9]) Cf. Stella Kramrisch, The Hindu Temple, Vol. 1, Calcutta 1946, p, 29ff.

īśo jayanta ādityo bhṛśāgnivitathas tathā |
yamabhṛṃgapitṛsugrīvā varuṇas saśoṣamarutaḥ ||
mukhyas somāditiś caiva bāhyadevāḥ prakīrttitāḥ |
āpavatsāryyasāvitrā vivasvāṃścendramitrakaḥ ||
rudrajaḥ pṛthivīdhārī maddhye brahmāṃgam iṣyate |
upapīṭhaṃ vāstuvinyāsam padam pīṭhaṃ vidhāsyate ||
caturmmukhaṃ caturbbāhu pītabhāvarṇasaṃyutaṃ |
jaṭāmakuṭasaṃyuktaṃ ratnakuṇḍalabhūṣitam ||
varadābhayahastaṃ ca akṣamālākamaṇḍalam |
sarvvābharaṇasampannaṃ śyāmavastreṇa bhūṣitam |
evan tu brahmarūpaṃ syān niṣaṇṇaṃ kamalāsane ||

Chapter 3 (*caityalakṣaṇa*) deals with all kinds of buildings belonging to a monastery and not only, as it may be assumed from the title, only with Dagobas. The buildings described are: *prāsāda* (confessional hall?), *sabhā* (assembly-hall), *pratimālaya* or *bimbālaya* (image-house), *bhaktaśālā* or *bhojanālaya* (dining-hall), *caitya*, *bodhiveśman* (enclosure-wall of the Bodhi-tree), *pratiharmya* (house of residence for the monks), *rogālaya* (hospital), *gavyaśālā* (cow-shed), *bherivāsa* (abode of the drums) and *kūpa* (well).

It depends on the type of monastery, where the buildings are situated. Example (*kḷ* R 2ff.):

brahmāṃśe pratimāvāsaṃ varuṇe prāsādam iṣyate |
yamāṃśe caityam ityuktam āditye bodhim ādriyet ||
somāṃśe tu sabhāṃ vidyād gavyaśālāgnibhāgike |
tatpāde bherivāsaṃ syād īśāne bhojanālayam |
tatpade bhaktaśālā syād vāte rogālayam bhavet ||
nirṛtāṃśe pratiharmmyaṃ syāc catuṣkoṇe kūpam ādriyet |
atra śālā na karttavyā navadevān tu vinyaset ||

The perimeter of each building has to be conformed to the *āyādi-ṣaḍvarga*, an astrological test to assure that the measurements of the building are auspicious.[10]) Inauspicious measurements will effect the ruin of the building and loss of wealth. Example (*ko* R 3):

āyādhike vyayāhīne sarvvasampajjayāvaham |
vyayādhikyād āyahīnaṃ vāstunāśan dhanakṣayam ||

The rest of the chapter prescribes the measurements of the buildings in detail.

Chapter 4 (*vṛkṣasaṃgrahavidhāna*) gives a classification of trees, the wood of which is suitable for various purposes as making door-frames,

---

[10]) See P. K. Acharya, An Encyclopaedia of Hindu Architecture. London etc. (1946), s.v. Ṣaḍvarga.

roofs, images, etc.[11]) It tells the way how the trees have to be selected and cut.

Chapter 5 (*vṛkṣasaṃcchedanavidhāna*) describes the methods of seasoning the wood and cutting it into pieces according to the various purposes it is needed for.

Chapter 6 (*garbhāgāravidhāna*). In the Śilpaśāstras usually the sanctuary of a temple is called *garbhāgāra* or *garbhageha*. In our text the *garbhāgāra* is probably the image-house and the same that is called *pratimālaya* or *bimbālaya* in chapter 3. This chapter mainly deals with the various ground-plans and the location of the Buddha- and Bodhisattva-images within the shrine. Example (*khau* V 1):

garbbhāgārasya vinyāsaṃ caturaśrāyatāśrakam |
aṣṭāśraṣoḍaśāśran tu vṛttavṛttāyatan tu ṣaḍ |
garbbhāgāram iti proktam ṣoḍaśāṃśaṃ diśe diśe ||

If the plan (*padavinyāsa*) is divided into 49 squares it is called *sthaṇḍila*.[12]) The square in the centre is occupied by Brahmā, the border of eight squares around the centre is occupied by the gods, the next border of sixteen squares by men, and the outer border of twenty-four squares by Piśācas. The central image, called *mūlabera* (*khām* R 7), is located in the Brahmapada or central square, while the Bodhisattva-images are situated around it. Example (*khām* R 7):

mānuṣyadvayapṛṣṭhāṃśe bodhisatvam pratiṣṭhitam |

Chapter 7 (*śūlalakṣaṇa*) and the following chapters are dealing with the technique of clay modelling. This technique of making images of unbaked clay is described in the Kāśyapaśilpa (ch. 79–86)[13]) and in Śrīkumāra's Śilparatna (pt. 2, ch. 83–94),[14]) a detailed study on this subject was made by K. M. Varma.[15]) The process begins with the cutting of the wooden parts for the armature (*śūla*). The wooden sticks are fixed together with clue (*aṣṭabandha*), the preparation of which is prescribed in chapter 9 (*aṣṭabandhavidhāna* . Ropes (*rajju*) are wound around the armature [cf. chapter 10 (*rajjukarmavidhāna*)] to support the clay which forms the body of the image. The preparation of the clay is described in chapter 11 (*mṛttikālakṣaṇa*). Chapter 12 (*kaṭaśarkaravidhāna* deals with the preparation of the limestone-paste used for the finish, and chapter 16 (*varṇalakṣaṇavidhāna*) with the preparation of paint.

---

[11]) See K. M. Varma, The Indian Technique of Clay Modelling, Santiniketan 1970, p. 30ff.

[12]) Cf. Stella Kramrisch, op.cit., p. 60.

[13]) Ānandāśramasaṃskṛtagranthāvaliḥ 95 (1926).

[14]) Ed. K. Sāmbaśiva Śāstrī, Trivandrum 1929 (TSS 98).

[15]) Op.cit. passim.

Chapter 8 (*ratnanyāsavidhāna*). The *ratnanyāsa*, the laying down of jewels, is a foundation ritual, which is to be performed before the armature is fixed in the pedestal. A similar ritual is described in the Rauravāgama and the Kāraṇāgama.[16]) Our text gives a detailed account of the ritual, including the measurements of the altar, and quotes the mantras to be recited. Example (*gī* V 3):

ekaikaṃ .... vastreṇa veṣṭayet kalaśaṃ kramāt |
brahmakumbhasya maddhye tu navaratnam pratiṣṭhitam ||
sadhūpagandhapuṣpaiś ca dīpaiḥ santoṣayet kramāt |
śilpācāryyaprasannātmā suviśuddhānulepanaḥ ||

Chapter 13 (*pramāṇalakṣaṇa*) gives a full length description of the canon of proportions. The system used is the 'uttamadaśatāla-system'.[17]) Example (*gṛ* R 1):

śreṣṭhan daśāṃgulasya mānamārggam pravakṣyate |
dvātriṃśallakṣaṇe yuktaṃ cāśītyaṃgam praśasyate ||
caturvvidham pramāṇaṃ ca saṃgaman divyabimbakam |
uṣṇīṣan triyavam bhāgan tasya keśāntam iṣyate |
tasyādho hanuparyyantan trayodaśarddhāṃgulam bhavet ||
keśāntād akṣisūtrāntāt triyavaṃ caturaṃgulam |
akṣisūtrāt puṭāntaṃ ca triyavam bhāgam iṣyate ||
puṭāntād hanuparyyantaṃ [ca] bhāgan triyavādhikam |
galam arddhāṃgulottuṃgaṃ kolakāyatavṛttakam ||
grīvodayan trimātrārddhan tato hṛnnābhisammitam |
saptaviṃśāṃgulākaṃ nābhyayonimūlatas trayo- |
daśārddhāṃgulam proktaṃ saptaviṃśorudīrghataḥ |
jānvodayan tu bhāgaṃ syāj jaṃghorusamam āyatam ||
caraṇocchrāyabhāgaṃ syād aṣṭādaśāṃgulāyatam |

In this system 1 tāla makes 13 1/2 aṅgulas (finger's breadth). 1 bhāga makes 4 aṅgulas, and 1 aṅgula 8 yavas (barley-corns). The vertical measurements of the body given in our text are the following:

	aṅgulas	yavas
Uṣṇīṣa ...	 0	3
Crown of the head ...	 4	0
From the end of the hair to the middle of the eyes ...	 4	3
From the middle of the eyes to the end of the nose ...	 4	3
From the nose to the end of the chin ...	 4	3
The fold below the chin (*gala*)	 0	4
Neck ...	 3	4
From the neck to the navel	... 27	0

---

16) Ed. N. R. Bhatt, Vol. 2, Pondichéry 1972 (Publ. de l'Inst. Français d'Indologie 18–2), p. 48.

17) See T. A. Gopinatha Rao, Elements of Hindu Iconography, Vol. I, Pt. 2, Appendix B. Madras 1914.

	angulas	yavas
from the navel to the pubic bone	... 13	4
Thigh ...	... 27	0
Knee ...	 4	0
Foreleg ...	... 27	0
Foot ...	 4	0
Total	124	0

Chapter 14 (*lambamānavidhāna*) forms the second part of the canon. The measurements given in this chapter are taken by means of plumb lines. The plumb lines are hanging down from a frame, which is fixed on the top of the image.[18])

Chapter 15 (*pañcabuddhendrādilakṣaṇa*) gives evidence of the Mahayanistic origin of our text. It contains an account of the pantheon with detailed iconographic descriptions of the Dhyānibuddhas and the Bodhisattvas. The text is in a bad condition. It is written in a poor style and has a number of metrical errors which, perhaps, go back to the original.

In the following, I shall give a list of names found in the text. The list, of course, is not complete.

The Dhyānibuddhas: Vairocana, Ratnasambhava, Amoghasiddhi, Akṣobhya (sometimes called Akṣodbhava), and Amitābha.

Bodhisattvas: Kṣitigarbha, Vajrapāṇi, Vyomagarbha, Avalokiteśvara (also called Avalokita and Lokanātha), Viṣkambha, Mañjughoṣa, Samantabhadra, and Maitreya.

Mortal Buddhas: Viśvabhū, Krakucchaṇḍa, Kanakamuni, Kāśyapa, Śākya(siṃha). They are described each with his Bodhi-tree. A part of the passage is illegible on the photographs. It possibly contains the description of two further Buddhas, i. e. of Vipaśyin and Śikhin.[19])

Gods: The eight Dikpālas: Āditya, Agni (Pāvaka), Yama, Nirṛti, Varuṇa, Vāyu, Soma, Iśa. Gandharvas: Citrasena, Mahāsena, Sumitra, Viśvāvasu, Indrota (?), Pañcaśikha (?). The eight Vasus: Vāsuki (?), Soma, Dhara, Uṣmapa, Nīlaka (?), Pratyūṣa, Prabhāsa, Āpa. Lakṣmī and some other goddesses are mentioned, the Brahmakāya-spirits, and some Yakṣas: Pūrṇabhadra, Maṇibhadra, and Jambhala.

Ṛṣis: Agastya, Bhṛgu, Aṅgiras, Bhārgava, Pulastya, and Gautama.

Some more names of divine or semi-divine beings seem to be mentioned in the text, but cannot be identified. Some passages of the text are badly corrupted.

---

[18]) Ibid.

[19]) Benoytosh Bhattacharyya, The Indian Buddhist Iconography, London etc. 1924, p. 10.

Example (*go* R 3):

ādityo yamanairṛtyau pāvako varuṇas tathā |
vāyuḥ someśau diśāṣṭau vāhanārūḍhakalpayat ||
gandharvvāś citrasenaś ca mahāsenaḥ sumitrakaḥ |
viśvāvasuś ca indrotaḥ pañcaśikhaḥ prakīrttitāḥ || [20]
vāsukiś caiva somaś ca dharoṣmapaś ca nīlakaḥ |
pratyūṣaś ca prabhāsaś ca āpaḥ śrīvāsavāṣṭakam ||

go V 2:

kṣitigarbbho vajrapāṇiś ca vyomagarbbhāvalokitaḥ |
viṣkambho mañjughoṣaś ca samantabhadraś ca maitreyaḥ ||

go V 8:

maitreyam pītavarṇṇaṃ ca dvibhujaṃ vā caturbbhujam |
varadābhayahastaṃ vā kathāvādābhayan tathā ||
† apare nāgapuṣpākṣanāvārddhakanakuṇḍalam | †
makuṭasya maddhyame sthitam akṣottamatathāgatam ||

Chapter 17 (*akṣimokṣaṇa*) gives detailed rules for the performance of a consecration ritual. This ceremony is exactly the same as described in chapter 30 of the Vaikhānasāgama [21]) and similar to the Ṣaḍaṅga-ceremony of the Sinhalese, which precedes the Netrapratiṣṭhāpana (see below, p. 318ff.).

The chapter begins (*ghī* R 5):

athedānīm pravakṣyāmi akṣimokṣaṇalakṣaṇam |
akṣimokṣadinät pūrvve aṃkurārpaṇam iṣyate ||

The *aṅkurārpaṇa* has the same function in the ceremony as the *indrakīla-sthāpana* in the Saḍaṅga-ceremony: it is the foundation of the ceremony. Subsequently the ground in front of the image is cleaned for the offerings (*ghī* R 6):

savastudakṣiṇe vāpi pramukhe vā viśeṣataḥ |
daṇḍamātran tu vistīrṇṇaṃ gomayālipya bhūmayaḥ ||

On bundles of Kuśa-grass an altar is made from rice with oil lamps at the four corners. The offering is a *kumbhasthāpana*, i. e. nine pots are established on the altar for the nine planetary deities. For carving the eyes a golden chisel or needle has to be used. After having carved the eyes the artist has to go to a near-by *snāna-maṇḍapa* for a ritual bath. Here the ritual differs from the Hinduistic *akṣimokṣaṇa*.

---

[20]) The MS reads: *sarvve* for *gandharvvāś*, *visvāprasū* for *viśvāvasuś*, *indrote* for *indrotaḥ*, *pañcasītā* for *pañcaśikhaḥ*.

[21]) Ed. Sāmbaśiva Śāstrī, Trivandrum 1935 (TSS 121).

The sources of the text

If we compare the sequence of chapters in the MC and in the Kāśyapaśilpa, we find a striking similarity. The MC follows the same pattern but has inserted some more details.

Mañjuśrībhāṣita-citrakarma-śāstra	Kāśyapaśilpa
4. vṛkṣasaṃgrahaṇavidhāna	79 vṛkṣasaṃgrahaṇa
7. śūlalakṣaṇa	80 śūlalakṣaṇa
8. ratnanyāsavidhāna	81 śūlapāṇilakṣaṇa
10. rajjukarmavidhāna	82 rajjubandhalakṣaṇa
11. mṛttikālakṣaṇa	83 mṛtsakāralakṣaṇa
12. kaṭaśarkaravidhāna	84 kalkasaṃskāralakṣaṇa
16. varṇalakṣaṇavidhāna	85 varṇasaṃskāralakṣaṇa
	86 varṇalepana

The canon of proportions is described in the Kaśyapaśilpa in chapter 50–57. But not only the sequence of the chapters is corresponding in both texts, the texts themselves are very closely related in a number of passages. An example is given in the following synopsis (page 99). We cannot draw any conclusions from a few verses compared, but it is possible that the Kāśyapaśilpa is one of the sources of the MC, though it is definitely not the only one, or, at least, the authors of Kāśyapaśilpa and MC have used the same source. The MC, on the other side, may be the source of the Śāriputra, a Sanskrit text on the proportions of Buddha-images, which is found in Sri Lanka.[22])

Despite the unsolved problem of the sources, we can say that the MC is of South Indian origin. The Kāśyapaśilpa is an Upāgama of the Aṃśumantamahātantra (the same as Aṃśumadbhedāgama?) and belongs therefore to the South Indian Āgamic literature. It is usually dated into the 11th or 12th century A. D. Though we fix the date of the MC not much later than that of the Kāśyapaśilpa, we are facing difficulties if we suppose that the text was composed in Sri Lanka or in South India. This problem, of course, cannot be discussed at length in a preliminary report like this. But it is one of the facts which make a more comprehensive study of this text desirable.

---

[22]) Partly transl. into English by Ananda K. Coomaraswamy, in: Mediaeval Sinhalese Art, New York ²1956, p. 150ff. Critical edition with German translation by the present author: Hans Ruelius, Śāriputra und Ālekhyalakṣaṇa, Zwei Texte zur Proportionslehre in der indischen und ceylonesischen Kunst, Göttingen 1974 (Phil. Diss.).

Kāśyapaśilpa 50, 92cff.	Mañjuśrībhāṣitacitrakarmaśāstra gṛ R 2ff.	Śāriputra 14cff.
triyavadhikacandrāṃśam	uṣṇīṣan triyavam	yavāṣṭa mūrddhni uṣṇīṣaś
uṣṇīṣoccam udāhṛtam		
tasmād āpūrvakeśāntam	bhāgan tasmāt keśāntam	śiromāṇaṃ tryaṃgulaṃ
aṅgabhāgam udāhṛtam	iṣyate	
keśāntād akṣisūtrāntaṃ	keśāntād akṣisūtrāntaṃ	keśāntād akṣisūtrāntāt
yugāṃśaṃ triyavādhikam	triyavaṃ caturaṃgulam	
akṣisūtrāt puṭāntaṃ ca	akṣisūtrāt puṭāntaṃ ca	
	triyavam bhāgam iṣyate	
puṭād dhanvantamānakam	puṭāntād hanuparyyantam	puṭāntād dhanum eva ca
pratyekaṃ triyavādhikyaṃ	bhāgaṃ [ca] triyavādhikam	bhāgabhāgas tathaivan tu
yugāṃśodayam iṣyate		
hanvādigalamānaṃ tu	galam arddhāṃgulottuṃgam	galam arddhāṃgulam matam
caturyavam udāhṛtam		

Kāśyapaśilpa 50, 139	Mañjuśrībhāṣitacitrakarmaśāstra gṛ R 5f.	Śāriputra 29
tato vai maṇḍalāt karṇa-	uṣṇīṣāt keśaparyyantaṃ	paryyantakeśam uṣṇīṣāt
keśāntaṃ ca navāṅgulam	navāṃgulārddham praśayaste	kalāpañca samunnatiḥ
maṇḍalāt pṛṣṭhakeśāntaṃ	uṣṇīṣam pārśvakeśāntād	tāvac ca pārśvakeśan tu
sārdham adhyaṅgulam bhavet	ekādaśāṃgulam bhavet	mānād ekādaśāṃgulam

II. BUDDHISM AND SOCIETY IN SRI LANKA

Kingship, the Sangha, and the Process of Legitimation in Anurādhapura Ceylon: An Interpretive Essay[1])

By BARDWELL L. SMITH

The process of legitimizing not simply power but authority in any society is a constantly evolving, complex and subtle phenomenon. While its configurations vary within all societies, the process reveals a number of interrelated features. This essay attempts to identify several of these features and to examine the process of legitimation within a particular society in its responses to opportunities and threats, both internal and external. The phenomena within this process are infinitely variable and the features selected, necessarily tentative. An interpretive essay of this sort seeks to highlight a few major ingredients of ancient Sinhalese history and test the usefulness of certain concepts in analyzing the legitimizing process itself.

The features examined are the following: one, the relationship between the precariousness of social and cosmic order as it is sensed by a tradition and the attempt to fashion forms of existence which appear less vulnerable to chaos or anarchy; two, the affirming of historical and even cosmic dimensions of legitimation, which provide the structures and values of a particular society with some transcending authority; three, the tensions existing between the claimants to legitimized power within any community, and the resultant balancing of power; four, the manner in which legitimation of authority is reinforced in symbolic, ritualistic and doctrinal modes; and, five, the validation of power through its ability to bolster a culture's "plausibility structure" in the face of crises threatening personal and communal existence and of pluralistic perceptions of reality. The interdependence of these features is clear, yet they hardly exhaust the theoretical possibilities. They serve simply as points of departure.[2])

---

[1]) The author's participation in the conference which resulted in this volume was made possible by a travel grant from the American Council of Learned Societies.

[2]) While the isolating of these particular features is my own, I am indebted to Peter Berger's discussion of the process of legitimation in his book "The Sacred Canopy: Elements of a Sociological Theory of Religion." Cf. pp. 29–51, and passim.

I. The precariousness of order

Historical and comparative studies reveal how all societies struggle to cope with threats of disorder and to create forms of order which lend meaning, cohesiveness and durability to social and personal existence. The potential chaos which lurks both outside and within the perceived orders of every cultural ethos occasions alarm about whether any structure of meaning can be an enduring safeguard against disintegration and anomie. From social conflict and political crisis to psychic disorder and death the evanescent nature of life and the relativity of all forms of order are constantly experienced. In the face of human avarice and stupidity, of institutionalized injustice, and of the seeming irrationality of existence itself men vacillate between simple but shallow assurances on the one hand and terror on the other. History may be viewed as a series of scenarios in which the symbols of order and disorder clash for allegiance in the minds of men and in which societies embrace chaos-averting forces through the legitimizing process. History is in part a search for frameworks of meaning both to endure the threat of non-being and to discover dimensions of order, however fragile and incomplete. Human beings remain vulnerable to attacks upon their perceived definitions of reality and cannot escape the dilemma of having to legitimize authority and power (to counter the forces of disintegration) without silencing challenges to their legitimacy.

In Sinhalese history the interplay between the monarchy, the Sangha, and society at large portrays a continuing awareness of the precariousness of order in every sense of the word: cosmic, social and personal. There is repeated testimony about the contagious nature of disorder, especially when manifested within the Sangha or by kings. Disorder breeds disorder, just as order can be promoted by order. A kind of inevitability is expressed by the tradition, if only to dramatize that men in the grips of selfishness create forms of evil which then ensnare other men in the process. The Sinhalese experience of political realism arose from the broader Indian doctrine of *matsyanyāya* ("law of the fishes"), which cautioned rulers and their ministers that power left to its own devices issues in the law of the jungle, in the strong consuming the weak. This perception of political mores was used by astute rulers in various ways, from crass opportunism to the responsible but realistic exercising of power. Legitimation of power and authority receives its warrant from the fact that, unless the power of others is checked, threats to order keep recurring. In any case, the doctrine of *matsyanyāya* was not only part of the Sinhalese heritage from India in general, but specifically of the early Buddhist recognition within the Indian setting. In the Dīgha-Nikāya there is extensive discussion of the theory of the "Great Chosen One" (*Mahāsammata*) to

---

For an astute critique of broader aspects of Berger's thought, see Van A. Harvey, Some Problematical Aspects of Berger's Theory of Religion, in: Journal of the American Academy of Religion, Vol. 41, No. 1 (March 1973), 75–93.

support the centralizing of power in kingly hands as a check to those who misappropriate power and in whose hands order becomes anarchy.[3])

The continuity between this theory and other teachings of the Buddha on the one hand and the manner in which power was said to be used by Aśoka is clear. The Buddhist doctrine of power and the Aśokan model were used repeatedly to alert later monarchs in Ceylon about the norms for legitimate authority. The *sine qua non* of all political legitimacy is protection from anarchy and its consequences.[4]) From the Manusmṛti and other Indian texts to the Chronicles of Ceylon this criterion is a constant. To the Sinhalese Buddhists this meant protection of the world (*loka*) from disorder, and of the *Sāsana* for the promotion of the *Dhamma*. Early in the Mahāvaṃsa the chronicler makes this clear as King Kālāsoka is first rebuked for being led astray by the Vesālī monks, prior to the Second Council, and then repents by promising to protect and further the doctrine.[5]) Even more significant is the Buddha's last will and testament to Sakka (Skt. Śakra), king of the gods: "In Laṅkā, O lord of gods, will my religion be established, therefore carefully protect him with his followers and Laṅkā."[6]) Association is repeatedly made between the welfare of the *Buddhasāsana* and the well-being of society as a whole. The king who internalizes this kind of legitimacy becomes the *Dhammarāja*, the protector of men from worldly harm and privation and the active agent in founding social order upon the order of the cosmos. His kingship becomes one with the lord of gods (Sakka), with the Conqueror himself (Buddha Gotama).

On a larger scale, an ontological interdependence between several modes of order is perceived. This assumes mythic proportions in the symbolism of the Yakkhas and the Nāgas who represent at the very least threats to the human order. "At the time the plane of Laṅkā had big forests and great horrors; different kinds of *Yakkhas*, greatly terrible, cruel, feeding on blood, furious, and demons of various forms having

---

[3]) Dialogues of the Buddha, tr. by T. W. and C. A. F. Rhys Davids. London, 1921, III, 77–94. See also Vishwanath Prasad Varma, Studies in Hindu Political Thought and Its Metaphysical Foundations, in: Journal of the Bihar Research Society, Vol. XXXVIII, Pts. 3–4, pp. 454–466. As Varma says, "The 'law of the fishes' symbolizes the sheer prevalence of the cult of naked and unashamed force." (p. 466) Or, from the Rāmāyaṇa, tr. by Griffith, ii, lxvii: "In kingless lands no law is known, / And none may call his wealth his own; / Each preys on each from hour to hour, / As fish the weaker fish devour."

[4]) The Laws of Manu, tr. by Georg Bühler, p. 238. See also J. Gonda, Ancient Indian Kingship from the Religious Point of View, pp. 3–6, 17–19.

[5]) Mahāvaṃsa, IV. 1–44. The transliteration of Aśoka (Sanskrit) or Asoka (Pāli) will vary here according to the content referred to or the text cited. Also true of Dharma or Dhamma.

[6]) Ibid., VII. 1–5. The person referred to is Vijaya, who is said to have landed on Ceylon that same day, that of the Buddha's *parinibbāna*. Sakka (Indra) then handed over the guardianship to Viṣṇu (Upulvan). Indra is also seen as the god who makes possible the fecundity of nature, as he supplies both light and water. Kingship in association with Indra becomes, therefore, the bestower of blessings.

different inclinations."[7]) "All the snakes were endowed with miraculous power, all were terribly poisonous, all were faulty, fierce, haughty and dependent. The snakes were quick, greatly powerful, wicked, rough, harsh, irritable, extremely angry, and desirous of destruction."[8]) On two of his legendary three trips to Laṅkā the Buddha encounters these forms of the demonic, reducing disorder to impotency, and ultimately enlists them in service to the Dhamma. Of one piece with this is the authority perceived by King Pasenadi of Kosala who marveled at how the Buddha "tames the untamed, calms the uncalmed," in reference to the dangerous robber Aṅgulimāla, "without stick or sword."[9]) In artistic and doctrinal form these lingering evidences of the demonic, now rendered benign, remind men not only of the Buddha's power in earlier days but of the power of the Dhamma to exorcize latter-day Yakkhas, to contain all forms of destruction.[10])

These acts of the Buddha are given temporal perspective within the tradition by being placed within a continuum from the remote past where three previous Buddhas are said to have visited Laṅkā (freeing it successively from pestilence, drought, and "a hideous and life-destroying war") to the time identified by the chronicler when the doctrine was established by the bhikkhu Mahinda, traditionally said to be Asoka's son.[11]) Each of these actions symbolically removes the consequences of disorder and bases the promise of order upon the implanting of the Dhamma in the minds and associations of men. The very establishing of the boundaries (*sīmā*) of the Mahāvihāra conterminous with those of the city, by Mahinda at the behest of Devānaṁpiyatissa, constitutes the conviction that earthly authority is grounded upon and gains legitimacy from a Dhamma having cosmic implications.[12]) Centuries later, in the reigns of Buddhadāsa (340–368) and his son Upatissa I (368–410), the theme is repeated as both kings are shown to display the power of genuine authority in healing the sick and driving plague and famine from the land.[13]) While the actions of virtuous men, the

---

[7]) Dīpavaṃsa, p. 135. Also, Mahāvaṃsa, XV. 160–165.

[8]) Ibid., p. 139. These mythic beings are to be seen not literally as beasts, but as symbols of disorder, whose power is sought in the Dhamma's behalf.

[9]) Middle Length Sayings, II, p. 288.

[10]) Cf. Walpola Rahula, History of Buddhism in Ceylon, pp. 39–41, for other examples in India and Ceylon of conquering and controlling "yakṣas and nāgas." See also Edward Conze's essay "Dharma as a Spiritual, Social and Cosmic Force" in Paul G. Kuntz, ed., The Concept of Order, Seattle: University of Washington, 1968. On page 241 he writes: "Those parts of the world which have escaped the control of Dharma are marked by strife (*raṇa*) and turmoil (*ḍamara*). On a more or less poetical and allegorical level this is often shown in the scriptures by contrasting the serenity, peace and harmony of the world which is dominated by the Buddhas and Bodhisattvas (who are channals through which the transcendental Dharma reaches the world) with what is going on in the hells or among Mara's hosts."

[11]) Mahāvaṃsa, XV. 56–172.

[12]) Ibid., XV. 180–194.

[13]) Cūlavaṃsa, 37. 105–198.

moral goes deeper than virtue; it points beyond the precariousness of order, beyond the readiness with which men revert to anomic existence, to the fundamental structure of reality which transcends yet makes possible the discovery of selfless freedom.

No less instructive, because equally part of the dialectic between order and chaos, is the insistence that the Dhamma's well-being depends upon the monarchy's residing in Buddhist hands. From the establishment of Sinhalese Buddhist kingship in the reign of Devānaṁpiyatissa to its final demise in the nineteenth century a continuing refrain attributes legitimacy only to monarchs who not only support the Sāsana but who perceive the Buddhadhamma as the essence of social order and harmony. "Just as religious legitimation interprets the order of society in terms of an all-embracing, sacred order of the universe, so it relates the disorder that is the antithesis of all socially constructed nomoi to that yawning abyss of chaos that is the oldest antagonist of all the sacred. To go against the order of society is always to risk plunging into anomy."[14]) In this vein one can appreciate the relief expressed within the Chronicles at the wresting of the monarchy from the Damiḷas by such kings as Duṭṭhagāmaṇī (161–137 B.C.), Vaṭṭagāmaṇī (89–77 B.C.), Dhātusena (459–477), and Vijayabāhu I (1055–1110), among others. The passages that "awaken serene joy (*pasāda*) and emotion (*saṃvega*)" in the minds of the faithful stress that the miseries of the world are healed only through the doctrine of the Saṃbuddha.[15])

II. The ontological status of legitimated authority

The safeguarding of authority rests not only with those who exercise power but with the institutions, laws and values of the society which sets criteria for legitimacy. While religious traditions are not unique in being engaged in the legitimation process, religion often invests social institutions with enduring significance, "bestowing upon them an ultimately valid cosmological status ... by *locating* them within a sacred and cosmic frame of reference."[16]) "The institutions are thus given a semblance of inevitability, firmness and durability ... Their empirical tenuousness is transformed into an overpowering stability as they are understood as but manifestations of the underlying structure of the universe."[17])

If the transcendent sacred reality in which society is believed to be rooted provides meaning to historic existence, it also challenges every

[14]) Berger, op.cit., p. 39.

[15]) Mahāvaṃsa, I. 3–4. See section III of this present essay for the way in which Sinhalese Buddhist ideology during this long period was strongly political in nature. See also an earlier essay by the author entitled "The Ideal Social Order as Portrayed in the Chronicles of Ceylon" (1972).

[16]) Berger, op.cit., p. 33.

[17]) Ibid., pp. 36–37.

conventional basis on which men claim status, wisdom and dignity. The ontological reality by which men endorse their claims to legitimacy remains a double-edged sword haunting those by whom power is abused. One clear facet of legitimated authority is thus its provisional nature, its susceptibility to using power for its own sake, and its final accountability to that which it purports to serve. Grounding authority in the structure of the universe makes it more, not less, vulnerable to attack, yet it is essentially the incumbent who is liable, more than the values and traditions he represents. These are undergirded with a kind of finality, with immense implications for the process of legitimation.

The history of Sinhalese Buddhism during the Anurādhapura period provides repeated instances of authority being perceived in ontological terms. Often, it is difficult to discern the uniquely Sinhalese features of this process because of the broader Indian texture (both Buddhist and Hindu) from which the heritage of Ceylon derives. In other respects, Ceylonese culture is distinctive and original, especially in the manner by which Sinhalese Buddhism has appropriated and modified various elements of Indian models. Three of these will be examined here: the envisioning of a universe in sacramental terms, the enthroning of the Buddha on the sacred lotus-seat of Brahmā, and the attempted elevation of the monarchy itself to comparable heights. While these fall outside orthodox teaching, they are part of a mythology which orthodoxy seldom discouraged and which supported the sacred reality affirmed by that tradition.

1. Throughout the Chronicles there is a poetic envisioning of an organic harmony within the universe derived from the turning of the Wheel of Law. Despite the acknowledgement that most men ignore or violate the teachings of the Dhamma, the ontological structure of existence was seen to remain unfragmented. In *sacramental* terms, evidences are educed from a host of worlds to promote a vision of reality which portrays men drawn by the power of the doctrine, enabled to participate in a universe of meaning beyond their separateness and outside the limits imposed by their fears. Early in the Mahāvaṃsa the stage is set for this vision as the chronicler, in reference to Asoka, writes: "Straightway after his consecration his command spread so far as a yojana (upward) into the air and downward into the (depths of the) earth."[18] Geiger's notes suggest that "not only men upon the earth but also the spirits of the air and the earth heard and obeyed Aśoka's command,"[19] the implication being that authority derived from faithfulness to the Dhamma elicits responses in kind from all corners of the universe. A similar notion emerges from the passage where Mahinda is depicted preaching to the devas, who, like his human congregations,

---

[18]) Mahāvaṃsa, V. 23. The following verses (24–33) are a delightful depiction of this organic harmony within the natural world.

[19]) Ibid., fn. 1.

are converted to the doctrine.[20] While these embellishments are partially to stress the Buddha's regnant status over gods as well as men, the coherent nature of reality is assumed and made vivid.

This last aspect is expanded in the many descriptions of wonders and miracles said to have occurred in the reigns of Devānaṁpiyatissa and Duṭṭhagāmaṇī. From the establishing of the Mahāvihāra to the coming of the Bodhi-tree, from the beginning of the Great Thūpa to the enshrining of the relics, the several events are depicted within a framework of cosmic majesty and as affirming the ontic unity within the universe. "Celestial instruments of music resounded, a celestial chorus pealed forth, the devatās let fall a rain of heavenly perfumes and so forth."[21] "All this was completed without hindrance by reason of the wondrous power of the king, the wondrous power of the devatās, and the wondrous power of the holy (theras)."[22] When one has seen the relics, in Mahinda's words, one has seen the Buddha. With their enshrinement in Laṅkā, the devotional transplanting of the Dhamma is complete. The transmission of the doctrine is not by words alone; what is really released is the empowerment to envision and make real dimensions of the sacred beyond the confines of our normal world. "There is, O bhikkhus, that which is not-born, not-become, not-made, and not-conditioned. If this not-born, not-become, not-made, and not-conditioned were not, then there would be no apparent release from that which is born, become, made and conditioned."[23] Whether in the logically clear, though cryptic language of the Buddha or in the allegorical flourishes of the chronicler, a continuity of perspective points to a universe which is sacramentally of one piece, beyond the divisions composing the history of mankind. The implications of this for the legitimation of power and authority are subtle, often unclear, and always indirect. The lesson is for each monarch, for the Sangha itself, and for all men to discover. But the assertion of the reality from which authority derives is a continuing theme in Buddhist doctrine and mythology.

2. If genuine authority is ontological by nature and if it embodies the truth of the Dhamma, then the Buddha himself is represented, whether in aniconic or image form, as *sovereign of the universe*. While the Chronicles speak from the vantage point of nearly 1000 years of Buddhist history (seven centuries within Ceylon alone), they strive to interpret the *meaning* of the relics, the Bodhi-tree, the stūpas, and the images for earlier generations as well as their own. Doubtlessly influenced by Mahāyāna symbolism and imposing later interpretations upon original forms, mid-Anurādhapura mythology was clearly in continuity with a progressively

---

[20]) Ibid., XIV. 38–40. Besides the devatās, nāgas and their mortal foes (the supaṇṇas) also heard and were converted.

[21]) Ibid., XXXI. 84.

[22]) Ibid., XXX. 99.

[23]) Udāna, VIII. 3 (Khuddaka-Nikāya).

expanding ontological picture of the Buddha's nature. From very early days the stūpa was regarded not simply as a repository for relics but as a symbol of the cosmos. "The relics enshrined within the *stūpa*, which at once symbolized the world and the Tathāgata, would convey the idea of the Tathāgata being immanent in the universe. The umbrella, the symbol of sovereignty, suggested to the faithful the idea of the Buddha being lord of the world." [24]) It was therefore in relationship to sovereignty of this sort that the authority and power of kings could be legitimated.

One intriguing rendering of this theme argues that in the early centuries of Buddhist iconography, perhaps first in Gandhāra but shortly afterwards throughout India and in Ceylon as well, there emerged the common representation of the Buddha in symbolical form as ascendant to the throne of ultimate power. "The Buddha was, according to the canonical texts, a great Being (Mahāpurisa) far above any God or Brahmā (Devātideva, Brahmātibrahma). Thus when the Buddha was taken as the tangible object of worship he had to be represented in supreme qualities that behove of a great Being. The obvious result was the creation, through art, of a supreme Being, who had surpassed earthly limits." [25]) This argument proceeds to analyze sculpture and architecture in early Ceylon, finally crystallizing in an artistic complex during the latter Anurādhapura period as well as at Polonnaruva which places the Buddha upon the sacred seat of Brahmā. While the chronology of this development is far from clear, a strong case is made for restructuring the Kailāsa myth whereby "the Buddha (Mahāpurisa) himself was enthroned thus making a suggestion that even the greatest Divine Being of the Hindu pantheon had succumbed before the Buddha by offering him his very lotus seat." [26]) Though space does not permit elaborating on this interpretation here, the author depicts in detail several elements of this sculptural portrayal, providing further insight into the meaning not only of the principal figure but of the Nāga guardians (*dvārapāla*), the moonstones (*sańdakaḍapahaṇa*), and the flight of steps leading to the cosmic mountain. In Mahāyāna imagery, especially in influencing Buddhist art among the Khmers, the Supreme Buddha takes on the abstract form of Vairocana. In Ceylon there is more a commingling of iconographic images (with primary stress upon the historic Buddha,

---

[24]) Senarat Paranavitana, Sinhalayo, revised second edition, Colombo 1970, p. 20.

[25]) A. D. T. E. Perera, Buddha on the Sacred Seat of Brahma, in: World Buddhism Vesak Annual, Colombo 1973, p. 38.

[26]) Ibid., p. 43. Kailāsa is the mountain paradise of Śiva, lying in Hindu cosmography to the east of Mount Meru. Cf. Himansu Bhusan Sarkar, The Evolution of Śiva-Buddha Cult in Java, in: Journal of Indian History, Vol. 45, 1967, pp. 637–646, for the opposite process, i.e., the adoption of Buddha into the Hindu pantheon as one of the ten Avatāras of Viṣṇu. This happened by the 11th century A.D., if not earlier. Cf. Senarat Paranavitana, Ceylon and Malaysia, Colombo, 1966, pp. 202–203, for an interesting statement on the development of the cosmic mountain theme in Southeast Asian Buddhist art.

drastically reinterpreted) with the essential theme of his ontological priority over all beings, spiritual and worldly, divine and human. Through understanding this fundamental priority one can appreciate the willingness of Buddhists in Ceylon and elsewhere not simply to be tolerant of Hindu gods and local deities but to convert them into service of the Dhamma, a point to be discussed in the final section.

3. A third feature of the ontological grounding of legitimated authority proceeds from the above, namely, the association of kingship with the sovereignty of the Buddha. Beyond the direct historical ties of Gotama with pious kings such as Bimbisāra and beyond the transmission of Buddhist kingship from Aśoka to Devānampiyatissa, there was the emerging conviction "that only a Buddhist had the legitimate right to be king of Ceylon," and by the 10th century that the king must be a Bodhisattva as well.[27] While the evolution of this is difficult to trace historically, there are nodal points along the way which suggest a definite elevation of kingship to divine status, or more precisely a direct ontological association between Buddhist kingship and the Lord Buddha. Canonical warrant for this is, of course, given in the *Cakkavatti* concept (Dīgha-Nikāya, II, 169f.; and III, 62f.) wherein the model of a World-ruler is one who presides "over the four quarters of the earth, righteous in himself, ruling righteously, triumphant, enforcing law and order at home, possessed of the seven jewels."[28] But this remains abstract until specific kings claim for themselves or have ascribed to them direct association with this status.

Though partial ascriptions are made throughout the Chronicles of various monarchs, the most deliberate early assertion of ontological parity with the Buddha as Lord of the universe is that of Kassapa (477–495), the famed parricide king, who built his palace atop Sīgiriya. "As the Cūlavaṃsa categorically states, Sīgiri was built as a replica of Ālakamandā paradise on the top of Mount Kailāsa; and Kassapa resided there as the embodiment of Kuvera on earth."[29] While the chronicler's account of the whole Dhātusena-Kassapa-Moggallāna saga hits the salient didactic keys, it is basically restrained on this score. A translation with commentary by Dr. Paranavitana of a purported fifteenth century Sanskrit history of Sīgiri, on the other hand, unfolds the story of Siṃhagiri as an Alakā (paradise) on earth and of the attempts by both Dhātusena and Kassapa to be proclaimed *Parvatarāja*. "When it was questioned by Dhātusena what purpose there was in administering the kingdom from a place on the summit of a rock, the Maga Brāhmaṇa replied that *Parvata* was a synonym of *Megha*, i. e. the Cloud, that the

---

27) Rahula, op.cit., p. 62.

28) U. N. Ghoshal, Principle of the King's Righteousness, in: Indian Historical Quarterly, Vol. 32, 1956, p. 309. One ruling over the four quarters was called *digvijayin*.

29) Paranavitana, op.cit., p. 26. Kuvera (Kubera) is the god of wealth, whose paradise is Alakā.

Cloud was the source of all prosperity, that if the Cloud did not rain, the whole world would be destroyed and that it would be possible for anyone who had made the world to accept that he himself was the Cloud, [to] bring the whole world under his subjection."[30]

Cynicism prompts one to reject the whole account, or at least to view what it portrays as a bald power play, basing legitimation upon hoodwinking of the populace. However specious the supposed Brāhmaṇa's reasoning and however transparent his motives, the account nevertheless suggests the lengths to which the legitimizing process could proceed and the delicate line between genuine and spurious legitimation. As it is said in the Manu-smṛti, the king should "emulate the energetic action of Indra, of the Sun, of the Wind, of Yama, of Varuna, of the Moon, of the Fire, and of the Earth."[31] Likewise, the Śukranīti emphatically states that "the king is made out of the permanent elements of Indra, Vāyu, Yama, Sun, Fire, Varuṇa, Moon, and Kubera, and is the Lord of both the immovable and movable worlds."[32] With these legitimating mythologies underwriting political authority and with the even more potent ontological association with the Buddha seated upon the sacred throne of Brahmā, the power of kingship gave the appearance of durability. "To repeat, the historically crucial part of religion in the process of legitimation is explicable in terms of the unique capacity of religion to 'locate' human phenomena within a cosmic frame of reference. All legitimation serves to maintain reality—reality, that is, as defined in a particular human collectivity. Religious legitimation purports to relate the humanly defined reality to ultimate and sacred reality. The inherently precarious and transitory constructions of human activity are thus given the semblance of ultimate security and permanence. Put differently, the humanly constructed nomoi are given a cosmic status."[33]

III. The extent and limitation of power

In traditional societies threatened by the continous spectre of disorder, authority and power must be buttressed by more than appeals to ontological legitimacy, however acknowledged these may be. Men do not live by ideology alone; agreement on that level does not preclude serious discord about particular issues. Authority is therefore legitimated

[30]) Senarat Paranavitana, The Story of Sigiri, Colombo, 1972, p. 22. In general, both the Buddhists and the Jains rejected the divinity of kings, though the evidence is less clear than orthodoxy implies. Paranavitana's speculations on this topic have been subject to much criticism. See Sirima Kiribamune, Some Reflections on Professor Paranavitana's Contribution to History, in: Ceylon Journal of the Humanities, Vol. I, No. 1 (January, 1970).

[31]) The Laws of Manu, p. 396.

[32]) Balakrishna, The Evolution of the State, in: Indian Historical Quarterly, Vol. 3, 1927, p. 325. The passage referred to is Śukranīti, I 375.

[33]) Berger, op.cit., pp. 35–36.

by the responsible exercise of power, not simply by where its ultimate grounding is perceived. In relatively stable social orders and within reasonably homogeneous communities, where traditions and values change gradually, concurrence about general goals comes more naturally. With the onset of social instability from whatever cause or with the absorption of heterogeneous sub-groups, basic agreements may dissolve and power is inevitably threatened. Appeals to legitimacy may then fall on deaf ears, of counterappeals may arise. At the very least, order again becomes a matter of highest importance and skill in political statecraft carries its own legitimation.

There is a political truism in the assertion that power seeks a vacuum. Maladministration, incompetence, or simply ignorance about the basic problems of a society finally undermine whatever ideological validation may exist. In a hierarchically structured body politic this means that leadership continues in name alone and that authority is retained only under duress. The fact that this authority is invested with ontological status may ironically become more of a liability than an asset, as blame is attached to those from whom benefits are supposed to flow. In a monarchy especially the kudos which attends kingship in times of plenty may suddenly collapse when conditions become critical, creating a crisis of confidence which places full responsibility upon the monarch in power. The jockeying for position which then emerges reveals the multiple loci of power comprising any society, however invisible these may be to the unsuspecting. In actuality, balancing of power occurs as much within a monarchy as in other forms of government. Attempts to secure absolute power are products of despair, resulting from the failure to extend legitimate authority throughout the system. Such efforts reveal that effective legitimation has been removed, that the mandate of authority is recalled, displayed as much by social disintegration as by inauspicious portents.

In this section the task is to examine the relationship between the concept of kingship and how kings actually exercised their legitimated power in ancient Ceylon. This does not mean ignoring the realms of ideology and rhetoric, since most of the source material is didactic by intention, but at least grains of realism become evident the more one explores the expansion, the use, and the curtailing of power. The areas to be viewed are the following: how the legitimation of authority is regularized and transmitted; how the actual power of kingship is expanded; how statecraft is envisioned and utilized; what bearing traditional expectations of kingship (stemming from legitimation) have for each monarch; and, what checks upon royal power effectually determine the shape and tenor of legitimacy.

1. In the entire history of Ceylon no event is accorded more importance for the establishment of legitimate political authority than the founding of Buddhist kingship upon the Aśokan model during the reign of Devānaṃpiyatissa (250–210 B. C.). This episode constitutes the classical designing

both of what kingship means and of how it is to be regularized. This story is so well known one needs only to mention the ingredients which became normative for the institution of the monarchy and how the Indian model of the ideal king, modified considerably by Aśoka, took root in Ceylon. If no direct lineage can be traced from the Mauryan dynasty to Ceylon, the fact that Aśoka's missionary, the bhikkhu Mahinda, is held responsible for Tissa's conversion to the Dhamma establishes a surrogate connection with the earliest of India's great empires. Laṅkā has, of course, related ambivalently throughout her history to this association with Indian prototypes, utilizing whatever served her own needs and becoming restive when threatened by political realities (especially from South India). In any case, the symbols of office, modes of consecration, and forms of administrative practice were largely Indian in origin.[34]) It would be naive to imply these arrived full-blown with the advent of Mahinda, unfolding immediately with the *abhiseka* of Devānaṃpiyatissa, but over the centuries the regalia, the titles, the ceremonies, and much of the exercising of authority became more Indian in complexion, without losing their central legitimating feature, i. e., the claim of the Dhamma.

2. More significant for our purposes than the acquiring and confirming of royal power are the means by which this power could be extended through a competent handling of the office. In line with the king's basic function of protection it is clear that military security and political stability were minimal conditions for the enhancement of the monarchy. As in the early days of any society, political leadership and military prowess were often merged. In India and Ceylon the caste basis of this solidified the connection even more. Among the greatest Sinhalese leaders were those whose strategic skills on the battlefield were noteworthy. The reverse is equally true, as many defeats by South Indian armies made clear. Without freedom from foreign attack or from civil strife legitimation was cast in doubt. The same was true with respect to economic welfare. Even with relative political stability the necessity of a productive agricultural base and a lucrative foreign trade regularly assumed major importance. The special climatic terrain, and soil features of Ceylon led eventually, with population increases, to the extensive irrigation system which began to develop under Vasabha (67–111) and continued, though with many interruptions, until the final collapse of the Rājaraṭṭha civilization in the fourteenth and fifteenth centuries.[35]) Safeguarding the economic base was therefore of no less consequence

---

[34]) This is fully discussed in a number of studies. Cf. Tilak Hettiarchchy, History of Kingship in Ceylon, pp. 6–64; Wilhelm Geiger, Culture of Ceylon in Mediaeval Times, pp. 111–132; H. C. Ray, ed., The University of Ceylon History of Ceylon, Vol. I, Part I, passim; H. Ellawala, Social History of Early Ceylon, pp. 11–27.

[35]) See K. Indrapala, ed., The Collapse of the Rajarata Civilization, Peradeniya 1971.

than political protection. In fact, the two were plainly intertwined, as was clear whenever foreign invaders took advantage of domestic unrest and weakness as the occasion to launch an attack.[36]) While kings had certain rights over land usage and ownership, and possessed the privilege to levy various kinds of taxation, there was an unwritten law that these rights were in jeopardy unless basic economic and political conditions were met. The lesson for each king was clear—unless legitimation is rooted in effective response to the everyday needs of society, its claims to cosmic status are of small comfort. The converse is equally true, i. e., with the maintenance of these benefits royal authority is enhanced.

3. On the other hand, it is obvious that social conditions are rarely ideal and that consummate skills in governance can turn relative losses into relative success. As we shall see, though power is regularly held in balance by the presence of contending factions, shrewd leadership can defuse factious elements, even convert discord into harmony. While the process is a never-ending dialectic and while it can easily backfire, there were carefully developed principles in the art of government (*daṇḍanīti*) which stood many a monarch in good stead. As Geiger indicates, the compiler of the first part of the Cūlavaṃsa (chapters 37–79) was well versed in Indian *nīti* literature, especially in the Arthaśāstra of Kauṭilya, and attributed not only detailed knowledge of this to Gajabāhu II (1132–1153) but also showed how it was put into practice.[37]) While earlier evidence of such statecraft is more fragmentary, one may find reference to it in the reigns of Kassapa V (914–923) and Dhātusena (459–477), whose bhikkhu uncle tutored him in these arts.[38])

Though few kings could meet Kauṭilya's high standards of intrigue and deviousness, rewarded by the successful manipulation of power, the evidence is considerable throughout the Chronicles that many Sinhalese monarchs were able practitioners of *Realpolitik*. The standard education of any prince included study of the arts of warfare and of *nīti* in general. Political marriages regularly took place with princesses from South Indian dynasties from the outset of Sinhalese history. Bhikkhus, as well, engaged themselves at times in direct political involvement. In reference to Dāṭhāsiva, whose position at the court of Aggabodhi I (575–608) was similar to that of the *purohita*, Geiger notes this as "the

[36]) As expressed in one famous maxim: "Watch for the weaknesses of others as a hawk watches its prey. And conceal your own weaknesses as a tortoise hides its soft body."

[37]) Cūlavaṃsa, 66. 126–158. Cf. also pp. vi and xiv.

[38]) Cf. Cūlavaṃsa. 52. 37–41, where it is said that Kassapa was "versed in statecraft" as well as being "a mine of virtues". Regarding Dhātusena, see Cūlavaṃsa, 38. 14–28, in which his uncle perceives that the boy Dhātusena "must be made a master in state-craft." The political aim of the chroniclers has been capably discussed by Heinz Bechert, who writes that "the basic idea of this ideology was that of the unity of nation and religion." See his paper "The Beginnings of Buddhist Historiography: Mahāvaṃsa and Political Thinking", to appear in: Religion and Legitimation of Power in Sri Lanka, ed. Bardwell L. Smith.

beginning of political influence on the bhikkhus."[39]) Long before this, however, in the late third century one can see in Saṃghamitta (during the reigns of Goṭhābhaya, Jeṭṭhatissa, and Mahāsena) a monk whose wiles and manipulation of power took second place to none, at least in the judgment of the Mahāvihāra.[40])

These examples should prove no surprise, for the climate of political practice in India and Ceylon made the knowledge of *daṇḍanīti* imperative. Even if Buddhist conscience did not normally approve of duplicity (*dvaidhībhāva*) or if circumstances did not always requires spies (*guḍha-puruṣas*), no leader could afford to be cavalier about the balancing of power (*āsana*), the prospect of anarchy (*matsyanyāya*), or the regularly practiced system of alliances (*maṇḍala*). While the influence of the Dhamma, as represented by the Sangha, doubtlessly exercised a moderating influence upon those who may have been tempted to excesses in statecraft, the Chronicles reveal that Sinhalese Buddhists in high places recognized that *daṇḍanīti* and tyranny did not need to be synonymous. Indeed, responsible statecraft and legitimation were more perceived to be hand and glove.[41])

4. In whatever ways a king's legitimacy is established and by whatever means he extends his authority, limits are set to his power both by the unpredictableness of circumstances and by other communities of power within his own society and beyond. As suggested earlier, the very inflation of status accompanying any ontological grounding of kingship produces a level of expectation and an automatic pinpointing of responsibility which ironically turn the monarchy into a precarious institution. When rainfall is sufficient and the crops flourish and the people prosper, the king may bask in the adulation of his citizens who, according to tradition, attribute all success to his righteousness, all bounty to his protection. When famine strikes, when plague decimates the populace, when a foe puts the king's troops to rout, blame is traditionally sought in the person of the monarch. "From Vedic times downwards the king has been regarded as the supporter and upholder of the law, the 'dharma'. It was believed that any unhappiness, misery and pestilence among the subjects were attributed to the failure of the king to conform to the duties (*rāja-dharma*) of the king. It is said that even sugar and salt lose their flavour during the rule of an unjust king."[42]) The very belief that kingly righteousness is the guarantee of heavenly blessing also attributes any nexus of afflictions to the absence of righteousness. "When kings become unrighteous, we are told in a canonical text (Aṅguttara-Nikāya, II, 74–76), the king's officers (*rājayutta*) also become unrighteous, this being so the

[39]) Ibid., p. 67, footnote 8.

[40]) Mahāvaṃsa, XXXVI. 110–XXXVII. 31

[41]) Extension of royal power came also through capable administration of justice, through the regular process of succession to the throne, through the power to make appointments to important positions and to make summary dismissals.

[42]) U. D. Jayasekera, Early History of Education in Ceylon, Colombo, 1969, p. 53.

Brāhmaṇas and the mass of ordinary freemen (*gahapati*), the townsfolk and the villagers in their turn become unrighteous, this being so the Sun and the Moon, the stars and the constellations go wrong in their courses; days and nights, months, seasons, and years are out of joint; the *devas* being annoyed do not bestow sufficient rain. This being so the crops ripen in the wrong season, and consequently men are short-lived, ill-flavoured, weak and sickly. Conversely, when kings become righteous all the reverse consequences follow."[43]) A good king is therefore an incalculable blessing; a bad king, a disaster. What legitimation bestows, circumstances may remove, for authority is not inherent in the king. It is provisional, arising largely from an effective use of power for the benefit of others.

5. Finally, what factors served to check royal power from becoming tyrannous and contribute to a balancing of power whereby the legitimacy of kingship was actually enhanced?[44]) First, on the level of theory, the fact that the king was supposed to rule according to the Dhamma created an image of sovereignty which had its effect upon incumbents, originally through their early education and later upon the throne. Secondly, there was always the threat of hostile public opinion, which could be capitalized upon by adversaries at home and abroad. Third, the lessons of history could provide sobering restraints as one reflected upon what happened when folly and injustice proceeded from the throne. Fourth, in the absence of instant communications and constant surveillance, local communities (the *gāma*, or basic unit of autonomy) and distant provinces (e. g., Rohaṇa) tended to promote a kind of functional independence within the general bounds of fealty. Fifth, the many centers of power within the court, the army, various corporations and guilds, all having their own diversity, were vehicles of support and potential threats to the king depending upon his ability to affect balances within and among these groups. Sixth, there was the factor of foreign mercenaries whose numbers grew in importance over the centuries and whose presence was ambiguous in relation to the various allies and foes among South Indian dynasties.

While all the above were important in limiting royal power, the most crucial factor was the bhikkhu Sangha. Because of the Sangha's closeness to the people and because of its rate in lending cohesiveness to the realm, a unified monastic community was an invaluable asset to effective kingship. On the other hand, from the reign of Vaṭṭagāmaṇī (89–77 B.C.) on the

---

[43]) U. N. Ghoshal, op. cit., pp. 306–307. See also John W. Spellman, Political Theory of Ancient India, pp. 211–219. Also, the Cakkavatti-Sīhanāda Sutta, in: Dialogues of the Buddha, Vol. IV, pp. 59–76; and, The Sutra of Golden Light, pp. 57–62.

[44]) Cf. B. P. Sinha, The King in the Kauṭilīyan State, in: Journal of the Bihar Research Society, Vol. 40, pp. 291–308; and, U. N. Ghoshal, An Aspect of State Administration in the Pre-Maurya Period—Influence of Public Opinion on Kingly Governments, Journal of Indian History, in: Vol. 40 (1962), pp. 551–555.

Sangha was not unified and was often seriously divided, a fact which regularly involved the king or his counsellors in disputes and which sometimes prompted them to take sides, creating further unrest. Kings were the primary patrons of the Sangha, but they could also become the target of abuse. The relationship between the monarchy and the monastic community deserves a great deal more attention than it has received thus far. The following summary at least begins to hint at the complexities at work and also suggests how royal power was both enhanced and limited in relationship to this community.

Conflicts arose between the king and the Sangha when the king carried his patronage too far and interfered in the affairs of *uposathāgāra*. The Sangha also started taking more interest in politics as they became a landed aristocracy, and the existence of a division within the order aggravated the situation so that the monks tried to put their favourites on the throne in order to secure material benefits. As the orthodox church grew in power the king was forced to take sides with them, but disputes arose regarding the respective fields of power of these two institutions which led to the ultimate clash in the reign of Mahāsena. When the king realized that his power was no match for that of the orthodox church he made a sudden reversal of policy and instead of attempting to maintain the unity of the Sasana tried to bring about and maintain as many rival Viharas as possible, thereby to redress the balance.[45])

IV. The nurturing of legitimation

As in the political realm where power arrangements continuously shift, legitimation of authority and power is a process needing regularly to be renewed by means of symbolism, mythology and ritual. It is no more true in a monarchy than in representative government that once legitimated, always legitimate. Because most legitimation is "pretheoretical in character," as Peter Berger indicates, the legitimating formulas of any community need reaffirmation. Even where no threat or challenge exists, the process must become real to new members of the society and kept alive among those already accepting it in theory. "There is both an objective and a subjective aspect to legitimation. The legitimations exist as objectively valid and available definitions of reality. They are part of the objectivated 'knowledge' of society. If they are to be effective in supporting the social order, however, they will have to be internalized and serve to define subjective reality as well. In other words, effective legitimation implies the establishment of symmetry between objective and subjective definitions of reality."[46])

A second ingredient of this process is the need for reciprocity between key elements in the society to be experienced and confirmed. Legitimation

[45]) Tilak Hettiarchchy, History of Kingship in Ceylon up to the Fourth Century, A.D., p. 143. This is a very capable study of this subject. Especially excellent is his chapter on "The Relationship between the King and the Sangha," pp. 116–143, which is one of the more perceptive analyses of this topic that exists. It restricts itself, however, to the period before the fourth century A.D.

[46]) Berger, op.cit., p. 32.

is not simply of kingship but of the entire structure of which kingship is the most prominent feature. Authority and power are not granted to the throne for its own sake, but to offset the precariousness of order and to ensure the possibility of stability and reasonable prosperity. The very concept of reciprocity suggests that communal existence is a fabric whose integrity depends upon the strength of all its parts. Even in a society organized along hierarchical lines, where overt political power is lodged at the top and where no regular procedures exist for influencing policy or removing those in power, the recognition that order is essentially indivisible remains imperative. While reciprocity takes different forms, with different meanings at various levels of society, it is necessary to the legitimation process. "Without integration among the elite, integration between the elite and the masses is difficult to achieve; without integration between the elite and the masses, there cannot be an integrated political community."[47]) The nurturing of legitimation remains, therefore, essential to any social organism.

Because most available source material from ancient Ceylon comes either from the bhikkhu community or from kings in the form of royal inscriptions, one would expect notions of reciprocity to dwell frequently on the relationship between the Sangha and the monarchy. While this is true, one may read between the lines for some picture of what was actually a more pluralistic reciprocity, with various groups within society and the populace in general being as central as the other two. Indeed, as recent anthropological studies of Ceylon, Burma and Thailand make evident, a rich heritage of ideology, symbolism, and ritual exists on the popular level throughout Theravāda societies. While present forms of these cannot be projected upon previous centuries without considerable qualification, it is clear that a host of pretheoretical legitimating phenomena has existed from early Sinhalese experience. The following discussion identifies three aspects of the nurturing of legitimation, each involving the king, the Sangha, and the people in various ways: the notion of the Sangha as a merit field (*puññakkhetta*) whose purity was essential to society at large; the normative qualities of kingship, centering primarily on its responsibility to protect and further the Dhamma; and, the role of ritual and ceremony in keeping alive not just the memory of the Buddha but faith in the doctrine's power. These aspects of legitimation go far beyond underwriting royal authority; they attest to and buttress the entire universe of belief which makes up Sinhalese Buddhism.

1. The stress upon the Sangha's purity has been central from the tradition's beginning; the relating of this to an *ideology of merit* grew gradually over the centuries. Throughout Theravāda Buddhism the injunction of the Buddha that "one of the six duties of a monk towards the

[47]) Ping-ti Ho and Tang Tsou, eds., China in Crisis, Vol. 1: China's Heritage and the Communist Political System, Chicago: University of Chicago Press 1968, p. 279.

laity is to show them 'the way to heaven' (*sagga*) . . . and not 'the way to emancipation' (*mokkhassa maggaṃ*)" has been taken seriously and helps to explain, with canonical support, the considerable encouragement given to pious practices of various sorts.[48]) If the path to Nibbāna is too arduous for those not seeking it directly, the Sangha accepts the task of assisting laymen to build up merit for their next existence and of becoming through the quality of its own life a source of merit to others. The reasons for the Sangha's purity are therefore twofold: one, that this may enhance the chances of its own membership for attaining Nibbāna; and two, that the merit accrued by this quest may be transferred to pious followers.

The modern dynamics of this have been carefully discussed by S. J. Tambiah, who shows how the ascetic monk becomes "an appropriate intermediary who can reach up to mystical powers associated with the Buddha and the sacred texts, and who can in turn transfer these powers to the layman in a form that can positively sacralize this life and the next."[49]) The doing of merit is thus accompanied by the receiving of merit, giving concrete form to the reciprocity which exists but needs actualizing to have meaning for the participants. As the king is ideally the mediator between the body politic and the cosmic realm, so the Sangha's mediatorial role helps to provide sacral meaning to mundane existence and the human odyssey. It is for this reason that the quality of bhikkhu life must ideally be *sans reproche*. Monks involved directly in political affairs, engaged in "monastic landlordism," or embroiled in strife among the nikāyas do not give the appearance of being merit fields for others. From the earliest days in India and Ceylon the king had an important role in prompting the Sangha to reform itself (*sodhana*) through a regulative act (*dhamma-kamma*) of the Vinaya. This did not place the king above the Sangha in ecclesiastical matters, but it reinforced the notion of reciprocity since the entire society had a stake in the Sangha's purity. Because the Sangha could be an effective check upon royal power that became tyrannous, a unified and healthy monastic community helped create political legitimacy. The ongoing process of purification was therefore a central ingredient in the nurturing of legitimation.

---

[48]) Rahula, op.cit., pp. 251–2. The reference here is to the Sigāla-sutta of the Dīgha-Nikāya, III, p. 117. The Sigāla Homily is, of course, one of the most important suttas for expressing the nature of true reciprocity, though it focusses on what it means for the layman in the relationships of the "six quarters"—i.e., between parents and children, teachers and pupils, husband and wife, friend and friend, master and servant, laymen and religious "recluses and brahmins."

[49]) S. J. Tambiah, The Ideology of Merit, in: E. R. Leach, ed., Dialectic in Practical Religion, p. 116. For the growth of the concept of merit in post-canonical Theravāda texts, see the article by Heinz Bechert entitled Notes on the Formation of Buddhist Sects and the Origins of Mahāyāna, in: German Scholars on India: Contributions to Indian Studies, Vol. I, Varanasi: Chowkhamba Sanskrit Series Office, 1973, pp. 16–17 especially.

2. The role of the king as protector of the Dhamma was in direct correlation with his role as chief patron of the Sangha, though it went beyond this as well. Aside from the direct advantages of various land grants and other endowments which kings made available to monasteries, without which they could not have flourished, royal beneficence was also seen as a model for others, in spirit if not in kind. The importance attached by the compiler of the Chronicles to the generosity of kings was not simply out of appreciation for what the Sangha received materially. It was also recognition that monarchs well disposed toward the livelihood of the bhikkhus furthered the Dhamma in a number of ways, beyond the maintaining of order and justice within society.

As in other respects, Aśoka was seen as a prime example. The Dīpavaṃsa records him as saying, "as much as the monks desire I give them whatever they choose."[50] It is also recorded that the monks had to restrain him in his liberality, though when he pressed the question to Moggaliputta as to whether there were "a kinsman of Buddha's religion like unto me," he received this response: "Even a lavish giver of gifts like to thee is not a kinsman of the religion; giver of wealth is he called, O ruler of man. But he who lets son or daughter enter the religious order is a kinsman of the religion and withal a giver of gifts."[51] It was only fitting then that Aśoka's purported son, the bhikkhu Mahinda, should be the one to tell Devānaṁpiyatissa that not until someone native to Ceylon be ordained will the doctrine be planted in that country. Both examples suggest the nature of true giving, of self more than substance. And yet the very prodigality of royal patronage was stressed in order to inspire later generations. In response to the lavish gifts of Duṭṭhagāmaṇī, the chronicler writes: "Merit, that a man has thus heaped up with believing heart, careless of insupportable ills of the body, brings to pass hundreds of results which are a mine of happiness; therefore one must do works of merit with believing heart."[52] Such performance of "pure deeds of merit" prompts others to "give alms lavishly, with a mind freed from the fetters (of lust), mindful of the good of beings."[53] It was this sort of monarch who was said to walk among men even as a bodhisatta (e. g., Buddhadāsa in the fourth century) and to be endowed with the ten qualities of kings (*dasa rājadhamma*) and the four heart-winning qualities (*cattāri saṃgahavatthūni*).[54] The models of exemplary kingship are threaded throughout the Chronicles, in contrast to others whose lives of evil are due warning. Also, the stories of holy monks and nuns, collected in the *Ariyavaṃsa*, were ordered by Vohārika Tissa (214–236) to be read

---

[50]) Dīpavaṃsa, p. 178. The gift in that particular instance, apparently unsolicited from the monks, was said to be 84,000 monasteries, a figure merely symbolic of his munificence.

[51]) Mahāvaṃsa, p. 43.

[52]) Ibid., p. 190

[53]) Ibid., pp. 219, 186.

[54]) Cūlavaṃsa, p. 10.

aloud for the edification of the people.[55]) Protection of the Dhamma obviously, therefore, took a number of forms, involving support of the Sangha, construction of stūpas, and especially lives founded upon the teaching. In the process, not only was the Dhamma enhanced and nurtured; the whole process of legitimation was deepened through this internalization.

3. The most standard and conspicuous way which society's roots in the sacred realm underwent reaffirmation was through ceremonies, festivals and other forms of ritual. While Aśoka's caution about the true nature of ceremony (*Dharmamaṅgala*) would rank proper respect for living creatures above the usual ceremonies people perform, he also placed "the gift of Dharma or the benefit of Dharma" above liberality.[56]) The Chronicles make vividly clear, however, that orthodoxy saw substantive benefits accruing to the Dhamma by the celebration of its power through ritual. Indeed, one of the more obvious emphases throughout the record of the Mahāvaṃsa, ending with the reign of Mahāsena (276–303), are its elaborate and unrestrained paeans in response to the rituals of stūpa-building, relic worship, reverencing of the Bodhi-tree, and other forms of paying homage to the Buddha. Unquestionably, the focus is upon the Buddha and the Dhamma, but it is upon their cosmic significance, not simply their historic features. Access to this realm comes preeminently perhaps through attitudes of reverence stimulated through symbolism, mythology and ritual. While many observers have suggested that these occasions were primarily for the populace, this argument is not convincing. The bhikkhu community was as much involved in the glorifying of the Buddha's relics and in celebrating the Wheel of the Law as any others. If the proper aspiration of each monk was the attainment of Nibbāna, paying homage to the Buddha formed an intrinsic avenue of approach even if the path finally required the extinction of all dependence.

It is true that the performance of ritual had its less elevated dimensions. Kings were often engaged in constructing dagobas and image houses, for instance, as much for their own merit as for the benefit these brought to the Dhamma. Political opportunism played its part as well, as a form of bread and circuses for the populace and building up credit with the Sangha. A touch of cynicism is appropriate in trying to assess motivations,

---

[55]) Mahāvaṃsa, p. 258. Cf. also Malalasekera, op.cit., p. 51, who says that this custom existed before this time and also continues to be practiced today. As he was dying, Duṭṭhagāmiṇī expressed his fear of death to the bhikkhu Therasutābhaya, who comforted him and assured him of his great merit. The catalogue of his good deeds was then read to him out of the "Merit Book" (*Puññapotthaka*), which kings and other laymen often kept. As Geiger indicates in his Introduction to the Cūlavaṃsa, the source materials available to the compiler were mainly *Puññapotthakāni*, that is, "registers of meritorious works by which the prince had furthered the Church (*sāsana*) and the laity (*loka*)." See pp. iv–v.

[56]) N. A. Nikam and Richard McKeon, eds. and trs., The Edicts of Asoka, pp. 46–47.

though there was undoubtedly sincerity in the intentions of many monarchs, with a mixture of motivations being perhaps the norm among most kings and other members of the lay elite. At any rate, the value of renewing legitimation liturgically was not lost to the ingenuous and the scheming alike. Because men forget or disregard the ontic dimensions of their social existence, they need to be reminded regularly. "Religious ritual has been a crucial instrument of this process of 'reminding.' Again and again it 'makes present' to those who participate in it the fundamental reality-definitions and their appropriate legitimations. The further back one goes historically, the more does one find religious ideation (typically in mythological form) embedded in ritual activity ... The performances of the ritual are closely linked to the reiteration of the sacred formulas that 'make present' once more the names and deeds of the gods ... They restore ever again the continuity between the present moment and the societal tradition, placing the experiences of the individual and the various groups of the society in the context of a history (fictitious or not) that transcends them all."[57])

The single most important festival was that of the Tooth Relic, brought to Ceylon in the reign of Sirimeghavaṇṇa (303–331), which became an annual event continued down to the present and now accompanied by the Kandy Perahära. While associated with the Abhayagiri-vihāra and not even mentioned by the Pāli commentaries of the fifth century, the Tooth and the Alms-bowl (*pātra-dhātu*) of the Buddha came to be considered "essential for a prince who wished to be the recognized king of Ceylon."[58]) Indeed, in an act of devotional symbolism Sirimeghavaṇṇa was said to have offered the whole kingdom to the Tooth Relic, whose annual festival scored the reliance of genuine sovereignty upon the sovereign rule of the Buddha in cosmic terms. Reinforced by the reverencing of the Hair Relic (*Kesadhātu*), begun in the reign of Silākāla (522–535), "there were also public festivals in connection with the older objects of religious veneration, the Bodhi Tree and the *stūpas*, in which the king and the people took part. A festival regularly celebrated in honour of the Bodhi Tree was known as *sinānāpūjā*, the ceremony of bathing the holy tree, still conducted in the height of the drought as a means of causing rain to fall."[59]) While it is not appropriate here to explore the vast subject of *pirit* (Pāli, *paritta*), it must at least be said that the importance of the Protection Suttas and their use in dealing with public and private calamity are central to the problem of evil which ensues when forms of anarchy threaten the cosmic order. While close to magic on one level, they may partake of spiritually more profound quests on another.[60])

[57]) Berger, op.cit., pp. 40–41.

[58]) Rahula, op.cit., p. 74.

[59]) Paranavitana, S., Civilization of the Period: Religion, Literature and Art, in: University of Ceylon History of Ceylon, Vol. I, Part I, p. 384.

[60]) For an extremely suggestive interpretation of the protection ceremonies and the cosmic calendrical rites, which aim to ensure both public and private benefits,

In conclusion, it should be stressed that all forms of ceremony and ritualistic action on the public level in ancient Ceylon were party to the nurturing of legitimation, provided one interprets this as legitimation of society's definition of reality and not simply of royal authority and power. In this vein, for example, one may see the wider significance of stūpa-building, which has always been regarded in Theravāda countries as the apogee of merit-making and which is also a form of ritual itself as well as the prime symbol of the Buddha's authority. The following comments by Edward Conze make this clear:

It was because Buddhism assured this harmony with the cosmos on which all social welfare depends that the laity was so eager to support the Order, house its members, and erect fine monuments in honor of their teachings. The world would not have put up for long with a community of monks which would merely turn their backs on those who fed them if they had not given something priceless to the world which it could not get in any other way. The visible manifestations of this concern for cosmic harmony are the magnificent stupas which adorn all parts of the Buddhist world and are the tangible focus of the religion. It was the business of the laity to build those stupas, though only the relics of the Lord Buddha could give them life. The stupas are as fundamental to Buddhism as the four holy truths, and it has been shown beyond doubt that they have a cosmic significance, that they are representative of the universe . . . This "cosmic architecture represents the world as a theatre for the working-out of the Dharma and for the awakening of all beings by its piercing rays." Each stupa is an "imitation" of the life, or rather lives, of the Tathagata . . ., they allowed a whole society to unite in one common celebration, and thus had not only great moral, but also political consequences.

It was the French scholar Paul Mus who in his monumental work on Borobudur proved that the works of architecture, properly interpreted, show that the Buddhists felt responsible for the welfare of society as a whole, and that the Samgha . . . aimed at fostering and maintaining that cosmic harmony which is the source and basis of all social prosperity.[61])

---

see Tambiah, op.cit., p. 118–120. In this section he writes: "Man, too, subjects himself to the moral order in these cosmic rites; his merit-making and selfless giving of gifts express this subjection; the Buddhist monk, through his form of ascetic subjection, appropriately chants and preaches about the Buddha's conquest of desire, pain and death. Perhaps at the back of these religious actions are the basic ethical ideas that man transcends his limitations by subjecting his animal nature, that it is by freely giving that he receives bountifully, that by refusing the grosser things in life he measures the value of life, and that by harnessing and releasing ethical energy, nature and agencies external to man can be brought into a single harmonious order. It is in this sense that Buddhist cosmic rites are not manipulative or instrumental in the manner of spirit cults of 'magical' rites. And this is why Buddhist values and action necessarily have a higher place in the hierarchy of values and acts that comprise the universe of religious action . . . On the other hand, a coercive relationship of bargaining with spirits, their placation or domination, is again a statement of power relations which are an extension of and a contrast to the socially normal manipulative behaviour . . . However ethically valued, both are stubbornly present in real life—for if either gains supremacy life will be heaven on earth or pure hell; both are improbable."

[61]) Conze, op.cit., p. 250.

V. The collapse of legitimation

It has been the thesis of this essay from the start that each human community requires for its social and psychic existence significant consensus about what Berger calls its "plausibility structure." This entails the definition of reality which that community uses to give ultimate meaning to its corporate life and to deal with the forces of disorder within and among people which make order itself seem precarious. The two most important ordering principles for human society are the political and the religious, both of which seek to relate the affairs of men, in different but complementary ways, to a perceived transcendent sacred reality. In this manner, genuine authority and power are identified and in various ways gain legitimacy, a legitimation more of the plausibility structure itself than of those comprising its leadership at any point in time. Furthermore, the structure by definition consists of whole cloth and cannot easily endure marked challenges to its authenticity without being radically affected. Lastly, the process of legitimation is a continuous one, needing reaffirmation regularly if its meaning is to persist.

A question which has become particularly acute in the second half of the twentieth century, as traditional forms of societies succumb to new means of ordering reality, is what happens to human communities in the face of immense pluralism when their plausibility structures are shattered or seriously threatened? The fact that we are more aware of this issue today does not mean the phenomenon is new. In the West, for instance, we have been dealing with this fact in a host of forms since the break-up of the Holy Roman Empire in the late Middle Ages. This does not suggest that new structures of meaning cannot emerge, for they obviously have. But they possess less scope and do not normally inspire the same confidence as those existing for centuries without successful challenge. On the other hand, history records successive efforts to weave new patterns from the ruins of the old, using many former threads but adding new ones besides. The process is thus no simple evolution from an originally affirmed plausibility structure, through its collapse, to the total absence of such a structure. More likely, the process is consensus, challenge, collapse, and attempts at new forms of consensus, ad infinitum. If consensus appears to be enduring, based indeed upon the perceived structure of reality, its collapse appears to preclude all possibility, at least until new visions become convincing.

The final section of a paper is no place to introduce new themes, but it is appropriate to suggest nuances of the original theme which could profit from further research and reflection. The history of the Anurādhapura period affords considerable evidence that the culture dominated by the ethos of Sinhalese Buddhism was in actuality remarkably diverse. This was somewhat true from the beginning, though it became more so through centuries of increased exposure to the political arenas of South India, the world trading community with which Ceylon was involved, and the changing patterns within Buddhism (in Therāvada and Mahāyāna circles alike). The traditional documents for studying the Ceylon scene are well known. While presenting an extraordinarily full picture, they would be enriched through comparative historical studies of other Theravāda cultures especially, as well as further anthropological case studies of the sort done by Hans-Dieter Evers on the interplay between the vihāra, dēvāle and palace systems in the Kandy District.[62]) This suggestion is made on the assumption that evidence for a fuller historic picture than we presently have of the diversity within the Sangha, the increasing influence of Purāṇic Brahmanism, and the impact of the national cults along with various forms of popular religion is obtainable.

The value of understanding this broader picture is obvious from a number of standpoints, but it is essential if one is to grasp more fully the factors leading to a radical challenge of the orthodox plausibility structure, beginning in the late Anurādhapura period. The final chapters of its collapse are not difficult to write, but to overstress the problems of this era when Ceylon fell victim to Cōḷa aggression would minimize the implications of expanding diversity over the centuries before. The main configurations of Mahāyāna history in Ceylon, from the reign of Vohārika Tissa (214–236) to the introduction of Vajrayāna and Tantrayāna in the ninth and tenth centuries, are well known, but detailed studies of nikāya history (involving the problems of schism, sectarianism and Sangha unity) have not yet been broached. Likewise, knowledge about the general patterns of Brahmanic culture, especially in the North, is available, but further historical and case studies which seek to appraise in depth the influence of Indian popular religion, Sanskritized Tamil Brahmanism, and the highly important Bhāgavata cult upon forms of Sinhalese Buddhist life and practice remain to be attempted. Finally, while recent anthropological work of increasing sophistication has been done on the national cults of Ceylon and on various indigenous types of popular religion, it is crucial that these be studied on a comparative basis and that we learn further about their role historically in affecting more orthodox forms of mythology, symbolism, ritual, and piety.

While traditional forms of legitimation may retain their credibility long past their zenith, unless they absorb creatively new elements into the plausibility structure they are destined to become unconvincing. At that point they cease to exist and are irrecoverable. Until we know more about the history of relationships between the major vihāras and the nikāyas, not to mention their associations with political figures in Rājaraṭṭha and the provinces, we are forced to speculate about the tensions involved in the constant struggle over legitimacy. Glimpses of the picture are available. We know the side several kings took in disputes between monastic communities. Evidence affords some insight into the role of bhikkhu influence upon affairs of state. But only a skeletal per-

[62]) Hans-Dieter Evers, Monks, Priests and Peasants: A Study of Buddhism and Social Structure in Central Ceylon, Leiden 1972.

spective is thus far possible. The same holds for the manner in which diverse branches of the Sangha responded to the mounting Indian influence in the last two or three centuries before what the Chronicles calls the "pillage of Laṅkā" (by Māgha in 1215). A synoptic account exists, but we learn little about the dynamics of a culture wrestling desperately to retain its definition of reality in the face of competing alternative views. Were there, for instance, important attempts to fashion new syntheses which were nipped in the bud and never even reported? Does the Sangha's livelihood, in fact, depend upon patronage from the political arm? What creative resources emerge in such a community when it becomes clear that this dependence is no longer possible? Obviously, there were many stages in the history of Sinhalese Buddhism, long before the colonial and modern periods, when royal patronage and political stability were precarious or non-existent. How did the bhikkhu community deal with these crises? One may suspect that during these times the plausibility structure was at most in abeyance, not extinct, but we have inadequate insight into what this actually meant for the life of monks. Moreover, the picture of lay Buddhism during the vast scope of ancient times is inadequately known. While this was often true in the records of early societies, it is particularly so in this case. Again, here is where comparative historical and case studies from other Theravāda societies might help speculation be more informed. To conclude, the process of legitimation involves the linking of mundane existence to a perceived sacred reality, indeed the perception of this reality within mundane existence. The more we discover about the dynamics of the process in detail, the more we see its fragile nature, its powers of renewal, its potential for accommodating new ingredients, the constant possibility of its collapsing, and the enduring importance of it for all communities.

References

1. Books

Adikaram, E. W.: Early History of Buddhism in Ceylon. Colombo 1946.

Arasaratnam, S.: Ceylon. Englewood Cliffs, New Jersey 1964.

Ariyapala, M. B.: Society in Mediaeval Ceylon. Colombo 1968.

Auboyer, Jeannine: Daily Life in Ancient India. London 1965.

Berger, Peter L.: The Sacred Canopy: Elements of a Sociological Theory of Religion. New York 1969.

Bhandarkar, D. R.: Aśoka. Calcutta 1969.

Cakkavattī-Sīhanāda Suttanta, in: Dialogues of the Buddha (Dīgha-Nikāya), Vol. III, tr. by T. W. Rhys Davids (Sacred Books of the Buddhists, Vol. IV). London 1965.

Choudhary, Radhakrishna: Kauṭilya's Political Ideas and Institutions. Varanasi 1971.

Cūlavaṃsa, tr. by Wilhelm Geiger and C. Mabel Rickmers, parts 1–2. Colombo 1953.

Devahuti, D.: Harsha: A Political Study. Oxford 1970.

Dīpavaṃsa, ed. and tr. by B. C. Law. Maharagama, Ceylon 1959.

Drekmeier, Charles: Kingship and Community in Early India. Stanford 1962.
Ellawala, H.: Social History of Early Ceylon. Colombo 1969.
Evers, Hans-Dieter: Monks, Priests and Peasants: A Study of Buddhism and Social Structure in Central Ceylon. Leiden 1972.
Geiger, Wilhelm: Culture of Ceylon in Mediaeval Times. Wiesbaden 1960.
Ghoshal, U. N.: A History of Indian Political Ideas. London 1966.
Gokhale, B. G.: Asoka Maurya. New York 1966.
— Samudra Gupta: Life and Times. New York 1962.
Gombrich, Richard F.: Precept and Practice: Traditional Buddhism in the Rural Highlands of Ceylon. Oxford 1971.
Gonda, J.: Ancient Indian Kingship from the Religious Point of View. Leiden 1969.
Hettiarchchy, Tilak, History of Kingship in Ceylon up to the Fourth Century A.D. Colombo 1972.
Indrapala, K. (ed.): The Collapse of the Rajarata Civilization in Ceylon and the Drift to the South-west. Peradeniya 1971.
Jayasekera, U. D.: Early History of Education in Ceylon. Colombo 1969.
Joshi, Lalmani: Studies in the Buddhistic Culture of India (During the 7th and 8th Centuries A.D.). Delhi 1967.
Katikāvatas, Laws of the Buddhist Order of Ceylon, ed. and tr. by Nandasena Ratnapala. München 1971.
Kosambi, D. D.: The Culture and Civilisation of Ancient India in Historical Outline. London 1965.
The Laws of Manu, tr. by Georg Bühler. New York 1969.
Leach, E. R. (ed.): Dialectic in Practical Religion. Cambridge 1968.
Ling, Trevor: The Buddha: Buddhistic Civilization in India and Ceylon. New York 1973.
Liyanagamage, Amaradasa: The Decline of Polonnaruwa and the Rise of Dambadeniya (circa 1180–1270 A.D.). Colombo 1968.
Ludowyk, E. F. C.: The Footprint of the Buddha. London 1958.
Mahāvaṃsa, tr. by Wilhelm Geiger. London 1964.
Mahā-Sudassana Sutta, in: Buddhist Suttas, tr. by T. W. Rhys Davids (Sacred Books of the East, Vol. XI). Delhi 1965.
Malalasekera, G. P.: The Pāli Literature of Ceylon. Colombo 1958.
The Middle Length Sayings (Majjhima-Nikāya), Vol. II, tr. by I. B. Horner. London 1957.
Mookerji, Radha Kumud: Ancient Indian Education (Brahmanical and Buddhist). Delhi 1969.
Mudiyanse, Nandasena: Mahayana Monuments in Ceylon. Colombo 1967.
Nicholas, C. W. and S. Paranavitana: A Concise History of Ceylon. Colombo 1961.
Nikam, N. A. and Richard McKeon (eds. and trs.): The Edicts of Asoka. Chicago 1959.
Nilakanta Sastri, K. A.: A History of South India. London 1966.
Paranavitana, Senarat: Ceylon and Malaysia. Colombo 1966.
— Sinhalayo. Colombo 1970 (rev. 2nd ed.).
— The Story of Sigiri. Colombo 1972.
— (ed.): The University of Ceylon History of Ceylon Vol. I, parts 1, 2. Colombo 1959–60.
Pāṭimokkha, tr. by Ñāṇamoli Thera. Bangkok 1966.
Raghavan, M. D.: India in Ceylonese History, Society and Culture. New Delhi 1969.
Rahula, Walpola: History of Buddhism in Ceylon: The Anurādhapura Period (3rd Century B.C.–10th Century A.D.). Colombo 1966.
Reynolds, C. H. B. (ed.): An Anthology of Sinhalese Literature up to 1815. London 1970.

Saletore, Bhasker Anand: Ancient India Political Thought and Institutions. London 1963.

Seligmann, C. G. and Brenda Z. Seligmann: The Veddas. Cambridge 1969.

The Sutra of the Golden Light, tr. by R. E. Emmerick. London 1970.

Shamasastri, R. (tr.): Kauṭilya's Arthaśāstra. Mysore 1967.

Sharma, Ramashraya: A Socio-Political Study of the Vālmīki Rāmāyana. Delhi 1971.

Sharma, Ram Sharan: Aspects of Political Ideas and Institutions in Ancient India. Delhi 1968.

Singh, Ram Charitra Prasad: Kingship in Northern India (c. 600–1200 A.D.). Delhi 1968.

Sinha, H. N.: The Development of Indian Polity. Bombay 1963.

Smith, Bardwell L. (ed.): The Two Wheels of Dhamma: Essays on the Theravada Tradition in India and Ceylon. Chambersburg, Pennsylvania 1972.

Spellman, John W.: Political Theory of Ancient India: A Study of Kingship from the Earliest Times to circa A.D. 300. Oxford 1964.

Spiro, Melford E.: Buddhism and Society: A Great Tradition and Its Burmese Vicissitudes. New York 1970.

Tambiah, S. J.: Buddhism and the Spirit Cults in North-east Thailand. London 1970.

Thapar, Romila: Aśoka and the Decline of the Mauryas. Oxford 1961.

Warder, A. K.: Indian Buddhism. Delhi 1970.

2. Unpublished Monographs

(These monographs are Ph.D. dissertations done at the University of London)

Adhya, G.: Studies in the Economic Life of Northern and Western India (200 B.C.–300 A.D.). 1962.

Gunawardana, R. A. L. H.: The History of the Buddhist 'Saṅgha' in Ceylon from the Reign of Sena I (833–853) to the Invasion of Māgha (1215). 1965.

Indrapala, K.: Dravidian Settlements in Ceylon and the Beginnings of the Kingdom of Jaffna. 1965.

Sinha, B. P.: Decline of the Kingdom of Magadha (c. 455–1000 A.D.). 1948.

Siriweera, W. I.: Economic Conditions of Ceylon (c. 1070–1344 A.D.). 1970.

Wijetunga, Mudalige Karunaratna: The Rise and Decline of Coḷa Power in Ceylon. 1962.

3. Further References

For further references (contributions to journals, etc.) see notes.

Fragen zum Problem des chronologischen Verhältnisses des buddhistischen Modernismus in Ceylon und Birma

Von EMANUEL SARKISYANZ

Von den Ländern des Theravāda-Buddhismus sind Ceylon und nach ihm Birma die frühesten. Auch der buddhistische Modernismus entwickelte sich in Ceylon und in Birma früher als in anderen Theravāda-Gebieten[1]). Doch ist nach wie vor die Frage von Entlehnungen bzw. analogen Parallelentwicklungen des buddhistischen Modernismus in Ceylon und Birma ein offenes Problem. Bekanntlich hat die Theravāda-Orthodoxie Birmas mehrmals in ihrer Geschichte auf Vorbilder Ceylons zurückgegriffen, im späten 12. Jahrhundert unter Narapatisithu, in den 1470er Jahren unter Dhammazedi von Pegu[2]). Seinerseits hat ein Teil des buddhistischen Ordens Ceylons in der Krisenzeit der ausgehenden politischen Unabhängigkeit von Kandy an Vorbilder aus Birma angeknüpft (Amarapura Nikāya seit 1802).[3]) Doch hat gerade in Südost-Asien die Fremdherrschaft europäischer Imperialismen die historischen Verbindungen zwischen den Ländern der Region gestört, wenn nicht weitgehend unterbrochen.

In Birma war ein Religionsgespräch bei Toungoo 1862 Anlaß zu — vielleicht nicht ohne indirekte christliche Einwirkungen erfolgten — deistischen Umdenkungsversuchen in buddhistischen Kreisen[4]). Jedenfalls entstand aus dieser Polemik mit dem katholischen Missionar De la Cruz angeblich laut Bastian die sogenannte Paramat-Sekte mit Vorstellungen von einem vor der Welt existierenden transzendentalen kosmischen Intellekt (*Shwe-nyan-do*), angeblich mit Tendenzen zu Entmythologisierung, Ikonoklasmus und sogar einer Art Antiklerikalismus[5]).

Dagegen hatte bekanntlich eine Wiederbelebung des Buddhismus in Ceylon gerade mit Auseinandersetzungen gegen die Fremdherrschaft von Mächten der Christenheit bzw. deren kirchlicher Mission begonnen. Als einer der Marksteine darin gilt das buddhistisch-protestantische Religionsgespräch von 1873 zwischen Guṇānandathera und dem wesleyanischen

---

[1]) H. Bechert, Buddhismus, Staat und Gesellschaft in den Ländern des Theravāda-Buddhismus, Band I (Institut für Asienkunde in Hamburg, Schriften, Band XVII/1), Frankfurt-Berlin 1966, S. 44–52.

[2]) Niharranjan Ray, An introduction to the study of Theravāda Buddhism in Burma, Calcutta 1946, S. 112ff., 184ff.

[3]) Koun: baun-ze' Maha Yazawin-to gyi:, Mandalay 1267/1905, S. 760ff.

[4]) A. Bastian, Reisen in Birma in den Jahren 1861 und 1862 = Die Völker des östlichen Asien, Band II, Leipzig 1866, S. 361ff.

[5]) Ibid.; Shway Yoe (James George Scott), The Burman, his life and notions, London 1896, S. 147f.

Pastor David de Silva, welches das intellektuelle Bewußtsein der Buddhisten stärkte. Es hat auch in Kreisen der englischsprachigen Theosophie dem Buddhismus zu Ansehen verholfen. Nicht ohne starke theosophische Anregungen hat dann Anagārika Dharmapala die erste große modernistische buddhistische Vereinigung, die Mahabodhi Society, gegründet. Bekanntlich arbeitete er ursprünglich mit Oberst Olcott zusammen[6]). Dieser hatte um dieselbe Zeit eine buddhistische Konferenz mit Vertretern aus Ceylon, aber auch Birma (sowie China, Japan und Ostbengalen) einberufen, welche 14 Artikel annahm, die den Buddhisten aller Länder annehmbar sein sollten. In seinem Monumentalwerk hat Heinz Bechert (im ersten Band, S. 96) auf diese Konferenz kurz verwiesen. Es ist möglich, daß aus der hier zugrundeliegenden Quelle „Mahabodhi Society of India, Diamond Jubilee" (Calcutta 1952, S. 72f.) aus der Identität der birmanischen Teilnehmer bzw. ihrem Verhältnis zu späteren Vereinigungen von buddhistischen Modernisten in Birma etwas über Einflüsse aus dem damaligen Ceylon nach dort geschlossen werden könnte.

Anscheinend war die früheste Vereinigung von buddhistischen Modernisten Birmas die Sāsanādhāra Society von Moulmein, welche 1897 gegründet wurde.[7]) Nachdem in Colombo ein ceylonesischer buddhistischer Jünglingsverein (Young Mens' Buddhist Association = YMBA) gegründet worden war, entstand erst 1906 eine entsprechende birmanische Vereinigung in Rangoon[8]). Beide Organisationen waren weitgehend Laienvereinigungen mit wenig Partizipation aus dem Mönchtum. Beide gingen von englischsprachig Gebildeten aus. Solche ceylonesischen Organisationen behielten diesen Charakter wesentlich länger als die birmanischen. So war auch bekanntlich der Einfluß angelsächsischer Theosophen im modernistischen Buddhismus Ceylons anfangs beträchtlich. Bei den birmanischen buddhistischen Modernisten spielte dagegen die Theosophie kaum eine Rolle und war kaum bekannt — wenn man von Maung Maung Ji (einem Mitglied der indischen Kongreßpartei) absieht. Überhaupt waren — aus dem ganzen historischen Hintergrund jahrhunderterlanger ceylonesischer Beziehungen mit dem Abendland — Ceylons modernistische Laien unvergleichlich kosmopolitischer als diejenigen Birmas. Im Falle von Ceylon hat wenigstens ein Teil des buddhistischen Mönchtums aus den Küstenprovinzen die modernistische Erneuerungsbewegung unterstützt, doch gibt Heinz Bechert (I, S. 68) hierüber wenig Einzelheiten[9]). Dagegen geht aus Becherts Darstellung hervor, daß in den

[6]) Bechert, I, S. 45, 49.

[7]) Bechert, I, S. 53.

[8]) E. J. Colston, Some recent social movements in Burma, in: The Imperial and Asiatic Quarterly Review, Third Series, Band XXIX, Nr. 57 (Januar 1910), S. 79f.; Annual Report for the Administration of Burma, Rangun, 1908, S. 88, zitiert in: J. Furnivall, Colonial policy and practice, A comparative study of Burma and Netherlands India, New York, 1956, S. 142f.; Government of Burma, Burma Handbook, Simla, 1943, S. 106.

[9]) Bechert, I, S. 68.

Kerngebieten des singhalesischen Buddhismus das Mönchtum außerhalb des Modernismus blieb. Gerade „Inlandsklöster", insbesondere das berühmte „Zahnheiligtum" von Kandy waren jedoch die wichtigsten Verbindungspunkte Ceylons mit Birma: Sie bildeten das Ziel buddhistischer Pilger aus Birma nach Ceylon. Soweit gerade diese traditionell gebliebenen Bereiche des singhalesischen Buddhismus vom Modernismus kaum erfaßt worden sind, erreichte er auch nicht die birmanischen Pilger in Ceylon.

Dies mag ein Faktor dafür sein, daß, obwohl Birmas Buddhisten noch in der spätenglischen Zeit nach Ceylon pilgerten, die bekannten modernistischen Bestrebungen in Birma nicht mit Vorbildern aus Ceylon assoziiert werden. Ein Beispiel ist Ledi Sayadaw (1846–1923): Soweit uns bekannt, ist er nicht außerhalb Birmas gereist, obwohl er enge Beziehungen mit der britischen Pali Text Society hatte. Endgültiges wird sich über die Einzelheiten seiner Rolle allerdings erst sagen lassen, wenn die zahlreichen Schriften von Ledi Sayadaw daraufhin kritisch untersucht sein werden. Aber schon jetzt läßt sich verallgemeinern, daß Ledi Sayadaw, weitgehend repräsentativ für semi-modernistischen Buddhismus Birmas — obwohl er untypischerweise Mönch blieb und nicht aus dem englisch ausgebildeten Laientum kam, ja nicht einmal Englisch beherrschte — hierin einen Gegensatz zu einer solchen Hauptfigur des buddhistischen Modernismus Ceylons darstellte wie David Hervavitarne Dharmapāla.

So fehlen einstweilen positive Anhaltspunkte für das Zurückgehen des buddhistischen Modernismus Birmas auf Anregungen aus Ceylon. Andererseits sind die Parallelen beider Bewegungen so offensichtlich, daß es schwerfällt, unabhängige, aber analoge Entwicklungen in beiden Theravāda-Ländern anzunehmen. Eine solche Analogie, wenn auch anscheinend mit beträchtlichem zeitlichen Unterschied, bieten die sozialfürsorgerischen Betätigungen von buddhistischen modernistischen Vereinen. In Ceylon beginnen solche Bestrebungen seit der Jahrhundertwende schon mit Dharmapāla und führen zu buddhistischer Laientätigkeit für Jugendvereine, Waisenhäuser, Blindenanstalten usw.[10]) In Birma dagegen entwickelt sich derartiges anscheinend erst in der zweiten Nachkriegszeit[11]), wenn auch diese Aspekte im einzelnen noch lange nicht genug sozialhistorisch erfaßt worden sind.

Eine — sonst naheliegende — Inspiration der Anfänge von buddhistischem Modernismus in Birma durch modernistische Buddhisten aus England dürfte jedoch kaum in Frage kommen: Die erste buddhistische Gesellschaft Englands wurde laut Christmas Humphreys erst 1906 bis

---

[10]) Anagārika Dharmapāla, in: Maha Bodhi and the United Buddhist World XIII, Nr. 5/6 (1904), S. 45; Bechert, I, S. 50f.

[11]) Das ohne Orts- und Jahresangabe (nicht später als 1959) erschienene Buch „Kappa pya thana" des Taun-twin Gyi: Sayadaw (U: Okkata) trägt auf der Titelseite in englischer Sprache das Motto, "Service to the Poor is service to the Buddha".

1907 gegründet[12]). Vielleicht wäre weiteren Arbeiten zu diesen Fragenkomplexen mit einer Unterteilung der Thematik gedient, weil einzelne Aspekte des Gedankenguts des modernistischen Buddhismus zu verschiedenen Zeiten in verschiedenen Richtungen entlehnt sein könnten.

Allerdings erheben die folgenden Beispiele keinen Anspruch darauf, mehr als einen nur vorläufigen Wissensstand wiederzugeben. Z.B. erscheint in voller Militanz das Bekenntnis zur Güte des buddhistischen Ostens gegenüber der Bosheit des antibuddhistischen Westens in Ceylon (vor dem Hintergrund jahrhundertelanger kreuzzugsartiger Religionskonfrontation) z.B. spätestens mit Dharmapāla, in Birma mit dieser Vehemenz eigentlich erst nach dem zweiten Weltkrieg.

Im einzelnen wird in Ceylon mit Dharmapāla eine militante Polemik gegen Praktiken und Ansprüche der historischen Christenheit, ihrer Missionstätigkeit und ihrem Imperialismus schon 1899 bis 1909 sozusagen journalistisch entwickelt[13]), wie sie in einer vergleichbaren birmanischen Presse erst in der Bürgerkriegs- und Kaltkriegssituation von 1948–1953 Ausdruck findet[14]). Ähnliches gilt für das typische Detail-Argument des buddhistischen Modernismus, der Buddhismus sei naturwissenschaftlich begründbar, die biblische Theologie aber nicht: Der Ceylonese Dharmapāla argumentierte (im Mahabodhi Journal, allerdings in Indien, mit einer Leserschaft auch außerhalb Ceylons) in dieser Richtung bereits 1904–1905[15]), ein birmanischer Unterrichtsminister außer Dienst eine Generation später, 1948 bzw. 1954[16]). Mit dem Angriff buddhistischer Modernisten gegen die biblische Theologie verbunden war ihre Kritik des Theismus auf Ceylon im Mahabodhi Journal 1905, in Birma durch U Ba Yin 1954[17]), durch den birmanischen sozialistischen Staatsmann Ba Swe auf einem Gewerkschaftskongreß von 1955[18]). Die These von der Gegenüberstellung des autoritären Gottesglaubens und eines demokratischen Buddhismus kam nach Ceylon nicht später als 1920[19]),

---

[12]) Christmas Humphreys, Sixty years of Buddhism in England, London, 1968, S. 4.

[13]) Journal of the Mahabodhi Society VIII, Nr. 2/3 (Juni/Juli 1899), S. 24; Maha Bodhi and the United Buddhist World XIII, Nr. 5/6 (1904), S. 47; XVII, Nr. 9 (September 1909), S. 236.

[14]) Po Yarzar (U Ba Yin), „Letters to a Communist Nephew. Letter IX", in: The Burmese Review vom 10. Januar 1949.

[15]) Anagārika Dharmapāla in: Maha Bodhi and the United Buddhist World XIII, Nr. 11/12 (März/April 1905), S. 86.

[16]) Po Yarzar, Letters to a Communist Nephew. Letter XI, in: The Burmese Review vom 24. Januar 1949; U Hla Maung, From Dogma, via Science to Truth, in: The Burman vom 3. Oktober 1953, S. 4.

[17]) Wie Anm. 15; U Ba Yin, „Buddha's Way to Democracy", in: The Burman vom 12. April 1954, S. 7; 19. April 1954, S. 8.

[18]) U Ba Swe-ị, Bama-to hlan-yei: hniṇ Bama lou'tha: lu-dụ, Rangun 1955, S. 27

[19]) Buddhism and Christian Missions, in: Maha Bodhi and the United Buddhist World XXIX, Nr. 10 (Oktober 1920), S. 213f.

wurde aber in Birma, soweit mir bekannt, erst 1954 ausgesprochen[20]): Das Verhältnis der Religionen in Birma ermangelt der kreuzzugsartigen Traditionen Ceylons seit der Portugiesenzeit (wenn sie dort gewissermaßen nicht schon auf Duṭṭhagāmaṇi[21]) zurückgehen). Dagegen wurde buddhistische Missionierung Englands aus Birma schon 1913 eingeleitet — bekanntlich nicht ohne Zutun von zum Buddhismus bekehrten Engländern[22]). Andererseits dürften Thesen von der antiimperialistischen Ethik des Buddhismus in Birma (spätestens 1923)[23]) früher formuliert und postuliert worden sein als in Ceylon (z.B. von Dharmapāla 1933)[24]): Dies ergab sich aus der unterschiedlichen sozialen Entwicklung der Unabhängigkeitsbewegung in beiden Ländern; in Birma hatte sie — buddhistischen Modernismus weitgehend absorbierend — als revolutionäre Massenbewegung die Unabhängigkeit erkämpft. Ceylon dagegen erhielt die Unabhängigkeit auf evolutionärem Wege, ohne daß vorher buddhistischer Modernismus als Teil einer militanten Massenbewegung aufgetreten wäre[25]).

Die inzwischen nicht mehr unbekannten politischen Thesen von sozialistischen Aspekten des Buddhismus werden zwar schon 1907 von einem indischen buddhistischen Naturwissenschaftler postuliert[26]). (Und etwa gleichzeitig auch im äußersten Norden der buddhistischen Welt, in Kreisen burjatischer Populisten unter russischen Einflüssen in Südsibirien ausgesprochen[27]), allerdings wohl ohne Auswirkungen außerhalb der Russisch lesenden Intelligenz.) Aber in den Ländern des Theravāda-Buddhismus dürften Ideologien eines buddhistischen Sozialismus erst durch die Anfänge des buddhistisch-marxistischen Synkretismus bei U Nu eingeleitet worden sein — allerdings schon in der zweiten Vorkriegszeit zwischen 1935 und spätestens 1938[28]). Der Gedankengang der Projektion des buddhistischen Ideals universaler Leidensüberwindung auf die Überwindung sozialer Leiden erscheint allerdings im politisierten birmanischen Buddhismus (im Kontext von *sa-upādisesa*

---

[20]) U Ba Yin, Buddha's Way to Democracy, in: The Burman vom 26. April 1954, S. 5, 8.

[21]) Mahāvaṃsa, XXV, 17: The Mahāvaṃsa or the Great Chronicle of Ceylon, translated by W. Geiger, London 1912, S. 171. Duṭṭhagāmaṇī wird mit 161–137 v.Chr. datiert.

[22]) Sarkisyanz, Buddhist backgrounds of the Burmese Revolution, s-Gravenhage 1965, S. 116.

[23]) Zeyawadi U: Thilasara, in: Pinnya Alin vom Wanin-Wagaung 1285 (d.h. vom 1. September 1923), übersetzt von U: Wan Nyunt, Rangun.

[24]) Anagārika Dharmapāla, in: Maha-Bodhi XLI (1933), S. 348.

[25]) Sarkisyanz, Südostasien seit 1945, München 1961, S. 16, 21, 76, 85.

[26]) Lakshmi Narasu, The Essence of Buddhism, Madras 1907, S. 45f.

[27]) Sarkisyanz, Narodnik-Einflüsse auf kulturpolitische Nationalbewegungen der orientalischen Völker des Russischen Reiches, in: Gottfried K. Kindermann (Herausgeber), Kulturen im Umbruch, Studien zur Problematik und Analyse des Kulturwandels in Entwicklungsländern, Freiburg im Breisgau 1962, S. 204.

[28]) Maung Nu (U Nu), Cun-do buthama, in: U: Thein: Pe Myiṇ ywei: hce ti: hpyat-tho, Hbun-wada hniṇ Dobama, Rangun 1954, S. 55, 57, 59, 66f.

nibbāna) schon 1923[29]) und kulminierte in sozialistisch entwickelten Vorstellungen eines Nirvāṇa in dieser Welt („Lokka Neibban") als Vision einer idealen Gesellschaft[30]). Zwar geht das Schlagwort des „Lokka Neibban", des weltlichen Nirvana schon auf den Titel eines birmanischen Filmes zurück, der anscheinend schon 1933 in Rangoon gelaufen war[31]) und unpolitisch-romantisch gewesen zu sein scheint. Doch entwickelte sich gerade dieser ursprünglich buddhistische Begriff zu einem typischen Schlagwort des birmanischen Marxismus bereits 1938[32]).

Im Kontext der mehr evolutionären Entwicklung des spätbritischen Ceylons wird in der Politologie Ceylons (anscheinend ohne Berücksichtigung Birmas) angenommen, erst nach 1943 hätten „die ersten asiatischen Marxisten begonnen, gewisse philosophische Affinitäten und sozialethische Annäherungen zwischen den Systemen" von Buddhismus und Marxismus zu behaupten. So steht es wenigstens bei Lerski in seiner Geschichte des Trotzkismus auf Ceylon[33]): Im Jahre 1943 veröffentlichte nämlich in Colombo der singhalesische Marxist S. N. B. Wijeyekoon (unter dem Pseudonym „Leuke") ein mir bisher nicht direkt zugängliches Buch unter dem Titel „Gautama Buddha and Karl Marx. A critical and comparative study of their system of philosophy", in welchem er versucht, durch materialistische Interpretation von buddhistischem Nicht-Theismus den Klassenkampf damit zu rechtfertigen, daß dessen Ergebnis, die sozialistische Gesellschaft, auch ein buddhistisches Anliegen, die Überwindung der Begierden, erst ermöglichen würde[34]). Zwar war es im selben Jahre 1936, als ein entscheidender Teil der birmanischen Unabhängigkeitsbewegung und des birmanischen modernistischen Buddhismus sich sozialistischer Orientation[35]) zuwandte, daß der nachmalige Theoretiker des ceylonesischen Trotzkismus N. M. Perera in der Legislative buddhistische Statuen gegen Beleidigungen durch Europäer verteidigte[36]). Dessen ungeachtet fehlt anscheinend in der diesbezüglichen Publizistik Ceylons Kenntnisnahme des buddhistisch-marxistischen Synkretismus der birmanischen Ent-

---

[29]) Wie Anm. 23.

[30]) Thakin Kudaw Hmain:, Thakin Ṭīkā, Rangun 1938, S. 181.

[31]) Dr. Hla Pe, London School of Oriental Studies, Burmese Dictionary Project, Schreiben vom 19. Februar 1961 an den Verfasser; Sarkisyanz, Buddhist backgrounds of the Burmese Revolution, S. 170.

[32]) Ba Swe, Lokka Nibban-te hsau-ne-thu Stalin, in: U: Thein: Pe Myiṇ ywei: hce ti: hpyat-tho, Hbun-wada hniṇ Dobama, Rangun 1954, S. 122.

[33]) G. J. Lerski, Origin of Trotskyism in Ceylon, A documentary history of the Lanka Sama Samaj Party, 1935–1942, Stanford 1968, S. 89.

[34]) Leuke (S. N. B. Wijeyekoon), Gautama the Buddha and Karl Marx: A critique and comparative study of their systems of philosophy, Colombo 1943, S. 67, 79, zitiert in: Lerski, S. 171.

[35]) Thakin Tin, Samāghaka Wada Sadaw (1936), Wahlkampagne-Broschüre nach Mitteilung von Thakin Thein: Maung Gyi:, Rangun, der in seiner 1959 geplanten Geschichte der Thakin-Partei Einzelheiten hierzu zu bringen gedachte.

[36]) Debates in the State Council of Ceylon, Colombo, London: Hansard Society for Parliamentary Government 1936, S. 259, nach Lerski, S. 88.

wicklung. Dies mag an der stärkeren Nationalisierung mit der damit verbundenen Säkularisierung der modernistischen Erneuerungsbewegung des Buddhismus auf Ceylon im Vergleich zum modernistischen Buddhismus Birmas liegen. Auch daran, daß die Heilsgeschichte des ceylonesischen Buddhismus auch traditionell als untrennbar mit dem Regionalschicksal des Dhammadīpa gedacht wurde. Die im frühen zwanzigsten Jahrhundert durch die Laienorientation des modernistischen Buddhismus verstärkte Verflechtung von ceylonesischem Buddhismus und singhalesischem Nationalismus[37]) verhinderte wahrscheinlich eine Berücksichtigung von birmanischen Vorbildern, etwas, was 1802 möglich gewesen war. Andererseits ist das buddhistische Ceylon unter allen Theravādabuddhistischen Ländern für birmanische Buddhisten das einzige fremde Land, dessen Buddhismus für Birma als relevant angesehen wird und aus welchem birmanischerseits traditionell buddhistische Modelle übernommen zu werden pflegen. Trotzdem fehlt auch in Birma ein Bewußtsein von ceylonesischer Beeinflussung modernistischer Ausrichtung des Buddhismus gerade in politisierten Aspekten. Dieser Gesamteindruck ist auch derjenige von U Tin Htway, M. A. unserem birmanischen buddhistischen Mitarbeiter.

---

[37]) Vijayavardhana, The Revolt in the Temple, Composed to commemorate 2500 years of the Land, the Race and the Faith, Colombo 1953, S. 3ff.

Religion and Social Position in British Times

By C. H. B. REYNOLDS

Under the heading 'Ecclesiastical', that most informative work, Arnold Wright's Twentieth Century Impressions of Ceylon (1907), provides articles on the Church of England, the Roman Catholic Church (comparatively long and informative), the Wesleyan Methodist Mission, Dutch Reformed Church, Baptist Missionary Society Ceylon, The Salvation Army, the American Mission, YMCA and YWCA, and finally an article on the principal religion of the country by the Anagārika Dharmapāla entitled 'Buddhism, Past and Present', followed by one by Hikkaḍuvē Sumangala on Buddhist Sects.

In the opening article, on the Church of England, the writer, Rev. W. Henly, says that when British power superseded Dutch in Ceylon, "the new Government very rightly did not continue the efforts of their predecessors to induce their subjects to profess any particular religion. Accordingly, though for some time the Dutch system of catechists and proponents (lay preachers) was continued, the number of Government Christians, as they were called, very rapidly decreased and has now long passed beyond vanishing point." This is somewhat disingenuous, since civil registration of births and marriages was not introduced into Ceylon till 1868, up till which time full civil status rights had to be secured by recorded baptism and marriage as before. Henly writes, of the baptized members of the Dutch church who existed at the end of Dutch rule, "many in heart were Roman Catholics; still more Buddhists or Hindus." (The Hindus here referred to are the Tamils of Ceylon.) Roman Catholics were given full civil rights in 1806, and the registered Roman Catholic population of the island increased from 50,000 in 1796 to 83,595 in 1809. Many of the remainder of the 300,000 Dutch Christians therefore presumably became registered Anglicans to start with.[1]

After 1868, it was no longer necessary for those who felt themselves Buddhists to register under Christian forms. However, many of the registered Christians continued to count themselves Christian. J. W P..,[2] the anonymous author of a pamphlet called Caste and Class: the Aristocracy of the Maritime Provinces of Ceylon, published in Colombo in 1887,

---

[1] J. S. A. Fernando says: "Most of the Moratuwa Dutch congregation had become churchmen after the British occupation of Ceylon." (Jubilee Memorials, 1860–1910, Holy Emmanuel Church, Moratuwa, p. 5). He adds that in the time of Proponent Adirian Perera (1802–1812) the majority of the congregation were accustomed to call themselves 'Buddhist Christians'.

[2] J. W. Perera.

makes a sustained attack upon the class of those who had held high office in the Low Country in Dutch times, and continued to hold it under the British. The author of this pamphlet is concerned to show "that a Native aristocracy in the Maritime Provinces never existed," i.e. that those who began in the latter part of the 17th century to hold high office in those areas were of no distinguished origin and that their families had not formed an aristocracy in the times of the Sinhalese kings of Kōṭṭē or earlier—or at the very least that there is no evidence to show that they had. This indeed may well be true. By 1887, however, such families were generally accepted by the Colonial authorities as "first-class Wellalas"; and of them the author writes: "The first class 'Wellalas' seem morally and socially separated from those on whom they contemptuously look down—the rest of the 'Wellalas.' Whether such indifference and contempt can be said to be compatible with a true Christian spirit we ask our readers to judge. But they are all Christians, or, as most of them would have it, 'first-class' members of the Church of England." He adds "We cannot forbear mentioning that not a few among them worship the *yellow robe*, and give alms to the Buddhist Priests, in the hope of prospective reward, or in expiation of their sins, notwithstanding their profession of Christianity." Here we see what has always been the religious tradition of Ceylon Buddhism, that it should not necessarily be considered incompatible with Christianity, and conversely that Christianity among the ruling classes of Ceylon should not be incompatible with certain Buddhist observances.

What then of those who were not first-class Wellalas (we would nowadays use the Sinhalese term Goyigama)? Here we may consider the history of the well-known de Soysa family. In Soysā Caritaya, C. Don Bastian's life of C. H. de Soysa, the first Sinhalese millionaire (1904), the matter of religious allegiance is treated rather quietly. We read that Susew de Soysa, younger brother of C. H. de Soysa's father, became Christian early in the century. The account is as follows:

"While Mr. Susew de Soysa was thus acquiring wealth as a good Buddhist, Christian teachers became friendly with him and made him a Christian. He was baptized in the Dutch church at Moraṭuva, with one Susew Perera as sponsor. After the baptism, he learnt the Christian religion and practised it, keeping God's commandments, but he would never have dreamt of doing anything contrary to his former religion of Buddhism, and sometimes he continued to assist it."

No date is given; indeed there are very few dates throughout the 900 pages of this book. But it was before his marriage in 1839.

In the chapter on C. H. de Soysa's father, Jeronis de Soysa, who started life with an ayurvedic training from the Buddhist temple, we read as follows:

"This same Mudaliyar had become rich by trade while he was a Buddhist. As he became wealthy, Christian teachers of the Anglican church became friendly with him and admitted him to their church. Nevertheless it is clear that he granted most of the requests for assistance made to him on various occasions by Buddhists from both Low Country and Up Country. He completely fulfilled all his obligations to his teacher Mäddegama thera and to his temple, and as long as that venerable monk was living, the Mudaliyar never went to him empty-handed when he called to enquire after his health, but continued unbroken the tradition of bringing him cakes and drink, betel and tobacco and the like."

No date, again, is given; but it seems to have been about the time of the controversial conferring of the rank of Gate Mudaliyar upon him in 1853.[3]) Up till then, he called himself a Buddhist. The biographer explains that Jeronis was only his 'church tombo' name; in his youth he was known as Babā Siñño. He was converted, according to J. S. A. Fernando, by the Rev. W. Oakley, who was the representative of the Church Missionary Society in Kandy from 1835 to 1867. His transfer of allegiance was thus very much later than that of his brother Susew (whose own Mudaliyarship, on the other hand, was given only in 1870). The author of Soysā Caritaya, who describes himself on the title-page as a pupil of Hikkaḍuvā Śrī Sumangala, presumably did not approve of such changes of religion, which nevertheless still appeared almost obligatory at the time for the holders of high office; but he found at least consolation in declaring that Jeronis de Soysa continued his support to Buddhist causes undiminished. It seems Jeronis, who spent much of his time Up Country, where Buddhism was least questioned, was reluctant to accept Christianity. Don Bastian reports that Buttala Punci Banḍāra Āracci told him that had Jeronis remained a Buddhist, he would have found the treasure hidden in Hañguranketa by the kings of Ceylon.

C. H. de Soysa himself, born in 1836, was baptized in 1837. He was educated at first in the temple, but spent his childhood in the Low Country with his uncle Susew, who was already an Anglican Christian; and he never seems to have considered himself anything but Christian, though this did not stop him from contributing to Buddhist causes from time to time.

Thus by the time JWP was writing in 1887, not only were the aristocracy of the Maritime Provinces, the 'first-class Wellalas', in general Christian, but the new rich, even when not Goyigama, sometimes also found it advisable to make a shift away from Buddhism, although they might still continue to support Buddhist causes. As a further mark of respectability, it is interesting to see that Jeronis de Soysa abandoned his arrack-renting activities about the middle of the century.[4]) Arrack-renting was not, apparently, felt to be inconsistent with the precept *surāmerayamajjappamādaṭṭhānā*, nor yet with the *sammā-ājīva* component of the Eightfold Path; but it did seem inconsistent with the contemptuous attitude

[3]) Soysā Caritaya seems to put it later than the conferral of the title; but J. S. A. Fernando, op.cit., says that Vīrahännädigē Alexander Fernando, Soysa's assistant, was converted by CMS missionaries before 1842.

[4]) J. S. A. Fernando, op.cit., and see Michael Roberts, Reformism, Nationalism and Protest in British Ceylon, unpublished paper presented to the seminar on Leadership in South Asia at SOAS, March 1974, note 52.

towards trade which the landowning Sinhalese upper classes shared with the upper classes of contemporary England.[5])

If now we seek to enquire into the somewhat less than 'first class' members of colonial society, we may again consult Twentieth Century Impressions, which gives a magnificent account of over 200 Sinhalese who were of importance in 1907, complete with photographs. (I exclude Tamils, Burghers and Muslims from consideration here.) Of 230 Sinhalese listed in detail in this work, 46 are said or known to be Buddhist, 73 Christian, and 110 are not specified. One (J. Kotalāvala) is described as a Rationalist. Of those specified as Buddhist, those in Colombo are mostly traders and large-scale shopkeepers, those in the provinces depend mostly on plumbago or arrack. A few are proctors (lawyers). Nearly all are also listed as land-owners, the purchase of an estate being one of the first signs of respectable wealth.

The Colombo list is divided into two sections, commercial (which stands first) and 'social.' The Buddhists here are mostly in the commercial list, where we find two ship-chandlers, two general merchants, a furniture store, a stationery store, a food store, a wine store, a woodcarver's and a timber merchant—totalling eleven, as against three businesses listed as Christian and nine unspecified (two of which seem not to be properly commercial).[6]) The social list has only two Colombo Buddhist names.[7]) Next follows a list of 23 plumbago merchants, of whom six appear to be Buddhist; in four other cases the religious affiliation is not stated. There follow the provincial lists, giving 13 Buddhists in the Western province outside Colombo. Those lists, however, are primarily social, and therefore trading businesses seldom figure in them, profitable trade being concentrated in Colombo, or at least moved from elsewhere (chiefly from Galle) to Colombo as the businesses expanded (e.g. Don Davit, Don Theodoris). Of the thirteen listed Buddhists in the Western province, five based their prosperity on arrack, and there is a sprinkling of doctors (D. J. A. Abeyratna) and lawyers (P. A. Gooneratna, S. H. B. Kuruppu). Outside the Western province, only eleven are listed as Buddhist, with three more in the supplement; but this is not surprising since purely commercial interests are here excluded.

Thus it seems that whereas the pressure on holders of Government office was still by the end of the 19th century to be at least nominally Christian, such pressures were not applicable to purely private sector traders, however rich they might become. Such men were almost all from the Low Country, and it is they who are referred to by L. A. Wickremeratne, who writing of the revival of Buddhism, "particularly after

[5]) Quite different is the attitude of Ceylon's neighbours, the totally Muslim Maldive Islands, where the aristocracy all practise trade (there being indeed little land to own) and find prejudice against it laughable. They do not, on the other hand, countenance alcohol.

[6]) James de Alwis and J. V. Atapattu.

[7]) The Census of 1911 puts Christians in Colombo as high as 28%, as against 10% for the population as a whole.

1865,"[8]) says "its real significance emerges from the fact that this revival was largely centred in the maritime districts, especially where certain castes were entrenched" (JRAS 1969, no. 2, pp. 123, 134–135). He asks why the Buddhist movement "despite its national appeal centred so much in the Southern and Western provinces. Education provides a plausible answer . . . Caste on the other hand throws a more penetrating light on the problem." When he speaks here of a Buddhist *movement*, this indicates an increased self-consciousness among existing Buddhists, rather than simply increased temple observances, or a movement for converting or reconverting Christians to Buddhism. Increase in temple observances seems to be an earlier phenomenon; according to R. S. Hardy (Jubilee Memorials [1864], p. 40), during the first ten years of British rule in Ceylon the number of Buddhist temples increased from between two and three hundred to twelve hundred. Conversions came much later, in the 1920s and 1930s, when 'Government Christians' of early British times became paralleled to some extent by 'Donoughmore Buddhists,' and E. W. Perera lost his seat in the Legislative Council. During the 19th century, conversions were still usually the other way, as in the case of the de Soysa family.[9]) The leadership of the post-1865 Buddhist 'movement' was in the hands of low-country traders, which indicates (a) that wealthy traders who were not substantial official figures had felt no irresistible pressure to conform to the Colonial religion, and (b) that the Kandyan territories were not yet capable of producing such leaders or such trading wealth.

It is not however the case that all—or even most—large-scale traders were Buddhist, nor that trade in Ceylon predisposed to self-conscious Buddhism rather than to Christianity. Much later, in the mid-20th century, H. D. Evers[10]) states that among the entrepreneurs he investigated, Roman Catholics are hardly to be found. This is, I think, surprising. C. H. de Soysa himself married a Roman Catholic wife; Roman Catholic also were the plumbago king N. D. P. Silva, and other traders of the colonial epoch such as Clovis de Silva, H. Bastian Fernando. Evers says his figures here were too uncertain to quote in detail, and I wonder if they should in fact be revised.

P. T. M. (Tissa) Fernando stresses a different aspect. He writes: "Developments in the 19th century brought about an unprecedented awareness that what the West could offer, including Christianity, was incompatible with the traditional Buddhist ethos of the country. It also made westernized Ceylonese to react against their political and emotional servility to the British, and helped to identify Buddhism as a rallying point in the struggle for Independence. I am not suggesting that the Buddhist revivalism of the second half of the 19th century brought about

---

[8]) Or 1868, when civil registration was introduced.

[9]) There were of course exceptions, e.g. Dandris de Silva.

[10]) Kulturwandel in Ceylon, Baden-Baden 1964, p. 82.

a change in élite ethos . . . What it did achieve was to show the potential of Buddhism for mobilising mass support for political purposes" (Contributions to Asian Studies, 4 [1973]). By the last sentence he indicates that it was not so much the heroes of the struggle for Independence who rallied to Buddhism, but rather that the success of hitherto secondary characters[11]) who had remained Buddhist, because of their comparative obscurity or their Upcountry origin, showed a new way to the élite, who had in fact remained still fairly substantially Christian.

The expression "incompatible with traditional Buddhism" indicates the bitterness that crept into the situation. It is no doubt typical of a colonial society that it accentuates the bitterness in unequal relationships. The famous remarks of R. E. Stubbs about those imprisoned after the 1915 riots—'a set of skunks—mostly I regret to say men educated in Europe—one or two Cambridge men amongst them if stories are true" — were not intended for public consumption, but many official remarks that were so intended appear equally unrestrained to us today; for instance Chalmers' statement, at the same period, that a person of the standing of E. W. Perera "would not expect to be received either by the Governor or by the Colonial Secretary of this colony." Or again, in the Archaeological Department what seems unnecessary acrimony is found in some of H. C. P. Bell's comments on the work of others (this tradition persists in archaeology into volume 5 of Epigraphia Zeylanica, where the late S. Paranavitana in turn reacts similarly). The caste dispute literature, which is inter-Sinhalese, is more unrestrained still. It may be, therefore, that the absurdly forceful language of some religious or semi-religious controversies was the normal coin for disputation in Ceylon (or even for disputation in general). But clearly some of the bitterness was due to the feeling that because Buddhism was the religion of 'inferiors', it was treated as an inferior religion.

It is hardly possible to deny that such feelings of inferiority were provoked by Christian missionaries. It is probably unavoidable that missionary Christianity should seem, and even should be, inextricably connected with western culture; it is after all the spiritual dimension of that culture.[12]) Thus when Thomas Moscrop writes: "When work began at Kurana, its name was one of evil . . . the people were idle, uncleanly, and worshippers of demons; the houses were coconut-leaf huts, and the food poor and scanty. Now there are manifest tokens of industry, cleanliness, comfort, and of ordered Christian living,"[13]) we can see that for him, as a Wesleyan missionary as well as an Englishman, not only

---

[11]) What Michael Roberts distinguishes as the 'local élite' (see University of Ceylon History of Ceylon, vol. 3 [1973], p. 264).

[12]) A phrase of Professor Z. Werblowski. Tennent speaks in 1850 of "Christianity and . . . that civilization which is its never-failing concomitant" (J. E. Tennent, Christianity in Ceylon, p. 175.

[13]) Moscrop and Restarick, Ceylon and its Methodism, 1906, p. 57.

idleness and uncleanliness, but even cadjan houses and scanty food are in some way unchristian. Herein is the relevance of the Weber-Tawney theory of protestant ethic to Ceylon, which Evers hesitates to apply to it, in that the missionaries who accepted this ethic were those who sought to provoke Sinhalese Buddhism to an encounter. That they did so seek has been pointed out by K. Malalgoda;[14]) Moscrop, again, writes "Besides faithful discipline, aggressive movements leading to controversy between the leaders of Christianity and Buddhism materially assisted the work of sifting and separation ... No one would arrange for similar public controversies today, but it is agreed that one invaluable result was an open avowal of one faith or the other" (p. 84). It was unfortunate for these men that their Fundamentalist approach left them very much at the mercy of the nineteenth-century spirit of scientific enquiry, which in this case harmonized well with the Buddhist outlook. It is in fact extraordinary to us today that such men as these missionaries could ever have expected to be able to pour contempt on the 'unscientific' religious presuppositions of Ceylon Buddhists without exposing themselves to the same criticisms of their own equally 'unscientific' religious presuppositions. Such controversies led eventually to Buddhist retorts such as D. B. Jayatilaka's Credentials of Christianity,[15]) 150 pages of reasonable and learned criticism of the Christian missionary and his preaching.

Another feature of non-conformist missions which was perhaps distasteful to Buddhists was the longing for revivalistic enthusiasm. "Our Ceylon churches," says Moscrop (p. 90), "now know and understand 'revivals'. The early missionaries used to pray and earnestly long for them, and their absence (for the most part) was mourned as a sore trial of faith ... Religion as ritual and routine, as custom and ceremony, the people understood; but it was a long and hard struggle to get the idea implanted that religion was experience and life ... The years 1865, 1866, 1869 and 1870 were years in which in many places there was a general awakening." "The Rev. Thomas Cook, in his book Days of God's Right Hand, says of one place 'It was almost too much like home. Their responses during prayer, their sparkling eyes and shouts of praise ... seemed more like Yorkshire than Ceylon.'" (Yet similar enthusiasm if observed in a purely Ceylon setting in a dancing ceremony would no doubt have incurred heavy censure.)

---

[14]) The Buddhist-Christian Confrontation in Ceylon, 1800–1880, in: Social Compass XX/2, 1973.

[15]) Young Men's Buddhist Association, Ceylon, 1909. There were of course also objective missionary assessments of Buddhism. Tennent wrote too early to be properly informed (he mentions "one of the early Buddhus, Sakya Muni", p. 329), but H. R. Reynolds, Principal of Cheshunt College, Buddhism: A Comparison and a Contrast, Present Day Tracts, 1886, is well informed. R. S. Hardy's Christianity and Buddhism Compared, 1874, on the other hand, is disappointingly without interest. It was posthumously published, perhaps by pious error.

The manifest differences between Christian sects were another obvious ground for Buddhist disapproval.[16] In the early days of the missionaries, the Roman Catholics, who were present already in Ceylon, were always helpful. Harvard, a Weslayan, tells how two Roman Catholic mission priests visited him when he was sick "with the kindest solicitude ... and, seated by my bedside, sympathized with me in my affliction, and earnestly prayed for my recovery. While I continued at Colombo, we regularly interchanged friendly visits."[17] Tennent generously allows that "The Roman Catholic converts are by far the most willing to contribute from their own means to the support of their clergy and churches, and their donations for these purposes are on a scale of extreme liberality" (op. cit., p. 299). But such a helpful attitude was seldom reciprocated. Ebenezer Daniel, a Baptist missionary, commenced a controversy against Roman Catholics as early as 1833.[18] Buddhists were also helpful to missionaries at the start.[19] Tennent reports of Oakley (CMS missionary in Kandy from 1835) that "the most numerous and apparently the most ingenious inquirers into the doctrine of Christianity have been the priesthood themselves. Mr. Oakley has been in the habit of visiting their temples ... and assemblies of fifty of their priests at a time ... They have come in numbers to his residence to ask for still further information." He adds that they had no serious doubts as to the authenticity of their own religion (op. cit., pp. 307–08). We need therefore feel little surprise at what Harvard writes earlier: "An aged Nāiaka came with great pomp and attended with a train of followers, bringing with him a nephew whom he desired should be made a Christian. In answer to our enquiry why he did not *himself* embrace the religion in which he wished to have his nephew instructed, he replied, that he felt he was too old to encounter the dificulties of so important a change; and on our bringing him into an argument, he attempted to defend his paganism, and departed as confirmed an Atheist as he came. The lad remained with us." Tennent also tells of a 'Sinhalese chief' who is reported to have said, in a similar context, that he considered Christianity" a very safe outrigger to Buddhism" (op. cit., p. 241). Such conduct was unintelligible to the missionaries, and it seemed to them wrong to enter into relationships of mutual respect. (Yet they had themselves no hesitation in visiting not only Buddhist temples but Buddhist and other ceremonies as well.)[20]

---

[16]) Inter-Buddhist abuse of Mahayana in Ceylon is mostly a twentieth-century phenomenon.

[17]) W. M. Harvard, Narrative of the Establishment ..., 1823.

[18]) J. A. Ewing, The Resplendent Isle, Baptist Missionary Society, 1912, p. 27. Daniel was however a real itinerant missionary preacher. Nor did such men confine their attentions to the Sinhalese as if the English were not also in need of them. Ewing says (p. 32), of Daniel's burgher colleague Siers, "several of the British soldiers owed their conversion to his ministry".

[19]) See Malalgoda, op.cit., pp. 185–86.

[20]) Callaway for instance visited a temple almost as soon as he arrived with the Methodist mission in 1816, and later that year "saw for the first time the cere-

It was not, however, every missionary who was unable to appreciate a Buddhist viewpoint. I take as one example the Rev. John Callaway, known as the author of Yakkun Nattanawā, who was with the Wesleyans in Ceylon from 1815 to 1826. He was a printer (the Methodist mission from the first laid great store by printers) and was originally encouraged to go out to Ceylon to act as mission printer, but found when he got there that someone else was given the job. He thereupon acted as a preacher for eleven years, though never with any great enthusiasm.[21]) In 1821, Callaway wrote: "However promising the face of things has been in Ceylon, the country has had a pretty fair trial; and if some other part of the world be more productive I should not regret to see Ceylon reduced to a moderate supply of efficient missionaries . . . With anything short of an express revelation from heaven I believe no Methodist missionary conceives himself doomed at all events to live and die in this part of the world . . . The adults appear as indifferent here as in the other stations I have been in. I converse with them frequently and am pleased with their attention, but they appear to think Buddhism is best for them and Christianity best for Europeans."[22]) Callaway in fact, being fairly devoid of expectations of revival or even of conversions, whiled away his time in Ceylon in writing and then printing sundry vocabularies and grammars of the Sinhalese and Ceylon Portuguese languages (an activity which his Mission in principle approved, though he himself incurred criticism for spending more of his time on it than on preaching). Callaway was an early missionary; the missionaries who came after him were less able to confess failures.

It was not only the non-conformist missions who came to connect Christianity so definitely with western culture. It was not even always Europeans who did so. In the introduction to Jubilee Memorials of Holy Emmanuel Church, Moratuwa, J. G. C. Mendis writes: "We cannot

---

mony of dancing the devil". A month later he watched two "bana manduas or preaching festivals", and the following month (Feb. 1817) two more.

[21]) It is interesting to note Harvard's version of these events. He says (p. 291): "The intelligence and application of our head-printer (Mr. Jantz) supplied my lack of service [i.e. Harvard was unwell], and enabled Mr. Callaway to enter upon the scene of his appointed labour at Matura; his absence from which had required no ordinary exercise of self-denial. The 'yearning charity' for the souls of the perishing heathen, which at first impelled him to Ceylon, was but partially satisfied, until he entered fully upon his beloved work". Callaway's own words are: "Thus diverted from the expectation of becoming an English itinerant and afterwards jostled out of a path of usefulness for which certainly my professional habits and natural genius had peculiarly fitted me [i.e. printing], I nevertheless bent my mind to the duties set before me . . . The experience of some years has convinced me that to the general labours of a Missionary my faculties are not well adapted'. (letter to Rev. J. Taylor, 28 Aug. 1821). And as for the 'yearning charity', he explains in the same letter that he had been asked to go to Ceylon as a printer, and had replied 'I would rather be employed at home for the present . . . especially as I have neither a deep or clear call to the work in my own mind".

[22]) Letter to Rev. J. Taylor, 14 June 1821.

be said to have done our duty till all our households are Christian. What effort is usually made in Christian families to influence for good those of their servants and dependents, who however humble they may be, are intimately connected with their welfare? The cook, the ayah, the groom or the cartdriver are indispensable adjuncts to our comfort and we know we cannot get on without them." This appears to take it for granted that the Christians of Moraṭuva are likely to be rich men, possessed of various trappings of western civilization. It is these two aspects, the implicit connection of Christianity, as displayed by the western missionaries, with (a) a claim to superior rational outlook and (b) wordly prosperity, that very naturally produced a bitterness among the Buddhists, who were conscious that in the first case they were perfectly equal to their opponents and in the second that the implied standards were irrelevant if not positively wrong. That Christians (other than Roman Catholics) should be usually of an upper social position might be a fact, but should not be elevated into a principle.

This is not to deny the social influence of leaders. Many western habits have percolated down to low strata of society through the examples of the upper classes. Christianity in its Roman Catholic form in Ceylon may have spread in such a way; but the diverse forms of non-Roman Christianity presented to the Ceylonese in the 19th century, the fact that those who first adopted these forms were usually either of a high social position or of a very low one (Baptists, for instance, early set up missions to Veddas, Rodiyas and gahalayas), the fact above all that those who came to spread these doctrines represented a totally alien way of life and society, made it certain that the mass of the people would not readily accept them at the time.[23])

The connection between Christianity and education has been stressed by Malalgoda.[24]) We may compare Harvard's somewhat naive words (p. 313): "At the school visitations, our bungaloes were generally surrounded by the parents of the children, who anxiously attended the result of the public examinations; and we invariably discoursed with them on the ways of God . . . The providence of God doubtless conducted us to this *effectual* mode of collecting congregations. Parents naturally esteem those who aim to advance the interests of their children." As late as 1890, according to the Rev. J. W. Balding,[25]) "the high-class Buddhists

---

[23]) Somewhat ironically, the last point, of alienation, is one which was also urged by colonial governors in the early part of the twentieth century as a reason against granting the franchise demands of the western educated Ceylonese.

[24]) According to Tennent, while education was regarded as the principal method of obtaining converts in the Hindu areas of Ceylon, it was given only second place to argument, expostulation, preaching and publication in the Buddhist areas (op. cit., pp. 249–50). Elsewhere he maintains that "of the whole number of real conversions in Ceylon, *five* at least have been made by means of preaching for one by the influence of the schools, or any other instrumentality" (ib. p. 279).

[25]) 100 Years in Ceylon, Madras 1922.

of the Kandyan country had seemed as inaccessible to ordinary methods of foreign missions as the rocky height of Adam's Peak"; in 1890, therefore, Hillwood School was founded to try to influence them through their children.

We may nowadays think of this as shocking cynicism. The Buddhist people of Ceylon, on the other hand, equally shocked the missionaries, for instance, by their insistence on preserving caste distinctions within Christian churches and schools. Harvard reports this as early as 1817, and Balding in 1822 at Mātara. There were also monastic disputes about *sīmās* and *nikāyas* going on throughout the first part of the nineteenth century, and some of these, I suggest, must have appeared similarly shocking to Colonel Olcott. K. Kariyawasam has commented with evident wonder (in an unpublished Ph. D. thesis, London 1973) on the way Olcott encouraged the replacement of members of the Sangha by laymen in most positions within the Buddhist Theosophical Society in Ceylon. It seems probable that Olcott, as an American, member of a nation which prided itself on emancipation from the social straitjackets of the Old World, would have been especially displeased to find similar divisiveness among the very Buddhists who had asked him to come over to Ceylon and help them. There was no reason why laymen should not act as apologists for a priesthood (they did, for example, in 19th-century Russia); while for Buddhist monks to engage themselves heavily in social controversies as did Migeṭṭuvattē Guṇānanda, may have seemed to Olcott to involve the abandonment of some of the best qualities of the monk. He probably failed to realize at first that laymen were equally divided in rather similar ways.

Olcott certainly inspired the Buddhist cause. By 1892, Miss C. F. Gordon Cumming could write 'At the present moment . . . a leaning to Buddhism and its twin brother Agnosticism has become a sort of fashion in England.'[26]) The Census of 1901 returned 8 male and 11 female British and American Buddhists in Ceylon. In 1903, the Church Missionary Society reported (1) A decrease in the number of conversions from Buddhism, and (2) Growing restlessness and discontent among Native Pastors.[27])

By 1922, after a century of work, the dangers of too close a connection between religious and secular in the mission field were at last beginning to be realized, and Balding writes[28]): "Among the masses of the Sinhalese there is a decided tendency to regard Buddhism as the national religion, while many, both Tamils and Sinhalese, regard Christianity as a religion of the West . . . For this reason, the missionary body as a whole would welcome a far greater measure of self-realization in the Ceylonese communities than has hitherto been reached."

---

[26]) Two Happy Years in Ceylon, p. 596.
[27]) See J. Ferguson, Ceylon in 1903, p. xciv.
[28]) Op.cit., p. 197.

Thus the missionaries eventually found themselves obliged to revise their ideas about Buddhism and its relationship with Christianity. Nowadays it is taken for granted that the 'Establishment' among both Christians and Buddhists in Ceylon have a place in national functions side by side. Even in 1945, before Independence, Professor Malalasekara officially attended the consecration of Bishop Lakdasa de Mel, to represent the All Ceylon Buddhist Congress. It will perhaps be necessary in the days to come for dhammadūtas to avoid similar causes of stumbling in their missionary dealings with the west, or they may also prove able to exert influence only over a very limited social and educational range.

III. A COMPARATIVE VIEW OF RELIGIOUS SYNCRETISM IN BUDDHIST COUNTRIES

Religionssynkretismus in Nepal

Von SIEGFRIED LIENHARD

Es ist eine natürliche Folge der geographischen Beschaffenheit Nepals, daß sich Geschichte und Geistesleben, sofern sie für Nepal wirklich kennzeichnend sind, stets auf engstem Raum abgespielt haben. Das von der Natur am reichsten gesegnete Tal, das Tal von Kathmandu, dem wir im Westen auch Navakoth und im Osten Palamcok hinzurechnen müssen[1]), repräsentiert das eigentliche Nepal. Es ist das Zentrum und der Schauplatz politischer Auseinandersetzungen, das Nepal der Geschichte, und erstellt, obwohl eines der kleinsten von indischer Lebensart und Kultur beeinflußten Länder, ein geradezu klassisches Beispiel des Religionssynkretismus. Die hier erfolgte Symbiose von Buddhismus und Hinduismus ist dem Fachmann seit langem geläufig, doch tritt die Verknüpfung beider Religionen in Nepal so deutlich zutage, daß dieselbe, wie zahlreiche Reiseberichte bezeugen, selbst dem Auge des Laien wahrnehmbar wird. So ist es in Nepal z.B. gewöhnlich, daß in buddhistischen Heiligtümern Bilder von Hindu-Göttern und Śivaliṅgas begegnen, in hinduistischen Tempeln buddhistische Caityas, daß einzelne Gottheiten die Verehrung sowohl von Buddhisten als auch Hindus genießen, daß zahlreiche große und kleine Feste gemeinsam gefeiert oder daß eine Vielzahl von Ritualen, die meisten hinduistischer Herkunft, von beiden Gruppen ausgeführt werden.

Obwohl nun das Phänomen des religiösen Synkretismus in Nepal fast überall und in manchmal krasser und verwirrender Weise hervortritt, sind die Vorstellungen und die komplizierten Vorgänge, die einer solchen Verschmelzung zugrunde liegen, noch wenig erforscht. Probleme verschiedenster Art greifen eng ineinander, und zu den zentralen Fragen der Annäherung von Buddhismus und Hinduismus, deren Ursachen und Ergebnis, reihen sich solche der Gesellschaftsform, des herrschenden Hauses, des Brauchtums und, nicht weniger wichtig, der Volksreligion und des Beitrags, den diese zu leisten vermocht hat.

---

[1]) Vgl. L. Petech, Mediaeval History of Nepal (ca. 750–1480), Serie Orientale Roma X, Materials for the Study of Nepalese History and Culture, 3, Rom 1958 (= Petech), p. 171.

Wie wir wissen, bildeten in den Jahrhunderten vor und auch lange Zeit nach der Eroberung des Kathmandu-Tals durch die Gurkhas (1768/69 n. Chr.) die Nevars die führende Bevölkerungsschicht des Landes. Obwohl wir nichts Sicheres über den Zeitpunkt ihrer Einwanderung aussagen können, gehören sie ohne Zweifel zu Nepals ältesten, auch heute noch lebenden Stämmen. Sie sind in ihrem Kern vielleicht Nachfahren der Kirātas, der Licchavīs oder eines anderen mongoloiden Volks, wurden im Laufe der Zeit aber stark indisiert und sind schon seit langem rassisch vermischt und in ein soziales Gefüge gegliedert, das äußerst komplex ist. Vom Anbeginn meist dem Buddhismus ergeben, bis in die Gegenwart aber mehr und mehr hinduisiert, zerfallen die Nevars — am deutlichsten in den höheren Schichten — in eine mehr oder weniger ausgeprägt buddhistische und eine hinduistische Gruppe, die Bauddhamārgins und die Śivamārgins. Die Berufs- und Kastenordnung des Landes wurde Ende des 14. Jahrhunderts von Jayasthiti Malla (1382–1395 n. Chr.), einem sehr reformfreudigen König, kodifiziert, doch ist sicher, daß die Änderung der Gesellschaft, die auch den buddhistischen Sektor in ein strenges System von Kasten hineinzwang, nicht das Werk eines Tages, noch eines einzigen Mannes sein konnte. Die Grundlagen dieses Wechsels waren vielmehr schon ein oder zwei Jahrhunderte früher und, wie weiter betont werden muß, nicht durch das Zutun der Obrigkeit ausgelöst worden.

Die Hindu-Kasten interessieren in diesem Zusammenhang wenig. Es versteht sich von selbst, daß die Minorität der nach Nepal immigrierten Brahmanen wie auch das nepalesische Herrscherhaus[2]) an der Kastenidee am stärksten festhalten mußten. Anders und weniger einfach war die Lage der buddhistischen Nevars, ja der Nevars überhaupt. Es ist anzunehmen, daß diese, wie andere mongoloide Himalaya-Völker, eine zu Anfang eher feudale Hierarchie der Gesellschaft besaßen. Doch war auch hier die spätere soziale Strukturierung in Kasten, deren einzelne Zweige noch heute Berufsgruppen sind, nicht von oben diktiert. Sie war, wie uns heute erscheint, das Ergebnis der Zerrüttung und der schließlichen Laisierung des Ordens: Die buddhistischen Klosterbewohner adaptierten sich rasch an die teils aus Laien bestehende, teils hinduistische Umwelt, und diese Anpassung war noch rascher und stärker, als die vielen *vihāras* Familienwohnstätten wurden[3]).

Es erübrigt sich, daß ich hier die Geschichte Nepals skizziere, doch sei festgehalten, daß Nepal schon früh mit sowohl dem Buddhismus als auch dem Hinduismus konfrontiert worden war. Obwohl die Legende und die Benennung mehrerer Stūpas als Aśoka-Stūpas oder Aśoka-Caityas einen Besuch Aśokas wahrhaben wollen, hat Kaiser Aśoka das Tal

---

[2]) Es ist von Bedeutung, daß die Nevars sowohl vor als auch nach der Gurkha-Eroberung einem Herrscherhaus hinduistischer Prägung gehorchten.

[3]) Vgl. D. Snellgrove, Buddhist Himalaya. Travels and Studies in Quest of the Origins and Nature of Tibetan Religion, Oxford 1957 (= Snellgrove 1957), p. 112.

von Kathmandu wohl niemals betreten. Dessen ungeachtet sind die ältesten uns erhaltenen Denkmäler Nepals buddhistisch, und die Vermutung liegt nahe, daß die Lehre Buddhas bald nach Aśoka nach Nepal eingeführt wurde. Die hinduistische Kunst dieser Epoche (und der noch älteren Zeiten) scheint verlorengegangen, denn Hindu-Kunstwerke begegnen relativ spät, erst seit dem 5. Jahrhundert n. Chr., jener Zeit, da hinduistische Könige auch Sanskrit-Inschriften im Gupta-Alphabet zu verbreiten beginnen. Schon dem 4. Jahrhundert entstammt die Säuleninschrift Samudraguptas (im heutigen Allahabad), die berichtet, daß Nepal, das in indischen Dokumenten erstmals im Arthaśāstra genannt wird, Tribut an das Großreich der Guptas entrichtet. Die Kontakte mit Indien waren rege, und zweifelsohne repräsentierte Nepals hinduistisches Königshaus, das nach indischem Vorbild einen Hofstaat von hinduistischen Priestern und Hindu-Beamten voraussetzen mußte, einen der einflußreichsten und mächtigsten Sammelpunkte brahmanischer Orthodoxie.

Es ist für uns sehr zu bedauern, daß die bekannten chinesischen Pilger und Verfasser von Reiseberichten nicht auch Stätten in Nepal aufgesucht haben, doch weiß Hsüan Tsang zu erzählen, daß, wie er gehört hat, in Nepal buddhistische Tempel in engster Nachbarschaft von hinduistischen Bauwerken stünden. Diese Koexistenz von Hinduismus und Buddhismus, die hierdurch für die Mitte des 7. Jahrhunderts dokumentiert ist, charakterisiert, wie wir wissen, auch Indien, doch allein bis ins 12. Jahrhundert. In Nepal sollten die beiden großen Religionen fortdauern können, ja einander so naherücken, daß, wie die verschiedenen Phänomene des Synkretismus erweisen, besonders geartete religiöse Strukturen Gestalt nehmen konnten. Nepal blieb vom Eroberungssturm des Islam verschont, erfuhr dagegen aufs stärkste die Auswirkungen der in Indien als hinduistische Renaissance in Bewegung gesetzten geistigen und politischen Kräfte. Wie Aśoka war auch Śaṅkara nie in Patan oder Kathmandu gewesen, doch berichten die nepalesischen Chroniken, insbesondere die buddhistischen Versionen der Vaṃśāvalīs, nicht umsonst vom verheerenden Aufenthalt Śaṅkaras, der nach Vernichtung der Buddha-Verehrung in Indien und der Zerstörung der dort befindlichen buddhistischen Texte die Schar der nepalesischen Buddhas empfindlich reduziert, die Śaiva-Religion eingeführt und die Heirat buddhistischer Bhikṣus stimuliert haben sollte. Beachtlich ist ferner, daß im Kastensystem König Jayasthiti Mallas die Brahmanen in die Pañca-Gauḍas, die dem Norden oder Nordosten entstammen, und die Pañca-Draviḍas, die dem Süden entstammen, eingeteilt werden, und daß die Tradition behauptet, daß die letzteren von Śaṅkarācārya nach Nepal gebracht worden seien. Gewiß, die Überlieferung übertreibt. Sie ist indessen, wie ich meinen möchte — und das ist vielleicht keine Tradition und keine Legende — nicht ganz ohne Wahrheit. Während zahlreiche Brahmanen teils als reine Glückssucher, teils im Gefolge von Königen, auch solchen südindischer Herkunft wie Nānyadeva, Someśvaradeva oder Harisiṃhadeva, nach Nepal gelangten, steht sicherlich fest, daß zu Beginn der hinduistischen Renaissance orthodoxe Hindus auch aus Glaubenseiferer ins Kathmandu-Tal kamen.

In einer Zeit, da der Buddhismus in Indien zu erlöschen beginnt, blühen Mahāyāna und Vajrayāna im Nepal-Tal weiter, ist Patan, die dort vermutlich älteste buddhistische Stadt, ein Zentrum klösterlicher und gelehrter Aktivität, die den alten Universitäten Indiens an Bedeutung nicht nachsteht, und wird der *saṃgha*, die buddhistische Glaubensgemeinschaft, durch Personen vermehrt, die ihre indische Heimat nicht allein, wie so gerne glaubhaft gemacht wird, aufgrund des Islam, sondern auch, und in wahrscheinlich noch größerem Umfang, aufgrund des orthodox-hinduistischen Machtspiels verlassen. Es fehlte somit nicht an Anlaß, daß sich der Eifer glaubensbeseelter indischer Brāhmaṇas auch auf Nepal erstreckte. Während im 13. Jahrhundert die Einwanderung indischer Buddhisten nach Nepal allmählich versiegte, fand der Hinduismus stets neue Verstärkung, indem, wie historische Dokumente, Kunstdenkmäler, Manuskripte und Nevārī-Volkslieder zeigen, auch weiterhin Śaivas, verschiedene Vaiṣṇava-Sekten und, gleichfalls schon früh von Bedeutung, dem Hinduismus aber meist lose verbunden, auch indische Yogins ins Nepal-Tal kamen. Indische Könige brachten Hindus auch aus ferneren Landstrichen mit, doch waren die Haupt-Zentren hinduistischen Zustroms die dem Königreich Nepal süd- und südöstlich vorgelagerten Länder, insbesondere Mithila, Bihar und Bengalen. So fand, um allein ein typisches Beispiel zu nennen, die *kṛṣṇabhakti* ihren Niederschlag auch in Liedern der Nevars, die unmittelbar von Vidyāpati inspiriert sind.

Die älteste uns erhaltene Nevārī-Handschrift, eine Abschrift (mit Nevārī-Übersetzung) des Hitopadeśa, entstammt erst dem Jahre 481 der nepalesischen Ära, d. h. dem Jahre 1360 n. Chr.[4]), doch verraten die Sprachform der Nevārī und die Kolophone der späteren Manuskripte, meist Sanskrittexte mit Nevārī-Paraphrase, daß man in Patan, dem kulturellen Mittelpunkt bis zur Zeit Jayasthiti Mallas, vorwiegend buddhistische Werke, in Bhatgaon hinduistische und in Kathmandu, der jüngsten der drei Städte, die erst nach 1500 n. Chr. politisch bedeutungsvoll wurde, sowohl buddhistische als auch hinduistische Werke studiert hat. Hiermit stimmt überein, daß Patan etwa einhundertdreiundfünfzig und Kathmandu dreiundfünfzig Haupt- und Neben-*vihāras* besitzen[5]),

[4]) Siehe H. Jörgensen, Versuch eines Wörterbuches der Nevārī-Sprache, in: Acta Orient. VI (1928), p. 26 und H. Jörgensen, A Dictionary of the Classical Newārī, Det Kgl. Danske Videnskabernes Selskab, Hist.-filologiske Meddelelser XXIII, 1, København 1936, p. 4.

[5]) Nach Angaben, die ich Herrn Dr. Niels Gutschow, Darmstadt, verdanke, verfügt Patan über 18 Haupt-, 32 Neben- und 103 sogenannte Zweigklöster (Nev. *kacābāhā*), Kathmandu über 18 Haupt- und 35 Nebenklöster. Die Ziffern in Snellgrove 1957, p. 102, wonach Patan ca. 120, Kathmandu ca. 80 Haupt- und Neben-*vihāras* besitzen, sind nicht richtig.

während die Zahl der in Bhatgaon erhaltenen Klöster auffällig klein[6]) ist. Diese religiöse Gruppierung der Nevars gilt in gewissem Ausmaß auch heute noch, trifft jedoch am genauesten für die Jahrtausendwende und für das mittelalterliche Nepal der Malla-Zeit zu, d. h. die Periode von ca. 1200 bis zum Schicksalsjahr 1768/69.

Nach dieser Zeitspanne, der eigentlichen Epoche des Nepals der Nevars, erfolgte eine weitere, diesmal mehr zielbewußte, gewissermaßen auch staatliche Hinduisierung, die, anders als frühere Strömungen, von den Eroberern ausging und den Gegensatz zwischen den Nevars und den rein hinduistischen Gurkhas bisweilen mit Schärfe hervortreten ließ. Diese Hinduisierung wirkte meist in die Breite, lag ihre Ansicht doch hauptsächlich darin, im Kathmandu-Tal jener Lebensart Geltung zu schaffen, die die Gurkhas Jahrhunderte vorher in den Bergen um Gurkha ausgeformt hatten. Hatten die Nevars schon früh eine rassische und kulturelle Indisierung erfahren, so wies die Entwicklung der arischen, ja vermutlich rājputischen Gurkhas in die andere Richtung. Sie vermischten sich rasch mit den Mongoloiden ihrer Rückzugsgebiete und lebten, wie andere Stämme der nepalesischen Bergwelt, geistig und religiös isoliert. Ihr Hinduismus tendierte von vorneherein nach sehr einfachen Normen, solchen der Lebensführung, der Kriegermoral und praktischen Zielen, wurde im Laufe der Zeit aber weiter vereinfacht, ja stützte sich letztlich bloß auf wenige Sittengesetze wie z.B. die Achtung der Brahmanen, die Gattinnentreue und die Rinderverehrung. Ein so beschaffener Glaube gereichte kaum zur Vertiefung, doch trug er wesentlich bei, in Vereinigung mit den alten, ständig genährten brahmanistischen Kräften, die politische und — seit Pṛthivī Nārāyaṇa — nationale Bedeutung des Hinduismus zu stärken. Die Hinduisierung kam am deutlichsten als Nepalisierung zum Ausdruck[7]).

Die Frage, ob nun die Religion (oder Religionen) der Nepalesen, d.h. der Bewohner des Tals von Kathmandu, als Buddhismus oder Hinduismus, als eine Mischform, ein korrupter Buddhismus oder korrupter Hinduismus charakterisiert werden kann, ist allein für die Malla-Zeit und die Neuzeit gegeben. Sämtliche Standpunkte wurden vertreten. In den Jahrhunderten vor der Malla-Herrschaft waren die religiösen Verhältnisse denen in Indien gleich, dessen geistiges Leben vor dem islamischen Einbruch zunächst in Nepal eine Fortsetzung fand. Ohne Zweifel waren die Grundlagen des buddhistisch-hinduistischen Synkretismus schon in dieser Epoche, ja bereits in Indien festgelegt worden. Die unvergleichlich bedeutendste Triebkraft zur Religionsannäherung war die wachsende Durchdringung des Mahāyāna mit dem Ideengut des Śivaismus, doch

---

[6]) Siehe D. Snellgrove, Shrines and Temples of Nepal, in: Arts Asiatiques VIII, 1 (1961), p. 116.

[7]) So beobachtet bereits F. B. Hamilton, daß „the changes in the names of places, since the Hindu conquest, has been rapid almost beyond conception" (An Account of the Kingdom of Nepal, London 1819, Reprint New Delhi 1971, p. 11 = Hamilton).

traten in Nepal Faktoren hinzu, die die Übereinstimmungen zwischen Hinduismus und Buddhismus noch weiter verstärkten und sich — der Gedanke ist reizvoll — ohne Islam und ohne brahmanistische Gegen-Renaissance vielleicht auch in Indien ausgeformt oder dort in ähnlicher Weise ausgewirkt hätten.

Wir können in Nepal die Beobachtung machen, daß die Grenzen zwischen Buddhismus und Hinduismus in verschiedener Weise verfließen. Es scheint mir angebracht, zwischen hauptsächlich drei Erscheinungen religiöser Überlagerung zu unterscheiden: einerseits der Übertragung religiösen Guts von der einen Religion in die andere, andererseits dem religiösen Parallelismus und drittens der Identifikation.

Die Übertragung besteht in der totalen Aufnahme von verschiedenen — kaum veränderten — Göttern und übrigen Elementen aus der anderen Religion und ist derart verbreitet, daß wir reiches Material auch aus nicht-indischen Religionen anführen könnten. Wichtig ist, und diese Tatsache gilt wohl für jede Art von Religionssynkretismus, daß der Prozeß kaum jemals vollständig ist, da bei weitem nicht sämtliche Gottheiten, Rituale, Verehrungsformen u. dgl. Aufnahme finden. Schon in Indien haben die hinduistischen Gottheiten Śiva, Kumāra, Viṣṇu, Gaṇeśa, Lakṣmī, Sarasvatī, ja auch Brahmā, die Dikpālas u. a. in das Vajrayāna-Pantheon Eingang gefunden und wurden die Praktiken des Vajrayāna, von śivaitischen, besonders tantrischen und śāktischen Riten, beeinflußt, mit stark hinduistischen Komponenten durchsetzt. In den meisten Fällen war der Śivaismus die gebende, der Buddhismus die entgegennehmende Religion.

Ich nenne das vorhin genannte zweite Phänomen Parallelismus, während Jan Gonda es vorzieht, dieselbe Erscheinung im vorislamischen Indonesien als „śivaitisch-buddhistische Koalition" zu bezeichnen[8]). Wesentlich ist jedenfalls, daß der religiöse Parallelismus nach der funktionellen Gleichschaltung von Göttern, Riten, Anschauungen usw. tendiert wie z.B. in der Gleichung Svayambhū (ist gleich:) Śambhu.

Für die Identifikation ist dagegen charakteristisch, daß dieselbe die Übertragung und die Analogie zwar meistens voraussetzt, doch darüberhinaus, wie dies in Nepal so deutlich der Fall ist, hinduistische, buddhistische und volksreligiöse Komponenten miteinander noch stärker verbindet und, eingeordnet in die Gestalt eines Gottes, eines Rituals oder Festes, religiöse Phänomene hervorbringt, die beide Gemeinden ansprechen können. So entstehen Formen gemeinnepalesischen Glaubens. Sie erfreuen sich, wie bei Übertragung und Parallelismus, des Zuspruchs sowohl des Buddhisten wie auch des Hindu, des Nevar wie auch des Gurkha. Sie bilden dagegen keine einfachen, kaum veränderten Formen, sondern sind immer komplex und werden — im praktischen religiösen

---

[8]) J. Gonda, Śiva in Indonesien, in: WZKS XIV (1970), p. 28. Wie J. Ensink hier (p. 182) mitteilt, gebraucht jedoch Th. G. Th. Pigeaud im selben Zusammenhang den Terminus Parallelismus (Java in the Fourteenth Century, etc., 5 vols., Koninklijk Inst. voor Taal-, Land- en Volkenkunde, Transl. Series 4, 1–5).

Leben — als weder eindeutig buddhistisch noch eindeutig hinduistisch erlebt. Kumārī und Matsyendranātha werden von beiden Parteien verehrt und ihre Feste, die Kumārīyātrā und die Matsyendra(nātha)yātrā, gemeinsam gefeiert.

Es ist eine Eigenart synkretistischer Prozesse, daß die Bestandteile, die sie miteinader verbinden, nach bestimmten Prinzipien ausgewählt werden[9]). Wie oben erwähnt, sind die Wandlungen selten total, sondern ergreifen hauptsächlich Elemente, die aufgrund gleicher Funktion, der Namensähnlichkeit oder Wesensgleichheit besonders leicht vereint werden können oder, was ebenfalls ins Gewicht fällt, ein spezielles Bedürfnis erfüllen. Der Synkretismus wählt aus, und mit diesem seinem selektiven Charakter hängt engstens zusammen, daß die Nepalesen zwar zahlreiche Götter gemeinsam verehren, verschiedene Riten gleich oder ähnlich vollziehen usw., in ihrem religiösen Selbstverständnis aber weitgehend Buddhisten oder Hindus verbleiben. Neben dem gemeinnepalesischen Glauben heben sich immer noch ausschließlich buddhistische und ausschließlich hinduistische Kultformen ab, und eine Bestätigung dieser Tatsache ist, daß zahlreiche Einzelpersonen, Clans, ja die Bewohner ganzer Ortschaften oder Gegenden ausdrücklich Wert darauf legen, als entweder Buddhisten oder Hindus zu gelten. Auch läßt sich die Beobachtung machen, daß das religiöse Selbstverständnis sich um so stärker behauptet und um so leichter orthodoxe Merkmale annimmt, je höher der Einzelne sozial eingestuft ist, während gesellschaftlich niedriger stehende Schichten sich des Unterschieds der Religionen in so manchen Belangen viel weniger deutlich bewußt sind.

Leicht erkennbar ist die Neigung zur Interpretation in die eine oder andere Richtung in verschiedenen Texten zur Landesgeschichte oder der religiösen Topographie. Während uns die Chroniken, die Vaṃśāvalīs, in sowohl buddhistischen als auch hinduistischen Fassungen[10]) vorliegen, ist das Svayambhūpurāṇa z.B. buddhistisch und das Nepālamāhātmya, das die Stationen einer hinduistischen tīrthayātrā darstellt, typisch śivaitisch. Die Distinktion der Religionen wird also aufrecht erhalten, doch treten mehr oder weniger zahlreiche Synkretismen in jedem dieser Texte zum Vorschein. Das Nepālamāhātmya, das die Dinge von śivaitischer Warte her sieht, inkludiert in den Pilgerweg auch den Besuch Buddhasthānas[11]), des Vajrayoginī-Tempels im Orte Sāṃkhu und eines

---

[9]) Vgl. G. Lanczkowski, Begegnung und Wandel der Religionen, Düsseldorf-Köln 1971, p. 107.

[10]) Die buddhistische Version der Vaṃśāvalīs benutzt verschiedene Quellen, folgt im legendarischen Teil aber meist dem Svayambhūpurāṇa (15. Jahrhundert). Von den neueren, teils buddhistischen, teils hinduistischen Vaṃśāvalīs (Ende des 18. oder Anfang des 19. Jahrhunderts) läßt sich eine ältere Gruppe, die Gopālavaṃśāvalīs der Malla-Zeit (Anfang des 15. Jahrhunderts), unterscheiden, die auf Sanskrit und Nevārī verfaßt worden waren, jedoch unvollständig nnd sprachlich sehr stark verderbt sind.

[11]) D.i. Svayambhūnāth; s. H. Uebach, Das Nepālamāhātmyam des Skandapurāṇam, Münchener Universitätsschriften 8, München 1970, p. 26 (= Uebach).

Tempels der Vajravārāhī, also buddhistischer Stätten, während andererseits das Svayambhūpurāṇa den bekanntlich größten und ältesten śivaitischen Schrein in Nepal, nämlich Paśupatināth, als auch für Buddhisten verehrbar erachtet.

Grundsätzlich für die religiöse Entwicklung in Nepal ist die Erscheinung, daß männliche Göttergestalten tendieren, in Lokeśvara-Matsyendranātha, einer Vermischung des hinduistischen Gottes Śiva (Paśupati), des Yoga-Heiligen Matsyendranātha und des buddhistischen Bodhisattva Avalokiteśvara, aufzugehen, während andererseits weibliche Götter darnach streben, in śivaitischer Sicht mit Kālī-Durgā, häufig Bhagavatī genannt, zu verschmelzen, in buddhistischer Sicht dagegen mit Tārā, dem bedeutendsten weiblichen Bodhisattva[12]). Zu den ältesten und populärsten hinduistischen Heiligtümern gehören das śivaitische Paśupati und die viṣṇuitischen Schreine des Nārāyaṇa von Caṃgu sowie des Jalaśayana Nārāyaṇa von Buṛā Nīlakaṇṭha, doch sagt das Svayambhūpurāṇa ausdrücklich, daß jene Götter, die die „Brahmanen und andere" unter dem Namen Paśupati und Nārāyaṇa ehren, in Wirklichkeit Lokeśvara sind[13]). So ist das Faktum nicht uninteressant, daß die Bevölkerung, an Synkretismen gewohnt, das Bild des Jalaśayana Nārāyaṇa in späterer Zeit Nīlakaṇṭha genannt hat[14]). Die Benennung ist, wie wir annehmen müssen, nicht höherer Einsicht, sondern simpler Verwechslung mit Śiva(-Nīlakaṇṭha) entsprungen, erscheint aber dennoch nicht völlig verfehlt, zumal Jalaśayana Nārāyaṇa in der Form des Nīlakaṇṭha-Lokeśvara in die Schar der einhundertundacht Lokeśvaras eingereiht wurde[15]). In der Kumārī und der Taleju-māju, die seit der Malla-Zeit Schutzgöttinnen der Königsfamilie und des Königtums sind, sieht das Volk teils Pārvatī-Durgā, teils Tārā, und erwähnenswert ist, daß die Könige Pratāpa Malla und Jagajjaya Malla in der tantrischen Vajrayoginī die Gemahlin Śivas erkennen, während Pratāpa Malla Svayambhū mit Gott Maheśvara gleichsetzt.

Weibliche Gottheiten gewinnen stark an Bedeutung. Schon in Indien zeigt sich, was in Nepal fortgeführt wird: Bestimmte Göttinnen (*devī*) entwickeln śāktische Züge, die ihnen von Anfang an durchaus nicht eignen. So ist die milde Sarasvatī, die Göttin der Gelehrsamkeit, der Polarität Śiva: Durgā von Haus aus entrückt, doch kennen sowohl Śivaismus

---

12) Ähnlich Snellgrove 1957, p. 115, doch ohne Differenzierung zwischen hinduistischer und buddhistischer Perspektive.

13) Siehe Rājendralāla Mitra, The Sanskrit Buddhist Literature of Nepal, Calcutta 1971 (reprint), p. 254 (= Mitra).

14) Die Statue, vom Wasser eines heiligen Teichs umgeben, zeigt Viṣṇu, der auf der Schlange Ananta ruht.

15) Es ist für den Synkretismus bezeichnend, daß zahlreiche Deutungsversuche nur zum Teil oder gar nicht Fuß fassen können. Eine bekannte Nevārī-Hymne aus der Zeit Jaya Bhāskara Mallas von Kathmandu (1700–1714) beschreibt den Gott von Buṛā Nīlakaṇṭha in ungetrübt viṣṇuitischer Andacht und verwendet den Anruf: *he Nārāyaṇaju guṁyā sisa rasana bijyāka*, „O Nārāyaṇa, (der du) glücklich am Fuße des Bergs (Śivapuri) residierst".

als auch Vajrayāna die dunkle Gestalt der Nīlasarasvatī, welcher vom Gläubigen, sei er Hindu oder Buddhist, die fast gleiche Verehrung und derselbe Rang zuerkannt werden wie der Vajravārāhī, der Vajrayoginī, der Chinnamastikā und der Kālī.

Man wird nun die Frage stellen, welche verschiedenen Göttergestalten es sind, die, bedingt durch Übertragung, Analogie oder Identifikation, einen gesicherten Platz im gemeinsam hinduistisch-buddhistischen Pantheon Nepals einnehmen konnten. Wir werden diese Frage erst sinnvoll beantworten können, wenn wir im Auge behalten, daß verschiedene Synkretismen verschiedene Wirkungskraft haben und die religiöse Situation einer Einzelperson oder Gruppe auch von außerreligiösen Faktoren abhängig ist. Die Anzahl und die Differenzierung der Gottheiten, die verehrt, und der Riten, die ausgeführt werden, schwanken nach Herkunft, sozialer Stellung, Familientradition, Beruf und Bildung. Von entscheidendem Einfluß ist weiter, daß, wie kürzlich erwähnt, das religiöse Selbstverständnis eine stärker hinduistische oder stärker buddhistische Färbung aufweisen kann. Der gesamte Vorrat an sowohl indischem als auch volksreligiösem Gut ist gewaltig, doch bilden allein Teile davon den Kern eines eigenen „nepalesischen" Glaubens und ist für den Religionssynkretismus in Nepal bezeichnend, daß der Gläubige die einzelnen Teile immer wieder aus eigener Warte betrachten und verschieden verwirklichen kann, ja daß er darüberhinaus — durch Tradition oder Selbstwahl — seinem eigenen individuellen Bereich auch mehr oder weniger unverändert hinduistische oder buddhistische Glaubensbereiche hinzuführen kann. Es wird nicht unrichtig sein, von einer Religion der Nepalesen zu sprechen, sofern wir nur ständig gewahr bleiben, daß diese Religion, ihre Mythologie usw. allein die vordergründigste und wichtigste Sphäre eines sehr viel größeren religiösen Ganzen bezeichnet, und wenn wir ferner beachten, daß die Grenzen dieser Sphäre nie völlig fixiert sind.

Aufschlüsse über den Glaubensbestand der nepalesischen Religion erhalten wir aus Texten wie den bereits genannten Vaṃśāvalīs und Māhātmyas, welche — unter gleichen oder verschiedenen Namen — gemeinsam verehrte Gottheiten nennen, aus Ortsnamen, Inschriften und Handschriftenkolophonen. Von besonderer Bedeutung sind Quellen, die volkstümlich sind. Diese haben den Vorzug der Unmittelbarkeit und verfolgen, im Gegensatz zu den Vaṃśāvalīs und Māhātymas, kaum jemals die Absicht, ihren Inhalt sektiererisch zu verfärben. Zu solchen Quellen dürfen wir vor allem die Nevārī-Volkslieder zählen, die auch heut noch gehört werden können, zumal die Nevars sehr singfreudig sind. Sämtliche Teile dieser Überlieferung nennen eine Vielzahl von Göttern und göttlichen Wesen, doch ist unverkennbar, daß gewisse Gestalten immer wiederkehren, von allen Texten aufgeführt werden, und daß diese, weil sie am populärsten sind und die Verehrung des ganzen Volkes genießen, den engeren Kreis des nepalesischen Pantheons bilden. Dabei ist bezeichnend, daß die Volkslieder auf Nevārī diese kleinere Gruppe am wenigsten überschreiten. Ihre Zusammensetzung mag willkürlich scheinen, doch gilt, wie vorhin gesagt, als ein wichtiges Merkmal des Religionssynkretismus, daß aus der Fülle der Gegebenheiten immer bloß einzelne Teile ausgewählt und ineinsgesetzt werden.

Eine Abgrenzung der nepalesischen Religion ist also möglich, wenn wir „gebundene“ (d. h. einseitig hinduistische oder einseitig buddhistische) Formen ausklammern, von rein lokalen Kulten absehen und, was die schriftlichen Quellen betrifft, allein die am häufigsten, allerorts und immer wieder erwähnten Gottheiten registrieren. Wie sich bei einem solchen Verfahren feststellen läßt, sind dem engeren Bezirk des eigentlich nepalesischen Olymps mit Sicherheit zugehörig: Lokeśvara, der auch Lokanātha genannt wird und mit Matsyendranātha zu einer Gottheit vereint ist, Svayambhū(nātha)[16]), Paśupati(nātha), Guhyeśvarī, Mañjuśrī, Sarasvatī(-Jayavāgīśvarī), Bhagavatī(-Durgā), Kumārī, Taleju, Vajrayoginī, Nārāyaṇa, Bhairava, Mahākāla, Bhīmasena und Gaṇeśa. In einem Liebeslied auf Nevārī[17]), das etwa ein halbes Jahrhundert alt ist, berichtet ein Mädchen, daß sie ein Gelübde (*vrata*) gehalten und sich am Vollmondstag zum Gott von Seṃgu[18]) begeben, daß sie am Dienstag gefastet und einen bestimmten Gaṇeśa[19]) verehrt und an einem weiteren Tag, einer *aṣṭamī*, den Gott von Cobhāra, d. i. Lokeśvara-Lokanātha, aufgesucht habe. Ein anderes Volkslied[20]) beschreibt die traurige Heimfahrt der in die Berge verbannten Gemahlin Raṇa Bahādur Śāhs (1777–1799), der Königin Rājarājeśvarīdevī, hier Bijyālakṣmī genannt[21]), welcher soeben die Nachricht von der Ermordung Bahādurs überbracht worden ist. Fest entschlossen, ihre Selbstverbrennung, die *satī*, zu vollziehen, unternimmt Bijyālakṣmī unverzüglich die beschwerliche Reise von Helambu nach Kathmandu und opfert unterwegs der Vajrayoginī des Ortes Sāṃkhu, dem Nārāyaṇa von Caṃgu, der Guhyeśvarī, dem Paśupatinātha und der (Jaya)vāgīśvarī[22]). Mit demselben König verknüpft ist ein Lied an die Śītalāmāju, die Göttin der Pocken[23]). Als eine Epidemie im Kathmandu-Tal wütet, läßt Raṇa Bahādur, um seinen Sohn und Thronfolger Girivān Yuddha Śāh zu schützen, alle an Pocken erkrankten Kinder aus dem Tal hinausjagen. Soldaten treiben die verzweifelten Eltern bis an das andere Ufer der Tamakosi, und in ergreifen-

---

[16]) Auf Nevārī Seṃgudya genannt.

[17]) Siehe S. Lienhard, Nevārīgītimañjarī. Religious and Secular Poetry of the Nevars of the Kathmandu Valley, Acta Universitatis Stockholmiensis, Stockholm Oriental Studies 10, Stockholm 1974, Nr. 43 (= Lienhard).

[18]) D.i. Svayambhūnātha.

[19]) In den Städten Nepals besitzt jeder Häuserblock einen Tempel oder Schrein, der Gaṇeśa geweiht ist, vgl. Seite 173.

[20]) Lienhard, Nr. 95.

[21]) Die einleitenden Bemerkungen zu Lienhard, Nr. 95 sind entsprechend zu korrigieren. Rājarājeśvarī(devī), die auch den Namen Vijayalakṣmī (Nev. Bijyālakṣmī, Vijyālakṣmī) trug, war Hauptgemahlin, nicht Konkubine Raṇa Bahādur Śāhs. Ein Verzeichnis der Rāṇīs des Raṇa Bahādur gibt B. J. Hasrat, History of Nepal, Hoshiarpur 1970, p. 132 (= Hasrat).

[22]) D.i. Sarasvatī.

[23]) Vgl. Lienhard, Nr. 96.

den Worten beschreibt uns das Volkslied, wie dieser schreckliche Zug an verschiedenen Heiligtümern Station macht: dem Schrein der Taleju in Bhatgaon, dem der Caṇḍeśvarī in Banepa, der Bhagavatī von Palamcok, des Bhīmasena in Dolakha und zuletzt dem des (Śiva) Mahādeva jenseits des Flusses. Zahllos sind die Gesänge, welche Lokeśvara(-Lokanātha-Matsyendranātha) anrufen, und eine Reihe von Liedern, die wir nach Melodie (*rāga*), Aufbau und Darbringungszeit einer eigenen Gattung, der der *sihnājyā*-Lieder, zuteilen können, nennen ebenfalls Lokanātha, weiterhin Indra, die Nāgas und einzelne „Mütter" (*māju*), d.h. Berge, die als Muttergottheiten aufgefaßt werden[24]). In vergangenen Zeiten wurden diese Lieder von Frauen und Männern, meist im Wechselchor, beim Reisumpflanzen gesungen. Diese Arbeit mußte vor dem Einbruch der Regenzeit, spätestens um die Mitte des Monats Śrāvaṇa, ausgeführt sein, und es ist offenbar, daß die genannten göttlichen und halbgöttlichen Wesen hier als Spender des Regens angefleht wurden.

Mit den Gestalten, die ich soeben vorgestellt habe, ist die zentrale Götterwelt Nepals umrissen. Im allgemeinen darf gelten, daß auf höherer, gebildeter Stufe dieses Pantheon auf der Interferenz hauptsächlich zweier Systeme, des Hinduismus und des späten Buddhismus, beruht, während wir auf breiterer, praktisch-kultischer Ebene einen entscheidenden Einfluß vor allem der Volksreligion werden zurechnen müssen, aus welcher Elemente u. a. in die Gestalt Lokeśvara-Lokanāthas einfließen konnten. Leider reichen unsere Kenntnisse der vorhinduistischen und vorbuddhistischen Glaubenssubstrate noch bei langem nicht aus, um die Überlagerungen gerade dieses — wohl ältesten — Religionsguts im einzelnen greifbar zu machen, doch kann a priori vorausgesetzt werden, daß eine Vielzahl von Synkretismen eben hierauf zurückführbar sind: Aus verschiedenen Gründen, nicht zuletzt aus Prestige, sind viele vorindische Götter und Rituale immer wieder neuinterpretiert und umbenannt worden, und letzten Endes läuft derselbe Prozeß, der ja nicht immer sehr tiefgreifen mußte, auch noch heutzutage fort[25]). Wesentlich ist, daß, wie schon früher erwähnt[26]), im Ineinandergreifen der beiden großen Religionen der Buddhismus die in der Regel überlagerte, der Hin-

---

[24]) Siehe Lienhard, Nr. 92–94.

[25]) Treffend bemerkt zu dieser Frage Prof. B. Kölver: „Unter den Phänomenen gibt es einige, die sich weder als hinduistisch noch als buddhistisch erklären lassen: die Nāsadyos mit ihren Wegen; die Gaṇeśas, die bloß amorphe Steine sind; auch Bhairavas erscheinen so und gehören wohl in denselben Kontext, bloß läßt sich das nicht mit der gleichen Sicherheit behaupten, weil sie eben ikonographisch nicht so festgelegt sind wie die Gaṇeśas. Bei solchen vom Hinduismus her gesehen anomalen Repräsentationen von Gottheiten liegt sicher eine nichtindische Wurzel zugrunde. Das erklärt auch die Vertauschbarkeit, den Mangel an Präzision, an ausgefülltem Inhalt: es wurden gewissermaßen bei der buddhistischen, der hinduistischen Mission immer neue Namen angeboten, verbunden mit Stiftungen, so daß (a) materieller Anreiz und (b) gelehrte und damit prestigebehaftete Interpretation die Bezeichnung der alten Götter änderten" (Mitteilung vom 11. 12. 1975).

[26]) Siehe Seite 151.

duismus die überlagernde Glaubensform darstellt. Auch läßt sich unschwer erkennen, daß die Interferenz der beiden großen Systeme im Kult und in der Ausgestaltung der einzelnen Götter in verschiedener Weise und mit verschiedener Stärke gewirkt hat.

Was die alten Heiligtümer Svayambhūnāth und Paśupatināth betrifft, ist die Verehrung hauptsächlich parallelistisch. Sie wird von einer deutlich monotheistischen Neigung gefördert, die auch bei Lokeśvara-Lokanātha sehr deutlich hervortritt. Wie man in Svayambhūnāth dem *dharmadhātu* oder dem Ādibuddha huldigt, wird in Paśupatināth der uranfängliche Gott, in śivaitischen Kreisen der Ādiśiva gefeiert. Der „Gott von Anbeginn", der *ādinātha*, ist die Quintessenz dieser Welt, die von beiden Gemeinden anerkannt wird. Seine Verehrung, von sowohl Buddhisten als auch Hindus vollzogen, durchbricht, da sie aus ein und demselben Antrieb erfolgt, weder das buddhistische noch das hinduistische Glaubensverständnis. Hindus huldigen dem Gott von Svayambhū als Śambhu, d.h. als Gott Śiva, während Buddhisten das *liṅga* des Paśupatinātha einmal im Jahr mit dem Kopfschmuck des Tathāgata Akṣobhya verzieren und denselben Phallus am Vollmondstag des Monats Kārttika als Bodhisattva verehren[27]. Dazu kommt, daß sich im Tempelbereich von Svayambhūnāth viele Śiva-Statuen und *Śivaliṅgas* befinden und andererseits das śivaitische Paśupatināth auch zahlreiche buddhistische Bilder beherbergt. Wie ich dafürhalten möchte, ist in der Gleichsetzung von Svayambhū mit Śambhu, die sicher nicht alt ist[28], auch der sprachliche Umstand ins Spiel gebracht worden, daß die nichtliterarische Nevārī längere Lehnworte gern reduziert. *svayambhū* wird in der Alltagssprache zu *saṁbhu* verkürzt, einer Lautform, die der phonotaktischen Struktur der Nevārī viel besser entspricht als die Sanskritbezeichnung. Die Identifikation mit Śambhu, einem der geläufigsten Beinamen Śivas, muß sich also fast aufgedrängt haben.

Während nun Svayambhūnātha und Paśupatinātha im Grunde genommen allein die Möglichkeit einer Gleichsetzung bieten, die dem Einzelnen freigestellt bleibt, ist eine gründliche Integrierung verschiedener Komponenten in der Gestalt Lokanātha-Matsyendranāthas erfolgt. Seine Verehrung ist ungeteilt, und nicht umsonst wird in Lokeśvara, in dessen Person Avalokiteśvara, Matsyendranātha und nicht zuletzt Śiva(-Paśupati) verschmelzen, der große Nationalgott Nepals erkannt. Seine weitgespannte Erscheinung ist die synkretistische Göttergestalt par excellence.

Es unterliegt keinem Zweifel, daß die Konzeption dieses Gottes auf śivaitischen Einfluß zurückgeht, doch ist gleichfalls gesichert, daß die Interpretation Avalokiteśvaras als Lokeśvara bereits auf indischem Boden vor sich ging und Avalokiteśvara selbst schon eine religionssynkre-

---

[27]) Siehe D. R. Regmi, Medieval Nepal, Part I (Early Medieval Period 750–1530 A.D.), Calcutta 1965, p. 557 (= Regmi I).

[28]) Vgl. H. Hoffmann, Die buddhistischen Heiligtümer des Nepal-Tales, in: Indologen-Tagung 1959, Göttingen 1960, p. 115.

tistische Überlagerung darstellt. Schon im Bengalen des 9., 10. und 11. Jahrhunderts standen zwei Bodhisattvas im Zentrum buddhistischer Laienfrömmigkeit, nämlich Mañjuśrī und Avalokiteśvara, und zahlreiche Texte bezeugen, daß das Volk mit Vorzug den letzteren, gewöhnlich Lokeśvara oder Lokanātha genannt, als den großen Erretter angefleht hat. Im 9. Jahrhundert schrieb Vajrasattva, ein Zeitgenosse König Devapālas, einen sprachlich sehr ausgefeilten Gedichtkranz, das Lokeśvaraśataka, das die Schönheit und die Größe Lokeśvaras feiert und das, poetisch gesehen, durch Bāṇas Caṇḍīśataka und Mayūras Sūryaśataka angeregt ist[29]), und aus der späteren Hälfte des 11. Jahrhunderts stammt die Anthologie Subhāṣitaratnakoṣa des bengalischen Buddhisten Vidyākara, der im zweiten Abschnitt (*vrajyā*) dieses Werks Gedichte verschiedener Dichter zum Thema „Lokeśvara“ kompiliert hat[30]). In zahlreichen buddhistischen Texten erscheint Lokeśvara als der allbarmherzige Helfer in Krankheit, Not und auf gefährlichen Reisen, und, wie die Nevārī-Volkslieder zeigen, erfüllt er dieselbe Funktion auch in Nepal. Für das Kathmandu-Tal ist charakteristisch, daß es diesen großen und attraktiven Gott zwar übernommen, seine Persönlichkeit aber weiter ausgebaut hat. Indem Avalokiteśvara-Lokeśvara mit Matsyendranātha und Mīnanātha ineinsgesetzt wurde, entstand eine typisch nepalesische Gottheit, die Züge erhielt, die sie leicht zum Gemeingut des ganzen Volks heranwachsen ließen. Die Buddhisten halten diesen Gott als die Lokanātha-Form des Avalokiteśvara heilig und rufen ihn häufig mit dem Namen „Mitleidvoll“, *Karuṇāmaya*, an. Er verbleibt auch in der Vermischung mit Matsyendranātha eine Emanation des Buddha „Unermeßliches Licht“ (Amitābha), der den Gläubigen ins Paradies Sukhāvatī heimführt, und es ist bemerkenswert, daß späte Nevārī-Hymnen den Gott auch aus dieser Schau her betrachten: Lokanātha, der während der Matsyendra(nātha)yātrā auf seinem prunkvollen Festwagen thront, ist mit dem Stirnschmuck einer Kleindarstellung des Tathāgata Amitābha geschmückt[31]). Gebildete Kreise erkennen in Lokeśvara — in Übereinstimmung mit der spätbuddhistischen Welterklärung — Padmapāṇi, d.h. jenen der fünf von den fünf Tathāgatas durch Meditation ins Leben gerufenen Bodhisattvas, der im Auftrage Śambhus (= Svayambhū) das Universum erschuf und deshalb zurecht der Weltenherr, Lokanātha, genannt wird[32]).

---

[29]) Vgl. S. N. Dasgupta and S. K. De, A History of Sanskrit Literature. Classical Period, Vol. 1, Calcutta 1962, p. 378.

[30]) Siehe The Subhāṣitaratnakoṣa. Compiled by Vidyākara, edited by D. D. Kosambi and V. V. Gokhale, Harvard Or. Series, 42, Cambridge, Mass. 1957, p. 4f. und An Anthology of Sanskrit Court Poetry. Vidyākara's "Subhāṣitaratnakoṣa", translated by D. H. H. Ingalls, Harvard Or. Series, 44, Cambridge, Mass. 1965, p. 62ff.

[31]) Vgl. B. Bhattacharyya, The Indian Buddhist Iconography, Calcutta 1958², p. 132 (= Bhattacharyya) und Lienhard, Nr. 8 und 9.

[32]) Vgl. B. H. Hodgson, Essays on the Languages, Literature and Religion of Nepal and Tibet, London 1874, Reprint Amsterdam 1972, p. 42.

Es ist offenbar, daß Lokeśvara kraft seines Namens auch śivaitischen und damit hinduistischen Zwecken dienstbar gemacht worden ist. Im Sanskrit sind die Benennungen Legion, welche Śiva als Weltenherrn, als Jagadīśa, Jagadīśvara usw. bezeichnen. Weiteren Vorschub leistete dieser Entwicklung die Identifikation mit Matsyendranātha. Sie war zu einem Zeitpunkt erfolgt, da der Nātha-Kult größtes Ansehen hatte, und war zweifellos dadurch begünstigt, daß die Nātha-Yogins, und sicherlich auch andere Wanderasketen und Mönche, besonders guten Kontakt mit den Volksmassen hatten. Die Nātha-Bewegung war in Indien über weite Gebiete verbreitet, und es verwundert wohl kaum, daß sie auch in Nepal und Tibet Fuß fassen konnte, zumal ihr Ursprung in mongoloiden Gegenden oder Bengalen gesucht werden muß. Wie wir wissen, repräsentiert ihr Asketismus einen der zahlreichen zeitgenössischen Siddha-Kulte, in dessen Mittelpunkt yogistische, tantrische, śāktische und den Körper verjüngende, alchemistische Praktiken standen. Doch war die Bewegung der Nāthapanthins sicherlich nicht, wie man vielfach geglaubt hat, eine buddhistisch gewordene, ursprünglich śivaitische Sekte, noch umgekehrt eine anfangs buddhistische Strömung, die sich später śivaitisch orientiert hat. Der Nāthismus hatte die verschiedensten Elemente in sich aufgesogen, war als typischer Yoga-Kult aber lang einer festen religiösen Bindung entgangen. Als er sich später systematisch festlegen sollte, assoziierte er sich nicht mehr mit dem Spätbuddhismus, der schon allzu geschwächt war, sondern dem Hinduismus, in dessen Rahmen er in Bengalen und in Nepal als eine Art Sonderform des Śivaismus hervortritt.

Innerhalb der nepalesischen Nātha-Bewegung übten besonders die Kanphaṭā-Yogins einen nachhaltigen Einfluß auf die Bevölkerung aus. Ihr Lehrmeister Gorakhanātha (Gorakṣanātha) wurde schon im frühen Mittelalter in Bhatgaon, Kathmandu, Pharping und anderen Orten verehrt, und ihre einst große Popularität bezeugt auch der Umstand, daß in Nevārī-Liedern das Wort Yogin oft Kanphaṭā-Yogin bedeutet. Bei der Vorliebe, an den Namen gewisser nepalesischer Heiligtümer oder göttlicher Gestalten wie Svayambhūnātha, Paśupatinātha, Buddhanātha (volkssprachlich inkorrekt: Bodhnātha), Bhairavanātha usw. den Ausdruck *nātha* anzuhängen, kann der Sprachgebrauch der Nāthapanthins mitgespielt haben[33]). Bekanntlich heben ihre Schriften die Existenz von vierundachtzig „Vollendeten“ (*siddha*) und eine Lehrtradition von neun im Himalaya lokalisierten Yoga-Meistern, den Nāthas oder „Beschützern“, hervor. An ihrer Spitze steht Ādinātha, der als Hevajra oder

[33]) Vgl. Snellgrove 1957, p. 114. Sicherlich beruhen nicht sämtliche, auch in Indien zahlreich vertretenen *nātha*-Benennungen auf dem Nāthismus. Eine Kartierung der indischen Ortsnamen auf *-nātha* wird von U. Schneider im Rahmen des Orissa-Projekts, Sonderforschungsbreich 16, geplant. Im ceylonesischen Buddhismus ist Nātha meist Kurzform für Lokeśvaranātha; die Rūpāvalī oder Rūpamālā (Śāriputra), ein auf Ceylon vielverwendetes ikonometrisches Handbuch, beschreibt den Gott in acht Formen: Śivanātha, Brahmanātha, Viṣṇunātha, Gaurīnātha, Matsyendranātha, Bhadranātha, Bauddhanātha und Gaṇanātha

Vajrasattva mit einerseits Śiva, andererseits Buddha identifiziert wird[34]) und der die Nātha-Lehre dem Heiligen Matsyendranātha (oder Mīnanātha), dem Lehrer des Gorakhanātha, kundgetan hat.

Was nun in Nepal auffällt, ist die totale Vergöttlichung des Yoga-Heiligen Matsyendranātha und die Tatsache, daß aus der Reihe der neun großen Nāthas gar nicht der Ādinātha, noch Gorakhanātha oder ein anderer, späterer Nātha mit Lokeśvara gleichgesetzt wurde, sondern daß eben Matsyendranātha und — in Verbindung mit Matsyendranātha — auch Mīnanātha[35]) ausgewählt wurden. Wie ich dafürhalten möchte, war diese Wahl vom Bedürfnis des Volkes diktiert, dessen Haupterwerbszweig die Landwirtschaft war und das, wie hier scheint, zu geeignetem Zeitpunkt zahlreiche Götter in eine Erscheinung aufgehen ließ und sich in Matsyendranātha, vereint mit Lokeśvara-Lokanātha, das Bild eines mächtigen, mitleidvollen Beschützers aufgebaut hat. Der große Gott stand in seinem Lokeśvara-Aspekt in Not und Krankheiten bei und segnete im Matsyendranātha-Aspekt Reisfeld, Acker und Ernte. Da die Hauptfunktion Matsyendranāthas (wie die Indras, der Nāgas und bestimmter Berg-Muttergottheiten) in der Spendung des jährlichen Regens besteht, scheint mir durchaus wahrscheinlich, daß Matsyendranātha und Mīnanātha aufgrund ihres Namens, „Beschützer Indra unter den Fischen“[36]) und „Beschützer Fisch“[37]) für diese Rolle ausgesucht wurden. Die indischen und die nepalesischen Erklärungen[38]) des Namens Matsyendranātha sind später erfundene mythologische Konstruktionen, die keinerlei Aufschlüsse bieten, doch ist von Bedeutung, daß Matsyendranātha mit Schlangenlegenden und -kulten verknüpft wird[39]), und interessant ist

(s. S. Paranavitana, Mahāyānism in Ceylon, in: Ceylon Journal of Science, Section G—Archaeology, Ethnology, Etc., Vol. II, 1928–1933, p. 53 und 60ff. Ich verdanke diesen Hinweis Herrn Dr. H. Ruelius, Göttingen, der mir auch freundlicherweise den Aufsatz beschafft hat).

[34]) In diesem Zusammenhang sei aufs neue beachtet, daß, wie S. 157 erwähnt, in Svayambhūnāth die Buddha-Essenz, die man sich in der Form des *svayambhū*, des *dharmadhātu*, Vajrasattvas, Vairocanas, Śākyamunis oder eines der vier Buddhas der Weltgegenden vorstellen kann, auch als der „Buddha von Anbeginn“, der Ādi-Buddha, verehrt wird. Dieser Kult entwickelte sich unter Einwirkung monotheistisch-hinduistischen Denkens und Einflüssen aus dem Westen, und bemerkenswert ist, daß die Zhang-zhung-Sprache Buddha mit dem Lehnwort *a-ti* (< Skt. *ādi*) bezeichnet; vgl. Erik Haarh, The Zhang-Zhung Language. A Grammar and Dictionary of the Unexplored Language of the Tibetan Bonpos, Acta Jutlandica, XL: 1, Hum. Serie 47, Aarhus-København 1968, p. 13.

[35]) In der Liste der „großen Vollendeten“ (*mahāsiddha*), welche die Haṭhayogapradīpikā gibt, werden u.a. Śiva, Matsyendra, Ānandabhairava, Mīna, Gorakṣa, Bhairava und Buddha genannt (I, 5–9).

[36]) Matsyendranātha.

[37]) Mīnanātha.

[38]) Siehe u.a. Haṭhayogapradīpikā of Svātmārāma Svāmin, translated by Yogī Śrīnivāsa Iyangār, Madras 1949³, Kommentar zu I, 27; D. Wright, History of Nepal, translated from Parbatiya, Calcutta 1958 (Reprint), p. 83 (= Wright) und M. M. Anderson, The Festivals of Nepal, London 1971, p. 53f. (= Anderson).

[39]) Siehe Anderson, p. 59ff.

ferner, daß Mīnanātha, den die Nepalesen teils als eine Manifestation des Matsyendranātha von Patan, des „Roten Matsyendranātha" (Nep. *rāto macchendra*)[40], teils als dessen Sohn oder Tochter erachten, auf Nevārī *cākuvādeo* genannt wird, d.h. „Gott süßer Regen"[41]) oder „Gott süßer Reis"[41]). Das große Fest des Gottes, die Matsyendrayātrā, zeigt tatsächlich den Beginn der Regenzeit an.

Eine Sage erzählt, daß Matsyendranātha einst von König Narendra aus Kāmarūpa herbeigeholt wurde[42]). Wie die Legende berichtet, wurde der Yogin Gorakhanātha vom Wunsche verzehrt, Lokanātha, den Schöpfer der Welt, mit eigenen Augen betrachten zu können. Da er wußte, daß Matsyendranātha-Lokanātha das hungernde Volk bemitleiden würde, veranlaßte Gorakhanātha, indem er Gewalt über die Nāgas ausübte, eine zwölf Jahre lang dauernde Dürre. In der Tat manifestierte sich Matsyendranātha als Retter: Von Narendra nach Nepal gebracht, erschien er dem Gorakhanātha, ließ Regen strömen und erfreute die Menschen mit reichlicher Nahrung. Ich habe den Eindruck, daß wir diese Legende nicht ganz als Erfindung[43]) abfertigen können. Einzelne Details mögen später erdacht und hinzugefügt worden sein, doch scheint der Kern der Erzählung doch insoweit richtig, als die Bewohner des Nepal-Tals Matsyendranātha zunächst wirklich als eine neugewonnene Gottheit empfanden. Die nepalesischen Quellen berichten, daß auch andere Götter, so z.B. die große Talejumāju, zu einem bestimmten Zeitpunkt nach Nepal „eingeführt", d. h. im Kathmandu-Tal propagiert und populär gemacht worden waren. Angaben dieser Art sind oft vage und selten verläßlich, doch scheint immerhin möglich, daß wir aus dem Hinweis auf die Herbeiholung Matsyendranāthas aus dem östlichen Kāmarūpa eine Anspielung auf die mongoloide, nord- oder nordostbengalische Heimat der Nāthapanthins herauslesen dürfen.

Sicher ist, daß Matsyendranātha eine Redundanz besaß, die so groß war, daß sie im Nepal-Tal inhaltlich aufgefüllt und zu besonderen Zwekken verwandt werden konnte. Daß in Lokeśvara-Matsyendranātha verschiedene lokale Götter vereint worden sind, verrät die Tatsache, daß sein Kult verschiedene örtliche Varianten umfaßt, und zwar, neben Mīnanātha, vor allem den Roten Matsyendranātha von Patan, den Weißen Matsyendranātha (Nep. *seto macchendra*) von Kathmandu und den Gott des Hügels Chobāra (oder Chobāla, mod. Nev. Chovā). In der zuletztgenannten Manifestation tritt die Verschmelzung mit Lokeśvara insoweit deutlich zum Vorschein, als (der Gott von) Chobhāra besonders bei Krankheit aufgesucht wird[44]). Er ist eine anfangs lokale Gottheit, ein Berggott. Wie oben erwähnt worden ist, ist Mīnanātha unter dem

---

[40]) Er wird rot dargestellt, um die Wesensgleichheit mit (dem gleichfalls roten) Avalokiteśvara zu betonen.

[41]) *vā*, Reis(schössling); Regen.

[42]) Vgl. Wright, p. 83ff. und Lienhard, Nr. 11.

[43]) Diese Auffassung vertritt Snellgrove 1957, p. 117f.

[44]) Siehe Lienhard, Nr. 24.

Nevar-Namen Cākuvādeo bekannt. Auch der Rote Matsyendranātha wird mit einem Lokalgott, dem Gott von Buga[45]), einem Ort südwestlich von Patan, identifiziert. Es ist zu vermuten, daß sich gerade in Buga(ma)-deo das wichtigste volksreligiöse — vorhinduistische und vorbuddhistische — Substrat des synkretistischen Matsyendranātha-Lokeśvaranātha verbirgt und daß dieser Bugadeo in früheren Zeiten einen alten Nevar-Regengott dargestellt hat[45a]). Bugadeo besitzt seinen Hauptschrein in Buga, wird aber, bevor die Matsyendrayātrā beginnt, im Januar oder Februar, nach Patan gebracht[45b]). Es ist offenbar, daß die Gestalt des Lokeśvara-Matsyendranātha dem stark gefühlten Bedürfnis nach einem mächtigen, durch die Verbindung mit sowohl buddhistischem als auch hinduistisch-śivaitischem Glauben verläßlich gesicherten Allgott entsprach. In Matsyendranātha-Lokanātha war dem nepalesischen Volk ein Heilbringer großen Formates erstanden, der in glücklichster Weise ein Bedürfnis des Volkes erfüllte und religiöse Diskrepanzen jeder Art ausglich. Nepal besitzt keinen anderen Gott, der ebenso einmütig und so begeistert verehrt wird.

Da den Nāthapanthins Wunder und Wunderkräfte (*siddhi*) zuerkannt wurden, ist es sicher kein Zufall, daß gerade einer ihrer neun Yogins, Matsyendranātha, der „Beschützer Indra unter den Fischen", in den großen, den Regen bringenden Gott transformiert worden ist. Es mußte dem Denken des Volkes wohl nahe liegen, den göttlichen Regenspender als eine barmherzige, mitleidvolle Gestalt zu verstehen, und es überrascht daher kaum, daß Matsyendra mit Lokanātha Karuṇāmaya gleichgesetzt wurde. Als Abschluß der Matsyendrayātrā und vielleicht als der einstige Höhepunkt dieses Festes wird eine Zeremonie ausgeführt, die auf Nevārī *bhote boyagu* heißt, d. i. das feierliche „Vorzeigen des Hemdes" Matsyendranāthas. Kanphaṭā-Yogins nehmen auch heute noch am Wagenfest teil, und die Annahme ist verlockend, daß die frühesten Jünger des Matsyendra das Hemd ihres Gurus als eine Art Reliquie aufbewahrt haben und die Nātha-Anhänger der ältesten Zeit, wann immer die Yātrā beendet war und der Regen bevorstand, diese Reliquie (oder einen Ersatz derselben) als ein Mittel des Regenzaubers vorgezeigt haben[46]). Im Zusammenhang mit der Matsyendrayātrā in Patan sei ferner erwähnt, daß der Balken, der vor dem Festwagen aufragt, ein geschnitztes Abbild des Schlangenkönigs Karkoṭa trägt[47]) und daß vorne, an der Wagenspitze, die Figur des Vajrasattva angebracht ist[48]).

Eine nahe Verbindung gingen im nepalesischen Glauben auch die Göttin (Jaya)vāgīśvarī, d.h. Sarasvatī, und Mañjuśrī ein. Ihre Verbindung

[45]) Auch Buṃga oder Bugama, Buṃgama.

[45a]) Vgl. hierzu J. K. Locke, Rato Matsyendranath of Patan and Bungamati, Tribhuvan University, Historical Series 5, p. 97.

[45b]) Auch Bhatgaon besitzt, im Westen der Stadt, einen Rāto Macchendra, dessen lokaler Nevārī-Name dort Laskudeo (auch Laskudyo) ist.

[46]) Bezüglich dieser scharfsinnigen Deutung siehe Snellgrove 1957, p. 117.

[47]) Vgl. Anderson, p. 58.

[48]) Siehe Snellgrove 1957, p. 117.

ist allerdings weniger fest als diejenige Lokanāthas mit Matsyendranātha. Der Hauptschrein der Vāgīśvarī liegt am westlichen Hügel hinter Svayambhū, derselben Stätte, die auch Mañjuśrī, ihrem buddhistischen Partner geweiht ist. Die Stellung Sarasvatīs ist im Hinduismus sehr schwankend, da sie einerseits als die Gattin Brahmās aufgefaßt, andererseits von den Vaiṣṇavas als die Gemahlin Viṣṇus und den Śaivas als die Tochter Śivas und Durgās und die Schwester Gaṇeśas verehrt wird. Ins Vajrayāna-Pantheon war Sarasvatī als die Gattin Mañjuśrīs eingeführt worden, doch gilt für die Weiterentwicklung in Nepal, daß der Kult der beiden eine weitgehend gleichgeschaltete Ausformung fand. In einfacheren Schichten des Volkes ist die synkretistische Ansicht verbreitet, daß Sarasvatī und Mañjuśrī überhaupt eins sind. Ikonographisch bemerkenswert ist, daß nepalesische Darstellungen die Göttin nicht bloß mit dem Buch und der Laute, sondern manchmal auch mit dem Schwert der Erkenntnis, dem Schwerte Mañjuśrīs, zeigen. Als ein für beide gemeinsames Fest wird am fünften Tag der hellen Monatshälfte des Māgha die Vasantapañcamī- oder Śrīpañcamī-Feier begangen, die nach śivaitischen Texten der Ehrentag der Sarasvatī, nach dem Svayambhūpurāṇa der Festtag des Mañjuśrī ist, weshalb sie auch Sarasvatī-Jayantī oder Mañjuśrī-Jayantī heißt. Die Funktion von sowohl Sarasvatī als auch Mañjuśrī ist der Schutz des geschriebenen Wortes, der Gelehrsamkeit und gewisser Handfertigkeiten, und wie man Sarasvatī als der Jayavāgīśvarī oder Vāgīśvarī huldigt, ehrt man Mañjuśrī als Jayavāgīśvara oder Vāgīśvara[49]). Beide Wesenheiten existieren im Ritus stets nebeneinander, und ihre Verbindung, die von Fall zu Fall teils loser, teils enger konzipiert werden kann, erlaubt eine sowohl parallelistische als auch eine identifikatorische Deutung: Mañjuśrī und Sarasvatī genießen entweder dieselbe Verehrung, wenngleich in gesonderter Form, oder verschmelzen mehr oder weniger stark ineinander.

Die Verknüpfung Sarasvatīs mit der śivaitischen Vorstellungswelt lebt insofern weiter, als hinduistische Zeremonien am Jayavāgīśvarī-Schrein auch blutige Opfer einschließen können. Solche Opfer wurden allerdings nicht der Vāgīśvarī selbst, sondern Gaṇeśa erbracht, auf dessen nahegelegenes steinernes Abbild man das Blut des Opfertiers, meist einer Ziege oder eines Huhns, herabtropfen läßt.

Wie schon erwähnt, waren Mañjuśrī, auch Mañjughoṣa genannt, und Lokeśvara die im Bengalen des 9. bis 12. Jahrhunderts populärsten Bodhisattva-Gestalten. Mañjuśrī fungierte nicht bloß als Gottheit der Weisheit, sondern wurde allmählich mit Eigenschaften versehen, die ihn in die Nähe sowohl des Kumāra als auch des Kāma, des Liebesgotts, rücken. Das vermutlich von einem Buddhisten, einem Autor namens Padmaśrī verfaßte Nāgarasarvasva, ein erotischer Text aus der Mitte des 14. Jahrhunderts, beschreibt Mañjuśrī in der Einleitungsstrophe als den „mit Blumenpfeilen (versehenen), in Schönheit strahlenden,

[49]) Vgl. Lienhard, Nr. 52 und 95.

mit leuchtenden Salben geröteten (Gott)“ [50]), der dem Liebenden, sobald er ihn anruft, die ersehnte Geliebte zukommen läßt. Im buddhistischen Tantrismus wurde dieser Aspekt des Mañjughoṣa in der Form des Vajrānaṅga verbildlicht, der eine wichtige Rolle in den Riten der Liebesnötigung, d. h. des Willfährigmachens (*vaśīkaraṇa*) von Frauen und Männern, gespielt hat [51]).

Die Varianten Mañjuśrīs sind ungemein zahlreich, doch besteht kein Zweifel, daß die Verehrung der breiteren Schichten der Nevars seinem Aspekt als Vāgīśvara vorbehalten sein sollte. In dieser Gestalt reitet Mañjuśrī auf einem Löwen und schwingt das Schwert Candrahāsa [52]). Die Sādhanamālā empfiehlt, daß sich der Gläubige den roten Vāgīśvara — es gibt daneben den gelben — als Kumāra und schön wie Kumāra (*kumārarūpeṇa*) vorstellen soll [53]), und es erstaunt daher nicht, daß der Eröffnungsspruch der im Tanjur [54]) enthaltenen tibetischen Version des Kāvyādarśa Mañjuśrī in der Form Kumāras beschwört [55]). Mañjuśrī besitzt damit heldische, Furcht einjagende Züge und wird von Buddhisten als Beschützer des Glaubens und Schutzgott Nepals erachtet. Seine Popularität war so groß, daß die buddhistische Fassung der Vaṃśāvalīs und das Svayambhūpurāṇa die Trockenlegung des Nepal-Tals, das in fernster Vergangenheit von einem großen See, dem Nāgahrada, ausgefüllt war [56]), dem Mañjuśrī zuschreibt [57]). In den hinduistischen Vaṃśāvalīs und im Nepālamāhātmya wird diese Großtat aber durch Viṣṇu-Kṛṣṇa besorgt, und es ist mehr als wahrscheinlich, daß diese brahmanistische Version nur eine rivalisierende Nachbildung der buddhistischen ist und daß auch die letztere, die buddhistische, keinen Anspruch auf Gültigkeit hat. Es bedarf kaum der Erwähnung, daß Mañjuśrī im nepalesischen, ja auch indischen Raum allzu jung ist, um in einem

---

[50]) *ullasitaḍambaraṃ sucirāṅgarāgāruṇaṃ ... sumanaḥśaraṃ ... ārya-mañjuśriyam.*

[51]) Vgl. Bhattacharyya, p. 114f. und H. v. Glasenapp, Buddhistische Mysterien. Die geheimen Lehren und Riten des Diamant-Fahrzeugs, Stuttgart 1940, p. 145.

[52]) Vgl. Lienhard, Nr. 12.

[53]) Vgl. Bhattacharyya, p. 116. Vgl. auch M.-Th. de Mallmann, Étude iconographique sur Mañjuśrī, Paris 1964, p. 17. Als ein früher Vorläufer sowohl des Avalokiteśvara als auch des Mañjuśrīkumārabhūta erscheint im Janavasabhasutta des Dīghanikāya die Gestalt des Brahmā Sanaṃkumāra, die dort als jugendlich und von lieblicher Stimme (*mañjusara*) vorgestellt wird; s. J. Filliozat, Un texte de la religion Kaumāra. Le TirumurukāRRupaṭai, Pondichéry 1973, p. XXXIV.

[54]) Narthang-Ausgabe.

[55]) *nama ārya-mañjuśrī-kumārabhūtāya.*

[56]) Es sei hier bemerkt, daß die moderne Naturwissenschaft dieses Faktum bestätigt. Die geologischen Formationen verraten, daß zwischen den Bergen einst ein See aufgestaut war, dessen Gewässer, als plötzlich ein Erdbeben ausbrach, nach dem Süden abgeströmt waren, worauf das fruchtbare Tal von Kathmandu entstand. Vgl. Pradyumna P. Karan, Nepal, A Cultural and Physical Geography, Lexington 1960, p. 4.

[57]) Siehe Wright, p. 45f. und Lienhard, Nr. 12 und 13.

Mythus der Vorzeit figurieren zu können[58]). Auch existierte dieselbe Legende in Khotan[59]). Sie war von Khotan nach Nepal eingeführt worden, und zwar durch Tibeter, die den Ausdruck *li.yul*, die alte Bezeichnung für Khotan, in späterer Zeit auf Nepal angewandt hatten. Es scheint mir plausibel, auch die Meinung der nepalesischen Überlieferung, daß Mañjuśrī aus China (*mahācīna*) herstamme, als eine Reminiszenz an Khotan zu deuten. Als eine Erinnerung an Khotan und eine direkte Übertragung auf das Kathmandu-Tal kann weiter die Tatsache gelten, daß der Wohnsitz Mañjuśrīs im Bereich Svayambhūnāths lokalisiert wird. Zweifellos ist Svayambhūnāth, das nach Auskunft des Svayambhūpurāṇa im Dvāparayuga *gośṛṅga* genannt worden ist, ein späteres, nepalesisches Gegenstück des Hügels Gośṛṅga in Khotan, dem Mañjuśrī seinen besonderen Segen verliehen haben soll[60]).

Wie Matsyendranātha war auch Mañjuśrī eine Göttererscheinung breitester Redundanz. Einen gewissen Ansatz, seiner Gestalt die Funktion eines landbebauenden Kultivators zu geben, verrät die buddhistische Version der Vaṃśāvalīs, die im Gott der Weisheit den ersten Besiedler des Nepal-Tals zu erkennen versucht[61]). Wie die nepalesische Religionsgeschichte zeigt, wurde diese Volkserwartung nach einem Gott des Ackerbaus und der Landwirtschaft aber nicht von Mañjuśrī, sondern der unvergleichlich größeren Gestalt des Lokeśvara-Matsyendranātha erfüllt.

Gegenstand intensiver Huldigung ist die rätselhafte Göttin Guhyeśvarī, deren Schrein sich am Ufer der Bāgmatī, nicht weit von Paśupatināth, befindet und täglich von zahlreichen Gläubigen aufgesucht wird. Die Grundlagen ihrer Gestalt sind im purāṇischen Śivaismus zu Hause, wo sie zunächst als die gattentreue Satī, die mit Rudra-Śiva vermählte Tochter des Dakṣa, erscheint. Tief betrübt, als eine unerbittliche Feindschaft zwischen ihrem Vater, dem listigen und Viṣṇu-freundlichen Dakṣa, und ihrem Gatten, Śiva, entsteht, überantwortet Satī ihren Körper dem Feuer, doch wird sie als Pārvatī wiedergeboren und so aufs Neue mit Śiva verbunden. Die Tatsache, daß das Heiligtum der Guhyeśvarī, wie nur wenige andere, auch von nepalesischen Mädchen und Frauen verehrt wird, beruht nicht zuletzt auf den Tugenden, die für Satī und Pārvatī kennzeichnend sind. Beide Erscheinungen komplettieren einander: Ist Satī das Symbol der Gattinnentreue, eines der wichtigsten Pfeiler im Sittenkodex der Gurkhas, so erscheint Pārvatī als eine jugendlich-schöne und sanfte Gestalt, die die Ehe beschirmt und Fruchtbarkeit schenkt. Aus diesem purāṇisch-śivaitischen Hintergrund erhebt sich Guhyeśvarī, die jedoch größere Dimensionen gewinnt. Anders als in der Purāṇa-Legende erzählen die Tantras, daß Śiva die tote Satī

---

[58]) Siehe Snellgrove 1957, p. 92.

[59]) Siehe John Brough, Legends of Khotan and Nepal, in: BSOAS XII (1948), p. 333ff. (= Brough) und E. Lamotte, Mañjuśrī, in: T'oung Pao XLVIII (1960), p. 49ff.

[60]) Vgl. Brough, p. 334 und 338.

[61]) Siehe Wright, p. 85 und Uebach, p. 19.

herumtrug, wobei einzelne Teile ihres Leichnams ausgestreut wurden. Im nepalesischen Guhyeśvarī-Heiligtum wird in der Form eines *kuṇḍa*, einer mit Wasser gefüllten, heiligen Öffnung, jener Stelle gehuldigt, an welcher das *guhya*, d.h. die Vulva, der Satī herabfiel[62]). Es ist auffällig, daß im Gegensatz zu anderen buddhistischen Stätten, die jedermann zugänglich sind, das Guhyeśvarī-*kuṇḍa* ein streng gehütetes Sanktuarium darstellt, dessen Zutritt nur Hindus und Buddhisten erlaubt ist. Die Guhyeśvarī, eine Erfindung des tantrischen Śivaismus, war offenbar auch von buddhistischen Tantrikern anerkannt worden, die sie zunächst in geheimen Riten verehrten, und wie Mañjuśrī war die Göttin schließlich so wichtig, daß die Legende auch sie in den Bericht von der Entstehung des Kathmandu-Tals eingebaut hat. Während die hinduistische Fassung der Vaṃśāvalīs um Paśupatinātha kreist, der der Anfang ist und das Ende der Dinge, und auf die Beschreibung Paśupatis die Sage von Dakṣa (-Prajāpati) und Satī (Guhyadevī, Guhyeśvarī) nachfolgen läßt, stehen im Mittelpunkt der buddhistischen Version das uranfängliche Licht von Svayambhū, der Nāgahrada und Mañjuśrī. Nachdem Mañjuśrī seine Großtat vollbracht und die Wasser freigelegt hat, erscheint ihm die Göttin Guhyeśvarī in der Form *viśvarūpas*, worauf Mañjuśrī an derselben Stätte den Svayambhū-Stūpa errichtet. Guhyeśvarī wird somit mit der Buddha-Essenz, dem *jyotīrūpa* oder *viśvarūpa* von Svayambhū verbunden, ein klares Zeichen dafür, in welch hohem Grad ihre Gestalt im Buddhismus Fuß gefaßt hat.

Dem gemeinen Mann war Guhyeśvarī eine Manifestation der großen erlösenden Mutter, der Erretterin ohnegleichen, die in den verschiedenen Formen der Durgā oder Tārā[63]) ein weibliches Gegenstück des Lokeśvara (-Paśupatinātha)-Avalokiteśvara bildet. Eine späte Nevārī-Hymne[64]) beschreibt sie als die schaurige Guhyakālī, die in wildem Tanz und umgeben von Bhūtas, Yoginīs und Vetālas, den übelgesinnten Daitya[65]) vernichtet. Ihr Kult ist aufs deutlichste mit dem Kult der Talejumāju, der Patronin des Königtums und des Thrones, verknüpft. Gleich wie die Gunst der Kumārī, die als die „keusche Jungfrau" eine zweite, den König und das Herrschertum beschützende Form der höchsten Devī repräsentiert, haben nepalesische Rājas und Rāṇas immer wieder den Segen der „Herrin des *guhya*" gesucht. Auf die Identifikation von Guhyeśvarī und Taleju weist u.a. die Tatsache hin, daß am Vorabend der Guhyeśvarīyātrā, also einmal im Jahr, ein die Göttin symbolisierender, glückbringender Krug (*kalaśa*) von seinem gewöhnlichen Standort, dem Taleju-Schrein in Kathmandu, nach dem Guhyeśvarī-Tempel gebracht wird. Wir dürfen vermuten, daß die Göttin aus Ostindien stammt. Ihre tantrische, nicht sehr früh belegte Erscheinung wird schon

---

[62]) Über eine Parallele zu diesem Kult in Assam siehe J. Gonda, Die Religionen Indiens, Bd. II, Stuttgart 1963, p. 211 und dort angegebene Literatur.

[63]) Prasannatārā, Ekajaṭā, Ugratārā, Vidyujjvālākarālī usw.

[64]) Vgl. Lienhard, Nr. 18.

[65]) D.i. Asura Mahiṣa.

zu Anfang sehr rasch vom hinduistischen Volksteil in Nepal akzeptiert worden sein, doch bewirkten, wie es scheint, Tantrismus und ähnliche Kräfte, daß Guhyeśvarī auch den Buddhisten nicht lange fremd bleiben sollte. Wie im Falle der Jayavāgīśvarī werden blutige Opfer auch in ihrem Heiligtum dargebracht, doch nicht der Guhyeśvarī selbst, sondern Bhairava, dessen Standbild im Tempelhof aufgestellt ist.

Dem Manifestationsbereich der Satī-Guhyeśvarī muß auch die Svasthānī Parameśvarī hinzugezählt werden. Wie die Guhyeśvarī genießt auch Svasthānī universale Verehrung. Die Svasthānī(parameśvarī)vratakathā, an deren Anfang die Legende von Dakṣa-Prajāpati und Satī gestellt ist, ist eine der populärsten Vratakathās auf Nevārī. Nach Aussage der Kolophone liegen diesem Text das Liṅga- und das Skandapurāṇa zugrunde. Svasthānī wird darin als die große, alle Wünsche gewährende, von allen Sünden — selbst denen der Tötung von Brahmanen, Kindern, Frauen und Kühen — befreiende Göttin gewürdigt, und es verdient der Erwähnung, daß Manuskripte dieses Textes auch von Vajrācāryas kopiert worden sind[66]).

Wie schon früher erwähnt, macht sich im nepalesischen Religionssynkretismus eine monotheistische Tendenz auch bei weiblichen Göttergestalten bemerkbar. Das Bestreben, verschiedene populäre Göttinnen mit Durgā und — weniger deutlich — Tārā zu assoziieren, war, wenn auch nicht allein von den Massen veranlaßt, so doch stark vom Volk unterstützt. Ich halte für wahrscheinlich, daß auch die Vajrayoginī und die Vajravārāhī[67]) in der volklichen Vorstellungswelt immer mehr als Varianten der höchsten Erretterin, der höchsten Mutter aufgefaßt wurden. Das große Heiligtum der Vajrayoginī ist der Tempel zu Sāṃkhu. Die Göttin wird dort weder in ihrer roten oder gelben Gestalt, noch in ihrer Manifestation ohne Kopf, sondern als Ugratārā verbildlicht.

Umgekehrt tritt im Volkskult der Ajimās, der „(Groß)mütter", die Erscheinung zutage, daß einheimische Bezeichnungen kraft hinduistischer Überlagerung stark zurückgedrängt werden und zahlreiche Ajimās, indem sie Sanskrit-Namen erhalten, als Varianten der Kālī-Durgā oder einer Mātṛkā dem śivaitischen Mutterkult einverleibt werden. So wird die Lumari Ajimā, die „alte Mutter Goldkuchen", auch unter dem Namen Bhadrakālī, die Luṭī Ajimā unter dem der Indrāṇī verehrt. Es kann kein Zweifel bestehen, daß die Wurzeln auch dieser Verschmelzung im tantrischen und śāktischen Śivaismus erblickt werden müssen.

Wie die Vārāhī und die eben genannte Indrāṇī gehört auch die Kaumārī, gewöhnlich Kumārī genannt, dem Kreis der hinduistischen Aṣṭamātṛkās an. Der Volksmund sieht den Stifter ihres Kults in König Jayaprakāśa Malla (1736–1768) von Kathmandu, doch ist zu vermuten,

---

[66]) Siehe Hs.or. 4283 und 4344 der orientalischen Handschriften der Staatsbibliothek der Stiftung Preußischer Kulturbesitz in Berlin.

[67]) Zur Stellung der beiden Gestalten im tantrischen Buddhismus vgl. u.a. Bhattacharyya, p. 217ff. und p. 247ff. und Shashi Bhushan Dasgupta, An Introduction to Tantric Buddhism, Berkeley and London 1974, p. 73 und 88.

daß Jayaprakāśa, den mehrere Sagen[68]) in Zusammenhang mit Kumārī, Taleju und Guhyeśvarī bringen, die Kumārī-Verehrung nur wiederbelebt und etwa als eine Erneuerung, wohl nachdem der König in schwerer Stunde Leben und Reich durch die Macht der Kumārī beschützt sah[69]), die Kumārīyātrā von Kathmandu eingeführt hat. Jayaprakāśa Mallas Regierungszeit liegt zu spät, um im Ernst mit der Einstiftung eines derart bedeutsamen, im Bewußtsein des Volkes so tief verwurzelten Kults verbunden zu werden[70]). In der Tat wird das sehr viel höhere Alter der Kumārī-Riten durch zwei Texte bestätigt, die Kumārīpūjā und das Kumārīpūjāvidhāna, die beide der Zeit Ananta Mallas (1274–1310) entstammen und das Datum 400 (= 1280 n.Chr.) bzw. 406 (= 1285 n.Chr.) der nepalesischen Zeitrechnung tragen[71]). Auf eine noch frühere Zeit, die Jahrtausendwende, weisen zwei Aussagen der Vaṃśāvalīs, die freilich unverbürgt sind: Bereits König Guṇakāmadeva (940–1008) soll während der Indrayātrā Kumārī-Bilder aufgestellt haben[72], während schon Lakṣmīkāmadeva (1018–1039) die Kumārī-Verehrung in der heute üblichen Form, der Anbetung eines *bandya*-Mädchens, der Tochter eines buddhistischen Nevar-Priesters, ausgeführt hat[73]). Wie dem immer auch sei, so ist durchaus wahrscheinlich, daß die Anfänge ihres Kults in den hierdurch gegebenen zeitlichen Rahmen, d.h. die religiös so produktive Epoche kurz nach der Wende des ersten Jahrtausends gesetzt werden können. Die nepalesische Kumārī entstammt dem Śivaismus tantrischer Prägung, doch fällt bei ihr auf, daß ihre Riten sowohl von Brahmanen als auch Vajrācāryas ausgeführt werden können. Wie zahlreiche den Nevars besonders heilige Tempel, so die Schreine der Brahmāṇī, der Indrāṇī oder der Mahālakṣmī, bewei-

---

[68]) Es existieren mindestens vier. Zur vermutlich geläufigsten Legende s. Regmi, Medieval Nepal. A History of the Three Kingdoms 1520 A.D. to 1768 A.D., Part II, Calcutta 1966 (= Regmi II), p. 602. Zwei weitere Sagen gibt Anderson, p. 132 wieder, eine davon auch D. Snellgrove 1957, p. 118.

[69]) Vgl. B. J. Hasrat, p. 87.

[70]) Snellgrove 1957 sieht dagegen den Ursprung der Kumārī-Verehrung in genau der Legende, die er p. 118 erzählt: Die Tochter eines *bandya* glaubt sich von der Göttin besessen und wird vom König aus Kathmandu verwiesen, doch annuliert Jayaprakāśa die Verbannung des Mädchens, als eine der Königinnen von Krämpfen heimgesucht wird, und stiftet ihm zu Ehren die alljährliche Yātrā. Snellgrove überschätzt den Wert dieser Sage, wenn er meint, daß die Kumārī uns zeige, in wie willkürlicher Weise ein Götterkult in Nepal entstehe. Ich halte dafür, daß die Legende bestenfalls die oben erwähnte Erneuerung des Kultes bestätigt und darüber hinaus, wie es scheint, auch die Praxis rechtfertigen will, welche darin besteht, daß man die menschliche Manifestation der Kumārī in einem noch nicht pubertätsreifen Mädchen aus einem Nevar-*vihāra* erkennt. Dasselbe gilt von der Sage, welche D. R. Regmi II, p. 602 berichtet: Jayaprakāśa verführt ein noch nicht geschlechtsreifes Mädchen und konsolidiert, nachdem ihm die Göttin im Traume erschienen, die Yātrā.

[71]) Siehe Petech, p. 95 und 97.

[72]) Indrayātrā, Kumārīyātrā und Bhairavayātrā sind bekanntlich miteinander vermengt.

[73]) Siehe Wright, p. 91ff.

sen, waren auch andere Mātṛkās dem Vajrayāna teils nahegerückt, teils als Śaktis ihm einverleibt worden. Ein fruchtbarer Nährboden für ihr Festwachsen im Herzen des Volks war weiterhin dadurch gegeben, daß, wie schon oben erwähnt, die Mātṛkās mit den Ajimās identifiziert werden konnten und diese nicht selten als die wichtigsten Gottheiten jedes Hauses aufgefaßt wurden.

Der besondere Erfolg und die so vorgeschobene Stellung, die der Kumārī zufallen sollte, ist auch hier wieder mehrfach bedingt. Einerseits bahnte bereits die śivaitische Schau[74]), die in Kumārī die göttliche Mutter (Ambikā, Durgā, Gaurī, Kālī, Pārvatī, Umā usw.) in Gestalt der Jungfrau (*kumārī*) erblickte, den Weg zur buddhistischen Perspektive, nach der die Kumārī mit Tārā gleichgesetzt wurde[75]). Andererseits war die Kumārī bei den Nevars dadurch verankert, daß die wichtigsten Klöster (*vihāra*), zu Beginn vielleicht alle, eine ursprünglich wohl tantrische Praxis fortgesetzt haben, die heute als die Institution der „lebenden Göttin" bekannt ist: Ein Nevar-Mädchen zwischen den Kindheitsjahren und der beginnenden Pubertät[76]) verkörpert die Kumārī jedes einzelnen Klosters. Reste tantrischer Riten sind noch heute in der Wahl der Kumārī bewahrt, die u.a. daran erkannt wird, daß die kleine Adeptin, die strengen Prüfungen ausgesetzt wird, ohne Angst über Schädel von eben geschlachteten Tieren hinwegschreiten kann[77]).

Es ist das Resultat günstiger Umstände und des Zusammenwirkens der eben genannten Ideen, daß die Kumārī-Verehrung gerade im Nepal-Tal blühte und eben dort festen Fuß fassen konnte. Doch wäre verfehlt, die Institution der Kumārī als ein einmalig nepalesisches Phänomen zu betrachten. Wie die Kumārī selbst ist die Sitte, daß ein reines Mädchen die Göttin verkörpert, von spät-śivaitischer Herkunft. Auch in der hinduistischen Durgā-Pūjā konnte die Göttin, in diesem Fall die (Durgā-)Rudrāṇī, durch ein elfjähriges Mädchen, das noch nicht menstruiert hat, dargestellt werden[78]). Es ist offenbar, daß sich die Kumārīyātrā in Nepal verselbständigt hat und, herausgelöst

---

[74]) Während Hemacandra in seiner Liste von insgesamt zweiunddreißig Namen von Śivas Gemahlin auch die Kumārī mitaufführt (Abhidhānacintāmaṇi 203), fehlt diese Bezeichnung im Amarakośa (I, 36–38).

[75]) Beachtet sei, daß Tārā auch in der Gruppe der tantrischen Daśa-Mahāvidyās, der zehn Transformationen der großen Göttin (d.i. Kālī, T., Ṣoḍaśī, Bhuvaneśvarī, Bhairavī, Chinnamastā, Dhūmavatī, Baglā, Mātaṅgī, Kamalātmikā) figuriert, deren Kult in Bengalen noch bis ins letzte Jahrhundert sehr populär war. Vgl. Ph. Rawson, Tantra. The Indian Cult of Exstasy, London 1973, Abbildung 17.

[76]) Jede Kumārī wird nach der ersten Menstruation durch ein jüngeres Mädchen ersetzt, das oft bloß drei oder vier Jahre alt ist.

[77]) Vgl. Anderson, p. 132f.

[78]) Zur Bedeutung von *rudrāṇī* als ein solches, die Durgā darstellendes Mädchen s. PW und Monier-Williams, Dict., sub verbo. Letzterer gibt als Quelle L(exicographers) an. Auf den Kumārī-Kult indischer Śivaiten (Bhairavas) verweist der Jaina-Autor Guṇacandragaṇi im 4. Buch seines Pāsanānacariya (Skt. Pārśvanāthacarita) aus dem Jahre 1111 n.Chr. Siehe Jagadīścandra Jain, *Prākṛt Sāhitya kā itihās*, Vārāṇasī 1961 (= Vidyābhavan Rāṣṭrabhāṣā Granthamālā 42), p. 549.

aus dem Durgā-Fest[79]), in einen religiös und sozial veränderten Kontext hineingestellt wurde. Ihre Verknüpfung mit dem engeren śivaitischen Götterkomplex erhellt aber daraus, daß eine wichtige Rolle in der Kumārīyātrā auch den Göttern Gaṇeśa und Bhairava zukommt, welche beide als Beschützer der Göttin fungieren und — wie die Kumārī — auf je einem Wagen plaziert sind.

Wie Matsyendranātha ist die Kumārī eine Gottheit der Masse, die, bei Gurkhas und Nevars gleich populär und in der Volksreligion auch als Ajimā interpretierbar, alle konfessionellen Beschränkungen weit überragt. Es ist bemerkenswert, daß ihrer Erscheinung, einer ursprünglich einfachen Übertragung, buddhistische Komponenten zwar eigentlich fehlen, doch ist gleichwohl kaum zu bestreiten, daß die lebhafte Pflege ihres Kults in den Nevar-Gemeinden der Kumārī eine dennoch so stark buddhistische Prägung aufdrücken konnte, daß die göttliche Jungfrau von zahlreichen Nevars als ihr eigenes Gut und somit als buddhistisch aufgefaßt wird. Es hängt nicht mit Jayaprakāśa zusammen, sondern der Weiterentwicklung vajrayānistischer Rituale, die späterhin freilich erstarrt sind, daß die Inkarnation der Kumārī noch jetzt aus dem Kreise der Bandyas, d.h., genauer, der Śākyabhikṣus[80]), einer Priesterkaste der Nevars, ausgesucht wird[81]).

Die Stellung der Kumārī innerhalb des nepalesischen Religionssynkretismus ist also insofern interessant, als ihre Wesenheit nicht wie Matsyendranātha-Lokeśvara-Lokanātha als eine vielfältig überschichtete, sehr komplexe Erscheinung hervortritt, sondern eine Übertragung darstellt, der, ohne Verlust oder Veränderung ihrer śivaitischen Züge, gerade aufgrund ihrer engen Verbindung mit den Wohngemeinschaften der *vihāras*, der Nachkommenschaft der verheirateten Mönche, eine besondere Durchschlagskraft zukam. Dazu trat als ein Zweites, daß ihre Gestalt noch weiter erhöht worden war, als neben den Kumārīs der Klöster die alle überragende Königs-Kumārī von Kathmandu eingesetzt wurde. Da die Gurkha-Eroberung der nepalesischen Hauptstadt genau zum Zeitpunkt der Kumārī-(und der Indra-)Yātrā erfolgt war, fällt diese Einrichtung in die Zeit vor den Śāhs[82]). Es ist, wie oben bemerkt, durchaus glaublich, daß es König Jayaprakāśa Malla war, der den Kult, wenn nicht etabliert, so doch wiederbelebt und der Königs-Kumārī einen eigenen Wohnsitz ganz nahe beim Königspalast, das Kumārīcheṁ[83]), eingeräumt hat. Pṛthivī Nārāyaṇa übernahm die Institution

---

[79]) Die Indra- und die Kumārīyātrā werden Mitte September gefeiert, die Durgā-Pūjā Ende September oder Anfang Oktober. In Bhatgaon ist die Kumārīyātrā aber noch heute sehr eng mit der Durgāpūjā verbunden.

[80]) Sie werden auch Banras genannt und sind heute meist Gold- oder Silberschmiede. Bezüglich ihres Ranges im Kastensystem siehe Petech, p. 186.

[81]) Beachtenswert ist, daß auch die Wahl der zwei Knaben, die in der Yātrā Gaṇeśa und Bhairava repräsentieren, in ganz ähnlicher Weise durchgeführt wird.

[82]) Zum Zweck klarerer Unterscheidung von den Mallas erscheint es mir praktisch, hier die Gurkha-Herrscher, ihrem Titel entsprechend, als Śāhs zu bezeichnen.

[83]) Auch Kumārībāhāla oder °bāhāra, mod. °bāhā.

schon vom Tag seines Überfalls an, und noch in jüngster Zeit ist die Staats- oder Königs-Kumārī, nicht aber die jeweilige Kumārī der einzelnen Klöster, aufs engste mit dem Herrscherhaus Nepals verbunden. Während des alljährlich stattfindenden Festzugs drückt die Kumārī eine *ṭīkā* auf die Stirne des Königs und erneuert kraft dieser Handlung ihren für König und Königtum unentbehrlichen Segen[84]).

Durch diese offizielle Funktion fand die Kumārī-Verehrung eine Wiederbefestigung innerhalb des Hinduismus, die sich um so stärker auswirken mußte, als sie von einem der wichtigsten hinduistischen Zentren in Nepal, dem Herrscherhaus, ausging. Sie verlieh der Kumārī nicht nur allnepalesische, sondern nationale Bedeutung, die sich gut in den immer stärkeren Hinduisierungsprozeß des Reiches eingefügt hat. Diese nationale Erhöhung ist allerdings nicht als Rückübertragung der in buddhistischer Lebensform so sehr heimisch gewordenen Göttin zu sehen. Vielmehr ist zu berücksichtigen, daß die Kumārī ihr śivaitisches Kleid nie abgelegt hat und sie auch bei den Hindus dauernd bedeutungsvoll blieb. Zahlreiche Inschriften und Handschriftenkolophone bezeichnen den Herrscher über Nepal als König von Paśupatis[85]) und, seit der Zeit Jayasthiti Mallas[86]), als König von Paśupatis und Māneśvarīs Gnaden[87]). Der Name Māneśvarī, während der Thākurī-Herrschaft erst noch sporadisch gebraucht[88]), läßt sich leicht als Variante von Caṇḍeśvarī deuten. Es überrascht somit kaum, daß sowohl Kumārī als auch Guhyeśvarī, die ja beide eine ungemein populäre Form der Pārvatī-Durgā-Caṇḍeśvarī[89]) sind, in den engeren Manifestationsbereich auch der höchsten staatsbeschützenden Göttin aufsteigen konnten.

Mit derselben Hausgöttin (*kuladevatā*) des Malla-Hofs wird die Tulajā Bhavānī oder Tulajā identifiziert, deren Kult auch in Tirhut (Mithila) geblüht hat und von dort im Winter 1324/25, als das Heer des Ghiyās ud-dīn Tughluq die Hauptstadt Simraongarh bedrohte, durch Harisiṃhadeva, einen König südindischer Herkunft, nach Nepal eingeführt wurde. Möglicherweise entstammt diese Göttin, eine Form der Durgā,

[84]) Auf die Möglichkeit, daß dieser hohe staatsbeschirmende Rang der Kumārī und der Taleju (vgl. weiter unten) erst von den Śāhs zugeteilt wurde, verweist mich Herr Prof. B. Kölver: Aus dem Bedürfnis, einen verstärkten, auch spirituellen Beweis ihres Status und Nachfolgerechts zu erbringen, übernehmen die Śāhs die beiden Göttinnen gänzlich, interpretieren deren Stellung aber insofern neu, als sie die einstige *kuladevatā*, das Familienattribut der Besiegten, nun auf das äußerste steigern und in ein Attribut des Staatsganzen, des Königtums und des Reiches, verwandeln.

[85]) *bhagavat-paśupati-bhaṭṭārakapādānugṛhīta*, s. R. Gnoli, Nepalese Inscriptions in Gupta Characters, Part I, Text, Serie Orientale Roma X, Materials for the Study of Nepalese History and Culture 2, Rom 1956, p. 68, 70f., 73f., 78 (Jiṣṇugupta); 81, 83 (Viṣṇugupta); 88, 90, 92, 99 (Narendradeva); 107, 109 (Śivadeva).

[86]) Zum ersten Mal 1354 erwähnt; siehe Petech, p. 123.

[87]) *śrīśrī-paśupati-caraṇāravindasevitaśrī-māneśvarī-varalabdhapratāpa-śrīśrī-jayasthitirāja*; s. Petech, p. 132.

[88]) Vgl. Petech, p. 173f.

[89]) Es beleuchtet die Stellung der Caṇḍeśvarī im allnepalesischen Glauben, wenn ein so ausgeprägt buddhistisches Werk wie der Vessantara-Fries im Indischen

überhaupt dem Dekkhan[90]), doch charakterisiert ihre Stellung in Nepal, daß in ihren Aspekten, die sowohl huldvoll sind als auch Schrecken einjagen, die śivaitischen und die buddhistischen Vorstellungsformen direkt konvergieren. Tulajā ist Pārvatī, Bhavānī oder Durgā, ist aber auch Tārā, Ugratārā, Nīlasarasvatī oder Ekajaṭā. Wiederum ist die Vieldeutigkeit śivaitisch, ja größtenteils śivaitisch-tantristisch begründet. Man nennt sie Ambikā, „(liebe) Mutter“, oder noch häufiger Talejumāju, „Mutter Taleju“, eine Bezeichnung, die, rein lautlich gesehen, mit Tulajā gut übereinstimmt. Nähere Prüfung erweist allerdings, daß die Gleichung *tulajā* = *taleju*[91]) eine vermutlich volksetymologische Gleichsetzung darstellt, da sich indisches *tulajā* nur mit Schwierigkeit in Nev. *taleju* umsetzen läßt. Gleich wie *māju*, das Nevārī-Beiwort der Göttin, aus *mā* und *ju*, d.h. Nomen und honorifischer Endung besteht, kann auch *taleju*, wenn aus der Sprachstruktur der Nevārī beurteilt, in *tale*, den eigentlichen Namen, und *ju*, das Honorificum, aufgelöst werden, eine Analyse, die insofern weiteste Perspektiven erschließt, als *tale/tare* eine unmittelbare Nevārī-Variante für Tārā ergibt und *tale* darüberhinaus, unter Berücksichtigung der vorhin genannten südindischen Relationen[92]), mit einem im Dravidischen vielverwendeten Ausdruck für Mutter, nämlich Telugu *tal(l)i*, Tamil *taḷḷai* u.a.m.[93]), in Verbindung gebracht werden kann.

Für die bedeutendsten Gottheiten des nepalesischen Pantheons gilt, daß sie ihren gesicherten Platz in dem neuen System auf dem Weg einer Umdeutung fanden; sie wurden als Emanationen anderer Götter erachtet oder konstituierten sich dadurch aufs Neue, daß sie teils identifiziert, teils, mit partiell neuem Inhalt erfüllt, in komplizierten Prozessen umgeformt wurden. Einer ganzen Reihe hinduistischer Übertragungen blieb jedoch weiter die Stellung erhalten, die ihnen von Anfang an zuerkannt war. Ihre Eingliederung war nicht fest, und wurde ihr Wesen auch manchmal verändert, so kam diesen Göttern doch ein- und dieselbe Aufgabe zu: die Buddhas und Bodhisattvas zu ehren[94]) und als Hüter von Lehre und

Museum zu Berlin (84 Bilder mit ebensovielen, von einem Vajrācārya verfaßten Nevārī-Inskriptionen) im Kolophon die *śrī-Caṇḍeśvarīdevī* anruft.

[90]) Ein Tempel der Ambā Bhavānī soll in Tulajāpura bei Hyderabad in Andhra Pradesh bewahrt sein; s. D. R. Regmi II, p. 593.

[91]) Vgl. R. L. Turner, Nepali Dict., s.v.

[92]) Schon der Gründer des Königtums Mithila, Nānyadeva (Thronbesteigung 1097), der Nepal nie wirklich beherrscht, aber sicherlich invadiert hat, war ein Karnatak (*karṇāṭakulabhūṣaṇa*). Hierzu und zur Frage des Cālukya-Anspruchs politischer Oberhoheit über Nepal s. S. Lévi, Le Népal. Étude historique d'un royaume hindou, Paris 1905–1908, Bd. II, p. 198ff. und Petech, p. 51f.; weitere Literatur ibid., p. 52, A. 1.

[93]) Siehe Burrow-Emeneau, A Dravidian Etymological Dict., Nr. 2560. Vgl. auch Petech, p. 111, A. 3 (Kolophon zum *Jātisaṃgraha*, India Office Libr., Hodgson 37/6): *karṇātasaṃjñanagarād[d] harisiṃhadevo nepāladeśam anayat talejumājum* (im MS fälschlich: *sajālejūmajū*).

[94]) Vgl. Lienhard, Nr. 1, ein Lied, das sehr anschaulich schildert, wie Brahmā, Sarasvatī, Kubera, Vāyu, Varuṇa und andere hinduistische Götter dem Tathāgata ihre Dienste erweisen.

Tempel, Gemeinde und Kloster, ja sogar König und Königspalast zu fungieren. Diese hütende Macht ist auch in Kumārī(-Taleju-Guhyeśvarī) noch erhalten, die, wie wiederholt bemerkt worden ist, dem König Erfolg und Reichtum verspricht, doch stellen die Schutzgottheiten par excellence die śivaitischen Götter Gaṇeśa, Mahākāla und Bhairava dar, die, ohne Rücksicht auf Herkunft, Kaste oder Glauben, ganz allgemein anerkannt werden. Ihre Übernahme in den Buddhismus war insoweit von Gewicht als buddhistische Inkorporierung auch größere Gültigkeit bei den Nevars bedeutet.

Auf eine ausführlichere Darstellung der genannten und ihnen verwandter Protektor-Gottheiten sei hier verzichtet, doch mögen im folgenden ein paar Einzelheiten vermerkt sein. Die Verehrung Gaṇeśas ist so stark verbreitet, daß jedes Stadtviertel (*tol*, *thāna*) einen Schrein für Vināyaka (> mod. Nev. Binā) hat und man den Gott auch als "Gott (jeder) Örtlichkeit", *thānadeo*, bezeichnet. Ein undatierter buddhistischer Text, das Gaṇapatihṛdaya, enthält Mantras, die die Gunst Gaṇeśas erzielen, und wie die Einleitung dieses Textes wahrhaben will, soll sogar Buddha selbst, in einer Mönchsversammlung zu Rājagṛha, dem Ānanda den Gebrauch dieser Formeln ans Herz gelegt haben [95]). Die ersten paar Strophen eines *sihnājyā*-Lieds [96]), welche Regen erbitten, beschwören die Nāginī des Teiches Tavadha, die Berg- und Muttergöttinnen Dudhana, Phulaco und Dhelāco, doch zugleich auch Gaṇeśa [97]), und ein Nevārī-Stotra datiert 1829 bzw. 1838 beschreibt Gaṇapati als ein Tigerfell und Nāga-Schmuckstücke tragend und weiter als den, „der zuerst die Pūjā empfängt" [98]). In der Kumārīyātrā erscheinen, wie schon oben erwähnt worden ist, Gaṇeśa und Bhairava als Beschützer der Göttin, und sowohl Gaṇeśa als auch M a h ā k ā l a, der auf Tibetisch *mgon.po*, „Beschützer" (Skt. *nātha*), genannt wird und den das nepalesische Mahākāladhyāna [99]), ein Stotra, bezeichnenderweise auch *buddhaśāsanarakṣaka* nennt, hüten Türen und Tore buddhistischer Klöster. Ein Zug, der Gaṇapati seinem indisch-hinduistischen Vorbild, einer stets gütigen, wohlgesonnenen Gottheit, entrückt und wie so vieles aus dem Tantrismus erklärt werden kann, ist die Tatsache, daß der elephantenköpfige Gott, wie derselbe in Nepal (und Tibet [100])) verehrt wird, ähnlich wie Durgā oder Śiva eine Bipolarität der Aspekte besitzt: er beseitigt die Hindernisse, erscheint andererseits aber auch als ein Hindernisbringer. Auch H a n u m a t figuriert als Beschützer, und zwar, als der treue Diener als welcher er

---

95) Siehe M i t r a, p. 88: *yaḥ kaścit kulaputra ānanda imāni gaṇapatihṛdayāni dhārayiṣyati vācayiṣyati paryyavāpsyanti te pravarttayiṣyanti tasya sarvvāṇi kāryyāṇi siddhāni bhaviṣyanti.*

96) Zu *sihnājyā* s. oben S. 156.

97) Siehe L i e n h a r d, Nr. 92, R, 1–3.

98) Siehe L i e n h a r d, Nr. 22: *nāga-tisā bāghambar ṅasā . . . pūjā hnāpā kāla.*

99) Siehe Hs. or. 4286 der orientalischen Handschriften der Staatsbibliothek der Stiftung Preußischer Kulturbesitz in Berlin.

100) Vgl. H. H o f f m a n n, Symbolik der tibetischen Religionen und des Schamanismus, Stuttgart 1967, p. 26f.

König Rāma im Epos zugetan ist, insbesondere in seiner Funktion als Hüter des Königspalastes[101]).

Interessanter und wichtiger als Hanumat ist eine zweite Erscheinung, die gleichfalls dem Epos entstammt: Bhīmasena. Wie der Yogin Matsyendranātha wurde Bhīmasena, der zweite der fünf Pāṇḍava-Brüder, vergöttlicht. Das Mahābhārata zeichnet ihn als den gefürchteten Krieger und den Beschützer der Draupadī, der gemeinsamen Pāṇḍava-Gattin: Bhīmasena rächt die Schandtat Duḥśāsanas an Draupadī und tötet Duḥśāsana. Von diesem epischen Hintergrund aus beurteilt, ist durchaus verständlich, daß Bhīmasena in Nepal als Protektor gerade der Ehe verehrt wird[102]). Interessanterweise schöpft diese Rolle das Bild Bhīmasenas aber keineswegs aus. Synkretistische Verflechtungen führten dazu, daß Gott Bhīmasena einerseits auch mit Bhairava(-Mahākāla) assoziiert wird, andererseits auch als Gott der Kaufleute (und folglich Beschützer besonders der Kaufmannsehe) anerkannt wird. Ich halte für möglich, daß die Verknüpfung mit Bhairava auf die sprachliche Gleichsetzung Bhīma(sena)s mit Bhairava, beide Derivate von *bhī-*, zurückgeführt werden kann. Licht auf den śivaitisch-tantrischen Aspekt Gott Bhīmasenas, dessen Idol im Kathmandu-Tempel, dem bekannten Bhīmasenathāna, zusammen mit Draupadī und Arjuna dargestellt wird, wirft das Faktum, daß Bhīmasena an dem Tag, welcher der Bhīmasena-*Ekādaśī*[103]) folgt, mit Huldigungsgaben, die auch Bhairava dargebracht werden, nämlich dem Blut von Büffeln, Ziegen usw. beschwichtigt wird[104]), während man Arjuna durch unblutige Opfer wie Blumen, Früchte, Süßigkeiten oder Tücher verehrt[105]). Pratāpa Malla (1641–1674) gibt Bhīmasena das Epithet Śivarūpa[106]). Sein Kult ist in Nepal seit etwa 1550 bestätigt, ist aber zweifellos älter. Der Ursprung ist ungewiß, wird letzten Endes aber wohl in der Gegend von Delhi und des nördlichen und nordöstlichen Uttar Pradesh[107]), von wo die Bhīma-Verehrung auch

---

[101]) Sehr schön illustriert diese Funktion die bekannte Hanumat-Statue vor dem Eingang zum alten Königspalast von Kathmandu.

[102]) Zur Gestalt Bhīmasenas in der Nevārī-Volksdichtung siehe Lienhard, Introd., p. 24f. und ibid. die Lieder Nr. 20, 21, 50, 61 und 87.

[103]) An sich ist jede *Ekādaśī* Fasttag. Auch die Bhīmasena-*Ekādaśī*, die in die helle Monatshälfte von Ende Januar oder Anfang Februar fällt, wird ganz allgemein, doch besonders von Kaufleuten, observiert.

[104]) Die Darstellungen Bhīmasenas bewahren völlig das heldische, aus dem Epos stammende Bild. Sein stämmiger Körper erscheint in heroischer, wie zum Kampf ausfallender Haltung, seine Rechte schwingt die Keule.

[105]) Siehe Anderson, p. 237.

[106]) Siehe Regmi II, p. 612.

[107]) Im Gebiet von Kedarkhand-Garhwal stellen die fünf Pāṇḍava-Brüder die am meisten verehrten Gottheiten dar. Jedes einzelne Dorf verfügt über einen eigenen Pāṇḍava-Schrein, in dem man auch Draupadī huldigt und auf einem Altar die Waffen der epischen Helden, nämlich hölzerne Keulen, Bogen, Eisenstangen und einen *triśūla* zur Schau stellt. Siehe G. D. Berreman, Hindus of the Himalayas, Bombay 1963, Appendix I, p. 381ff. Gewisse Aufschlüsse über die Verbreitung der Bhīmasena-Verehrung gäbe u.a. die Kartierung einzelner Ortsnamen wie Bhimpedi in Nepal, Bhimsen in Uttar Pradesh oder Bhimbar in Jammu und

nach Gurkha und von dort ins Kathmandu-Tal ausstrahlen konnte, gesucht werden müssen[108]).

Obwohl hinduistischer Herkunft, erfreut sich Bhīmasena universaler Beliebtheit. Später als das śivaitische Element floß in das Wesen des Gottes jene zweite synkretistische Komponente, die Bhīmasena zum Gott der Kaufleute macht, und zwar insbesonders jener, die — zum größten Teil Nevars — Handel mit Tibet betrieben. Ich habe bereits anderenorts die Vermutung geäußert[109]), daß die Zuschreibung dieser Funktion auf einer volkstümlichen Kontamination Bhīmasenas mit Bhīmamalla (oder Bhīmalla), dem bekannten Minister (*kāji*) König Lakṣmīnarasiṃha Mallas (Thronbesteigung 1631), des Vaters Pratāpa Mallas, basiert. Wie verläßliche Quellen erweisen, war Bhīmamalla ein Diplomat von Format, der ein Handelsabkommen mit Tibet erzielt hat, daneben aber auch selbst als ein kluger und erfolgreicher Kaufherr gewirkt hat, der in Lhasa und an anderen Orten Tibets eine Vielzahl von Umschlageplätzen, insgesamt zweiunddreißig Geschäfte (*koṭhi*), etabliert haben soll[110]). Die späten Vaṃśāvalīs beziehen Bhīmasena sogar in die Sagen vom Ursprung des Kathmandu-Tals ein[111]). Diese Nachkonstruktion, die den Gott in den Rang eines der ersten Kulturbringer hebt, hat geringe Bedeutung, zeigt aber immerhin, eine wie wohl unterbaute und gesicherte Stellung Bhīmasena im Volksglauben zuerkannt wurde.

Kashmir. Nach W. Crooke, Religion and Folklore of Northern India, Reprint New Delhi o.J., spielt Bhīma(sena) die Rolle des "*chief rain-god in the Central Provinces. Gonds celebrate a festival in his honour at the close of the monsoon, when two poles are erected and boys with the aid of a rope climb to the top and slide down—possibly a magical device to promote the sprinkling of the crops and the fall of the rain*" (p. 70).

[108]) Es ist erstaunlich, daß ein Kult Bhīmasenas auch auf Java belegt werden kann; s. W. F. Stutterheim, Studies in Indonesian Archaeology, Den Haag 1956, p. 107ff. (späte Majapahit-Periode). Die Verehrung Bhīma(sena)s war dort äußerst lebendig, doch verdient Beachtung, daß die indonesische Mythe von Bhīma(sena) drei verschiedene Versionen umfaßt: die Bhīmaruci-, die Devaruci- und die Navaruci-Fassung. Auch wurde, wie das Bhīmastava verrät, Bhīma(sena) mit Vajrasattva identifiziert. An weiterer Literatur über Bhīmasena in Indonesien sei hier vermerkt: R. Goris, Storm-kind en Geestes Zoon, in: Djåwå VII (1927), p. 110ff.; Prijohoetomo, Nawaruci. Inleiding, Middel-Javaansche prozatekst, vertaling, vergeleken met de Bimasoetji in Oud-Javaansch metrum, Groningen-Den Haag-Batavia 1934 (Diss.); W. F. Stutterheim, Een Oud-Javaansche Bhīma-cultus, in: Djåwå XV (1935), p. 37ff.; Poerbatjaraka, Dewaroetji, in: Djåwå XX (1940), p. 7ff.; F. D. K. Bosch, The Bhīmastava, in: India Antiqua (= Festschrift J. Ph. Vogel), Leiden 1947, p. 57ff.; K. W. Lim, Studies in later Buddhist iconography, Bijdragen tot de Taal-, Land- en Volkenkunde, deel 120 (1964), p. 327ff.; T. Goudriaan and C. Hooykaas, Stuti and Stava (Bauddha, Śaiva and Vaiṣṇava) of Balinese brahman priests, Amsterdam-London 1971 (Freundliche Mitteilung von Prof. J. Ensink, Groningen, vom 14. 8. 1974). Vgl. auch Rajeshwari Ghosh, Bhīma in Indonesia, in: JASB 10/11 (1968–69), p. 49ff.

[109]) Lienhard, Introduction, p. 25, note 3.

[110]) Vgl. Wright, p. 144; Hasrat, p. 73.

[111]) Siehe Wright, p. 57; Hamilton, p. 9f.

Ich enthalte mich der Aufgabe, im Rahmen dieser Darstellung die beinahe totale Durchdringung des religiösen Lebens in Nepal mit dem hinduistischen Ritual zu erörtern. Wie wir wissen, hat die Überführung hinduistischer Riten in den Buddhismus schon sehr früh begonnen, wurde im weitesten Ausmaß aber erst im Vajrayāna vollzogen. *pūjā* und *homa* bilden seit langem die Grundpfeiler eines zum größten Teil gemeinsamen Rituals, das sowohl von Vajrācāryas als auch Brāhmaṇas und zu sowohl buddhistischen als auch hinduistischen Zwecken praktiziert werden kann. Die beiden Gemeinschaften waren in der Ausübung ihres Kults noch enger aneinandergerückt als in der Frage der Götterverehrung, wobei auch die Tatsache mit ins Gewicht fällt, daß die verschiedenen Observanzen nicht immer nur rein religiöse, sondern bisweilen auch soziale Funktionen erfüllten. Die Pflege der Kultbilder, ihre Waschung, Bekleidung und Ausfahrt, fand weite Verbreitung, und es ist geradezu typisch, daß, wo ein Unterschied der Behandlung erfolgt, der Offiziant nicht so sehr von hinduistischen oder buddhistischen Merkmalen ausgeht, sondern hauptsächlich zwischen tantrischen und nichttantrischen Gottheiten differenziert. Während die letztgenannten eine *pañcāmṛta*-Waschung und die üblichen Gaben wie Blumen, Lampen, Weihrauch, Kleider, Reis oder Butter empfangen, werden die erstgenannten, die tantrischen Götter, in Branntwein (Nev. *elā*) gebadet und erhalten blutige Opfer[112]). Sowohl die Nevars, die buddhistisch orientiert sind, als auch Gurkhas und übrige Hindus vollziehen Gelübde (*vrata*), üben Freigebigkeit (*dāna*), praktizieren *nyāsa*, baden an Tīrthas[113]), veranstalten Yātrās und applizieren die *ṭīkā*. Ein von Amṛtānanda auf Sanskrit verfaßter Abriß[114]) der Hauptrituale des nepalesischen Buddhismus faßt die täglich zu vollziehenden Zeremonien in der Gruppe dreier Saṃdhyās zusammen und nennt als Teile der Morgen-Saṃdhyā u.a. *japa*, *nyāsa*, *dhyāna*, *prāṇāyāma* und *triratnapūjā* und als solche der Nachmittag- und der Abend-Saṃdhyā *triratnapūjā*, *prāṇāyāma* und Rezitation des *ṣaḍakṣarīmantra*[115]).

In den Grundlagen ist die Darstellung des nepalesischen Religionssynkretismus hiermit abgeschlossen. Notwendigerweise mußte sich diese zum Großteil den Hauptgottheiten des Pantheons widmen, an denen, da sie volknahe sind, die einzelnen die Gestalten vereinenden Kräfte am klarsten zur Auswirkung kommen. Im zusammenfassenden Rückblick ergibt sich, daß die Entstehung synkretistischer Phänomene im Gebiet des Kathmandu-Tals durch Faktoren verschiedenster Art in Gang gesetzt wurde. Ein gemeinsamer Nenner für die beiden großen Religionen und zum Teil auch den Volkskult war vor allem durch Tantrismus, Śāktismus und Vajrayāna geboten, doch wurde die śivaitisch-spätbud-

---

112) Vgl. als Beispiel dieses Unterschieds Arjuna und Bhīmasena, oben p. 174.

113) Siehe S. Lienhard, Nr. 44, 1f.

114) Hodgson Papers; siehe J. Brough, in: BSOAS XII (1948), p. 668ff. (Herausgabe und Übersetzung).

115) D.i. *oṃ maṇipadme hūṃ*.

dhistische Annäherung auch noch später, ja in noch relativ neuer Zeit (Bhīmasena), durch Übertragungen, Synthesen oder Teilsynthesen bereichert, deren Ursachen vielfältig sind. Übertragungen und Verschmelzungsprozesse waren von Haus aus begünstigt, wenn zwei oder mehrere populäre Strömungen gleichzeitig blühten und religiöse Vermittler aufgetaucht waren, die guten Kontakt mit den Volksmassen hatten (Yogins, Vratins u.a.). Wie wir beobachtet haben, ergaben sich Identifikationen auch dann, wenn sprachliche Gleichheit entdeckt werden konnte (Svayambhū : Śambhu; Bhīma : Bhairava), ein Bedürfnis vorlag (Matsyendranātha-Mīnanātha) oder ein Kult die Form sozialer Funktionen annehmen konnte (Yātrās). Bedeutung muß auch dem Umstand zuerkannt werden, daß das Königreich Nepal ein stets hinduistisches Herrscherhaus hatte, das zwar halbstaatliche synkretistische Kulte befördern konnte, aber nie einen Glauben als Staatsreligion zur Vorschrift gemacht hat.

Erscheinungen, die auf die religiöse Entwicklung Nepals aufs stärkste eingewirkt haben, sind der Verlust der buddhistischen Lehre und die völlige Laisierung des Buddhismus, die mit jenem Augenblick eintrat, als verheiratete Mönche ihre Klöster in Großfamilienheime zu verwandeln begannen und der dogmatische Kern fast gänzlich durch Riten abgelöst wurde[116]); weiter die ständige Hinduisierung, die um so schneller vor sich ging, als, nach dem 12. Jahrhundert, dem Buddhismus jede geistige Neubelebung versagt war, während der Hinduismus, sei es kraft des hinduistischen Hofes, sei es durch neue Einwanderergruppen, stets lebendig gehalten und stimuliert werden konnte; und schließlich die immerzu starke Tendenz zu doppelter Monotheisierung, die eine Symbiose der Götter und Göttinnen in je eine Gestalt (Durgā : Tārā; Paśupatinātha : Matsyendranātha) und eine Symbiose der *śūnyatā* des Vajrayāna mit dem *ātman-brahman* des Vedānta zu erzielen bestrebt war. Alle diese Kräfte waren selten vereinzelt, sondern meist in Bündnissen wirksam.

Wie meine Ausführungen gezeigt haben werden, sind buddhistische Glaubensformen in der einen oder anderen Weise bis auf heute erhalten, doch ist unverkennbar, daß Nepal in steigendem Maß hinduisiert worden ist[117]).

[116]) M. Allen erklärt die Tatsache, daß das Vajrayāna der Nevars mehr als siebenhundert Jahre ohne Mönchstum und Kloster fortdauern konnte, in der Hauptsache dadurch, daß die politische Beschirmung reduziert worden war und der Vajrayāna-Buddhismus, der größere Dienste auch der Laienschaft bot, einen statt dessen viel festeren Rückhalt in den Volksmassen fand (Buddhism without Monks: The Vajrayana Religion of the Newars of Kathmandu Valley, in: South Asia, Journal of South Asian Studies III, 1973, p. 1, 4 und 13f.).

[117]) Es verdient Beachtung, daß, zu Anfang des vorigen Jahrhunderts, B. H. Hodgson, der ja lange in Nepal gewirkt hat, das Kathmandu-Tal als ein „*Bauddha country*" betrachtet (Hodgson, p. 35), während Colonel Kirkpatrick, dessen An Account of the Kingdom of Nepaul im Jahre 1811 in London erschien, Nepal als „Hindoo country" bezeichnet (ibid., p. 185). F. B. Hamilton sagt von den Newars, daß „*a very small portion has forsaken the doctrine of Buddha, while by far the most numerous class adhere to the doctrines taught by Sakya Singha*" (Hamilton, p. 29).

Śiva-Buddhism in Java and Bali

By JACOB ENSINK

The first to introduce Indian culture in Indonesia must have been brahmans and monks and priests of different sects from India, who followed the routes of maritime trade.[1]) But, as soon as they had won a certain number of followers, another movement must have set in and Indonesian converts must have sailed to visit India as pilgrims and students and returned with deep impressions and a store of new knowledge.[2])

Indian culture must have been accepted eagerly. Bosch (1952, p. 20) says that "points of similarity and affinity of Indo-Javanese and Indian art cannot be reduced to one period, one region or one style, but appear to be spread over nearly the whole of India." The same may be said with regard to Old-Javanese and Balinese literary tradition, religious as well as secular. As to religion there is only one of the major Indian teachings of which no trace has been found in Java and Bali or anywhere else in the Archipelago: that is Jainism.

Yet, though they have had a very wide knowledge of what India had to offer, this does not mean that the Javanese and Balinese have applied their knowledge in the same way as the Indians did, nor do they appear to have applied all of it. One might say that, though they had nearly all Indian building materials at their disposal, they never erected an Indian building. While this is almost literally true of architecture, the metaphor also applies to religion. Javanese-Balinese tradition includes many teachings and cults that are composed completely of Indian elements, yet anything exactly corresponding is hard to find in India. In the selection and combination of the elements the national character obviously has had its say. And how the selection and combination were made and why is one of the central and most interesting problems for the student of Javanese and Balinese culture.

Buddhism must have come to the Archipelago rather early and most information about its first spreading there we derive from Chinese sources. Fa hsien, who, coming from Ceylon in 414, was driven by storm to *Yeh p'o t'i* (*Yavadvīpa*; whether Java or Sumatra is not certain), was disappointed by the poor state of his religion there in comparison with 'the brahmans and heretics.' But before 424—again according to a Chinese source—Buddhism was spread throughout the country *Shê p'o* (Java). The missionary who accomplished this is said to be Guṇavarman,

---

[1]) Van Leur 1967, pp. 96–109; Bosch 1946.

[2]) Bosch 1952, pp. 16ff.

a prince's son from Kaśmīr. He came from Ceylon to Java[3]) and left it in 424 for China, where he died seven years later. He translated a text of the Dharmagupta school.[4])

In the seventh, eighth and ninth century the Indonesian Buddhists, or at least some Buddhist centres in Sumatra and Java, seem to have had a full share in the cosmopolitan character of the religion. This is the picture we derive in the first place from I ching's works. In his Mémoire[5]) he tells us that pilgrim Hui ning broke his journey in Java for three years (664/5–667/8) in order to translate a—probably Hīnayāna—sūtra on the Great Nirvāṇa together with a Javanese scholar Jñānabhadra. I ching's own high regard for the Buddhist seats of learning in Sumatra is evident from the fact that he stayed six months in Śrīvijaya (nowadays Palembang) and two in Malāyu (Jambi) on his way to India (671)[6]) and altogether ten years (685–695) in Śrīvijaya after his pilgrimage.[7])

He also mentions the schools that in his time were followed in "the islands of the Southern Sea," i.e. the Indonesian Archipelago: ". . . The Mūlasarvāstivādanikāya has been almost universally adopted, though occasionally some have devoted themselves to the Sammitinikāya; and recently a few followers of the other two schools (viz. the Mahāsaṅghikas and the Sthaviravādins[8])) have also been found."[9]) A few lines further

[3]) The evidence of relations between Java and Ceylon is scanty. Dupont (1959, pp. 633f.) supposed that two bronzes from Java, probably dating from the fifth or the sixth century, emanate from a local school in which Ceylonese influences combine with those from Central India. De Casparis (1959) discussed an inscription from the Ratu Baka plateau (Central Java; 792/3 A.D.) which records the foundation by king Samaratuṅga of "the Abhayagiri monastery for the Sinhalese (*Abhayagirivihāraḥ kāritaḥ Siṅhalānām*)." He preferred the explanation that these 'Sinhalese' were Javanese monks returned from a visit to the Ceylonese Abhayagirivihāra rather than Sinhalese monks from that monastery. In any case there must have been a rather close tie between both foundations. De Casparis in passing (p. 245, note 14) referred to *vĕḍihan siṅhal*, mentioned in Old-Javanese inscriptions from the ninth century onwards, which according to him is a term for a special kind of textile imported from Ceylon. Inscriptions (OJO LVIII back 14/124; LIX back 15/126f.; LXIV front 28/146) issued by king Airlaṅga (1019–1049) mention Sinhalese (*Siṅhala*) among the foreigners who resided in the country. They belonged to the *varga kilalan*, who have been a topic for much discussion. See Van Naerssen 1941, pp. 11–19 and Pigeaud 1960–1963, 4, pp. 422f., 476, 499 and 530.

[4]) Lévi - Chavannes 1916, p. 46.

[5]) Chavannes 1894, pp. 60–62.

[6]) Chavannes 1894, p. 119.

[7]) Chavannes 1894, pp. VI–VIII.

[8]) There is little evidence of Pāli, Pāli literature and Theravāda Buddhism in the whole of the Indo-Javanese and Indo-Balinese culture. OJav. *viku* is, as Pigeaud 1924, p. 28 puts it, "the most general term for an ordained clergyman." The same author (ibid., p. 36, note 2) expresses some doubt as to the Indian provenance of the word. But probably it is a very early loan, the origin of which (Pāli *bhikkhu*) was forgotten. Cp. Gonda 1973, pp. 158, 202 and 274. OJav. *palaṅka*, 'throne, seat for a priest' (KBW 4.259b s.v.) and Bal. *pĕlaṅkan*, the word for the bench of the brahman priest (Ensink 1967a., p. 401) stem from Pāli *pallaṅka*. The flat,

on he summarizes: "Buddhism is embraced in all these countries, and mostly the system of the Hīnayāna is adopted,' but adds: 'except in Malayu (i.e. Sumatra), where there are a few who belong to the Mahāyāna."

But in Java less than a century after I ching's time the form of Buddhism we find is a combination of Mahāyāna and Vajrayāna. In fact in Old-Javanese *Mahāyana* (consistently with *ya* short) comes to stand for 'Vajrayāna.' Barabuḍur, which as a whole is a colossal maṇḍala, on its thousands of sculptured panels illustrates a number of Sanskrit texts emanating from or adopted by Mahāyāna: Mahākarmavibhaṅga, Lalitavistara, Jātakamālā, Divyāvadāna, Gaṇḍavyūha.[10])

With Barabuḍur we have come to the flourishing period of Indo-Javanese culture in Central Java (beginning eighth century — 929). It is the age that has left us the temples of Kalasan, Mendut, Sewu, Plaosan, Lara Jonggrang and many smaller monuments besides Barabuḍur. And a probably still greater number has been lost. For our subject it is important that, as far as our evidence goes, all of them are either Buddhist or Śivaite. Buddhism seems to have been favoured by the Śailendra dynasty (about 750–about 850) and Śivaism by the Mataram dynasty, which succeeded the Śailendras and probably has preceded them. But no doubt both religions coexisted throughout the whole period.

It hardly needs any comment that at the same time more forms of religion must have been practised than those of which the monuments give evidence. The life-cycle of the common man and the cycle of agriculture must have been attended by ritual; to ward off the threat of demonic forces recourse may have been had to exorcists; in short we may suppose a similar variety of religious practice as Pigeaud (1960–1963, 4, pp. 480–484) has described for fourteenth century Java and as we find alive in present-day Bali. In the inscriptions, which, apart from the monuments, are our sole source for this period, it is seldom that something transpires about these other aspects. Conceivably it was only the official cult of the ruler, his house, the high officials and the high clergy that required building and engraving in stone, even if other people could have afforded it. We might however wonder why among the remains of the Central-Javanese culture there is no trace of Viṣṇuism. As early as 450 king Pūrṇavarman of Tārumā in West-Java in an inscription bore testi-

---

square cushion on which the Balinese Buddhist priest is seated while performing his ritual is called *luṅka-luṅka* or *pataraṇa* (KBW 4.184a s.v.; Purvaka E 17f./60), the last term probably continuing Pāli *pattharaṇa*. The Old-Javanese poet Tantular in calling the Man-eater much more frequently *Poruṣāda* than *Puruṣāda* may have been influenced by Pāli and in writing his Sutasoma kakavin may have been inspired by the Mahā-Sutasoma-jātaka (J 537), but whether directly or by some intermediary is not certain. Cp. Ensink 1967b, p. 59, note 3 and p. 61, note 30a, and my forthcoming paper 'The Man-eater converted' in Ṛtam.

[9]) I ching, Record 10.

[10]) Krom - Van Erp 1, pp. 47–635 and plates series O–IV; Bernet Kempers 1970. On the Gaṇḍavyūha reliefs Fontein 1966, pp. 116–174.

mony to his worship of the feet of Viṣṇu. But Viṣṇuism has always been considerably less important than Śivaism and Buddhism in the Archipelago.

So apparently Śivaism and Buddhism were supported by the rulers alternately or even simultaneously. Though the two religions seem to have been tolerant towards each other, there is not the slightest hint at a relation of a theological nature between the two: Śivaite monuments are Śivaite without any reference to Buddhism and vice versa; and likewise the inscriptions.

The situation is different at a later time (after 929), when the royal court has shifted to East-Java. We are also better informed on this period, as Bali has preserved a good number of texts that date back to it.

Two categories of these texts are most important for our purpose. In the first place the religious treatises called *tutur*,[11]) produced by Buddhists as well as Śivaites. Some of these, probably the oldest, are in fact Old-Javanese commentaries on Sanskrit verses, others are Old-Javanese treatises interspersed with a few ślokas, still later ones leave the Sanskrit verses out altogether. Though this relative chronology—which was first formulated by Goris (1926, pp. 69ff.)—has remained undisputed until now, an absolute dating of the texts is very difficult. A Buddhist tutur which will prove essential for our subject, the Saṅ hyaṅ Kamahāyānikan (SHK) or "Divine Mahāyāna religion," until recently was considered one of the oldest, if not the oldest one of the genre—mainly on account of the fact that the first king of the East-Javanese period, Siṇḍok (929–947), is mentioned in one of its manuscripts. This seemed to tally with Goris's chronology as at least the first part of it was clearly of the oldest type: Old-Javanese commentary on what appears to be a coherent text in Sanskrit ślokas. But Wulff (1935) showed that this first part is really a separate text entitled Saṅ hyaṅ Kamahāyānan Mantrānaya (SHKM) or "the Divine Mahāyāna Doctrine; the Formula Method." Wogihara and Sakai[12]) have identified several of its verses in Chinese and Tibetan texts and De Jong is of the opinion that it cannot be dated earlier than in the tenth century. It is however with the second part that we will be concerned and here the reference to king Siṇḍok is found. Mrs. Soebadio (1971, pp. 60f.) has stressed that the mention of the king's name only constitutes a terminus post quem and she is inclined "to place the SHK in approximately the same period as the Sutasoma kakavin, that is in the second half of the fourteenth century." Anyhow the formation of this part of SHK must lie somewhere between the first half of the tenth and the second half of the fourteenth century.

In the second place the genre of the *kakavin* provides important material for our subject. The word *kakavin* is the Old-Javanese equivalent for Sanskrit *kāvya* and usually denotes what in alaṃkāraśāstra is called *mahākāvya* or *sargabandha*. The prescriptions of the Indian ars poetica

[11]) Goris 1926, p. 54; Soebadio 1971, pp. 3f.
[12]) De Jong 1974.

are followed in detail—but for the language, which is Old-Javanese. The Sutasoma kakavin (Sut. K.) written by the poet Tantular between 1365 and 1389 is most explicit on the relation between Śiva and Buddha, Śivaism and Buddhism. The other work of the same poet that has come down to us, the Arjunavijaya, also mentions the identification of forms of Buddha with forms of Śiva.[13] The Nāgarakṛtāgama (Nāg.) of Prapañca will also prove an important source for us. It is a description of the kingdom of Java during the rule of king Rājasanagara or Hayam Vuruk (2nd half 14th century) of the dynasty of Majapahit. The author was a high dignitary of the Buddhist clergy at the royal court. His work sheds light on the religious institutions of his time and country as well as the monuments of the preceding period, in which the Siṅhasāri dynasty ruled from 1222 till 1292 and the Majapahit dynasty from 1293 onwards. Other kakavins that mention the identity of Śiva and Buddha are much later and at least one of them has been written in Bali.[14]

As for the Siṅhasāri and Majapahit periods we have well dated and detailed texts at our disposition and as some monuments from that time illustrate the relation between Śivaism and Buddhism, I now first propose to try and draw a picture of that relation in that period.

The relation has been variously characterized. Kern—who was the first[15] to discuss it circumstantially—spoke of 'blending,' Zoetmulder (1965, p. 269) of 'syncretism,' Pigeaud (1960–1963, 4, pp. 3f.) preferred 'parallelism,' which refers to one of the most striking features, Gonda (1970, p. 28) 'coalition,' which stresses the historical aspect.

The texts often designate Śivaism and Buddhism as *pakṣa*. They belong together on account of the identity of the Supreme Gods Śiva and Buddha.

In the Sutasoma kakavin, when the army that has undertaken the defence of king Sutasoma has been completely defeated, the king—who is a bodhisattva—goes to surrender himself to the Man-eater, who in the course of the battle has transformed himself into Rudra. But then it appears that Rudra cannot capture nor kill Sutasoma, all missiles aimed at the bodhisattva turning into flowers. Utterly furious Rudra takes on his world-consuming form of Kālāgni-Rudra. Now the gods and seers come to beseech Rudra not to destroy the world and they say: "You will not by far overpower the king, for he is an incarnation of Buddha. God Buddha is not different from god Śivarāja . . . Buddhahood is one with Śivahood, *bhinneka tuṅgal ika*, they are distinct, yet they are one."[16]

---

[13]) Zoetmulder 1965, p. 269; Supomo 1972, pp. 281f. Supomo's Canberra thesis, Arjunawijaya, a kakawin of mpu Tantular (1971) [text and translation], is as yet unpublished.

[14]) Ensink 1965, p. 104 and 1967b, p. 12.

[15]) In 1888, second edition 1916.

[16]) Sut.K., pp. 139.4cff. Cp. Kern 1916, p. 172; Zoetmulder 1965, p. 269. Here we find the words that have become the motto of the coat of arms of the

The identity of the two Supreme Gods also applies to the pantheons emanating from them: each emanation of Buddha is identical with one of Śiva. This is explicitly stated of four pairs: Akṣobhya is Īśvara, Ratnasaṃbhava Brahmā, Amitābha Mahādeva, Amoghasiddhi Viṣṇu. And obviously we have to infer that this holds good for any god in either of the pantheons. In the kakavin it especially has its bearing on Rudra, who—as an emanation of Śiva—is ultimately one with his opponent, the Bodhisattva.

In the Old-Javanese tale of Kuñjarakarṇa[17])—which, according to Kern, might date as far back as the twelfth century—Vairocana and the four Buddhas are identified with the five Kauśikas, a specially Javano-Balinese group of aspects of Śiva, which has recently been discussed by Hooykaas (1974, esp. p. 135f.).

The implication of the identity is that there is only one Supreme God, worshipped by the Buddhist under the Buddha aspect and by the Śivaite under the Śiva aspect. Indeed Tantular,[18]) Prapañca[19]) and others[20]) name Him Śiva-Buddha and so the term Śiva-Buddhism for this doctrine seems to be justified.

It should however be observed that in the Sutasoma kakavin sometimes Brahmā and Viṣṇu together with Śiva and Buddha seem to form a group of four. In the beginning of the poem[21]) it is said that in the Kṛta, Traita, and Dvāpara yugas Īśvara, Viṣṇu and Brahmā respectively were born as kings in the world of men, but now, in the Kaliyuga, Buddha (Jinapati) was incarnated to defeat Kāla. Two great heroes, Daśabāhu of Kāśī and Jayavikrama of Siṃhala are said to be incarnations of Brahmā and Viṣṇu respectively. Daśabāhu is a cousin on the mother's side and a brother-in-law of Sutasoma and both Daśabāhu and Jayavikrama valiantly oppose the Man-eater—who is possessed by Rudra—in battle.

This group of four is however far less important than the dual group Śiva-Buddha.

We find the doctrine of the identity of Śiva and Buddha applied in the cult of the deified deceased king. This is a prominent feature in the religion of Siṅhasāri and Majapahit. From the Nāgarakṛtāgama and the chronicle Pararaton (Par.) we learn that it was customary to worship a deceased king or other member of the royal family as identical with a god and for that purpose erect a sanctuary (*dharma*) with a statue (*pratiṣṭhā*) of the god over part of his ashes.[22]) It is even supposed that

---

Republic Indonesia. *Bhinneka tunggal ika* is now applied to the various components of the nation.

[17]) Kuñjarakarṇa 36 and 68. Cp. Kern VG 10 (1922), pp. 14–16. English translation 121.

[18]) Sut.K. 139.7b.

[19]) Nāg. 1.1b and 43.5cd.

[20]) Cp. Brandes - Krom 1920, p. 82.

[21]) Sut.K. 1.4bcd; see Kern 1916, p. 168.

[22]) Stutterheim 1931; Pigeaud 1960–1963, 4, pp. 113 and 490.

the temple Lara Jonggrang (early tenth century) in Central Java was devoted to the posthumous worship of King Balituṅ.[23])

Now from the beginning of the Siṅhasāri dynasty onwards it appears to be the rule that deceased kings were given a Buddhist as well as a Śivaite sanctuary. The last king of Siṅhasāri, Kṛtanagara—who died in 1292—in his divine character was styled Śiva-Buddha and his ashes were entombed in two temples, each of which had a Śivaite statue in the central cella of the ground-floor and a Buddha image in the first floor. Probably one of these is candi Siṅhasāri, which has been preserved; the other one is candi Jawi, of which the remains are still there. Prapañca[24]) describes this last monument: the Buddha image in the top floor—he says—represented Akṣobhya. He also tells us that a Buddhist clergyman of high rank worshipped the Śiva image in the ground floor, to the great wonder of the temple priest, who did not know about the Buddha image.[25])

The identity of the gods implies that both the Śivaite and the Buddhist way to release lead to the goal. But Tantular[26]) says: "The sage of the Buddhist denomination will fail, if he does not know about the way to Śiva-hood, which is the highest reality, and likewise the excellent sage who follows the yoga of Śiva-hood, if he does not know about the essence of Buddha-hood, which is the highest reality." This seems quite in keeping with the doctrine of identity, but is not borne out by the tuturs, which seldom refer to the other denomination. They do however contain some passages which are curiously illustrative of the parallelism of both religions; one might describe these as 'translations' of Buddhist teachings into Śivaite terms or vice versa. Mrs. Soebadio (1971, pp. 12ff.) has signalized some such adaptations. The Śivaite tutur Jñānasiddhānta proved to include a passage which runs parallel with one in the Buddhist Saṅ hyaṅ Kamahāyānikan. It deals with a yoga method which we will discuss later on in its Buddhist form of *advaya-yoga*. For the greater part the passages correspond word for word; the main difference is in the names of gods and technical terms. Let us suppose for the time being that the Śivaite borrowed from the Buddhist (which is probable, but not certain), then *advaya* has been replaced by *paraṃ brahma*, *advayajñāna*

---

[23]) Bernet Kempers 1959, p. 61. Cp. Krom 1924, p. 23.

[24]) Nāg. 56f.

[25]) Other kings deified both in a Buddhist and a Śivaite form: Rājasa (of Siṅhasāri; † 1227) 'given a double—Śivaite-Buddhist—shrine in Kagĕnĕṅan' (Nāg. 40.5d); Viṣṇuvardhana (of Siṅhasāri; † 1268) 'given a Śiva image in Valeri and a Sugata image in Jajaghu' (Nāg. 41.4b; Jajaghu is now known as Candi Jago; its central image represents Amoghapāśa); Kṛtarājasa (of Majapahit; † 1309) as Jina in Majapahit, as Śiva [Harihara] in Simpiṅ (Nāg. 47.3b); Jayanagara (of Majapahit; † 1328) as Viṣṇu in three shrines, as Amoghasiddhi in one (Nāg. 48.3bcd; the relation Viṣṇu-Amoghasiddhi we also have found in Sut.K.; see p. 183 of this paper). Berg (1962 and 1969) has connected a comprehensive theory on the history of Java with the divine character of the members of the dynasty.

[26]) Sut.K. 42.2; Ensink 1974, pp. 220f.

by *saṅp hyaṅ praṇavajñāna*, Prajñāpāramitā by Vāgīśvarī, alias Praṇavatridevī, alias Sarasvatī,[27]) Divarūpa by Parañjyotirūpa, and, of course, Buddha by Śiva. Another passage in the Jñānasiddhānta stands in the same relation to a Buddhist text, Kalpabuddha.[28]) In the Śivaite version it is said to be the common possession of Śivaite and Buddhist priests.

Correspondences like these give the impression that the way to release of the Śivaite and that of the Buddhist run exactly parallel, and only differ in that they are directed to different aspects of the Supreme God. However Tantular in his Sutasoma kakavin[29]) describes two materially different ways and he implies that also the practical attitudes of Śivaite and Buddhist are different, a view which we also find in other texts and which is widely spread in Bali.

The exposition has the form of a teaching given by Sutasoma to three disciples, the demon Gajavaktra, a snake and a tigress. In order to suit the tale it has been given a special arrangement, which—for the sake of clarity—I shall not follow here.

The Śivaite way then is the yoga of six stages (*ṣaḍaṅgayoga*).[30]) This yoga method seems to have become more current in Java than it was in India and to have superseded the eight stage yoga nearly completely. The tuturs seem to confirm that this is the Śivaite way, for it is repeatedly discussed in Śivaite tuturs and I have not found it in a really Buddhist context. The tuturs as a rule follow the same tradition as we find in the Amṛtanādopaniṣad. The ślokas quoted and the sequence of the stages are indeed the same as given in that text. It is noteworthy that the Buddhist poet speaks of the Śivaite way with obvious courtesy. Sutasoma characterizes the Śivaites as *nirmalabhava*, "of pure character;" the pupils speak of the Śivaite way as "the excellent way" (*mārga viśeṣa*) and the teacher reacts by calling their attention to the six stages, which he considers "truly most important" (*mahottama tĕmĕn*).

The Buddhist way is in the first place described as *paratramārga*. Here *paratra* should be understood in its Javanese sense of 'to die'. In the discussion of this "way of dying" evidently there is an allusion to the preceding episode, which in fact is the well-known Vyāghrījataka. Sutasoma had sacrificed himself to the hungry tigress, who was on the point of devouring her own cubs, and only on the repeated supplications of the repentant tigress had he been restored to life by Indra. The "way of dying" combines two ideals, renunciation (*tyāga*) and service to the wellbeing of the world (*jagaddhita*)—both in their most radical form. The

---

27) On the identification Prajñāpāramitā = Sarasvatī Hooykaas 1964a, pp. 31f.

28) Soebadio 1971, pp. 14f. This Kalpabuddha is different from the text of the same title edited by Bosch 1961, pp. 132f.

29) Sut.K. 38.1–42.4; ed. and transl. Ensink 1974, pp. 212–221.

30) Ensink 1974, pp. 198f. and 211. I did not yet know Grönbold's thesis (1969) on the subject when I wrote that paragraph.

recluse should see to it that at the hour of death his soul is as easily separated from the body as "the kris (the Javanese dagger) drawn freely from its sheath." But to this end yet another element seems to be required. This is styled "the esoteric knowledge of the yoga of non-duality" (*advayayogasandhi*); it is the method discussed in the passage of the Saṅ hyaṅ Kamahāyānikan[30a]) which—as we have seen—has a Śivaite parallel. Probably this passage was Tantular's source and it is of much help for the understanding of his poetic version. To Tantular this obviously was a central doctrine, as he refers to it in the opening verse of the Sutasoma kakavin and comes back to it in the end (145.6d and 147.5c).

The method proceeds from a double symbolism of the syllables *aṃ* and *aḥ*. These stand in the first place for the absolute reality, 'non-duality' (*advaya*), in the second place *aṃ* stands for inhalation and *aḥ* for expiration. This is applied in a steady exercise of inhalation and expiration, once more symbolized by sun and moon respectively. When this exercise has been carried to perfection, it is said that 'the knowledge of non-duality' (*advayajñāna* or *advayacitta*) arises and that from the meeting of non-duality and knowledge of non-duality Buddha Divāṅga is born. *Divāṅga* is one of the variants which Tantular—as a good kavi—coins to avoid wornout technical terms; the Saṅ hyaṅ Kamahāyānikan spoke of—and the Balinese priests still speak of—*Divarūpa*. The birth of this 'Buddha as clear as daylight'—that is how the name should be understood—is meant to be the realization of Buddhahood by the yogin. Buddha Divāṅga—we may say—is the yogin become Buddha. Indeed non-duality, knowledge of non-duality—personified in Prajñāpāramitā—and Buddha Divāṅga are said to stand in the relation of father, mother and son.

So much about the Sutasoma kakavin. It is interesting to compare a tale which must have been current in the same time and deals with the same subject, but in a different form and under a rather different aspect. This is the tale of Bubhukṣa, which on archaeological evidence[31]) was known in Tantular's time and has been preserved in Bali.[32]) So far it has not yet been edited, but a condensed rendering has been given by Poerbatjaraka.[33]) Van Stein Callenfels[34]) observed that it is a tale of the prototypes of the Buddhist and Śivaite priests.

I summarize that part of the story which is of direct interest for our subject. Two brothers, Gagaṅ Akiṅ, 'Dry Stalk,' and Bubhukṣa, 'Glutton', retired to a mountain as hermits. Gagaṅ Akiṅ led a pious life and only took pure food, Bubhukṣa on the other hand did not stop eating and

[30a]) SHK 46ff.

[31]) Van Stein Callenfels - Poerbatjaraka 1919.

[32]) Pigeaud 1967–1970, 1. §§ 13000 and 13020.

[33]) Van Stein Callenfels - Poerbatjaraka 1919, pp. 351–358, abridged by Rassers 1959, pp. 79–83.

[34]) ibid., p. 359.

drinking, taking everything he caught in his snares, even men if it so happened. Gagaṅ Akiṅ repeatedly remonstrated with his brother on his way of life, but in vain. Now the gods became aware that the brothers disputed the question who had made most progress on the way to beatitude. Therefore they sent the white tiger Kālavijaya to test both of them and find out who really was free from attachment to life (*tyāga*). The tiger first met Gagaṅ Akiṅ and asked him for his body as food. Gagaṅ Akiṅ excused himself on account of his leanness and referred the tiger to his brother. Bubhukṣa however was very happy to have the opportunity to sacrifice himself, he only asked for some delay so that he might check his snares and no animal would be slowly tortured to death in any of them. He also explained that he ate all living beings he caught in order to help them to a favourable rebirth. When he had made the round of his snares and eaten all creatures he found in them, he offered himself to the tiger and was not at all scared even when the tiger jumped at him with wide-open mouth and out-stretched clutches. As Bubhukṣa thus had given proof of his being tyāga, the tiger took him on his back, while Gagaṅ Akiṅ was allowed to hold his tail. In this way the brothers ascended to heaven—a striking scene, which has inspired the artist in present-day Bali[35]) as much as in medieval Java.[36]) Both Bubhukṣa and Gagaṅ Akiṅ were received into heaven—only Gagaṅ Akiṅ was given a smaller share in all enjoyments.

A curious illustration of the paratramārga with the sacrifice to the great feline as a test—as in the kakavin. The matter of diet—which Tantular does not mention—obviously carries much weight here and this is in accordance with the situation in Bali.

We have seen already that the deceased rulers of Siṅhasāri and Majapahit were worshipped both under a Śivaite and a Buddhist aspect. Though this cult appears to be very important to the dynasty, it is only one of the functions at the court in which the two religions had a share. On every occasion we find the Śivaite as well as the Buddhist clergy (*Śaiva Bauddha*, or *Śaiva Saugata*) present, or at least their bishops (*dharmādhyakṣa riṅ kaśaivan,—kasaugatan.*[37]) This is the situation according to inscriptions and Prapañca's Nāgarakṛtāgama, which describes the Majapahit court. The other kakavins—which take their subject as a rule from the Sanskrit epics—also mention the twofold clergy at court on every occasion: evidently to the Old-Javanese poet their presence was as it should be, for all times and countries. The institution indeed is older than the Siṅhasāri period: two inscriptions of

---

[35]) Paintings by I Wj.Durus, reproduced by Hooykaas 1962, opp. p. 325, and by I Tawang, reproduced in Bali kringloop, pl. 19.

[36]) Van Stein Callenfels - Poerbatjaraka 1919, pl. II.

[37]) Decree Jaya Soṅ, plate 3 recto, line 4f., ed. and transl. Pigeaud 1960–1963, 1. p. 104 and 3. p. 152; Ferry charter, plate 3 verso, line 1f., ed. and transl. Pigeaud ibid. 1, p. 109 and 3, p. 158.

king Airlaṅga (1030[38]) and 1041[39])) mention *Saugata Māheśvara* and *Śaiva Saugata*. Often, but not always, there is yet another group, usually the *ṛṣi*. These seem to be representatives of the monks in monastical communities throughout the country. Once[40]) the term *tripakṣa* is used for the three groups: monks, Śivaites and Buddhists. In a few cases brahmans (*mahābrāhmaṇa, vipra*) are mentioned in the same breath with the Śivaites and Buddhists. And only once[41]) have I found all four groups together. The members of these Śivaite and Buddhist clergies were married and their office was hereditary. A text which seems to have been issued by king Kṛtanagara[42]) prescribes: "The Śivaite's son shall be a Śivaite, the Buddhist's son a Buddhist, the rāja's son a rāja, the manuh's (common layman's) son a manuh, the śūdra's son a śūdra, and so on all classes shall follow their own avocations and ceremonies."[43])

So much about Java. In Bali we find evidence of Buddhism and Śivaism as early as the ninth century. The island may have undergone direct influence from India, but the contacts with Java were naturally intense. In 1343 it became a province of the Majapahit kingdom and the three highest orders in Balinese society refer their ancestry to priests and administrators from Majapahit. Old-Javanese literary tradition has been continued in Bali and to the Balinese we owe nearly all Old-Javanese texts that have come down to us.

It would be difficult to analyse how much in the cult of the Buddha priest and the Śiva priest in Bali goes back to pre-Majapahit Balinese tradition and how much stems from the Javanese metropolis. Anyhow in Bali today we see the Buddha priest and the Śiva priest (*padanda Buddha,-Śiva*) officiating in one and the same religion, the Āgama Tīrtha, "religion of holy water," or Āgama Hindu Bali. Both belong to the highest class, the brahmans. Outwardly they are distinguished—among other things—by the way they wear their hair, the Śivaite tying it in a knot on the crown of his head, the Buddhist combing his locks backwards and down to the neck. Each has his rules (*brata*) and the rules pertaining to food remind us of Bubhukṣa and Gagaṅ Akiṅ, for the padanda Buddha is allowed to eat everything, while the diet of the padanda Śiva is subject to many restrictions.[44])

Hooykaas (1973 and 1966) has made the daily ritual of both Buddhist and Śivaite priest accessible in text and translation. Usually every

---

38) OJO LX, front and right hand side, 7/129.

39) OJO LXII. 15/138; Kern VG 7, pp. 104 and 108.

40) Nāg. 51.5a.

41) Nāg. 81.2ab.

42) Rājapatiguṇḍala, ed. Pigeaud 1960–1963, 1, pp. 87–90.

43) Translation Pigeaud 1960–1963, 3, p. 130.

44) Van Eerde 1911, pp. 8–12. Cp. the quotations from Usana Java and Saṅ hyaṅ Kamahāyānikan, ed. Sugriwa, by Hooykaas 1973, pp. 50f. Not all in Hooykaas's note on *āhāra-lāghava* pertains esp. to the brata of the Buddhist. *āhāra-lāghava* is a rule that Śivaite and Buddhist have in common.

padanda officiates alone, his chief task in society being the preparation of holy water, which is indispensable in every ritual. To the common Balinese it makes no difference whether the holy water is prepared by a padanda Śiva or a padanda Buddha. Family tradition seems to decide from whom one should obtain it.

Only in great rituals more priests cooperate and then often one Buddhist together with several Śivaites. In a description of the consecration of a Balinese king, performed in 1903, we find the leading padanda Śiva together with a padanda Buddha seated in the centre and one padanda Śiva in each of the cardinal points.[45]) The Buddha priests nowadays form a small minority as compared to the Śiva priests. Hooykaas (1973, pp. 250f.)—who made enquiries in 1967—found that in the whole of Bali only ten Buddha priests officiate and six more among the Hindus in the island of Lombok. Of Śiva priests there are several hundreds. One of the Buddha priests, a lady (*padanda istri*), originated from a Śivaite family, but had assumed what is called the *gama Bauddha*, "the Buddhist religion." This is an exception.

Among the Balinese brahman priests there are various conceptions of the relation between Śiva and Buddha, which is not radically distinguished from the relation between padanda Śiva and padanda Buddha. Van Eerde (1911, p. 13) heard the saying: *Buddha sakiṅ niṣkala ṅĕrĕrĕh sakala, Śiva sakiṅ sakala ṅĕrĕrĕh niṣkala,* "Buddha, starting from the non-manifest, seeks the manifest; Śiva, starting from the manifest, seeks the non-manifest." A learned padanda Śiva[46]) told me: *Buddha sakiṅ sor, Śiva sakiṅ luhur,* "Buddha comes from beneath, Śiva comes from above." It is pointless to enter into speculations about such sentences as long as we have not more material at our disposal.

This is a short survey of what I think are the main facts relating to the history of Buddhism—and especially its coalition with Śivaism—in Java and Bali. How should we interpret that history? Should we see this Śiva-Buddhism mainly as a result of the interaction of the two and so not essentially determined by the Javanese-Balinese situation or is it by its nature an expression of the culture of the two islands?

Kern in his article (1916) in what he termed the blending of Śivaism and Buddhism in Java explained the phenomenon as a result of developments in the religions themselves, developments that could take place—and to a certain extent did take place— in any country where there were Śivaism and Buddhism. Accordingly he thought it justified to adduce data from the Sutasoma kakavin to explain the occurrence of Śivaite images

---

[45]) Schwartz - Swellengrebel 1947. 6f. The arrangement reflects a constellation which we also find in a temple group in Sut.K. 67. 2f. Also cp. Friederich 1849–1850, 1, p. 29.

[46]) Ida Padanda Made Sidemen of Sanur, whom I met in 1964. For the opportunity given me to work in Indonesia for more than three months I am indebted to the Netherlands Foundation for the Advancement of Pure Research (Z.W.O.) Cp. Ensink 1965.

in Buddhist temples in Nepal. Obviously he took no account of the possibility that the Javanese background played an important part in the blending.

In 1926 Rassers on this point criticized Kern and other writers who in the main had adopted Kern's views. He based himself on the Bubhukṣa legend, which he considered a variant of the myth of the tribe, Bubhukṣa and Gagaṅ Akiṅ being the prototypes of the two phratries of which the tribe is composed. This theory on the myth of the tribe, supposed to date back to a post-totemistic prehistory of the Javanese people, has been explained more in detail in Rassers's papers (1925 and 1931) on the Javanese shadow theatre, the wayang.

Pigeaud (1960–1963, 4, p. 3) speaking of the parallelism of Śivaism and Buddhism, said: "It is beyond doubt that this pair is related to very old conceptions of dualism belonging to a mode of thought which has been characterized as 'classification,' for its tendency to place all beings and things in classes that stand in fixed relations one to another."

Zoetmulder (1965, pp. 270f.), though not fully subscribing to Rassers's theory, is of the opinion that especially in the Siṅhasāri—Majapahit period, primeval autochthonous elements to a great extent have determined the special form of Javanese culture and religion.

While admitting the possibility that primeval concepts have exercised influence, Gonda (1970, pp. 30f.) is sceptical about Rassers's theory and stresses the fact that similar processes of blending occur in Kamboja and Nepal as well as in India.

Gonda refers to a Saṅ hyaṅ Kamahāyānikan passage which speaks of Divarūpa.[47]) It runs: "He is the supreme God of the Buddhists, he is called the Lord Supreme Void, he is called Paramaśiva (by the Śivaites), he is the Lord Puruṣa to the followers of the reverend Kapila, he is the divine ātman to the followers of Kaṇabhakṣa,[48]) Lord Nirguṇa is his name to the Viṣṇuites ..." This has a parallel in the opening stanzas of Prapañca's Nāgarakṛtāgama, where Śivabuddha is said to be Niguṇa to the Viṣṇuites, Īśvara to the yogins, Poruṣa to (the followers of) Kapila, etc., etc. These places are interesting in that they mention some schools with which we seldom meet in Old-Javanese sources. The teaching of Kapila, that is to say the Sāṃkhya, we find sometimes—in the Nāgarakṛtāgama and inscriptions—together with the Nyāya as a specialism mastered by high clergymen at court. Kaṇabhakṣa is a variant of Kaṇāda and so his followers are the Vaiśeṣikas. I do not know any other reference to them in Old-Javanese sources. Divarūpa in the Saṅ hyaṅ Kamahāyānikan and Śivabuddha in the Nāgarakṛtāgama are said to be identical

[47]) Gonda 1970, p. 27. SHK 50 and 100. Whether one adopts the reading of MS C, which mentions Divarūpa explicitly, or the shorter one of the other MSS, from the context it is clear that Divarūpa is meant.

[48]) Thus with MS C.

with the Supreme Being as taught in each of the sects and schools. Kern (1916, p. 155) quoted a śloka from a Nepalese inscription which forms a striking parallel to this identification:

> *Matsyendraṃ yogināṃ mukhyāḥ Śāktāḥ Śaktiṃ vadanti yam |*
> *Bauddhā Lokeśvaraṃ tasmai namo Brahmasvarūpiṇe ||*
> "Honour to Him whom the best of Yogins call Matsyendra, the Śāktas Śakti and the Buddhists Lokeśvara, who by His own nature is brahman."

And Gonda (1970, pp. 30f.) has pointed out more parallels from different countries. The idea that the gods worshipped by different sects are identical may well have been among those that were borrowed from India.

In the Sutasoma kakavin to my mind it is important that the identification is limited to two Supreme Gods and their pantheons and the two aspects are each other's complement: the Buddhist must know the Śivaite way and vice versa. This conception also seems to underlie the religious practice at the court of Siṅhasāri and Majapahit: at least most kings are deified both in a Śivaite and a Buddhist form and Śivaites as well as Buddhists have to be present at every official function. It is true that sometimes other groups of clergymen are mentioned along with them, but of these the monks (*ṛṣi*), as representatives of the monasteries, had a different status and they had no houses in the royal compound. The brahmans (*vipra*)[49]) appear to be Viṣṇuites. I shall come back to them in the end.

Though one may be sceptical about Rassers's speculations on the origin of concepts of bipartition in Javanese culture, the importance—stressed by Pigeaud—of these concepts and similar classifications can hardly be denied. Bipartition may affect every sphere in cosmos and society and expresses itself in different oppositions: non-manifest—manifest; mountains—seaside; right—left; younger—older; winning—losing; etc., etc.

To give only a few examples. According to Pigeaud[50]) the two halves Jaṅgala and Kaḍiri, into which the Javanese kingdom was traditionally considered to be divided, formed such an opposition, Kaḍiri being the mountainous country and Jaṅgala the lowland. During the reign of king Hayam Vuruk the king's grandmother was given a temple at the end of the legendary dividing line. The śrāddha ritual which accompanied the inauguration of the temple is one of the main subjects described by Prapañca in his Nāgarakṛtāgama (Nāg. 63–69). He says: "The reason for it to be fashioned as an eminent dharma was: in order that again

[49]) Nāg. 8.4b and 81.2b; Pigeaud 1960–1963, 4, pp. 15 and 492. Stutterheim (1948, pp. 50f.) has made plausible that they were Viṣṇuites. According to Pigeaud they came from India.

[50]) Pigeaud 1960–1963, 4, pp. 202ff. I prefer his explanation to that of Berg 1953.

the land of Java might become one, that orderly it might have a King, that as one country it would be known in the world in future, not going to deviate."[51]) The kingdom—we are given to understand—flourishes through the harmonious cooperation of the two halves, it is the ruler's task to see to it that they do not fall apart.

The opposition mountains—sea (*kaja—kělod*) is very important in Bali; it corresponds to the opposition of the gods of heaven and those of earth and is a vital force in the organisation of many villages.[52])

The concept of bipartition is very marked in the world shown in the wayang. This form of theatre goes back to the tenth century A. D. or earlier. Its apparatus is so arranged as to fit the opposition of the two sides: all puppets of the right hand party standing on the right of the puppeteer, all those of the left hand side on his left. Much has been written on the individual characters in wayang as well as the general characteristics of the parties.[53]) Suffice it here to say that the opposition of right and left is not the opposition of good and bad. The general theme of the plays may be said to be the conflict between right and left, which ends in the victory of the right. Yet the left is never annihilated. The victory must rather be understood as a restoration of harmony.

There is a curious story told in two texts (Koravāśrama and Cantakaparwa), which evidently are narrowly related to the wayang plays. After the great battle of the Mahābhārata Vyāsa restores the Kauravas to life: "For," he says, "how could it be all right if there were not both Kauravas and Pāṇḍavas! For they are the content of the world."[54]) Later on, after the Kauravas have performed austerities, Duryodhana, Śakuni and Bhagadatta ask the death of the Pāṇḍavas as a favour from Brahmā, Mahādeva and Viṣṇu respectively, but in every case the answer is that the Pāṇḍavas as well as the Kauravas are essential in the world.[55])

In all varieties of bipartition a certain tension between the opposites seems essential. In some cases it is no more than a mild rivalry, in some it may lead to bitter war, but the balance is restored ever again. There also may be a periodical change in the supremacy.

Now does the relation between Śivaism and Buddhism which we have styled Śiva-Buddhism fit in the frame of a bipartition such as we have described? For a test let us see whether the texts from which we learned about this Śiva-Buddhism show features that are typical of such a bipartition.

In the Bubhukṣa legend Gagaṅ Akiṅ, the loser, is the older brother, Bubhukṣa, the winner, the younger one. There is a continued rivalry

---

[51]) Nāg. 68.5bc. The translation is Pigeaud's. Cp. Berg 1953, p. 37 and Teeuw-Uhlenbeck 1968, 2, p. 37.

[52]) Grader 1937.

[53]) Cp. Ensink 1968, pp. 412f. and 424f.

[54]) Krvś. 14.8.

[55]) Krvś. 162.30ff., 164.32ff. and 168.1ff. A parallel in the Cantakaparwa; see Ensink 1967b, p. 9.

over the question what is the right way of life for the recluse, but in the end each gets his due. These are indeed elements that are characteristic of a dualist classification.

In the Sutasoma kakavin right from the beginning the whole world is threatened by the increasing power of the king who has become a Man-eater, Poruṣāda, and who has won the demons as his allies. He is possessed by Rudra and in the course of the tale makes a vow to Kāla to offer him a hundred kings, later on to be exchanged for king Sutasoma. The Boddhisattva is born as Sutasoma with the express object of curbing the Śivaite power in its demonic form and in the end does so, not by force of arms, but by his spiritual power; Rudra realizes his error and withdraws to heaven; the Man-eater and Kāla hear the teaching of Sutasoma —on the Śivaite way as well as on the Buddhist way— and then Kāla becomes Īśvara and Poruṣāda stops being a Man-eater. Sutasoma obtains the release of the kings who have been captured by Poruṣāda, but he binds them over not to take revenge on him: "For," he says, "it is not he who caused your suffering, but this is the requital of your misbehaviour" (141.4c). And he follows this up with a severe predication. In the end former friends and foes, men and demons join in a happy feast, where various strong drinks flow abundantly and each makes his contribution in song or dance.

The main theme of the kakavin is the conflict between the Buddhist and the Śivaite sides. Really this conflict is impossible, because the parties are fundamentally one and stand in need of each other. Only through blindness—in this case on the Śivaite side—is a rupture possible. So by removal of that blindness harmony is restored. This fits in very well with the concept of bipartition; actually it gives the concept in a sublimated form.

An indication that at least later generations saw the kakavin in the general dualistic frame we may find in the fact that it has been staged in the wayang,[56] where naturally Sutasoma is placed on the right hand side. In this connection a slight change which later tradition made in the tale is interesting. Tantular, following the Indian tradition, designated Sutasoma as a scion of the Kauravas. Later generations may have found it difficult to accept this. In the prose version of the tale in the Cantakaparva—which may well have served the wayang puppeteer—Sutasoma through his mother is linked up with the Pāṇḍavas, while his father's descent is passed over in silence.[57]

I hope to have made plausible that a dual system has been a formative force in the development of Śiva-Buddhism. Dual systems are not the only type of classification in Javanese and Balinese culture, but other types were not much in evidence in the sources we have discussed. Only we may find a system of quadripartition in the group Brahmā—Viṣṇu—

---

[56]) See Ensink 1968, pp. 432f. The text of the play written down by I Wayan Mendra is MS 2290 of the Gedong Kirtya in Singaraja, Bali.

[57]) Ensink 1967b, pp. 22f.

Śiva—Buddha, which plays a part in the Sutasoma kakavin.[58]) From the point of view of Indian tradition we might say that it has been formed through extension of the triad Brahmā—Viṣṇu—Śiva by adding Buddha. If we accept that older Javanese-Balinese concepts have been at work, we should rather say that the opposition Śiva—Buddha has been combined with another one of Brahmā and Viṣṇu. For a parallel we might refer to the Balinese cosmic system, where the opposition East—West (*kaṅin—ka-uh*) is added to the opposition mountains—sea (*kaja—kĕlod*).[59])

In a tripartite system Viṣṇuism has a place beside Śivaism and Buddhism. Thus at the court of Majapahit (Viṣṇuite) brahmans[60]) had their shrines in a row with those of the Buddhist and Śivaite priests; moreover they had a place for offerings to chthonic deities. There is again a parallel in Balinese ritual, where sometimes the sĕṅguhu priest—who calls himself Vaiṣṇava[61])—officiates together with the padanda Śiva and the padanda Buddha.[62]) But Viṣṇu is also worshipped as an aspect of Śiva with the Amoghasiddhi aspect of Buddha as a counterpart.[63])

In conceiving Śiva-Buddhism the Javanese and the Balinese have in the main followed the traditions, originating from India, of the two religions involved. The steps that have led to the new form seem essentially consistent with those traditions. Yet it depends on older Javanese-Balinese concepts that they took these very steps. They have acted likewise with other elements of the Indian tradition. It is only natural that a people should act thus with what it borrows from a foreign culture.

References

1. Abbreviations

Bali kringloop = Bali, kringloop van het leven. Tentoonstelling . . . 17 december 1965–31 mei 1966. Ethnographisch Museum, Delft.

B.Indon. = Bibliotheca Indonesica.

BKI = Bijdragen tot de Taal-, Land- en Volkenkunde (till 104/1948: van Nederlandsch-Indië).

I ching, Record = I tsing. A Record of the Buddhist Religion as practised in India and the Malay Archipelago, transl. J. Takakusu. Oxford 1896. Reprint Delhi 1966.

J = Jātakatthavaṇṇanā. The Jātaka together with its commentary, ed. V. Fausbøll. Index by Dines Andersen. London 1877–1897. 7 vols. Reprint 1963. (Nr. of jātaka.)

JA = Journal Asiatique.

[58]) See p. 183 of this paper.
[59]) Grader 1937.
[60]) See p. 182f. of this paper.
[61]) Goris 1931, pp. 45–49; Hooykaas 1964b.
[62]) Schwartz - Swellengrebel 1947, p. 15; Swellengrebel 1960, pp. 44f.
[63]) Cp. Hooykaas 1966, pp. 182–185. Cp. note 25 to this paper.

KBW = H. N. van der Tuuk. Kawi-Balineesch-Nederlandsch Woordenboek. Batavia 1897–1912. 4 vols.

KITS = Koninklijk Instituut voor Taal-, Land- en Volkenkunde, Translation Series (Nr.).

Krvś. = Korawāçrama. Een Oud-Javaansch prozageschrift, uitgegeven, vertaald en toegelicht door Jan Lodewijk Swellengrebel. Santpoort 1936. Thesis Leiden.

Kuñjarakarṇa = De legende van Kuñjarakarṇa volgens het oudst bekende handschrift, met Oud-javaanschen tekst, Nederlandsche vertaling en Aanteekeningen door H. Kern. Reference is to page of VG 10, pp. 1–76. First published Amsterdam 1901, VKAWLNR dl. 3, nr. 3. Translated from the Dutch of Professor Kern by L. A. Thomas, in: Indian Antiquary, March 1903, pp. 111–127.

MK = Mededeelingen van de Kirtya Liefrinck-van der Tuuk. (Instalment and p.)

MK(N)AWL = Medede(e)lingen der Koninklijke (Nederlandse) Akademie van Wetenschappen, afd. Letterkunde.

Nāg. = Prapañca, Nāgarakṛtāgama, ed. and transl. Pigeaud 1960–1963.

OJO = Oud-Javaansche Oorkonden. Nagelaten Transscripties van wijlen J. L. A. Brandes. Uitgegeven door N. J. Krom. Batavia-'s Hage 1913. VBG 60. (Inscription, line and p.)

Par. = Pararaton, ed. and transl. Brandes - Krom 1920.

Purvaka = ed. and transl. Hooykaas 1973, pp. 47–115. (Paragraph, line and p.)

SHK = Sang hyang Kamahâyânikan. Oud-Javaansche Tekst met Inleiding, Vertaling en Aanteekeningen door J. Kats. 's-Gravenhage 1910.

SHKM = Saṅ hyaṅ Kamahāyānan Mantrānaya. SHK 17–30. German translation with emended Sanskrit text of the ślokas: Wulff 1935.

SSI = Selected Studies on Indonesia by Dutch Scholars.

Sut.K. = "Sutasoma." Ditulis dengan huruf Bali dan Latin. Diberi arti dengan bahasa Bali dan bahasa Indonesia. Denpasar 1959. 22 fasc. — Soewito-Santoso. Boddhakawya-Sutasoma, a study in Javanese Wajrayana. The Australian National University, Canberra 1968. Unpublished Ph. D. thesis.

TBG = Tijdschrift voor Indische Taal-, Land- en Volkenkunde.

VBG = Verhandelingen van het Bataviaasch Genootschap van Kunsten en Wetenschappen.

VG = H. Kern. Verspreide Geschriften. 's-Gravenhage 1913–1929. (Vol. and p.)

VK(N)AWLNR = Verhandelingen der Koninklijke (Nederlandse) Akademie van Wetenschappen, afd. Letterkunde. Nieuwe Reeks. (Pt. and nr.)

VKI = Verhandelingen van het Koninklijk Instituut voor Taal-, Land- en Volkenkunde.

2. Research Publications

(The titles quoted here are referred to by name of the author and year of publication only)

Berg, C. C.: Herkomst, vorm en functie der Middeljavaanse rijksdelingstheorie. Amsterdam 1953. VKNAWLNR 59, 1.

— Het Rijk van de Vijfvoudige Buddha. Amsterdam 1962. VKNAWLNR 69, 1.

— Māyā's hemelvaart in het Javaanse Buddhisme. Amsterdam 1969. VKNAWLNR 74; 1, 2.

Bernet Kempers, A. J.: Ancient Indonesian Art. Amsterdam 1959.
— Borobudur. Mysteriegebeuren in steen. Verval en restauratie. Oudjavaans volksleven. Wassenaar 1970.

Bosch, F. D. K.: Het vraagstuk van de Hindoe-kolonisatie in den Archipel. Leiden 1946. Inaugural address Leiden.
— "Local genius" en oud-Javaanse kunst. Amsterdam 1952. MKNAWL, Dl. 15, No. 1.
— Buddhist Data from Balinese Texts and their contribution to archaeological research in Java, in: F. D. K. Bosch: Selected Studies in Indonesian Archaeology. The Hague 1961. KITS 5, pp. 109–133.

Brandes, J. L. A. en N. J. Krom: J. L. A. Brandes. Pararaton (Ken Arok), of het Boek der Koningen van Tumapĕl en van Majapahit. 2e druk, bewerkt door N. J. Krom, met medewerking van J. C. G. Jonker, H. Kraemer en Poerbatjaraka. 's-Gravenhage-Batavia 1920. VBG 62.

Chavannes, Édouard: Mémoire composé à l'époque de la grande dynastie T'ang sur les religieux éminents qui allèrent chercher la Loi dans les pays d'Occident par I-tsing, traduit en français. Paris 1894.

De Casparis, J. G.: New evidence on cultural relations between Java and Ceylon in ancient times, in: Artibus Asiae 24, 3–4 (1961), pp. 241–248.

De Jong, J. W.: Notes on the sources and the text of the Sang hyang Kamahāyānan Mantranaya, in: BKI 130 (1974), pp. 465–482.

Dupont, Pierre: Variétés archéologiques III. Les Buddhas dits d'Amarāvatī en Asie du Sud-Est, in: Bulletin de l'École Française d'Extrême-Orient 49 (1959), pp. 631–636.

Ensink, J.: Het Oudjavaanse gedicht Sutasoma. Onderzoek op Java en Bali, in: ZWO-Jaarboek 1964 ('s-Gravenhage 1965), pp. 103–106.
— Paṅhiḍĕp hati. Some notes on the worship of Sarasvatī in Balinese Hinduism, in: Kavirāj Abhinandana Grantha (Akhila Bhāratīya Saṃskṛta Pariṣad, Lakhnaū) 1967, pp. 400–404 (Quoted: Ensink 1967a).
— On the Old Javanese Cantakaparwa and its tale of Sutasoma. 's-Gravenhage 1967. VKI 54. (Quoted: Ensink 1967b).
— Rekhacarmma. On the Indonesian Shadow-Play with special reference to the Island of Bali, in: Adyar Library Bulletin 31–32 (1968), pp. 412–441.
— Sutasoma's Teaching to Gajavaktra, the Snake and the Tigress (Tantular, Sutasoma kakavin 38, 1–42, 4), in: BKI 130 (1974), pp. 195–226.

Fontein, Jan: The Pilgrimage of Sudhana. A study of Gaṇḍavyūha illustrations in China, Japan and Java. 's-Gravenhage 1966. Thesis Leiden.

Friederich, R.: Voorloopig verslag van het eiland Bali, in: VBG 22–23 (1849–50). (Pt. and p.)

Gonda, Jan: Śiva in Indonesien, in: Wiener Zeitschrift für die Kunde Süd-Asiens und Archiv für Indische Philosophie 14 (1970), pp. 1–31.
— Sanskrit in Indonesia. 2nd ed., International Academy of Indian Culture, New Delhi 1973. Śata-Piṭaka Series vol. 99.

Goris, Roelof: Bijdrage tot de kennis der Oud-Javaansche en Balineesche theologie. Leiden 1926. Thesis Leiden.
— Secten op Bali, in: MK 3 (1931), pp. 37–53.

Grader, C. J.: Tweedeeling in het Oud-Balische dorp, in: MK 5 (1937), pp. 45–71.

Grönbold, Günter: Ṣaḍ-aṅga-yoga. Raviśrījñāna's Guṇabharaṇī nāma Ṣaḍaṅgayogaṭippaṇī mit Text, Übersetzung und literarhistorischem Kommentar. München 1969. Thesis München.

Hooykaas, C.: Śaiva-siddhānta in Java and Bali, in: BKI 118 (1962), pp. 309–327.
— Āgama Tīrtha. Five Studies in Hindu-Balinese religion. Amsterdam 1964. VKNAWLNR 70, 4. (Quoted: Hooykaas 1964a).
— The Balinese Sengguhu-Priest, a Shaman, but not a Sufi, a Saiva, and a Vaisnava, in: Malayan and Indonesian Studies. Essays presented to Sir Richard Winstedt . . ., ed. by John Bastin and R. Roolvink. Oxford 1964, pp. 267–281. (Quoted: Hooykaas 1964b).
— Surya-Sevana. The way to God of a Balinese Śiva priest. Amsterdam 1966. VKNAWLNR 72, 3.
— Balinese Bauddha Brahmans. Amsterdam-London 1973. VKNAWLNR 80.
— Cosmogony and Creation in Balinese Tradition. The Hague 1974. B. Indon. 9.

Kern, H.: Over de vermenging van Çiwaïsme en Buddhisme op Java, naar aanleiding van het Oud-Javaansch gedicht Sutasoma, in: VG 4 (1916), pp. 149–177. (First published Amsterdam 1888 in Verhandelingen en Mededeelingen der Koninklijke Akademie van Wetenschappen, 3, 5, pp. 8–43).

Krom, N. J.: Over het Çiwaïsme van Midden-Java. Amsterdam 1924. MKAWL 58, B. 8.
— en T. van Erp: Beschrijving van Barabuḍur. Den Haag 1919–1930. 2 vols. and 3 portfolios.

Lévi, Sylvain et Édouard Chavannes: Les seize arhats protecteurs de la Loi (premier article). I. La relation de Nandimitra, in: JA 11e série, 8 (1916), pp. 5–50.

Pigeaud, Theodoor Gautier Thomas: De Tantu Panggĕlaran. Een Oud-Javaansch Prozageschrift, uitgegeven, vertaald en toegelicht. 's-Gravenhage 1924. Thesis Leiden.
— Java in the Fourteenth Century. The Nāgara-Kĕrtāgama by Rakawi Prapañca of Majapahit, 1365 A.D. 3rd. ed. revised and enlarged by some contemporaneous texts, with notes, translations, commentaries and a glossary. The Hague 1960–63. 5 vols. KITS 4.
— Literature of Java. Catalogue raisonné of Javanese manuscripts in the Library of the University of Leiden and other public collections in the Netherlands. The Hague 1967–70. 3 vols.

Rassers, W. H.: Over den zin van het Javaansche tooneel, in: BKI 81 (1925), pp. 311–384 (Translation: Rassers 1959, pp. 1–61).
— Çiwa en Boeddha in den Indischen Archipel, in: Koninklijk Instituut voor de Taal-, Land- en Volkenkunde van Nederlandsch Indië, 's-Gravenhage. Gedenkschrift uitgegeven ter gelegenheid van het 75-jarig bestaan, 's-Gravenhage 1926, pp. 222–253 (Translation: Rassers 1959, pp. 63–91).
— Over den oorsprong van het Javaansche tooneel, in: BKI 88 (1931), pp. 317–450 (Translation: Rassers 1959, pp. 93–215).
— Pañji, the Culture Hero. A structural study of religion in Java. The Hague 1959. KITS 3.

Schwartz, H. J. E. F. en J. L. Swellengrebel: Een vorstenwijding op Bali, naar materiaal verzameld door de heer H. J. E. F. Schwartz †, bewerkt door J. L. Swellengrebel. Leiden 1947. Mededelingen van het Rijksmuseum voor Volkenkunde te Leiden No. 2.

Soebadio, Haryati: Jñānasiddhânta. Secret Lore of the Balinese Śaiva priest. 's-Gravenhage 1971. Thesis Amsterdam. B. Indon. 7.

Stutterheim, W. F.: The meaning of Hindu-Javanese caṇḍi, in: Journal of the American Oriental Society 51 (1931), pp. 1–15.
— De kraton van Majapahit. 's-Gravenhage 1948. VKI 7.

Supomo: "Lord of the Mountains" in the fourteenth century kakavin, in: BKI 128 (1972), p. 281–297.

Swellengrebel, J. L.: Introduction, to: Bali. Studies in Life, Thought and Ritual. The Hague-Bandung 1960. SSI 5, pp. 1–76.

Teeuw, A. en E. M. Uhlenbeck: Over de interpretatie van de Nāgarakṛtāgama, in: BKI 114 (1958), pp. 210–237.

Van Eerde, J. C.: Hindu-Javaansche en Balische eeredienst, in: BKI 65 (1911), pp. 1–39.

Van Leur, J. C.: Indonesian Trade and Society. Essays in Asian Social and Economic History. The Hague 1967. SSI 1.

Van Naerssen, F. H.: Oudjavaansche Oorkonden in Duitsche en Deensche verzamelingen. Leiden 1941. Thesis Leiden.

Van Stein Callenfels, P. V. en Poerbatjaraka: Verklaring van Basreliefseries. A. De Bubukṣah-serie aan het pendapa-terras te Panataran, in: TBG 58 (1919), pp. 348–361.

Wulff, K.: Sang hyang Kamahāyānan Mantrānaya. Ansprache bei der Weihe buddhistischer Mönche, aus dem Altjavanischen übersetzt und sprachlich erläutert. København 1935. Det Kgl. Danske Videnskabernes Selskab. Hist.-filol. Meddelelser 21, 4.

Zoetmulder, Piet: Die Hochreligionen Indonesiens, in: Waldemar Stöhr und Piet Zoetmulder: Die Religionen Indonesiens. Stuttgart 1965. Die Religionen der Menschheit 5, 1, pp. 223–354.

Buddhistisch-schintoistischer Synkretismus in Struktur und Praxis des Tempels Rinnōji in Nikkō, Japan

Von ROBERT K. HEINEMANN

Kōbōdaishi Kūkai (774–835), der Begründer der japanischen esoterischen Sekte Shingon-shū, hat uns aus dem 5. Jahr Kōnin, 814, folgende, den Mönch Shōdō-Shōnin betreffende biographische Notiz hinterlassen:

„Im 3. Monat des 2. Jahres Tennō (782) kopierte der Mönch Shōdō Sūtren, malte Buddhabilder und brachte beides den himmlischen und irdischen Gottheiten dar; er trennte den Saum seines Gewandes ab, umwickelte damit seine Füße und machte sich unter Verachtung des eigenen Lebens auf den Weg. Sūtren und Bilder mit Schnüren auf den Rücken gebunden, erreichte er den Fuß einer Berggruppe. Sieben Tage lang rezitierte er dort Sūtren und übte sich in buddhistischer Ehrfurchtsbezeugung; dann äußerte er folgende inständige Bitte: ‚Wenn es möglich ist, mich Euch, Göttern, mitzuteilen, so bitte ich, schaut in mein Herz! Die von mir kopierten Sūtren und gemalten Bilder sollen, wenn ich den Gipfel des Berges erreiche, den Göttern dargebracht werden, ihre Würde zu preisen und das Glück aller Wesen zu mehren. Demütig bitte ich: Entfaltet Eure Macht, ihr guten Götter! Umhüllt mich mit Nebel, ihr Giftdrachen! Weist mir den Weg, ihr Berggeister! Laßt so meinen Wunsch in Erfüllung gehen! Sollte ich den Gipfel des Berges nicht erreichen, so möge ich auch nicht zur Erleuchtung gelangen!'"[1]

Shōdō-Shōnin, der ehrwürdige Mönch Shōdō, von dem hier die Rede ist, gilt als der Gründer des etwa 120 km nördlich von Tōkyō liegenden Tendai-Tempels Rinnōji bei der Stadt Nikkō. Er lebte von 735 bis 817, gehörte den uns bekannten Quellen[2] nach nicht fest einer der damaligen japanischen buddhistischen Schulen oder Sekten an, sondern übte sich frei in buddhistischen Praktiken wie Sūtrenrezitation und hingebungsvoller Verehrung des Bodhisattva Avalokiteśvara (jap. Kannon). Bemerkenswert an der uns überlieferten, oben zitierten Notiz des Kōbōdaishi Kūkai ist, daß der Mönch Shōdō die ursprünglich im Hinblick auf die drei buddhistischen Kostbarkeiten, Buddha, Lehre und Gemeinde, geübten Praktiken hier den „himmlischen und irdischen Gottheiten" (jap. *jingi*) widmet, um sie gewogen zu machen, ihm Beistand bei der Erfüllung seiner Gelübde zu leisten. Kūkai, Begründer und erster Höhepunkt des buddhistischen Esoterismus in Japan, tadelt den Mönch Shōdō wegen seines Einsatzes buddhistischer Praktiken zur Ehre der einheimischen

---

[1]) Shamon Shōdō, sansui wo he, genju wo migaku no hi („Inschrift über den buddhistischen Mönch Shōdō, der Berge und Gewässer überquert und das wunderbare Juwel blank schleift"); in: Nikkōsan-Rinnōji-shi („Geschichte des Tempels Nikkōsan-Rinnōji"), Nikkō 1966; Shiryōhen (Quellen), S. 3f.

[2]) Gesammelt in dem in Anm. 1 genannten Werk.

Gottheiten und seines gläubigen Vertrauens, das er in sie setzt, keineswegs; im Gegenteil, an anderer Stelle der zitierten Schrift lobt er seine unermüdliche religiöse Praxis und seine Entschlossenheit, zur Erleuchtung zu gelangen.[3])

Shōdō-Shōnin steht als Buddhist, der zu asketischem Üben in die Berge geht, nicht allein in seiner Zeit. War während der ersten zwei bis drei Jahrhunderte nach dem Eindringen des Buddhismus nach Japan die neue Religion in der Hauptsache eine Angelegenheit des Adels bei Hofe und innerhalb der religiösen Zentren, der Tempel, so scheint es bereits um das 8. Jahrhundert zu den gewohnten Praktiken gehört zu haben, daß Anhänger der vom Festland übernommenen Lehre zur Stärkung der Willenskraft und Abhärtung von Körper und Geist in unwegsame Berggebiete eindrangen und dort buddhistische Sūtren sowie magische Silben und Sprüche, *dhāraṇī*, rezitierten.[4]) Es war jene Zeit, in der sich der Buddhismus zunehmend mit einheimischen Glaubensformen, bis heute häufig mit „Ur-Shintō" bezeichnet[5]), vermischte. Die Wahl eines ruhigen, abseits vom störenden Treiben der Menschen gelegenen Orts zu religiösem Üben entspricht durchaus den bekannten Idealen des indischen[6]) und chinesischen[7]) Buddhismus. Auch in esoterischen Schriften ist es nicht schwer, Stellen zu finden, die dem Gläubigen nahelegen, in den Bergen zu leben und dort zu praktizieren.[8]) Dem kam gewiß die japanische Tradi-

[3]) Op. cit., S. 10f.

[4]) Siehe dazu z.B. G. Renondeau, Le Shugendō, histoire, doctrine et rites des anachorètes dits yamabushi; Cahiers de la Société asiatique, XVIII, Paris 1965, S. 18ff., sowie das Kapitel über En no gyōja, S. 26ff.

[5]) Zur Frage des „Ur-Shintō" siehe die kritische Abhandlung von Nelly Naumann, Einige Bemerkungen zum sogenannten Ur-Shintō; in NOAG 107/108 (1970), S. 5–13.

[6]) So nennen z.B. die allgemein bekannten Läuterungsübungen (Skrt. *dhūta*) zur Reinigung von Körper und Geist durch das Ablassen vom Haften an den Dingen unter anderem das Üben im Wald, an einem ruhigen, fern von menschlicher Behausung liegenden Ort.

[7]) Der chinesische Buddhismus hat die indischen Übungsideale, wenn auch teilweise den eigenen Systemen angepaßt und umstrukturiert, weitgehend übernommen. So findet sich z.B. im Hsiu-hsi-chih-kuan-tso-ch'an-fa-yao nach Chih-i (538–597), dem sogenannten Hsiao-chih-kuan (der „Kleinen *śamatha-vipaśyanā*") die Aufforderung, an einem ruhigen Ort: „tief in den Bergen", „im Wald" oder „in einem reinen Tempel", zu weilen und zu üben. Cf. Taishō-shinshū-daizōkyō (fortan T.), Bd. 46, Nr. 1915, S. 463b.

[8]) G. Renondeau, op. cit., S. 41f., nennt das So-shijji(kara)-kyō (chin. Su-hsi-ti-chieh-lo-ching, Skrt. Susiddhikaramahātantrasādhanopāyikapaṭala; übers. von Śubhakarasiṃha (637–735); T. Nr. 893) und das Fudō-shisha-(darani-)himitsuhō (chin. Pu-tung-shih-chê-(t'o-lo-ni-)pi-mi-fa, übers. von Vajrabodhi (671–741); T. Nr. 1202). Es ist mir nicht gelungen zu verifizieren, an welche Stelle in der zweiten der beiden Schriften Renondeau gedacht haben mag. (Meint er T. Bd. 21, S. 23b, Z. 10?) In der ersten finden sich diesbezügliche Stellen u. a. in T. Bd. 18, S. 605c–606a und S. 626b–c. Vgl. auch das Bontenchakujihō (chin. Fan-t'ien-tsê-ti-fa, „Regeln zur Wahl der (Übungs-)Stätte des Bonten [= Brahman]"), vermutlich von Vajrabodhi (671–741), in T. Bd. 18, S. 924c–926a: Dort sind 42 Übungsstätten genannt, davon die ersten 31 in den Bergen.

tion einer Art primitiver Bergverehrung, heute geläufig mit dem Fachwort „Bergglauben“ (jap. *sangaku-shinkō*) bezeichnet, in Verbindung mit dem Glauben an die Kraft der einheimischen Naturgötter entgegen. Schon in der ältesten uns erhaltenen Anthologie japanischsprachiger Gedichte, der Sammlung Man'yōshū[9]), findet sich ein Gedicht, das zeigt, daß Japaner der Narazeit, des 8. Jahrhunderts, den Berg Fuji als Gottheit, die für Ruhe und Frieden des Landes sorgte, verehrten[10]). Eine beachtliche Zahl von Mythen, Ritualen, Festen und Volksglaubensformen steht noch heute in engem Verhältnis zu den Bergen. Von China übernommene taoistische Elemente, besonders das Bild des Eremiten, *shinsen* (chin. *shên-hsien*), der sich zur Erlangung übernatürlicher Fähigkeiten und Lebensverlängerung durch asketische Übungen in die Berge zurückzog, lieferte den Bergpraktiken zusätzliche rituale Elemente als auch eine gewisse spekulative Stütze[11]). So bildete sich bis zum japanischen Mittelalter langsam aus einheimischen, buddhistischen und taoistischen Traditionselementen ein Glaubens- und Übungssystem heraus, das seit dem 9. Jahrhundert unter dem Namen *shugendō*, wörtlich „Weg der Wunderwirkungen durch Üben“, bekannt ist. Seine Anhänger werden als *yamabushi*, Bergasketen, bezeichnet. Die Hauptzentren ihres Übens lagen in den Bergen von Yamato[12]) und Kii[13]). Im Laufe der Zeit übernahmen die *yamabushi*, in teilweise abgewandelter Form, Magie und Beschwörungspraxis der esoterischen Sekten Shingonshū und Tendai-shū und spalteten sich um die Mitte des 12. Jahrhunderts in zwei Richtungen auf, deren jede sich an eine der beiden Sekten anlehnte[14]). Unter Einfluß der genannten beiden Esoterismen stellten sie den schreckenerregenden, flammenumloderten Lichtgott Acala, japanisch Fudō-myōō, und seinen Kult, besonders das ursprünglich brahmanische, später vom esoterischen Buddhismus umgestaltete und umgedeutete *goma* (Skrt. *homa*), in die Mitte ihrer geheimen Praktiken[15]).

Bis zum 13. Jahrhundert, zum Beginn der Kamakurazeit, hatten sich die Organisationen dieses synkretistischen Übungssystems so gefestigt und verbreitet, daß nun im ganzen Land Shugendō-Berge eröffnet wurden und die *yamabushi* im religiösen Leben, ja sogar teilweise bis in die Politik hinein, eine gewichtige Rolle spielten[16]). In der Edozeit, dem

---

[9]) Engl. Übersetzungen von J. L. Pierson, The Manyosu, Translated and Annotated, Leiden 1929–1969, und Nihon-gakujutsu-shinkōkai, The Manyōshū, Tōkyō 1940[3].

[10]) Gedicht Nr. 319; in der japanischen Iwanami-Bunko-Ausgabe, Shintei-Shinkun-Man'yōshū, Bd. 1, S. 127.

[11]) G. Renondeau, op. cit., S. 5ff.

[12]) Op. cit., S. 44ff.

[13]) Op. cit., S. 53ff. Zu anderen, hier nicht genannten Zentren siehe dort auch S. 59ff.

[14]) Op. cit., S. 66ff.

[15]) Op. cit., S. 133f.

[16]) Siehe dazu H. O. Rotermund, Die Yamabushi, Aspekte ihres Glaubens, Lebens und ihrer sozialen Funktion im japanischen Mittelalter (Reihe „Mono-

17., 18. und den ersten zwei Dritteln des 19. Jahrhunderts etwa, gelangten sie unter den Herrschaftseinfluß der Militärregierung, des *bakufu*[17]), und ihre Organisationen wurden zwischen 1868 und 1872, nach Wiedereinsetzung der Staatsgewalt des Tennō, abgeschafft[18]). Diese Maßnahme ging einher mit dem Bestreben, die japanische Nationalreligion (Shintō), deren Struktur theoretisch die Göttlichkeit und weltliche Macht des Tennō begründete, von allem Fremden, namentlich buddhistischen Elementen, zu befreien und auf eine — zumindest vermeintlich — ursprüngliche, rein japanische Form zurückzuführen. Es war ein Teil jener groß angelegten Religionsreform, die unter dem Namen *shinbutsu-bunri*, „Trennung von Göttern und Buddhas", bekannt ist, und die — besonders in der ersten, fanatischen Zeit — von einer Unterdrückung des Buddhismus, dem sogenannten „Abschaffen des Buddha und Zertrümmern des Śākya(muni)" (*haibutsu-kishaku*) und einer absoluten Vorrangstellung des Shintō als Staatsreligion bis zum Ende des 2. Weltkrieges begleitet war.

Wir wissen, daß der Shintō durchaus nicht in einer rein japanischen Form — wenn es eine solche als „Shintō" überhaupt jemals gab[19]) — wiederhergestellt wurde und werden konnte; denn was durch eine über tausendjährige Symbiose geworden ist, läßt sich schwerlich auf eine sogenannte ursprüngliche, im übrigen vergessene Grundform zurückführen. Wichtig war es für das damalige Staatssystem, beide Religionen politisch-ideologisch und verwaltungsmäßig scharf voneinander zu trennen und den Staatsshintō von allen äußeren Zeichen fremden, sprich buddhistischen Einflusses zu „reinigen".

Mit weniger Gründlichkeit verfuhr man bei der Säuberung des Buddhismus. Hier überlebten nicht nur in buddhistischer Assimilierung und Namensgebung schintoistischer Gottheiten, sondern auch in bestimmten Praktiken wesentliche und als spezifisch japanisch erkennbare Elemente einer über tausendjährigen schintoistisch-buddhistischen Verschmelzung (jap. *shinbutsu-shūgō*). Auch gewisse Praktiken des eben skizzenhaft angedeuteten Übungssystems des *shugendō*, des „Wegs der Wunderwirkungen durch Üben", sind dort lebendig geblieben.

Die vielfältigen Möglichkeiten der Bezüge zwischen beiden Religionen sollen hier an einem verhältnismäßig einfachen, in seinen Grundzügen durchsichtigen Fall eines solchen Synkretismus paradigmatisch dargestellt werden. Der von dem eingangs erwähnten Mönch Shōdō gegründete Tempel Rinnōji in Nikkō[20]) eignet sich gut zu einer leicht überschaubaren

graphien zur Völkerkunde", hrsg. vom Hamburgischen Museum für Völkerkunde, Bd. 5), Hamburg 1968.

[17]) G. Renondeau, op. cit., S. 79ff.

[18]) Op. cit., S. 86.

[19]) Siehe H. O. Rotermund, Les croyances du Japon antique; in: Histoire des Religions 1 (Encyclopédie de la Pléiade), Paris 1970. Vgl. auch Anm. 5.

[20]) Tempel der Tendai-Sekte. Er ist, neben dem Haupt-Tempel der Sekte, dem Enryakuji auf dem Berg Hieizan bei Kyōto, einer der Tempel, die sich unter anderem der Ausbildung von Novizen widmen.

Darstellung: Der Aufbau seiner synkretistischen Entsprechungen beruht auf einer klaren, durchgehenden Dreiteilung. Sie ist aus dem Schema auf Seite unten ersichtlich und wird im folgenden erläutert werden. Die Entsprechungstypen sind grundsätzlich auch in anderen Gebieten und

3 Berge	3 schintoistische Gottheiten	3 schintoistische Schreine	3 buddhistische „Verehrungswürdige"	3 *ten* (*devāḥ*)
Nyohōzan	Tagorihime no mikoto	Takinoo-jinja („Wasserfallschweifschrein")	Amidabutsu (Amitābha)	Benzaiten (Sarasvatī)
Nantaizan	Ōnamuchi no mikoto	Shingū („Neuer Schrein")	Senjukannon (Sahasrabhujārya-avalokiteśvara)	Daikokuten (Mahākāla)
Tarōzan	Ajisukitakahikone no mikoto	Hongū („Ursprünglicher Schrein")	Batōkannon (Hayagrīva)	Bishamonten (Vaiśravaṇa)

Tempeln Japans wiederzufinden und bedeuten nichts Neues dem, der den Fragen schon anderswo im Land nachgegangen ist. Weniger bekannt mag sein, daß die synkretistischen Züge dort auch der Praxis anhaften. Besondere Betonung verdient, daß es sich hier nicht um synkretistische Formen etwa im Volksbrauchtum und -glauben handelt — was nähmen diese nach so langem Nebeneinander und Miteinander der Religionen wunder! —, sondern um Praktiken, dem Einblick der Öffentlichkeit verschlossen, im streng orthodoxen Rahmen einer der großen buddhistischen Sekten Japans, der Tendai-Sekte — trotz staatlich dekretierter „Trennung von Göttern und Buddhas".

Das Schema veranschaulicht die heutige Struktur des Pantheons des Tempels Rinnōji in Nikkō[21]). Die darauf erkennbare Dreiergruppierung entspricht derjenigen vieler buddhistischer „Verehrungswürdiger" (jap. *honzon*). Wie in zahlreichen Tempelhallen nicht eine einzelne Buddhastatue verwahrt ist, sondern ihr zur Seite zwei andere stehen, so findet der Besucher auch hier in der Haupthalle des Tempels eine Triade: Amidabutsu (Amitābha) in der Mitte und ihm zu Seiten zwei Bodhisattvas — links Senjukannon, den Tausendarmigen Kannon (Sahasrabhujāryāvalokiteśvara), und rechts Batōkannon, den Pferdekopf-Kannon (Hayagrīva). Der um die Kamakurazeit (etwa 13.—14. Jh.) zu einem System ausgebauten Lehre vom „eigentlichen Stand und der herabgelassenen Spur" (jap. *honji-suijaku*)[22]) zufolge wurde jede einzelne japanische einheimische Gottheit als Erscheinung einer Gestalt aus dem

[21]) Ein ähnliches, weniger vollständiges Schema findet sich in dem japanischen Werk von R. Hoshino, Nikkō-Kaisan Shōdō-Shōnin („Der Gründer des Tempels in Nikkō, Shōdō-Shōnin"), Nikkō 1954; S. 161.

[22]) Deutsche Übersetzung des Ausdrucks *honji-suijaku* in W. Gundert, Japanische Religionsgeschichte, Stuttgart 1943, S. 76f.

buddhistischen Pantheon verstanden[23]). So hat man die drei schintoistischen Gottheiten Tagorihime no mikoto, Ōnamuchi no mikoto und Ajisukitakahikone no mikoto in Nikkō als Erscheinungen der drei genannten buddhistischen Verehrungswürdigen angesehen und mit ihnen identifiziert. Diese Gottheiten werden in den im Schema aufgeführten drei schintoistischen Schreinen Takinoo („Wasserfallschweif"), Shingū („Neuer Schrein") bzw. Hongū („Alter Schrein", wörtlich „Ursprünglicher Schrein"), alle dem Tempelgebiet von Nikkō zugehörig, verehrt. Als Besonderheit des japanischen Bergglaubens tritt in Nikkō hervor, daß die genannten schintoistischen Gottheiten mit den „drei Bergen" identifiziert werden: Nyohōzan, der „Berg des weiblichen Schatzes", ist Tagorihime no mikoto; Nantaizan, der „Berg des männlichen Körpers", ist Ōnamuchi no mikoto; Tarōzan, der „Berg des ältesten Sohnes", ist Ajisukitakahikone no mikoto.

Im allgemeinen besteht ein Shintō-Schrein aus einem Doppelbau: Im Hintergrund liegt als Allerheiligstes die Haupt- oder Götterhalle (jap. *honden* oder *shinden*) mit dem Gegenstand der Verehrung, dem *shintai*, wörtlich dem „Gottesleib", und davor steht, mit der Götterhalle meist durch einen Laufgang verbunden, die etwas größere, etwa quadratische Kulthalle (*haiden*), in der die Priester die Riten verrichten und die Gläubigen die Götter verehren. Entsprechend der Identifizierung der „drei Gottheiten" mit den „drei Bergen" weisen die „drei Schreine" von Nikkō jedoch eine wesentliche Abweichung von dieser Norm auf: In ihren Haupthallen befindet sich kein „Gottesleib" (*shintai*). Stattdessen ist in der Rückwand der Halle eine nach außen zu öffnende Tür eingebaut. Das Schreingebäude ist im Grundriß so orientiert, daß der dem betreffenden Schrein entsprechende Berg vor der hinteren Tür der Haupthalle liegt: der Nyohōzan vor der Tür des Schreins Takinoo, des „Wasserfallschweifs", der Nantaizan vor der Tür des Shingū, des „Neuen Schreins", und der Tarōzan vor der Tür des Hongū, des „Alten" oder wörtlich „Ursprünglichen Schreins". Diese Bauweise zeigt klar, daß der Gegenstand der Verehrung, der „Gottesleib" (*shintai*), der betreffende Berg selbst ist[24]).

In Übereinstimmung mit der Dreiteilung und zur Einhaltung der Parallelität dazu wurde in späterer Zeit bei der Einrichtung von kleinen Heiligtümern für buddhistische Gottheiten, von *ten* (Skrt. *deva*), darauf geachtet, daß auch sie in einer Gruppe von dreien hinzugefügt wurden. Alle drei gehören übrigens zu den Sieben Glücksgöttern (jap. Shichi-

[23]) Mit „Gottheit" ist hier das japanische Wort *kami* übersetzt. Vgl. H. O. Rotermund, La conception des kami japonais à l'époque de Kamakura: Notes sur le premier chapitre du "Sasekishū"; in: Revue de l'histoire des religions, CLXXXII, 1 (Juli 1972), S. 3–28, und R. E. Morrell, Mujū Ichien's Shinto-Buddhist Syncretism: Shasekishū, Book 1, Einleitung; in: Monumenta Nipponica, XXVIII, 4 (Winter 1973), S. 447–454. Vgl. auch A. Matsunaga, The Buddhist Philosophy of Assimilation; Tokyo 1969.

[24]) Vgl. dazu oben die Bemerkung zum Berg Fuji, der, dem Gedicht Nr. 319 im Man'yōshū zufolge, schon im 8. Jh. als Gottheit verehrt wurde.

fukujin)[25]), die sich in Japan seit dem Mittelalter bis heute großer Popularität erfreuen.

Die einfachen, klaren Entsprechungen in Dreiergruppen, die für den Tempel in Nikkō heute zwar zu einer Selbstverständlichkeit geworden sind, entbehren, wie es scheint, jedoch logischer Notwendigkeit. Der Buddhologe muß sich fragen, ob eine Parallelität besteht zwischen den Entsprechungen Amitābha-Sarasvatī, Sahasrabhujāryāvalokiteśvara-Mahākāla und Hayagrīva-Vaiśravaṇa. Er muß sich auch fragen, warum gerade diese drei buddhistischen Verehrungswürdigen als Hypostasen der genannten schintoistischen Gottheiten eingesetzt worden sind. Schließlich muß er sich die Frage stellen, wie es dazu kam, daß gerade diese drei Berge mit gerade diesen schintoistischen Gottheiten identifiziert worden sind. Authentische historische Quellen, die uns glaubhaft über das Entstehen der Entsprechungen und seine Gründe unterrichten, liegen uns nur in geringer Zahl vor[26]). Die vielen Legenden, die sich später darum gewunden haben, scheinen zu zeigen, daß man sich erst nachträglich bemüht hat, die Entsprechungen — eben weil sie logischer Notwendigkeit entbehren — zu rechtfertigen.

Die eingangs zitierte biographische Notiz des Kōbōdaishi Kūkai über den Tempelgründer Shōdō-Shōnin ist das einzige uns überlieferte authentische zeitgenössische Dokument. Zwar ist darin noch nicht eine Dreizahl schintoistischer Gottheiten genannt, ganz zu schweigen von ihren Namen; es läßt jedoch eine gewisse, wenn auch noch nicht systematisierte Form der gegenseitigen Durchdringung von japanischem Götter- und Naturglauben und Buddhismus schon in jener Zeit der Tempelgründung durch Shōdō-Shōnin, der späten Narazeit, erkennen. Berichtet die Schrift doch von dem Einsatz buddhistischer Praktiken zur Erlangung der Gunst der einheimischen himmlischen und irdischen Gottheiten und ihres Beistands zur Erfüllung der von Shōdō-Shōnin ausgesprochenen Gelübde.

Der erste Bericht mit Ansätzen einer konkreten Beschreibung von drei schintoistischen Gottheiten liegt uns in einer Schrift aus dem Jahre 818, dem Hodarakusan-konryū-shugyō-nikki[27]), vor. Diese stammt dem Kolophon zufolge von vier Schülern des Shōdō-Shōnin und berichtet von einer Begebenheit aus dem Jahre 816. Damals habe der Mönch einen der Berge bei Nikkō bestiegen, wobei ihm drei Gottheiten erschienen seien: Die erste, eine weibliche Gottheit im Alter von etwa 30 Jahren, sei von auffallender Schönheit gewesen; die zweite, eine männliche um 50 Jahre, habe ihm einen kraftvoll-majestätischen Eindruck gemacht; die dritte sei ein schöner Jüngling im Alter von etwa 15 oder 16 Jahren gewesen. Die Echtheit dieser Schrift wird heute bezweifelt, und man ver-

[25]) Die Sieben Glücksgötter sind: Daikoku(ten), Ebisu, Bishamon(ten), Benzaiten, Fukurokuju, Jurōjin und Hotei(oshō).

[26]) Gesammelt in dem in Anm. 1 genannten Werk, Nikkōsan-Rinnōji-shi. Dort finden sich auch kritische Bemerkungen zur Echtheit der Quellen und ihrer Entstehungsdaten.

[27]) Nikkōsan-Rinnōji-shi, Shiryōhen (vgl. Anm. 1), S. 72–81, und Zoku-gunshoruijū, Bd. 813 (Shakke-bu).

mutet, daß sie, wie viele andere, irgendwann in späterer Zeit als legendäre Rechtfertigung der parallelen Triaden dieses Tempels entstanden ist[28]).

In einer anderen, angeblich aus dem Jahre 825 stammenden Quelle zur Tempelgeschichte, dem Nikkōsan-takinoo-konryū-sōsōki[29]), wird berichtet, Kōbōdaishi Kūkai sei im Jahre 820 in das Gebiet des Tempels gekommen und habe dort den Takinoo-jinja, den Wasserfallschweif-Schrein, zur Verehrung einer namentlich nicht genannten weiblichen Gottheit errichtet. Auch dieses Dokument ist offenbar erst bedeutend später entstanden und gehört damit nicht nur zu den zahlreichen Kūkai-Legenden, sondern auch zu den nachträglichen Rechtfertigungen zur Entstehungsgeschichte des Tempels[30]).

Die erste verläßliche Aufzeichnung über eine Dreiteilung der Struktur des Pantheons von Nikkō ist uns in dem Bericht über den Besuch des dritten Patriarchen (jap. *zasu*) der japanischen Tendai-Sekte, Jikakudaishi Ennin (794—864), im Jahre 848 im Tempel in Nikkō überliefert. Diese Schrift, das Ennin-oshō-nyū-tōzan-ki[31]), 855 von dem Mönch Sonchin, einem Schüler des Shōdō-Shōnin, verfaßt, berichtet davon, daß Ennin anläßlich seines Besuchs die Statuen der drei im Schema aufgeführten buddhistischen Verehrungswürdigen errichtet habe. Die Schrift belehrt uns nicht darüber, warum Ennin dem Hauptverehrungswürdigen, das heißt der mittleren Statue, dem Amidabutsu (Skrt. Amitābha), nicht, wie allgemein üblich, die Bodhisattvas Seishi und Kannon (Skrt. Mahāsthāmaprāpta und Avalokiteśvara) zur Seite gestellt, sondern statt deren den Tausendarmigen Kannon, Senjukannon (Skrt. Sahasrabhujāryāvalokiteśvara), und den Pferdekopf-Kannon, Batōkannon (Skrt. Hayagrīva), gewählt hat. Zur Wahl des Senjukannon ließe sich als mögliche Begründung anführen, daß der Legende zufolge der Mönch Shōdō in einem benachbarten Tempel im Jahre 784 bereits einen Senjukannon errichtet habe, wobei freilich recht fraglich bleibt, wieviel Wirklichkeitswert dieser Legende zugrunde liegt[32]). Daß Ennin die drei buddhistischen Verehrungswürdigen, deren Statuen er errichtet hat, tatsächlich als Hypostasen in drei in Nikkō verehrten einheimischen Gottheiten verstanden hat (wenn uns deren damalige Namen auch nicht überliefert sind), geht zweifellos aus der Bezeichnung, die er dem dafür errichteten Tempelbau gab, hervor. Er nannte ihn Honji-jingū-ji, „Schrein-Tempel des ursprünglichen Stands", wobei mit „ursprünglichem Stand", der Gundertschen Übersetzung für *honji*, gemeint ist, daß es sich um Hypostasen in einheimischen Gottheiten handelt.

Die Triade der schintoistischen Schreine sei, nicht veröffentlichten Tempelchroniken zufolge[33]), auf folgende Weise entstanden: Nachdem

---

28) Z.B. K. Fukui im Nachwort des Nikkōsan-Rinnōji-shi.
29) Op. cit., Shiryōhen, S. 82–86, und Zoku-gunsho-ruijū, Bd. 813 (Shakke-bu).
30) Vgl. Anm. 28.
31) Nikkōsan-Rinnōji-shi, Shiryōhen, S. 19–21.
32) Nach S. Sekiguchi, Nikkō, Tōkyō 1964, S. 88.
33) Nach K. Fukui in Nikkōsan-Rinnōji-shi, S. 26.

Shōdō-Shōnin im Jahre 790 einen ersten Schrein, den sogenannten Futarasan-jinja, gegründet hatte, wurde dieser im Jahre 827, nach dem Tode des Mönchs Shōdō, ein erstes Mal und im Jahre 850 ein zweites Mal an eine andere Stelle verlegt. Der Bau des 850 entstandenen Schreins wurde als „Neuer Schrein" (Shingū) bezeichnet, während der 790 gegründete erste Schrein gleichzeitig als selbständig anerkannt wurde und den Namen Hongū, „Alter" oder „Ursprünglicher Schrein", erhielt. Zusammen mit dem von Kōbōdaishi Kūkai im Jahre 820 errichteten Schrein Takinoo-jinja ist somit die Entstehung der drei schintoistischen Schreine belegt.

Es ist nicht bekannt, wann die im Schema aufgeführten Namen der drei schintoistischen Gottheiten zu Gegenständen der Verehrung der drei schintoistischen Schreine wurden. Vermutlich wird es nicht vor der Kamakurazeit gewesen sein, der Zeit nämlich, in der die Lehre des *honji-suijaku* systematisiert wurde, indem klare und konkrete Beziehungen zwischen den einzelnen Gestalten des schintoistischen Pantheons einerseits und des buddhistischen andererseits festgelegt wurden. Wir kennen die drei Gottheiten aus der klassischen japanischen Mythologie, wie sie im Kojiki[34]) und Nihongi[35]) dargestellt sind. Demnach sind Tagorihime no mikoto und Ōnamuchi no mikoto ein Paar, das Ajisukitakahikone no mikoto gezeugt hat. Ōnamuchi no mikoto ist identisch mit der Gottheit Ōkuninushi no mikoto. Es ist bekannt, daß Ōkuninushi no mikoto häufig mit der buddhistischen Gottheit Daikokuten (Skrt. Mahākāla) in Verbindung gebracht wird: Die Zeichen für Ōkuni werden in sino-japanischer Lesung *daikoku* ausgesprochen und sind gleichlautend mit dem Daikoku für Mahākāla, dem „Großen Schwarzen". So ist es verständlich, wenn Daikokuten der Reihe zugeordnet worden ist, in der auch Ōnamuchi no mikoto steht.

Zur Entsprechung zwischen Tagorihime no mikoto und Benzaiten (Skrt. Sarasvatī) läßt sich folgendes schließen: Erstens ist Benzaiten die einzige weibliche Gottheit innerhalb der Sieben Glücksgötter (jap. Shichifukujin). So müßte es erstaunen, wenn nicht sie es wäre, die der Reihe zugeordnet worden ist, in der auch Tagorihime no mikoto, die einzige weibliche schintoistische Gottheit der Triade, steht. Zweitens ist die jüngere Schwester der Tagorihime no mikoto, die Ichiki-shima hime no mikoto, der japanischen Mythologie zufolge eine Göttin des Wassers und entspricht darin der buddhistischen Benzaiten, die unter anderem auch als Wassergöttin gilt.

---

[34]) Engl. Übers. von B. H. Chamberlain, Translation of "Kojiki" or "Records of Ancient Matters"; 2. Aufl, Kōbe 1932. Von den drei genannten Gottheiten und ihrem Verhältnis zueinander ist die Rede in Bd. 1. Japanischer Text in Shinten, Yokohama 1936, S. 41.

[35]) Engl. Übers. von W. G. Aston, Nihongi; Reprint London 1956. Das Nihongi berichtet nicht vom Verhältnis der drei Gottheiten zueinander, wohl aber werden ihre Namen in anderem Zusammenhang genannt: Tagorihime no mikoto und Ōnamuchi no mikoto in Bd. 1 (in Shinten [vgl. Anm. 34] S. 196 et pass. bzw. S. 209 et pass.), Ajisukitakahikone no mikoto in Bd. 2 (in Shinten S. 218 et pass.).

Es ist mir noch nicht gelungen, einen einleuchtenden Bezug zwischen dem dritten der drei *ten* (Skrt. *deva*) und irgendeinem anderen der in gleicher Reihe stehenden Elemente aufzudecken. Freilich bliebe nun nur noch diese dritte Reihe zur Besetzung mit einer buddhistischen Gottheit offen. Die Frage aber, warum gerade Bishamonten (Skrt. Vaiśravaṇa) gewählt wurde, ist damit nicht beantwortet. Folgende Beobachtung bietet vielleicht einen ersten Hinweis zur Lösung der Frage, wenngleich ihr, solange nur einen Einzelfall betreffend, noch keine Beweiskraft zukommt: Bishamonten ist mit einem peripher im Tempelgebiet liegenden Berg identifiziert. Vergleicht man nun die geographische Karte dieses Gebiets mit dem esoterischen Maṇḍala der Mutterschoßwelt, dem Taizōkai-mandara (Skrt. Mahākaruṇāgarbhadhātumaṇḍala), so stellt man fest, daß die Richtung von der Haupttempelhalle, in der die Statue des Amidabutsu (Amitābha) als Hauptverehrungswürdiger (*honzon*) steht, hin zu dem Berg, der den Bishamonten verkörpert, etwa die gleiche, nämlich annähernd NNW, ist wie diejenige vom Amidabutsu zum Bishamonten innerhalb des Taizōkai-mandara. Zu dem Maṇḍala ist zu erklären, daß entsprechend seiner früheren Aufhängeweise in japanischen Tempeln die linke Seite Norden entspricht, während die linke Seite des Kongōkai-mandara (Skrt. Vajradhātumaṇḍala), das ihm gegenüber hing, nach Süden gerichtet war. Im übrigen beginnt der japanische Name für das äußerste Feld dieses Maṇḍalas, Gekongōbu-in[36]), mit demselben chinesischen Zeichen wie der Name des Berges, Toyama, der „Äußere Berg", mit dem Bishamonten identifiziert ist: mit dem Zeichen für „außen". Da der Richtungssymbolismus im esoterischen Buddhismus stark ausgeprägt ist, wäre es durchaus möglich, daß die genannte Entsprechung bei der Wahl des Bishamonten eine Rolle gespielt hat. Ein Beweis für die Richtigkeit dieser Hypothese steht jedoch noch aus, solange nicht eine überzeugende Zahl von Parallelfällen in Nikkō entdeckt ist.

Auch die Identifizierung der drei Berge mit den drei schintoistischen Gottheiten ist mit hoher Wahrscheinlichkeit nicht vor Mitte der Kamakurazeit anzusetzen. Jedenfalls sind die Namen dieser Berge, die ja als Berge von Frau, Mann und Sohn den drei Gottheiten entsprechen, vorher nicht belegt[37]).

Die bisherige Darstellung zeigt, wie wenig positive Beweise uns in verläßlichen schriftlichen Dokumenten zur Entstehung der Triaden und ihrer Entsprechungen überliefert sind. Es scheint, daß heute kaum mehr mit einer sicheren Rekonstruktion des historischen Ablaufs gerech-

---

[36]) Siehe dazu R. Tajima, Les deux grands maṇḍalas et la doctrine de l'ésotérisme Shingon, Tōkyō und Paris 1959, S. 127ff.

[37]) Nach T. Wakamori, Nikkōsan no mukashi — sangaku-shinkō to nichirinsūhai („Der Berg Nikkō in früheren Zeiten — Bergglaube und Verehrung der Sonnenscheibe"); in: Zauhō-kankō-kai, Hrsg., Nikkō-Oze, Tōkyō 1970, S. 47ff. Die Datierung stützt sich auf Inschriften auf bronzenen und goldenen Ausgrabungsgegenständen (*fuda*, Amuletten, Erinnerungsmünzen von Pilgern u. a.), die in den letzten Jahren auf dem Berg Nantaizan gefunden wurden.

net werden kann. Welche aber auch immer die Abfolge bei der Genese des Systems gewesen sein mag, das Ergebnis einer wahrscheinlich langen Entwicklung, nämlich die Identifizierung der drei buddhistischen Verehrungswürdigen mit den drei schintoistischen Gottheiten und deren Identifizierung wiederum mit den drei Bergen, dürfen wir als besonders klares Schulbeispiel für den buddhistisch-schintoistischen Synkretismus in Japan werten. Daß die Berge Nyohōzan, Nantaizan und Tarōzan im Endergebnis nichts anderes sind als Amitābha, Sahasrabhujāryāvalokiteśvara und Hayagrīva, wird dem indologisch orientierten Buddhologen durchaus keine Selbstverständlichkeit sein, so sehr die Identifizierung konkreter Naturerscheinungen mit buddhistischen Symbolen andererseits dem Kenner japanischer Religion gewohnte Tatsache ist.

Eines darf nicht unerwähnt bleiben: Die Identifizierungen im Rahmen der dargestellten Beziehungen gelten fast nur von buddhistischer Sicht aus; auf schintoistischer Seite stößt, auch wenn der Staatsshintō seit Ende des letzten Krieges abgeschafft ist, eine Deutung der einheimischen, schintoistischen Gottheiten als Erscheinungen von Figuren des buddhistischen Pantheons meist auf Ablehnung.

Es mag die Frage aufgeworfen werden, inwieweit es in der heutigen religiösen Situation überhaupt noch von praktischem Belang ist, ob ein Berg oder eine mit ihm identifizierte Gottheit als Erscheinung eines buddhistischen Verehrungswürdigen angesehen wird oder nicht. Man sollte erwarten, daß Reminiszenzen einer solchen „Verschmelzung von Buddhas und Gottheiten" (jap. *shinbutsu-shūgō*) allenfalls noch im Volksglauben und -brauchtum erkennbar sind. Daß in einem Rahmen, in dem strengste Orthodoxie zum Ausdruck kommt, während der Ausbildung der buddhistischen Novizen, die genannten Relationen praktisch weiterleben, verdient durchaus der Aufmerksamkeit. Ein einfaches, das oben dargestellte Schema — wenigstens in wesentlichen Teilen — betreffendes Beispiel liefert die esoterisch-buddhistische Ausbildungspraxis *shidokegyō* (etwa „vorbereitendes Üben in vier Phasen") der Tendai-Sekte im Tempel Rinnōji. Wenn diese Praxis dem Wort „Esoterismus" entsprechend auch „geheim" ist, so liegt der eigentlich geheime Teil der Lehre doch außerhalb dessen, was direkt auf das hier besprochene Schema zu beziehen ist. Diejenigen Handlungen, die dafür als belangvoll gelten können, erfolgen während des ersten Teils des Tagesablaufs des Novizen, zwischen Aufstehen und Sonnenaufgang. Davon soll im folgenden die Rede sein.

Nach etwa sechsstündiger Ruhe steht der Übende morgens um 2 oder 3 Uhr[38]) auf und beginnt seinen Tagesablauf damit, daß er seinen Körper zur — realen und symbolischen — Reinigung mit kaltem Wasser übergießt. Dies ist eine leicht veränderte Art asketischen Übens, der man heute in verschiedenen Formen auch in nicht esoterischen Sekten des japanischen Buddhismus begegnet. Ich selbst habe sie als sogenanntes

---

[38]) Die Stunde variiert je nach dem Stadium der Ausbildung.

taki no gyō („Wasserfall-Üben") in der Nichiren-Sekte und als Wechselbäder in kaum erträglich heißem und abschreckend kaltem Wasser in der Rinzai-Sekte des Zen-Buddhismus erlebt. Einen synkretistischen Zug erlangt diese „Wasser-Übung" in Nikkō dadurch, daß der Übende dabei einen aus der esoterischen Übungsanleitung stammenden Vers in Sino-japanisch und eine aus dem Sanskrit übernommene *dhāraṇī* (in japanisierter Aussprache) rezitiert: So wird die Naturkraft des Wassers, die in japanischen Glaubensformen und Praktiken, namentlich dem *shugendō*, eine Rolle spielt, esoterisch-buddhistischer Symbolik dienstbar gemacht[39]).

Die nächste Handlung des Übenden besteht in der Zelebration des Feuerritus *goma* (Skrt. *homa*). Wahrscheinlich wurde ein ursprünglich aus vorbuddhistischer Tradition stammendes Ritual, in dem zur Aufhebung des Bösen und Erlangung von Glück dem Feuergott Agni geopfert wurde, vom esoterischen Buddhismus übernommen und dahingehend umgedeutet, daß das Feuer der buddhistischen Weisheit alle Besudelungen und Unwissen (jap. *mumyō*, Skrt. *avidyā*) verbrennt. Das höchste Ziel des Ritus liegt in der Identifizierung des Übenden mit dem Verehrungswürdigen, vor dem der Ritus stattfindet, meist, wie hier in Nikkō, dem Lichtkönig Fudō-myōō (Skrt. Acala), und über diesen mit dem Dainichi-nyorai (Skrt. Mahā-vairocana-tathāgata), der symbolisch dargestellten letzten, höchstens Realität. In dieses Ritual, das sich aus einer komplizierten Reihe symbolhafter Handlungen: Feuerspeisung, Hand- und Fingerstellungen (Skrt. *mudrā*) und Rezitation einer großen Zahl aus dem Sanskrit stammender *dhāraṇī*, zusammensetzt, sind in Japan an einheimische Gottheiten gerichtete Gebetsformeln aufgenommen. Auch hier zeigt sich die Durchdringung von buddhistischen und schintoistischen Elementen. Im übrigen wird die Ausführung des Ritus durch den Novizen zu Zeiten noch von einer asketischen Praxis begleitet: In das Feuer werden feuchte Blätter und Zweige geworfen, um die Rauchentwicklung so bis aufs äußerste zu verstärken. Mit großen Fächern wird dem Übenden dann der Rauch minutenlang ins Gesicht gefächelt, bis er nahe einer Ohnmacht ist. Es versteht sich von selbst, daß diese zweifellos harte asketische Übung nichts mit dem ursprünglichen buddhistischen „mittleren" Übungsweg, bei dem Extreme vermieden werden sollen, zu tun hat. Vielmehr handelt es sich um ein spezifisch japanisches Element, das ganz dem Charater der asketischen Praktiken der *yamabushi* entspricht: eine Praxis zur Stärkung von Mut, Ausdauer und Widerstandskraft. Vom alten *shugendō* ist uns überliefert, daß das Ertragen körperlicher Härten und Schmerzen dazu diente, die Qualen der untersten der sechs Daseinsebenen, der Hölle, auszukosten[40]).

---

[39]) Zur engen inneren Verwandtschaft von *shugendō* und Esoterismus vgl. G. Renondeau, op. cit., S. 92ff. (Kap. „La doctrine du Shugendō et celle du Bouddhisme ésotérique") und S. 103ff. (Kap. „La bouddhéité atteinte dans la vie présente").

[40]) Vgl. op. cit., S. 126ff.

Nach Beendigung des Feuerritus beginnt, etwa gegen 3 Uhr morgens, die Begehung der Berge des Tempelgebiets, diejenige Übung, die am meisten an die bekannte Praxis der Bergasketen, das *kaihōgyō*, „Üben durch Umwandern des Gipfels", erinnert. In der rechten Hand hält der Übende einen Rasselstab, *shakujō* (Skrt. *khakkhara*), zur symbolhaften Vertreibung ihm unter Umständen begegnender wilder Tiere, in der linken einen Fächer, auf dem die Stationen seines Wegs und die dort jeweils zu rezitierenden Sūtren und *dhāraṇī* eingetragen sind. Der Tempelbegründer Shōdō-Shōnin ist auf den meisten uns — wenn auch aus späterer Zeit — überlieferten Bildern und Statuen mit dem *shakujō* abgebildet, zum Gedenken an sein erstes Eindringen in das unwegsame Berggebiet, von dem die eingangs zitierte biographische Notiz spricht. Von unwegsamen Bergen kann heute zwar nicht mehr die Rede sein. In diesem Sinn bildet die Begehung auch keine eigentlich asketische Praxis mehr. Die Schwierigkeit der Übung wird jedoch dadurch künstlich ersetzt, daß der Übende gezwungen wird, einen Weg, für den er einschließlich aller Rezitationen an den vorgeschriebenen Stationen normalerweise gut zwei Stunden benötigen würde, in etwa einer Stunde zurückzulegen.

Sein Weg nun ist folgender: Zuerst begibt er sich zu der Stelle, an der der Tradition zufolge der Tempelgründer Shōdō-Shōnin seine erste Unterkunft und eine kleine Tempelhalle mit einem Tausendarmigen Kannon errichtet hat. Hier rezitiert der Übende einmal das Sūtra Hannyashingyō (Skrt. Prajñāpāramitā-hṛdaya-sūtra) und dreimal den *mantra* des Tausendarmigen Kannon: *on-basara-kiri-sowaka* (Skrt. *oṃ vajra hrīḥ svāhā*)[41]. Die zweite Station ist der „Alte Schrein", Hongū. Auch hier rezitiert er einmal das Hannyashingyō und, wie aus dem Schema oben zu schließen ist, ein *mantra* des Pferdeköpfigen Kannon, Batōkannon (Hayagrīva): *on-amirito-dohaba-unpatta-sowaka* (Skrt. *oṃ amṛtodbhava hūṃ phaṭ svāhā*)[42]. Nach zwei weiteren Stationen, ohne Belang für das dargestellte Schema, gelangt er nun zur Haupthalle des Tempels, in der die Statuen der drei buddhistischen Verehrungswürdigen stehen. Es versteht sich von selbst, daß er hier, neben dem Hannyashingyō, die *mantra* aller drei Verehrungswürdigen rezitiert, nämlich die bereits genannten für den Tausendarmigen und für den Pferdeköpfigen Kannon und dazu den für den Buddha Amitābha: *on-amirita-teze-kara-un* (Skrt. *oṃ amṛta teje hara hūṃ*)[43].

Nach vier weiteren Stationen, die wiederum in keiner direkten Beziehung zum Schema oben stehen, gelangt der Übende in die Nähe des

---

[41]) In der Version der anderen der zwei japanischen esoterischen Sekten, der Shingon-Sekte, lautet der *mantra*: *on-basara-darama-kiriku* (Skrt. *oṃ vajra-dharma hrīḥ*).

[42]) Die Version der Shingon-Sekte lautet: *on-amirito-dohanba-unhatta* (Skrt. *oṃ amṛtodbhava hūṃ phaṭ*).

[43]) Die japanische Lesart dieses *mantra* lautet in der Shingon-Sekte: *on-amirita-teisei-kara-un*.

Berges Nantaizan. Neben dem Hannyashingyō und einigen anderen kurzen Anrufungsformeln rezitiert er hier dreimal den *mantra* des Tausendarmigen Kannon: Der Berg ist, wie schon erwähnt, mit diesem Bodhisattva identifiziert.

Die nächsten vier Stationen des Weges stehen wieder außerhalb des dargestellten Schemas. Danach, nach fast einstündiger Rundwanderung und schon wieder nahe des Ausgangspunkts, steht der Übende jetzt —, durch eine Schlucht getrennt — dem Berg Toyama, dem „Äußeren Berg", gegenüber, jenem Berg, der — aufgrund der analogen Lage des Vaiśravaṇa im Maṇḍala der „Mutterschoßwelt"? — als Erscheinung dieser buddhistischen Gottheit gewählt worden ist. Zum Berg gewandt rezitiert der Übende den *mantra* dieser Gottheit: *on-bei-shira-manaya-sowaka*, entsprechend der Sanskrit-Form: *oṃ vaiśravaṇāya svāhā*.

Noch zwei letzte Stationen auf dem Weg, und der Übende ist wieder in sein Quartier zurückgekehrt. Dort erwartet ihn die Pflicht, ein einstündiges exoterisches Ritual im buddhistischen Zeremonialgesang *shōmyō* durchzuführen. Dann hat er sich etwa eine Stunde lang mit Abschreiben von Sūtrentexten und ähnlichem zu beschäftigen, bis er, genau um 7 Uhr, sein Frühstück serviert bekommt: eine Schüssel Reis mit 2 dünnen Scheiben Gurke und einer gesalzenen Pflaume (jap. *umeboshi*) und einer kleinen Schale *misoshiru*, einer aus gegorenem Bohnenmus hergestellten, würzigen Brühe. So wie sich die *yamabushi* anderen leiblichen Härten und Schmerzen unterzogen, um die Qualen der untersten der sechs Daseinsebenen auszukosten, so hungerten sie freiwillig, um die Qualen der nächsthöher gelegegen Daseinsebene, der der hungrigen Geister, *gaki* (Skrt. *preta*), kennenzulernen[44]). Während der Übungszeit des Novizen wird dementsprechend die Nahrungsration nicht zu reichlich bemessen, damit er Gelegenheit hat, die Qualen dieser zweitniedrigsten Daseinsebene, wenn auch in geringeren Dimensionen, kennenzulernen.

Dem unkritischen Beobachter müssen die buddhistisch-schintoistischen Entsprechungen und Identifizierungen in Nikkō erscheinen, als existierten sie seit eh und je, gewissermaßen als natürliche, zeitlose Gegebenheit. Die oben skizzierte Studie der historischen Quellen zeigt, daß die schriftliche Tradition diesen Eindruck zwar bestärkt und rechtfertigt, sie aber dabei so verfährt, daß sie den wahren Anfang der konkreten synkretistischen Entsprechungen weit in die Vergangenheit zurückverlegt. Der Vorgang ist durchaus verständlich und von geradezu paradigmatischem Wert: Mit der Entstehung einer von religiösem Glauben erfüllten Doktrin ist bereits die Zeit ihres Entstehens transzendiert, und als bequemste rationale Ausdrucksform eines solchen irrationalen Ereignisses bietet sich das Zurückprojizieren auf den ersten Anbeginn oder eine anfanglose Vergangenheit an. Historischer Ablauf und religiöser Gehalt können sich dank der Einsicht in diese Tatsache gegenseitig

[44]) Vgl. G. Renondeau, op. cit., S. 128.

erhellen. Wenn heute im streng orthodoxen Rahmen buddhistischer Novizen-Ausbildung trotz offizieller „Trennung von Göttern und Buddhas" wesentliche Elemente eines buddhistisch-schintoistischen Synkretismus lebendig geblieben sind und sich harmonisch in das Ganze fügen, so darum, weil sie als Praktiken und Glaubensinhalte einer die Zeit transzendierenden Tradition außerhalb dieser ihnen nicht entsprechenden historischen Entwicklung geblieben sind: der „Trennung von Göttern und Buddhas".

Hindu Elements in the Religion of the Buddhist Baruas and Chakmas in Bengal

By HEINZ BECHERT, AMIT DAS GUPTA
and GUSTAV ROTH

(Summary)

The contribution on religious syncretism among the Buddhist Baḏuẏā[1]) or Barua and Cākmā (Chakma) communities of Bangla Desh presented to and discussed during the symposium deals with the religious history of these communities in general and with the Bauddharañjikā, a Bengali Buddhist text handed down in the tradition of the Baruas and Chakmas in particular. Work on this Bengali text was done in cooperation with Dr. Amit Das Gupta (then Lecturer of Hindi and Bengali at the University of Göttingen) who was to be the third co-author of the final version of the contribution, but unfortunately was prevented from continuing participation in the project by other obligations. A collection of material in East Bengal by the present authors in 1967/8 has been made possible by a grant of the Deutsche Forschungsgemeinschaft, and reports on other aspects of Buddhism in East Bengal were and will be published elsewhere[2]). A more detailed study of the Bauddharañjikā, along with other new material for the study of Buddhism in Bangla Desh, will be published separately so that only a short summary is included in the present volume.

The Buddhist Baruas live mainly in the Chittagong District of Bangla Desh. Buddhist monasteries of Indian tradition have existed here until the 15th century. It seems that during the period of strong Arakanese influence which ended with the annexation of Chittagong to the Moghul Empire in 1666 A. D. most surviving groups of Buddhists in Southeastern Bengal were converted to Theravāda. The ancestors of the Chakmas, one of the „hill tribes“ of Chittagong Hill Tracts, on the other hand, originated from Burma, and are related to the Sak (Thet), one of three main ethnical groups of Tibeto-Burman immigrants into the Irrawaddy plains. Sak are referred to in Old Burmese inscriptions of the Pagan

---

[1]) Baḏuẏā is the transliteration recently established for German libraries; the name is spelt Baṛuẏā in the transliteration used by the Library of Congress, and Barua in the usual English orthography.

[2]) See Heinz Bechert, Contemporary Buddhism in Bengal and Tripura, in: Educational Miscellany, Tripura 4 (1967/8), pp. 1–25; ib., Zur Geschichte des Theravāda-Buddhismus in Ostbengalen, in: Beiträge zur Indienforschung, Berlin 1977 (Veröffentlichungen des Museums für Indische Kunst Berlin, vol. 4), p. 45–66.

period. Chakmas were converted to Theravāda Buddhism long before they migrated to Chittagong Hill Tracts, but during centuries of isolation their form of Buddhism has much degenerated.

Since 1856 A. D., under the leadership of Sāramedha or Sāramitta Mahāthera (1801–1882), an Arakanese bhikkhu, a reform of Buddhism of the Baruas and Chakmas was achieved. In the course of this reform, Buddhist literary works in Bengali were composed, and the Bauddharañjikā which is also called Tātuhāṃ or Tādubāiṃ written by Bābu Nīlakamala Dāsa (ca. 1870 A. D.) in Bengali verse is by far the most important text of this literature. Due to its archaic language and difficult style, it was not widely read and it was erroneously dated in a much earlier period by the authors of the standard histories of Bengali literature.[3]) The Bauddharañjikā is a biography of the Buddha. It is based on Burmese sources, and its alternative title Tādubāiṃ is derived from the title of a Burmese work named Dhātuvaṃsa (Dhātuvaṅ) which was used as a source.

In the context of our symposium, the particular way was stressed in which certain elements of Hindu religious and philosophical thought were used by its author in order to introduce his Buddhistic message to a community which, in spite of its ability to preserve its identity as a Buddhist community during long periods of isolation, was remarkably influenced by the culture and by the ways of thinking of their Hindu neighbours. The printed version of the Bauddharañjikā[4]) contains an introductory chapter named *Icchāmatīra bandanā* (obeisance to Icchāmatī i.e. Kālī) in 22 stanzas, and it includes the sections *Jagadīśvarera bandanā* (obeisance to the Lord of the world i. e. Śiva) in 23 stanzas and *Sarasvatīra bandanā* (obeisance to Sarasvatī) in 11 stanzas. These portions devoted to Hindu deities are, however, not found in the two manuscripts of the Bauddharañjikā which we had at our disposal. In our opinion, this difference can be explained by the fact that the printed version was published by the order of Kālindī Rāṇī, then Rāja of the Chakmas,[5]) whereas the manuscripts represent the version used by the monastic tradition. We observe how particular conditions favourable to the spread of syncretistic tendencies could exercise their influence upon the presentation of a basically Buddhist text when it was edited for the religious public of East Bengal. Kālindī Rāṇī was a devoted Buddhist, and she followed the Aśokan example of tolerance when she felt responsible for the welfare of all her subjects, Hindus and Moslems

[3]) e. g. Dinesh Chandra Sen, History of Bengali Language and Literature, Calcutta 1911, p. 802.

[4]) Bauddharañjikā arthāt Bauddhadigera mūla Dharmmasaṃgraha Bauddharañjikā, Caṭṭagrāma 1890. The book is listed by J. F. Blumhardt, A Supplementary Catalogue of Bengali Books in the Library of the British Museum acquired during the years 1886–1910, s.v. Kālindī Rāṇī.

[5]) The Rāja or Chief of the Chakmas had a personal rather than a territorial jurisdiction over the Chakma community which was exercised, of course, under the overlordship of the British colonial administration of Bengal.

included, as recorded by historical sources, and thus she had invocations of Hindu gods included in the text of the Bauddharañjikā.

The manuscript version of the Buddharañjikā which excludes the three sections devoted to Hindu gods, is not free from Hindu influences either. Thus in the very first stanza, obeisance is not only paid to the Buddha, but also to the well-known three guṇas of Sāṃkhya philosophy.[6])

The discussion on the interpretation of these facts in the context of the general theme of syncretism is summarized above, pp. 23f.

---

[6]) Text of this stanza:

pranamāmi Nirañjana Sammāsambuddha
sattva rajaḥ tamo guṇa haẏa suprasiddha.

On the Popular Religion of the Sinhalese

By HEINZ BECHERT

The first comprehensive account of the religion of the Sinhalese is found in Robert Knox' Historical Relation of Ceylon (1681). His description is not correct in all details, but for its time it is astonishingly unprejudiced. Knox describes Buddhism and folk religion in their parallel existence, and he informs his readers of the different classes of gods, of the rituals for the "demons" as well as of the more important festivals of Buddhism and of the cult of the gods. Knox had little knowledge of the teachings of Buddhism, and his description is most accurate where the religious practices and social position of the different "orders of priests", viz. the "Tirinanxes" (*terunnānsē* i.e. *bhikkhu*), the "Koppuhs" (*kapuvā*), and the "Jaddeses" (*yakädurā* or *kaṭṭādiyā*; see below, p. 232) are concerned. It is, however, clear from his description that the religion of the Sinhalese appeared to him what we would now describe as a "loose system" consisting of several subsystems.

The position of Dandris de Silva Gooneratne, a scholar who contributed more to the knowledge of the popular beliefs of the Sinhalese than any other scholar of the 19th century, was a quite different one. He sees the practices of "demonology" in sharp contrast with Buddhism, but he also stresses the tendencies towards systematization within the sphere of folk cults and magical practices. In his famous study "On Demonology and Witchcraft in Ceylon", published in the Journal of the Ceylon Branch of the Royal Asiatic Society 4, No. 13 (1865–66), reprint, Colombo 1954, pp. 1–117, he remarked (p. 2):

> "And although there is scarcely a single country in the world, in which this belief (i.e. belief in spirits) does not more or less prevail in some form or other, yet we do not think there is any in which it has developed itself in such gigantic proportions, or such hideous forms, as in this beautiful Island. Elsewhere it may sometimes exercise considerable influence and even command many devoted votaries; but here it has been moulded into a regular religion, arranged and methodized into a system, and carefully preserved in writing: so that the amount of influence, which it exercized over the thought, the habit, the every day life of a Sinhalese, is such as can hardly be believed by a stranger to the character of a genuine Sinhalese Buddhist."

Gooneratne's description of the "demon" cult has remained one of the most valuable source books for our knowledge of the popular beliefs of the Sinhalese. Hugh Nevill, Paul Wirz and Otakar Pertold were three later scholars who immensely enriched the amount of available information on this subject. The Buddhologists who have undertaken to describe the religious life of the island, on the other hand, have neglected this aspect, and this can also be said of the writers of Buddhist modernism who have stressed the purity of the Buddhist tradition of Ceylon.

In recent ethnological and sociological studies the question of the relation of Buddhist and non-Buddhist elements has been raised in a systematical way. Michael M. Ames' study on "Magical-animism and Buddhism: A structural Analysis of the Sinhalese Religious System", in: Religion in South Asia, ed. E. Harper, Seattle 1964, pp. 21–53, has decisively influenced later work in the field by his attempt to describe the structures underlying the "system"[1]). Gananath Obeyesekere had already done this a few years earlier in a review published in the Ceylon Journal of Historical and Social Studies 2 (1958), pp. 259–262, when he argued against the separation of "Buddhist" and "non-Buddhist" beliefs and described both as parts of "one interconnected system which may profitable be studied as Sinhalese Religion" (so Obeyesekere, loc. cit., p. 259). "Buddhist" tradition and "popular beliefs" are divided in accordance with their functions as *lokottara* (supra-mundane) and *laukika* (worldly) respectively (see below). Though most publications on this subject by anthropologists since 1964 are based on eclectic samples of material and tend to draw far-reaching conclusions from what may represent the opinion of only one or a few informants rather than the prevalent form of the traditions, remarkable methodological progress has been achieved in the last decade.

An important step forward was taken by Richard F. Gombrich in his "Precept and Practice" (Oxford 1971) which provides a detailed and reliable study of both sides of the picture—the Buddhist one and that of the popular cults—based on a thorough observation of the situation in a particular region of the highlands. Gombrich also discusses the problem of "orthodoxy or syncretism" (loc. cit., pp. 40–56), and he is very emphatic in his refutation of the use of the term "syncretism" to describe the religious situation in Ceylon, because "the presence of 'Hindu' or 'animist' supernaturals in the Buddhist's universe is not a novel or syncretistic feature, but has always been the case" (loc. cit., p. 48f.). Gombrich arrives at the conclusion that traditional Sinhalese Buddhism is not "syncretistic" but "surprisingly orthodox". As I have remarked earlier (see above, Introduction, pp. 20–24), there is no universally accepted use of the term "syncretism", so that the question whether the correlation between "Buddhist" and "non-Buddhist" (or not strictly "Buddhist") elements in the system of traditional Sinhalese religion may be described as "syncretistic" or not depends on the terminology adopted by the particular author, but basically I agree with the main points presented in Gombrich's work.[2]) Conclusions drawn from an

---

[1]) For a critical evaluation of the study by M. M. Ames, see my Einige Fragen der Religionssoziologie und Struktur des südasiatischen Buddhismus, in: International Yearbook for the Sociology of Religion 4 (1968), pp. 267–275.

[2]) See also my review of Gombrich's work in: Indo-Iranian Journal 18 (1976), pp. 145-149.

observation of the traditional religion of a particular region of the highlands of Ceylon are, of course, not always necessarily valid for Sinhalese religion in general. I have undertaken to provide readers with a comprehensive survey of Sinhala popular religion in my Mythologie der singhalesischen Volksreligion (published in: Wörterbuch der Mythologie, ed. H. W. Haussig, I. Abt., Lieferung 15, Stuttgart 1976, pp. 509–656). The material is arranged under 207 catch-words, and a bibliography of publications on the subject in Western languages is added. For information underlying the following remarks including bibliographical references, I will, therefore, largely refer to this work which is quoted as „Mythologie" (with reference to the entries where the reader will find material on the particular god, demon, ritual etc.).

Any attempt at a satisfactory analysis of the Sinhalese "popular religion" has to tackle the problem from various points of view. To begin with the "systematic" view, we can safely assume, that "popular cults" have existed side by side with Buddhism in all periods since the introduction of Buddhism to Ceylon, because they form part of the "structure" or "system" of thought and behaviour in all Theravāda countries.[3]) The Buddhist sāsana is defined as an instrument towards a "supra-mundane" (*lokottara*) goal i.e. for progress on the way to final salvation or *nibbāna*. Buddhism was traditionally institutionalized in the sangha, and from a study of the relations between state and sangha we observe the central conceptions by which the transformation of Buddhism from the religion of a rather small section of the élite into the religion of whole nations could take place. The functional division of "mundane" and "supra-mundane" aims and activities was one of the decisive factors. In the relation of state and religion, the "mundane" sphere was in principle the sphere of the state, whereas the "supra-mundane" sphere was that of the sangha. Consequently, the traditional rituals at the royal courts were to be performed not by bhikkhus, but by court brahmins which remain in charge of these functions in the Buddhist kingdom of Thailand until today.

A closer observation of the relations of sangha and state, however, raises doubts about the universal validity of this formula. On the one hand, with its mission for preserving and spreading the dhamma, the sangha could not remain neutral towards political events under all circumstances, and in Ceylon the sangha has also accepted responsibility for the continuity of a Buddhist as well as a national identity from a very early period, as can be seen from the Sinhalese chronicles (see Heinz Bechert, Zum Ursprung der Geschichtsschreibung im indischen Kulturbereich, in: NAWG 1969, pp. 33–58, and The Beginnings of Buddhist Historiography: Mahāvaṃsa and Political Thinking, in: Religion and the Legitimation of Power in Sri Lanka, ed. Bardwell

---

[3]) A comparative view of the relation of Buddhism and popular cults in Burma and in Ceylon with a discussion of the differences is found in Bechert, Einige Fragen der Religionssoziologie (see above, note 1), pp. 287–293.

L. Smith, in the press). On the other hand, the political authority tended to legitimize its power by religious arguments i. e. by arguments derived from Buddhist tradition (see Bardwell L. Smith, Kingship, the Sangha, and the Process of Legitimation in Ancient Ceylon, in this volume, above, pp. 100–126). The division into a "mundane" and a "supra-mundane" sphere was, however, used by the political power to justify the particular way in which the sangha was integrated into the political system and placed under the control of the state; the kings explained their actions for the reform of the sangha by emphasizing the need to protect the sangha from meddling in the "mundane" sphere. I need not to go into more detail here (see also my Theravāda Buddhist Sangha: Some General Observations on Historical and Political Factors in its Development, in: Journal of Asian Studies 29, 1969/70, pp. 761–778), because these remarks will suffice to show that, though in theory, Theravāda Buddhists always accepted the dualism of a "mundane" and a "supra-mundane" sphere, in practice they only applied it to a limited degree.

The lines between Buddhism and what we may call "non-Buddhist elements" are clearly drawn by the definition of "orthodoxy" which has been accepted by traditional Buddhists in Ceylon for many centuries. According to this definition, the canonical scriptures (*tipiṭaka*), the classical commentaries (*aṭṭhakathā*) and the Pāli chronicle Mahāvaṃsa are considered as sources of orthodoxy i. e. the information derived from these sources is considered as authoritative. There are many other works of Buddhist literature in Pāli and in Sinhalese, but unlike these authoritative sources, they are not necessarily accepted as unchallengeable.

These observations will help us to arrive at an adequate understanding of the relations between "Buddhist" and "non-Buddhist" elements in the traditional religion of the Sinhalese. By "Buddhist" in this context is meant the sphere of the sāsana in the narrower sense of the term i. e. the teachings of the dhamma as well as the institutions of traditional Buddhism viz. the sangha, the vihāras, the relics etc. which form part of the sāsana in the wider sense of the word. The sāsana is, as we have seen, ultimately directed towards salvation from rebirth in saṃsāra. In Buddhist terminology, this is expressed by the above-quoted formula that the sāsana is "supra-mundane" (*lokottara*). Of course, the so-called religious needs of men often refer to problems of mundane life in this world, but in the "mundane" sphere Buddhism in its original and orthodox form does not provide its followers with relief, except by an explanation of their sufferings in terms of the Buddha's teachings about the origin of suffering and the way to salvation which, however, implies leaving the world (*pabbajjā*). The Buddha, as is well known, never denied the existence of gods, but described them as impermanent beings (cf. Helmuth von Glasenapp, Buddhism: A Non-Theistic Religion, London 1970, pp. 19–34). Therefore, it was possible for a layman to seek help from gods in mundane affairs without running any risk of a conflict with professing Buddhism, as long as the ritual did not violate Buddhist ethics. For monks, the participation in the cult of gods was, of course, out of the question, because any such practice would be a relapse into worldly entanglements which were to be strictly avoided by bhikkhus. In practice, however, this was not always followed by the bhikkhus, and in Ceylon there are groups of monks who consequently avoid participation in the cult of the gods, and other bhikkhus who participate in rituals of the "folk religion" in varying degrees. We shall see later on that this question has been of considerable importance in recent times.

Gods are considered as beings with limited power and limited lifespan, subject to the law of karma and rebirth like any other being, but able to offer help to human beings under certain conditions, in a relation which is somewhat similar to the relation of a king to his subjects. On the other hand—and this, too, is not dissimilar from the relation between state and individual person—the gods are in a position to cause considerable harm to men, if their displeasure is caused willingly or unwillingly. The same can be said of other "supernatural"—or, more exactly, "superhuman"—beings.

Thus, these "superhuman" beings and the rituals and customs connected with them are not part of the sphere of the sāsana, but belong to the mundane sphere. If the word *sāsana* is translated by "religion"—and this is the accepted English translation used in Sri Lanka—it is possible to formulate that "gods are nothing to do with religion" as a senior monk is quoted by Gombrich (loc. cit., p. 46), but this understanding of the word "religion" is then, of course, quite different from the definition of religion current in Western culture and religious science.

Another terminological problem is created by the words "popular religion" or "folk religion" if used in this context. Some of the cults of the gods in Sinhalese tradition were definitely not "popular" cults, but formed part of the established system of state ceremonies and state ritual of the Sinhalese kingdom. This does not contradict the fact that Buddhism was the state religion, because—as we have seen earlier—such rituals, though considered essential for the prosperity of king, state and nation, could not be performed by bhikkhus because of the "supra-mundane" function of the sāsana. For practical purposes I have, however, retained the term "popular religion" as a conventional term for the "non-Buddhist" elements in the religion of the Sinhalese.[4])

There are, however, certain Buddhist practices which can help in the solution of "mundane" problems and thus belong to an intermediate sphere between Buddhism, if strictly defined in the way described above, and "popular religion". The most important of these practices is the *paritta* (Sinh. *pirit*) in its use as a ritual for protection from all kind of misfortune. This rite is a very ancient one and it is regularly practiced in all countries where Theravāda has spread (see Mythologie, s. v. Pirit; cf. also above, introduction, p. 27f., and the summary of the contribution

[4]) See also above, Introduction, p. 24f.

by Peter Schalk, below, pp. 339–341). Not less important is the *pattā-numodanā* which implies the transference of merit. It was recently discussed by R. F. Gombrich (Merit Transference in Sinhala Buddhism: A Case Study of the Interaction between Doctrine and Practice, in: History of Religions 11, 1971, pp. 203–219, and ib., Precept and Practice, pp. 226–241) and, with a different explanation of its origin, by me (H. Bechert, Buddha-Feld und Verdienstübertragung: Mahāyāna-Ideen im Theravāda-Buddhismus Ceylons, in: Bulletin de la Classe des Lettres et des Sciences Morales et Politique de l'Académie Royale de Belgique 1976, pp. 27–51). Gombrich hinted at the "intermediate" function of this practice when he remarked that it affords "some psychological relief from the oppressive doctrine of man's total responsibility for his own fate" (Precept and Practice, p. 242). Both practices are fully accepted by orthodoxy, but, at the same time, they belong to a sphere which may be termed "popular Buddhism". There are some other practices of popular Buddhism, and we get a very good picture of this sphere from some of the mediaeval Buddhist literature of Ceylon, particularly from Vedeha's Rasavāhinī (13th cent.).

In *paritta* and in *pattānumodanā*, gods also play an important role, but a very different one from that in the popular religion in the stricter sense of the term. The gods are solemnly invited at the end of the *mahā-paritta* ceremony, a "gods' messenger" (*devadūtayā*) recites a text about the arrival of the gods, and finally a bhikkhu reads out an admonition (*anusāsanāva*) to the gods (see Ernst Waldschmidt, Das Paritta, Eine magische Zeremonie der buddhistischen Priester auf Ceylon, in: Von Ceylon bis Turfan, Schriften ... von Ernst Waldschmidt, Göttingen 1967, pp. 474–476). In the practice of the *pattānumodanā*, the invitation of the gods to participate in the religious merit (p. *puñña*, Sinh. *pin*) occupies a prominent position.

Whereas these practices are universally accepted as part of Theravāda Buddhism, we observe some other important relations of the Buddhist sāsana and the "popular religion" which are restricted to Ceylon. Already in the Mahāvaṃsa (7.1ff.) it is said that the Buddha entrusted god Sakka (Śakra) with the protection of Vijaya and his followers and of the island of Lankā, and that Sakka handed over the guardianship of Lankā to god Uppalavaṇṇa (Upulvan, since the 16th century identified with Viṣṇu). In a similar way, the cults of the other gods are directly related to Buddhism by the belief that the activities of the gods depend on a commission or at least a permission (*varaṃa*) granted by the Buddha (see Mythologie, s. v. Götter). Thus the numerous gods and godlings of the Sinhalese pantheon form a complicated system of hierarchical dependences which, in the last instance, is always traced back to such an order by the Buddha.

This type of relationship could, of course, give opportunities for syncretistic tendencies which are further enhanced by the coexistence of Buddhistic and non-Buddhistic elements in the state cults already mentioned. The cult of the great gods who served as "guardian gods" of the island was heavily influenced by Hinduistic rituals at least from the later mediaeval period, if not earlier. These rituals have in turn influenced the particular form of the cult of relics, especially the Tooth Relic (which serves to represent the Buddha) as performed in the Temple of the Holy Tooth (described in the Daḷadā sirita and in A. M. Hocart, The Temple of the Tooth in Kandy, London 1931; see Mythologie s. v. Zahnreliquie), as well as the rituals performed before Buddha images in other "royal monasteries" (*rājamahāvihāra*) before the Buddha images, the structure of which shows its indebtedness to mediaeval Hinduism of South India, though, of course, the texts recited during these rituals are all purely Buddhist in content.

The greatest religious festival of the island, the yearly Äsaḷa Perahära (see Mythologie, s. v. Perahära) in Kandy, which consists of a great procession of the Tooth Relic and the insignia of the "Four Guardian Gods" of Lankā (Upulvan or Viṣṇu, Kataragama, Pattini and Nātha), is an impressive exemplification of this integration of Buddhism and cults of gods, though it is not very ancient in this form, the procession of the Tooth Relic being included in the Perahära only since 1775 A.D. Here, the cult of the most important Buddhist relic of the island and of the guardian gods of the island form part of the state cult of the Sinhalese, and this understanding has survived the breakdown of the Sinhalese monarchy and the colonial period. It is difficult to avoid a description of this aspect of Sinhalese religion as "syncretistic", because it is evident that the afore-mentioned division of the Buddhist sphere and the "mundane" cults of the gods has lost its validity in this context. Similar "syncretistic" tendencies can be observed in Kataragama and a few other places of pilgrimage. Another clear case of a syncretistic ritual is the *netrapratiṣṭhāpana*, the consecration of Buddha images, which forms the subject-matter of two contributions in this volume (by H. Ruelius, and by R. F. Gombrich, below, pp. 304–338; see also above, Introduction, p. 26). In all these instances, the intrinsic interrelation between religion and society did not allow a consistent application of the dividing-line between sāsana and mundane sphere.

Another type of relation between Buddhism and basically non-Buddhist traditions originated from the identification of a given god as a bodhisattva (Sinh. *bōsat*; see Mythologie, s. v. Bōsat). In this way, Upulvan and even Pattini were integrated into the realm of Buddhism by many Buddhists, though this belief was never accepted as part of orthodoxy as defined above. Historically, this form of integration of gods into the system of Buddhist beliefs originated from the opposite process, viz. the acceptance of certain bodhisattvas of Mahāyāna Buddhism into the pantheon of Sinhalese gods when Mahāyānistic tendencies as such were finally superseded. The most conspicuous example of this development is the god Nātha, who is no other than Avalokiteśvara, the most important of the bodhisattvas of Mahāyāna (see Mythologie, s. v. Nātha).

In these ways, the "popular religion" of the Sinhalese is integrated into the greater "system" of religious beliefs and practices to such an extent that it is impossible to imagine its separate existence outside the system of interrelations with Buddhism. The "popular religion" is subordinate to Buddhism in a hierarchical way, whereas this correlation is of a rather casual nature if viewed from the "Buddhist" point of view i.e. from the point of view of orthodox Buddhism as defined before. This is obvious from the fact that Theravāda Buddhism "coexists" with completely different "folk religions" in other Buddhist countries, but no differences worth mentioning in the theory and practice of Buddhism itself result from these differences. Thus, popular beliefs and cults were always considered as beliefs and practices of a lower order which loose their importance if viewed from the higher level of Buddhism.

Buddhist tradition is incorporated in a well defined corpus of scriptures and commentaries as we have seen. The situation of the popular religion is quite different. There is a rich literature of the popular cults (see Mythologie, Einleitung), but there was no authority which could achieve a canonization and codification of particular beliefs and practices. Thus there is no "canon" of texts of the cult of the gods in Ceylon. Most traditions remained regional or local, and many are related to one particular temple only and unknown a few miles away. The popular religion is subject to constant development and change, and the variability of its traditions increases with the lessening of its relations with Buddhism, so that it is much greater in the sphere of lower gods than in that of the old state cults. We observe rather similar and consistent traditions relating to the most important gods like Upulvan, Kataragama and Saman in all parts of the island, whereas traditions concerning lower gods like the *baṇḍāra deviyō* remain in many cases mere local myths.

For an adequate analysis of Sinhala folk religion, its historical development must be taken into consideration. There is no doubt that several elements of Sinhalese beliefs of the pre-Buddhist period survive in the popular religion, but the information provided by the historical sources is too scanty to enable us to attempt a full description of the pre-Buddhist religion of Ceylon. The scarcity of information on the popular beliefs of earlier periods may be explained by the fact that Buddhist monks were the authors of most works of early Sinhalese literature, and they, of course, saw no point in writing down details of the cult of popular gods and related traditions. Thus we find in the early literature not more than a few rather unconnected data on the cult of gods (for such information, see Wilhelm Geiger, Culture of Ceylon in Mediaeval Times, Wiesbaden 1960, pp. 164–179). Popular myths on the Buddha, on his visits to Lanka and on the immigration of Vijaya and his followers are, on the other hand, well documented since an early period, but only in the particular form in which they have been incorporated into the official historiography of the Sinhala nation. There were other variants of these ancient myths, but they are not documented by earlier sources, but only by comparatively recent texts of the popular religion (see Mythologie, s.v. Divi dos, Mala raja, Vijaya).

More information about the cult of gods is available since the 14th and 15th centuries, when the earliest Sinhalese *sandeśa* poems preserved were composed. This poetry, written on the model of the Meghadūta of Kālidāsa, has the conveyance of messages to particular beings as its theme (see C. Godakumbura, Sinhalese Literature, Colombo 1955, pp. 183–208). In most of the Sinhalese *sandeśa* poems, a god is the addressee, and a bird serves as the messenger. In some cases, the connection with the cult of a god is more indirect, e.g. in the Tisarasandēśaya (14th cent.), the oldest of the existing Sinhalese *sandeśa* poems, where a message is sent through a swan from Devinuvara (Dondra) to the king residing in Dädigama, with the information that a monk in Devinuvara was praying to the god Upulvan for the king's protection and success etc. The Mayūrasandēśaya (14th cent.), the Parevisandēśaya (15th cent.) and the Kōkilasandēśaya (15th cent.) are also connected with the cult of god Upulvan, the Sälalihiṇisandēśaya (15th cent.) with that of god Vibhīṣaṇa, the Girāsandēśaya (15th cent.) with god Nātha, the Sävulsandēśaya (16th cent.) with god Saman, and the Kahakurulusandēśaya (18th cent.), the Nīlakobōsandēśaya (18th cent.), the Käṭakirilisandēśaya (dated 1788 A. D.), the Diyasävulsandēśaya (composed in 1813 A. D.), the Kēralasandēśaya (1815 A. D.) and a number of others describe the sending of messages to the god Kataragama or Mahasena, whereas only the Haṃsasandēśaya (15th cent.) and a few recent *sandēśa* poems have a purely Buddhist theme. This *sandeśa* poetry provides us with detailed descriptions of the temples of the gods and other related information, and thus enables us to trace at least some aspects of the history of the cults of the main gods of the Sinhalese during the last five centuries.

We would expect to obtain more knowledge of the early history of these cults from archaeological sources, but unfortunately most of the temples of gods discovered from before the 14th century were built during the Cola occupation of the island, and the same must be said of the origin of most of the earlier images of gods, so that this material is not of much help for our purpose, because it represents the purely Hindu religion of Tamil invaders and immigrants in mediaeval Ceylon. There seem to be, however, a few exceptions, e. g. the famous Isurumuniya sculpture of man and horse, if the identification as Aiyaṉār (Sinh. Ayiyanāyaka) by W. A. de Silva and recently by J. E. van Lohuizen de-Leeuw is correct (see Mythologie s. v. Ayiyanāyaka). For the period from the 15th century on there is, fortunately, no want of sources for Sinhala folk religion, because we know an immense multitude of relevant texts which were composed during the last few centuries. Most of these texts are poems used during rituals, for the praise of particular gods etc., but much of this vast literature has not yet been evaluated. No serious study of the Sinhala folk religion can, however, neglect this important source of information.

With all the material which is available to us, it is now possible to recognize various strata of cults and myths of different origin. We begin here with the gods of canonical Buddhist tradition. Since the canonical texts have been handed down in Ceylon as they were introduced from India without major alterations, we can infer that the concepts of the gods as incorporated in the Pāli canon were codified in India during the Maurya period. Certain features of Vedic religion survive in this "Buddhist pantheon" which do not seem to have been preserved in Brahmanical literature of the same period, e.g. the leading role played by Indra, who is named Sakka (Śakra). On the other hand, Brahmā is also an important god in the pantheon of the early Buddhist texts. In the Tevijjasutta (Dīghanikāya I, p. 244) Inda (Indra), Soma, Varuṇa, Īsāna (Īśāna i.e. Śiva), Pajāpati (Prajāpati), Brahmā, Mahiddha and Yama are enumerated as the main gods of the Brahmanical cult during the time of the Buddha, but Varuṇa is rarely mentioned in other Buddhist works in this important function, and Śiva as well as Viṣṇu (Pāli Veṇhu), the two main gods of Hinduism, do not yet seem to have reached their later leading positions. Thus, while the cult of the gods as represented in the early Buddhist texts cannot be described as a form of Vedic religion, it must be characterized as still pre-Hindu. The question remains, whether the pantheon found in early Buddhist texts is identical with that of the main stream of religious life in the country where Buddhism originated shortly before and during the Maurya period, and whether the cult of Viṣṇu was not yet prominent at that time. While some argue that the Buddhist texts have purposely ignored the prominent position of Viṣṇu, I tend to accept that the texts give a generally reliable picture of the religious situation during the Maurya period.[5])

The Buddhists integrated the Brahmanic gods into their own cosmography by assigning them particular roles as followers and servants of the Buddha, and they described the gods as converts and followers of the true dhamma. The gods were also subjected to the Buddhist view of ethics. Some gods were believed to exist in higher spheres of existence which may be reached by meditating Buddhists in deep concentration, and new Buddhist gods were described as inhabitants of yet higher meditative spheres of existence.

It is in thus transformed that the gods of the pre-Hindu Indo-Aryans of Northern India survive in the mythology of the Buddhists of Ceylon and Southeast Asia. In Burma, Sakrā[3] (Śakra) is the highest of the *nat* i. e. the gods of the popular cults of the Burmans, and in his function as overlord of the local gods he serves as a link between the cosmography of Buddhism and the local pantheon. In a similar way, Sakka (Skt. Śakra, Sinh. Sak; cf. Mythologie, s. v. Sak) is the highest god who was first entrusted by the Buddha with the protection of the Sinhalese and he

[5]) In discussion at the symposium, Prof. Härtel stressed that the iconography of Śiva and Viṣṇu develops only from the 2nd century B. C. on. This would fit in well with the suggestion formulated here. See also above, Introduction, p. 26.

still has this function in some Sinhalese myths, but there Sakka was replaced by Upulvan, who took over the responsibility for the island and its people as recorded in the afore-mentioned passage of the Mahāvaṃsa. Sakka thus remains a good-natured but remote god, who is not feared by anyone, and consequently does not need to be placated by any rituals or sacrifices. It is thus evident that Sakka's function for the pantheon of the Sinhalese is essentially the same as in the popular religion of the Burmese i. e. to serve as a link between the cosmography of the canonical texts and the local pantheon. From a historical point of view, we can say that in Ceylon as well as in Burma the pantheon of Indian Buddhism i. e. that of the canonical texts was replaced by the local pantheon with the sole exception of Sakka, the highest god.

In spite of this replacement, the "canonical" gods remain, of course, known to the Sinhalese and we find them depicted in temple paintings illustrating the life of the Buddha, Jātakas and other Buddhist tales, but they do not play any active role in the popular religion. No more cult or ritual is devoted to any of them. The true rulers of the pantheon of the Sinhalese are the guardian gods of the island (see Mythologie, s. v. Götter, vier große). These gods appear as a group of four gods (*satara varam deviyō*), and Upulvan and the god of Kataragama have been included in this group since the earliest period. We have seen that Upulvan (Pāli Uppalavaṇṇa) has been assigned the status of a guardian of the island already in the Mahāvaṃsa, so his cult is more integrated into the Buddhist literary tradition than that of the other Sinhalese gods (see Mythologie, s. v. Upulvan). The group of four gods was subject to change with regard to the identity of the other two gods. In Mahanuvara (Kandy), the last in the succession of royal cities of the island, Pattini and Nātha are considered to be the third and fourth of the four guardian gods, but we can prove from literary and inscriptional sources that Saman and Vibhīṣana occupied these positions in earlier periods.

Each of the four gods is considered the protector of a particular part of the country. It seems that this particular concept can be traced back to a very early form of South Indian Religion (see H. Bechert, Eine alte Gottesvorstellung in Südindien und Ceylon, in: Wiener Zeitschrift für die Kunde Süd- und Ostasiens 12/13, 1968/69, pp. 33–42). Thus there is a strong element of religious belief belonging to a stratum of common South Indian and early Ceylonese culture. The immigrants from Northern India who brought the Proto-Sinhalese language to the island must also have brought with them some elements of the early Aryan religious tradition, but it does not seem that they imported and retained the tradition of brahmanical religion in the strict sense of the word. The religious beliefs brought to Ceylon by these immigrants have merged with and were assimilated to the religious traditions of earlier inhabitants of the island.

Later on, cultural influence from South India had a strong impact on the popular religion of the Sinhalese in consequence of the cultural and economic relations between Ceylon and South India. Cultural relations were particularly strong during the period when Theravāda Buddhism was widespread in South India, as was the case during the period of the great Pāli commentators, 5th to 8th century A. D. Pattini, the heroine of the Tamil epic Cilappatikāram of Ilaṅkovatikaḷ, was incorporated into the pantheon of the Sinhalese as the most powerful goddess (see Mythologie, s. v. Pattini). It is very difficult to determine the date of the introduction of her cult into Ceylon, and I would like here to draw the reader's attention to the convincing analysis of the myths about Gajabāhu by Gananath Obeyesekere (Gajabahu and the Gajabahu Synchronism, in: The Ceylon Journal of the Humanities 1, 1970, pp. 25–56). Obeyesekere has shown that the socalled "Gajabāhu synchronism" is of a purely mythological nature and so has no historical value. As a consequence of this important discovery, the chronology of early Tamil literature so far accepted by most scholars, which is largely based on this synchronism, needs revision.

In the course of time, not only Dravidian religious traditions, but also brahmanic traditions in their particular South Indian form, influenced the cults of the gods in Ceylon. This was a result of the process of Hinduization and Sanskritization of South India which had, of course, begun at a much later date than that of the immigration of the proto-Sinhalese in Ceylon. In the course of time, many local gods merged with Hindu gods.[6]) In this way, Upulvan and Saman, two of the most important figures of the pantheon of the Sinhalese, were identified with the Hindu gods Viṣṇu and Lakṣmaṇa respectively at a comparatively late period.[7])

Some Sanskritization resulted from the influx of brahmanical refugees fleeing from the conquering Muslims, but the impact of Sanskritization remained a limited one, so that these Brahmins were largely assimilated to the Sinhalese goyigama caste and did not preserve a separate literary tradition. The descendants of the brahmins who officiated at the temple of Upulvan (Viṣṇu) in Devundara (Dondra) and in other places became Sinhalese Buddhists, and consequently they transformed themselves from brahmanic priests into Buddhists who acted as priests of the cults of Sinhalese gods. A further source of the tendency towards Sanskritization was the royal court of the last dynasty of Sinhalese kings, which descended from South India, so that some of its connections with the

---

[6]) Hans-Dieter Evers, Monks, Priests and Peasants, A Study of Buddhism and Social Structure in Central Ceylon, Leiden 1972, has tried to show that strong religious influences from Southeast Asia can be traced in the religion of the Sinhalese. I have dealt at length with his theory, which cannot be accepted in this form, in my forthcoming review of his book in: Orientalistische Literaturzeitung, and it seems innecessary to repeat my arguments here.

[7]) The fact that the identification of Upulvan with Viṣṇu is of comparatively recent origin was first observed by S. Paranavitana. I cannot, however, accept Paranavitina's theory that Upulvan was originally Varuṇa and Saman originated from Yama; see my Mythologie, s. v. Upulvan and s. v. Saman.

Vaiṣṇava renaissance were retained in spite of the acceptance of Buddhism as the official creed of the rulers.

Apart from this impact of South Indian Hinduism on the development of beliefs and practices amongst the higher social strata, the taking over of popular cults of the lower social strata can be observed, often as a result of the immigration of population groups from South India who were then linguistically and culturally assimilated by the Sinhalese, but contributed some of their traditions to Sinhala folk religion. Several of the castes of the low-country Sinhalese can be described as descendants of such assimilated immigrants, and many of the demons known and the rituals practiced by the Sinhalese living in the coastal areas are clearly of South Indian origin (cf. Mythologie, s. v. Yakā). These traditions could easily be incorporated because, as explained, Sinhalese popular mythology was not codified. As one can see from many examples, the South Indian origin of many of the lower gods is still recognized by their devotees, and recorded in the myths about the immigration of those gods to the island. Very often it is also related that the local gods tried to prevent the landing of a foreign god in Ceylon. After they were accepted, a particular place in the hierarchical system of the gods of Ceylon was allocated to these gods and they were made ministers or servants or at least members of the retinue of one of the higher gods.

Another category of superhuman beings consists of gods of a definitely local origin. Many of these are deifications of men who have died an unnatural death. In a way which is quite similar to the Burmese cult of the nats, in some cases a cult was instituted for the atonement of collective guilt. As an example, the cult of Galē baṇḍāra deviyō in Kurunāgala (see Mythologie, s. v. Galē baṇḍāra) may be mentioned; in this case the elevation of a Muslim prince, who was murdered by the Sinhalese Buddhists to prevent the ascent of a Muslim to the throne, to the status of a god served to resolve conflicts between Sinhalese Buddhists and Muslims, who have lived together in this region for many centuries. Sinhalese Buddhists and Muslims both participate in rituals for Galē baṇḍāra, and the most important oracle of Ceylon is connected with this temple. Many other gods of a purely local character belong to the category of the Yakṣas (Sinh. *yakā*, pl. *yakku*), but there are many Yakṣas of South Indian origin too.

The Pretas (p. *peta*, Sinh. *pretayō*) are derived from Buddhist canonical belief (see Mythologie, s. v. Ahnenkult), the cult of the planets (Sinh. *grahayō*) which plays a major role in the rituals of the Sinhalese (see Mythologie, s. v. Planeten) is of clearly Hinduistic origin. Astrology is, of course, of the greatest importance, and it is interwoven with the popular religion in many ways, though it must be described rather as a "science" than as belonging to the sphere of popular religion.

Some of the gods and demons can be identified as personifications of rituals, of diseases etc. Thus, Hūniyam (see Mythologie, s. v.) is nothing but a personification of the magic ritual *hūniyama* or *sūniyama* (originally *hū-niyam*, derived from skt. **sūtraniyāma* "string-procedure" by Wilhelm Geiger in 1916; see Wilhelm Geiger, Kleine Schriften zur Indologie und Buddhismuskunde, Wiesbaden 1973, pp. 414–425), and the dangerous disease-spreading eighteen Sanni yakku (see Mythologie, s. v. Sanni yakā) represent *sannipāta* which is the ayurvedic technical term for the concurrence of all three humours and the resulting diseases, as already recognized by Albert Grünwedel in 1893 (see A. Grünwedel, Sinhalesische Masken, in: Internationales Archiv für Ethnographie 6, 1893, pp. 86–88).

In our short survey of the main elements which have contributed to the pantheon and to the mythology of Sinhala popular religion, we have been able to observe strongly syncretistic features in the sense of the term defined in the introduction (above, pp. 20ff.) in so far as the difference of origin of the concepts is still clearly visible, and in many instances even known to the practitioners of these cults. There are, however, strict limits to such syncretistic tendencies, and these limits are set by the identity of the Sinhala Buddhists. As I have said before, the popular cults occupy a position "below" the Buddhist dhamma, and, though contradictions between the folk beliefs and Buddhist teachings could not always be avoided, they are not tolerated, if essentials of the Sinhala-Buddhist identity are affected. Thus, any attempt to replace Buddhism with Hinduism was met with the most determined resistance by the Sinhalese, as is exemplified by the reaction to the religious policies of Māgha (1215–1236) and of Rājasiṃha I (1581–1592). Hinduism was considered as a potential danger only in its South Indian Śaivite form, and therefore it is by no means accidental that Śiva, who is called Isuru (i. e. Īśvara) or Mehesura (i. e. Maheśvara) by the Sinhalese, was not assigned a prominent role in their popular cults, but is a god of minor importance only (see Mythologie, s.v. Īśvara).

The problem of the reception of the Rāmāyaṇa must be seen in this context (cf. Mythologie, s. v. Rāma). Versions of the Rāmāyaṇa are well known in all countries to which Indian culture has spread, and the story of Rāma is popular not only with Hindus, but also with Buddhists. Lankā being the scene of the Rāmāyaṇa, we would expect it to be even more popular with the Sinhalese than it is in Laos or Thailand, but we soon discover that the classical literature of the Sinhalese has not incorporated any version of the Rāmāyaṇa. From the Jānakīharaṇa, a Sanskrit kāvya based on the Rāmāyaṇa story which was composed by a Ceylonese author of the later Anurādhapura period (see The Jānakīharaṇa, ed. S. Paranavitana and C. E. Godakumbura, Colombo 1967, pp. LI–LXXII), and from the fact that Vibhīṣaṇa was one of the guardian gods of the island during late mediaeval times (see Mythologie, s. v. Vibhīṣaṇa), we can conclude that the Rāmāyaṇa story occupied a rather important place in certain periods of the history of Sinhala culture. But the Rāmāyaṇa was not allowed to retain such a position in the long run. In Sinhalese literature, a version of the story of Rāma is only met with in some popular poems connected with the mythology of the Kohoṁbā kankāriya ritual (see Mythologie, s. v. Mala raja), but in a form which is very different from the standard Rāmāyaṇa. Not a single manuscript of the Rāmāyaṇa is found among the many Sanskrit texts preserved in Sinhalese tradition. The non-existence of the Rāmāyaṇa in the main cultural tradition of the Sinhalese must be explained as a consequence of the fear that it could endanger the exclusive validity of the traditions on the early history of the island found in the Ceylonese chronicles. The very idea of a different version of the early history of the island which could contradict the traditions on which the ideology of the national identity of the Sinhalese was based, was so abhorrent to the Sinhalese literati that the Rāmāyaṇa was not allowed to become part of their established literary tradition. What remained in terms of popular versions became part of the lower level of popular mythology, and the Jānakīharaṇa, though a work composed in the island, was no longer copied, so that only a fragment of its Sinhala translation (*sannaya*) was preserved in a Sinhalese manuscript, while the complete text was handed down only in Indian tradition.

The tendency to reassert the Buddhist identity remains very strong, of course, in all forms of the Buddhist revival movement. In my description of the modern history of Buddhism in Ceylon (Buddhismus, Staat und Gesellschaft in den Ländern des Theravāda-Buddhismus, vol. 1, Frankfurt 1966), I have stressed the importance of the traditional reform movements which preceded the origin of Buddhist modernism (loc. cit., pp. 43f.). The monks of the socalled "Burmese Sects" (Amarapura Nikāya with its sub-sects and Rāmañña Nikāya) which were formed from the beginning of the 19th century, did not allow in their temples that coexistence of Buddhism with popular cults which was customary in the older monasteries of the Siamese Sect (Syāma Nikāya), where often small temples of gods (*dēvālaya*) were erected within the boundaries of the vihāra. The rejection of any connection with the cults of the gods by the newer sects was, of course, based on the grounds that temples of the gods have no place in an institution devoted to the sāsana.

The Buddhist modernists went even further in their attempts to eliminate popular religion in the course of their efforts to modernize Buddhist thought. Many educated Sinhala Buddhists, therefore, do not accept any form of the cult of gods in their religious thought and practice. But with the transformation of the Buddhist renaissance from an élitist into a mass movement, such consistency was soon the exception rather than the rule. In the urbanized and semi-urbanized new Sinhala middle class we witness a strong revival of the cult of the gods and other elements of the popular religion, but this part of the population has largely forgotten the complicated traditions of the old mythology, so that in these circles we meet with a simplified version of the popular religion. The god Kataragama has become the most popular figure of the pantheon now, and he has grown into a kind of symbol for the identity of the nationalist middle class. There are also political overtones in this revival when politicians send a formal message (*sandēśaya*) to the god to achieve particular aims, and the new role of this god can be explained in the context of social changes that have taken place during the last decades (see also Gananath Obeysekere, Religious Symbolism and Political Change in Ceylon, in: The Two Wheels of Dhamma, ed. Bardwell L. Smith, AAR Studies in Religion, No. 3, Chambersburg, Penn., 1972, pp. 73–75). The cult of Hūniyam has also seen a considerable revival, and contains a peculiar mixture of ecstatic and shamanistic elements with rationalistic and symbolic interpretations (see Obeyesekere, loc. cit., p. 75f.; Bechert, Buddhismus, Staat und Gesellschaft, vol. 1, p. 365). The aforementioned installation of new cults for the atonement of acts of violence can be witnessed in the case of the deification of S.W.R.D. Bandaranaike under the name of Horagollē devatā baṇḍāra which was also accepted by some sections of the urban population (see Mythologie, s. v. Horagollē devatā baṇḍāra).

The simplification of the pantheon and its reduction to a few important gods by the urban "middle class" is the last stage of a process of assimilation of different local traditions which we observe since the island has been progressively opened up to traffic by road and rail. It must be added, however, that many ancient traditions are still preserved in rural areas, not only in remote parts of the island, but also in the densely populated South-west.

The existence of more or less professional "specialists" for the performance of the various rituals is one of the factors which guarantee the preservation of the traditions. The priests of the gods are termed *kapuvā* or *kapurāḷa*. The exorcism of the Yakṣas is performed by the *yakädurā* or *kaṭṭādiyā*, and the rituals connected with the cult of the planets are carried out by the *balädurā* or *balikārayā*. The exact knowledge of the rituals and mantras is kept secret and handed down mostly in a family tradition, in some instances from teacher to pupil. The performance of the cult for higher gods is traditionally reserved to members of the goyigama caste, whereas the cult of certain lower gods is only performed by members of particular lower castes. Other complicated interrelations of social structure and cult result from the traditional obligations of the tenants of temple land. There are many services to be rendered by temple tenants, e. g. temple music, production of offerings, cleaning of the temple and its surroundings etc.

The popular religion of the Sinhalese proves to be an extremely complicated "system", and the "structural" models proposed for its description, though very helpful for the understanding of some important features of and interrelations within Sinhalese religion, do not suffice for a description of this religion in its totality. It is for this reason that I do not propose a new structural analysis here, but have contented myself with a more conservative type of descriptive and historical survey of my subject.

For further research, the systematic study of the popular religion in particular regions of the country seems urgent in view of the progressive assimilation and simplification of the folk religion, with the resulting loss of many traditions. A systematic collection and evaluation of the literary sources is imperative for a better understanding of the details and of the historical developments. Last not least, a comparative study of the relation of Buddhism and popular cults as attempted during this symposium should be useful for an adequate understanding of the religion of the Sinhalese.

Kataragama: Das Heiligtum im Dschungel Südost-Ceylons — aus geographischer Sicht[1])

Von KLAUS HAUSHERR

1. Lage und Bedeutung des Heiligtums Kataragama

In der einförmigen Dschungelwildnis des Flachlands von Südost-Ceylon liegt eines der bedeutendsten Heiligtümer der Insel: Kataragama, nach Wirz (1954), die „heiligste Stätte Ceylons" (Abb. 1). Vor wenigen Jahren noch hat nichts in der die Kultstätte umgebenden Landschaft auf das Bestehen einer Siedlung oder eines Heiligtums hingewiesen, kein Bauwerk den Buschwald überragt. Heute läßt sich — scheut man die Mühe nicht, auf einen der zahlreichen Inselberge in der Umgebung zu steigen — der wiederhergestellte, weißleuchtende große Stūpa, das Kirivehera, inmitten einer graugrünen Vegetationsdecke schon von weitem erkennen.

Dieser Stūpa aber ist nur einer der Sakralbauten der drei an diesem Ort vertretenen Religionen; denn sowohl Buddhisten wie Hindus und Muslim sehen und haben in Kataragama eine Stätte der Verehrung. Allerdings deuten außer dem Stūpa keine aufragenden Hindutempel südindischer Prägung oder Minaretts äußerlich auf die Bedeutung und Wichtigkeit dieser Dschungelsiedlung im Glaubensleben der Inselbewohner hin.

Die hervorragende Stellung des Heiligtums erahnt erst, wer sich etwas intensiver mit der Insel und besonders mit dem Südosten beschäftigt; denn „Kataragama" begegnet man buchstäblich auf Schritt und Tritt in den verschiedensten Zusammenhängen.

Da ist 1. das Tempelland, das zu einem großen Teil den Tempeln von Kataragama gehört und auf dem häufig Chena (Brandrodungsfeldbau) betrieben wird, während das umliegende Waldland unberührt zu bleiben scheint (Hausherr, 1971a). Weite Dschungelflächen werden zuweilen als „Deviange Kelle", „Dschungel Gottes" (d. h. Gott Kataragama), bezeichnet (Spittel, 1933, S. 281) oder sind in Karten als „Kataragamakele", „Dschungel von Kataragama", eingetragen. Da sind 2. die

---

[1]) Verfasser ist der Deutschen Forschungsgemeinschaft für die Unterstützung seiner Arbeiten auf Ceylon (1970) und dem Südasien-Institut, Heidelberg, für die Ermöglichung von Archivarbeiten in London (1971) zu Dank verpflichtet. — Für Ortsangaben wird die in den amtlichen topographischen Karten verwendete Schreibweise benutzt. Den Professoren H. Bechert, Göttingen, und S. Lienhard, Stockholm, danke ich für ihre Hilfe bei der Schreibung singhalesischer und tamilischer Namen und Begriffe.

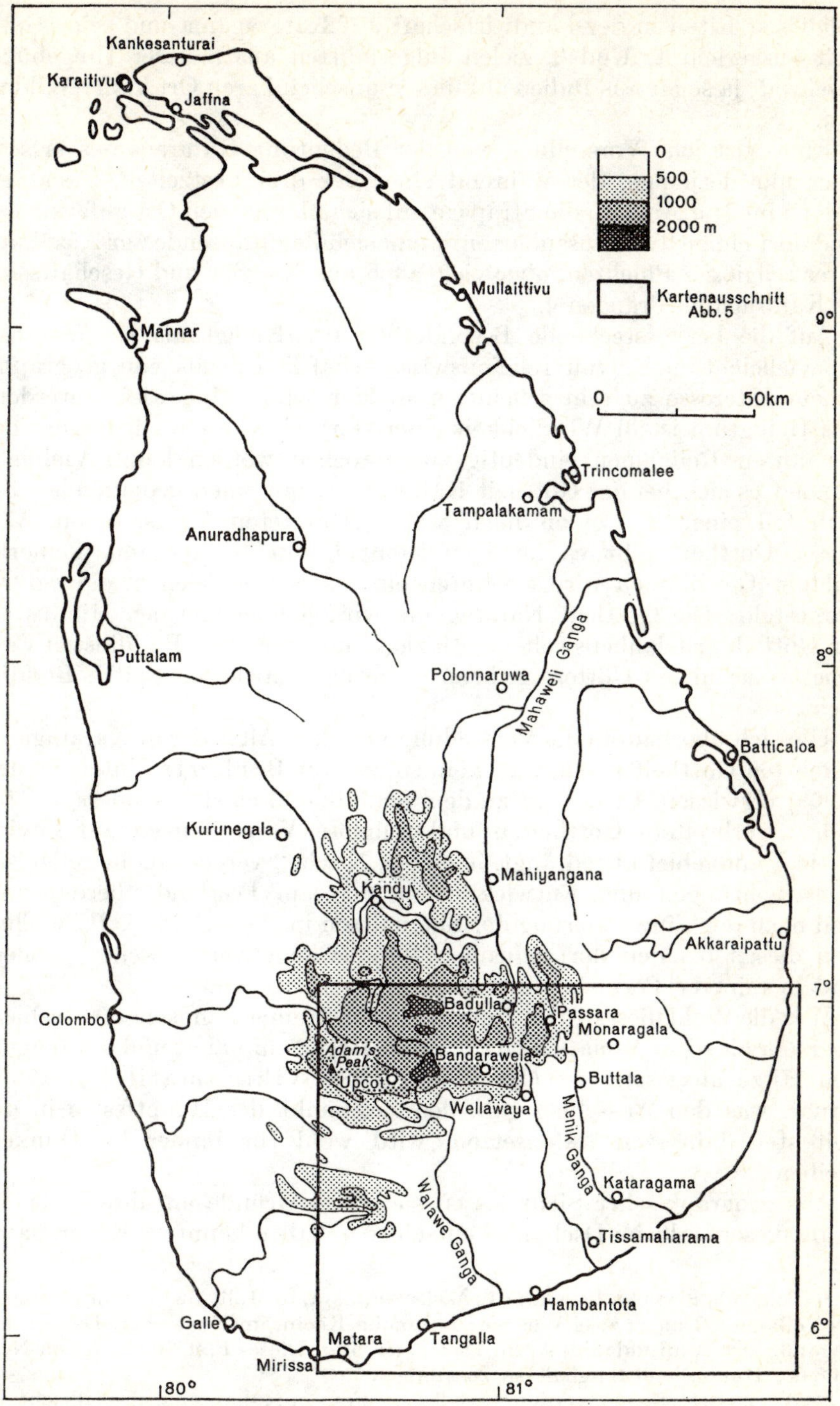

Abb. 1: Übersichtskarte von Ceylon.

religiösen Riten in der Landwirtschaft auf Kataragama und seine Gottheit ausgerichtet. Und 3. zielen Pilgerfahrten aus näherer Umgebung, inselweit, ja sogar aus Indien auf diesen unscheinbaren Ort in der Wildnis hin.

Eine wirkliche Vorstellung von der Bedeutung Kataragamas erfährt aber nur derjenige, der während einer der drei Festzeiten, besonders jedoch im Juli/August, die Strapaze auf sich nimmt, den Ort aufzusuchen und dort einige Tage auszuharren, wenn sich Zehntausende zur Ausübung ihrer religiösen Pflichten, aber viele auch aus Neugier und Geschäftssinn in Kataragama drängen[2]).

Auf die hervorstechende Besonderheit des Heiligtums Kataragama, die vielleicht mehr von religionswissenschaftlichem als von geographischem Interesse zu sein scheint, muß hier schon hingewiesen werden: das Heiligtum ist in Wirklichkeit einer Gottheit geweiht, die keiner der genannten Religionen eindeutig zugesprochen werden kann. Vielmehr handelt es sich bei der Gottheit Kataragama um einen bedeutenden Bestandteil einer in Ceylon noch weit verbreiteten Volksreligion. Von dieser Gottheit gibt es im Haupttempel von Kataragama keinerlei Bildnis. Gewöhnlich wird sie durch ein magisches Zeichen, ein *yantra*, dargestellt. Die Gottheit Kataragama wird jedoch von den Hindus als ein Gott ihrer Glaubenswelt identifiziert, und von den Buddhisten Ceylons ist sie in ein Götterpantheon eingefügt, an dessen Spitze Buddha steht.

Um sich überhaupt eine Vorstellung von dem Alter der in Kataragama verehrten Gottheit machen zu können, sei auf Becherts Untersuchung (1968) verwiesen. Er kommt zu dem Schluß, daß einst besonders in Südindien verbreitete Gottheiten und religiöse Vorstellungen auf Ceylon in ein Randgebiet abgedrängt, in einer „Nische" vergessen, die religiösen Umschichtungen und Entwicklungen auf dem Festland überdauerten und nach der Einwanderung der Singhalesen in Ceylon (im 6. Jh. v. Chr.) von diesen bei den dort lebenden Väddas angetroffen, weiter gepflegt und in reinerer Form bewahrt wurden als in Indien.

Was die Wahl dieses Ortes zum Heiligtum in einer Landschaft entschied, die mehr als sechs Monate im Jahr kaum Regen empfängt und der sengenden Hitze ausgesetzt ist (Domrös, 1968; Wikkramatileke, 1956), ferner, was den Ausschlag gab, den Zeitpunkt des Hauptfestes in der heißesten Jahreszeit festzusetzen, wird wohl für immer im Dunkeln bleiben[3]).

Aus geographischer Sicht lassen sich zwei Gründe anführen, die die Wahl dieser Stelle im Dschungel entschieden haben könnten: Kataragama

[2]) Folgende Feste finden statt: 1. Äsala Perahära, im Juli/August von Neumond bis Vollmond, Dauer: zwei Wochen; 2. Ilmaha Kachi, im November, Dauer: drei Tage; 3. Alut Avurudda, im April, Dauer: ein Tag. Dieses Fest fällt mit dem Neujahr der Hindus und Singhalesen zusammen.

[3]) Wirz (1941, S. 166) vermutet, daß dem Fest „. . . ursprünglich vielleicht der Gedanke einer Sommersonnenwendfeier zugrunde lag . . ."

liegt an einem Fluß, dem Menik Ganga („Juwelenfluß"), dem heiligen Fluß der Insel, der, von wenigen Ausnahmen abgesehen, das ganze Jahr über Wasser führt, eine „Oase" also im trockenen Südosten Ceylons. Dies schon könnte zu einer Siedlungsgründung geführt haben. Es gibt aber keinerlei Hinweise darüber, was die Wahl der Ortslage bestimmte. Nicht der Fluß allein, auch der südlich des Ortes sich erhebende, in west-östlicher Richtung verlaufende, rund 9 km lange Bergzug, der im Wedahitikanda (Kataragama Peak) mit 417 m die höchste Erhebung im Umkreis aufweist und damit die flache Umgebung um 350 m überragt, muß wohl in die Überlegungen zur Auswahl dieses Ortes als Heiligtum mit einbezogen werden. Nicht von ungefähr ist der Berg heute einer der drei heiligen Bezirke des Heiligtums Kataragama. Möglicherweise hat hier schon in vorgeschichtlicher Zeit Sonnenverehrung stattgefunden, wie sie z. B. noch andeutungsweise auf dem Adam's Peak, dem von drei der vier großen in Ceylon vertretenen Religionen — Buddhismus, Hinduismus und Islam — verehrten Berg zu finden ist (Cartman, 1957, S. 126)[4].

Auf einen anderen geographischen Anhaltspunkt deutet Wirz (1954, S. 141) hin: Kataragama bildet den südlichen Endpunkt einer Achse, die im Norden bis zum Berg Kailasa, dem Sitz Śivas, einem der höchsten Götter der Hindus, im Himalaya reicht (geographische Längen: Kailasa 81°10'; Kataragama 81°20'). Ob die Übereinstimmung in der Lage beider heiliger Berge auf einem Zufall beruht oder nicht, wird wohl ebensowenig nachzuweisen sein wie die Hintergründe, die zur Entstehung des Heiligtums führten.

2. Heilige Bezirke und Verehrungsstätten

Das Heiligtum Kataragama besteht aus insgesamt drei heiligen Bezirken, in denen sich wiederum zahlreiche Stätten der Verehrung befinden, die aus Tempeln, Schreinen und heiligen Bäumen bestehen. Diese drei sind: Sella Kataragama, der Berg Wedahitikanda und der Ort Kataragama[5]) (Abb. 2).

In Sella Kataragama (= Kleines Kataragama) stehen ein alter Tempel, der dem Elefantengott Gaṇeśa geweiht ist, ferner neuere Tempel zu Ehren der Gottheiten Pattini und Kataragama, sowie ein Stūpa.

Auf dem heiligen Berg Wedahitikanda ist man noch dabei, die Verehrungsstätten auszubauen. Neben einem alten Schrein und einer Lanze, Zeichen der Verehrung Gott Kataragamas, waren 1970 eine buddhistische Verehrungsstätte mit einem Bo-Baum (*Ficus religiosa*) und ein im Bau

---

[4]) Christen beteiligen sich entgegen anderslautenden Darstellungen nicht an den Pilgerfahrten zu diesem Berg (P(erera?), 1919).

[5]) An der Straße Beragalla (Haputale)–Wellawaya steht zwischen Meilenstein 134 und 135 ein kleiner Opferschrein, der Punchi Kataragama genannt wird. Angeblich kann man von hier aus erstmals das Heiligtum von Kataragama erblicken.

befindlicher Tempel, der einer hinduistischen Gottheit geweiht ist, bereits vorhanden[6]).

Der heilige Bezirk Kataragama zerfällt in zwei bauliche Komplexe, die sehr ungleichmäßig mit Tempeln ausgestattet sind (Abb.3). Wegen der mit ihnen verbundenen Riten, aber auch wegen ihrer getrennten Lage müssen sie gesondert betrachtet werden.

Der größere Tempelbezirk umfaßt praktisch die Siedlung (Abb. 4). Am nördlichen Ende von drei parallel verlaufenden Straßen, bzw. Wegen liegen zwei Einfriedungen, in denen mehrere Tempel und Schreine stehen. Der bedeutendste in der einen der beiden Umwallungen ist das Ruhuṇu Mahā Kataragama dēvālē[7]), im folgenden als Haupttempel

Tab. 1: Tempel und Schreine im Ort Kataragama

a–b: in Abb. 3 c–x: in Abb. 4

a	Kirivehera; Stūpa
b	Däḍimuṇḍa dēvālē
c*)	Ruhuṇu Mahā Kataragama dēvālē; Mahādēvālē
d*)	Gaṇeśa kōvila; Gaṇapati kōvila; Māṇikka Piḷḷaiya kōvila
e*)	Viṣṇu-Temple; Perumāḷ kōvila (enthält Buddhastatue)
f	Pattini kōvila
g	Mānākāra kōvila
h	Kaliamma kōvila
i	Budugē (Buddhaschrein)
j	Śrī Bhairava
k	Viṣṇu kōvila; Śrī Mahā Viṣṇu
l	Śiva kōvila
m	Teyvāṇiammā kōvila; Śrī Mahā Viṣṇu
n	Palni kōvila; Śrī Palani Aniandavar
o	Skanda kōvila; Shrine of God Kataragama
p	Hatara mahā dēvālē
q	Abhinavārāma
r	Katiresan kōvila
s	Kolanda kōvila; Kulandaivadivel kōvila
t	Kali kōvila
u	Īśvara kōvila; Īśvara Mahā dēvālē; Mutuliṅgam Svāmī kōvila; Śiva-Temple
v	Vaḷḷīammā kōvila
w	Moschee; Khizar Thakkiya
x	Kaṇṇakaiammā kōvila; Angha Pattini Amman kōvila

*) Davy (1969, S. 313) nennt: c) Katragam Dewale, d) Ganna Dewale, e) Boodhoo Wihare, sowie sechs kleine ‚Kovillas', eine davon als ‚Patine'. Bei White (1893, Fußnote S. 39) werden diese sechs kleinen kōvila genannt: Pattini Dewale, Ganadewi Kowila, Alutdeyianne Kowila, Basnairadeyianne Kowila, Parakasadeyianne Kowila und Kumeradeyianne Kowila.

Quellen: Hassan (1968); Spittel (1933); Wirz (1954); verschiedene Unterlagen in der Kachcheri Monaragala; eigene Befragungen

[6]) Wirz (1954, S. 156) nennt zwei Berge, den Kataramalai und den Vedahitiya Kanda. Er unterlag wahrscheinlich einer Täuschung, denn beide von ihm genannte Berge sind identisch.

[7]) *Dēvālē* ist die Bezeichnung für den Tempel einer Gottheit der Volksreligion. *Vihāra, Dāgoba, Stūpa* weisen immer auf eine buddhistische Kultstätte hin. *Kōvila* ist eine andere Bezeichnung für einen hinduistischen Tempel. In der Lite-

Tab. 2: Unterkunftshäuser (*madam*) in Kataragama

Nummer in Abb. 3 u. 4	Namen der *madam*	andere Namen	Bedeutung des durch *) gekenn-zeichneten Namens	Baujahr	Wohnsitz des Grund-stückspächters oder Institution	Räume (R) bzw. Fassungsvermö-gen (Pilger; P) (1970)
1	Chetti*)	Nagaratar	Geldverleiher	ca. 1866	Trustees of the Katiresan kōvila	22 R
2	Markandan		angeblich von reichem Reishändler gestiftet	ca. 1881	Batticaloa	?
3	Sadai Amma	Gurunatan*)	Gründer	ca. 1886	Kankesanturai	?
4	Teyvaniamma			vor 1900		ca. 200 P
5	Pasupaty*)	Kolanda; Kulandaivadivel	Gründer	ca. 1911	Tissamaharama	3 R
6	Ponampalam Svami*)		Gründer	1924	Jaffna	ca. 300 P
7	Tambaiya*)		Gründer	1925	Jaffna	?
8	Barber*)	Maritua; Marutuvar	angeblich von Friseuren finanziert	1926	Mirissa	?
9	Galkanda	Kalkandusamy		ca. 1926	Jaffna	?
10	Dr. Appuswami*)		Gründer	1928	Kotahena (Colombo)	?
11	Arunashalampillai*)		Gründer	1928	Bandarawela	?
12	Kamala Circus	Narayanaguru	angeblich von Artisten aus Kerala (Indien) gestiftet	1928	?	?
13	Dhobi*)		*madam* der Wäscher	1929	Jaffna	?
14	Mauna Svami*)		Gründer	ca. 1930	?	?
15	Puvalingam	Pullingam Chettiar*)	Gründer	1931	Peliyagoda (Colombo)	?
16	Tambusamy*)		Gründer	1931	Ponnaturai-Kalady	?
17	Malaiamma			1931	?	?
18	Variya*)		Steuererheber (?)	1935	Tampalakamam	?
19	Ponnaturai*)		Gründer	1935	Upcot-Maskeliya	?
20	Sattu Saddichami	Shaddy Sami		1936	?	?
21	Dr. Kanagasabai*)		Gründer	1936	Ratmalana (Colombo)	?
22	Madanaguru	Kortagala; Kottukola Kankani		1936	Kotapola	?
23	Gnanapandita		Gründer	1941	Badulla	?
24	Ramakrishna Mission*)			1953	Trustees of the Rama-krishna Mission	1000–2000 P
25	Leo*)	Palu	Gründer	nach 1960	Bandarawela	?
26	Government's Pilgrims Rest			1965	Regierung	200 P
27	Kataragama Visrama-sala Sadhaka Bauddhasamitiya			ca. 1965	?	?
28	Ceylon Transport Board			1969	Regierung	500–600 P
29	Murughananda Svami			ca. 1969	?	?
30	Mutulingam Svami			?	?	6 R
31	Moschee	(Khizar Thakkiya; Masjidul Hilri)		?	?	80 P

Quellen: Unterlagen der Kachcheri Monaragala;
Mr. V. Sabaratnam, Ramakrishna Mission Madam, Kataragama;
eigene Befragungen

oder Mahādēvālē bezeichnet; in der anderen steht der Teyvāṇiammā-Tempel. Am südlichen Ende der Straßen befindet sich der Vaḷḷiammā Tempel und in dessen unmittelbarer Nähe die Moschee und das Īśvara kōvila.

---

ratur wird nicht immer klar zwischen *dēvālē* und *kōvila* unterschieden. Das hängt damit zusammen, daß z.B. eine Gottheit der Volksreligion in den hinduistischen Glaubensvorstellungen integriert worden ist.

Der zweite bauliche Komplex wird von dem Stūpa, dem Kirivehera, und den um ihn herum stehenden Gebäuden und Schreinen gebildet. Der Stūpa liegt am Ende eines Weges, etwa 560 m von dem großen Tempelkomplex im Ort entfernt.

Die Lage aller Stätten der Verehrung im Ort Kataragama — soweit zu erfahren war — ist zusammen mit ihren Namen in den Abbildungen 3 und 4, bzw. in Tabelle 1 eingetragen.

In der räumlichen Verteilung der heiligen Bezirke und der in ihnen befindlichen Kultstätten lassen sich nicht für alle von ihnen bestimmte Ausrichtungen untereinander oder nach einer Himmelsrichtung erkennen. Ohne sichtbaren Bezug zu den anderen liegt Sella Kataragama am weitesten nördlich auf einer Insel im Menik Ganga (Abb. 2). Eine, wenn auch nur am Wegenetz erkennbare Ausrichtung (eine etwa N-S verlaufende Achse) besteht zwischen dem am weitesten südlich gelegenen heiligen Berg Wedahitikanda und dem Stūpa. Diese Achse durchschneidet den einen Endpunkt des sich NNW—SSO über 330 m erstreckenden Tempelkomplexes im Ort Kataragama. Die Moschee ist wie alle islamischen Gotteshäuser nach Mekka ausgerichtet.

3. Legenden um Kataragama und ihre Bedeutung für das Heiligtum

Obwohl der Tempelkomplex im Ort selbst alle anderen Bezirke bei weitem an Bedeutung überragt, wurde die Aufzählung der heiligen Bezirke absichtlich in dieser Reihenfolge vorgenommen, um der Darstellung in mehreren Legenden zu entsprechen. Es gibt einen ganzen Schatz davon, der sich fast ausschließlich aus Elementen des Hinduismus und der singhalesischen Volksreligion zusammensetzt. Auf sie soll zunächst eingegangen werden, schon deswegen, weil sie sehr viel über die Bedeutung der einzelnen heiligen Stätten und ihre Rolle im Gesamtkomplex des Heiligtums Kataragama aussagen. Ein kurzer Überblick über die Legenden scheint berechtigt zu sein, weil sie in gewissem Sinn den Ablauf des Besuches der Gläubigen vorzeichnen und z. T. auch deren Verhalten in den einzelnen heiligen Bezirken beeinflussen und damit wiederum — vereinzelt zwar, aber doch bemerkenswert — das Ortsbild geprägt haben. Ferner bestimmen die Legenden weitgehend den täglichen Ritus und den Ablauf der Prozessionen während der großen Feiern.

Der Kern der Legenden um Kataragama hat als Zentralfigur einen Gott, der unter verschiedenen Namen, z. T. auch verschiedenen Funktionen über den gesamten indischen Subkontinent vom Himalaja bis nach Ceylon bekannt ist. So weisen die Namen Skanda, Murukaṉ, Subrahmaṇya, Kārttikeya u.a. alle auf ein und dieselbe Gottheit hin. Bechert (1968) hat den Zusammenhängen eine ausführliche Untersuchung gewidmet, auf die hier hingewiesen werden soll. In Ceylon hat dieser Gott seinen Namen von dem Ort Kataragama, dem Zentrum und Ausgangspunkt seiner Verehrung auf der Insel bekommen. Der Name wird

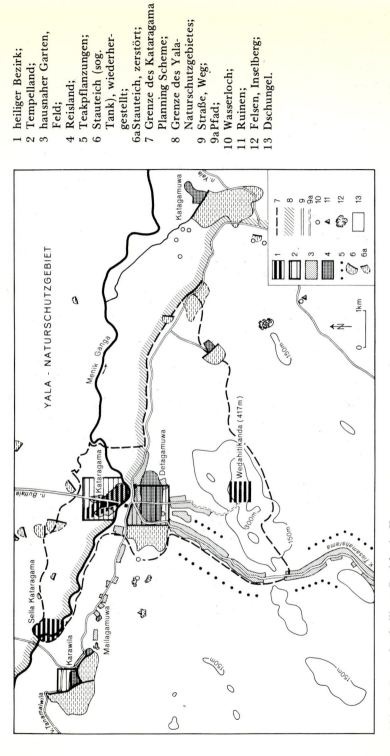

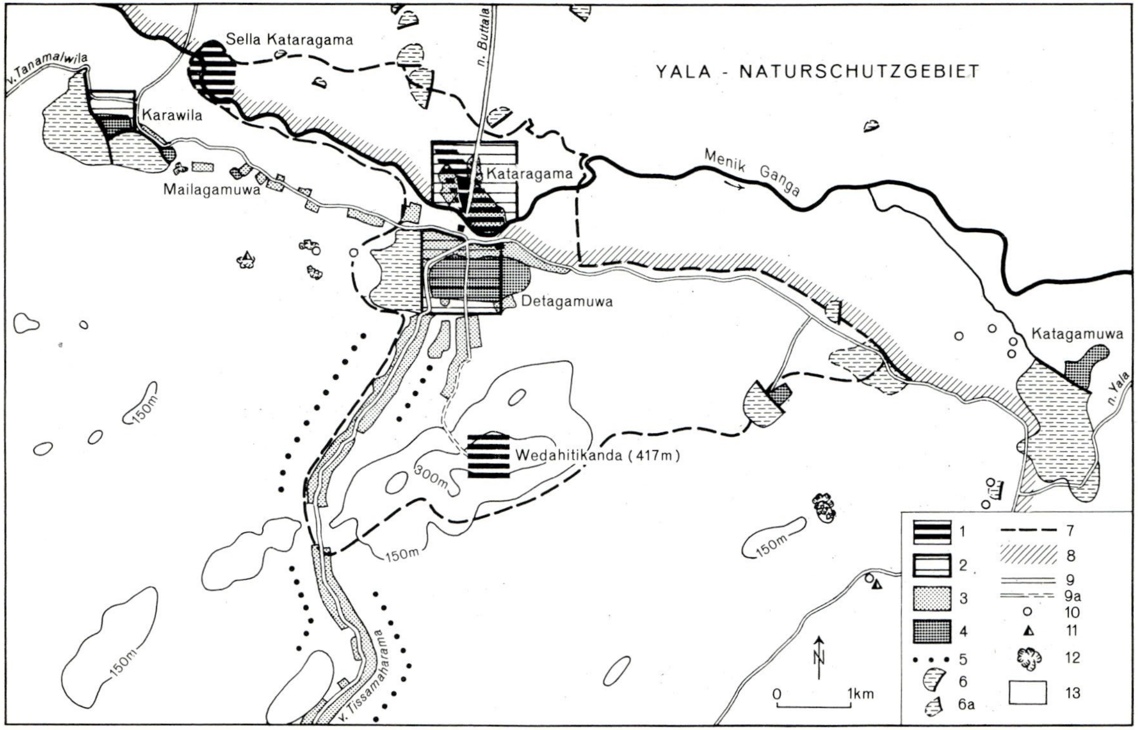

1 heiligen Bezirk;
2 Tempelland;
3 hausnaher Garten, Feld;
4 Reisland;
5 Teakpflanzungen;
6 Stauteich (sog. Tank), wiederhergestellt;
6a Stauteich, zerstört;
7 Grenze des Kataragama Planning Scheme;
8 Grenze des Yala-Naturschutzgebietes;
9 Straße, Weg;
9a Pfad;
10 Wasserloch;
11 Ruinen;
12 Felsen, Inselberg;
13 Dschungel.

Abb. 2: Lage der heiligen Bezirke in Kataragama.

Quellen: Topographische Karte 1 : 63360 (one inch to one mile), Blatt Kataragama, sheet P 3, 4, 8, 9, (1968); Unterlagen der Kachcheri Monaragala.

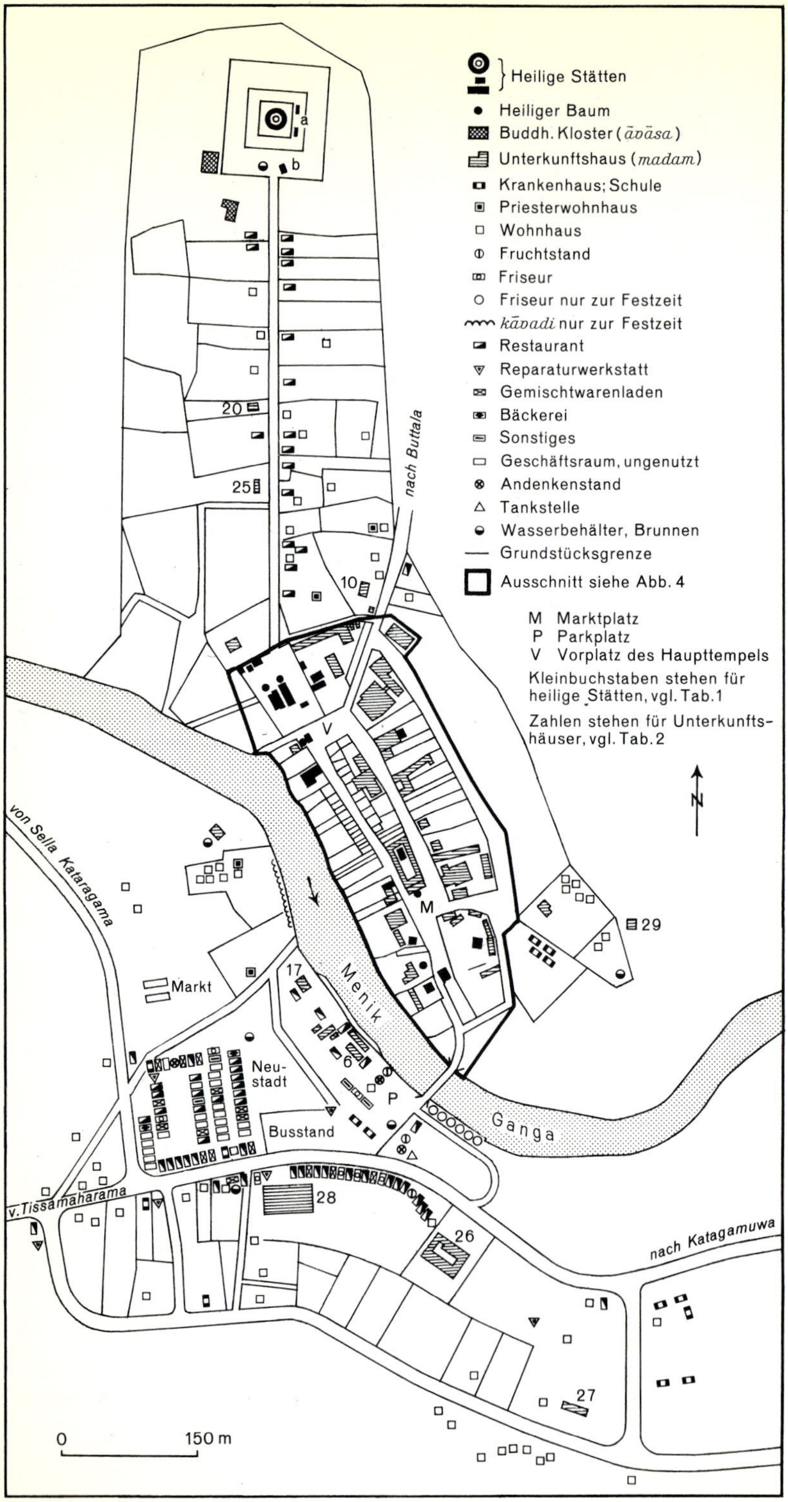
Heilige Stätten
Heiliger Baum
Buddh. Kloster (āvāsa)
Unterkunftshaus (madam)
Krankenhaus; Schule
Priesterwohnhaus
Wohnhaus
Fruchtstand
Friseur
Friseur nur zur Festzeit
kāvadi nur zur Festzeit
Restaurant
Reparaturwerkstatt
Gemischtwarenladen
Bäckerei
Sonstiges
Geschäftsraum, ungenutzt
Andenkenstand
Tankstelle
Wasserbehälter, Brunnen
Grundstücksgrenze
Ausschnitt siehe Abb. 4
M Marktplatz
P Parkplatz
V Vorplatz des Haupttempels
Kleinbuchstaben stehen für heilige Stätten, vgl. Tab. 1
Zahlen stehen für Unterkunftshäuser, vgl. Tab. 2
N
a
b
20
25
10
nach Buttala
V
M
29
von Sella Kataragama
Markt
17
Menik
6
P
Neu-stadt
Busstand
Ganga
v. Tissamaharama
28
26
nach Katagamuwa
27
0
150 m

Abb. 3: Funktionalkartierung von Kataragama und Detagamuwa (1970).

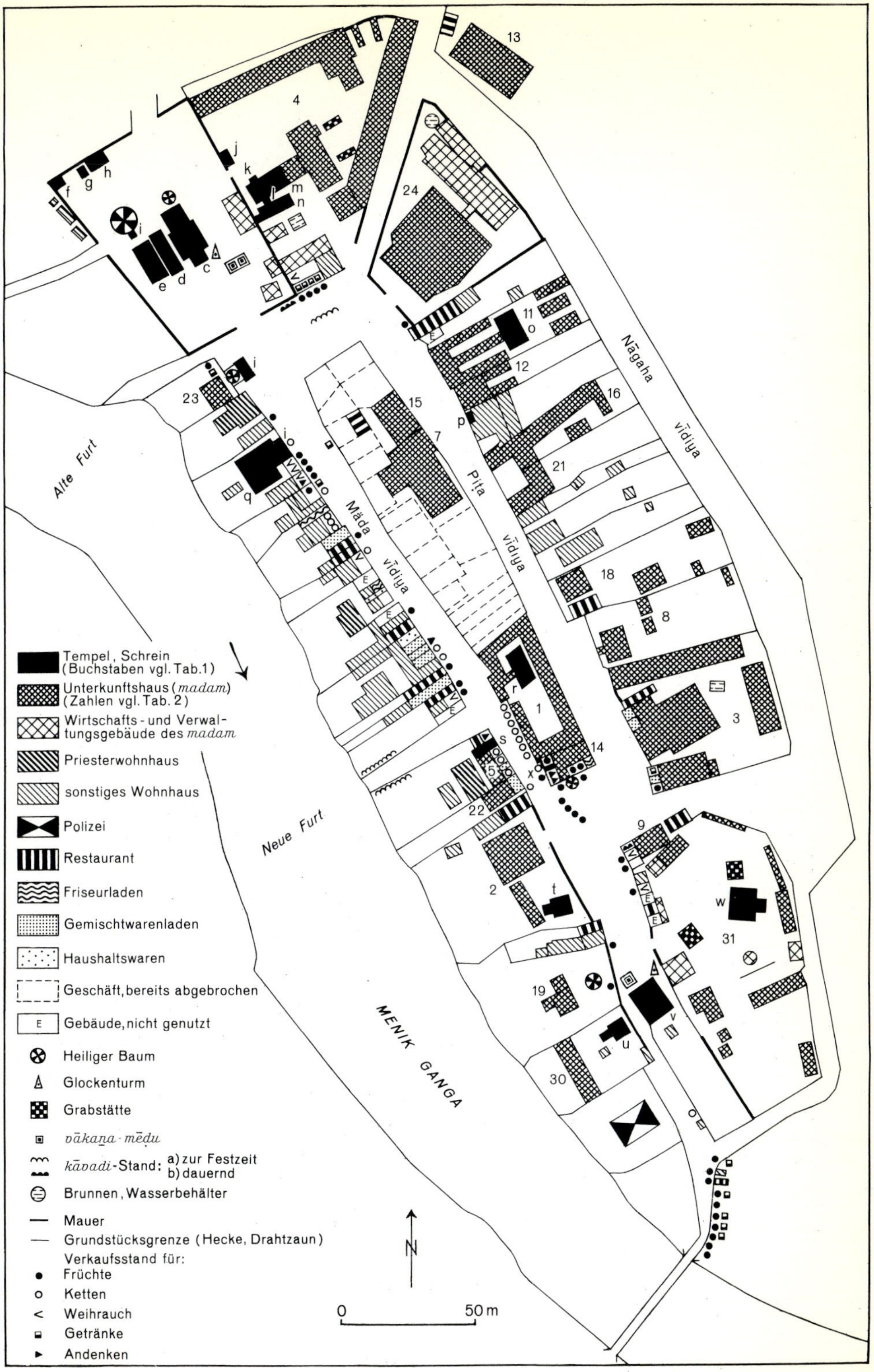

Tempel, Schrein (Buchstaben vgl. Tab. 1)
Unterkunftshaus (*madam*) (Zahlen vgl. Tab. 2)
Wirtschafts- und Verwaltungsgebäude des *madam*
Priesterwohnhaus
sonstiges Wohnhaus
Polizei
Restaurant
Friseurladen
Gemischtwarenladen
Haushaltswaren
Geschäft, bereits abgebrochen
Gebäude, nicht genutzt
Heiliger Baum
Glockenturm
Grabstätte
vākaṉa-mēḍu
kāvadi-Stand: a) zur Festzeit b) dauernd
Brunnen, Wasserbehälter
Mauer
Grundstücksgrenze (Hecke, Drahtzaun)
Verkaufsstand für:
Früchte
Ketten
Weihrauch
Getränke
Andenken
Alte Furt
Neue Furt
MENIK GANGA
Māda vīdiya
Piṭa vīdiya
Nāgaha vīdiya
N
0
50 m

Abb. 4: Funktionalkartierung von Kataragama (1970).

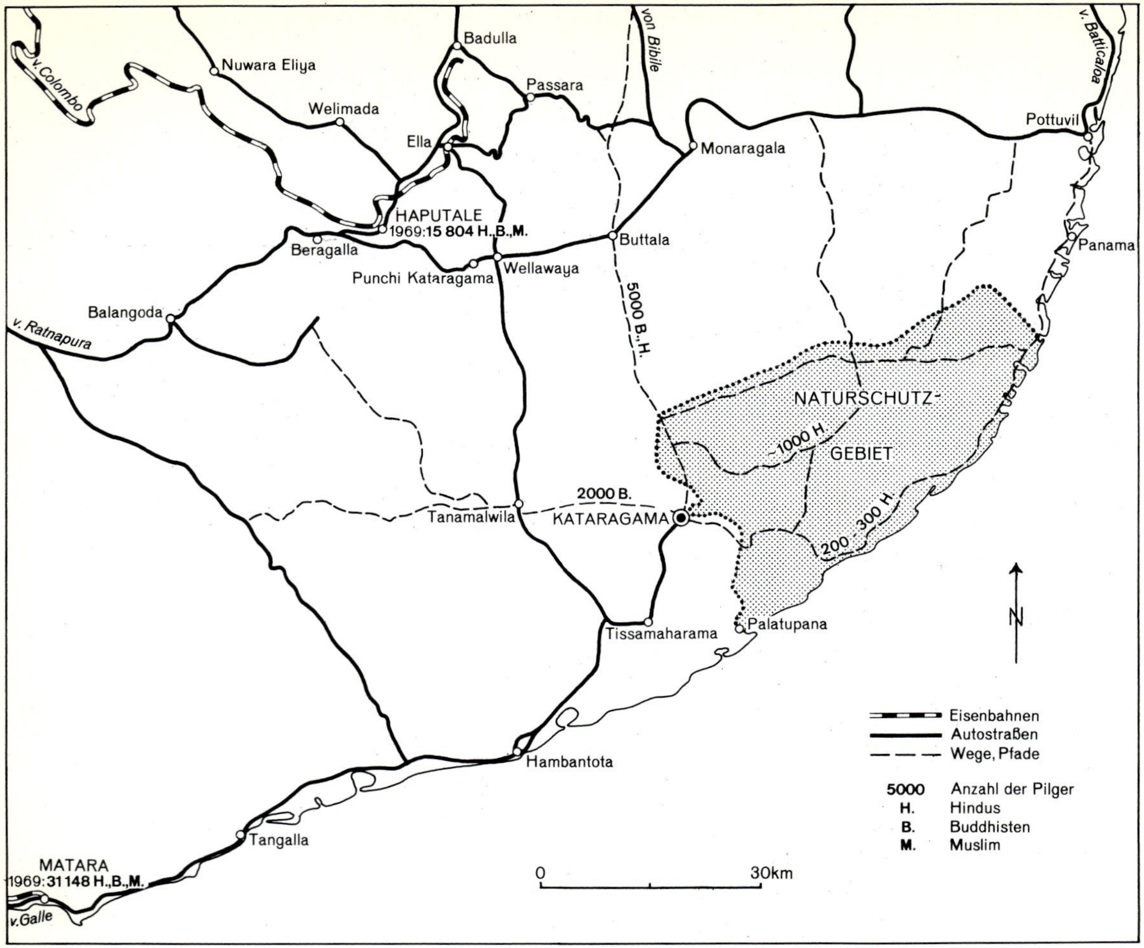

Abb. 5: Pilgerwege nach Kataragama.

Quellen: Report of the Ceylon Transport Board 1966/67, Colombo 1969; Unterlagen der Ceylon Government Railway für 1969; Mr. K. S. *Perera* (Angaben über Fußpilger)

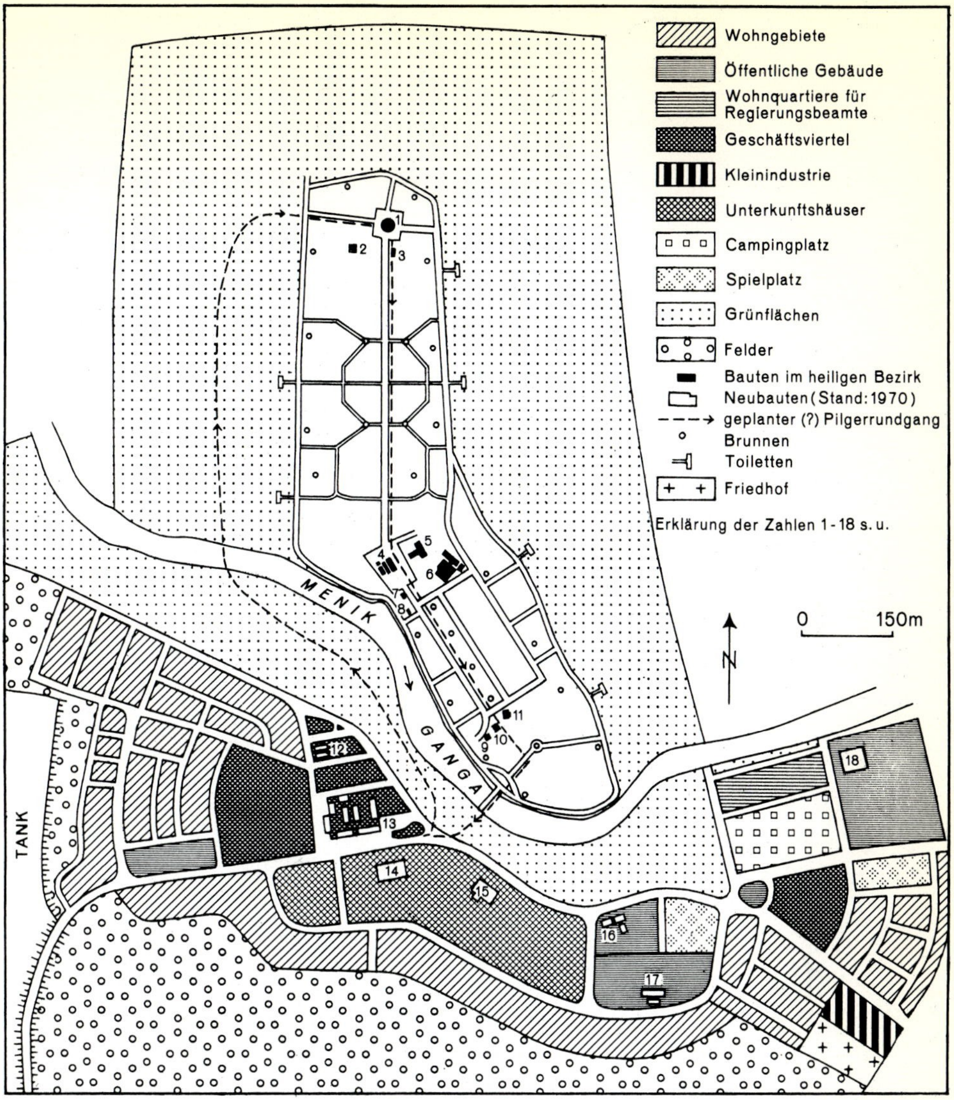

Abb. 6: Neuplanung von Kataragama

1 Kirivehera; 2 buddhistisches Kloster (*āvāsa*); 3 Däḍimuṇḍa dēvālē; 4 Haupttempel (Ruhuṇu Mahā Kataragama dēvālē, Gaṇeśa kōvila, Viṣṇu-Tempel u.a.); 5 Teyvāṇīammā kōvila; 6 Ramakrishna Mission Madam; 7 Budugē; 8 Abhinavārāmā; 9 Īśvara Mahā dēvālē; 10 Vaḷḷīammā kōvila; 11 Moschee; 12 Markt; 13 'New Town'; 14 Ceylon Transport Board Madam; 15 Government's Pilgrims Rest; 16 Schule; 17 Hospital; 18 Ceylon Transport Board (C. T. B.) Busdepot.

Quellen: Heiliger Bezirk Kataragama (nördl. Menik Ganga) nach einem Plan des Dept. of Archaeology: Colombo, 21.9.65/14.5.69; Kataragama Town (südl. Menik Ganga) nach Kataragama Planning Scheme (under the Town and Country Planning Ordinance No. 13 of 1946), 1964; Unterlagen der Kachcheri Monaragala.

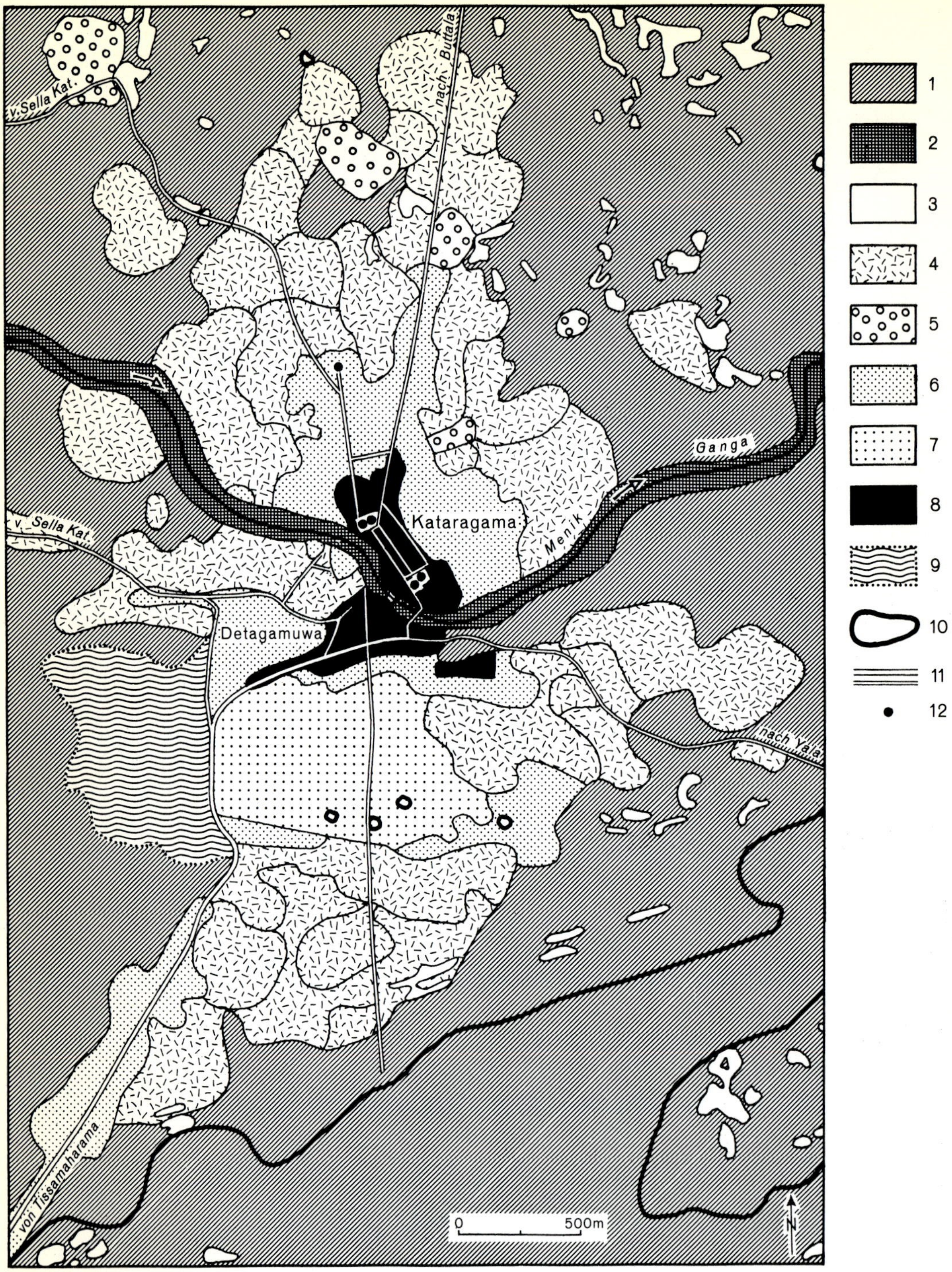

Abb. 7: Interpretationsskizze zum Luftbild Kataragama.

1 trockener Monsunwald; 2 hoher Baumwuchs (entlang Menik Ganga); 3 'damana'-Grasland (geringer Busch- und Baumbestand); 4 Chena (Brandrodung), aufgegeben; 5 Chena, in Nutzung; 6 Feld; 7 Reisland; 8 Siedlung und hausnaher Garten; 9 Tank (mit Bäumen bestanden); 10 Bergland, Inselberg; 11 Straße, Weg; 12 Kultstätte.

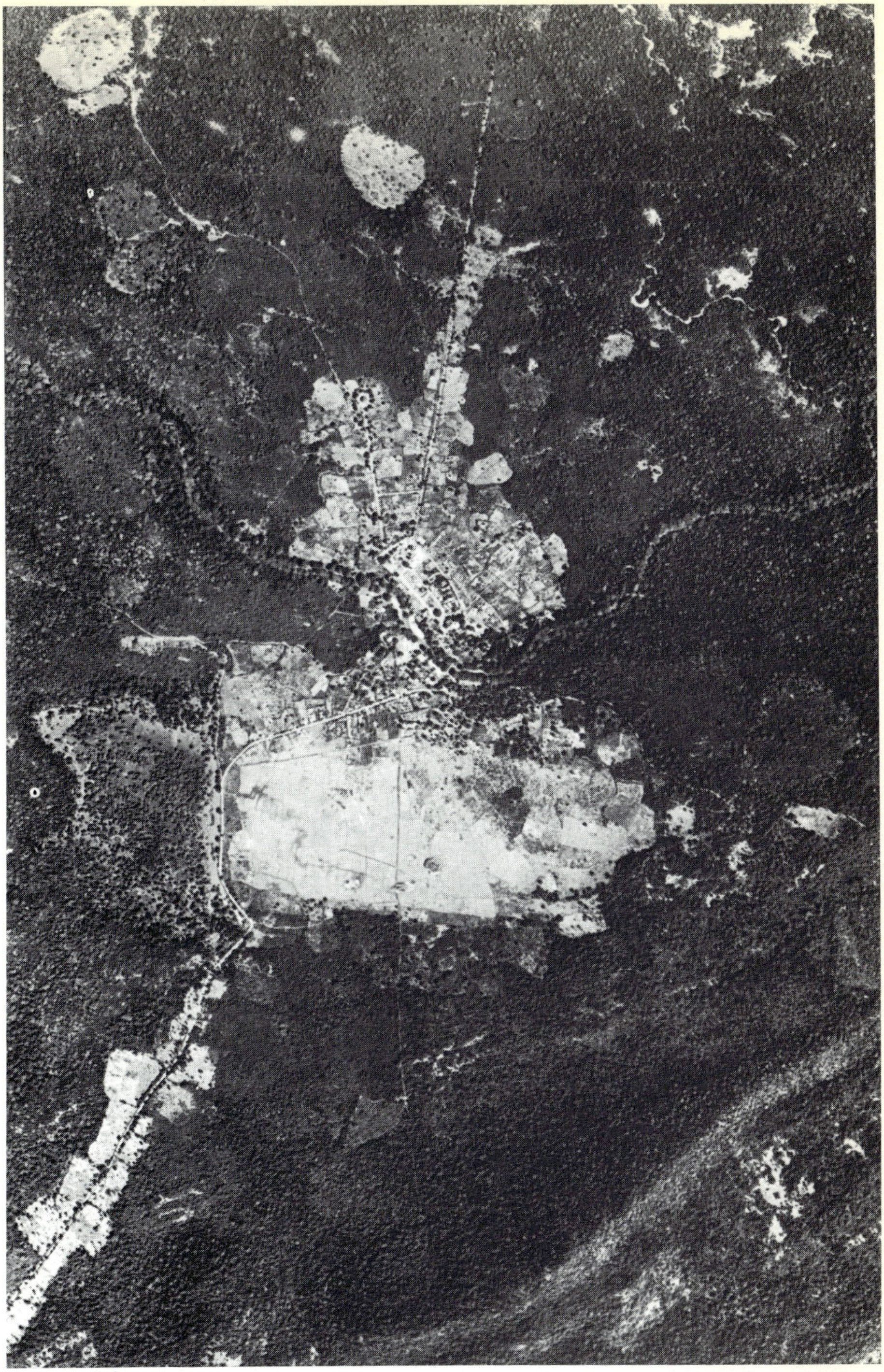

Kataragama: Ausschnitt aus Luftbild P 9/A 9, Bild 153, 1956; Originalmaßstab ca. 1 : 40000, genauere Aufnahmedaten unbekannt; aufgenommen von: The Photographic Survey Corporation, Limited, Toronto, Canada, in co-operation with the Surveyor General of Ceylon.

Bild 1: Blick vom Wedahitikanda auf den Detagamuwa Tank (links) und dem dazugehörigen, sich nach rechts anschließenden Reisfeld. Hinten rechts: die Siedlung Detagamuwa und Kataragama mit dem Stūpa (14.6.70).

Bild 2: Restaurants ('hotels') gegenüber dem Busbahnhof (1971 abgerissen) (14.6.70).

Bild 3: Hinterhof eines typischen Neubaublocks in der 'New Town' von Kataragama mit Blick auf einen der Kataragama-Berge (14.6.70).

Bild 4: Pilger am Menik Ganga während des Hauptfestes (15.7.70).

Bild 5: Neue Verkaufsstände der aus dem heiligen Bezirk ausgesiedelten Händler am Zugang zur Brücke über den Menik Ganga (28.9.73).

Bild 6: Stände für Schmuckketten, Andenken und Fruchtschalen im heiligen Bezirk von Kataragama (1971 abgerissen) (14.6.70).

Bild 7: Blick über die neuerbaute Plattform zwischen den Prozessionswegen Mäda vīdiya und Piṭa vīdiya. Hinten: Umwallung und Eingangstor des Haupttempelkomplexes (28.9.73).

Bild 8: Die Haupttempel von Kataragama (von rechts): Ruhuṇu Mahā Kataragama dēvālē, Gaṇeśa kōvila und Viṣṇu-Tempel. Links vorn: Opferstein zum Zerschlagen von Kokosnüssen (28.9.73).

Bild 9: Der wiederaufgebaute Stūpa (Kirivehera) von Kataragama; vorn: Restaurants (15.6.70).

Bild 10: Gaṇeśa kōvila in Sella Kataragama mit Opferstein für Kokosnüsse, rechts: Arm des Menik Ganga zur Trockenzeit (13.6.70). Alle Aufnahmen: K. *Hausherr*.

verschiedentlich als ‚Karthigeya grama', d. h. das Dorf Kārttikeyas oder Gott Kataragamas, gedeutet (Spittel, 1933, S. 282; u.a.).

Eine der Legenden, die die meisten Stätten der heutigen Verehrung und andeutungsweise einen großen Teil des im Zusammenhang mit diesem Gott in Kataragama vollzogenen Rituals in sich vereinigt, lautet folgendermaßen: Dem Gott Skanda wird in seiner indischen Heimat von einem schönen Mädchen, Vaḷḷīammā, Tochter eines Häuptlings des Dschungelvolkes der Väddas, berichtet, das bei Kataragama lebt. Er beschließt, dieses Mädchen zu suchen, findet es in der Höhle des Häuptlings in der Nähe des heutigen Sella Kataragama und gewinnt es zur Frau, der zweiten, denn er ist bereits mit Teyvāṇīammā verheiratet. Der Gott und seine junge Frau lassen sich auf einem in der Nähe gelegenen Berg, dem Wedahitikanda, nieder. Nach Bekanntwerden seiner Vermählung mit dem jungen Vädda-Mädchen folgte dem Gott die erste Frau, begleitet von zahlreichen Brahmanen. Ihr gelang es schließlich, ihren Mann zum Verlassen des Bergdomizils zu bewegen und sich in der Ebene, im heutigen Kataragama, niederzulassen[8]). Im Ort selbst wohnten alle drei getrennt. Neben dem Hause Skandas, nun Kataragama genannt, stand das der Teyvāṇīammā, der Eingang jedoch abgekehrt vom Hause des Gottes. Sein Hauseingang lag jedoch der in einiger Entfernung errichteten Wohnstätte der Vaḷḷīammā, seiner zweiten Frau, gegenüber. Vaḷḷīammā wird von dem Gott in der Folgezeit besucht, nicht aber seine erste Frau Teyvāṇīammā.

Nach Sella Kataragama, der Stätte der Vereinigung zwischen Gott Kataragama und dem Vädda-Mädchen, pilgern heute vor allem jungverheiratete, meist hinduistische Paare, verbringen hier oft eine Nacht und erflehen Segen für ihre Ehe[9]). 1969 sollen angeblich 50000 Pilger das Heiligtum aufgesucht haben. Die in der Legende erwähnte Höhle existiert nach Spittel (1933, S. 296) noch, konnte vom Verfasser selbst aber nicht lokalisiert werden.

Für den Wedahitikanda, dem zweiten genannten heiligen Bezirk in Kataragama, lassen sich aus der kurz geschilderten Legende keine besonderen Motive für den immer mehr zunehmenden Pilgerstrom entnehmen. Hinweise für die Verehrung des Berges sind in einer anderen Legende enthalten. Hier heißt es, daß Gott Skanda einen Kampf mit Dämonen bestanden habe und als Zeichen des Sieges seine Lanze auf einem Berg aufpflanzte. Als dieser wird der Wedahitikanda identifiziert; eine Lanze wird noch heute auf dem Gipfel verehrt.

Neben der Lanze gibt es ein weiteres wichtiges Attribut des Gottes, das ebenfalls im Heiligtum und bei den Prozessionen im Ort von großer

---

[8]) Ausgerechnet in Kataragama, dem Hauptsitz der Gottheit für Ceylon, wird der Gott nicht, wie von Bechert (1968, S. 34f.) für Südindien dargelegt, auf einem Berg, sondern im flachen Land verehrt.

[9]) Senaveratne (1919, S. 92) erwähnt, daß Pilgerfahrten zwar nicht speziell nach Sella Kataragama, aber nach Kataragama durchgeführt werden, um für männliche Nachkommen zu bitten.

Bedeutung ist: der Pfau. Er gilt als der von Gott Kataragama besiegte Herrscher der Dämonen, der seither in der Vogelgestalt den Gott begleitet (Asangananda, 1964, S. 8f.; u.a.).

Nach Mitteilung eines Einheimischen von Kataragama erhebt der Priester des buddhistischen Schreins auf dem Berg unter Berufung auf eine angeblich gefundene Inschrift den Anspruch, daß der Berg das eigentliche „alte" Kataragama gewesen sei.

Die meisten Aussagen enthält die Legende in bezug auf die in der Aufzählung der heiligen Bezirke zuletzt genannte Ortschaft Kataragama. Die drei für den Hinduismus und den Volksglauben wichtigsten Tempel sind darin in ihrer Lage beschrieben, und der Verlauf eines Teils des Rituals wird angedeutet, soweit er sich auf die Besuche des Gottes bei seiner zweiten Frau bezieht; denn die großen Prozessionen lassen den Tempel der Teyvāṇīammā aus und finden nur zwischen dem Haupttempel und dem Tempel der Vaḷḷīammā statt[10]). Der Stūpa und die Moschee werden bei diesen Umzügen ebenfalls nicht besucht.

Von den „offiziellen" Umzügen sind die von — meist hinduistischen — Pilgern durchgeführten zu unterscheiden, die einzeln oder in Gruppen, oftmals unter ekstatischen Tänzen, von wilder, sich steigernder Musik begleitet, alle Verehrungsstätten in diesem Teil des heiligen Bezirks aufsuchen, gleichgültig, ob es sich um Verehrungsstätten für die Götter der Volksreligion, des Buddhismus oder Hinduismus handelt. Sogar die Moschee wird dabei nicht ausgelassen. Später statten die Pilger auch dem Stūpa einen, wenn auch stillen und ohne von Tanzvorstellungen begleiteten Besuch ab. Buddhisten besuchen den Haupttempel, um dort ihre Opfer darzubringen, und anschließend den Stūpa. An den Tänzen und Umzügen scheinen sie sich nicht zu beteiligen. Muslim suchen angeblich nur die Moschee auf.

Die in der Legende dargestellte Beziehung zwischen dem Gott Kataragama und dem Vädda-Mädchen äußert sich neben den zwischen beiden Tempeln durchgeführten Prozessionen bis zum heutigen Tag in einer Hervorhebung der Väddas im Ritual des Haupttempels. Seine Priester, die *kapurālas*, berufen sich auf ihre Abstammung von dieser ältesten bekannten Bevölkerung der Insel, sind aber Singhalesen. Ebenso werden die dem Tempel zugeordneten Dienerinnen als Väddas oder wenigstens als Abkömmlinge dieses mehr und mehr verschwindenden Volkes bezeichnet. Schließlich pflegten bei den Prozessionen zwischen dem Haupttempel und dem Tempel der Vaḷḷīammā vor Jahren Väddas dem Zug voranzugehen.

Diese bei Wirz (1954) ausführlich beschriebenen Zusammenhänge sind hier nur kurz erwähnt, um anzudeuten, wie vielschichtig die Kulthandlungen in Kataragama sind und wie weit in die Kulturgeschichte der Insel sie zurückzureichen scheinen. Die Aussagefähigkeit der Legenden

---

[10]) Nur vor diesen beiden Tempeln befindet sich ein *vākaṉa-mēḍu*, eine Rampe für den Priester zum Besteigen des Prozessionselefanten (vgl. Abb. 4).

in ihrem religiösen und kulturgeschichtlichen Gehalt vermag nur vergleichende Legendenforschung zu überprüfen. Wieweit überhaupt in den religionsgeschichtlichen und mythologischen Hintergrund eingedrungen worden ist, kann an den Ergebnissen bei Bechert (1968), Cartman (1957), Spittel (1933) und Wirz (1954) nachgeprüft werden.

Zum geschichtlichen Fragenkreis im Zusammenhang mit den Legenden haben zahlreiche Wissenschaftler darauf hingewiesen, daß zumindest Teile der Legende erst in jüngerer Zeit eingeflochten worden sind. So ist die Ankunft der die Göttin Teyvāṇīammā begleitenden Brahmanen in der hier geschilderten Version der Legende ein Vorgang, der auf den Anfang des 17. Jahrhunderts festgelegt werden kann. Hier liegt wahrscheinlich die Ursache dafür, daß noch heute Brahmanen des Puri-Ordens aus Benares die Betreuung des Teyvāṇīammā-Tempels in der Hand haben (Spittel, 1933, S. 286, 291)[11]). Die in der Legende erwähnte Ankunft der Göttin Teyvāṇīammā mag als bildliche Darstellung der Einführung ihrer Verehrung oder als die Erneuerung ihrer Verehrung durch die mit ihr in Ceylon eingetroffenen Brahmanen zu sehen sein.

Wie anfangs erwähnt, bestehen neben den Legenden, die aus Elementen des Hinduismus und der Volksreligion aufgebaut sind, auch buddhistische und muslimische Legenden über Kataragama. Sie sind — soweit bekannt — weniger vielschichtig. In der ceylonesisch-buddhistischen Tradition bildet Kataragama eine der Stellen in Ceylon, an denen Buddha auf einer seiner drei „magischen" Besuchsreisen auf der Insel eine Ruhepause eingelegt hat.

In der dritten, im Heiligtum Kataragama vertretenen Religion, dem Islam, galt Kataragama besonders bei den indischen Muslim, von denen auch die Moschee erbaut wurde, als eine Stelle, an der „die Quelle des ewigen Lebens" zu finden sei. Diese Versinnbildlichung wurde von zahlreichen Muslim mißverstanden. Hudson, Government Agent in Hambantota, somit der leitende Beamte des gleichnamigen Distrikts, schrieb (nach Hassan, 1968, S. 6) in seinem Verwaltungsbericht für das Jahr 1870, daß viele Muslim von Hambantota und anderen Dörfern in der Umgebung des Heiligtums nach Kataragama zogen, um nach einer tatsächlichen Quelle zu suchen und durch das Trinken ihres Wassers die Unsterblichkeit zu erlangen.

Die von dem Assistant Government Agent in Hambantota, Steele, 1873 niedergelegte Beobachtung, daß „Fakire" aus Indien, nicht aber ceylonesische Muslim das Heiligtum am Menik Ganga besuchten (nach Hassan, 1968, S. 7), darf wohl mit auf religiöse und kulturelle Unterschiede bei den Muslim beider Länder zurückzuführen sein.

Für die indischen Muslim dürfte die Pilgerfahrt nach Kataragama die Fortsetzung einer vorislamischen Tradition ihrer Heimat darstellen und das Heiligtum jetzt in die islamische Glaubensvorstellung integriert sein.

---

[11]) Arunachalam (1924, S. 244): '... the Teyva yānai amman temple and monastery ... belongs to a section of the Dasanāmi order of monks founded by the great Sankarāchārya of Sringeri Matt (Mysore).'

Bei den ceylonesischen Muslim mögen kulturelle Unterschiede zu ihren indischen Glaubensbrüdern eine Rolle spielen. Die um Hambantota ansässigen Muslim werden z. B. als ‚Malays' bezeichnet. Sie stammen aus den früheren holländischen Kolonien in Indonesien, wo das Heiligtum Kataragama nicht bekannt gewesen zu sein scheint. Darüber hinaus kann angenommen werden, daß zumindest diese muslimische Gruppe in Ceylon kaum mit den Geistesströmungen des Islam in Indien in Berührung gekommen ist und somit wenig Gelegenheit gehabt hat, deren Ansichten zu übernehmen. Dagegen dürften wohl die ‚Ceylon Moors', die am Galēbaṇḍāra-Kult in Kurunegala teilnehmen, unter den Kataragama-Pilgern angetroffen werden (freundliche Mitteilung von Prof. Bechert).

Aus der Legendenbildung der drei Religionen um das Heiligtum im Dschungel lohnt sich festzuhalten, daß dieser Ort eine Ausstrahlungskraft besitzt, die weit in die Geschichte zurück- und auch weit über die Insel hinausreicht. Diese Kultstätte konnte auch über Glaubensänderungen und -schranken hinweg ihr Anziehungsvermögen erhalten, im Grunde allerdings eine Erscheinung, die für viele Heiligtümer zutrifft.

4. Zur Geschichte Kataragamas bis zur Übernahme durch Großbritannien

Die besondere Stellung Kataragamas im religiösen Leben der Insel schlägt sich zwar nicht in einer Fülle historischer Daten nieder, wird aber doch schon aus der Tatsache ersichtlich, daß dieses Heiligtum bis zum heutigen Tag erhalten blieb, wenn auch in seiner Bedeutung im Laufe der Geschichte wohl oft nachlassend, während andere, bedeutende Stätten geistlicher und weltlicher Machtausübung im Südosten der Insel heute als Ruinen, z.T. weit entfernt von Zugangswegen im Dschungel verborgen liegen.

Einige Daten seien vorgelegt. Im Jahre 246 v. Chr. läßt König Devanampiya Tissa einen Setzling des heiligen Bo-Baumes von Anuradhapura nach Kataragama bringen und dort pflanzen. Von dieser Zeit an galt Kataragama als Ziel buddhistischer Pilger. Die Erbauung des Kirivehera wird gewöhnlich in das 3. Jh. v. Chr. oder auch in die Regierungszeit des Königs Dutthagamani (161–137 v. Chr.) gelegt (Wirz, 1954, S. 154). Archäologische Funde — mit Stempeln versehene Ziegeln aus dem oberen Teil des Stūpa — lassen das Bauwerk mit Gewißheit bis in das 1. Jh. v. Chr. datieren (Nicholas, 1963, S. 51). Mit dem König Dutthagamani werden in Kataragama noch andere Ereignisse verbunden, so der Bau des Mahādēvālē, des Haupttempels von Kataragama, und auch Landschenkungen an den Tempel.

Nach dem Tode dieses Königs, der als Zentralfigur zahlreicher wahrer, noch mehr aber legendärer Ereignisse in der ceylonesischen Geschichte steht, ist ein Rückgang der Bedeutung Kataragamas bis in das 11. Jahrhundert zu verzeichnen. Zwischen 1050–1056 wird Kataragama als Königsstadt erwähnt, die von eindringenden Chola-Heeren aus Südindien geplündert und verwüstet wurde. Auch dieser Vorgang hat das Heiligtum nicht in Vergessenheit geraten lassen; denn nach dem 11. Jahrhundert machten angeblich Tausende aus Indien und Ceylon Pilgerfahrten zu dem Heiligtum im Dschungel, das (so Wirz, 1954, S. 140f.; ähnlich Asangananda, 1964, S. 3) in seiner Bedeutung auf gleicher Stufe mit den indischen heiligen Stätten wie Benares, Puri und Rameswaram stand.

Aus der Zeit der Besetzung Ceylons durch die Portugiesen und Holländer, die sich, ausgenommen die Südwestküste, nur auf Küstenstreifen und dort oft sogar nur punktartig auswirkte, liegen über Kataragama bisher nur geringe Angaben vor. Rasanayagam (nach Hassan, 1968, S. 12) gibt an, daß während der Herrschaft der Portugiesen (1505–1656) muslimische Pilger aus Indien zunächst ungehindert über Jaffna nach Kataragama gezogen seien. Diese Route wurde unterbrochen, als die Portugiesen mit dem König von Kandy im Krieg lagen (seit 1594) und aus militärischen Gründen die Wege in den Süden sperrten. In die portugiesische Zeit fällt auch die Ankunft der in der Legende erwähnten Brahmanen, die von dieser Zeit an(?) den Teyvāṇiammā-Tempel betreuen. Navaratnam (1964, S. 76) erwähnt, daß die Erbauung des gegenwärtigen Haupttempels von Kataragama dem König Rajasinha I (1581–1593) zugeschrieben wird (vgl. auch Arunachalam, 1924, S. 251).

Der den Tempeln von Kataragama nachgesagte Reichtum veranlaßte 1642 die Portugiesen zu einer Expedition zu diesem Heiligtum. Es wurde aber trotz seiner Nähe zur Küste von ihnen wegen Unkenntnis der Wegeverhältnisse und der genauen Lage nie erreicht. Über diese gescheiterte Unternehmung nach ‚Catérgao‘ berichtete Ribeiro (Pieris, 1909, S. 174f.).

Die Aufzeichnungen des Engländers Knox (1681; 1966), der 20 Jahre lang (von 1659 bis 1679) Gefangener am Hofe des singhalesischen Königs Rajasinha II war, enthalten einen Hinweis auf das Heiligtum: ‚. . . of a great God, who dwelleth near by in a Town they call Cotteragom, standing in the Road to whom all that go to fetch Salt both small and great must give an Offering.‘ (Knox, 1966, S. 12).

Diese kurze Notiz bei Knox zusammen mit den übrigen spärlichen Angaben bieten eine gewisse Aufhellung des heute noch weithin unklaren Entwicklungsstandes im Südosten der Insel, seit das singhalesische Königreich im trockenen Tiefland Ceylons nach Wirren im Inneren, Kriegen von außen (mit Südindien) und Krankheiten (Malaria etc.) zusammengebrochen und der Sitz des Königreiches in das Hochland verlagert worden war. Die Gebiete der früheren Hochkultur galten jahrhundertelang als verödet.

Die Gründe für die Erhaltung Kataragamas über mehr als 2000 Jahre sind ohne Zweifel in der großen religiösen, aber wohl auch in der — seit der portugiesischen Landung auf der Insel — strategischen Bedeutung dieses Ortes zu sehen. Kataragama liegt an einer sehr alten Heerstraße, die einst von Mahagama (Tissamaharama) über Kataragama, Buttala und Mahiyangana nach Polonnaruwa führte.

Das Heiligtum war wie alle bedeutenden Kultstätten der Insel im Laufe der Zeit von den singhalesischen Königen mit Länderein ausgestattet worden[12]). Aus der Lage des heute noch existierenden Tempellandes läßt sich nach vorläufigen, noch unveröffentlichten Untersuchungen der vorsichtige Schluß ziehen, daß den Tempeln von Kataragama und ihrer Verwaltung Grenz- und Gebietsüberwachungs-, aber vielleicht auch Wegeschutzfunktionen übertragen worden waren (Hausherr, 1971 b)[13]).

Diese Feststellung läßt sich anhand eines englischen Verwaltungsberichtes belegen, in dem es heißt, daß die Könige von Kandy den großen *dēvālē*, zu denen auch das Kataragama *dēvālē* gehört, mehr aus finanziellen und politischen als aus religiösen Gründen große Ländereien übereignet und darüber hinaus mit besonderen Rechten ausgestattet hatten. Aus finanziellen Gründen deswegen, weil der höchste Verwalter des *dēvālē*, der *basnāyake nilamē*, bei seiner Ernennung und dann fortlaufend monatlich eine recht erhebliche Geldsumme an den Herrscher abzuführen hatte, aus politischen insofern, als durch die Tempel ein Gegengewicht zu den Fürsten und Adligen, den *dissāvas*, sozusagen deren Überwachung, bestand[14]). Im Falle Kataragama kam der vorgeschobenen Lage des *dēvālē* im Tiefland eine besondere strategische Bedeutung zu. Denn über diesen Ort verlief die Verbindung zwischen dem Hochland und den Salzgewinnungsstätten in den Lewayas, den natürlichen Salzpfannen an der Südküste (von Hambantota ostwärts), von denen schon Knox berichtete.

5. Kataragama während der britischen Kolonialherrschaft

a) *Entwicklungspläne für die Wirtschaft Südost-Ceylons und ihre Gefährdung durch den Krankheitsherd Kataragama*

Ausführlichere Berichte über das Heiligtum liegen erstmals aus britischer Zeit vor. Als früheste bekannte Darstellung hat die von Davy (1821; 1969) zu gelten, der 1819 das Heiligtum aufgesucht hatte, zwei

---

[12]) Vom Ruhuṇu Mahā Kataragama dēvālē, dem Haupttempel in Kataragama, wurden im letzten Jahrhundert im Zuge der Grundbesitzfeststellung durch die Kolonialverwaltung über 145000 acres im Tiefland der Uva-Provinz beansprucht. Nach einem über 50 Jahre dauernden Verfahren erkannte die Kolonialverwaltung nur einen Bruchteil der Forderung an. Das unmittelbar um Kataragama herum verstreut liegende Tempelland ist in Abb. 2 eingetragen.

[13]) Ribeiro (Pieris, 1909, S. 174) berichtet, daß in Kataragama ständig 500 Mann zur Verteidigung des Heiligtums und seiner Schätze bereitstanden.

[14]) Report of the Temple Land Commissioners, 1858/59, S. 15ff.; Section V auch in: Evers (1972, S. 112–121; Appendix 2).

Jahre nach dem Ende der Uva-Rebellion. Seine Beschreibung zeigt Kataragama an einem allgemeinen Tiefpunkt, eine Folge der politischen Wirren jener Zeit.

Der Ort Kataragama war nach Davy (1969, S. 313ff.) von geringer Größe. Er berichtet von zwei Tempeleinfriedungen, in denen der Haupttempel und der Tempel der Teyvāṇīammā im Zustand des fortgeschrittenen Verfalls liegen, ferner von dem Tempel der Vaḷḷīammā südlich davon und dem zerfallenen Stūpa. Das Dorf, das sich am linken Ufer des Menik Ganga befand, umfaßte nur wenige Hütten und war zu seiner Zeit mit 40 Soldaten belegt, die hier als Folge der Uva-Rebellion unter zwei einheimischen Offizieren mit Einwilligung der Tempelbehörden zur Sicherung der wichtigen Straße von Hambantota ins Hochland stationiert worden waren (White, 1893, S. 39, Fußnote).

Das von Davy erwähnte Nachlassen des Pilgerzustroms nach Kataragama ist lediglich als Auswirkung der politischen Verhältnisse zu sehen, denn in den folgenden Jahrzehnten kam es zu einer erheblichen Steigerung der Pilgerzahlen. Leider liegen darüber bis zum Eingriff der britischen Verwaltung nur wenige Unterlagen vor. Baker (1892, S. 152) schätzt, daß um 1847 etwa 18000 Pilger zu erwarten gewesen waren. Diese Angabe ist wahrscheinlich zu hoch gegriffen. Genauere Schätzwerte liegen vor, seit sich die Kolonialverwaltung mit Kataragama befaßt.

Der Südosten der Insel geriet wie auch der Osten nach der Niederschlagung des Uva-Aufstandes von 1817 für lange Zeit in den Schatten des Interesses der Kolonialverwaltung. Erst als sich im Hochland der großflächige Anbau von Kaffee ausbreitete und besonders als mit dem Aufbau der Plantagen der Bedarf an Arbeitskräften wuchs, der nicht aus dem einheimischen Angebot, sondern nur durch den Einsatz von Südindern (Tamilen) gedeckt werden konnte, geriet Kataragama in den Gesichtskreis der Verwaltung und zwar deswegen, weil viele tamilische Hindus das von ihren Arbeitsplätzen auf den Plantagen nicht weit entfernte, ihnen aus Indien überdies bekannte Heiligtum des Gottes Kataragama aufgesucht haben und krank zu ihren Arbeitsplätzen zurückkehrten (dazu auch: Bastiampillai, 1968). Kataragama war schließlich mit dem stärkeren Zustrom von Pilgern ein die gesamte Insel gefährdender Krankheitsherd.

Der enge Zusammenhang zwischen Plantagenausbreitung, Einsatz tamilischer Arbeiter und deren Pilgerfahrt zu dem Heiligtum in der Trockenzone des Südostens bildete aber nur einen Teil des sich entwickelnden Problems, mit dem sich in der Folgezeit die Kolonialverwaltung zu beschäftigen hatte. Es erfuhr eine Erweiterung durch die Entwicklungsarbeiten im Süden der Insel, die z.T. in unmittelbarer Umgebung von Kataragama ausgeführt wurden.

Im Tiefland, das damals noch wenig erschlossen war — das alte Bewässerungssystem um Buttala war 1869 gerade erst wieder instand gesetzt worden — wirkte sich die Pilgerfahrt nach Kataragama in zweierlei Weise auf die Wirtschaft und die geplante Entwicklung aus: Arbeiten an Straßen und Bewässerungsanlagen, die in der trockenen Jahreszeit besonders gut durchgeführt werden konnten, mußten unterbrochen werden, sobald das große Fest in Kataragama näherrückte, weil die Arbeiter aus Angst vor ansteckenden Krankheiten der durchziehenden Pilger in ihre Dörfer zurückkehrten und eine Rückkehr zu ihren Arbeitsplätzen verweigerten, solange noch das Land von den Pilgern gefährdet wurde. Die Reaktion der ansässigen Bevölkerung ließ die Verwaltung für die Zukunft befürchten, daß wegen dieses Risikos nur wenige Siedler sich in den unter großen Anstrengungen und finanziellen Opfern wiedereingerichteten Bewässerungsprojekten um Tissamaharama niederließen oder daß sie von den Pilgern ebenfalls mit Krankheiten infiziert werden und dadurch diese Projekte fehlschlagen könnten [15]).

Eine erhebliche finanzielle Einbuße drohte durch die Pilgerfahrt und deren Begleiterscheinungen aber regelmäßig der wirtschaftlich wichtigsten Quelle des Südostens, den natürlichen Salzpfannen um Hambantota, denn, falls die „Ernte“ nicht rechtzeitig einsetzt, beginnt das Salz (Natriumchlorid) zu „blühen“ und geht in wertloses Natriumsulfat über. So verdarb 1872 während des Festes in Kataragama die Salzernte in Palatupana, östlich von Tissamaharama (Steele, nach White, 1893, S. 43), weil die Arbeitskräfte aus dem genannten Grund ihre Arbeitsstelle verlassen hatten [16]). In einem Bericht des Assistant Government Agent von Hambantota, Steele, heißt es denn auch (Ceylon Administration Reports [17]), 1871, S. 146; Berichterstatter: O'Brien): 'The pilgrimage to Kataragama which, without any prejudice, may be briefly described as one of the greatest pests the people of the Southern Province have undeservingly to suffer from, in that it frequently sows disease broad-cast among them, and works incalculable mischief throughout the country, takes place every year in July.'

Die Feststellung der Verwaltung trifft zu, betrachtet man allein die Tatsache, daß 1858 an der Straße zwischen Hambantota und Tangalla 76 Choleratote gefunden und wesentlich mehr noch im Dschungel vermutet wurden. Neben der Gefährdung und Beeinträchtigung der Wirtschaft drohte also auch eine Ausbreitung und Verschleppung der Seuche (Gordon-Cumming, 1892, vol. 2, S. 224ff.; Steele, nach White, 1893, S. 43).

Als Gründe für die wiederholten Ausbrüche von Cholera und anderen, in den Berichten nicht näher genannten Krankheiten, wurden damals angeführt:

---

[15]) Die Rückständigkeit und Notlage dieses Gebietes ist eindrucksvoll im Tagebuch von Leonard Woolf nachzulesen. Er war von 1908–1911 Assistant Government Agent im Hambantota Distrikt (Woolf, 1962).

[16]) Die Angst der Arbeiter vor Ansteckungen durch die Pilger und deshalb die zeitweilige Aufgabe ihrer Arbeitsstätte kann dabei nur als ein Faktor für mögliche Fehlernten angesehen werden. Gordon-Cumming (1892, vol. 2, S. 213) führt als weitere Möglichkeit unerwartete Regenfälle an, die zur Zeit der Ernte im August die Ausbeute erheblich verringern oder, wie 1878, völlig vereiteln können.

[17]) Im folgenden als C.A.R. zitiert.

1. die „ungesunde“ Lage des Heiligtums;
2. die Dauer des Festes. In Kataragama zieht es sich über 14 Tage hin, in anderen Pilgerstätten der Insel sind derartige Festlichkeiten auf drei Tage beschränkt;
3. die Herkunft der Pilger, die — was immer das auch bedeuten mag — nicht ‘of respectable class’ waren.

Pilger, die nach Kataragama zogen, waren sehr oft schlecht mit Nahrungsmitteln und Trinkwasser ausgerüstet. Das führte gewöhnlich schon auf dem Hinweg zu Erschöpfungen, die dann die Gläubigen in Kataragama sehr leicht für Krankheiten anfällig werden ließen (Steele, nach White, 1893, S. 43).

b) *Regulierung der Pilgerfahrt und Überwachung des Heiligtums Kataragama durch die britische Verwaltung*

Die Kolonialverwaltung ordnete schließlich Maßnahmen an, um das Heiligtum überwachen und die möglicherweise von der Pilgerfahrt ausgehenden und im Ernstfall die ganze Insel bedrohenden Seuchen unterbinden zu können. 1870 wurde die Kontrolle des Ortes angeordnet, 1873 ein Gesetz erlassen, das entscheidende Maßnahmen vorsah (Ordinance No. 14 of 1873). Es erlaubte der Regierung unter anderem: 1. die Zahl der Pilger zu beschränken, 2. auf die Gruppierungen und Zusammensetzung der Pilgerzüge an den Ausgangsplätzen und auf dem Marsch nach Kataragama Einfluß zu nehmen und 3. einzugreifen, um die Hygiene zu fördern und den Ausbruch und die Verbreitung von ansteckenden Krankheiten zu verhindern.

Die Entwicklung des Pilgerverkehrs nach Kataragama unter staatlicher Überwachung sollen einige Zahlen verdeutlichen, die auf der Durchsicht verschiedener Verwaltungsberichte und Literatur beruhen. Für die Zeit vor der Regulierung der Pilgerfahrt konnte nur für das Jahr 1868 — sieht man von der Schätzung Bakers (1892, S. 152; 1847: 18000) einmal ab — eine Angabe gefunden werden.

In dem Auf und Ab der Pilgerzahlen nach 1873 ist deutlich die Anwendung der vom Staat beschlossenen Regulierungsmaßnahmen zu erkennen, vor allem die Einführung des ‘ticket-system’. Danach wurde jedesmal, wenn in Kataragama der Ausbruch einer Krankheit zu befürchten war, die Zahl der Besucher des Heiligtums z.T. drastisch kontingentiert[18]). Im Jahr 1884 glaubte man, Anzeichen für den Ausbruch von Cholera in

[18]) Eine Ausnahme bildete das Jahr 1874, in dem die ‚Colombo Chetties‘ aus Protest gegen das Gesetz der Pilgerfahrt nach Kataragama fernblieben (C.A.R. 1874, S. 108). Die ‚Colombo Chetties‘, auch ‚Colombo Tamils‘ genannt, sind reiche Geldverleiher, die, nach den Berichten zu urteilen, im letzten Jahrhundert die jährliche Pilgerfahrt von Colombo nach Kataragama anführten und darüber hinaus durch Schenkungen an religiöse Institutionen bekannt waren. Ihr Eintreffen am Menik Ganga bedeutete oft den eigentlichen Beginn des Festes (Covington, 1885, S. 153; Spittel, 1933, S. 301). Zu diesem Thema auch: Weerasooria, 1973.

Tab. 3: Entwicklung des Pilgerverkehrs nach Kataragama zwischen 1868 und 1925

Jahr	Zahl der Pilger	Quelle
1868	3–4000	Covington, 1885, S. 154
1871	3500	C.A.R. 1872
1872	ca. 5000	„ 1874
1873	7–8000	„ 1874
1874[19])	1200	„ 1874
1875	60	Gordon-Cumming, 1892
1876	107	„ 1892
1877	44	C.A.R. 1877
1878	15	Gordon-Cumming, 1892
1883	1000	„ 1892
1884	150	Cartman, 1957, S. 124
1889	‘a mere handful’	White, 1893, Fußnote S. 42
1906	2256	C.A.R. 1906
1910	3–4000	Woolf, 1962, S. 168
1919	0	C.A.R. 1919
1920	ca. 13000	„ 1920
1922	über 10000	„ 1924
1923	über 1000	„ 1924
1924	unter 10000	„ 1924
1925	15000	„ 1925

Kataragama gefunden zu haben. Daraufhin wurden nur 150 Pilgerpässe ausgegeben, je 30 für Colombo, Kandy, Galle, Kurunegala und Batticaloa. Für das Jahr 1877 liegt ebenfalls ein Verteilungsplan der ‚tickets‘ vor. Es fehlen zwar Angaben, welche Gründe zu dieser Einschränkung Anlaß gaben, es werden aber wahrscheinlich ebenfalls medizinische gewesen sein. Danach standen der Central Province 26, der Western Province 3, der Southern Province 10 und der Eastern Province 5 ‚tickets‘ zu.

Dem C.A.R. von 1906 sind noch weitere, aufschlußreiche Details in bezug auf die staatlichen Kontrollmaßnahmen bei der Pilgerfahrt nach Kataragama zu entnehmen. Demnach wurden während der Pilgerzeit an den Straßen zum Heiligtum im Dschungel ständige Wachen aufgezogen. Alle Pilger, die z.B. Hambantota passierten, wurden auf ihren Gesundheitszustand hin untersucht und endgültige ‚tickets‘ nur den Gläubigen ausgehändigt, die sich in guter körperlicher Verfassung befanden. Um einem Mißbrauch der ‚tickets‘ vorzubeugen, wurde der Name des Pilgers eingetragen. Kontrollen überwachten ferner die beiden von Westen nach Kataragama führenden Straßen über Katagamuwa und die neue, heutige Straße von Tissamaharama zu dem Heiligtum

[19]) Während des Kataragama Festivals 1874 war ein gewisser Spittel der ‚Medical Officer in Charge‘ (C.A.R. 1874, S. 108).

am Menik Ganga, und schließlich war auch Buttala mit einer Meldestelle ausgestattet, um alle Pilger ohne 'tickets' abzufangen. In Kataragama ohne Passierschein angetroffene Gläubige mußten mit einer Gefängnis- oder Geldstrafe rechnen.

1919 war in Kataragama die Cholera ausgebrochen; in diesem Jahr wurde die Pilgerfahrt verboten. 1920 schließlich schaffte man das ‚ticket-system' und andere Kontrollmaßnahmen ab, mit der Folge, daß die Pilgerzahlen kräftig anstiegen. Ohne Erfolg wurde nach dem Ausbruch von Malaria im Jahre 1923 von den Pflanzern die Wiedereinführung des ‚ticket-system' gefordert (C. A. R. 1923, S. H8). 1924 beeinflußten unerwartete, starke Regenfälle in der zweiten Hälfte des Festes nachteilig die Zahl der Pilger (C. A. R. 1924, S. H10).

c) *Kataragama als medizinisches Problem*

Das Verlangen der Pflanzer nach Kontrollen ist zu verstehen; denn seit der Aufgabe des Kaffeeanbaus — er fiel seit etwa 1869 der Ausbreitung einer Pilzkrankheit (*Hemileia vastatrix*) zum Opfer — waren sie mehr und mehr zum Aufbau von Teepflanzungen übergegangen, die jetzt im Gegensatz zum Kaffee einer ganzjährigen Pflege bedurften (Schweinfurth, 1966).

Die Arbeiter und Arbeiterinnen dieser Plantagen schlossen sich oftmals organisierten Pilgerfahrten an und kehrten im Anschluß an ihre Wallfahrt nach Kataragama erschöpft, von Malaria und anderen Krankheiten befallen, zurück und verursachten dann einen Arbeitsausfall, der zur Zeit der Saisonarbeit im Kaffee die Pflanzer nicht weiter störte, da sie nicht auf diese Arbeitskräfte angewiesen waren (Pelzer, 1935, S. 42).

Die stärkste gesundheitliche Gefährdung in Kataragama verursachte wohl nicht so sehr die Cholera als vielmehr Malaria. Dieser Schluß drängt sich auf, wenn man Verwaltungsberichte durchsieht und hin und wieder auf die Bezeichnung ‚Kataragama Fever' stößt. Lange Zeit herrschte Ungewißheit darüber, wodurch das Fieber ausgelöst wurde. An den Mutmaßungen über seine Art und Entstehung läßt sich — wenn auch in bescheidenem Rahmen — ein Stück Geschichte der Tropenmedizin demonstrieren.

Bei White (1893, S. 42) wird der für den Hambantota Distrikt zuständige leitende Verwaltungsbeamte Steele zitiert, der über Kataragama aussagt, daß der Ort während des Festes im Juli/August '. . . is exposed to strong land winds, laden with malaria the prolific source of disorders in Ceylon'. Erst 1924 wurde auf langjähriges Drängen von Pflanzern aus der Uva-Provinz, deren tamilische Arbeitskräfte nach der Pilgerfahrt erkrankt waren und einen geregelten Ablauf der Arbeiten auf den Teepflanzungen unmöglich machten, eine Untersuchung eingeleitet, die nachweisen sollte, um welche Art von Fieber es sich in Kataragama eigentlich handele, das sich dort besonders bei trockenem Wetter ausbreite. Dabei wurde der Verdacht geäußert, daß es sich nicht um Malaria, sondern um ‚sand-fly fever', also um Erkrankungen handele, die durch ‚sand-flies' (Schmetterlingsmücken, *Phlebotomus*) übertragen werden. Unter die von diesen Mücken übertragenen Krankheiten fallen z. B. alle Leishmanien.

Mit der Durchführung der Untersuchung — als Sessional Paper XXXVII–1925 veröffentlicht — wurde der Entomologe Carter betraut, der zunächst feststellte, daß ‚sand-flies' in Kataragama völlig fehlen. Dagegen ergab eine Untersuchung bei Pilgern und Bewohnern aus der Umgebung des Heiligtums, daß abgesehen von den Pilgern, die aus endemischen Malariagebieten, z. B. Mullaittivu, Batticaloa, Orten an der Ostküste, stammten, besonders die Händler aus Tissamaharama stark unter Malaria litten. Vorgefunden wurde vor allem *Malaria quartana*. Die entomologischen Untersuchungen erbrachten, daß in den um Kataragama vorhandenen offenen Wasserflächen nur im Menik Ganga Mückenlarven lebten.

Eine wertvolle Differenzierung erfuhren diese Arbeiten Carters durch den Umstand, daß zwischen dem 20. Juli und dem 1. August 1924 der Wasserstand des Menik Ganga stark abnahm und dadurch die Veränderungen im Mückenbestand beobachtet werden konnten. Es ergab sich, daß bei genügend hohem Wasserstand und bei frischem Wasser vor allem Larven der Arten *Anopheles funestus* und *A. barbirostris* sich hielten, später dagegen, als der Wasserstand wegen der anhaltenden Trockenheit sank und sich Tümpel bildeten, *A. culcifacies* und *A. subpictus* verstärkt auftraten. Als die wahrscheinlichen Hauptträger der Malaria im Tiefland Ceylons sah Carter *Anopheles funestus* und *A. culcifacies* an, wobei er die letztere für die gefährlichere Moskitoart hielt und sie wegen ihres Vorkommens bei Niedrigwasser und zunehmender Tümpelbildung als ‚sandbank breeder' bezeichnete[20]).

Bei seinen Untersuchungen in Kataragama hatte Carter aber auch die Gelegenheit, die zufällige Verhinderung der vollständigen Entwicklung der Larven durch die Natur zu beobachten. Er berichtete, daß am 1. August der Fluß seinen tiefsten Wasserstand erreicht hatte und die zuvor genannten Moskitoarten erheblich entwickelt waren, als durch Regenfälle im Hochland, um Passara, der Menik Ganga anstieg und die Larven der Moskitos wegschwemmte.

Die während der Festlichkeiten mitunter auftretenden Malariaepidemien, z. B. im Jahre 1916, erklärt Carter mit einem Zusammentreffen bestimmter klimatischer und hydrologischer Verhältnisse. Herrscht nämlich in den Wochen vor dem Beginn des Festes Trockenheit im Einzugsbereich des Menik Ganga und somit niedriger Wasserstand im Fluß bei Kataragama, so haben die Anophelesmücken genügend Zeit, sich zu entwickeln und sich vor dem Eintreffen der ersten Pilger an den Einheimi-

---

[20]) *Anopheles culcifacies* hat sich als der einzige Überträger von Malaria in Ceylon herausgestellt (vgl. Gill, 1935, S. 15; Rodenwaldt, 1937, S. 332).

schen mit Malariaparasiten zu infizieren. Die Ansteckungsgefahr der Pilger besteht somit vom ersten Tag ihres Aufenthaltes in Kataragama und kann bei der Länge des Festes von 14 Tagen unter den Gläubigen zu epidemiehaftem Umfang anschwellen. Vom medizinischen Standpunkt ist daher nicht nur die Länge des Festes, sondern vor allem der Monat August denkbar ungünstig. Die Empfehlungen Carters lauteten denn auch, daß

1. die Festlichkeiten in Kataragama verkürzt oder in einen gesünderen Monat, z.B. September, verlegt werden sollten; ein Vorschlag, der wegen der jahrtausendealten Tradition nicht durchführbar ist;
2. alles Buschwerk im Umkreis von 200 m um die Lagerplätze entfernt und zusätzliche Schutzhütten für die Pilger errichtet werden sollten;
3. die Moskito-Brutplätze im Abstand von 4–5 Tagen durch eine künstlich erzeugte Wasserwelle von den Larven befreit werden sollten.

So hat Kataragama als Herd von Krankheiten die britische Kolonialverwaltung zum Eingreifen veranlaßt. Damit war der Grundstein gelegt zu den weiteren Entwicklungen; denn von der zeitweiligen Überwachung geriet Kataragama im 20. Jahrhundert mehr und mehr zu einem Objekt der Verwaltung, um schließlich in gewisser Hinsicht auch von der Politik „übernommen" zu werden. Auf diese Entwicklung wird noch später hingewiesen.

Kataragama ist bis heute ein potentieller Seuchenherd geblieben. Es kommt immer wieder einmal zum Ausbruch einer Krankheit, obwohl durch verschärfte Sicherheitsvorkehrungen auf dem sanitären Sektor die Gefahr so gut wie gebannt zu sein scheint[21]). Ein weiteres bewirkt die Einstellung der Bevölkerung. Nur noch bei wenigen dürfte die früher verbreitete fatalistische Auffassung zu finden sein, auch der Tod durch eine auf der Pilgerfahrt nach Kataragama erworbene Krankheit bedeute eine Glaubensleistung. Bei der überwiegenden Zahl der Bevölkerung, die das Heiligtum Kataragama aufzusuchen beabsichtigt, braucht die Regierung bei Verdacht eines Krankheitsausbruchs nicht erst abwehrend einzugreifen, die Gläubigen sind sich selbst der Gefahren bewußt. Als 1967 (nach Auskunft Einheimischer) Zeitungen über das Auftreten von Diarrhöe in Kataragama berichteten, hatte diese Meldung einen Rückgang von Pilgern in jenem Jahr zur Folge.

Ein weiteres Beispiel soll die Komplexität des „medizinischen Problems" Kataragama aufzeigen. 1948 erkrankte eine ganze Reihe von Menschen, die „heiliges Wasser" aus dem Menik Ganga getrunken hatten, an Typhus, ohne selbst in Kataragama gewesen zu sein. Das Wasser hatten ihnen Freunde von der Pilgerfahrt mitgebracht (Cartman, 1957, S. 123).

---

[21]) 1974 fanden sich wegen des Auftretens von Cholera in der Umgebung von Kataragama nur wenige Pilger zum Hauptfest ein.

d) *Wasserversorgung — Existenzgrundlage des Heiligtums*

Die Darlegungen Carters weisen, wenn auch aus einem medizinischen Blickwinkel, auf das Wasser als das Hauptproblem der Trockenzone Ceylons hin. Die Bedeutung einer gesicherten Wasserversorgung und damit die Abhängigkeit vom Menik Ganga war den Tempelbehörden von Kataragama wohl schon immer bekannt gewesen. Wie weit die Interessen der Tempel in diesem Punkt reichten und wie sehr die Zusammenhänge gesehen wurden, erhellt eine Notiz bei White (1893, Fußnote S. 41). Er berichtet, daß eine Abordnung der Kataragama-Tempelverwaltung vorstellig wurde und auf die Auswirkungen für die Wasserversorgung des Heiligtums hinwies, als 1841 in der Nähe von Badulla (Maussagala Estate) Land vermessen wurde und der darauf befindliche Wald geschlagen werden sollte[22]).

Ein weiteres Beispiel soll die ohne künstliche Eingriffe labile Stellung Kataragamas im natürlichen Gesamtgefüge des Südostens aufzeigen: Kurz vor dem Kataragama Festival 1873 trocknete der Menik Ganga aus. Pilger, obwohl unter den bereits verordneten, aber erstmals angewandten Regulierungen reisend, ließen sich nicht aufhalten, und es schien sich eine Katastrophe anzubahnen. Da wurde von Hambantota aus eine Eilbotschaft nach Badulla entsandt, mit der Bitte, die Schleusen des 1869 wiederhergerichteten Bewässerungswerkes von Buttala zu öffnen, um die Wasserversorgung Kataragamas sicherzustellen und damit die 7–8000 Pilger vor möglichen Folgen zu bewahren (C. A. R. 1873, nach White, 1893, S. 41).

1906 war der Menik Ganga bei Kataragama wieder ausgetrocknet. Zunächst ließ man Wasserlöcher im Flußbett graben, dann, nach einer Woche, kurz vor dem Eintreffen der Hauptmasse der Pilger, wurden in Buttala die Schleusen geöffnet und so vermutlich — ohne es zu wissen — ein Malariaausbruch verhindert (C. A. R. 1906, S. H8).

6. Die Entwicklung des Ortes Kataragama seit dem Eingriff der britischen Kolonialverwaltung (ca. 1870) bis zum Zweiten Weltkrieg

a) *Temporäre Pilgerlager*

Die Überwachung der Pilger erstreckte sich aber neben Gesundheitskontrollen entlang der Anmarschwege auch auf das Lager selbst, das gewöhnlich auf der rechten Seite des Menik Ganga lag. Mit Hilfe von Strafgefangenen aus Hambantota wurden jedes Jahr Dschungelareale

[22]) Daß die Abholzung der Wälder im Hochland und die Umwandlung des gewonnenen Terrains in Kaffee- und später in Teepflanzungen zu Störungen des Wasserhaushaltes führte, ist aus den Aufzeichnungen verschiedener hoher Beamter

freigeschlagen, Laubhütten in Reihen aufgebaut, Toiletten eingerichtet und auf ihre Benutzung geachtet. Die Anlage des Pilgerlagers erfolgte gewöhnlich unter Berücksichtigung der starken Winde, die zu dieser Jahreszeit aus Westen wehen, viel Staub aufwirbeln, aber die einzige Abkühlung in der Hitze des Tages und der Nacht bringen. Es handelt sich hierbei um den am Sabaragamuwa-Bergland abgeregneten SW-Monsun, der dann als trockener Wind weht und unter der Bezeichnung ‚Kachchan' bekannt ist. Den Pilgerkontingenten aus den einzelnen ‚ticket'-Bezirken waren bestimmte Stellen im Lager zugewiesen. Es wurde auf strikte persönliche Sauberkeit, Übernachtungsmöglichkeiten und reichliche Versorgung mit Nahrung und vor allem Wasser gedrungen. Hierzu unterteilte man den Fluß in Abschnitte für Trink- und Badezwecke und zur Tränkung des Viehs, eine Maßnahme, die bis zum heutigen Tag beibehalten worden ist.

Zu Beginn ist das Fest meist schwach besucht. In der zweiten Woche erst drängen sich die Pilger in Kataragama. Fällt das Fest dazu mit den Zahltagen auf den Teeplantagen zusammen (zwischen dem 5.–10. eines jeden Monats), dann kann man mit einer größeren Zahl von Hindus rechnen[23]). Der zur zweiten Festwoche hin ansteigende Pilgerzustrom, von zahlreichen Beobachtern beschrieben, läßt sich anhand einer Statistik aus dem Jahre 1906 belegen. Diese Feststellung gilt nicht nur für die in Kataragama eintreffenden Pilger, auch Tempeldiener und Händler finden sich erst während der letzten zehn Tage, an denen täglich Prozessionen veranstaltet werden, in dem Heiligtum ein. Vor allem waren Händler, die das Zusammentreffen so zahlreicher Menschen zu Geschäften zu nutzen suchten, immer vorhanden (Tab. 4).

Es entwickelte sich dann im wahrsten Sinne des Wortes jedesmal ein Jahrmarkt. Covington (1885, S. 154) berichtet, daß seinerzeit in Kataragama einschließlich der ‚hopper'-Frauen, d. h. Frauen, die am Straßenrand ein speziell ceylonesisches Teiggericht zubereiteten, mehr als 200 ‚boutiques' aufgestellt waren, die von Moors, Malays (beides Muslim), Singhalesen und Tamilen geleitet wurden. Nicht nur Lebensmittel, sondern auch Messinggegenstände, die man in großen Mengen aus Galle, Tangalla und Batticaloa herantransportiert hatte, wurden zum Verkauf angeboten. Eine Schilderung aus dem 20. Jahrhundert, von Cook (1931; 1953, S. 323), erwähnt, daß sich neben Händlern auch Bettler entlang des Weges von Kataragama nach Buttala niedergelassen hatten, um an den Gläubigen etwas zu verdienen.

---

zu entnehmen (vgl. Wesumperuma, 1967, S. 136f. Er weist auf die Berichte von Moir, Le Mesurier und Baumgartner hin). — Diese Auswirkungen gelten im gleichen Ausmaß auch für das Tiefland.

[23]) Quelle: Notice of the Government Agent, Monaragala, June 9, 1961, über das Kataragama Äsala Festival 1961. — Die Bezahlung der Plantagenarbeiter hat nach dem Gesetz spätestens bis zum 10. eines jeden Monats zu erfolgen.

Tab. 4: Pilger in Kataragama
während des Festes vom 21. Juli bis zum 5. August 1906

Tag der Ankunft		Pilger mit/ohne ‚ticket‘		Tempel-diener	Händler	Beamte	Diener, Fuhr-leute	andere	insgesamt
Juli	21	46	—	—	—	10	11	4	71
	22	42	—	—	—	—	—	—	42
	23	42	—	—	—	1	3	—	46
	24	58	—	—	—	—	—	—	58
	25	39	—	—	—	—	—	—	39
	26	69	—	113	9	—	—	—	191
	27	44	3	—	21	2	3	—	73
	28	199	2	—	3	—	—	—	204
	29	266	34	—	—	—	13	1	314
	30	424	—	—	—	—	5	—	429
	31	420	—	—	2	—	—	—	422
August	1	255	—	—	—	—	—	—	255
	2	48	—	28	—	—	—	—	76
	3	23	—	—	—	—	—	—	23
	4	13	—	—	—	—	—	—	13
		1988	39	141	35	13	35	5	2256

Quelle: C.A.R. 1906

Eine recht aufschlußreiche Mitteilung in bezug auf Fleischverkäufer ist dem C. A. R. 1874 zu entnehmen. Hierin wird ausdrücklich darauf hingewiesen, daß sie in einem eigenen Viertel ihre Stände aufzuschlagen hatten und dort Wildbret, jedoch kein Geflügel anboten. Das einseitige Fleischangebot hängt wahrscheinlich mit der Tatsache zusammen, daß der Pfau das Begleittier des Gottes Kataragama ist, Fleisch von Geflügel aus diesem Grunde zumindest im Heiligtum des Gottes zu verzehren, abgelehnt und als pietätlose Handlung angesehen wurde.

Diese Maßnahmen im Pilgerverkehr nach Kataragama, nach den Verwaltungsberichten von den Pilgern mitunter als besondere Schirmherrschaft der Regierung über ihre Wallfahrt empfunden[24]), führten, das kann heute wohl gesagt werden, mit zum erfolgreichen Abschluß der Entwicklungsarbeiten um Tissamaharama, auch zum geregelten Ablauf der für die Wirtschaft der Insel so wichtigen Arbeiten in den Salzgewinnungsstätten und legten letzten Endes auch einen Grundstein zu einer Angliederung des bis dahin ganz abseits gelegenen Heiligtums an das Wirtschaftsleben der Insel.

b) *Die Ortschaft*

Nach Davys kurzer Schilderung gibt Covington (1885), der um 1868 in Kataragama gewesen war, eine Beschreibung des Ortes außerhalb der Festzeit, wie sie wohl im großen und ganzen bis weit in unser Jahr-

[24]) Daß nicht alle Pilger vom Eingriff der Verwaltung angetan waren, zeigen die Proteste der ‚Colombo Chetties‘ (C.A.R. 1874, S. 108). Eine Folge der Restriktionen war allerdings auch, daß sich z.B. in Colombo separate Prozessionen zu Ehren der Gottheit Kataragama entwickelten (Cartman, 1957, S. 124f.).

hundert hinein zutraf. Entlang der beiden Prozessionswege, zwischen dem Mahādēvālē — dem Haupttempel in Kataragama — und dem Tempel der Vallīammā, waren Lehmhütten errichtet und teilweise mit Ziegeln gedeckt. Er zählte 15 Wohnhäuser und gab als Einwohnerschaft 40 Personen an. Damals wie heute verbargen zu beiden Seiten des Menik Ganga stehende hohe und weitausladende Kumbuk-Bäume (*Terminalia arjuna*) dem von Westen oder Süden nach Kataragama reisenden Besucher die Sicht auf die Siedlung und ihre Tempel.

Wie geringfügig Kataragama und sein Umland trotz des anschwellenden Pilgerverkehrs bis in die 30er Jahre dieses Jahrhunderts besiedelt war, darüber geben — wenn auch lückenhaft — statistische Angaben Auskunft (Tab. 5).

Tab. 5: Bevölkerungsentwicklung von Kataragama und umliegenden Siedlungen

Siedlung	1901 a)	1911 b)	1921 a)	1931 a)	1935 a)	1968 c)
Kataragama	97	?	103	181	?	1240
Detagamuwa	0	?	20	0	?	2947
Karawila	17	?	0 [25])	0	?	402
Sella Kataragama	?	?	?	?	?	132
Mailagamuwa	?	?	?	?	?	180
Katagamuwa [26])	?	?	?	?	?	5
Personen	114*)	159	123*)	181*)	102	4906
Familien	31*)	38	?	?	?	906

*) Diese Angaben beziehen sich lediglich auf die Siedlungen Kataragama, Detagamuwa und Karawila.

Quellen: a) Mapping Out Report of F.T.P.P. No. 25, 1935
b) Final Report on the Area of T.P.P. No. 25, 1923
c) Angaben des Grama Sevaka, Kataragama, 1970.

Trotz der geringen Einwohnerzahl hatte Kataragama um 1923 eine recht komplexe Sozialstruktur. Nach dem Begleittext des Final Report on the Area of T. P. P. No. 25, 1923, gehörten die Bewohner des Ortes der Goiwansa-(Bauern-), Karawa-(Jäger- und Fischer-), Durawa-(Palmsaftzapfer-) und Nawandanna-(Handwerker-)Kaste an; auf sie entfiel die überwiegende Zahl der singhalesischen Bevölkerung [27]). Daneben gab es aber auch einige indische Brahmanen, Tamilen und Moors (Muslim).

[25]) Um 1920 gab die Bevölkerung von Karawila ihre Siedlung auf und zog nach Kataragama und Detagamuwa, obwohl der Bewässerungsstauteich (sog. ‚Tank') nach den topographischen Karten von 1902 noch intakt war.

[26]) 'There used to be 13 families in Katagamuwa: the population now (i.e. 1910, Anm. d. Verf.) consists of 3 women, a girl of 17, a few children and 2 game watchers . . .' (Woolf, 1962, S. 171).

[27]) Nach Geiger (1960, S. 32) bilden die Goiwansa die höchste Kaste; alle anderen sind ihr untergeordnet.

Die Abgelegenheit des Ortes auch in verwaltungsmäßiger Hinsicht zeigt die Entfernung von folgenden Einrichtungen: Die nächste Schule, Post und ‚dispensary', d.h. ärztliche Beratungsstelle und Medikamentenausgabe, befanden sich 1923 16 km entfernt in Tissamaharama, das Meldeamt für Geburten, Heiraten und Sterbefälle gar in Buttala, etwa 40 km von Kataragama gelegen. Einmal im Monat wurden die Amtshandlungen der genannten Behörden allerdings in Kataragama vorgenommen. Ein weiteres Indiz für die Abgeschiedenheit des Heiligtums mag auch darin gesehen werden, daß bis 1935 kein Land an Ortsfremde veräußert oder verpachtet worden war. Es muß jedoch darauf hingewiesen werden, daß das Land um Kataragama und Detagamuwa zum Besitz des Ruhuṇu Mahā Kataragama dēvālē, dem Haupttempel von Kataragama, gehört. Ein ‚sub-post office' wurde erst 1939 eingerichtet (Asangananda, 1964, S. 4). Der Detagamuwa Tank, in den topographischen Karten von 1902 als verfallen vermerkt, ist auch in der Kartenausgabe von 1936 als noch nicht wiederhergestellt eingetragen.

c) *Feste Unterkunftshäuser* (*madam*)

Trotz dieser isolierten Lage und der Stagnation in der Bevölkerungsentwicklung bis nach dem Zweiten Weltkrieg fanden in Kataragama einige Entwicklungen statt, die für die bauliche Gestaltung des Ortes von besonderer Bedeutung sind. Sie müssen im Zusammenhang mit geistigen Bewegungen gesehen werden, die sich aus dem Kontakt Ceylons mit westlichen Kultureinflüssen im Laufe des letzten Jahrhunderts besonders stark herausgebildet hatten und die zu einer ‚Buddhist-' und vor allem zu einer ‚Hindu revival' führten, einer Rückbesinnung auf eigene geistige und kulturelle Werte[28]) (Bechert, 1966, S. 37ff.). Nicht die Hintergründe, sondern nur die für Kataragama als Ortschaft bedeutsamen Auswirkungen dieser Bewegungen seien hier angeführt.

Am sichtbarsten zeigen sie sich im Heiligtum wohl in den Unterkünften für die Pilger, den *madam*, auch *chattram* genannt, die z.T. von reichen Gläubigen, den Führern der 'revival' oder auch von einzelnen Kasten errichtet wurden und nach und nach die temporären Lager ablösten. Einige von ihnen kann man nur als luftige, wellblechgedeckte Schutzhallen bezeichnen, andere dagegen sind festgebaute Häuser. In allen *madam* können Pilger und andere Besucher des Ortes kostenlos übernachten und Essen erhalten. Unterhalten werden sie heute meist durch Spenden, um die die Nutznießer dieser Einrichtungen gebeten werden. Bei einigen *madam* lassen die Namen erkennen, daß sie auf bestimmte Kasten ausgerichtet sind (z.B. Dobhi-(Wäscher-), Barber-(Friseur-)*madam*). Da aber Hindus und Buddhisten ohne Unterschied Unterkunft gewährt

[28]) Mit den von den ‚revival'-Bewegungen verbreiteten Ideen ziehen wohl auch die Streitigkeiten zwischen Hindus und Buddhisten (Tamilen und Singhalesen) in Kataragama ein. 1897 wird von Unruhen im Ort selbst, 1928 von Streitereien zwischen diesen Gruppen um den Wehahitikanda berichtet (Report on Wellawaya Division, ca. 1967, S. 39).

wird, ist heute kaum, wenn überhaupt, eine Betonung der Kastenzugehörigkeit zu spüren. Ortskundige erklärten, daß diese *madam* von Angehörigen dieser Kasten gestiftet worden seien und nichts mit irgendwelchen Restriktionen zu tun hatten.

Von den 31 *madam*, die es 1970 während der Kartierung des Heiligtums gab, ist die große Mehrheit in den ersten 50 Jahren unseres Jahrhunderts entstanden (Tab. 2). Covington (1885, S. 151) berichtet von der ‚Chetties Chattram' gegenüber der neuen Furt, die den Ort mit der Straße nach Tissamaharama verbindet. Weitere Angaben über die Errichtung von *madam* sind in Tabelle 2 enthalten. Nach dem Grundbuch sind 18 Grundstücke, auf denen ein *madam* errichtet wurde, von Personen oder Institutionen gepachtet, die nicht in Kataragama ansässig sind. Zwei *madam* befinden sich in Regierungsbesitz. Der Rest (11) steht auf Grundstücken, die an Einwohner von Kataragama verpachtet worden sind. Das läßt vermuten, daß zumindest einige dieser Unterkunftshäuser aus finanziellen Überlegungen erbaut wurden und die Erbauer hofften, durch Spenden der Benutzer ein Geschäft zu machen.

d) *Sonstige Entwicklungen*

Die Maßnahmen der Kolonialverwaltung förderten unbeabsichtigt die Entwicklung des Ortes und riefen auch andere Initiativen als den Bau von *madam* hervor. Ob die Errichtung der zum Ort hin mit Elefantenköpfen und Pfauen — als Wahrzeichen der im Heiligtum besonders verehrten Götter Gaṇeśa und Kataragama — geschmückten Umwallung des Haupttempels mit Maßnahmen der Verwaltung zusammenhängt oder, was eher zu vermuten ist, eine erste Auswirkung der ‚revival'-Bewegung in Kataragama darstellt, ließ sich nicht in Erfahrung bringen. Die nach allen vier Seiten mit Toren und Pforten versehene Umwallung des Haupttempels z.B. wurde um 1872 von den ‚Colombo Chetties' erbaut (C. A. R. 1873, S. 145).

Der Aufschwung im Pilgerzustrom hat neben der Einbeziehung Kataragamas in das Geschehen der Insel auch dazu geführt, daß 1897 die Trasse für die heutige Straße von Tissamaharama nach Kataragama, die den Hauptstrom der Pilger trägt und die älteren Pfade z.T. ablöste oder allmählich in ihrer Bedeutung einschränkte, von einem gewissen Sirivaddana Upasaka angelegt wurde (C. A. R. 1906, S. H 8). Mit diesem Wegebau war Kataragama an das für den Südosten wichtige Verkehrsband angeschlossen, das nach der Vollendung der Verbindungsstraße zwischen dem Hochland über Wellawaya nach Hambantota (um 1890) und von dort nach Galle führte und zusammen mit dem wiederhergerichteten Bewässerungsgebiet um Tissamaharama zur starken Belebung dieses Teils der Insel beitrug.

Die heute fast ausschließlich benutzte Verbindung nach Kataragama über Tissamaharama war zunächst mehr ein Weg als eine Straße. Bis in die 50er Jahre vermochten außer Fußgängern meist nur ‚bullock carts', Ochsenkarren, den Zugang zu meistern. Erst bei den Ausbauarbeiten um 1960 wurde der Weg der Aufnahme des stark gestiegenen Pilgerverkehrs angepaßt und erhielt eine feste Decke.

7. Entwicklungen nach dem Zweiten Weltkrieg

a) *Anstieg des Pilgerstroms*

Seit dem letzten Krieg bahnt sich in bezug auf Kataragama eine Entwicklung an, die nicht nur zu einer Einbeziehung des Ortes in das Leben des südöstlichen Landesteils über die Festzeit hinaus mit sich bringt, sondern — das muß man aus der bevorzugten Förderung des Ortes schließen — die Siedlung und das Heiligtum zu einem der wichtigsten religiösen Zentren der Insel werden läßt.

Als auslösende Faktoren für diese neue Entwicklung und für den starken Anstieg der Pilgerzahlen müssen u. a. genannt werden:

1. die besseren Verkehrsbedingungen; es werden heute Omnibusse eingesetzt;
2. eine Umbewertung des ceylonesischen Götterpantheons und die damit verbundene Hervorhebung des Gottes Kataragama.

Zu 1.: Heute ist Kataragama das Ziel zahlreicher Pilger, die das ganze Jahr über den Ort aufsuchen, obwohl zur Hauptfestzeit im Juli/August der Zustrom weitaus am stärksten ist. Hindus, Buddhisten und Muslim bilden die Hauptmasse der Besucher, die zu diesem abseits, in der Wildnis der südöstlichen Trockenzone gelegenen Ort wallfahrten, aber auch Christen kann man vereinzelt antreffen. Ihre Zahl ist zwar verschwindend gering im Vergleich mit den übrigen Gruppen, doch war bis 1970 einer der Führer bei dem am Ende des Festes veranstalteten Feuerlaufes ein Katholik. Von anderen Christen hört man folgende Begründung für ihre Wallfahrt: Gott Kataragama werde von ihnen wie ein Heiliger um Fürsprache bei Gott gebeten.

Besucht wird der Ort während der großen Feier im Juli/August allein von etwa 100000 Menschen. Über die Gesamtzahl liegen lediglich Schätzungen vor. Daß diese aber eher als zu niedrig angesehen werden muß, läßt sich der Tatsache entnehmen, daß allein mit der Bahn pro Jahr durchschnittlich 60000 Gläubige (1964–66: 65529, 56004, 65459)[29] die größte Strecke des Pilgerweges bis Matara, bzw. Haputale zurücklegen, von wo aus sie den während des Festes eingerichteten ‚shuttle service', den Pendelverkehr der Busse der staatlichen Straßentransportmittel C.T.B. (Ceylon Transport Board) zwischen den Endpunkten der Bahn und Kataragama benutzen (sog. ‚coordinated service').

Die staatlichen Buslinien befördern seit 1969 mindestens 55% aller Pilger. Für 1966 zählte die Eisenbahn in beiden Endpunkten Haputale

[29]) Administration Report, Ceylon Government Railway, 1969.

und Matara 65459, der koordinierte Verkehr zwischen diesen Orten und Kataragama jedoch insgesamt 118417 Pilger[30]). Da in der koordinierten Beförderung sowohl Reisende, die nur den Bus benutzen, als auch Pilger, die erst von den beiden Bahnendpunkten aus die Busse nehmen, eingeschlossen sind, läßt sich die nur mit Bussen des koordinierten Verkehrs anreisende Pilgerschar für dieses Jahr auf 52958 festlegen. Zu diesen muß aber noch eine unbekannte Zahl von Pilgern gezählt werden, die mit Bussen direkt von ihren Heimatorten oder dem nächsten Verwaltungs- oder Hauptort nach Kataragama reisen, so z.B. von Kandy, Batticaloa, Colombo, Jaffna etc.

Pilgerfahrten sind in Ceylon durch moderne Transportmittel — Eisenbahn und Omnibus — wesentlich vereinfacht worden. Vor Jahren noch bedeutete eine solche Reise eine physische Leistung, da man — um bei dem Beispiel Kataragama zu bleiben — meilenweit bei großer Hitze und mangelnder Wasserversorgung durch Dschungelgebiete laufen mußte, wobei nicht selten zusätzlich zu Moskitos noch mit Bedrohungen durch Elefanten, Leoparden und anderen wilden Tieren zu rechnen war.

Die Benutzung moderner Transportmittel ließ die Pilgerzahlen hochschnellen, bewirkte aber gleichzeitig teilweise eine Umwandlung der Pilgerfahrt in jährlich wiederholbare und oft auch wiederholte Wallfahrten. Heute veranstalten Reiseunternehmen sogar außerhalb der eigentlichen Festtage Touren zu den heiligen Stätten, besuchen aber auch andere auf dem Wege liegende religiöse, historische und touristische Stätten von einiger Bedeutung.

Wie einige Informanten meinten, ist der „Umschlag" von Pilgern gestiegen, mehr Menschen sehen mehr heilige Stätten, aber Gläubigkeit und Ernsthaftigkeit haben dadurch nicht zugenommen, eher darunter gelitten. Musik und Transistorradios zeigen an, daß es sich oftmals mehr um Ausflüge handelt. Die Gruppenfahrten nach Kataragama außerhalb der großen Festzeiten haben, soweit beobachtet werden konnte, sehr oft eine starke touristische Komponente. Die Fahrten zu den großen Festen sind dagegen in den meisten Fällen von religiöser Ehrfurcht und Überzeugung geprägt. Zur Festzeit in Kataragama im Juli/August sind die Busse hinduistischer (tamilischer) Pilger häufig von den Rufen ‚*haro, hara*!' erfüllt; nach Spittel (1933, S. 292) ist dies das *mantra*, der Zauberspruch zur Anrufung des Gottes Kataragama.

In Abbildung 5 wurde versucht, für 1969 den zur Hauptfestzeit auf Kataragama ausgerichteten Pilgerstrom zu zeigen. Leider waren Angaben über Pilger, die die staatlichen oder die wenigen privaten Transportunternehmen benutzen, überhaupt nicht oder — ausgenommen die Eisenbahn — nicht aufgeschlüsselt zu erhalten. So läßt sich nur das vom motorisierten Pilgerverkehr benutzte Verkehrsnetz eintragen; eine Aussage über die Frequenz ist nicht möglich.

Anders sieht es mit den Angaben über Pilger aus, die mit der Eisenbahn bis zum jeweiligen End- oder Umsteigepunkt reisten, Matara 31148

[30]) Report of the Ceylon Transport Board, 1969.

bzw. Haputale 15804, von wo aus Omnibusse den Weitertransport übernehmen. Die Differenz in der Zahl der Pilger im Vergleich zu früheren Jahren (1964–66) muß nicht unbedingt einen Abfall der Beteiligung an der Pilgerfahrt bedeuten; denn die vorher angeführten Daten für die Jahre 1964–66 umfassen die Besucher Kataragamas für das gesamte Jahr. Die Zahlen für 1969 beziehen sich dagegen nur auf das Fest im Juli/August. Diese Pilger wurden von der ceylonesischen Eisenbahnverwaltung genau registriert und sind in die Abbildung eingetragen worden.

Im Verhältnis zu der großen Pilgerschar, die öffentliche Transportmittel benutzt — der Anteil der mit privaten Fahrzeugen dürfte kleiner sein, obwohl viele Plantagen ihren Arbeitern für die Pilgerfahrt Lastwagen zur Verfügung stellen — hält sich die wesentlich geringere Zahl der Pilger zu Fuß angeblich konstant. Hierin eingeschlossen sind allerdings auch diejenigen, die nur etwa einen Tagesmarsch, die letzten 20–30 km zum Heiligtum, zu Fuß zurücklegen. Unter konservativen Gläubigen gilt es heute noch als eine besonders verdienstvolle Glaubenstat, eine Pilgerfahrt zu Fuß zu absolvieren.

Verschiedene Anmarschwege und zahlreiche Dschungelpfade führen sternförmig nach Kataragama. Von Westen zog sich früher eine Pilgerroute von Tissamaharama über Katagamuwa nach Kataragama (Länge 24 km) hin. Sie wurde von den Gläubigen, die an der dicht besiedelten Westküste leben, für ihre Anreise zu dem Heiligtum gewählt. Dieser Pilgerweg verlor aber nach der Öffnung des heute benutzten wichtigsten Zugangs fast alle Bedeutung. Aus dem Norden der Insel und aus dem Hochland zieht die alte Heerstraße über Buttala nach Kataragama (Länge 42 km). Auf ihr wanderten nach Aussagen Einheimischer im Jahre 1969/70 etwa 5000 Pilger, Hindus und Buddhisten, entlang. Ein anderer von Westen auf Kataragama zulaufender Weg beginnt in Tanamalwila. Er hat eine Länge von 24 km und passiert Pewuwewa und Sella Kataragama. Ihn bevorzugten in dem angegebenen Jahr etwa 2000 vornehmlich buddhistische Pilger. Schließlich ist eine nicht genau zu übersehende Zahl von Dschungelpfaden zu nennen, die das menschenleere östliche Waldgebiet — heute zu großen Teilen von Naturschutzgebieten eingenommen[31]) — durchqueren. Über diese Pfade — einige von ihnen sind in der Abbildung eingetragen — ziehen entlang der Küste oder durch das Landesinnere alljährlich etwa 1300 Hindus, die zu Fuß von Jaffna, sogar von Indien aus ihre Pilgerfahrt antreten. Diese Angaben beruhen auf Schätzungen Ortskundiger.

Der Anstieg des Pilgerstromes nach Kataragama läßt sich allerdings nicht nur mit der leichteren Erreichbarkeit des Heiligtums dank verbesserter Verkehrseinrichtungen erklären; die Pilgerfreudigkeit der Ceylonesen ist schon immer groß gewesen. Sie wurde durch die besseren Verbindungen vielleicht „sichtbarer“, sowohl am Ziel der Pilgerfahrt in

[31]) Ruhunu National Park, Yala Strict Natural Reserve, Yala East und Yala North Intermediate Zone u. a.

der größeren Zahl der Gläubigen wie auch auf den Anfahrtwegen, wo Sonderbusse und Sonderzüge z.T. mit Spruchbändern auf eine Wallfahrt hinweisen. Die Steigerung der Pilgerzahlen darf ohne Zweifel auch mit der seit einigen Jahren stärker um sich greifenden Siedlungsbewegung zusammenhängen, die in den bisher wenig erschlossenen Räumen der südlichen Trockenzone stattfindet und damit in der näheren Umgebung des Heiligtums einen lokalen Pilgerstamm herangebildet hat.

Zu 2.: Ein wesentlicherer Grund für den verstärkten Zustrom von Pilgern nach Kataragama zu jeder Zeit des Jahres, wenn auch besonders stark während der Festzeiten, dürfte wohl in einer religiösen Verhaltensänderung liegen. Obeyesekere (1970, S. 58f.) kommt zu dem Schluß, daß es sich um ein religiöses und zugleich um ein soziologisches Problem handelt. In dem ceylonesischen Götterpantheon, an dessen Spitze Buddha steht und dessen nächsttiefere Stufe von den regionalen Schutzgottheiten, zu denen auch die Gottheit von Kataragama zählt[32]), gebildet wird, hat sich in den letzten Jahren eine Umbewertung vollzogen, dergestalt, daß heute die Gottheit von Kataragama in weiten Teilen Ceylons als die „geeignetste" Schutzgottheit angesehen wird, an die man sich mit seinen Problemen wenden kann[33]).

Diese Hervorhebung der Gottheit Kataragama über ihren in Ceylon auch regionalen Bedeutungsbereich hinaus hat denn auch zu einer Veränderung der sozialen Zusammensetzung seiner Verehrer geführt. Heute gibt es vor allem unter der Stadtbevölkerung und den Intellektuellen eine größere Zahl von Gruppen, die besonderen Belastungen und Problemen ausgesetzt sind. Geschäftsleute, vor Wahlen vor allem Politiker, Studenten, viele, die ins Ausland reisen, seien es Buddhisten, Hindus oder vereinzelt auch katholische und protestantische Christen, pilgern nach Kataragama, um diese Gottheit um Erfolg für ihre Pläne zu bitten. Aus Gesprächen mit Pilgern und Einheimischen, aber auch aus eigenen Beobachtungen läßt sich die Feststellung von Obeyesekere bestätigen.

Leider liegen keine genauen Untersuchungen über die soziale Zusammensetzung der Pilgergruppen in Kataragama vor. Ihrem Äußeren nach gehören die Pilger allen Gesellschaftsschichten an: Ärmlich gekleidete mischen sich mit sehr wohlhabend aussehenden.

Der große soziale Wert, die beruhigenden Auswirkungen der Wall- und Pilgerfahrten zu den zahlreichen Heiligtümern der Insel, ist von den Politikern klar erkannt worden. Religiöse Überzeugung, aber auch die

---

[32]) Der Gott von Kataragama wurde bekanntlich sehr früh mit dem indischen Gott Skandakumāra identifiziert (vgl. Bechert, 1968, S. 37ff.), so daß Kataragama auch als Pilgerstätte für Hindus aus vielen Teilen Indiens von großer Bedeutung ist. Auf Ceylon hat die Gottheit Kataragama im Gebiet zwischen dem Walawe Ganga und Mahiyangana noch eine zusätzliche Funktion: Sie wird hier als die oberste Schutzgottheit, z.B. in der Landwirtschaft, verehrt.

[33]) Obeyesekeres Darstellung trifft nicht ganz zu; es ist eher von einer „,revival' des Kataragama-Kultus" zu sprechen (briefl. Mitteilung von Prof. Bechert).

Überlegung, die Pilgerfahrten als ‚psychological soother', als Auffänger oder als Katalysator für die wirtschaftlichen und sozialen Schwierigkeiten des Landes zu nutzen, werden daher verschiedentlich als Gründe für ihre Förderung durch die Regierung genannt. Durch Ausgabe verbilligter Rückfahrkarten (Colombo—Kataragama 1970: Rps. 11.20; eine Rupie entsprach damals etwa DM 0.40) und sonstige, allgemeine Verbesserungen in den Heiligtümern werden sie gefördert[34]).

b) *Wandlungen im Ortsbild und in der Umgebung*

Im Ortsbild haben der starke Zustrom von Pilgern und die seit etwa 1965 stattfindenden, geplanten Arbeiten für das Heiligtum Kataragama zu ersten Umwandlungen geführt.

Zu Beginn der britischen Kontrolle (um 1870) bildeten der Haupttempel mit dem nahebei stehenden Tempel der Teyvāṇiammā und dem in 330 m Entfernung gelegenen Tempel der Vaḷḷiammā den Kern der heiligen Stätten. Es gehörten dazu auch der Prozessionsweg, d. h. die beiden heute von ‚boutiques' und *madam* eingerahmten Straßen, die Piṭa vīdiya und Mäda vīdiya, und der am Ende eines etwa 560 m langen Verbindungsweges noch in Trümmern liegende Stūpa. Unter der britischen Verwaltung entwickelten sich entlang des Prozessionsweges die Unterkunftshäuser für die Pilger, die *madam*, in denen sich oft kleine Tempel und Schreine befinden. Die *madam* kann man neben den alten Tempeln als das zweite den Ort bestimmende Bauelement bezeichnen.

Das allmähliche Wachsen der Siedlung jener Zeit und der Übergang zur Ortsplanung läßt sich vielleicht am besten an der schrittweisen Verlagerung und Entwicklung des Krankenhauses darstellen. Das erste Hospital lag unmittelbar an der Mauer, die den Haupttempel umgibt, nahe der alten Furt durch den Menik Ganga (Spittel, 1933, S. 300). Das bis in die Zeit nach dem Zweiten Weltkrieg benutzte Krankenhaus steht in der Nähe der Fußgängerbrücke am südlichen Ortseingang, am Menik Ganga. Das heute betriebene Hospital wurde schließlich am Westufer des Flusses, auf einem von der Planung festgelegten Areal errichtet.

Den stärksten Anstoß zur baulichen Neugestaltung, aber auch der Gesamtentwicklung erhielt der Ort und seine Umgebung, nachdem das 1955 erstmalig vorgeschlagene ‚Kataragama Planning Scheme' nach der ‚Town and Country Planning Ordinance No. 13 of 1946' beschlossen

---

[34]) Inwieweit die Darstellungen zutreffen, daß im Fall von Kataragama von der Regierung bewußt der Versuch unternommen wird, die Gläubigen — Hindus und Buddhisten — von dem gegenwärtig im Zentrum der Verehrung stehenden Haupttempel als primärem Ziel der Wallfahrt abzuziehen und sie als erstes dem Stūpa zuzuführen, muß die Zukunft erweisen. Geplant ist angeblich, bei der Neuordnung des Heiligtums die Pilger von dem Busbahnhof oder den Parkplätzen für die privaten Wagen so zu leiten, daß sie den Menik Ganga etwas nördlicher als heute auf einer Brücke überschreiten, dann als erstes den Stūpa und erst auf dem Rückweg und nicht wie bisher auf dem Hinweg den Haupttempel besuchen (Abb. 6).

wurde und ab 1964 zur Ausführung gelangte. Mit diesem ‚Planning Scheme' hat es sich die Regierung zum Ziel gesetzt, eine Entflechtung und „ordentliche" Trennung von Heiligtum und Geschäft vorzunehmen. Die Aufmerksamkeit, die Kataragama seit dieser Zeit durch die Öffentlichkeit und die Regierung erfährt, hat zu einem ähnlichen Entwicklungsanstoß geführt wie nach dem Eingreifen der britischen Kolonialverwaltung. Nur handelt es sich heute um einen sehr umfassenden Vorgang, der zudem wesentlich schneller abläuft als die Entwicklung des Ortes in der britischen Zeit, als die Verwaltung ihre Aufgabe allein in der Überwachung sah und die Neuerungen sich nach und nach dem Bedarf anpaßten.

Heiligtum, Siedlung und Umgebung werden heute geplant (Abb. 6). Nur noch an wenigen Stellen ist Platz für private Initiativen. Zu diesen zählt vor allem der Ausbau des Wedahitikanda, dem heiligen Berg, der vor 1960 wegen Unwegsamkeit nur mühsam und unter Gefahren bestiegen werden konnte. Ein gewisser Ratmalana Sri Siddhartha hatte damals begonnen, mit gespendeten Geldmitteln einen Weg zum Gipfel auszubauen, eine Schutzhütte zu errichten und Mahlzeiten zu verteilen. Heute (1970) ist auf dem Gipfel der Bau eines *madam* weit fortgeschritten, ein hinduistischer Schrein errichtet und ein Bo-Baum gepflanzt. Sogar elektrisches Licht ist bis auf den Gipfel verlegt.

8. Funktionalkartierung von Kataragama und Detagamuwa (1970)

a) *Stand der Bebauung*

Die 1970 durchgeführte Kartierung (Abb. 3, 4) zeigt die Ortsteile Kataragama, links des Menik Ganga, und Detagamuwa, auf der rechten Seite des Flusses gelegen, zu Beginn der Umwandlung, der Trennung zwischen heiligem Bezirk und Geschäfts- und Wohnviertel. Bis auf den fast abgebrochenen Gebäudekomplex zwischen beiden Prozessionswegen war Kataragama noch weitgehend in seiner Vermischung von Heiligtum und Siedlung erhalten.

In einigen verstreut liegenden Neubauten deutet sich die in Zukunft auf dem rechten Ufer des Menik Ganga entstehende Neustadt schon an. So wurden bereits zwei zweistöckige Wohn- und Geschäftsblöcke fertiggestellt und teilweise bezogen (bei den Einheimischen ‚New Town' genannt). Sie dienen zur Aufnahme der Händler, die aus dem zum heiligen Bezirk ernannten Geschäftsviertel, das 1970 noch überwiegend am östlichen Ufer lag, ausgewiesen werden sollen, z. T. aber auch schon umgesiedelt worden sind. In der Neustadt sind außerdem folgende zentrale Einrichtungen errichtet worden: Krankenhaus, Schule, Busbahnhof, Busdepot, Post und Markthallen. Ferner wurden bereits zwei staatliche *madam* als Ersatz für die im alten Kataragama abgerissenen Unterkunftshäuser, ein Wasserhochbehälter, der durch einen im Bett des Menik Ganga abgesenkten Tiefbrunnen gespeist wird, ein Dieselgenerator zur Erzeugung von Strom und ‚circuit bungalows‘ verschiedener Behörden in Colombo aufgebaut.

Bei den Gebäuden im 1970 noch bestehenden alten, aber auch bei den genannten im neuen Kataragama handelt es sich um dauerhafte, feste Bauten[35]). Daneben haben sich mit dem verstärkten Einstrom von Pilgern an verschiedenen Stellen des Heiligtums in schnell errichteten Ständen und barackenartigen Bauten Geschäftsleute niedergelassen. Diese Läden hätten ohne das ‚Kataragama Planning Scheme‘ und den in dessen Rahmen ausgeführten Arbeiten bei dem immer stärkeren Einstrom von Pilgern wahrscheinlich noch lange Zeit gestanden. Jetzt können sie aber nur die Gunst des Augenblicks nutzen. Alle in Abbildung 3 eingetragenen Geschäfte zwischen den beiden neuen *madam* am rechten Ufer gegenüber dem Busbahnhof wurden im Frühjahr 1971 abgerissen. Die übrigen werden im Laufe der Ausbauarbeiten ebenfalls eingeebnet.

Diese Holzhütten liegen alle an verkaufsgünstigen Stellen entlang der Wege, die die Pilger normalerweise nach ihrer Ankunft am Busbahnhof bis zum Stūpa zurücklegen, und überall dort, wo vorher Geschäfte im alten und neuen Kataragama aus den verschiedensten Gründen nicht eingerichtet wurden oder errichtet werden konnten.

Auf der rechten Flußseite sind hier zu nennen: das Gebiet um den Busbahnhof und um den Übergang über den Fluß (Gründe des Verbots: Uferschutz und geplante Grünanlagen und Neubebauungspläne); am linken Ufer des Menik Ganga einmal das nicht bebaute Ufer am Fuß der Brücke (Uferschutz) und vor allem das Wegestück zwischen dem Haupttempel und dem Stūpa, das bis zur Wiederherstellung des Stūpa ohne wirtschaftliches Interesse war.

b) *Geschäftsausstattung des Heiligtums während der Kartierung*

Die Kartierung des Ortes wurde bewußt zu einem Zeitpunkt durchgeführt, an dem kein Fest stattfand. Sie umfaßt die zukünftige heilige Stadt und die Neustadt, soweit sie 1970 bereits besiedelt war. Die Kartierung erfolgte außerdem zwischen Poya-Tagen[36]), um zu zeigen, daß trotz des relativ geringen Zustroms von Pilgern außerhalb der großen Feste der gesamte Ort auf die Tempel, auf das Heiligtum, ausgerichtet ist und von ihm geprägt wird.

Die Geschäftsausstattung Kataragamas außerhalb der Festzeit läßt sich in drei Gruppen gliedern:

---

[35]) Neben der zweistöckig errichteten ‚New Town‘ (Erdgeschoß: Geschäfte, Obergeschoß: Wohnungen) ragen nur der Stūpa, die verzierten Aufbauten des Teyvāṇīammā-Tempels und der neue Wasserhochbehälter gegenüber der alten Furt aus der ebenerdigen Baumasse Kataragamas heraus, werden z. T. aber selbst von heiligen Bo-Bäumen oder den hohen Kumbuk-Bäumen, die den Menik Ganga säumen, überragt.

[36]) Buddhistische „Sonntage“; monatlich vier, den Mondphasen entsprechend.

I. Geschäfte für religiösen Bedarf (a, b) und/oder mit religiöser Funktion (c)
   a) Devotionalien (religiöse Andenken; Buddhastatuen, Bilder usw.)
   b) Opfergaben (Kampfer, Lotosblüten, Kokosnüsse, Fruchtschalen usw.)
   c) Friseure, *kāvadi*-Verleih

II. Geschäfte zur Pilgerversorgung
   a) Restaurants, Gemischtwarenläden usw.
   b) Stände für Schmuckketten
   c) Reparaturwerkstätten (Autos und Fahrräder)

III. Geschäfte für den normalen täglichen Bedarf

   Geschäfte, die nichts oder nicht überwiegend mit der Funktion des Ortes als Heiligtum zu tun haben, sondern mehr oder weniger zur normalen Ausstattung eines Ortes von der Größe Kataragamas gehören.

Eine Erweiterung erfährt diese Ausstattung jeweils während der Festzeit. Dann kann man neben den genannten z. T. ganz neue Geschäftsarten antreffen, oder es erfolgt eine starke Vermehrung einiger in Tabelle 6 schon enthaltener, während der normalen Zeiten oft sehr schwach vertretener Läden. Neben solchen, die der Versorgung der Pilger dienen, seien hier vor allem Geschäfte genannt, die eine religiöse Funktion erfüllen. Zu diesen gehören Friseure und Verleiher von *kāvadis* und die dazu gehörenden Musiker, auch Verkäufer heiliger Asche. Von den profanen „Geschäftszweigen", die während der Festzeit in Kataragama hervortreten, müssen Verteiler von Trinkwasser und besonders Bettler erwähnt werden. Kaum zu erfassen sind ambulante Händler, Quacksalber usw.

Die hier genannten Geschäftszweige werden einschließlich der Friseure im Anschluß an die Beschreibung der normalen Geschäftsausstattung, d. h. der Ausstattung außerhalb der Festzeit, etwas eingehender behandelt.

Von insgesamt 227 Geschäften und Ständen in Kataragama z. Zt. der Kartierung entfielen nur 11 auf die Kategorie III, d.h. diese Geschäfte entsprachen an Zahl dem Bedarf einer Siedlung von der Größe Kataragamas (Kataragama und Detagamuwa, 1968: 4187 Einwohner). Einige Geschäfte aus den Gruppen I und II müssen zweifellos mit zur Normalausstattung einer Siedlung von der Größe Kataragamas gezählt werden (z. B. Gemischtwaren, Restaurants, Friseure, Reparaturwerkstätten). Leider verhindert der Mangel an Vergleichsuntersuchungen festzustellen, wie stark die Mehrausstattung mit Geschäften dieser Gruppen wirklich ist.

Das Heiligtum läßt sich nach seinem Dienstleistungs- und Warenangebot in drei Teile gliedern: das alte und neue Kataragama sowie der

Tab. 6: Geschäfte und Stände in Kataragama und Detagamuwa (1970)

	Weg zwischen Stūpa und Haupt-tempel	Altstadt (Kataragama)				Neustadt (Detaga-muwa)	Gesamtzahl der Geschäfte und Stände
		Mäda vīdiya (Markt bis Vorplatz des Haupt-tempels	Piṭa vīdiya	Markt bis Brücke	insgesamt		
I. Geschäfte für religiösen Bedarf (a, b) und/oder mit religiöser Funktion (c)							
a) Devotionalien (religiöse Andenken)	—	7	—	3	10	4	14
b) Opfergaben							
Fruchtstände	—	17	1	20	38	3	41
Kampfer-, Weihrauchstände	—	6	—	2	8	1	9
c) Friseure	—	2	—	1	3	7	10
kāvadi-Verleih	—	1	—	1	2	—	2
Insgesamt (I.)	—	33	1	27	61	15	76
II. Geschäfte zur Pilgerversorgung							
a) Restaurants	13	8	3	5	16	40	69
Getränkebuden	6	—	—	—	—	3	9
Getränkestände	—	7	—	6	13	—	13
Gemischtwarenläden	—	7	2	1	10	13	23
b) Schmuckketten	—	20	—	1	21	—	21
c) Reparaturwerkstätten (Autos, Fahrräder)	—	—	—	—	—	5	5
Insgesamt (II.)	19	42	5	13	60	61	140
III. Geschäfte für den normalen täglichen Bedarf							
Bäckerei	—	—	—	—	—	2	2
Haushaltswaren	—	1	—	—	1	1	2
Schneider	—	—	—	—	—	2	2
Textilgeschäfte	—	—	—	—	—	1*)	1
Fotoatelier	—	—	—	—	—	1*)	1
Wäscherei	—	—	—	—	—	1**)	1
Billardhalle	—	—	—	—	—	1**)	1
Tankstelle	—	—	—	—	—	1	1
Insgesamt (III.)	—	1	—	—	1	10	11
Insgesamt (I.–III.)	19	76	6	40	122	86	227

*), **) diese Geschäfte sind in Abb. 3 unter „Sonstiges" zusammengefaßt

*) in der Neustadt gelegen
**) am Parkplatz (‚P') gelegen

Weg zwischen dem Haupttempel und dem Stūpa. Auf das alte Kataragama — 122 Geschäfte und Stände — entfallen relativ wenig Restaurants, dafür aber zahlreiche Getränkestände und -buden, die vielfach mit dem Verkauf von religiösem Bedarf wie Fruchtschalen, Kampfer, Lotosblüten, z.T. auch Kokosnüssen, gekoppelt sind, aber auch mit Ständen, die Schmuckketten oder Andenken aller Art anbieten.

Religiöse Artikel werden in Kataragama auf folgende Weise verwendet: Kampfer liegt in kleinen Würfeln zum Kauf aus und dient als Weihrauchspender. Auf dem Weg zu den Stätten der Verehrung und vor Schreinen zünden die Gläubigen die Kampferstücke an, die einen recht intensiven, aromatischen Geruch verbreiten. Die Fruchtschalen sind Opfergabe für den Haupttempel. Dort werden die Früchte von den *kapurālas*, den Priestern, geweiht, zur Hälfte dem Gott gereicht und zur Hälfte dem Gläubigen zurückgegeben, der die gesegneten Früchte selbst verzehrt oder mit anderen teilt. Die Lotosblüten kaufen vor allem die Buddhisten, die sie am Kirivehera oder anderen Buddhaschreinen als Opfergabe niederlegen. Die Kokosnüsse werden auf einem Steinblock vor dem Tempel des Elefantengottes Gaṇeśa innerhalb der Umwallung des Haupttempels zerschmettert. Aus der Art wie die Nuß zerspringt und wie die Schalen zu liegen kommen, meint der Gläubige, eine Antwort auf sein Anliegen ablesen zu können.

Von allen anderen Geschäften im alten Kataragama zeigen nur noch die für Gemischtwaren eine auffällige Verdichtung. Die Zahl der Friseure hält sich in Grenzen.

In Altkataragama läßt sich, anders als in den übrigen Ortsteilen, in der Verteilung der Funktionen eine räumliche Differenzierung feststellen: In der flußnahen Straße, der Mäda vīdiya, dominiert das Geschäft, in der anderen, der Piṭa vīdiya, überwiegen die *madam*, die Unterkunftshäuser. Die dritte Straße, die Nāgaha vīdiya, ist außerhalb der Festzeit bedeutungslos und kaum als Straße zu erkennen. Nur zur Hauptfestzeit im Juli/August werden hier am Rande der Ortschaft temporäre Bauten zur Betreuung und Versorgung der Pilger errichtet.

Eindeutig heben sich die Wege heraus, die von den Gläubigen zum Heiligtum benutzt werden, d.h. der Zugang von der Fußgängerbrücke bis zum Haupttempel, die Mäda vīdiya. Am stärksten drängen sich hier die Geschäfte allerdings in dem Abschnitt vom Markt bis zum Haupttempel. Der Grund dafür liegt in der Tatsache, daß besonders zu Festzeiten die Gläubigen es vorziehen, den heiligen Fluß an der neuen Furt zu durchwaten als die Fußgängerbrücke zu benutzen. Die große Zahl von Ständen für Fruchtschalen und Getränke an dem Wegstück zwischen Brücke und Markt, meistens ‚encroachments', d.h. Geschäfte ohne Genehmigung für diesen Standort, ist auf die Pilger ausgerichtet, die nicht den Fluß durchqueren.

Auf der Piṭa vīdiya fehlen Geschäfte fast völlig. Die wenigen, die es dennoch gibt, liegen an beiden Enden der Straße, also in dem Bereich um den Markt oder um den Vorplatz am Haupttempel. Diese Straße wird durch die hohe Zahl an *madam* charakterisiert.

Insgesamt prägen Geschäfte für religiösen Bedarf und kleinere Andenkenstände das Gesicht der Altstadt Kataragamas außerhalb der Festzeit.

Eine ganz andere Zusammensetzung kennzeichnet die Geschäfte auf dem Zugangsweg zum Stūpa und in der Neustadt. Zum Kirivehera hin sind vor allem auf der ersten Wegstrecke hinter dem Haupttempel Getränkestände aufgestellt, Restaurants drängen sich kurz vor dem Stūpa. Diese ‚hotels' zeichnen sich durch besondere Größe aus. Pilger kehren nach Verrichtung ihrer Opfer und Gebete auf dem Rückweg oft hier ein, um einen Imbiß zu sich zu nehmen.

Auch in der Neustadt sind Restaurants das kennzeichnende Element. Sie machen die Hälfte aller hier vorhandenen Geschäfte aus und dienen der Versorgung der Pilger und Besucher mit fertigen Speisen und Getränken. 1970 verteilten sich die ‚hotels' in der Neustadt auf drei Punkte:

a) auf die Neubaublöcke (sog. ‚New Town'), heute eine sehr schlechte Geschäftslage, da die Hauptzahl der Pilger noch im alten Kataragama versorgt wird;

b) auf das Areal gegenüber dem Busbahnhof. Sie wurden vorwiegend zwischen 1955 und 1961 errichtet;

c) auf den Uferstreifen oberhalb der Brücke und um den Parkplatz.

Diese Restaurants scheinen noch aus der Vorkriegszeit zu stammen. Sie dürfen mit zu den lukrativsten Geschäften der Ortschaft gezählt werden. Eine besondere Ausweitung und Belebung erfuhren sie, seit die Badetreppen am rechten Ufer des Menik Ganga (1965?) beiderseits der Brücke gebaut wurden.

Neben den Restaurants fällt in der Neustadt die hohe Zahl der Gemischtwarengeschäfte auf. Sie ist zweifellos damit zu erklären, daß sich hier auf dem rechten Flußufer die Pilger, die nicht in ein *madam* ziehen, lagern und in den Geschäften die zahlreichen Zutaten zu den selbstbereiteten Speisen, den ‚curries', kaufen. Zu erwähnen sind noch die Friseure und die Reparaturwerkstätten für Autos und Fahrräder. Bei letzteren handelt es sich um kleinere Betriebe. Ihre Zahl läßt erkennen, daß ein gewisser Prozentsatz der Pilger mit eigenen Fahrzeugen — Pkw, Lkw oder mit Bussen privater Gesellschaften — nach Kataragama reist, deutet aber auch auf den baufälligen Zustand der meisten dieser Fahrzeuge hin.

Gering ist die Zahl der Geschäfte in der Neustadt, die Artikel für Kultzwecke anbieten. Sie konzentrieren sich auf den Parkplatz oder in der Nähe der Brücke. Die übrigen Geschäfte am rechten Flußufer, die zur normalen Geschäftsausstattung einer Siedlung von der Größe Kataragamas gezählt werden können, weisen eine beträchtliche Vielfalt auf.

Die auffallend hohe Zahl leerer Läden im Neubaublock rührt daher, daß einmal die Räume für weitere Umsiedlungen von Händlern aus dem zukünftigen heiligen Bezirk vorgesehen sind, zum anderen, daß einige Geschäftsleute ihre neuen Läden noch nicht besetzt haben, da sich ihrer Ansicht nach ein Geschäft unter den augenblicklichen Bedingungen nicht rentiert. Sie versuchen, in der Nähe der Pilgerwege eine ‚boutique' aufzuziehen.

c) *Zusätzliche Geschäftsausstattung während des Festes*

Die kurz geschilderte normale Geschäftsausstattung Kataragamas erfährt regelmäßig eine Ausdehnung, sobald die Festzeit im Juli/August herannaht. Dann werden zahlreiche Verkaufsstände errichtet. Eine besonders sprunghafte Zunahme läßt sich bei den Friseuren und den *kāvadi*-Verleihern beobachten. Daneben sollen hier noch drei „Geschäftszweige" vorgestellt werden, von denen zwei für Kataragama, der andere für alle bedeutenden Pilgerstätten in Ceylon als charakteristisch zu gelten haben. Es handelt sich um Getränkeverteiler, den Verkauf heiliger Asche und Bettler.

Zur Festzeit in Kataragama tritt ein besonderer ‚zoning plan‘ für die Benutzung des Menik Ganga in Kraft. Er soll verhindern, daß der Fluß willkürlich und unkontrolliert genutzt wird und schließt sich an die Regelung der britischen Kolonialverwaltung von 1870 an. Seit der Einrichtung eines modernen Wasserversorgungsnetzes spielt der Menik Ganga als Trinkwasserquelle nur mehr eine untergeordnete Rolle. Auch die früher bestehende Gefahr einer Verschmutzung des Flusses durch Rinder ist weitgehend beseitigt, seitdem Ochsen als Zugtiere für den ‚bullock cart‘ oder ‚bullock bandy‘, mit dem früher bessergestellte Pilger von Tissamaharama nach Kataragama reisten, kaum noch Verwendung finden.

In die gewerbliche Nutzung wird der Fluß heute im wesentlichen durch die Friseure und *kāvadi*-Verleiher einbezogen, an die alljährlich zur Festzeit besonders am rechten Ufer des Menik Ganga gewöhnlich 10 × 10 Fuß große Flächen versteigert werden.

An den Friseuren, auf die hier zunächst eingegangen werden soll, läßt sich am besten die religiöse Funktion des an sich profanen Berufes darstellen. Sie hängt mit dem hinduistischen Brauch zusammen, das Haar eines neugeborenen Kindes einer von den Eltern ausgewählten Gottheit zu opfern, um dadurch den Schutz des Gottes für das Kind zu erhalten. Um das Gelübde zu vollziehen, werden Kinder manchmal auf die Pilgerschaft mitgenommen, sei es nach Kataragama, zum Adam's Peak oder sogar nach Indien. Angeblich ist das Gelübde besonders gut erfüllt, wenn das Haar beim Schneiden am Heiligtum in das Wasser eines heiligen Flusses fällt. Neben Kindern, nach Aussagen Einheimischer besonders männlicher, unterziehen sich aber auch Erwachsene dieser Handlung.

Die heute bestehende Regelung der Versteigerung von Stellflächen, besonders für Friseurstände, ‚barber saloons‘, wurde erst vor einigen Jahren eingeführt. Davor war es üblich, die Flächen dem Pächter aus dem vorangegangenen Jahr zur erneuten Übernahme anzubieten. Die Verwaltung fand jedoch bald heraus, daß die Umsätze in den temporären Friseurständen ganz erheblich waren. Daraufhin wurden die Ausgangspreise für die Versteigerung aufgrund von Schätzungen des vorjährigen Umsatzes festgelegt. Trotz einer fortlaufenden Erhöhung der Ausgangspreise bei der Versteigerung brachte der ständig steigende Pilgerstrom immer noch so großen Gewinn, daß bei einzelnen, günstig gelegenen Blöcken für die zweiwöchige Veranstaltung mitunter die kaum glaubliche Summe von Rps. 25000 gezahlt wurde, wobei allerdings zweifelhaft ist, daß diese Summe für einen einzelnen ‚block‘ von 10 × 10 Fuß entrichtet werden mußte.

Mit dem Anstieg des Auktionspreises erhöhten sich dann allerdings auch die Preise für die gebotenen Leistungen. Bis um 1962 bestand noch eine sehr starke Konkurrenz der Friseure um die Blöcke, obwohl die Verwaltung durchschnittlich bis zu Rps. 1000 als Ausgangspreis der Versteigerung ansetzt. Damals verlangten Friseure bis zu Rps. 5 für einen

Haarschnitt, es wurden aber auch Preise bis Rps. 15–20 für einen Haarschnitt und Rps. 3–5 für eine Rasur gefordert[37]).

Aufgrund von Protesten seitens der Öffentlichkeit wurden schließlich die Ausgangspreise für die Versteigerung auf Rps. 400 und die Preise für einen Haarschnitt auf Rps. 2.50 festgesetzt. Um bei diesen Reglementierungen trotzdem noch ein gutes Geschäft machen zu können, sprachen sich die Friseure untereinander ab und boten nicht mehr als Rps. 401 für einen Stellplatz.

Auffällig ist, daß die meisten der während der Festzeit in Kataragama tätigen Friseure von der Ostküste und von Jaffna stammen, auch wenn sie zum Fest in Kataragama nicht direkt von dort kommen, sondern von Buttala, Wellawaya oder anderen Siedlungen der südlichen Trockenzone, wo sie ihrer Tätigkeit nachgehen. Herkunftsort (z. B. Akkaraipattu, Karaitivu), z. T. auch ihre Namen, weisen auf Tamilen, d. h. Hindus, hin. Der Brauch, das Haar zu opfern, ist, wie zuvor dargelegt wurde, ein Bestandteil des hinduistischen Glaubens.

Für die auf den Blöcken errichteten ‚barber saloons‘ werden dann wiederum Friseure angeworben. Nach Unterlagen im District's Revenue Office in Buttala gab es 1960 in Kataragama 11 ‚barber saloons‘, an denen mindestens 17 „Manager“ beteiligt waren. 1966 waren es 10 Friseurstände. Gewöhnlich arbeiteten in jedem Stand 10–15 Mann, die eigentlich zu den Belegschaften von Plantagen des Hochlandes gehören und als Pilger oder aus Verdienstgründen während der Festzeit nach Kataragama ziehen. In Kataragama hat ihre Herkunft von den Plantagen zur Folge, daß sie von mit ihnen befreundeten oder bekannten Pilgern aufgesucht werden, die sie von ihrem, außerhalb der Festzeit, täglichen Arbeitsbereich kennen. Durch diesen Zusammenhang ist ihnen ein bestimmter Kundenkreis gesichert. Für jeden Haarschnitt erhalten die Friseure Rps. 0.80–1.00, den Rest verdienen die Manager, die Pächter der Blöcke.

Das zweite hier zu behandelnde Geschäft mit religiöser Funktion ist der *kāvadi*-Verleih. Bei den *kāvadis* handelt es sich um mit Pfauenfedern geschmückte, jochähnliche Bögen, die von den Gläubigen während eines Rundganges durch den Ort zwischen dem Haupttempel und dem Tempel der Vaḷḷiammā auf der Schulter getragen werden. Unterbrochen wird der von einer Musikgruppe begleitete Rundgang vor jedem Schrein, wo dann unter immer schneller werdender Musik ein manchmal ekstatischer ‚peacock dance‘ (Pfauentanz) von den *kāvadi*-Trägern aufgeführt wird.

Die *kāvadi*, die in indischen Legenden um Gott Skanda erwähnt werden, fehlen in den ceylonesischen um Gott Kataragama. Die Verwendung der *kāvadi*, eigentlich eine indische Tradition, wurde von hinduistischen Pilgern und Svamis, d. h. frommen Männern, erst auf Ceylon eingeführt und ist so nach Kataragama gekommen.

---

[37]) Im Jahre 1970 kostete in Ceylon ein Haarschnitt zwischen Rps. 1–1.50.

Die Entstehung der Legende um das Joch kann bei Jagadissa Ayyar (1922, S. 476) oder Wirz (1954, S. 162) nachgelesen werden. Auf sie wird hier nicht weiter eingegangen, da sie keinerlei direkte Beziehung zu dem Heiligtum hat.

Während zur Zeit der Kartierung — also außerhalb der Festzeit — lediglich zwei *kāvadi*-Verleiher im Ort anwesend waren, steigt ihre Zahl während des Festes ganz beträchtlich an. 1961 waren in Kataragama 43 *kāvadi*-Stände zugelassen. Sie standen fast alle am rechten Ufer des Menik Ganga. Über einen direkten Zusammenhang zwischen der *kāvadi* und dem Wasser ließ sich, wie z. B. beim Haareschneiden, nichts in Erfahrung bringen. Daß es sich beim Verleih von *kāvadis*, der meist von Svamis betrieben wird, um ein recht einträgliches Geschäft handelt, ist daraus zu ersehen, daß das Leihen einer *kāvadi* für einen 45–60 Minuten dauernden Rundtanz durch den Ort für jeden Teilnehmer Rps. 3 kostet. Gewöhnlich aber nehmen ganze Gruppen, Familien, an dem Rundtanz teil. Jeder Einzeltänzer, aber auch jede *kāvadi*-Gruppe wird von einer Musikgruppe begleitet. Über Zahl und Herkunft der Musiker konnte nichts in Erfahrung gebracht werden. In den Verleih eingeschlossen sind, sofern von den Gläubigen verlangt, auch das Durchstechen der Haut an den Armen, auf dem Rücken und auf der Brust mit silbernen Pfeilen und das Durchbohren der Wangen. Nach der Prozession werden den Beteiligten die Pfeile, auch die mitunter durch die Haut getriebenen Haken entfernt und die Wunden mit heiliger Asche eingerieben.

Mit dieser heiligen Asche wird ein anderes Geschäft gemacht. Viele Pilger, aber auch zahlreiche Priester nehmen auf dem Rückweg von Kataragama Asche mit nach Hause. Die Priester verwenden sie über das Jahr hinweg in ihren Tempeln zu rituellen Zwecken. Normalerweise erwirbt man die Asche auf dem Wedahitikanda, neuerdings ist sie aber auch im Ort erhältlich (Cartman, 1957, S. 123; Wirz, 1954, S. 161).

Nach Wirz besteht unter den Pilgern der Glaube, daß sich diese Asche im Lauf der Jahrhunderte als Rest verbrannten Kampfers, der den Göttern als Weihrauchopfer dargebracht wurde, auf dem Berg angesammelt hat. Sehr wahrscheinlich handelt es sich aber um eine kaolinartige Erde. Sie wird sich aus dem kristallinen Kalkstein, der in die aus Charnockiten bestehenden Gesteine der Kataragama-Berge eingebettet ist, gebildet haben. Zu Beginn der Festzeit werden davon beträchtliche Mengen in den Ort gebracht, zerkleinert und dann den Pilgern als heilige Asche verkauft.

Kurz sei noch auf die beiden anderen genannten „Geschäftszweige“ hingewiesen, das kostenlose Verteilen von Getränken (Tee oder Wasser) und das Betteln. Die Verteiler von Getränken, die dafür bei der Verwaltung ebenfalls eine Lizenz einholen müssen, stellen sich meist an den Wegen auf, die von Kataragama zu den anderen heiligen Bezirken führen: nach Sella Kataragama und zum Wedahitikanda. Die Stände (1960: 10 Stück) sind eine Notwendigkeit; denn über einige Meilen gibt es bei sengender Hitze keine Wasserstellen. Als Gegenleistung erwarten die

Getränkeverteiler eine Geldgabe. Dieser Dienst muß recht lohnend sein, sonst gäbe es nicht diese Einrichtung.

Das Betteln ist ein besonderer „Geschäftszweig“ in Kataragama; es gehört heute bereits zu den ständigen Einrichtungen des Heiligtums. Alljährlich mit den großen Festen strömen zu den bereits dauernd anwesenden Bettlern aus allen Teilen der Insel, vereinzelt sogar aus Indien, Bettler in großer Zahl nach Kataragama. 1956 wurden in dem Heiligtum am Menik Ganga über 700 Bettler gezählt (Sessional Paper 1956–XI). Man begegnet ihnen nicht nur entlang der Wege zu den heiligen Stätten, nach dem Untersuchungsbericht traf man auf sie sogar auf beiden Seiten des Weges nach Sella Kataragama, der durch dichten Dschungel führt. Bei der 1956 durchgeführten Untersuchung traf man neben Krüppeln, die wohl kaum eine andere Möglichkeit zum Gelderwerb gefunden hätten und die sich ohne Hilfe von Gesunden überhaupt nicht fortbewegen konnten, viele mit vorgetäuschter Invalidität. Es existierten in Kataragama regelrechte Bettlerorganisationen, deren Manager in dem Bericht als ‚beggar mudalalis‘ (*mudalali* = „reicher Mann“) bezeichnet wurden.

Einer dieser mudalalis leitete eine Gruppe von über 200 Bettlern in Kataragama. Die einzelnen Gruppen hatten festgelegte Bezirke, aus denen nicht organisierte Bettler oder Angehörige anderer Gruppen vertrieben wurden.

9. Kataragama als Ausgangspunkt zur Erschließung des Umlandes

Seit dem Niedergang des singhalesischen Reiches im Tiefland der Insel bildete nach den vorliegenden Unterlagen Kataragama die am weitesten nach Südosten vorgeschobene Siedlung, die stärker in das Geschehen der Insel einbezogen und mit den Zentren der Macht im Hochland durch eine Straße verbunden war. Um die Siedlung herum dehnte sich meilenweit Dschungel aus. Trotz der seit dem letzten Jahrhundert immer stärker fortschreitenden Angliederung des Ortes an das kulturelle und wirtschaftliche Leben hat er bis heute noch den Charakter eines, wenn auch gut ausgebauten und versorgten Vorpostens und wird ihn wohl noch für einige Zeit behalten (Abb. 2, 7 und Luftbild).

Nach Osten wird eine zukünftige Ausdehnung des Siedlungsraumes um Kataragama durch das Naturschutzgebiet, dessen westliche Grenze dem Menik Ganga folgt, eingeschränkt. Eine Entwicklung ist also nur westlich dieser Linie möglich. Ansätze dafür sind zweifellos vorhanden. Zieht man den desolaten Entwicklungsstand des Heiligtums aus der Zeit vor 30 Jahren heran, so muß die heutige Situation bereits als ein großer Fortschritt angesehen werden. Der Aufschwung des Heiligtums Kataragama blieb nicht nur auf den Ort beschränkt. 1961 begann die Regierung entlang der Straße nach Tissamaharama ein ‚highland project‘ zu entwickeln, das die Ansiedlung von 353 Siedlern auf je zwei acres nicht bewässerbarem Land zum Ziel hatte. Ein weiterer Ausbau in der näheren Umgebung des Heiligtums fand in Karawila bei Sella Kataragama statt, wo 1968 eine Fläche von 96 acres bewässerbaren Reislandes unterhalb des hier gelegenen Tanks ebenfalls an Siedler übergeben worden ist.

Anfang der 60er Jahre begann auch die Forstverwaltung ein Projekt, das im Abstand von knapp einem Kilometer zu beiden Seiten der Straße Kataragama-Tissamaharama zur streifenförmigen Aufforstung mit Teak (*Tectona grandis*) führte (Gesamtfläche: 600 acres).

Eine Erweiterung des Siedlungslandes werden in Zukunft wahrscheinlich die Straßen- und Wegebauten bringen, die von Sella Kataragama auf beiden Seiten des Menik Ganga nach Norden und auch nach Westen das Land öffnen helfen. Allerdings muß der Versuch einer Vergabe von großen Landflächen an finanzstarke Gesellschaften zur Urbarmachung und damit vielleicht auch als Anreiz für Siedler, der seit 1967 eingeleitet worden war, als gescheitert angesehen werden. Schon vor dem Regierungswechsel im Jahre 1970, mit dem auch diese großen Projekte endgültig zum Stillstand gelangten, waren die meisten der Unternehmungen nach Ausschlagen der Holzvorräte und kurzfristiger Nutzung durch Brandrodung aufgegeben worden.

Den Fortschritt der Besiedlung in der näheren Umgebung des Heiligtums lassen aber einmal die Angaben über den starken Anstieg der Bevölkerung seit 1935 (Tab. 5), zum anderen Zahlen aus einer Statistik über das Ausmaß von Chena (Brandrodung) im Raum um Kataragama erkennen (Tab. 7).

Tab. 7: Chena-Nutzung im Raume Kataragama

Siedlung	Chena auf Staatsland (‚Crown Land') 1969/70 in acres: mit Erlaubnis	ohne Erlaubnis
Kataragama	53	315
Detagamuwa	29	175
Detagamuwa Janapadaya[38]	16	100
Mailagamuwa	18	125
Karawila	125	725
Sella Kataragama	25	150

Quelle: Chena-Survey of the Monaragala District, Maha-Periode 1969/70, Dept. of Census and Statistics, Colombo (unveröffentlicht)

10. Schluß

Das Heiligtum Kataragama kann als Beispiel dafür dienen, wie sich im Laufe von etwa 100 Jahren aus der Verbindung politischer, wirtschaftlicher, religiöser und anderer Interessen in kolonialer und nachkolonialer

[38]) *janapadaya* = ‚scheme', Entwicklungsprojekt; an der Straße nach Tissamaharama gelegen.

Zeit eine Entwicklung herausbildete, die zunächst zur Hervorhebung eines an und für sich mehr regionalen Heiligtums der südlichen Trockenzone und schließlich seit einigen Jahren zu seiner Eingliederung in das kulturelle und wirtschaftliche Gesamtgefüge der Tropeninsel Ceylon führte.

Aus diesem komplexen Vorgang sei nochmals auf zwei Aspekte hingewiesen, die als Ende und Anfang von Entwicklungstendenzen betrachtet werden können: einmal der vorläufige Schlußpunkt in der Entwicklung des religiösen Zentrums, zum anderen ein Beginn für die zukünftige wirtschaftliche Erschließung des Raumes um Kataragama.

Staatliche Initiativen haben dazu geführt, daß in Kataragama Entflechtung und „ordentliche" Trennung von Heiligtum und Geschäft vorbereitet wurden und z.T. auch schon durchgeführt worden sind. Ohne Zweifel wird das Heiligtum durch dieses Vorhaben an Ruhe und Erhabenheit gewinnen, gewiß geht aber auch ein Stück orientalischen Lebens verloren. Beim Abschluß dieses Prozesses wird Kataragama dann dem großen Pilger- und Wallfahrtszentrum im Norden der Insel, der alten Königsstadt Anuradhapura, ähneln, wo ebenfalls Stadt und Heiligtum, zuvor ineinander verschachtelt, getrennt wurden.

Der zweite Aspekt, unter dem die Entwicklung des Heiligtums Kataragama gesehen werden muß, steht im Zusammenhang mit den Erschließungsversuchen in den „Entwicklungsgebieten" der Insel, als welche die zwei Drittel der die gesamte Insel einnehmende Trockenzone zu betrachten sind. Spontane private und staatlich gelenkte Erschließungen in größerem Umfang setzten besonders in der südlichen Trockenzone erst nach dem letzten Krieg ein, verspätet im Vergleich mit anderen Landesteilen, vor allem dem Norden, wo mit Erschließungsansätzen in größerem Umfang bereits vor etwa 100 Jahren begonnen wurde.

Die Bewältigung einiger großer Probleme Ceylons, z.B. die Umverteilung der Bevölkerung aus der dicht besiedelten Feuchtzone, die, grob umrissen, die Südwestküste und das Hochland umfaßt, eine Begegnung des Landmangels und der Arbeitslosigkeit und die Erzeugung zusätzlicher Nahrungsmittel, lassen sich in Ceylon nur durch die Erschließung der Trockenzone bewältigen. Sie könnten in der südlichen Trockenzone neben den nur kurz erwähnten privaten und staatlichen Erschließungsansätzen indirekt durch die Förderung der Pilgerstätte Kataragama vorangetrieben werden.

Kataragama könnte einmal als Stütze für die dringend notwendigen Urbarmachungen in der Trockenzone dienen, es könnte auch, wie die Ansätze erkennen lassen, zu einem weiteren Kern für die Erschließungsbemühungen werden und somit neben seiner geistigen und religiösen Bedeutung seine, wie es scheint, durch die gesamte Geschichte hindurch gehaltene, zumindest in diesem Teil der Insel, bestimmende Bedeutung wieder zurückgewinnen.

Literaturverzeichnis

Administration Report of the General Manager, Ceylon Government Railway for 1966–67; Colombo (?), Jan. 1969, (B. D. Rampala).

Ameresekere, H. E.: The Kataragama God, shrines and legends; in: Ceylon Literary Register, vol. 1, no. 7, 1931, S. 289–292 und vol. 1, no. 8, 1931, S. 356–360.

Arunachalam, P.: The worship of Muruka or Skanda (the Kataragama God); in: J. Roy. Asiat. Soc., Ceylon Branch, vol. XXIX, no. 77, 1924 (1925), S. 234–261.

Asangananda, Swami: Kataragama — the holy of holies of Sri Lanka, Colombo 1964, 4. Aufl.; Nachdruck aus: The Kalyana-Kalpataru, Gorakhpur 1935.

Ayyar, P. V. J.: South Indian shrines, Madras 1922.

Baker, S. W.: The rifle and the hound in Ceylon, London 1857, 2. Aufl.

Bastiampillai, B.: The administration of Sir William Gregory, Governor of Ceylon 1872–77, (The Ceylon Historical Journal, vol. 12) Dehiwala 1968.

Bechert, H.: Buddhismus, Staat und Gesellschaft in den Ländern des Theravada-Buddhismus, Bd. I: Allgemeines und Ceylon, Frankfurt 1966.

—: Eine alte Gottheit in Ceylon und Südindien; in: Beiträge zur Geistesgeschichte Indiens, Festschrift für Erich Frauwallner, Wiener Zeitschrift für die Kunde Süd- und Ostasiens, Bd. XII–XIII (1968/69), 1968, S. 33–42.

—: The cult of Skandakumara in the religious history of South India and Ceylon; Vortrag: IIIe Conférence Internationale d'Études Tamoules, Paris 1970, 8 S. mimeo.

—: Contradictions in Sinhalese Buddhism; in: Contributions to Asian Studies, vol. IV, 1973, S. 7–17.

Brohier, R. L.: Ancient irrigation works, Part 3 (Western, Southern and Eastern areas of the island), Colombo 1935.

C.A.R. (Ceylon Administration Reports), Public Record Office, Dokumente des Colonial Office (C.O.), London
1871 (Colombo 1872; C.O. 57/54)
1873 („ 1874; C.O. 57/62)
1874 („ 1875; C.O. 57/63)
1877 („ 1878; C.O. 57/72)
1906 („ 1907; C.O. 57/166)
1919 („ 1920; C.O. 57/200)
1920 („ 1922; C.O. 57/201)
1923 („ 1925; C.O. 57/210)
1924 („ 1926; C.O. 57/213)
1925 („ 1927; C.O. 57/216).

Carter, H. F.: Report on "Kataragama Fever"; its nature, causes, and control; Sessional Paper XXXVII - 1925, Colombo.

Cartman, J.: Hinduism in Ceylon, Colombo 1957.

Clothey, F.: Skanda-Ṣaṣṭi: a festival in Tamil India; in: History of Religions, vol. 8, no. 1, 1968, S. 236–259.

Cook, E. K.: Ceylon; its geography, its resources and its people, Madras, Bombay, Calcutta, London 1953.

Covington, M.: Hindu Kataragama; in: The Orientalist, vol. III, 1888–89, S. 149–156.

Davy, J.: An account of the interior of Ceylon and of its inhabitants with travels in that island, London 1821, (The Ceylon Historical Journal, vol. 16) Dehiwala 1969.

Domrös, M.: Untersuchungen der Niederschlagshäufigkeit auf Ceylon nach Jahresabschnitten; in: Jahrbuch des Südasien-Instituts 1967/68, Bd. II, Wiesbaden 1968, S. 70–84.

Evers, H.-D.: Monks, priests and peasants. A study of Buddhism and social structure in Central Ceylon, Leiden 1972.

Festing, R. A. G.: Administration report of the Government Agent, Province of Uva, for 1923; in: C.A.R. 1923.

—: Administration report of the Government Agent, Province of Uva, for 1924; in: C.A.R. 1924.

Final Report on the Area of Topo Preliminary Plan No. 25 comprising the villages of Kataragama, Detagamuwa and Karawilagama and its settlement by the Land Settlement Department; Acting Settlement Officer: Wedderburn, M. M.; Sept. 18, 1923.

Geiger, W.: Culture of Ceylon in mediaeval times, Wiesbaden 1960.

Gill, C. A.: Report on the malaria epidemic in Ceylon in 1934–35 together with a scheme for the control of malaria in the island; Sessional Paper XXIII – 1935, Colombo.

Godakumbura, C. E.: The Kirivehera of Kataragama; in: Ceylon Today, vol. XII, no. 4, 1963, S. 24–29.

—: Kataragama and Kirivehera; in: Ceylon Today, vol. XIV, no. 6, 1965, S. 7–14.

Goonewardene, E. T.: The story of Kataragama: a result of research; in: The Maha Bodhi, vol. 60, no. 8, 2496/1952, S. 290–293.

Gordon-Cumming, C. F.: Two happy years in Ceylon, Edinburgh und London, 2 Bde., 1892, 2. Aufl.

Gunaratna, N.: Kataragama planning scheme; in: Ceylon Today, vol. 11, no. 6, 1962, S. 23–24.

Guruge, A. W. P.: Kataragama, a jungle shrine; in: Ceylon Today, vol. 16, no. 8, 1967, S. 17–19.

Hassan, M. C. A.: The story of the Kataragama mosque and shrine, Colombo 1968.

Hausherr, K.: Traditioneller Brandrodungsfeldbau (Chena) und moderne Erschließungsprojekte in der „Trockenzone" im Südosten Ceylons. Versuche der Wiederherstellung alten Kulturlandes um Buttala, Monaragala Distrikt; in: Landschaftsökologische Forschungen auf Ceylon, Geogr. Zeitschrift, Beihefte, 27, Wiesbaden 1971 (a), S. 167–204.

—: Bericht über Untersuchungen auf Ceylon 1970; in: Arbeitskreis Ceylon-Forschung. Zweite Arbeitssitzung über Ceylon-Forschung in Reinhausen bei Göttingen am 10.–12. Juni 1971 (b), Anlage 4, S. 25–36, masch.schriftlich.

Hellings, R. B.: Administration report of the Government Agent, Southern Province, for 1919; in: C.A.R. 1919.

Jagadiswarananda: Pre-Buddhistic Hindu shrines in Ceylon; in: The Calcutta Review, June 1933, S. 285–295.

King, A. A.: Report upon the Kataragama pilgrimage 1877; in: C.A.R. 1877.

Knox, R.: An historical relation of Ceylon, London 1681, (The Ceylon Historical Journal, vol. 5) Dehiwala 1966, 2. Aufl.

Kurukkal, K. K.: A study of the Karttikeya-cult as reflected in the epics and the puranas; in: University of Ceylon Review, vol. XIX, no. 2, 1961, S. 131–137.

Mapping Out Report of Final Topo Preliminary Plan No. 25 Kataragama, Detagamuwa and Karawilagama, Sept. 2, 1935.

Marby, H.: Tea in Ceylon. An attempt at a regional and temporal differentiation of the tea growing areas in Ceylon, Geoecological Research, vol. 1, Wiesbaden 1972.

Meaden, H. A.: Note on the kāvadi ceremony among the Hindus in Ceylon; in: J. Roy. Asiat. Soc. (Great Britain and Ireland), 1908, S. 848–850.

Murty, J. O'K.: (Bericht über Kataragama) unter: Report of the Government Agent, Province of Uva, for 1906; in: C.A.R. 1906.

Navaratnam, C. S.: A short history of Hinduism in Ceylon and three essays on the Tamils, Jaffna 1964.

Nicholas, C. W.: Historical topography of ancient and mediaeval Ceylon; in: J. Roy. Asiat. Soc., Ceylon Branch, N.S. vol. VI, Special Number, 1963.

Obeyesekere, G.: Religious symbolism and political change in Ceylon; in: Modern Ceylon Studies, vol. I, no. 1, 1970, S. 43–63.

O'Brien: (Bericht über Kataragama) unter: Report on the Hambantota District for 1871; in: C.A.R. 1871.

Peiris, W.: The esala festival at Kataragama; in: Ceylon Today, vol. 8, no. 7, 1959, S. 17–20.

Pelzer, K. J.: Die Arbeiterwanderungen in Südostasien. Eine wirtschafts- und bevölkerungsgeographische Untersuchung, Hamburg 1935.

P(erera ?), S. G.: Adam's Peak; in: The Ceylon Antiquary and Literary Register, vol. V, pt. 1, 1919, S. 6–11.

Pieris, P. E.: Ribeiro's history of Ceilao with a summary of De Barros, De Couto, Antonio Bocarro and the Documentos Remettidos with the Parangi Hatane and Kostantinu Hatane, Colombo 1909.

Pytlik, G.: Der Reisanbau im unteren Kirindi Oya-Becken. Analyse einer Reisbaulandschaft im Südosten der Insel Ceylon, Diss. nat. wiss. Gesamtfak. Heidelberg 1972.

Raghavan, M. D.: Kataragama—the sylvan shrine of Ceylon; in: Ceylon Today, vol. 5, no. 4, 1956, S. 6–11.

Rasanayagam, C.: Kataragama, Colombo 1935; Nachdruck aus: Hindu Organ, Jaffna o. J.

Report of the Ceylon Transport Board 1966/67, Colombo 1969.

Report of the Temple Land Commissioners, on the progress and results of the commission, from its constitution, in Feb. 1857, to the end of 1858; Ceylon-Minutes of the Legislative Council 1858/59 (C. O. 57/26); auch in: Evers, 1972: Appendix 2, S. 112–121.

Report on Wellawaya Division (um 1967), District Revenue Officer (D.R.O.) Office Buttala, masch.schriftlich (singhalesisch).

Rodenwaldt, E.: Die Malariaepidemie auf Ceylon 1934/35 als geomedizinisches Problem; in: Koloniale Rundschau, 28. Jg., 1937, S. 330–344.

Sarasin, F.: Reisen und Forschungen in Ceylon, Basel 1939.

Schweinfurth, U.: Die Teelandschaft im Hochland der Insel Ceylon als Beispiel für den Landschaftswandel; in: Heidelberger Geogr. Arbeiten 15, Heidelberger Studien zur Kulturgeographie, Festgabe für G. Pfeifer, Wiesbaden 1966, S. 297–310.

Senaveratne, J. M.: Sex in offspring—the pumsavana ceremony; in: The Ceylon Antiquary and Literary Register, vol. V, 1919, S. 91–92.

Sessional Paper XVI–1873: Kataragama pilgrimage bill, Colombo.

Sessional Paper XI–1956: Report on the beggar problem in Ceylon, Colombo.

Spittel, R. L.: Far-off things, Colombo 1933.

Steele, T.: Memorandum on Kataragama festival 1874, unter: Report on the Hambantota District for 1874; in: C.A.R. 1874.

Swettenham: Report on the Kataragama festival of 1873, unter: Annual report on the Hambantota District for 1873; in: C.A.R. 1873.

Thaine, R. N.: Administrative report of the Government Agent, Province of Uva, for 1920; in: C.A.R. 1920.

Weerasooria, W. S.: The Nattukottai Chettiar merchant bankers in Ceylon, Dehiwala 1973.

Wesumperuma, D.: The evictions under the paddy tax, and their impact on the peasantry of Walapane, 1882–1885; in: The Ceylon Journal of Historical and Social Studies, vol. 10, nos. 1–2, 1967, S. 131–148.

White, H.: Manual of the Province of Uva, Colombo 1893.

Wikkramatileke, R.: Climate in the south-east quadrant of Ceylon; in: Malayan Journal of Tropical Geography, vol. 8, 1956, S. 55–72.

—: Southeast Ceylon: trends and problems in agricultural settlement, Dept. of Geography, Research Paper no. 83, Univ. of Chicago, Chicago 1963.

Wirz, P.: Die kultische Bedeutung der Kokosnuß bei den Singhalesen; in: Verhandlungen der Naturforschenden Gesellschaft in Basel, Bd. LI, 1. Teil, 1940.

—: Ceylon — Exorzismus und Heilkunde, Bern 1941.

—: Kataragama, die heiligste Stätte in Ceylon; in: Verhandlungen der Naturforschenden Gesellschaft in Basel, Bd. LV, 1954, S. 123–177; Übersetzung: Kataragama—the holiest place in Ceylon, Colombo 1966.

Woolf, L.: Diaries in Ceylon 1908–1911. Records of a colonial administrator being the official diaries maintained by Leonard Woolf while Assistant Government Agent of the Hambantota District, Ceylon, during the period August 1908 to May 1911; in: The Ceylon Historical Journal, vol. 9, July 1959 to April 1960, nos. 1–4, Dehiwala 1962.

Weitere Literatur über Kataragama in:

Goonetileke, H. A. I.: A bibliography of Ceylon, 2 Bde., Bibliotheca Asiatica 5, Zug 1970.

Kosala-Bimba-Vaṇṇanā

By RICHARD F. GOMBRICH

Introduction

"The Laudatory Account of the Kosalan Image" (KBV) is a Pali text in both prose and verse from mediaeval Ceylon. It is an aetiological myth, providing justification for the practice of making Buddha images. Pasenadi, King of Kosala, a canonical figure, calls on the Buddha one day only to find that he is out. When he repeats the call the next day he mentions his disappointment, and asks if the Buddha would allow an image of himself to be set up at his monastery to provide against such contingencies: visitors not finding the Buddha could then worship him in effigy. The Buddha not only agrees, but declares that the merit to be acquired by making a Buddha image of any size or material is incalculably great. The king has an image made of sandal-wood and set in a gorgeous shrine, and invites the Buddha and his monks. When the Buddha arrives, the image begins to rise and greet him; the Buddha stops it and predicts a long life for it. The earth quakes and other miracles of that order mark the moment. After a seven-day donation of food to the monks, King Pasenadi requests the Buddha to tell him what merit he has acquired, and Ānanda, the Buddha's favourite disciple, asks also to be told what merit lies in copying a Buddhist text. The Buddha responds to Ānanda's question with a series of verses: copyists and image-makers will not be reborn in unpleasant states, but will be reborn, free from congenital defects, in good families, and lead prosperous lives. Ultimately they will attain nirvana. Five thousand of the listeners attain nirvana on the spot. The Buddha and his company are escorted back to the Jetavana monastery. The next day the king has the image in its jewelled shrine installed there.

When, at the very beginning of the fifth century A. D., Fa Hsien visited Śrāvastī, the scene of this story, he heard and recorded the story like this:

"When Buddha went up to heaven for ninety days to preach the Faith to his mother, king Prasenajit, longing to see him, caused to be carved in sandalwood from the Bull's-head mountain an image of Buddha and placed it where Buddha usually sat. Later on, when Buddha returned to the shrine, the image straightway quitted the seat and came forth to receive him. Buddha cried out, 'Return to your seat; after my disappearance you shall be the model for the four classes of those in search of spiritual truth.' At this, the image went back to the seat. It was the very first of all such images, and is that which later ages have copied. Buddha then moved to a small shrine on the south side, at a spot about twenty paces away from the image."[1])

I know of no other reference to this story outside Ceylon, but it would be surprising if none existed. Perhaps further research will produce other versions, and throw light on our text.

Our text cannot be close in date to the first Buddha images in Ceylon; in fact it probably post-dates them by at least a millennium. The Mahāvaṃsa (xxxvii, 102) tells us that in the reign of King Mahānāma (334-362) his younger son Jeṭṭha-Tissa carved an ivory image of the Bodhisattva. This is worth mention because it is nearly a contemporary record. But the Buddha image in Ceylon is much older. We may not believe that the „great stone image" which the Mahāvaṃsa several times refers to and which Fa Hsien perhaps saw early in the fifth century had in fact been made for King Devānampiya-Tissa (247–207 B. C.). But there seems to be little reason to doubt the record that King Duṭṭha-Gāmaṇī (101–77 B. C.) towards the end of his reign had a golden Buddha-image put inside the Mahācetiya (now known as the Ruvanvälisāya) (Mahāvaṃsa xxx, 72–3).

At the symposium my colleagues objected that the Mahāvaṃsa account of the shrine which King Duṭṭha-Gāmaṇī had put inside the Ruvanvälisāya was not credible, on two grounds: it is not in the earlier chronicle, the Dīpavaṃsa; and the mention of a Buddha image must be an anachronism, as no Indian Buddha image is dated so early. This is of course the *idée reçue* among art historians. The Ruvanvälisāya is still in worship and cannot be excavated, so the matter cannot be finally settled. But what is the chronicle's probable source at this point? Like many Sinhalese since his day, the king kept, or caused to be kept, a record of his meritorious deeds, a *puñña-potthaka*. When he was on his deathbed he had the book read to him (Mhv. XXXII, 25), and the chronicle quotes a lengthy extract from it. That the quotation is verbatim is unlikely, if only because the book was probably not in Pali verse; but the passage very strongly suggests that the chronicler had access to the book. The Ven. Dr. Walpola Rahula, who drew my attention to this, thinks that the detailed account of the shrine, including the Buddha image, was probably drawn from that book. I agree; and would add that the account is so circumstantial that it somewhat strains credulity to posit that it is sheer invention.

We know of no iconoclastic movement in Ceylon (or elsewhere in Buddhism), and it is obscure what could have given the impetus for the retelling of a story justifying a practice so well established. Perhaps it is significant that chapter XI of the Sad-dhamma-sangaha, a related text

---

1) The Travels of Fa-hsien, trans. H. A. Giles, Cambridge 1923, pp. 30–31. My attention was drawn to this passage by its mention in Dr. Ruelius' paper on the *netrapratiṣṭhāpana* ceremony in this volume.

(see below), begins with the verse: "He who sees my true doctrine (*saddhamma*) sees me, Vakkali; if he does not see the true doctrine, even though he see me, he does not see." This is a versification of a canonical dictum of the Buddha's (Saṃyutta-nikāya III, 120), a dictum with which the most ancient phase of Buddhist art has been thought to harmonize. Possibly some religious teacher or party had made it too popular for the comfort of image-makers, and a counterweight was needed. Certainly its spirit is directly contrary to the spirit of our text.

The KBV has attracted little scholarly attention. Malalasekera made passing mention of it in his Pali Literature of Ceylon (London 1928, p. 246) and repeated the same information in his Dictionary of Pali Proper Names (London 1937). There is no evidence that he had seen the text, and his statement that it is quoted in the Sad-dhamma-sangaha (published in the Journal of the Pali Text Society, 1890, pp. 23–90) is not quite accurate. Chapter X of that work is devoted to describing the merit to be gained from copying or having copied even the smallest part of the three Piṭaka (i. e. the Pali canon), and most of it is in bad verse, probably made worse by textual corruption, which is very close to our work in style, and even in content. Between verses 10 and 11 it says in prose: "The advantages of images, which the Blessed One taught at length in the Kosala-bimba-vaṇṇanā, should be inserted here, and the advantage of writing the three Piṭaka related." There do not seem to be any actual quotations, though some phrases in the verses do recall some phrases in the final sequence of KBV verses. Malalasekera ascribes the Sad-dhamma-sangaha to the fourteenth century, and the KBV, on the basis of this mention, to the thirteenth or fourteenth.

The Sinhalese version of the same story, the Kōsala-bimba-varṇanāva, is slightly better known. It is summarily described by Ananda Coomaraswamy in Mediaeval Sinhalese Art (Broad Campden, Glos., 1908, footnote to p. 71); he calls it "a sixteenth or seventeenth century work in Sinhalese prose." He says that it was recited at the start of the ceremony of painting in the eyes of a Buddha image (*nētra pinkama*); this would account for the frequency of manuscripts of the Sinhalese version. Coomaraswamy was apparently unaware of the existence of our text. The Sinhalese version has been printed in Ceylon at least five times, of the first four of which the last was in 1927. I have not been able to find a copy (there is none in the library of the University of Ceylon at Pērādeṇiya). Professor Bechert has kindly given me a photo-copy of an edition in pamphlet form by M. Sudharmā Karuṇātilaka (Kāgalla, 1939); it consists of just over seven pages of closely printed Sinhalese prose. Dr. Ruelius has provided me with photographs of a manuscript containing a truncated version in Sinhalese prose which includes five of the Pali verses of our text (further details below). I have cursorily inspected some other MSS of Sinhalese versions. They differ widely; moreover, Dr. Ruelius has confirmed my impression that some of them contain Pali verses which are not in our text. The version I have seen which is closest to the Pali as a whole is the Kāgalla pamphlet; in places it is almost a word for word translation. Yet it misses out some passages in the Pali, and amplifies many others almost beyond recognition, inserting innumerable clichés. Just where we hope for help in resolving a crux, this version invariably fails us, omitting the doubtful words or drifting off into vague periphrasis. This need not surprise us. The multiplicity of Sinhalese versions (which contrasts with the unity of the Pali tradition) suggests that they arose on different occasions, and their prolixity corroborates the thesis that they arose from the Pali, not vice versa. There is nothing about their language which would tell against Coomaraswamy's dating, though that may have been little better than a guess. Therefore the author of a Sinhalese version was probably faced with a Pali text already corrupt and obscure at the very points which puzzle us. In any case the status of a given Sinhalese version as independent testimony is bound to be problematic. I fear, therefore, that we can expect little help from Sinhalese versions in establishing our text. The only one which has deserved mention in our apparatus is the Kaṭārangala *sanne*—of which more below.

The KBV is in poor Pali, and devoid of literary merit. The form chosen is that of the Jātaka story, though it is inappropriate to the content. (In fact in Dr. Somadasa's handlist of Ceylon manuscripts (see below) a Sinhalese version is listed with the title Kōsala-bimba-jātakaya.) Like a Jātaka story, the text begins by citing the first words of the first verse, and then says in the standard formula that the Teacher preached this story concerning *x* while staying in the Jetavana monastery. In the Jātakas, the story concerning *x* which follows is a story about one of the Buddha's former lives. Here *x* is the King of Kosala, an older contemporary of the Buddha's, and the story does not concern earlier events; the preaching referred to in the rubric is directed *to* the king, not *about* him. At the end of each Jātaka the Buddha gives the key to (*samodhāneti*) the story, identifying the characters of the past with people in the present; here the same technical term is used, but the "key" is just a summing up: "Meritorious people who desire their own welfare should have a book copied or an image made." The Jātaka form is presumably adopted to convey an impression of canonical authority.

The language contains many solecisms, not all of which are likely to be due to textual corruption. There are several examples of false gender: *vihāra* appears as neuter (p. 289 l. 6), *paṭimā* as neuter (p. 289 l. 24), *phusita* as masculine (p. 290 l. 8), *toraṇa* as masculine (p. 291 l. 11), and *dassento* (p. 291 l. 24) seems to be in agreement with a neuter noun. Some cases are odd: *ṭhapetvā* takes the ablative in *-to* (p. 290 l. 13) and *pūjetvā* governs *Satthu* where one expects *Satthāraṃ* (p. 290 l. 22). Final *anusvāra* is dropped *metri gratia*, leaving no case ending at all (p. 291 l. 19). *Seyyathā* is incorrectly used (p. 290 l. 7, 9, 11) in a context where one can only translate it as "if"; and the same may be said of *yathā* (p. 290 l. 3). As all these forms, and other solecisms, are readily intelligible, I have not often emended against the authority of all the manuscripts; but occasionally one can do so with confidence: the author can hardly have been so incompetent as to write the first person where the second is required (p. 289 l. 20). Unfortunately some of the verses in the final sequence are so corrupt, and the exigencies of the metre so afflict the author's grammar, that one hardly knows what requires emendation.

I first came upon the KBV at Kaṭārangala Raja Mahā Vihāra, Halloluva, near Kandy, through the kindness of the incumbent, the Ven. Meḍērigama Paññāsāra Mahā Thero, who also drew my attention to a manuscript of a Sinhalese paraphrase (*sanne*) of part of the text. I then consulted the handlist of manuscripts in Ceylon[2]) compiled by Dr. K. D. Somadasa, then Librarian of the University of Ceylon at Pērādeṇiya. The publication of the text owes much to the help and interest of these two learned Buddhists. I was able to investigate all the manuscripts listed by Dr. Somadasa as Pali, and two of them turned out to be in Sinhalese. From the handlist I learnt of five manuscripts (including the four which turned out to be the most important) in Sinhalese monasteries, one in the university library at Pērādeṇiya, and one in the British Museum; from W. A. de Silva's Catalogue of Palm Leaf Manuscripts (Colombo 1938) I learnt of three manuscripts in the library of the Colombo Museum. I was able to copy all these ten manuscripts, and also to have copied for me the Kaṭārangala *sanne*.

The sigla and locations of the ten KBV manuscripts are as follows:

K — Kaṭārangala Raja Mahā Vihāra, Halloluva, Central Province.

M — Sangharājārāmaya, Väliviṭa Pansala, Malvatta, Kandy, Central Province.

N — Nāgollē Raja Mahā Vihāra, Bōyagaṇē, North-Western Province. Library no. 135.

C — Colombo Museum. W. A. de Silva no. 2347, library no. Y 11.

P — Pälmadulla Purāṇa Vihāra, Sabaragamuva Province. Library no. 80 in first list.

Z — Colombo Museum. W. A. de Silva no. 2344, library no. $\frac{AV}{7}$.

T — Puṣpārāmaya, Tāvalla, Dummalasūriya, North-Western Province. Library no. 77.

B — British Museum. Neville Collection. Library no. BM Or. 6601 (24).

U — University of Ceylon, Pērādeṇiya. Library no. Univ. MS 153.

Y — Colombo Museum. W. A. de Silva no. 2340, library no. $\frac{85}{K\ 31}$ (963.)

K + M + N + C = *K*   P + Z + T + B + U + Y = *P*

T + B + U + Y = *T*

The manuscripts fall clearly into two groups, and the above sigla are arranged accordingly: the first four listed fall together, and so do the

[2]) Lankāvē Puskola Pot Nāmāvaliya, Colombo, part 1 1959, parts 2 and 3 1964.

last six. I am not certain that any one of the manuscripts is a direct copy of any other, but four pairs seem very close: N is probably descended from M, Z from P, B from T, and Y from U. At least it is clear that the relationships are not the other way, as N, Z, B, Y all have serious gaps. (I reserve the term *lacuna* for a gap caused by damage to the MS; only B and Z have damage, and that is slight.) N, Z, B and Y are unlikely to have much independent value; but the complexity of the situation may be exemplified by pointing out that in one place, on p. 290 footnote 97, N clearly sides with the larger group against KMC. Within the larger group T, B, U and Y constitute a sub-group, of which T is the best (though it is inferior to P). Within the smaller group, K, M and N perhaps constitute a sub-group; C is slightly inferior to K and M (and much more recent) but has a few independent readings of interest. The following chart shows approximate relationships; the lines do not indicate direct and uncontaminated descent.

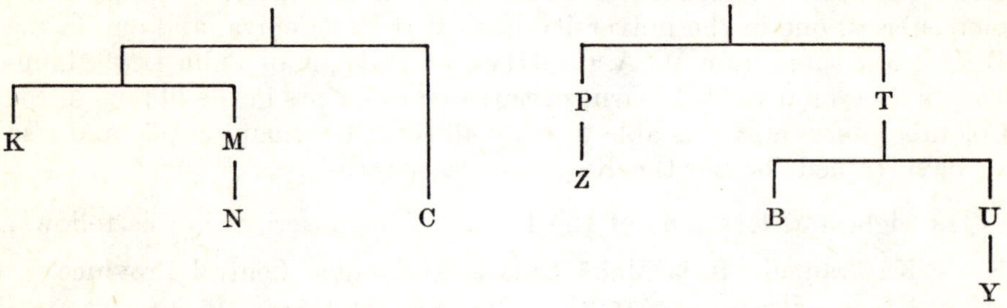

In compiling the apparatus criticus, I have thought it necessary to include every variant, since my work in consulting them all is unlikely soon to be repeated and one cannot foresee what questions future scholars may wish to ask of the material. However, those variants which I judge to be of no importance for establishing the text — variations in spelling, slips of the pen, and most of the readings occurring only in the inferior MSS NZBUY—are bracketed. The unbracketed apparatus concentrates on KMCPT, though the readings of the other MSS are reported where they coincide with those and in the few cases where they may have independent value.

After the symposium, Dr. Hans Ruelius was kind enough to send me photographs of a Sinhalese version which occurs as part of a larger text which he is studying, the Ṣaḍaṃgam Vīdiya. In this version are included four Pali verses, numbers 2 to 5 of our text. Though there are no new readings of value—they generally follow our group *K*—I have included the testimony of this MS for those four verses, with the siglum R. Dr. Ruelius writes, "According to the language this version must be older than 14th century," but I can see no basis for this claim.

R — Colombo Museum. W. A. de Silva no. 2357, library no. 7 H. 4.

The Kaṭārangala *sanne* purports to be a *sanne* of the KBV *ānisaṃsa*, i. e. the passage (principally the final verse sequence) in which the Buddha recites the advantages to be gained by copying texts or making images; and it does roughly cover our text from the prose after verse 6 to the end of verse 25. But it is very free and often prolix. It is obviously glossing a text diverging considerably from ours; it includes almost all our verses, though in a garbled order, but adds many more, including perhaps some from Sad-dhamma-sangaha X. Where our text is difficult the *sanne* is hardly ever close enough to be useful. In the two places where it has provided superior readings it is quoted in the apparatus as *Sanne*. I am grateful to Mr. K. G. Senaratne for copying out this *sanne*, and to my learned friend Mr. U. A. Gunasekara for helping me to understand it.

I must also record here my gratitude to colleagues at the symposium for their helpful suggestions, and in particular to my teachers, Mr. C. H. B. Reynolds and Mr. K. R. Norman. It is a rare encouragement to have one's work so carefully read. Though most of my specific debts are acknowledged in the text, it would have been too cumbrous to indicate there all the improvements in the translation which I owe to Mr. Norman.

Notes on the manuscripts

K. 4 leaves, 7 sides, starts on verso of first leaf; ka—kī (except that ka not marked). 7 and 8 lines to a page. Punctuation at end of *gāthā* etc. in black and red. Fine round hand, letters medium size, well differentiated except for cca/ḍa. At end of colophon there is incised, but not inked in: "Karaṃvilagala unnasse visin Galagedara unnassēṭa pūjā karaṇa lada Kōsalabimbavarṇṇanāvayi." So the manuscript was given to a monk from Galagedara by a monk from Karaṃvilagala. Date: late Kandyan period.

M. 3 leaves, 4¼ sides, part of larger MS. Beautiful hand, small letters, absolutely clear. Text ends "Bimbavaṇṇanā niṭṭhitā." Colophon, after next text, probably in another hand, gives measurements of MS and adds "Välivita Saranaṃkara unvahansēgē pota." So the book belonged to the great Sangharāja. Date: mid 18th. century.

N. 4 leaves, 8 sides, third text in MS; ka—kī. 7 and 8 lines to page. Several corrections. Fairly clear hand, letters medium size, well differentiated except for i/ī and ta/na. Colophon: "Bimbavarṇanāva niṭṭhitā." Date: probably 19th. century.

C. 6 leaves, pages numbered 60–65; title p. 60 recto, text starts centre p. 60 verso, ends middle p. 65 verso. 8 lines to a page. Glossy pages in mint condition. Fairly large letters, generally clear, but ta/na poorly differentiated. Colophon: "Kosalabimbavaṇṇanā samattā.

Vaṇṇi hat patuvaṭa ayiti Beruvuve pansale pote piṭapataya liya nima kalē 1897.3.21." So MS is from Kegalle District. Date: 1897.

P. 3 leaves, 4⅔ sides; third and last text in MS; ḍe—ḍo. Clear hand, small letters, well differentiated. Colophon: "Bimbavaṇṇanā niṭṭhitā." Date: probably 18th. century.

Z. 3 leaves, just over 5 sides, ending top line of third leaf verso; ka—ki. 7 lines to a page. Fairly clear hand, letters medium size, differentiation of ta/na very slight, of ca/ma even slighter. Damaged at one edge throughout, including colophon, which begins, "Bimbavaṇṇanā ..." The name Ovilānē Atthadassi is then added, probably in a different hand, and the MS ends with a Sanskrit verse and Sinhalese prose which are so corrupt as to be completely unintelligible. Date: 19th. century.

T. 4 leaves, 7½ sides; ka—kī. 6 and 7 lines to page. Fine hand, letters medium size, well differentiated. Colophon: "Bimbavaṇṇanā niṭṭhitā." Date: late Kandyan period.

B. 4 leaves, 8 sides; ka—kī. 8 lines to page. One edge damaged. Generally clear hand, letters medium size, ca/va and bha/ha sometimes poorly differentiated. Colophon: "Bimbavaṇṇanā niṭṭhitā." Date: probably early 19th. century.

U. 3 leaves, just under 4 sides, starting on verso; part of longer MS; ko—kām. 9 lines to page. Generally good hand, letters rather small, tend to be squashed together, ca/ma/va not always well differentiated, especially first two. Long colophon at end of whole MS gives precise date, beginning, "Sakavarṣa ekvā dahas sat siya hatalih aṭa pämiṇi varṣayehi", and ending, "Nettipolagedara Vipassī terunnassa livū potayi." Date: 1826.

Y. 3 leaves, 4½ sides, part of longer MS; ku—kṛ (from ku recto line 2 to kṛ recto line 6). 9 lines to page. Careless MS, full of corrections and deletions. Fairly good hand, but poor spacing, letters squashed but fairly well differentiated. Text ends, "Kosalabimbavaṇṇanā niṭṭhitā." Whole MS incomplete, lacks colophon. Date: 19th century.

R. Good hand, letters well differentiated. The four Pali verses occur as follows:

v. 2 - folio 8 recto lines 1–2
v. 3 — folio 8 verso lines 5–6
v. 4 — folio 9 verso line 8 to folio 10 recto line 1
v. 5 — folio 10 recto line 3.

Date: 1914.

All MSS are on palm leaves. The initial conventional salutations to the Buddha, and remarks in the colophon such as "Siddhir astu", have been disregarded.

Text of the Kosala-bimba-vaṇṇanā

Karoti kārāpayatī ti. Imaṃ dhammadesanaṃ Satthā Jetavane[1] viharanto Kosalarājānaṃ ārabbha kathesi. Ekadivasaṃ hi Satthā paccūsasamaye[2] katābhinīhāraṃ[3] puggalaṃ disvā tassânuggahatthāya[4] dīgham addhānam agamāsi. Tadā Pasenadi[5] Kosalarājā[6] mahantena parivārena[7] Jetavanaṃ gantvā tattha Sammā-Sambuddhaṃ adisvā "Aho vihāraṃ suññam iva[8] khāyatī" ti domanassaṃ[9] patvā[10] ānītaānītāni[11] gandhamālādīni apūjetvā[12] dhammasabhāyam eva pātetvā nagaram eva gato. Tesaṃ gatakāle Satthā vihāraṃ paccāgami.

Dutiyadivase Kosalarājā[13] gandhamālādīni ca[14] gilānapaccayādīni[15] ca[16] gāhāpetvā[17] mahantena[18] parivārena[19] Satthu[18] santikaṃ[18] gantvā[20] Sammā-Sambuddhaṃ[21] gandhamālādīhi[22] pūjetvā[23] pañcapatiṭṭhitena[24] vanditvā ekam[25] antaṃ nisīdi[26]. Ekam[27] antaṃ[27] nisinno kho[28] Bhagavantaṃ etad avoca: "Bhante, hiyyo[29] Sāvatthivāsino[30] bahū[31] manussā[32] gandhamālādīni gahetvā vihāraṃ gantvā[33] Sammā-Sambuddhaṃ adisvā[34] ativiya[35] anattamanā hutvā nagaram eva gatā[36]. Tasmā sabbalokahitatthāya ahaṃ Tathāgatasadisaṃ paṭimaṃ kārāpetukāmo[37] 'mhī" ti āha. Satthā taṃ[38] sutvā[39], "Sādhu sādhu, mahārāja, tayā cintitam eva[40] varataran"[41] ti vatvā, "Paṭimaṃ kātuṃ anuññāto 'sī"[42] ti āha. Atha rājā "Mayā[43] paṭimaṃ kīdisaṃ[44] kātuṃ vaṭṭatī"[45] ti pucchi. "Yena kena ci, mahārāja, hitakāmena[46] kulaputtena kaṭṭhamayaṃ vā selamayaṃ vā dantamayaṃ vā mattikāmayaṃ[47] vā rajatamayaṃ[48] vā kaṃsamayaṃ vā tambamayaṃ vā tipumayaṃ vā vālukamayaṃ[49] vā Tathāgatasadisaṃ paṭimaṃ[50] kātabbaṃ, dīghaṃ[51] vā rassaṃ vā aṇuṃ[52] vā thūlaṃ[53] vā antamaso yavappamāṇam[54] pi vidatthippamāṇam[55] pi[56] yāva purisappamāṇam[57] pi kattabbaṃ. Appameyyaṃ[58], mahārāja, paṭimākaraṇaṃ[59] asaṃkheyyaṃ mahānisaṃsan"[60] ti vatvā imaṃ gātham āha:

---

[1] [Jetavaṇe C]. [2] -yaṃ *K* [paccūṣa- N]. [3] [kathā- CN]. [4] [tassânuggāh- N]. [5] [Pasenadī M, Pasenādī Y]. [6] Kosalo *P*. [7] [parivāreṇa PC]. [8] [eva N]. [9] [domaṇassaṃ C]. [10] pavedetvā *P*. [11] ānītāni *P* [ānitāni TBYZ, ānitaānitāni C]. [12] *om. P* [apujetvā N]. [13] [Kosaḷa- C]. [14] ce K, ceva *P*C. [15] [giḷāṇa- C]. [16] *om.* P*T*. [17] *om.* PTU. [18] *om.*; vihāraṃ g. *K*. [19] *om. K* [parivāre Y]. [20] [ganvā Z]. [21] *om. P*, pañca P. [22] mālādīni *K*, gandhamālādīni *P*. [23] [pujetvā N]. [24] [paca- C]. [25] [ekām U]. [26] *om.* PZ [nīsīdi B, nisīdī M]. [27] *om. P*. [28] *om.* PZ [rāja Kosalo Bh. N]. [29] [hīyyo C, hiyo Y, hīyo MPZ, bhiyo U, bhiyyo B]. [30] [Sāvatthiyaṃ vāsino Z]. [31] bahu- *K*UYZ. [32] [maṇussā C]. [33] [ganvā Z]. [34] [disvā Y]. [35] [ativiya *bis* Y]. [36] gato *T*. [37] [kārāpetuṃ- Y]. [38] naṃ TB. [39] *om. P except* T. [40] *om. K* [cintitaññeva P*T*, cintitaṃñeva Z]. [41] [varaṃtaran M, varataraṃ C]. [42] 'mhī MSS. [43] *om. K*. [44] [kīdisaṃ *om.* Z]. [45] [vandhatī UY]. [46] attano h. *P*. [47] mattika- *P except* B. [48] rūpimayaṃ vā raj. *P* [seḷamayaṃ vā mattikamayaṃ vā dantamayaṃ vā Z]. [49] vālukā- KMCPZUY [vāḷu- MC*T*Z]. [50] [paṭimaṃ *om.* Y]. [51] [kātabbaṃ dīghaṃ *om.* Y]. [52] [anuṃ *K*ZUY]. [53] [thulaṃ N]. [54] [-ppamānam NZUY]. [55] [vidatthippamānam NZUYB]. [56] [pi ti UY]. [57] purisassa pamāṇam TB [purisaṃ- Z; -ppamānam NZUY]. [58] [appameyya M]. [59] [paṭimaṃ UY]. [60] [-samsaṃ C, -saṃsaṃn N]. [61] [kārāpayatī C]. [62] [Jiṇa- C, nija- Y]. [63] [ti *om.* Z]. [64] [-kā-

(1) "Karoti kārāpayati[61] Jinabimbaṃ[62] naro idha
Sele lepe paṭe kaṭṭhe mahantaṃ khuddakam pi vā" ti.[63]

"Mahārāja, paṭimākārāpaṇe[64] pamāṇātikkantaṃ[65] phalaṃ hoti. Yathā[66] iddhimanto puriso imasmiṃ cakkavālagabbhe[67] pūritāni[68] tilasāsapabījāni attano[69] iddhibalena[70] gaṇetuṃ[71] kusalo[72] bhaveyya, tādiso[72] pi 'ekasmiṃ Jinabimbe[73] phalaṃ[74] ettakappamāṇan'[75] ti[76] vattuṃ[77] cheko na[78] bhaveyya. Puna[79] seyyathā pi, mahārāja, catusu samuddesu vārirāsiṃ phusite[80] katvā minituṃ[81] kusalo[82] bhaveyya, asmiṃ phalaṃ vattuṃ[83] asamo[84] bhaveyya. Seyyathā pi, janādhipa, assaṃ[85] vasudhāyaṃ pulinapaṃsuṃ[86] māsamuggappamāṇe[87] katvā gaṇetuṃ caturo[88] bhaveyya[89], imaṃ vipākaṃ na sakkā kathetuṃ. Seyyathā pi, mahārāja, 'ekasmiṃ Jinabimbe phalam ettakan'[90] ti sace vattabbaṃ bhaveyya[91], ṭhapetvā Sammā[92]-Sambuddhato aññe[93] mukhasatam[94] pi sahassam pi māpetvā tato uttarim pi attano iddhibalena[95] anekāni mukhāni māpetvā[96] vattuṃ[97] na[97] sakkontī"[97] ti.

Saṃkhepena[98] ānisaṃse kathite rājā taṃ[99] sabbaṃ Satthu santikā[100] sutvā vanditvā saparivāro attano nivesanaṃ gantvā[101] mahagghaṃ[102] candanasāraṃ āhārāpetvā[103] salakkhaṇam[104] paṭimārūpaṃ[105] kāretvā kañcanakhacitaṃ[106] katvā mahagghaṃ kāsāvaṃ pārupāpetvā ekasmiṃ patirūpaṭṭhāne ṭhapāpesi[107]. Tato Kosalarājā[108] gandhamālādīni gāhāpetvā[109] mahantena parivārena[110] Jetavanaṃ gantvā Satthu[111] pūjetvā[112] vanditvā evam āha[113]:

(2) "Jinassa[114] bimbaṃ tava[115] sāsanena[116]
Kārāpito candanasārakena[117]
'Tat⟨r⟩opagantvā[118] Sugato sunetto[119]
Passeyya ce taṃ[120] pavaran' ti maññe" ti[121].

Tadā[121] Satthā evaṃ yācite[122] tuṇhībhāvena[123] adhivāsesi.

---

rāpane NZTBY]. [65] pamāṇaṃ kittakaṃ *K* [pamān- UY]. [66] tathā C. [67] [cakkavāḷa- CNPB]. [68] pūritā KMC. [69] attano *bis* *K*U [tilasāsapamattāni bījāni atta id. Z]. [70] [-baleṇa C]. [71] [ganetuṃ NUY]. [72] na so (*for* tādiso) TB [ku . . . diso *lacuna* Z]. [73] [Jiṇa- CY]. [74] [phalam ZB]. [75] ettikaṃ *P*, ettakaṃ p. *K* [pamānan CNYZ]. [76] [ti ca U]. [77] om. PZ [vacanattuṃ Y]. [78] *om. P.* [79] [puṇa YC]. [80] [phusitake N]. [81] milituṃ K, mīlituṃ C, militaṃ MN [miṇituṃ TBU]. [82] kātuṃ k. *all except* Z. [83] [vattum TBZ, vatthum Y]. [84] asamaṃ *P.* [85] assa PZ, ayaṃ *K.* [86] [puḷiṇa- C; pu . . . gappamāṇe *lacuna* Z]. [87] [samugga- C; -ppamāne T, -ppamānena N]. [88] [kusalo bh. N]. [89] [bhaveyiya M]. [90] ettikan *P.* [91] [bhayya UY]. [92] [Sammā *om.* N]. [93] [añña U, añño B, *om.* Y]. [94] [mukhatāsatam UY]. [95] [iddhi . . . anek. *lacuna* Z]. [96] m. pi *P* [mācetvā Y]. [97] vattuṃ ma sakkotī KMC, vattum asakkontī *P*N. [98] [saṃkhepeṇa C]. [99] [rājānaṃ U, rajānaṃ Y]. [100] santikaṃ *P.* [101] [ganvā Z]. [102] mahaggha- C. [103] āharāpetvā MSS. [104] [salakkhanam U, -ṇaṃ CN, -ṇa T, -ṇā YB]. [105] [paṭirūpaṃ UY]. [106] kañcanacittaṃ *K* [kañcaṇa- T]. [107] ṭhapāpetvā KMC, ṭhāpetvā N, ṭhapetvā *P.* [108] [Kosaḷa- NZ]. [109] [gāhapetvā YB]. [110] [parivāreṇa PC]. [111] [Satthū M]. [112] [pujetvā CN]. [113] [āhā CUY]. [114] [Jiṇassa C]. [115] viya C. [116] dassanena C. [117] candanakena ratnakena TU, candanaratnakena BY. [118] tatop. *KP*, tathūp. R [ganvā Z]. [119] [suteto N]. [120] [naṃ N]. [121] *om.* PZ. [122] yācitena *K.* [123] [tunhī- N; -bhāve Y, -bhāveṇa C]. [124] *om. T.* [125] ñatvā

Rājā Satthu[124] adhivāsanaṃ viditvā[125] attano nivesanaṃ gantvā rājaṅgaṇe[126] sattaratanamaṇḍapaṃ[127] kāretvā suvaṇṇiṭṭhikāhi[128] chādāpetvā[129] suvaṇṇa[130]-rajatatārakādi[131]-vicittavitānaṃ bandhitvāgandhadāmapupphadāmādīni olambetvā[132] antarantarā[133] suvaṇṇādikiṃkiṇikajālaṃ[134] bandhitvā bhūmiṃ[135] catujātigandhena limpāpetvā[137] samantato[136] anagghapaṭṭasāṇiyo[137] bandhetvā[138] dakkhiṇapasse[139] mahārahaṃ āsanaṃ paññāpetvā[140] paṭimārūpaṃ[141] tattha patiṭṭhāpetvā tato paṭṭhāya yāva[142] Jetavanadvāraṃ[143] tāva maggaṃ visamaṃ samaṃ katvā rajatavaṇṇam[144] atidhavalaṃ[145] vālukaṃ[146] okiritvā tasmiṃ pañcavaṇṇāni[147] vatthāni attharitvā[148] lājapañcamāni[149] pupphāni okiritvā ubhosu[150] passesu suvaṇṇarajatāditoraṇe[151] uṭṭhāpetvā[152] antarantarā[153] nānāvidhāni[154] dhajāni ussāpetvā antarantarā puṇṇaghaṭāni[155] c'eva[156] ⟨ṭhapetvā⟩[157] gandhatelapadīpāni[158] jālāpetvā evaṃ maggaṃ sabbālaṃkārehi alaṃkaritvā vihāraṃ gantvā[159] Satthāraṃ vanditvā[160] evam āha.

(3) So Kosalo[161] bhūpati bhūmipālo
Sajjetva[162] panthaṃ Sugatassa tassa
Gantvā tato[163] Jetavanaṃ vihāraṃ
Idam[164] abravī[164]: "Bimba vilokayassū"[165] ti.

Tato Satthā "Sādhū"[166] ti paṭisuṇitvā[167] uṭṭhāyâsanā[168] sāvakagaṇaparivuto[169] gantvā Kosalena[170] kārāpita⟨ṃ⟩[171] ratanamaṇḍapaṃ mahatā sirisobhaggena[172] pāvisi. Tasmiṃ khaṇe taṃ[173] acetanaṃ paṭimārūpaṃ sacetanaṃ Sammā-Sambuddhaṃ disvā Satthu ādarena[174] uṭṭhānākāraṃ[175] dassento vyākato[176]. Satthā tadākāraṃ disvā, "Āvuso, tvaṃ mam'[177] accayena mama sāsanaṃ jotessasi[178]. Sāsanatthāya[179] pañca vassasahassāni tiṭṭhā"[180] ti[181] Erāvaṇasoṇḍasadisaṃ[182] dakkhiṇahatthaṃ[183] pasāretvā nivāresi. Taṃ[184] garukaraṇatthaṃ[185] suma-

---

vanditvā *P*. [126] [-angane KNTUY]. [127] [-paṇḍapaṃ N]. [128] [svaṇṇiṭṭhikāhi N; -iṭṭhikāyahi U]. [129] [chadāpetvā Y]. [130] [svaṇṇa- Y]. [131] [-tārakādī- Z]. [132] [olambitvā Y]. [133] antarantaraṃ K. [134] jālā *PT* [suvaṇṇādiṃ K, -dī- Y; -kiṃkinika- KCTBUZ]. [135] bhūmiyaṃ MSS [bhūmiyañ M]. [136] [sammantato U, sammāntato Y]. [137] [limpāpe . . . sāniyo *lacuna* B; sāniyo CNTBU, sāni Y]. [138] bandhitvā KMC, bandhi N. [139] passena *KT* [dakkhina- TYZ]. [140] [paṃñāpetvā P; *all after* paññāpetvā *up to* -ni attharitvā *om.* N]. [141] [patimā- CZ]. [142] [tato Y]. [143] [Jetavaṇa- C; -dvāra Y, dvāraṃ *bis* Z]. [144] [-vaṇṇaṃ PZTUY]. [145] atidhavala *PT* [atidhavaḷa U]. [146] vāḷukā *T* [vāḷukaṃ MCZ]. [147] [-vannāni Y]. [148] [see 140]. [149] lājañcapañcamāni KC. [150] [usobhāsu Y]. [151] -rajatāṇi t. *T*, rajatādīni t. C. [152] ussāpetvā *K*. [153] [antarantara M]. [154] nānāvidha- *P*. [155] [punna- Y; -gaṭāni N]. [156] [meva TB]. [157] *om.* MSS; *suggerit* Norman. [158] -telappadīpāni *P*. [159] [gaṇatvā N]. [160] [vandhitvā Y]. [161] [*nothing before* salo N]. [162] sajjetvā K, sajetvā UY. [163] gantvān' atho R. [164] idhabravī PZ, idham abruvī UY, idam abruvī MN, abbravī TB. [165] [vilokayassu NUY]. [166] [sādhu NY]. [167] [paṭisunitvā NTYZ]. [168] [vuṭṭhā- C]. [169] [-gana- NPZUY]. [170] [Kosaleṇa N]. [171] kārāpita MSS [kārāpīta T]. [172] [-sogaggena Y]. [173] [taṃ *om.* Z]. [174] [ādareṇa CN]. [175] [uṭṭhānaṃkāraṃ N]. [176] viya kate MSS [viyakakate N]. [177] [mama M]. [178] jotessati KMN, jotessatisi C. [179] sāsanantaṃ ṭhatvā yāva *K*. [180] [niṭṭhā M, tiṭṭha NU]. [181] [ni M]. [182] Erāvaṇahatthisoṇḍa-*K*PZ [Erāvana- MNBUYZ]. [183] [dakkhina- Y, dakkhinā- N]. [184] [naṃ napupphamuṭṭhīhi[186] pūjesi[187], pañcasatā[188] khīṇāsavā pi puthujjanā pi nānāsugandhapupphehi[189] tath' eva pūjesuṃ. Tasmiṃ khaṇe Sakka[190]-Suyāma-Santusita-Brahmādayo[191] attano attano[192] pūjābhaṇḍehi taṃ paṭimaṃ[193] pūjesuṃ. Cattāro mahārājāno[194] catuddisaṃ[195] ārakkhaṃ gaṇhiṃsu[196]. Sabbe devā[197] manussā[198] ca sādhukārasahassāni[199] pavattesuṃ. Taṃ abbhutaṃ disvā[200] mahāmahī chambhi[201], mahānādam[202] akāsi, mahā Meru naṭako naccanto[203] viya[204] namassi[205], satta kulapabbatā pi tath' eva akaṃsu, catusu mahāsamuddesu[206] udakaṃ saṃkhubhitvā[207] ratanāni[208] matthakaṃ pattā[209], sakalacakkavāḷaṃ[210] nānāpupphehi[211] samalaṃkataṃ[212] pupphāsanaṃ viya ahosi, catusu mahādīpesu[213] mahāmegho[214] uṭṭhahi[215].

Rājā imāni acchariyāni disvā pītiyā phuṭasarīro[216] hutvā tasmiṃ maṇḍape mahantaṃ Buddhāsanaṃ paññāpetvā Satthāraṃ tattha[217] nisīdāpetvā[218] nānāvidhehi yāgukhajjakādīhi[219] Buddhapamukhaṃ[220] bhikkhusaṃghaṃ[221] sakkacca[221] parivisitvā iminā[222] niyāmena sattāhaṃ mahādānaṃ[223] datvā sattame divase[223] pacchābhatte Satthāraṃ vanditvā[224] ekam antaṃ ṭhito rājā paṭimākārāpaṇe[225] ānisaṃsaṃ[226] pucchanto imaṃ gātham[227] āha[228]:

(4) "Yo jīvaloke paṭimaṃ kareyya
Kim ānisaṃsaṃ labhate, muninda?
Pucchāmi taṃ, sādhu vadehi mayhaṃ"[229],
Idam[230] abravī[230] Kosalabhūmipālo.

Taṃ sutvā[231] tam atthaṃ pakāsento Satthā[231] āha:

(5) "Sādhu sādhu, mahārāja, yaṃ mayhaṃ pucchitaṃ[232] tayā[233].
Pavakkhāmi[234] phalaṃ[235] tassa; suṇohī[236] ti, mahīpati."[236a]

TB]. [185] [-karanatthaṃ Z]. [186] [sumaṇa- CNBUZ, suma- K; -pupphaṃmuṭṭhīhi Z; -muṭṭhīṇi N]. [187] [pūjehi Z]. [188] pañcasata *all except* C. [189] [nāṇāvidhasug. UY; -puppehi N]. [190] Sakkha P, Sakya TBZ. [191] [-Brahmāda N]. [192] *om.* T. [193] patimaṃ *all except* ZU. [194] [mahārājā UY]. [195] [catudisaṃ N]. [196] [ganhiṃsu Y, ganhisuṃ N]. [197] deva *K*UY. [198] [maṇussā C]. [199] [sākāra- Y]. [200] [dasvā N]. [201] chambhī MN, chabbi TB, chabbī UY, chabbidhā P, chabbidā Z. [202] mahānādakam C, nādam *P except* U, nāndam U. [203] *om. P.* [204] *om. K.* [205] namakkāram akāsi *T*, nādamakkāram akāsi PZ. [206] [-samuddasu C]. [207] [saṃkkhubhitvā U]. [208] [rathanāni N]. [209] [patta B]. [210] [sakaṃlacakkavalaṃ Y, -cakkavālaṃ MNTU]. [211] [-puppehi C]. [212] samalaṃkata *all except* KZ. [213] [mahadipesu Y; dīpesu . . . megho *lacuna* Z]. [214] [see 213]. [215] [uṭṭhāhi BY]. [216] [phuṭha K]. [217] vanditvā t. KMC. [218] [nisīdapetvā Y]. [219] [yābhu- N]. [220] Buddhappamukhaṃ BUY. [211] sakkaccaṃ KC, nimantetvā sakkaccaṃ N, -saṃghassa kattabbaṃ *P except* Z, -saṃghaṃssa kattabbaṃ Z. [222] [imiṇā Y]. [223] [mahā . . . pacchā *lacuna* Z]. [224] [Sattāraṃ ditvā N]. [225] kārāpane *all except* C. [226] [ānisaṃse N]. [227] [gāthām KC]. [228] [āhā C]. [229] [mahiyaṃ N]. [230] idhabravī PZ, idham abruvī UY, idham abbravī T, idam abbravī B, idam abruvī M. [231] [su . . . Satthā *lacuna* Z]. [232] pucchito MSS. [233] mayā UY, *corrected to* tayā B [tayo C]. [234] vakkhāmi taṃ *K*R. [235] phalan KMPT. [236] [sunohi R]. [236a] [mahīpatī Z]. [237] -samujjalita KMC. [238] [añjali M]. [239] *om. P.* [240] [āhā

Tato Ānandatthero dasanakhasamujjalitaṃ[237] añjaliṃ[238] sirasi ṭhapetvā namassamāno Satthāraṃ pucchanto[239] evam āha[240]:

(6) "Munindarājena[241] sudesitena
Dhammena lekheyya[242] pan' ekadesaṃ.[243]
Kim ānisaṃsaṃ[242] paṭimāphalañ[244] ca?
Desetum icchāmi"[245] ti ajjhabhāsi[246].

Taṃ sutvā, "Sādhu sādhu, Ānanda, tayā cintitam eva varataran" ti aṭṭhaṅgasamupetamadhurassarena[247] dvīsu pi [248]phalaṃ[248a] vaṇṇento[249] cātuddīpikamahāmegho[250] ⟨. . .⟩[251] viya ca yojanappamāṇaṃ[252] madhupaṭalaṃ cakkayantena[253] pīḷetvā[254] madhuṃ pāyento viya ca dhammaṃ desento, "Ānanda[255], imasmiṃ loke ye[256] puññavantā[257] sattā[257a] paṭimaṃ[258] karonti kārāpenti potthakaṃ likhanti likhāpenti te ubho pi anopamaṃ[259] sampattiṃ anubhavantī"[260] ti vatvā imā gāthā abhāsi:

(7) "Bhayānakāpāyikasattasaṃkule[261]
Durāsade aggisikhānirantare
Mahaṭṭhapāyesu ca soḷasussade[262]
Na jāyare lekhakabimbakārakā[263].

(8) [264] "Buddhantare[265] bhattudake[266] ṭhapetvā
Siṃghānikaṃ[267] nāpi labhanti semhaṃ. —
Etādise petabhave bhayaṃkare
Na[267a] jāyare lekhakabimbakārakā[268].

(9) "Kappam pi āloka-m[269]-adassanīye
Lokantare niraye ghorarūpe[270]
Te kāla[271]kañja[272]vhayadānavāsure
Na jāyare lekhakabimbakārakā[268].

(10) "Acintiyānekasudukkhabhājane[273]
Bhave tiracchānabhave suvādike[274]
Mahattabhāvā[275] jalajā pi hutvā
Na jāyare lekhakabimbakārakā[276].

C]. [241] [muṇinda- U]. [242] [lekhe . . . saṃsaṃ *lacuna* Z]. [243] [pana desaṃ C]. [244] patimā- MSS, [245] [enemi N]. [246] [ajjhabhāsī T, ajjhabhāsatāni N]. [247] [-ssareṇa CUY, -ssare N]. [248] *om.* M. [248a] [phalena N]. [249] [vaṇento T, vannento N]. [250] [-dīpaka- N]. [251] *no sign of lacuna in* MSS. [252] tiyojana- P*T* [-ppamānaṃ TUYZ, -ppamāṇa M]. [253] [-yanteṇa Y]. [254] [pīletvā MCNBUY]. [255] [Ānande BU, Ānandena Y; Y *then illegible, inserts* cintitam?]. [256] [yeva Y]. [257] [puṃñavantā N]. 257[a] [satthā Z]. [258] patimaṃ MSS. [259] anopama KMN, anopa C [aṇopama- N]. [260] anubhavatī *T*. [261] [bhayānakāvārsiyika- N; satta *bis* K]. [262] [solas- MNUY]. [263] lekhika- *all except* C, lekkhika- C. [264] *Before stanza* (8) *P reads stanza* (10). [265] [Buddhāntare N]. [266] jann- C, can- T, cann- *all other* MSS, batpàn tabā *Sanne*. [267] [siṃghāṇikaṃ PN, siṃghānikan UY]. [267a] [bhayaṃkare . . . mbakārakā *lacuna* B; -limba- N]. [268] lekhika- *all except* C. [269] mālokam *K*. [270] [-rūpo U]. [271] [kāḷa- CTB]. [272] -kaja- K. [273] acittiyā- M, C? [-kārakā . . . sudukkha- *lacuna* B; -bhājaṇe Y]. [274] [tiracchāṇa- Y; -bhāve K]. [275] mahanta- MCNUYZ [-bhāvaṃ C]. [276] lekhika- *all except* C, lekaka- C,

(11) "Āruppāsaññasattesu[277] cakkavāḷantaresu[278] ca
Īdisesu[279] na jāyanti[280] paṭimākārā ca lekhakā[281].

(12) "Imamhā cakkavāḷā[282] pi sesadīpattayesu[283] ca
Paccantesu na jāyanti[284] paṭimākārā ca[285] lekhakā[281].

(13) "Buddha-pacceka-Sambuddhâsekkhānaṃ[286] cakkavattinaṃ
Uppattiṭṭhānabhūtamhi[287] majjhadese[288] va[289] jāyare.

(14) "Micchādiṭṭhiṃ[290] na gaṇhanti[291] sammādiṭṭhiṃ[292] ca[293] gaṇhare[294];
Ubhatovyañjan'[295] itthī[296] ca[297] paṇḍakā[298] ca[299] napuṃsakā,

(15) "Jātyandhā[300] ca[301] jalummattā[302] mūgā[303] badhirakhañjakā[304]
Pīṭhasappī[305] na jāyanty āpasmārā[306] jātijātiyaṃ[307].

(16) "Dudikkhā[308] gaṇḍapilakā[309] kaṇḍukacchuvaṇādayo[310]
Kilāsā[311] ca[312] vivajjanti[313] uppannuppannajātiyaṃ[314].

(17) "Suvaṇṇakkhandhasaṃkāsā[315] honti tesaṃ tanū[316] sadā.
Ravîva tejasā honti paṭimākārā ca lekhakā[317].

(18) "Na papponti sapattānaṃ[318] bhayaṃ tāsaṃ[319] kadā ci pi.
Ucce kule pajāyanti mahāsāle[320] mahaddhane[321],
Aññe[322] kule na jāyanti paṭimākārā[323] ca lekhakā[324].

(19) "Yadā mātūdare[325] jāye[326] soṇṇarūpaṃ[327] va[328] nimmalaṃ[329]
Bahiddhā pi padissanto toseti[330] mātarādayo[331].

(20) "Dasamāsaccayen' evaṃ sotthinā janito[332] susu.
Kamena[333] abhivaḍḍhanti dutiyan[334] tithimā[335] viya[336].

(21) "Tass' uppannakule[337] niccaṃ dasadhā ratanehi ca
Dhanadhaññasamiddhīhi[338] anūnaṃ hoti sabbadā.

---

[277] -saññā- KUY [aruppa- Z, āruppa- N]. [278] [cakkavāl- MNUY]. [279] īdise ti C. [280] [jānayanti Z]. [281] lekhikā *all except* C. [282] [cakkavālā MNY]. [283] -ttaye pi *K*. [284] [jāyante Z]. [285] [*om.* Z]. [286] sambuddha-sāvakānaṃ *K* [sāvakānañ K]. [287] -bhūmimhi *P* [uppati- C; -bhūtam pi N]. [288] mandhadese *P*. [289] ca CNPZ. [290] [micchādiṭṭhi UY]. [291] [ganhanti N]. [292] -diṭṭhī K [-diṭṭhiñ M, -diṭṭhi N]. [293] va CZTBY. [294] gayhare *K*. [295] -vyañjanan' KZ, -bbyañjanan' TUY, -byañjana- M [byañjan' N, -bbyañjan' B]. [296] -tthī M, ītthī B. [297] [vā *T*]. [298] [pakā Y]. [299] vā *P*. [300] jātyāndhā C, jatyāndha- Y, -andha- PZTBY. [301] *om. P*. [302] jaḷu- N, jāḷummattā Y, jāmattā U. [303] [mugā CN]. [304] badhirā ca khañjakā *K*. [305] [-sappī *om.* Z, sappi CNPU]. [306] jāyanti 'pasmārā *K*. [307] [*extra* jāti KNB]. [308] [dudikkha N]. [309] gandha- KT [gaṇda- U; -piḷakā KTU]. [310] kāḍu- C. kacchukaṇḍū v. P, kacchukaṇḍu Z; -van- *all except* KB. [311] kilesā MSS, kilāsa *Sanne* [kiḷesā C]. [312] va *P*. [313] [vivajanti Y]. [314] [uppaṇṇuppaṇṇa- C]. [315] [suvaṇṇakhandha- C]. [316] nanū U, nanu KCN. [317] lekhikā *all except* C. [318] pasannānaṃ UY [sapattāhaṃ na (*correction intended?*) N]. [319] tesaṃ KMC, *corrected to* trasaṃ P. [320] tayosāle *all except* C, so sāḷe C [tayosāḷe B]. [321] mahaddhano CN [-dhaṇo N]. [322] [aṃñe T]. [323] [patimā- N]. [324] lekhikā MSS. [325] mātudare MSS [mātudaro Z]. [326] jāto KC. [327] [sonna- N]. [328] ca KCPU. [329] [*extra* va *at end of line* Z]. [330] tosotu K. [331] mātuādayo *K*PZ. [332] [jānito N]. [333] [kameṇa CN]. [334] dutiyat M*P*, adutiyat N. [335] thitimā PTUY, thītimā Z, thuni N. [336] viyaṃ UY. [337] [uppaṇṇa- C]. [338] -samuddhīhi *all except* C. [samuddhihi M]. [339] [koṭihī P]. [340] [-gavādihi KMB].

(22) "Khomakoseyyakādīhi nānāsāṭakakoṭihi[339]
Hatthiassagavādīhi[340] khettavatthūhi[341] ijjhati[342].

(23) "Vacanakkhamabhūtāni[343] dāsīdāsāni[344] labbhati
Tath' eva puttadārādi[345] parivāre ca sabbadā.

(24) "Devaloke manusse[346] vā yattha yatth' ūpapajjati[347]
Sabbasampattirūpehi sabbe abhibhavissati.

(25) "Dharaṇūpamāya[348] paññāya[349] sabbasippamhi[350] kovido
Bhaveyya sabbadā dhīro lekhako[351] bimbakārako[352].

(26) "Iti vibhavasiriṃ[353] so sādhu sampāpuṇitvā[354]
Vipulataramanuññe[355] pañca kāme bhujitvā
Atha nikhilakilese[356] sosayitvā[356] visesaṃ[357]
Vajati[358] tividhabodhyā[359] ekam[359a] ekaṃ[360] tato[360] so" ti.

Evaṃ Bhagavā Ānandattherena[361] ca[362] Kosalena ca[362] yācito ākāsagaṅgaṃ[363] otārento viya ca amatavassaṃ vassento[364] viya ca anekākārena[365] vipākaṃ vaṇṇetvā[366], "Mahārāja[(367)], attano hitakāmehi puññavantehi[367] potthakaṃ[368] likhāpetabbaṃ paṭimā kārāpetabbā"[369] ti[370] vatvā imaṃ dhammadesanaṃ samodhānesi[371]. Desanāvasāne pañcasahassapurisā[372] saha paṭisambhidāhi arahattaṃ pāpuṇiṃsu[373], ekacce sotāpannā[374] ekacce sakadāgāmino[375] ekacce[376] anāgāmino[376] ahesuṃ[377]. Atha[378] Kosalarājā ca devamanussā[379] ca[362] mahantaṃ pūjāsakkāraṃ[380] karontā[381] Buddhapamukhaṃ[382] bhikkhusaṃghaṃ Jetavanavihāram[383] eva nesuṃ. Punadivase[384] taṃ[385] candanapaṭimārūpaṃ[386] sattaratanamaṇḍapena saddhiṃ vihāre yeva patiṭṭhāpesī ti.

Translation: The laudatory account of the Kosalan image

"A man makes or causes to be made . . ." This sermon the Teacher preached while living at Jetavana with reference to the king of Kosala. For one morning at dawn the Teacher saw an individual who had made

---

[341] [-vatthuhi CNY]. [342] [ijjati MC, icchati N]. [343] [-kkhaca- U]. [344] dāsi- MSS; -dāsādi U, -dāsānidi *with* -ni- *deleted* Y. [345] [-dhārādi N, -dārādī CY]. [346] [maṇusse C]. [347] [upapajjati N]. [348] [dharan- KCNZ]. [349] [saññāya N, paṃññāya T]. [350] -sippehi *K*. [351] lekhiko KMNPZ, lekhikā *T*. [352] bimbakārakā *T*. [353] tibhava- *P* [-sirī UY]. [354] [sampāpunitvā CNU, pampāpunitvā Y]. [355] [-makuññe Y, -manuṃñe Z]. [356] [-kileso sesayitvā N]. [357] visesā PZTB. [358] [vajata N]. [359] tividhabodhiṃ *K*, tidivabodhyā UY [tividhaboddhyā Z, -baudhyā T]. [359a] [ekaṃ KUY]. [360] ekaṃta C, ekantato PZ, ekantaro UY, ekantiro TB. [361] [-ttherena CN]. [362] *om. P*. [363] [gaṃgaṃ *T*]. [364] vassāpento N, vassanto MCPZTB. [365] [-ākāreṇa C]. [366] [vannetvā UY]. [367] puññavanto va PZTB [mahā . . . puñña- *lacuna* Z; puṃñavantehi T]. [368] [pottakaṃ N]. [369] kāretabbā *P*. [370] [ni B]. [371] [samodhāṇesi Y, samodānesi TB]. [372] -parisā *P*. [373] [pāpunimsu CNY]. [374] sotāpannaṃ PUY [sotāpaṇṇā C]. [375] [sakadāgāmiṇo CY]. [376] [anāgāmiṇo Y]. [377] ekacce arahattaṃ pāpuṇiṃsu *P*. [378] [ekacce (as in 377) . . . tha *lacuna* Z]. [379] dibba- *P* [dibbaṃ- Y; -maṇussā C]. [380] [pujā- C, sakkāra M]. [381] kārentā KM, kārento NC. [382] Buddhappamukhaṃ TB [Buddhaṃ- Z]. [383] Jetavanam *P*, Jetavanaṃ vihāraṃ N. [384] [puṇa- C]. [385] *om*. C. [386] -patimā- MSS.

a religious aspiration, and to favour him he went on a long journey. Then Pasenadi, king of Kosala, went with a great retinue to Jetavana, and on not seeing the fully Enlightened one there he thought, "Alas, the monastery appears to be empty," and so became sad; without making any offering he had all the perfumes, garlands and the rest which had been brought dropped right there in the preaching hall, and returned to the city. When they had gone the Teacher came back to the monastery.

Next day the king of Kosala had perfumes, garlands and the rest, and requisites for the sick etc. taken along, and with a great retinue went to the Teacher. When he had offered them to the fully Enlightened one he prostrated himself completely[1]) and sat down to one side. When seated to one side, he said this to the Blessed one: "Your reverence, yesterday many of the inhabitants of Sāvatthi went to the monastery with perfumes, garlands and the rest, but did not see the fully Enlightened one, and so returned to the city exceedingly dissatisfied. So for the benefit of the whole world I would like to have made an image in the likeness of the Tathāgata"—so he said.[2]) On hearing this the Teacher said, "Very well, great king, your idea is excellent." Then he said, "You are[3]) permitted to make an image." Then the king asked, "What kind of image is it right for me to make?" "Great king, any man of good family who desires his well-being should make an image in the likeness of the Tathāgata of wood, stone, ivory, clay, silver, bronze, copper, tin or sand, and make it long or short, tiny or large, even the size of a barley-corn, a span long, or up to life size.[4]) Making an image, great king, is immeasurable, incalculable in the advantage it brings." So saying, he spoke this verse:

(1) "A man makes or causes to be made in this world an image of the Conqueror, in stone, in[5]) plaster, on cloth, in wood, great or even small."

"Great king, the advantage in having an image made is beyond measure. If[6]) a man of supernormal powers were able through the efficacy of those powers of his to count the sesamum or mustard seeds which could be[7]) packed inside this world system, even such a man would not be clever enough to say just how much benefit accrues from one image of the Conqueror. Again, great king, were he able to make all the water in the four

[1]) The five-fold prostration, in which forehead, elbows, waist, knees and feet touch the ground.

[2]) There is a redundant "he said" in the text: possibly an interpolation, more likely a defect of the original.

[3]) The MSS read, "I am permitted."

[4]) Literally: "up to man-size". Sinhalese tradition holds the Buddha to have been about 9 metres tall. Statues were sometimes far larger: the recumbent Buddha at Gal Vihāra, Poḷonnaruva (12th century) is 46 feet long; the standing statue at Avukana (8th century?) is 39 feet tall.

[5]) Or "on", if painting is meant.

[6]) Literally: "as"; see Introduction.

[7]) The literal translation, "seeds filled inside . . .", makes no sense.

oceans into drops and measure them, he would not be equal to saying the benefit of this. Were he clever enough, O lord of men, to make all the dust and sand on this earth into measures of a *māsa* bean[8]) and count them, he could not relate the good result of this. If, great king, one had to say just how much benefit accrues from one image of the Conqueror, except for the fully Enlightened one, others could not say it after creating by supernormal power many mouths—a hundred, a thousand, or even more."

When the advantage had been described in brief the king, having heard it all from the Teacher, paid homage to him and went home with his retinue. He had valuable fine sandalwood brought, and had a statue made with the distinctive characteristics;[9]) he had it inlaid with gold and clothed in valuable yellow robes, and had it set up in a suitable place· Then the king of Kosala had perfumes, garlands and the rest taken along, and with a great retinue went to Jetavana. He offered them to the Teacher, paid him homage, and spoke thus:

(2) "Caused by your command to make an image of the Conqueror out of finest sandalwood, I think it would be excellent if the Well-gone one of fine vision were to approach there and see it."

Then upon this request the Teacher consented by his silence.

On realizing the Teacher's consent the king went home and had a shrine[10]) of seven jewels made in the palace courtyard. He had it covered with tiles of gold, and put up an awning brightly decorated with gold and silver stars and so forth; he had garlands of perfume, garlands of flowers, etc. hung up, and in the interstices put up a network of bells made of gold etc.; the ground he had sprinkled with perfumes of four kinds[11]); all around he had hung curtains of priceless cloth; and on the right side he had a costly seat[12]) prepared, and the image set upon it. From there all the way to the gate of Jetavana he levelled the road where it was uneven and scattered extremely brilliant silvery sand; on it he spread stuffs of the five colours and scattered puffed rice and four kinds of flowers[13]); on both sides he had erected[14]) arches made of gold,

---

[8]) *Māsa* and *mugga* are both kinds of bean, but *māsa* is also the name of a small measure, "said to be equal to 7 lice" (PTS dictionary).

[9]) I.e. the 32 distinctive features of a Buddha.

[10]) A *maṇḍapa* is a temporary structure, especially one put up for a ritual. In this case it is a temporary shrine which, we learn at the end of the text, was moved to Jetavana.

[11]) "These 4 ingredients of perfume are saffron, jasmine, Turkish (*tarukkha*) and Greek incense (*yavana*)." PTS dictionary, *s.v. catujāti*.

[12]) The "seat" is the term in Sinhalese Buddhism for the slab on which images are set and offerings of flowers etc. are laid.

[13]) This literally translates the conventional phrase; but according to Sinhalese tradition the other four items are broken rice-grains, white mustard, jasmine buds, and panic grass.

[14]) The reading *ussāpetvā*, "had hoisted", is probably due to the appearance of that word in the next clause.

silver, etc., and between them at intervals had various banners hoisted, and between them at intervals had full vessels placed, and torches blazing with perfumed oil. Having thus adorned the road with every adornment, he went to the monastery, paid homage to the Teacher, and spoke thus:

(3) He, the king of Kosala, protector of the earth, having prepared the road for that Well-gone one, then went to Jetavana monastery and said this: "Behold the image."

Then the Teacher assented, "It is well," and rose from his seat, and surrounded by a group of his disciples went and entered with great pomp and splendour the jewelled shrine made on the orders of the king of Kosala. At that moment that non-sentient statue, on seeing the sentient fully Enlightened one, out of regard for the Teacher showed that it was rising to greet him, and received a prediction.[15] The Teacher, seeing its appearance, said, "Reverend sir, after me you will illumine my Teaching. For the sake of the Teaching endure five thousand years."[16] He extended his right arm, which was like Erāvaṇa's[17] trunk, and restrained it. To do it honour he offered it handfuls of jasmine flowers, and likewise both five hundred whose defilements were destroyed and the ordinary unenlightened people offered various fragrant flowers. At that moment Sakka, Suyāma, Santusita, Brahmā and the rest[18] offered that image their own respective material offerings. The Four Great Kings[19] took up guard on all four sides. All gods and men shouted thousands of hosannas.[20] On seeing that marvel the great earth quaked and gave a great roar; great Meru bowed like a performing dancer,[21] and the seven lesser mountain ranges[22] did the same; in the four great oceans the water

---

[15]) The text is ungrammatical (*dassento* masculine agreeing with a neuter subject) whether we read with the MSS or emend. The MSS *viya* means that the statue *seemed* to rise to pay homage (we may deduce that it was a seated image), and leaves *kate*, which is meaningless. The usage *vyākaroti* + acc. of person, "to make a prediction about (someone)", is not in the PTS dictionary but occurs several times in the Nidāna-kathā, e.g. p. 39 § 2 line 5. I know of no example elsewhere of this usage in the passive, but it does not seem illogical or implausible.

[16]) This is the time which, it is traditionally held, will elapse before the Buddha's teaching is forgotten.

[17]) The white elephant who is the mount of Sakka, an important god.

[18]) Representatives of the various heavens.

[19]) Rulers of the lowest heaven, who guard the four cardinal points.

[20]) Thus I translate *sādhu*, which is a cry of joy and participation on a religious occasion.

[21]) Dancers begin and end each performance with a deep and supple obeisance.

[22]) The world on our plane is complex. At its centre stands Mt. Meru *alias* Sineru. It is bordered at the four cardinal points by four continents which are peninsulas, each with its own ocean. All Buddhas are born in the southern one, Jambudīpa (i.e. India). Beyond these oceans are seven concentric mountain ranges called *kula-pabbatā*. These in turn are encircled by the *cakkavāḷa* range at the rim. The term *cakkavāḷa* also denotes the whole of a world system thus enclosed; there are

was stirred up as the jewels came[23])to the top; the whole world system was decorated with various flowers till it looked like a flower altar; and over the four great continents a great cloud arose.

When the king saw these wonders his body thrilled with pleasure, and in that shrine he had prepared a great seat for the Buddha, on which he had the Teacher sit down. He attentively served the Buddha and the monks whom he headed with rice gruel, food to bite, and so forth. In this way he gave a great donation of food to the monks for a week. On the seventh day after the meal he paid homage to the Teacher[24]); then, standing to one side, the king said this verse to ask about the benefit accruing from having an image made:

(4) "Who in the world of the living should make an image, what benefit does he derive, lord of sages? I ask you, please tell me." Thus said the king of Kosala.

Hearing this, the Teacher expounded that matter by saying:

(5) "It is very good, great king, that you asked me. I shall proclaim its result; listen, lord of the earth."

Then the elder Ānanda put together his hands, blazing with his ten nails, and put them on his head; thus worshipping the Teacher, he questioned him, saying:

(6) "Of[25]) the doctrine well taught by the king of lords of sages one may moreover copy a passage. What is the benefit, and the reward for an image? I wish you to teach." So he addressed him.

Hearing this he said, "Very well, Ānanda, your idea is excellent," and in a voice sweet with all the eight qualities he described the good results of both, teaching the doctrine as if a great cloud over the four continents were . . .,[26]) or as if he were giving mead to drink by expressing with a circular instrument[27]) a honeycomb a league across. "Ānanda," he said, "those meritorious creatures who in this world make

---

infinitely many of them, and the spaces between them are hells. Many other hells lie below the earth.

[23]) Presumably *pattā* is for *pattāni*.

[24]) The sense is complete, but the repetition of the subject (*rājā*) makes me suspect a trivial lacuna, probably after either *datvā* or *vanditvā* (where *ekam antam aṭṭhāsi* could have fallen out by haplography).

[25]) The meaning of this verse seems clear, but it is either corrupt or inept. (i) *sudesitena dhammena*: the instrumental case seems to occur by attraction to *-rājena*; emend to *sudesitassa dhammassa*? (ii) The construction of the last line is very elliptical. (iii) The final vowel of *icchāmi* is kept short before *ti metri gratia*.

[26]) I suspect a lacuna, because the great cloud should do something, e.g. rain down ambrosia.

[27]) Probably a centrifugal press. (Information supplied by Mr. U. A. Gunasekara).

an image or have one made, copy a book or have one copied, both of them experience incomparable bliss." Then he spoke these verses:

(7) "In[28]) a place crowded with frightening hellish creatures, unapproachable, chock full of fiery flames, in the eight great hells and sixteen projecting hells, copyists and image-makers are not born.

(8) "For Buddha-eons they do not even get snot or phlegm, let alone food and water[29])—in such a frightening existence as ghosts copyists and image-makers are not born.

(9) "Where for a whole eon one cannot see the light,[30]) in between worlds in a hell of horrible form, copyists and image-makers are not born as ghouls and demons[31]) called black hobblers.

(10) "In a receptacle of many unthinkable great woes, in existences as animals such as parrots, copyists and image-makers are not born, nor even as water-born creatures with large bodies.[32])

(11) "Among creatures without form or consciousness,[33]) or in the interstices between world systems, in such conditions image-makers and copyists are not born.

(12) "Even within this world system image-makers and copyists are not born in the other[34]) three continents or in remote regions.

---

[28]) The first four verses describe avoidance of the four kinds of bad rebirth (*duggati*) envisaged in the Canon: in nether hell, as a hungry ghost (*peta*), as a demon (*asura*), or as an animal. These and the following verses contain several echoes of the verses in the Nidāna-kathā (the introduction to the Jātaka book) which describe the advantages of Bodhisattvas. See Jātaka (ed. Fausbøll), vol. 1, pp. 44–5. Similar subject matter (the 18 conditions in which no Bodhisattva can be born) in Paramattha-jotikā II (= Sutta-nipāta-aṭṭhakathā), PTS ed., p. 50.

[29]) All the MSS are astray here. Probably the syllable *bha* was lost and *tt* then misread as *nn*, with *ca* being added to fill out the line. *Bat* in Sinhalese means both "food" and "cooked rice", the typical food; the same applies to Pali *bhatta*. A *Buddhantara* is the interval between the appearances of Buddhas, an immensely long time; though it is normally neuter, an accusative plural makes better sense here than a locative singular.

[30]) Literally: "not to be seen in the light for even an eon". Mr. Norman has pointed out to me that the *m* is a sandhi consonant.

[31]) Asura and dānava are archaic kinds of demon. They are not usually denizens of the interstitial hells, but that is poetic license. The black and the lame may be separate groups or the same: cf. Nidāna-kathā p. 44 v. 253d.

[32]) Both parrots and large aquatic beasts are unexpected in this context. The meaning may simply be that they are not reborn as animals, birds or fishes. But the allusion may be more precise. The Paramattha-jotikā (loc. cit., see note 28 above) says that Bodhisattvas reborn as animals are not smaller than quails or larger than elephants. (This is an *ex post facto* statement, based on what happens in the Jātaka stories). Our author may be making the same point, and trying to express in Pali the one creature larger than the elephant: the whale.

[33]) The planes (*āyatana*) without form or consciousness are the highest forms of phenomenal existence—in theory; but who wants to be reborn in them?

[34]) Other than Jambudīpa—see note 22 above.

(13) "They are born in the very middle region which is the area of provenance of those who need no further training: ordinary, lone, and fully Enlightened Buddhas[35]); of those on the way to Buddhahood; and of world rulers.

(14) "They do not acquire wrong views, but acquire right views[36]); as hermaphrodites, women, eunuchs and neuters,

(15) "Blind from birth,[37]) with water on the brain,[38]) dumb, deaf, lame, as crutched cripples, epileptic[39]) from birth to birth—thus they are not born.

(16) "In their every birth unsightly[40]) leprosy, boils and pimples, itches, scabs, wounds, etc., and skin diseases are avoided.

(17) "Their bodies are always like nuggets of gold. Like the sun in splendour are image-makers and copyists.

(18) "They never become frightened or terrified of rivals. Image-makers and copyists are born in a high family of great halls and great wealth, not in any other family.[41])

(19) "When born in the mother's womb their golden form, spotless, delights the mother and others even when seen from the outside.

(20) "Thus at the end of ten lunar months the baby is produced in safety. They grow in due course, like the moon on the second day of the lunar fortnight.[42])

---

[35]) The three types of Enlightened person are mentioned in ascending order: the one who has heard the Teaching from another; the one who has realized it unaided but has not taught it; and the one who has realized it unaided and then taught it. Only this last is normally called a Buddha in English. The unmetrical reading *sāvakānaṃ* has arisen because someone has not understood that *Buddha-* at the beginning of the line stands for the first type.

[36]) I.e. become Buddhists.

[37]) Normal Pali phonology would require *jaccandhā* (as in Nidāna-kathā v. 254a), but I have not removed the Sanskritism against the authority of all the MSS.

[38]) Literally: "water-crazy". Possibly *jal'* "water" is a mistake for *jaḍ'* "inert", i. e. moronic.

[39]) K's reading is an attempt to save the metre.

[40]) *Dudikkhā*, "hard to look at"; cf. Sanskrit *-dṛkṣa*. I owe this interpretation to Dr. Jothiya Dhirasekera.

[41]) *Aññe* can hardly be nominative plural here.

[42]) This line has puzzled the copyists. Perhaps we have here a coinage on the analogy of *puṇṇamā*, "the night of the full moon". The baby grows like the new moon; my cumbrous translation keeps close to the Pali to remind us that the moon only becomes visible on the second day of the lunar month. The *n* at the end of *dutiyan* may be wrong, but could be inserted to avoid a run of four short syllables. Mr. Norman makes the soberer suggestion that we read *thitimā* with P etc., deriving the word from Skt. *sthitimat*, "having stability". Then the line would mean, "In due course they double in size, like what is stable." But what would that be—a mountain?

(21) "In the family in which he is born there is never a lack of wealth[43]) in money and grain, with jewels ten-fold always.

(22) "He prospers with tens of millions of various cloths—linens, silks and so forth, with elephants, horses, cattle and so forth, with fields and building land.

(23) "He acquires male and female slaves who are obedient to his word, and similarly wife and children, and dependants always.

(24) "Wherever he is born, in the world of gods or men, he will surpass all others with all forms of wealth.

(25) "With wisdom like the earth, skilled in every craft, the copyist, the image-maker would always be steadfast.

(26) "Having[44]) thus properly attained the splendour of riches,[45]) having enjoyed exceedingly delightful pleasures of the five senses, then having dried up all defilements, he then by the triple Enlightenment attains each single spiritual distinction."[46])

Thus at the request of the elder Ānanda and of the Kosalan the Blessed one gave a laudatory account in many a way of the results, as if he were causing the celestial river to descend to earth, or causing a shower of ambrosia to rain down. Then he gave the key[47]) to this sermon, saying, "Great king, those meritorious people who desire their own welfare should have a book copied or an image made." At the conclusion of the sermon, five thousand men attained arhatship with the discriminating insights; some became stream-enterers, some once-returners, and some non-returners. Then the king of Kosala and the gods and men made great offerings in worship, and conducted the Buddha and the monks whom he headed to the Jetavana monastery. The next day he had that sandal-wood statue with the shrine of seven jewels set up right there in the monastery.

---

[43]) The reading *samuddhīhi* reflects Sinhalese pronunciation of Sanskrit *samṛddhi*; if it is original, and C represents a correction, this sheds interesting light on the author's Pali.

[44]) This final verse follows the tradition of elaborate poetry (*kāvya*) rather than of Buddhist scriptures, in that it is in a different and more elaborate metre than its predecessors. The more difficult metre is so smoothly handled as to make one wonder whether in previous verses the textual tradition may have failed to do the author justice, or alternatively whether he borrowed this verse from elsewhere.

[45]) The reading *tibhava*, equally possible, would mean "the three forms of phenomenal existence", i.e. in the worlds of desire, of form and of non-form. Cf. Sad-dhamma-sangaha X, 24.

[46]) *K*'s reading could be right, but *visesaṃ vajati* is probably a periphrasis modelled on *visesa-gāmin* etc. To take *visesaṃ* as an adverb is comparatively awkward.

[47]) See Introduction p. 281.

Appendix: Metre

1. *Vatta.*

17 verses, of which 16 have 4 *pāda* and 1 has 6.

35 prior *pāda*, with cadences as follows: 33 *pathyā*, 1 first *vipulā*, 1 second *vipulā*.

The openings all conform to the rule that the second and third syllables should not both be short.

There is resolution of the first syllable in 1 case.

The caesura between prior and posterior *pāda* is violated in 2 cases (13 ab and 15 cd), though the *K* MSS try to mend this.

35 posterior *pāda*, with regular cadences.

The openings conform to the rule that the second and third syllables should not both be short; but two *pāda* end in a triple iambus.

There is resolution of the first syllable of the *pāda* in 4 cases, but all 4 are the same word, *paṭimākārā*.

2. *Tuṭṭhubha.*

4 whole strophes and 5 *pāda* in mixed *tuṭṭhubha-jagatī* strophes: total 21 *pāda*.

20 *pāda* conform to the classical *upajāti* scheme, except that 2 of them have resolution of the first syllable.

1 *pāda* (v. 9 b) is of the older type with a caesura after the fourth syllable followed by ⏑⏑– (rather than –⏑⏑).

Noteworthy instances of metrical license are *sajjetvă* (3 b), *bimba* (for *bimbaṃ*) (4 d), and *icchāmĭ ti* (6 d).

3. *Jagatī.*

1 whole strophe and 7 *pāda* in 3 mixed strophes (see above): total 11 *pāda*.

All conform to the classical *upajāti* scheme.

4. *Mālinī.*

1 strophe. Regular.

Netrapratiṣṭhāpana — eine singhalesische Zeremonie zur Weihe von Kultbildern

Von HANS RUELIUS

Sowohl die Weihe von Buddhastatuen im singhalesischen Buddhismus als auch die der Götterbilder der singhalesischen Volksreligion geschieht durch das rituelle Einsetzen der Augen, das Netrapratiṣṭhāpana[1]). Diese Zeremonie ist spätestens seit dem 5. Jh. n. Chr. in Ceylon bekannt[2]). Zu Zeiten der singhalesischen Könige bestanden die Augen besonders kostbarer Statuen in den großen Klöstern aus Edelsteinen, die vom König eigenhändig eingesetzt wurden[3]). Bei den vollständig bemalten Statuen, wie sie heute fast ausschließlich in Ceylon üblich sind, wird bei der Weihe lediglich die Pulpille in den weißen Untergrund des Auges gemalt. Das ist Aufgabe des Künstlers, der die Statue hergestellt hat.

Bei der Weihe von Buddhastatuen wird das Netrapratiṣṭhāpana heute nicht mehr in jedem Falle durchgeführt. Moderne singhalesische Buddhisten halten es meist für überflüssig. In solchen Fällen geschieht die Weihe lediglich durch eine ,,Prathamapūjā“, eine erste, besonders feierliche Verehrung der Statue, der in der Regel eine Paritta-Zeremonie vorausgeht. In ländlichen Gegenden ist die Weihe von Buddhastatuen in Form eines Netrapratiṣṭhāpana aber noch immer die Regel.

Dabei ist das Einsetzen der Augen Teil und Kernstück einer längeren Zeremonie. Die gesamte Zeremonie, von den Singhalesen als ,,Netra maṅgalya“ oder ,,Netra pinkama“ bezeichnet, besteht aus zwei deutlich voneinander unterschiedenen Teilen, die nur locker miteinander

---

[1]) Die Zeremonie wurde bereits zweimal beschrieben. S. Ananda K. Coomaraswamy, Mediaeval Sinhalese Art, 2. Aufl., New York 1956, S. 70–75 und Richard Gombrich, The Consecration of a Buddhist Image, in: Journal of Asian Studies, Vol. 26, No. 1 (1966), S. 23–36. Sie unterscheidet sich sehr wesentlich vom hinduistischen Netronmīlana bzw. Netramokṣaṇa, das dort nur Teil sehr viel komplizierterer Weihezeremonien ist. Siehe dazu: Vaikhānasāgama, hg. v. K. Śāmbaśiva Śāstrī, Trivandrum 1935 (Trivandrum Sanskrit Series 121), Kap. 30 (S. 103ff.) und Rauravāgama, Vol. 2 (Kriyāpāda), hg. v. N. R. Bhatt, Pondichéry 1972 (Publications de l'Institut Français d'Indologie 18–2), Kap. 11, V. 12–16 (S. 49), Kap. 12, V. 16–21 (S. 58), Kap. 14, V. 14–17 (S. 70f.).

[2]) Als Akkhipūjā ist die Zeremonie bereits in Buddhaghosas Samantapāsādikā (5. Jh. n. Chr.) erwähnt (hg. v. J. Takakusu und M. Nagai, Bd. 1, London 1924, S. 44), ebenso im Mahāvaṃsa (hg. v. Wilhelm Geiger, London 1908, V. 94). Vgl. Richard Gombrich, op. cit. (s. Anm. 1), S. 26.

[3]) Cūḷavaṃsa, hg. v. Wilhelm Geiger, Bd. 1, London 1925, Bd. 2, London 1927. Kap. 37, V. 123; Kap. 38, V. 62; Kap. 73, V. 78. Vgl. Coomaraswamy, op. cit, (s. Anm. 1), S. 72 und Gombrich, op. cit. (s. Anm. 1), S. 26.

verknüpft sind: Den ersten Teil bildet eine komplizierte Opferzeremonie, das Ṣaḍaṅga-Opfer. Ihm folgt die eigentliche Netrapratiṣṭhāpana-Zeremonie, die auch ohne das vorhergehende Ṣaḍaṅga-Opfer durchgeführt werden kann[4]). Diese Zeremonie besteht wiederum aus zwei Teilen: dem Einsetzen der Augen und einem anschließenden Reinigungsritual.

Wenn eine neue Buddhastatue fertiggestellt ist, wird der günstige Zeitpunkt für die Weihezeremonie von einem Astrologen berechnet. In der Nacht vor dem festgesetzten Zeitpunkt findet die Ṣaḍaṅga-Zeremonie statt.

Die Ṣaḍaṅga-Zeremonie ist ihrem äußeren Hergang nach eine magische Opferzeremonie. Dabei wird vor dem Sockel der Statue ein Altar aus Reis aufgeschichtet, auf dessen Oberfläche mit Hilfe von Betelnußblüten ein Diagramm ausgelegt wird. Dieses Diagramm hat die Form eines Quadrates oder Rechtecks, das in eine bestimmte Zahl von Feldern eingeteilt wird. In die einzelnen Felder werden irdene Töpfe mit Opfergaben gestellt. Schon die Errichtung des Opferaltars und das Aufstellen der Töpfe sind Teil der Zeremonie. Der weitere Fortgang der Zeremonie ist relativ handlungsarm. Er besteht im wesentlichen aus Rezitationen von Mantras und Stotras. Die beiden Bali-Spezialisten (Ädurās), von denen der eine ein rotes und der andere ein blaues Tuch über der Schulter trägt[5]), rezitieren zeitweise abwechselnd und zeitweise gemeinsam. Die Rezitation wird nur durch ein Räucheropfer und mehrmaliges Besprengen der Opfergaben mit Wasser unterbrochen. Eine genaue Beschreibung der Ṣaḍaṅga-Zeremonie ist ohne eine genaue Kenntnis der zu rezitierenden Texte nicht möglich. Auf die bei seiner Untersuchung auftretenden Schwierigkeiten werde ich weiter unten nochmals ausführlicher eingehen[6])

Nach Beendigung des Ṣaḍaṅga-Opfers tritt meist eine längere Pause ein. Einige Minuten vor dem für das Einsetzen der Augen vorausberechneten astrologisch günstigen Zeitpunkt betritt der Künstler den Schrein, in dem die Statue steht. Er wird nur von seinem Gehilfen begleitet; denn außer diesen beiden darf sich während der Zeremonie niemand in dem Gebäude aufhalten. In dem Augenblick, in dem er die Tür hinter sich verschließt, beginnen draußen, von einem klarinettenähnlichen Blasinstrument begleitet, die Trommeln zu schlagen. Sie ändern genau zu dem vorausberechneten günstigen Augenblick ihren Rhythmus und verstummen erst, wenn sich die Tür wieder öffnet und der Künstler nach Vollendung seiner Arbeit den Schrein wieder verläßt[7]).

Im Inneren des Schreins findet in der Zwischenzeit der wichtigste Teil der Zeremonie statt. Der Künstler und sein Gehilfe bereiten zunächst

---

[4]) So z.B. bei einer von mir beobachteten Zeremonie in Nugegoḍa bei Colombo. Siehe unten S. 308 und S. 319.

[5]) Rot ist die Farbe des Kataragama, Blau die des Viṣṇu.

[6]) Siehe unten S. 318ff.

[7]) Zu den wechselnden Trommelrhythmen, die die singhalesischen Rituale häufig begleiten, siehe A. M. Hocart, The Temple of the Tooth in Kandy, London 1931 (Memoirs of the Archaeological Survey of Ceylon 4), S. 18ff.

die schwarze Farbe zu, die zum Malen der Pupillen benötigt wird. Zu diesem Zweck wird ein Stück Sandelholz verbrannt. Die dabei entstehende Holzkohle wird zerrieben und auf einem Betelblatt mit etwas Kokosnußöl vermischt. Die so zubereitete Farbe wird in ein kleines goldenes Schälchen gefüllt. Zum Malen benutzt der Künstler einen in Gold gefaßten Pinsel.

Beim Einsetzen der Augen muß der Künstler mit großer Sorgfalt vorgehen; denn der Blick aus den gerade eingesetzten Augen eines Kultbildes gilt als äußerst gefährlich. Es wird behauptet, daß ein Blick in die Augen einer gerade geweihten Statue Erblinden oder gar den Tod zur Folge haben kann. Der Künstler schaut deshalb nicht direkt in die Augen der Statue, sondern benutzt zum Malen einen Spiegel, der von seinem Gehilfen gehalten wird. Er selbst steht dabei mit dem Rücken zur Statue.

Eine ähnlich gefährliche Wirkung wie dem Blick der eben geweihten Statue wird auch dem des Künstlers zugeschrieben, nachdem er seine Arbeit beendet hat. Sein Blick, von dem man sagt, daß er alles zerstört, was er trifft, wird ängstlich gemieden. Er muß sein Gesicht so lange mit einem Tuch verhüllen, bis er ein Reinigungsritual vollzogen hat, d.h. bis er die gefährliche Kraft aus seinen Augen gewaschen hat. Erst dann ist die Gefahr gebannt.

Das Reinigungsritual läuft folgendermaßen ab: Der Künstler wird mit verdecktem Gesicht aus dem Schrein herausgeführt zu der Stelle, an der die für das Ritual benötigten Gegenstände schon vorbereitet sind. Dort steht eine Schüssel mit Milch, auf deren Boden ein Goldstück liegt. Neben der Schüssel ist ein Schwert bereitgelegt, und einige Schritte daneben steht ein junger Bulle, der an einen Baum oder einen Pfahl angebunden ist.

Von dem Augenblick an, in dem der Künstler den Schrein verläßt bis zur Beendigung des Reinigungsrituals wird peinlich darauf geachtet, daß alle anwesenden Zuschauer den vorher festgelegten Abstand zum Ort des Geschehens einhalten und dem Künstler nicht zu nahe kommen.

Wenn der Künstler an der vorbereiteten Stelle angekommen ist, schlägt er das Tuch von seinem Gesicht zurück. Dabei fällt sein Blick zuerst auf einen Baum. Er ergreift das bereitliegende Schwert und schlägt es in den Stamm des Baumes. Danach wäscht er sich über der Schüssel mit der Milch das Gesicht. Anschließend soll er, wie einige Informanten berichten, die volle Schüssel auf den Hörnern des Bullen zerschlagen. Aus verständlichem Grund geschieht dies in der Praxis meist nicht, sondern der Künstler greift hier zu einer Ersatzhandlung, indem er etwa seine Hände zwischen den Hörnern des Bullen trocknet. Der Bulle wird dann weggetrieben.

Die Tatsache, daß die Netrapratiṣṭhāpana-Zeremonie auch der Weihe von Buddhabildern dient, hat verschiedentlich zu Mißdeutungen geführt. So erscheint die Vorstellung, der Blick einer Darstellung des Buddha könne eine gefährliche, ja sogar tödliche Wirkung besitzen, dem unbefangenen Beobachter in der Tat zunächst als Widerspruch: Nach der

Lehre des Theravāda-Buddhismus war der Buddha eine historische Persönlichkeit. Er war ein Mensch, der die Erleuchtung erlangte und damit den Weg ins Nirvāṇa gefunden hat. Er nahm die Mühe auf sich, das gefundene Wissen weiterzugeben, d.h. zum Heile aller Wesen seine Lehre zu verkünden, um auch ihnen den richtigen Weg zur Erlösung zu zeigen, damit sie vom Leiden befreit werden.

Die Verehrung des Buddhabildes soll ebenso wie die seiner Reliquien der Erinnerung an den Buddha und der Vergegenwärtigung seiner Lehre dienen. Der Buddha, der das Nirvāṇa erlangt hat, kann nach der Lehre in keiner Weise mehr als existent angesehen werden. Aber er wird verehrt als ob er gegenwärtig wäre[8]).

Und von dem Bild dieses Buddha sollte Gefahr drohen? Wie ich im folgenden zeigen werde, ist dies nur scheinbar ein Widerspruch zur buddhistischen Lehre, der seinen Grund nicht in der Sache selbst hat, sondern in den bisherigen Deutungsversuchen.

Ananda K. Coomaraswamy, der die Netrapratiṣṭhāpana-Zeremonie zum ersten Male ausführlich beschrieben hat, sieht hier Gemeinsamkeiten zwischen Hinduismus und Buddhismus: "But the ceremony no doubt dates back to the time when Buddhism and Hinduism were more distinctly recognized as two aspects of one faith, which historically and fundamentally they are. Some idea of danger (as of 'playing with fire', or 'calling down lightning from heaven') appears to attach to this consecration of the image, whereby it is made a medium between the worshipper and his god (which would be a Hindu not a Buddhist idea); and the object of the ceremonial is, in this connection, to avert misfortunes, akin to those resulting from a glance of the 'evil eye', which might otherwise afflict the presumptious builder and artist."[9]) Diese sehr stark vom Neohinduismus geprägte Auffassung Coomaraswamys ist sicher nicht haltbar. Mit der Möglichkeit eines gemeinsamen historischen Ursprungs des singhalesischen Netrapratiṣṭhāpana und des hinduistischen Netramokṣaṇa werden wir uns weiter unten noch befassen müssen[10]).

Richard Gombrich in seiner Studie über die Netrapratiṣṭhāpana-Zeremonie widerspricht zwar der Meinung Coomaraswamys, die Zeremonie sei eher hinduistisch als buddhistisch, hält aber daran fest, daß beim Netrapratiṣṭhāpana die Buddhastatue im Widerspruch zur buddhistischen Dogmatik als belebtes Abbild eines Gottes aufgefaßt wird[11]).

Gombrich weist darauf hin, daß der singhalesischen Volksreligion die Vorstellung des „bösen Blicks" durchaus geläufig ist. Er kommt daher zu der Auffassung, das Einsetzen der Augen diene dazu, die Statue zum Leben zu erwecken: "That the circumstances of a nētra pinkama imply

---

[8]) Siehe Dieter Schlingloff, Die Religion des Buddhismus, Bd. 2, Berlin 1963 (Sammlung Göschen 770), S. 63.

[9]) Op. cit. (s. Anm. 1), S. 71.

[10]) Siehe unten S. 329f.

[11]) Op. cit. (s. Anm. 1). Siehe auch: Richard Gombrich, Precept and Practice, Oxford 1971, S. 138ff.

the attribution of life to the image cannot be and was not denied; ... In the terms of my analysis, the ceremony treats the Buddha as a god. But what is especially striking is that the gaze is treated as dangerous, potentially maleficient. It is not an excess of holiness which the craftsman fears from the new-born gaze ... But the totally undoctrinal danger of the nētra pinkama is clear and unambiguous."[12])

Es gibt keinerlei Anhaltspunkt dafür, daß dem Netrapratiṣṭhāpana der Gedanke des Zum-Leben-Erweckens der Statue zugrunde liegt. Die Verehrung des Buddhabildes, die Buddhapūjā, auch wenn sie in der Form eines Opfers auftritt, setzt keineswegs die Vorstellung einer belebten Statue voraus. Die Möglichkeit der Ritualisierung des Sich-Erinnerns an den Buddha ist nach der buddhistischen Lehre durchaus gegeben. Somit ist es nicht verwunderlich, ja eigentlich selbstverständlich, wenn man dabei auf ein vorhandenes und vertrautes rituelles Repertoire zurückgreift.

Es wäre deshalb nicht sehr sinnvoll, anzunehmen, die Netrapratiṣṭhāpana-Zeremonie, hätte den Sinn, die Statue zu Leben zu erwecken. Es geht vielmehr um die Fertigstellung der Statue, um den letzten Handschlag bzw. um den letzten Pinselstrich, der in ritualisierter Form als Weiheritual dient.

Wir können also nicht davon ausgehen, daß der Buddha im Weiheritual die Bedeutung eines Gottes hat, sondern wir müssen uns hier mit der Feststellung begnügen, daß Buddhabild und Götterbilder bei der Weihe gleich behandelt werden. Und eines ist ihnen ja auch gemeinsam: Sie sind beide Kultgegenstand. Als Kultgegenstand bedürfen sie einer Weihe. Die Netrapratiṣṭhāpana-Zeremonie gilt also nicht dem Buddha oder dem Gott, sie gilt auch nicht dem Buddhabild oder dem Götterbild als belebtem Repräsentanten des Buddha oder des Gottes, sie gilt dem Kultgegenstand Buddhabild und dem Kultgegenstand Götterbild.

Wenn wir eine Erklärung für den Verlauf der Netrapratiṣṭhāpana-Zeremonie suchen, so müssen wir von der Funktion des Buddhabildes als Kultobjekt ausgehen und nicht von einem angenommenen Glauben der Beteiligten über die Natur des Buddha. Nicht die intuitive Rekonstruktion etwaiger Motive der Beteiligten führt zu einer brauchbaren Deutung des Rituals, sondern wir müssen das vorhandene Material einer gründlichen Analyse unterziehen. Eine mögliche Deutung kann nur durch den Hinweis auf das vorhandene Material gerechtfertigt werden.

1. Das Material

Als Quellen für diese Untersuchung standen mir zur Verfügung:

1. Protokolle eigener Beobachtungen zweier Netrapratiṣṭhāpana-Zeremonien, die ich während eines Studienaufenthaltes in Ceylon 1968/69 machen konnte — die erste Zeremonie fand am 23. Januar 1969 im Isi-

[12]) Precept and Practice (s. Anm. 11), S. 139.

patanārāma in Yaṭihalagala bei Kandy statt, die zweite am 24. Februar 1969 im Vikramasiṃhārāma in Nugēgoḍa bei Colombo —,

2. eine Beschreibung der Zeremonie von Ananda K. Coomaraswamy in seinem Buch „Mediaeval Sinhalese Art“[13]),

3. der detaillierte Bericht Richard Gombrichs über eine von ihm beobachtete Netrapratiṣṭhāpana-Zeremonie im ceylonesischen Hochland[14]),

4. einen Text mit dem Namen „Ṣaḍaṅga vidhiya“, der den Beginn der Zeremonie und das dem Einsetzen der Augen vorausgehende Opfer, das Ṣaḍaṅga, beschreibt[15]).

2. Aufbereitung des Materials und Methode der Beschreibung

Mit der Niederschrift von Schilderungen unserer Informanten und den Protokollen eigener Beobachtungen besitzen wir noch kein brauchbares und vollständiges Material, um eine Zeremonie zu beschreiben. Das Material muß zunächst einmal aufbereitet werden; es muß auf seine Vollständigkeit und seine Brauchbarkeit für eine Beschreibung und Deutung des Geschehens hin untersucht werden.

In unserem Falle müssen wir davon ausgehen, daß die Rituale der singhalesischen Volksreligion und des volkstümlichen Buddhismus, sofern es sich nicht um regelmäßig durchgeführte Tempelzeremonien handelt, nicht nach absolut bindenden, genau festgelegten Regeln ablaufen. Der äußere Ablauf ist häufig von den jeweiligen Bedürfnissen und Möglichkeiten des Auftraggebers oder des Durchführenden abhängig. Das bedeutet selbstverständlich nicht, daß es keine Regeln gibt, nur werden diese Rituale durch Abweichungen von der Norm nicht ungültig oder unwirksam. Es gibt keine kanonisierte Ritualliteratur und keine Zentralinstanz, die über die Richtigkeit von Regeln entscheidet und ihre Befolgung durchsetzt. Diese Aufgabe lag früher teilweise in den Händen der singhalesischen Könige, doch ihre Aufmerksamkeit galt in der Hauptsache nur dem Staatskult und bestimmten regelmäßig wiederkehrenden Zeremonien in einigen großen Tempeln[16]).

Wenn wir also eine Zeremonie oder ein Ritual der singhalesischen Volksreligion beschreiben wollen, müssen wir in jedem Falle berücksichtigen, daß deren konkrete Durchführung in ihren Details sehr stark von Zufällen bestimmt sein kann.

[13]) Siehe Anm. 1.

[14]) Siehe Anm. 1.

[15]) Nr. 2357 in W. A. de Silva, Catalogue of Palm Leaf Manuscripts in the Library of the Colombo Museum, Bd. 1 (alles erschienene), Colombo 1938 (Memoirs of the Colombo Museum, Ser. A, No. 4). Dort: Saḍamgam Vidiya (sic!). Die unter Nr. 2358 beschriebene Handschrift enthält einen anderen Text.

[16]) Wie dies im Falle der Rituale um die Zahnreliquie geschah. Zu den durch König Parākrama Bāhu IV erlassenen Vorschriften siehe Hocart, op. cit. (s. Anm. 7), S. 34ff. Ähnliches gilt für die Perahäras.

Was für unsere eigenen Beobachtungen gilt, gilt auch in gewissem Grade für die Berichte unserer Informanten, sofern sie den Verlauf der Zeremonie betreffen. Sonstige Schwierigkeiten, die bei der Befragung einheimischer Informanten auftreten, brauchen hierwohl nicht gesondert erörtert zu werden.

Das Material, das wir aus eigenen Beobachtungen und aus Berichten von Informanten erhalten, muß also keineswegs repräsentativ sein. Wir müssen mit Varianten rechnen. Das Auftreten solcher Varianten kann die unterschiedlichsten Ursachen haben. Es können technische Gründe vorliegen: Soll z.B. im Verlaufe des Rituals eine Schüssel zerschlagen werden, so ist das nicht durchführbar, wenn nur eine Blechschüssel zur Verfügung steht statt der vorgesehenen irdenen Schüssel. Wenn ein weißer Bulle benötigt wird und ein solches Tier nicht beschafft werden kann, wird man sich auch mit einem braunen begnügen. Häufig sind es auch die beschränkten finanziellen Möglichkeiten, die zu Improvisationen zwingen: Ist z.B. die Verwendung von goldenem Gerät oder eine aus Gold und Edelsteinen bestehende Opfergabe gefordert, wird man sich oft mit einem billigeren Ersatz behelfen müssen. Mitunter hängt der Verlauf eines Rituals — und hier besonders die Auswahl der rezitierten Texte — auch von den jeweiligen Kenntnissen des Durchführenden ab. Hervorragende Experten verlangen auch eine entsprechend hohe Bezahlung.

Solche Varianten müssen wir bei unserer Beschreibung berücksichtigen, d.h. wir müssen versuchen, Ersatzhandlungen als solche zu erkennen und ihre Ursachen festzustellen; denn für die Deutung eines Rituals oder einer Zeremonie genügt uns nicht die Beschreibung des tatsächlichen Verlaufs in einem oder mehreren konkreten Fällen, sondern wir müssen den Ablauf so rekonstruieren, wie er beabsichtigt war bzw. wie er zustande gekommen wäre, wenn äußere Umstände nicht zu Änderungen gezwungen hätten. Unsere Aufbereitung des Materials besteht zunächst also darin, aus dem sichtbaren tatsächlichen Verlauf einer Zeremonie oder eines einzelnen Rituals den idealen Verlauf zu rekonstruieren.

Zur Rekonstruktion des idealen Verlaufs benötigen wir Vergleichsmaterial. Es ist deshalb wichtig, das gleiche Ritual mehrmals an verschiedenen Stellen und unter verschiedenen Bedingungen zu beobachten. Ein erster Vergleich ermöglicht dann häufig schon, eine Reihe von Varianten zu erkennen und auszuscheiden.

Darüber hinaus sind uns hier die Schilderungen der einheimischen Informanten eine wertvolle Hilfe. In vielen Fällen beruhen diese Schilderungen nämlich gar nicht auf eigenen Beobachtungen, sondern sie geben das wieder, was der betreffende Informant über das Ritual gehört oder gelernt hat. Sie beschreiben das Ritual dann häufig so, wie es verlaufen sollte, nicht wie es gewöhnlich tatsächlich verläuft. Dieselben Informationen erhält man nicht, wenn man nach den Regeln fragt, die dem Ritual zugrunde liegen. Diese Regeln sind zwar bekannt, doch sie sind nirgends genau und im Zusammenhang formuliert.

Bei der Rekonstruktion des idealen Verlaufs muß natürlich gewährleistet sein, daß nicht auch bewußt herbeigeführte Veränderungen, die ihre Ursache in einem Wandel von Funktion und Bedeutung des Rituals haben, als Varianten ausgeschieden werden. Bevor wir Varianten aus unserer Beschreibung ausscheiden, muß also in jedem Falle der Nachweis erbracht werden, daß es sich dabei um zufällig zustande gekommene Varianten handelt.

Die Berichte einheimischer Informanten enthalten neben einer Beschreibung des Verlaufs meist auch noch andere Informationen, wie z.B. Erläuterungen über den Zweck einzelner Ritualhandlungen, Geschichten über Vorkommnisse bei früheren Zeremonien der gleichen Art, Angaben über Gefahren bei der Durchführung und über den Zweck oder Nutzen der ganzen Zeremonie sowie häufig auch eine Kultätiologie.

Trennen wir diese Aussagen von der eigentlichen Beschreibung des Rituals oder der Zeremonie, in die sie eingeflochten sind, so erhalten wir eine Darstellung des Geschehens, die ich hier als mythischen Begleittext bezeichnen will[17]). Dieser mythische Begleittext stellt für die Beteiligten eine Erklärung bzw. Rechtfertigung des Rituals dar. Für uns aber kann sie keine Erklärung sein, sondern sie bedarf selbst der Deutung. Der mythische Begleittext wird dem außenstehenden Beobachter so lange unverständlich bleiben, wie er den Hergang des Rituals nicht kennt. Aber nicht nur die mythologische Ausdrucksweise bereitet hier Schwierigkeiten. Ebenso wie die Regeln für die Durchführung der Rituale ist auch der mythische Begleittext nirgendwo als autoritativer Text formuliert. Er muß also in der gleichen Weise rekonstruiert werden wie der ideale Verlauf, d.h. wir müssen ihn aus den Angaben unserer Informanten zusammensetzen.

Die singhalesische Volksreligion besitzt zwar keinen Kanon von Ritualtexten, doch es gibt in der singhalesischen Literatur zahlreiche Werke über Rituale. Da diese Texte nicht kanonisiert und somit auch nicht autoritativ sind, können wir sie nicht als Vorschriften für die Durchführung der Rituale werten, sondern nur als Beschreibungen ihres Verlaufs. Diese Beschreibungen sind allerdings nicht sehr ins einzelne gehend und für den, der den Ablauf der Rituale nicht kennt, kaum verständlich. Sie nennen zwar die einzelnen Ritualhandlungen beim Namen und legen deren Reihenfolge fest, doch über die Art und Weise der Durchführung geben sie wenig Auskunft. Daneben enthalten sie die im Verlaufe der Zeremonie oder des Rituals zu rezitierenden Texte und Mantras. Ermöglichen diese Ritualtexte alleine auch keine Beschreibung des jeweiligen Rituals, mit dem sie sich befassen, so geben sie uns im Zusammenhang gesehen mit unseren eigenen Beobachtungen und den Auskünften unserer Informanten doch sehr wichtige Aufschlüsse.

---

[17]) Ich habe diese Bezeichnung gewählt, da es sich hier nicht um eine vollständige mythische Erzählung handelt, sondern um einzelne in die Beschreibung des Rituals eingeflochtene, mythologisierende Erläuterungen.

Im Falle der Netrapratiṣṭhāpana-Zeremonie besitzen wir einen solchen Ritualtext, nämlich das oben erwähnte Ṣaḍaṅga vidhiya. Dieser Text beschreibt zwar nur den Beginn der Zeremonie und das Ṣaḍaṅga-Opfer, das dem Einsetzen der Augen vorausgeht, aber wir müssen ihn als zusätzlichen Zeugen heranziehen.

Beschreibung und Deutung einer religiösen Zeremonie sind in den seltensten Fällen voneinander zu trennen. Bei der Beobachtung laufen wir ständig Gefahr, Einzelheiten zu übersehen, weil wir ihre Bedeutung nicht kennen. Wenn wir den Zusammenhang des ganzen nicht überschauen, nehmen wir an bestimmten Stellen häufig bestimmte Dinge nicht wahr, weil wir sie dort nicht erwarten.

Um solche Fehler zu vermeiden, müssen wir schon zur Beobachtung der Zeremonie oder des Rituals, das wir untersuchen wollen, eine Vorstellung von dem mitbringen, was uns erwartet. Wir müssen den voraussichtlichen konkreten Verlauf schon kennen. Hierzu verhilft uns der mythische Begleittext; denn er stellt durch seine Erklärung des Geschehens die Zusammenhänge zwischen den einzelnen rituellen Handlungen her. Denselben Zusammenhängen, die wir im mythischen Begleittext finden, folgt auch der Verlauf des Rituals. Wenn wir davon ausgehen, daß im Ritual reales Geschehen symbolisch dargestellt wird, so müssen dieselben Zusammenhänge auch in der Wirklichkeit zu finden sein. Ist dies der Fall, d.h. wenn sich im mythischen Begleittext, im idealen Verlauf des Rituals und im tatsächlichen Geschehen innerhalb des sozialen Systems dieselben Strukturen auffinden lassen, so haben wir die gesuchte Erklärung gefunden.

Wenn wir nun das dramaturgische Konzept, das dem Ritual zugrunde liegt, kennen, sind wir in der Lage, festzustellen, ob unsere Beschreibung des Rituals lückenlos ist. Andererseits können wir aber auch anhand unserer Beobachtungen die Richtigkeit der aus dem mythischen Begleittext erschlossenen Dramaturgie und damit die Vollständigkeit der von unseren Informanten erhaltenen Schilderung überprüfen. So ist es nun auch möglich, durch gezielte und entsprechend formulierte Fragen an unsere Informanten den mythischen Begleittext wenn nötig zu vervollständigen.

3. Der mythische Begleittext

Im mythischen Begleittext zum Netrapratiṣṭhāpana haben wir keinen durchkomponierten Mythos vor uns. Er besteht vielmehr aus einzelnen Aussagen, die wir den Berichten unserer Informanten entnehmen können. Er läßt sich folgendermaßen darstellen:

Der Künstler vollendet die Statue, indem er die Augen einsetzt. Der Blick der frisch eingesetzten Augen hat eine überaus gefährliche Wirkung. Würde er das Auge des Künstlers treffen, kann dies zu dessen Erblinden oder gar zu seinem Tod führen. Deshalb benutzt der Künstler beim Einsetzen der Augen einen Spiegel. Obwohl der Künstler nicht direkt in die Augen der Statue schaut, geht die gefährliche Wirkung nun auch auf seine Augen über. Auch von seinem Blick geht nun Gefahr aus. Der Künstler verhüllt sein Gesicht, um seine Umgebung vor dieser gefährlichen Wirkung zu schützen. Sein Blick würde sonst alles vernichten, was er trifft. Erst wenn der Künstler den gefährlichen Blick aus seinen Augen gewaschen hat, ist sein Blick wieder erträglich. Die Gefahr befindet sich nun im Wasser, das deshalb auf einen Bullen geladen wird, der es wegträgt.

Das ist eine Zusammenfassung dessen, was ich den Berichten meiner Informanten entnehmen konnte und was im wesentlichen auch mit dem übereinstimmt, was Coomaraswamy und Gombrich berichten[18]). In einem Falle fügte ein Informant noch eine Geschichte an: Der Künstler, der die große sitzende Buddhastatue des Gaḍalādeṇiya Vihāra[19]) in der Nähe von Kandy errichtet hat, ist nach der Durchführung des Netrapratiṣṭhāpana erblindet. Auf meine Frage meinte der Informant, er müsse wohl in die Augen der Statue geblickt haben, aber der wahre Grund sei darin zu suchen, daß er die Augen der Statue nicht den Vorschriften entsprechend proportioniert habe[20]). Es wird häufig berichtet — und solche Angaben finden wir auch in der Śilpa-Literatur —, daß Fehler bei der Errichtung von Kultbildern oder sakralen Bauwerken üble Folgen nach sich ziehen. Einige Künstler behaupten deshalb, die Netrapratiṣṭhāpana-Zeremonie diene dazu, solche Folgen möglicherweise unbewußt gemachter Fehler bei der Arbeit zu vermeiden[21]).

Der mythische Begleittext läßt sich, wie wir gesehen haben, nicht völlig von der Beschreibung des Rituals trennen. Als mythologisch kann man eigentlich nur die Aussage bezeichnen, der Blick der neu eingesetzten Augen der Statue und der des Künstlers nach dem Einsetzen der Augen sei gefährlich, sowie die Angaben darüber, wie man sich vor dieser Gefahr schützt und wie man sie beseitigt. Über die Natur des „gefährlichen Blicks“, d.h. darüber, ob er als Substanz oder als eine Kraft zu denken ist, werden keine Angaben gemacht. Auch beschäftigt sich der mythische Begleittext nicht mit dem Ṣaḍaṅga-Opfer und kaum mit dem Einsetzen der Augen selbst. Sein Gegenstand ist das Reinigungsritual, das dem Einsetzen der Augen folgt. Dieses Ritual bedarf offensichtlich einer besonderen Erklärung. Es scheint wichtig zu sein. Die Auffassung Gombrichs, dieses Reinigungsritual, das er „śānti karaṇaya“ nennt, sei für eine Netrapratiṣṭhāpana-Zeremonie nicht typisch, ist offensichtlich nicht richtig[22]).

---

[18]) Op. cit. (s. Anm. 1).

[19]) Beschreibung der Statue in: Nandasena Mudiyanse, The Art and Architecture of the Gampola Period (1341–1415 A. D.), Colombo 1963, S. 73–77.

[20]) Die auffällig weit geöffneten Augen der Statue sind ein Stilmerkmal der Kunst der Gampola-Periode. Dies widerspricht der Auffassung der heutigen Künstler.

[21]) Tatsächlich hat die Ṣaḍaṅga-Zeremonie eine Funktion, die diesem Bedürfnis Rechnung trägt. Siehe unten S. 322.

[22]) Op. cit. (s. Anm. 1), S. 36. Möglicherweise meinte der Informant mit „Śāntikaraṇaya“ gar nicht dieses Ritual, sondern einen Teil der Ṣaḍaṅga-Zeremonie.

Das Thema des „gefährlichen Blicks“ zieht sich wie ein roter Faden durch die Erzählung des mythischen Begleittexts und die Handlung des rituellen Dramas. Er entsteht beim Einsetzen der Augen der Statue. Durch den Spiegel schirmt sich der Künstler gegen die Gefahr ab. Trotzdem geht die gefährliche Wirkung auf die Augen des Künstlers über. Dieser schützt seine Umgebung vor der Gefahr, indem er sein Gesicht mit einem Tuch bedeckt. Er bringt den „gefährlichen Blick“ zu der Stelle, an der er das Reinigungsritual vollzieht. Dort wäscht er ihn aus seinen Augen und lädt ihn zusammen mit dem Wasser, mit dem er sich gewaschen hat, dem Sündenbock auf. Der Sündenbock trägt die Gefahr davon.

Der mythische Begleittext rechtfertigt das rituelle Geschehen und interpretiert das Problem der Gesellschaft, das unter Zuhilfenahme des Rituals gelöst werden soll. In diesem Sinne wird er von den Beteiligten auch verstanden. Obwohl die Funktion des Rituals selbst nicht Gegenstand des mythischen Begleittexts ist, sind sich die Beteiligten doch darüber im klaren, daß die Beseitigung des „gefährlichen Blicks“ der Buddhastatue nicht das eigentliche Problem ist. Die Frage nach der Wahrheit der im mythischen Begleittext gemachten Aussagen über den „gefährlichen Blick“ wird infolge dessen auch gar nicht gestellt.

Auch die buddhistischen Mönche wissen meist sehr genau, worum es geht. Dies zeigen m. E. die Antworten, die man häufig erhält, wenn man Mönche oder gebildete buddhistische Laien nach dem Sinn des Netrapratiṣṭhāpana befragt: Sie halten die Zeremonie für sinnlos und nutzlos. Ähnliches berichtet auch Gombrich: Die von ihm befragten Mönche hielten das ganze für eine sinnlose (aber harmlose) Tradition[23]). Die Betonung liegt hier auf *sinnlos* und *nutzlos,* nicht auf *falsch.*

Worum es geht, wird durch folgenden Zwischenfall deutlich, der sich während einer von mir beobachteten Netrapratiṣṭhāpana-Zeremonie ereignete[24]): Als ich um Erlaubnis bat, während der Zeremonie zu fotografieren, wies mir der Künstler mit Einverständnis der Mönche des Klosters einen Platz vor der Tür des Schreins zu, in dem die zu weihende Buddhastatue stand. Auf diese Weise konnte ich ihn beim Verlassen des Schreins nach dem Einsetzen der Augen und bei der Durchführung des anschließenden Reinigungsrituals aus unmittelbarer Nähe fotografieren. Die übrigen, singhalesischen Zuschauer mußten dagegen einen vorgeschriebenen weiten Abstand zu der Stelle des Geschehens einhalten. Als der Künstler aus dem Schrein heraustrat, blieb er einen Augenblick in der Tür stehen und schlug das Tuch vor seinem Gesicht zurück, um sich fotografieren zu lassen.

Wenn man davon ausgeht, daß der Blick des Künstlers nach dem Einsetzen der Augen als äußerst gefährlich gilt, erscheint diese Handlungsweise als ein schwerer Verstoß gegen die Regeln. Man könnte dem

---

[23]) Precept and Practice (s. Anm. 11), S. 139.

[24]) In Nugegoḍa (s. oben S. 309).

Künstler hier natürlich Eitelkeit unterstellen und sein Verhalten damit erklären, daß er nicht an die Gefährlichkeit seines Blickes glaubte, ja, daß schließlich die ganze Zeremonie nur noch leere Tradition ist. Das ist möglich, doch das erklärt nicht, warum dann die singhalesischen Zuschauer den vorgeschriebenen Abstand einhalten mußten. Auch wenn der Künstler selbst nicht an die Gefährlichkeit seines Blickes glaubte, mußte er annehmen, daß einige der singhalesischen Zuschauer die taten und daß er damit deren Zorn auf sich zog. Er hätte damit seinen Ruf und sein Ansehen als Künstler gefährdet. Aber keiner der Zuschauer protestierte.

Die Erklärung ist folgende: Ich wurde als Fremder betrachtet, den das, was hier geschah, nicht betraf. Die Zeremonie betraf nur die Laiengemeinde des Klosters, d.h. nur die Gesellschaft, in deren religiösem Mittelpunkt eine Buddhastatue geweiht wurde.

Nunmehr wird auch klar, warum Coomaraswamy und Gombrich in der Anwendung des Netrapratiṣṭhāpana auf das Buddhabild einen Widerspruch zur buddhistischen Dogmatik sehen: Hier sind zwei völlig verschiedene Dinge verglichen worden, Dinge, die man nicht vergleichen kann. Der Inhalt eines Mythos auf der einen Seite und auf rationales Denken gegründete Dogmatik auf der anderen Seite sind nicht vergleichbar. Der Widerspruch liegt also nicht in der Sache, sondern hat seinen Ursprung in den Untersuchungsmethoden.

4. Beschreibung und Deutung

Mit Hilfe der oben entwickelten Methode kann die eingangs gegebene Beschreibung der Zeremonie ergänzt und präzisiert werden. Beschreibung und Deutung laufen dabei parallel.

Die Weihe der Statue geschieht durch das Einsetzen der Augen. Damit wird sie, zunächst Gegenstand handwerklicher und künstlerischer Arbeit, d.h. profaner Tätigkeit, in einen anderen Status übergeleitet. Sie wird zum Kultobjekt, zum Gegenstand religiösen Handelns. Der Engländer Robert Knox, der zwischen 1660 und 1679 als Gefangener im Königreich von Kandy lebte, hat dies sehr treffend beschrieben: "Before the Eyes are made, it is not accounted a God, but a lump of ordinary Metal, and thrown about the Shop with no more regard than any thing else ... The Eyes being formed, it is thenceforward a God."[25]) Die Weihe ist somit ein Überleitungsritual.

Überleitungsrituale, sofern sie der Überleitung von Personen aus einem Status in einen anderen dienen, sind seit Arnold van Genneps berühmten Buch „Les rites de passage"[26]) bekannt und häufig untersucht worden. Sie dienen der Bewältigung von Lebenskrisen, d.h. von problema-

[25]) Robert Knox, An Historical Relation of Ceylon, Originalausgabe: London 1681, Neuausgabe, 2. Aufl., Dehiwala (Ceylon) 1966. Zitat: S. 155 (Originalausg. S. 81f.).

[26]) Paris 1909.

tisch gewordenen Statusübergängen wie Pubertät, Heirat etc. und begleiten den Menschen von seiner Geburt bis zu seinem Tode. Vor allem in weniger differenzierten, d.h. primitiven Gesellschaften spielen sie eine wichtige Rolle. Sie sind weniger wichtig und teilweise entbehrlich in hochdifferenzierten, modernen Gesellschaftssystemen. Überleitungen müssen nicht in jedem Falle unter Zuhilfenahme religiöser Riten vollzogen werden. In modernen Gesellschaften haben Überleitungsrituale oft auch äußerlich profanen Charakter[27]). Solche Rituale sollen Orientierungsschwierigkeiten beheben, die beim Statuswechsel auftreten, und haben dabei einen doppelten Zweck: Sie helfen dem Überzuleitenden, sich über seinen jeweils geltenden Status klar zu werden und ermöglichen der Gesellschaft, den betreffenden entsprechend einzuordnen.

Dabei reicht eine rein zeitliche Zäsur zur Klärung der Situation offenbar nicht aus. Es scheint nicht möglich zu sein, die Beendigung des alten Status und den Beginn des neuen im Bewußtsein gleichzeitig zu vollziehen. Beides muß getrennt geschehen. So entsteht eine Übergangslage, für die keine statusbezogenenen Verhaltensregeln vorliegen. „Der Überzuleitende ist ‚sowohl — als auch' oder ‚weder — noch', und zwar gleichzeitig! Seine Identität wird unklar und unbestimmbar"[28]) Der Überzuleitende muß deshalb zumindest symbolisch für die Dauer der Übergangsphase verschwinden, um mit Beginn des neuen Status wieder zu erscheinen[29]).

Die Anwendung von Überleitungsritualen ist allerdings nicht auf Personen beschränkt. Rituale gleichen Typs können auch der Überleitung von Gegenständen dienen, die eine fest umrissene Funktion im Leben des Einzelnen oder der Gesellschaft einnehmen und die deshalb einen bestimmbaren Status besitzen müssen. Auch solche Rituale treten sowohl im religiösen als auch im alltäglichen Bereich auf. Beispiele sind die „Einweihungsparty" beim Beziehen einer neuen Wohnung, die Einweihung eines Denkmals oder die Weihe einer Kultstätte oder eines Kultbildes wie in unserem Falle. Die Übergangsphase ist dabei meist sehr deutlich gekennzeichnet. So wird ein Denkmal z.B. nach Fertigstellung mit einem Tuch verhüllt, um dann feierlich enthüllt zu werden. Auch im Falle des Netrapratiṣṭhāpana ist die Übergangsphase deutlich erkennbar: Die Statue wird wegfingiert dadurch, daß man zum Einsetzen der Augen einen Spiegel benutzt.

---

[27]) Siehe dazu: Anselm Strauss, Spiegel und Masken. Die Suche nach Identität [Übers. aus dem Amerikanischen]. Frankfurt 1968.

[28]) Niklas Luhmann, Religiöse Dogmatik und gesellschaftliche Evolution, in: Karl-Wilhelm Dahm/Niklas Luhmann/Dieter Stoodt, Religion – System und Sozialisation, Darmstadt und Neuwied 1972 (Sammlung Luchterhand 85). Zitat: S. 48. Victor W. Turner, Betwixt and Between: The Liminal Period in Rites de passage, in: June Helm [Hrsg.], Symposium on New Approaches to the Study of Religion, Proceedings of the 1964 Annual Spring Meeting of the American Ethnological Society, Seattle 1964, S. 4–20.

[29]) Turner: „structurally, if not physically ‚invisible'". Op. cit. (s. Anm. 28), S. 6.

4.1 Beginn der Zeremonie

Die Zeremonie beginnt mit der dreimaligen Rezitation der buddhistischen Verehrungsformel „Namo tassa Bhagavato Arahato Sammāsambuddhassa“ und der Zufluchtsformel „Buddhaṃ saraṇaṃ gacchāmi, Dhammaṃ saraṇaṃ gacchāmi, Saṅghaṃ saraṇaṃ gacchāmi ...“ So beginnen in der Regel alle Zeremonien der Singhalesen, seien sie buddhistisch oder der Volksreligion zugehörig[30]).

4.2 Die Kultätiologie

Wahrscheinlich gehörte zur Einleitung der Zeremonie ebenfalls die Rezitation der Kosalabimbavaṇṇanā als Kultätiologie. Dieses Werk ist in Ceylon in drei Versionen überliefert: in einer Pali-Version, sowie in mehreren singhalesischen bzw. gemischten Pali-singhalesischen Versionen[31]). Der Text erzählt zu Beginn die Legende von der Entstehung der ersten Buddhastatue. Diese soll auf Geheiß des Königs Prasenajit von Kośala errichtet worden sein. Der Buddha hat nach der Legende die Verehrung seines Abbildes ausdrücklich gutgeheißen und prophezeite, die Buddhaverehrung in dieser Form werde 5000 Jahre lang fortdauern. Anschließend gibt er Belehrungen darüber, welches Verdienst man erlangt, wenn man Buddhastatuen in Auftrag gibt, errichtet oder verehrt. Ein Fragment der gemischten Version ist im Ṣaḍaṅga vidhiya enthalten[32]).

Aus dem Ṣaḍaṅga vidhiya geht jedoch nicht hervor, ob der vollständige Text der Kosalabimbavaṇṇanā zu Beginn der Zeremonie rezitiert werden soll. Bei der von Coomaraswamy geschilderten Zeremonie war das offensichtlich der Fall[33]). Zu Beginn der von Gombrich beschriebenen und der beiden von mir beobachteten Zeremonien wurde der Text nicht rezitiert[34]). Meinen Informanten war auch nicht bekannt, daß die Rezitation der Kosalabimbavaṇṇanā zur Zeremonie gehört. Nach dem Ṣaḍaṅga vidhiya wurde jedoch mit Sicherheit beim Aufstellen des Indrakīla, das die folgende Ṣaḍaṅga-Zeremonie einleitet, folgender Satz rezitiert: „So vollziehe ich diese als Indrakīlaya bezeichnete Aufstellen der Säule zum Zwecke der Duchführung des Netrapratiṣṭhāpana an der Statue des Allwissenden [d.h. des Buddha], die zu Lebzeiten des Buddha mit dessen Zustimmung zum ersten Male in Śrāvastī auf Geheiß des Königs von Kośala angefertigt wurde, die von Zeichen und Wundern und einer

[30]) Vgl. auch Gombrich, op. cit. (s. Anm. 1), S. 34. Zu den zu Beginn singhalesischer volksreligiöser Zeremonien rezitierten Texten siehe Jē. Ī. Sēdaraman, Laṃkāvē bali upata, Teil 1, Colombo 1964, S. 20ff.

[31]) Siehe den Beitrag von R. F. Gombrich in diesem Band, oben, S. 281–303. Singhalesische Version: Kosalabimbavarṇanāva, hg. v. Em. Sudharmā Karuṇātilaka, Kägalla (Ceylon) 1939. Handschriften verschiedener Versionen u. a. beschrieben in: W. A. de Silva, op. cit. (s. Anm. 15), unter N. 2336–2348.

[32]) Siehe unten S. 330ff.

[33]) Op. cit. (s. Anm. 1), S. 71.

[34]) Siehe Gombrich, op. cit. (s. Anm. 1), S. 34.

unermeßlichen Zahl von Verehrungen durch unzählige Götter und Menschen, angeführt von Śakra, Suyāma und Santuṣita, begleitet, sogar von dem Buddha, dem einzigen Lehrer der gesamten Welt, mit Lobreden und Jasminblüten verehrt wurde und die, den Göttern und Menschen das Erlangen des Himmels und der Erlösung ermöglichend, fünftausend Jahre überdauert.“[35])

Dieser Satz faßt den Inhalt des Textes zusammen. Die Kosalabimbavaṇṇanā ist nicht die Kultätiologie der Netrapratiṣṭhāpana-Zeremonie, sondern der Buddhaverehrung. Durch den oben zitierten Satz wird sie zur Kultätiologie des Netrapratiṣṭhāpana umgedeutet.

Der Wegfall der Rezitation der Kosalabimbavaṇṇanā bzw. der auf die Kultätiologie hinweisenden Formel ist möglicherweise darauf zurückzuführen, daß hier zwei Zeremonien verschiedener Funktion und verschiedener Herkunft künstlich zusammengefügt wurden[36]). Die Rezitation der Kultätiologie sollte offensichtlich als Rahmen dienen, der beide zusammenhalten mußte. Dieser Rahmen hat seine Bedeutung verloren. Das bedeutet, der Aufbau der Zeremonie wurde einem Wandel unterzogen, der die Abfolge von Ṣaḍaṅga-Opfer und Netrapratiṣṭhāpana sinnvoll erscheinen ließ und verständlich machte, ohne daß eine notwendige Einheit beider Zeremonien konstruiert werden mußte.

Diese Veränderung ist im Verlauf der Ṣaḍaṅga-Zeremonie zu suchen. Die Ṣaḍaṅga-Zeremonie, die aus dem hinduistischen Ritual übernommen wurde und in ihrer ursprünglichen Form dem Kumbhapratiṣṭhāpana der hinduistischen Weihezeremonien glich, wurde den singhalesischen Śānti-Zeremonien angeglichen. Diese Angleichung an die vertrauten astrologischen Rituale hat die zunächst fremde Zeremonie verständlich gemacht. Auf diese Weise wurde aus dem künstlichen Zusammenhalt ein verständlicher Zusammenhang, der allerdings keine notwendige Einheit darstellte. Dadurch wurde es möglich, in einzelnen Fällen die Ṣaḍaṅga-Zeremonie wegfallen zu lassen oder sie durch ein anderes Ritual zu ersetzen[37]).

4.3 Die Ṣaḍaṅga-Zeremonie

Eine exakte Analyse und Bestimmung der Funktion der Ṣaḍaṅga-Zeremonie ist hier nicht möglich. Das vorliegende Material reicht dazu

[35]) „Mesē Kosol maharajahu visin jīvamānakālayehi Budungē anumatiyen Śrāvastīpurayehi-dī prathamayen karavana-lada āścaryya adbhūta dharmayangē pahaḷavīmen hā Śakrasuyāmasantuṣitādi apramāṇadivyamanuṣyayangen pramāṇātikrānta pūjā ladin tava-da samastalokaikaguru vū Budungenu-du pavā stutipūjā hā samanmalin pūjā läba divyamanuṣyayanṭa svarggasampat sādhā demin pasvādahasak havuruda pavatnā Sarvajña pratibimbayehi netrapratiṣṭhāpanaya karanu piṇisa indrakīlaya-yi kiyanu-lada mē stambhapratiṣṭhāpanaya kerem.“ Ṣaḍaṅga vidhiya (s. Anm. 15), Blatt 10 R, Zeile 6ff.

[36]) Siehe unten S. 330.

[37]) Dies war bei der von mir in Nugegoḍa beobachteten Zeremonie der Fall (s. oben S. 309). Zu den Śānti-Zeremonien siehe Paul Wirz, Exorzismus und Heilkunde auf Ceylon, Bern 1941, S. 133ff.

nicht aus. Die Angaben Coomaraswamys und Gombrichs weichen sehr voneinander ab[38]). Meine eigenen Aufzeichnungen sind lückenhaft und ungenau, da ich zu der Zeit, als ich die Zeremonie beobachten konnte, keinerlei Vorstellung von ihrer möglichen Bedeutung hatte.

Auffällig ist, daß Ṣaḍaṅga-Opfer und Netrapratiṣṭhāpana-Zeremonie im engeren Sinne nicht als Einheit betrachtet werden. In dem einen von mir beobachteten Falle gab es eine mehrstündige Pause zwischen beiden Zeremonien, und es war keinerlei Überleitung zu erkennen. Im zweiten Falle fiel die Ṣaḍaṅga-Zeremonie ganz weg und wurde durch ein einfaches Bhairava-Opfer ersetzt[39]). Auch wird das Ṣaḍaṅga-Opfer von Bali-Spezialisten (Ādurās) durchgeführt, das Netrapratiṣṭhāpana hingegen von dem Künstler, der die Statue errichtet hat.

Das Kernstück der Ṣaḍaṅga-Zeremonie ist, wie oben schon erwähnt, seinem äußeren Hergang nach ein magisches Opfer. Die Fläche des aus Reiskörnern aufgeschütteten Opferaltars wird in der Form eines magischen Diagramms (Yantra) in einzelne Felder aufgeteilt. In jedem der Felder befindet sich ein Topf mit Opfergaben. Ähnliche Diagramme hat Paul Wirz beschrieben[40]). Sie finden bei den singhalesischen Malbali- und Śānti-Zeremonien Anwendung. Nach dem Muster solcher Diagramme werden auch einige bei Bali-Zeremonien verwendeten Bilder komponiert[41]). Über das Aussehen des beim Ṣaḍaṅga-Opfer verwendeten Diagramms besteht Unklarheit, ebenso über die Zahl der aufgestellten Töpfe und die vollständige Reihe der Götter, die angerufen und mit Opfergaben bedacht werden. Aus der Beschreibung Coomaraswamys läßt sich kein genaues Bild der Zeremonie gewinnen. Die Schilderung Gombrichs ist zwar anschaulicher, führt aber ebenfalls nicht zu einer endgültigen Klärung[42]).

Das Ṣaḍaṅga vidhiya führt zwar in der Reihenfolge, in der sie rezitiert werden, die an die verschiedenen Götter gerichteten Mantras und

---

[38]) Loc. cit. (s. Anm. 1).

[39]) In Nugegoḍa (s. S. 309).

[40]) Op. cit. (s. Anm. 37), S. 134. Siehe auch Sēdaraman, op. cit. (s. Anm. 30), S. 10.

[41]) Jē. Ī. Sēdaraman, Baliyāga vicāraya nohot Laṃkāvē bali upata, Colombo 1967 [= Teil 2 zu Laṃkāvē bali upata (s. Anm. 30)], passim.

[42]) Coomaraswamy, op. cit. (s. Anm. 1), S. 72, Gombrich, op. cit. (s. Anm. 1), S. 33ff. Das von Coomaraswamy beschriebene Aṭamaṅgalya wird offensichtlich auf den Boden unter dem Altar aufgezeichnet (siehe dazu die Beschreibung des Hūnyam vīdiya bei Wirz, op. cit. (Anm. 37), S. 87). Auf dem Altar aber wird ein Diagramm in der von Gombrich beschriebenen Form ausgelegt. Gombrichs Beschreibung der Verteilung der Opfertöpfe auf dem Diagramm ist ungenau. Es bleiben nur acht Felder für die Opfergaben der Planetengötter am Rande. Das Opfer für Ketu, den neunten der Planetengötter, soll in der Mitte aufgestellt werden (vgl. Sēdaraman, op. cit., Teil 1 (s. Anm. 30), S. 104). Es ist ebenfalls unwahrscheinlich, daß die Opfer für die Götter Śakra, Brahmā, Viṣṇu und Maheśvara an den vier Ecken des Altars niedergestellt werden; denn dort werden gewöhnlich die Opfer für die Hatara varan deviyō (Dhṛtarāṣṭra, Virūḍha, Virūpākṣa und Vaiśravaṇa) plaziert. Die Opfer für die oben genannten Götter gehören in den Brahmapada, das innere Feld des Diagramms.

Stotras an, macht aber kaum Angaben über die praktische Durchführung des Opfers. Es nennt zuerst die Erdgöttin (Bhūmidevī) und Brahmā. An anderer Stelle werden Indra, Ātmabhū (Brahmā), Kṛṣṇa, Maheśvara, Nāgānana (Gaṇeśa), Skanda und Bṛhaspati aufgezählt. Gesondert werden dann Viṣṇu und die zehn Viṣṇu-Avatāras genannt sowie die Beherrscher der Himmelsrichtungen (Dikpālas) Indra, Agni, Yama, Nirṛti, Varuṇa, Vāyu, Soma, Īśāna und Hiraṇyagarbha (Brahmā) als Beherrscher des Zenits. Neben den Beherrschern der Himmelsrichtungen sind die neun Planetengötter (Navagraha-Devatās) Ravi (Sonne), Candra (Mond), Guru (Jupiter), Śukra (Venus), Kuja (Mars), Budha (Merkur), Śani (Saturn), Rahu und Ketu besonders wichtig. Es folgen Anrufungen der die Dikpālas und Planetengötter begleitenden Gottheiten (Parivāra-Devatās). Am Ende wird schließlich Gaṇeśa noch einmal gesondert verehrt.

Ein während der von mir beobachteten Zeremonie rezitierter Text enthielt auch noch eine Anrufung des Viśvakarman. Nach Aussage eines Informanten sollte allerdings das Opfer an Viśvakarman dem Ṣaḍaṅga-Opfer vorausgehen. Coomaraswamy und Gombrich erwähnen außerdem noch ein Opfer bzw. eine Anrufung einer Khaḍgapāla-Devatā[43]).

Aufgrund der Bezeichnung Ṣaḍaṅga sollte man annehmen, daß es sich dabei um ein sechsgliedriges Opfer handelt. Es ist aber nicht mit Sicherheit festzustellen, welches die sechs Teile der Zeremonie sind. Die Kenntnis darüber scheint verlorengegangen zu sein. Die Auskünfte, die ich auf die Frage nach den sechs Teilen der Zeremonie erhielt, waren größtenteils Ad-hoc-Erfindungen. Dasselbe trifft für die Informationen zu, die Gombrich erhalten hat. Man erkennt solche Antworten häufig schon daran, daß die Befragten sich über die Reihenfolge der aufzuzählenden Begriffe nicht im klaren sind. Sie müssen zuerst überlegen. Handelt es sich dagegen um traditionelles Wissen, steht die Reihenfolge fest. Wenn solche Dinge für wichtig gehalten werden, wird die Aufzählung auswendig gelernt. Ich gebe hier nur ein Beispiel einer solchen Aufzählung wieder: 1. Devapūjā, 2. Navagrahapūjā, 3. Bhairavapūjā, 4. Indrakīlapūjā, 5. Khadgapālapūjā, 6. Kalasthāpanapūjā[44]).

Teilt man die Opferzeremonie nach den jeweils mit Opfergaben bedachten Göttern oder Göttergruppen auf, so erhält man stets mehr als sechs Teile, zumal, wenn man die von Coomaraswamy genannten Opfer hinzunimmt, die außerhalb des Schreins stattfinden. Es ist kaum anzunehmen, daß man die Zeremonie in sechs wichtige und eine Reihe von

[43]) Gombrich, op. cit. (s. Anm. 1), S. 34, Coomaraswamy, loc. cit. (s. Anm. 1), S. 72. Coomaraswamy nennt Opfer für Dvārapālas (Türhüter des Schreins), den Kṣetrapāla (lokale Schutzgottheit) und einen Khaḍgapāla. Mir wurde von einem Informanten erklärt, bei den Khaḍgapālas handle es sich um die Türhüter. Ich konnte dies allerdings nicht nachprüfen.

[44]) Gombrich zählt folgende sechs Teile auf: „... drumming (*magul bera*), worship of the gods (*dēviyanṭa pūjāva*), setting pots (*kumbhasthāpanē*), Indrakīlaya, worship of the statue(s) (*mūrta pūjāva*), ‚making peace' (*śānti karaṇaya*)". Siehe op. cit. (s. Anm. 1), S. 33f.

unwichtigen Teilen einteilt und entsprechend benennt. Die oben angeführte Aufzählung der Teile entspricht zudem einer Einteilung der Zeremonie nach unterschiedlichen Gesichtspunkten: Einige Teile sind nach den Adressaten der Opfer, andere nach der Art und Weise der Opferhandlung benannt. Wenn man davon ausgeht, daß sie wenigstens einen Rest traditioneller Kenntnis enthält und daß die Bezeichnung Ṣaḍaṅga auch noch im Zusammenhang mit anderen Bali-Zermonien gebraucht wird[45]), kann man vermuten, daß die Zeremonie nicht nach den Adressaten, sondern nach der Funktion der Opferhandlungen in sechs Teile eingeteilt wird. So wäre eine Unterteilung folgender Art vorstellbar: 1. Aufstellen des Indrakīla, der das Zentrum des Opferaltars markiert, 2. Herrichten des Opferaltars (Auslegen des Diagramms), 3. Zubereitung der Opfergaben (Kalaśasthāpana), 4. Verehrung der Götter (Namaskāra), 5. Einladung der Götter zur Annahme des Opfers (Diṣṭi), 6. Versöhnung mit den Göttern (Śānti). Möglicherweise kann eine gründliche Bearbeitung des Ṣaḍaṅga vidhiya und ein Vergleich mit dem hinduistischen Kumbhasthāpana hier weiterhelfen[46]).

Dasselbe gilt für die Aufteilung der Altarfläche, d.h. für das Diagramm. Auch darüber kann uns sicher ein Vergleich mit dem hinduistischen Kumbhasthāpana mehr Aufschluß geben. Eine eingehende Analyse des Ṣaḍaṅga-Opfers setzt die Verwendung des Ṣaḍaṅga vidhiya und des hinduistischen Materials voraus. Zusätzliche Feldstudien nach der oben beschriebenen Methode müßten eine solche Analyse ermöglichen. Dabei kann die Opferhandlung ebenso wie die rezitierten Texte so in ihre einzelnen Elemente zerlegt werden, daß die logische Struktur des Opfers sichtbar wird[47]).

Die Ähnlichkeit der Ṣaḍaṅga-Zeremonie mit dem Kumbhasthāpana der hinduistischen Weihezeremonien ist auffällig. Im Vaikhānasāgama steht dieser Teil der Zeremonie sogar in engem Zusammenhang mit dem Öffnen der Augen (Netronmīlana) der Statue[48]). Doch das Ṣaḍaṅga-Opfer hat offensichtlich eine Umformung erfahren, die es möglich machte, es in das System der astrologischen Rituale d.h. der Śānti- bzw. Bali-Zeremonien einzuordnen[49]). Dies zeigt z.B. die Tatsache, daß einmal bulat taṭuva puda als Opfer für die Erdgöttin und ein Aṣṭamaṅgala im Ṣaḍaṅga vidhiya als Teile der Zeremonie genannt werden. Beide sind auch Bestandteil verschiedener Bali-Zeremonien[50]). Ein weiteres An-

---

[45]) Die zweite von de Silva beschriebene Handschrift mit dem Namen Ṣaḍaṅga vidhiya (s. Anm. 15) enthält einen Ritualtext für eine solche Zeremonie.

[46]) Vorschriften für dieses Ritual finden sich u. a. in: Vaikhānasāgama, Kap. 30 (s. Anm. 1) und Rauravāgama (s. Anm. 1), Kap. 11, V. 32–34; Kap. 12, V. 16–21; Kap. 14, V. 24–26.

[47]) Zur Methode siehe H. Hubert et M. Mauss: Essai sur la nature et la fonction du sacrifice, in: Année Sociologique 1897–1898, S. 29–138.

[48]) Loc. cit (s. Anm. 1).

[49]) Zu diesen Zeremonien siehe Paul Wirz, op. cit. (s. Anm. 37), passim.

[50]) Beide werden von Coomaraswamy als Bestandteile des Ṣaḍaṅga genannt (loc. cit. [s. Anm. 1], S. 70 und 72). Sie werden ebenfalls im Ṣaḍaṅga vidhiya er-

zeichen für diese Umwandlung ist die Änderung der Funktion des Indrakīla im Ṣaḍaṅga-Opfer. Der Indrakīla wird nach Angaben des Ṣaḍaṅga vidhiya in der Mitte des Altars aufgestellt. Er besteht aus einem Stock, der in ein weißes Tuch mit einem eingenähten Goldstück eingehüllt ist. Er markierte ursprünglich das Zentrum des Diagramms und wurde als erstes aufgestellt. Heute steht er gewöhnlich am Rand des Altars an der Seite zur Statue hin und wird an die Statue bzw. deren Sockel angelehnt[51]). Er dient dabei nicht als Sündenbock, wie Coomaraswamy vermutet, sondern hat die Funktion der Schnur in den Bali- und Śānti-Zeremonien übernommen[52]). Ebenso wie dort die Schnur soll er schlechte Einflüsse der Sterne und auch die durch mögliche Fehler bei der Arbeit drohenden Gefahren ableiten.

Solche Fehler bei der Arbeit können zweifacher Art sein: Sie können erstens Verstöße gegen ikonographische Regeln und gegen Regeln der Proportionslehre darstellen. Ein Beispiel dafür ist die oben erwähnte Geschichte über die sitzende Buddhastatue von Gaḍalādeṇiya. Die üblen Folgen solcher Verstöße treffen nicht nur den Künstler. Nach dem Śāriputra, einem in Ceylon überlieferten Lehrbuch der Proportionslehre der Buddhastatue, können Verstöße gegen die Regeln auch Hungersnöte, den Sturz des Königs und die Verwüstung des Landes durch Feinde nach sich ziehen[53]). Damit ist die ganze Gesellschaft, deren religiösen Mittelpunkt die jeweils betroffene Statue darstellt, gefährdet.

Aber nicht nur Fehler in den Proportionen und den ikonographischen Merkmalen der Statue können sich unheilvoll auswirken, sondern auch falsch gewählte äußere Abmessungen. Die in den jeweils üblichen Maßeinheiten gemessenen Maße der Statue werden mit Hilfe der sog.

---

wähnt (Blatt 11 V). Zu ihrer Verwendung in Bali-Zeremonien vgl. Wirz, op. cit. (s. Anm. 37), passim und Sēdaraman, op. cit., Teil 1 (s. Anm. 30), S. 12ff.

[51]) Siehe auch Coomaraswamy, loc. cit. (s. Anm. 1), S. 72 und Gombrich, op. cit. (s. Anm. 1), S. 33. Die Bedeutung der Form des Indrakīla ist mir nicht klar. Nach Auskunft eines Informanten soll er die Gestalt eines Menschen besitzen. Ein Indrakīla — dort auch „Rājagaha" genannt — wird auch bei der Paritta-Zeremonie verwendet. Er hängt dort unter dem Dach des Paritta-Maṇḍapa und bildet das Zentrum, von dem die Paritta-Schnur nach verschiedenen Richtungen hin ausgelegt wird. Ich bin nicht sicher, ob dies allgemein üblich ist. Waldschmidt (Das Paritta. Eine magische Zeremonie der buddhistischen Priester auf Ceylon, Baessler-Archiv 17 (1934), S. 139–150) erwähnt den Indrakīla nicht.

[52]) Zur Verwendung der Schnur in Bali- und Śānti-Zeremonien siehe Paul Wirz, op. cit. (s. Anm. 37), passim.

[53]) Śāriputra, hg. v. M. Sirivimala, Alutgama (Ceylon) 1924, auszugsweise ins Englische übersetzt von Ananda K. Coomaraswamy, op. cit. (s. Anm. 1), S. 154–163. Kritische Ausgabe mit deutscher Übersetzung des Verf.: Hans Ruelius, Śāriputra und Ālekhyalakṣaṇa, Zwei Texte zur Proportionslehre in der indischen und ceylonesischen Kunst, Göttingen 1974 (Phil. Diss.). Beispiel: „Durch eine Statue, die mit einem Hohlraum versehen ist, entstehen Zwistigkeiten und Verlust von Hab und Gut. Nicht lange danach wird eine Hungersnot ausbrechen, Handel und Wandel werden zum Erliegen kommen und der Sturz des Königs wird folgen." (Vers 12)

Ṣaḍvarga-Kalkulationen auf ihre heilbringende Größe hin untersucht[54]). Bei diesen Berechnungen werden die Maße der Statue wie Zeitangaben behandelt, aus denen man ähnlich wie bei der Erstellung eines Horokops günstige oder ungünstige Konstellationen errechnet. Ist das Ergebnis ungünstig, müssen die Maße geändert werden.

Die Ṣaḍvarga-Berechnungen haben also offensichtlich den Zweck, eine Harmonie zu ermöglichen zwischen der äußeren Beschaffenheit des vom Menschen hergestellten Gegenstandes[55]) einerseits und den kosmischen Ordnungsprinzipien andererseits.

Diese Harmonisierung geschieht auf ritueller Ebene offensichtlich durch das Ṣaḍaṅga-Opfer. Dieses Opfer kann somit als Überleitungsritual aufgefaßt werden, das die Aufgabe hat, das Artefakt — das ist in unserem Falle die Buddhastatue — in die bestehende kosmische Ordnung zu integrieren. Der Zustand vorher, d.h. der Zustand der noch nicht vollzogenen Integration, ist gleichzeitig Zustand drohender Konflikte mit den Göttern. Die Integration wird erreicht durch Versöhnung mit den Göttern. Der zunächst nicht einzuordnende Gegenstand wird dadurch bestimmbar. Er war bis zu seiner Fertigstellung Gegenstand handwerklicher und künstlerischer Tätigkeit. Als fertiges Produkt muß er in ein neues Handlungsschema eingelgliedert werden, das durch die Zeremonie selbst allerdings nicht näher bestimmt ist. Diese Aufgabe hat das folgende Netrapratiṣṭhāpana.

Durch die Ṣaḍaṅga-Zeremonie wird das Werkstück zum brauchbaren Gegenstand, durch das Netrapratiṣṭhāpana wird der profane Gegenstand zum Kultobjekt. Dabei ist in beiden Fällen für die Prozedur nicht entscheidend, ob es sich um eine Buddhastatue handelt oder um etwas anderes. Entscheidend ist, daß die Buddhastatue hier zunächst als Werkstück und dann als Artefakt auftritt und Kultobjekt sein soll. Sie bedarf also jeweils einer Überleitung.

4.4 Der günstige Augenblick

Der für das Einsetzen der Augen günstige Augenblick wird von einem Astrologen berechnet. Die Konsultation eines Astrologen vor dem Beginnen einer wichtigen Unternehmung ist heute in Ceylon sehr weit verbreitet, um nicht zu sagen, allgemein üblich. Selbst die erste Mönchsweihe findet häufig zu einem astrologisch günstigen Zeitpunkt statt. Somit braucht die Beachtung des günstigen Augenblicks für den Beginn des Netrapratiṣṭhāpana nicht als für diese Zeremonie typisch angesehen werden.

[54]) Siehe dazu Prasanna Kumar Acharya, An Encyclopaedia of Hindu Architecture, London usw. 1946, S. 500ff. Diese Methode wird im Śāriputra auch für die Buddhastatue vorgeschrieben (V. 15–19).

[55]) Dieses Bestreben liegt möglicherweise auch dem metrologischen System der späteren indischen Śilpaśāstras zugrunde. Siehe Hans Ruelius, Tālamāna — Metrologie und Proportionslehre der Inder, in: Der ‚vermessene' Mensch, München 1973, S. 75–83.

Das Ṣaḍaṅga-Opfer findet gewöhnlich in der Nacht vor dem eigentlichen Netrapratiṣṭhāpana statt. Die Angabe Coomaraswamys, wonach das Netrapratiṣṭhāpana bei der Buddhastatue in der Regel morgens gegen fünf Uhr durchgeführt werden soll, kann durchaus zutreffen. Er berichtet, dies geschehe eingedenk der Überlieferung, nach der der Buddha um diese Tageszeit die Erleuchtung erlangt haben soll[56]). In dem einen von mir beobachteten Falle fand das Netrapratiṣṭhāpana auch zu diesem Zeitpunkt statt[57]), im anderen Falle dagegen erst am späten Vormittag.

4.5 Das Einsetzen der Augen

Die Angaben über den technischen Vorgang des Malens weichen voneinander ab. Einige Informanten berichten, der Künstler stehe dabei mit dem Rücken zur Statue, während sein Gehilfe mit verdecktem Gesicht den Spiegel halte. Bei einer Demonstration der Technik in Yaṭihalagala[58]) hielt der Künstler selbst den Spiegel waagerecht vor die Statue und konnte so auf den Spiegel schauend aber zur Statue gewandt leichter arbeiten. Da durch die Verwendung des Spiegels die Statue wegfingiert werden soll, ist wohl die erstere die ursprünglichere Version. Nach Beendigung der Arbeit bedeckt der Künstler sein Gesicht mit einem Tuch und wird von seinem Gehilfen aus dem Schrein geführt.

Das rituelle Einsetzen der Augen besteht hier aus dem Malen der Pupillen. Das ist der „letzte Pinselstrich". Die Statue ist damit vollendet. Durch die Verwendung einer goldenen Farbschale und eines in Gold gefaßten Pinsels sowie durch die besondere Art der Farbzubereitung wird diese rituelle Arbeit von der vorhergehenden profanen Arbeit unterschieden.

Die Statue, die *vorher* Gegenstand künstlerischer Tätigkeit war — und das ist profane Arbeit —, ist *nachher* Kultobjekt. *Dazwischen* liegt der in ritueller Form durchgeführte „letzte Pinselstrich". Das ist also die Zwischenphase des „Weder — noch" bzw. des „Sowohl — als auch". Diese Zwischenphase ist auf zweierlei Weise gekennzeichnet: Für die Zuschauer außerhalb des Schreins geschieht dies auf sehr unproblematische Weise. Die Zwischenphase beginnt mit dem Verschließen des Schreins, nachdem der Künstler hineingegangen ist, und endet mit dem Öffnen der Tür nach Ende der Zeremonie. In dieser Zeit ist die Statue nicht sichtbar, sie ist „verschwunden". Sie verschwindet als profaner Gegenstand und erscheint wieder als Kultobjekt. Die Zeit des Wandels wird markiert und „dramatisiert" durch die Trommeln.

Schwieriger ist die Situation des Künstlers. Er muß an der Statue arbeiten und muß sie deshalb sehen. Dadurch, daß er sie nicht direkt,

---

[56]) Op. cit. (s. Anm. 1), S. 71.

[57]) In Yaṭihalagala (s. oben S. 309). Ebenso die von Gombrich beschriebene Zeremonie. Siehe Gombrich, op. cit. (s. Anm. 1), S. 36.

[58]) Durch Herrn Sunil Premadāsa, der das Netrapratiṣṭhāpana in Yaṭihalagala (s. oben S. 309) durchführte.

sondern durch den Spiegel sieht, unterscheidet sich die Situation von dem Vorher und dem Nachher. Die Statue wird auf diese Weise wegfingiert [59]). Damit ist der Übergang geregelt. Würde dies nicht geschehen, so wäre der Zustand vorher und der Zustand nachher für den Künstler nicht mit der geforderten Klarheit zu unterscheiden. Die spätere Verehrung seiner eigenen Schöpfung als Kultgegenstand würde für ihn problematisch. Deshalb ist der Blick in die frisch geweihten Augen der Statue gefährlich. Der mythische Begleittext bringt diesen Zusammenhang dadurch zum Ausdruck, daß er der Statue einen „gefährlichen Blick" zuschreibt.

4.6 Das Reinigungsritual

Bei der Wahl der Bezeichnung „Reinigungsritual" für das nun folgende Ritual habe ich mich am äußeren Hergang orientiert. Etwas abwaschen heißt reinigen. Dem Vollzug eines Reinigungsrituals muß keineswegs immer die Auffassung zugrunde liegen, daß das, wovon man sich reinigt, an sich negativ ist. Der Begriff sagt nichts über Funktion und Bedeutung des Rituals aus. Deshalb ist seine Anwendung aus Gründen der Zweckmäßigkeit hier gerechtfertigt.

Zu Beginn des Reinigungsrituals, nachdem der Künstler von seinem Gehilfen mit bedecktem Gesicht zu der vorbereiteten Stelle geführt worden ist, fällt sein Blick zuerst auf einen Baum. Dies soll nach Aussage einiger Informanten ein Baum sein, der eine milchige Flüssigkeit absondert, wenn man ihn verletzt (sgh. *kiri gaha*). Der Künstler ergreift nun das Schwert und schlägt es in die Rinde des Baumes. Während in dem einen von mir beobachteten Falle das Schwert in den Stamm eines dickeren Baumes geschlagen wurde [60]), schlug der Künstler in dem anderen Falle einige Äste eines kleineren Baumes ab. Der Unterschied ist sicher ohne Bedeutung. Der Baum soll hier symbolisch vernichtet werden. Die Forderung nach der Verwendung eines Baumes, der milchige Flüssigkeit absondert, ist sicher sekundär. Ein ähnlicher Fall liegt vor beim Fällen des Äsaḷa-Baumes zu Beginn der Zeremonien im Zusammenhang mit dem Äsaḷa-Perahära in Kandy. Auch dort wird der Äsaḷa-Baum durch einen „Kiri gaha" ersetzt [61]). Das Fällen eines solchen Baumes ist ein Ritual, das auch als Bestandteil von Bali-Zeremonien vorkommt [62]). Dieses Ritual bot sich hier als Ersatz für das Fällen des Äsaḷa-Baumes an. Im Falle unseres Reinigungsrituals wird der „Kiri gaha" wohl deshalb gefordert, weil hier jede Handlung nicht nur im Zusammenhang, sondern auch für sich alleine rituellen Charakter tragen muß, gleichsam wie für eine besondere Rede besondere Vokabeln nötig sind. So hat man hier auf das vertraute rituelle Repertoire zurückgegriffen, indem man nicht einen gewöhnlichen Baum, sondern einen

[59]) Siehe oben, S. 17.
[60]) In Yaṭihalagala (s. oben, S. 309).
[61]) Richard Aluvihare, The Kandy Perahera, Colombo [2]1964, S. 4.
[62]) Laut mündlicher Auskunft von Herrn Frank Perera, z. Z. Göttingen.

„Kiri gaha" benutzt. Aus demselben Grunde wird auch die Verwendung eines weißen Bullen gefordert anstelle eines gewöhnlichen braunen. Doch dieser Forderung ist in der Praxis schwer nachzukommen, weshalb man dann doch ein gewöhnliches Tier benutzt.

Nachdem er das Schwert zur Seite gelegt und sich über der Schüssel mit der Milch oder dem Wasser das Gesicht gewaschen hat, soll er, wie einige Informanten berichten, die Schüssel zwischen den Hörnern des Bullen zerschlagen. Dies geschieht in der Praxis meist nicht. Der Grund dafür ist verständlich; denn man möchte das Tier nicht verletzten oder wild machen. Man greift also zu Ersatzhandlungen. So trocknete er in einem von mir beobachteten Falle[63]) seine Hände zwischen den Hörnern des Bullen. Im anderen Falle zerschlug er eine Kokosnuß auf dem Boden und warf die Teile dem Bullen zum Fressen vor. In beiden Fällen ist so die Verbindung zwischen Schüssel und Bullen hergestellt und damit der Dramaturgie des Rituals genüge getan. Das Zerschlagen der Kokosnuß ist ein häufiges Opferritual, das gewöhnlich vor dem Eingang von singhalesischen Göttertempeln vollzogen wird[64]). Der Künstler hat also auch hier eine Ersatzhandlung aus dem allen vertrauten rituellen Repertoire gewählt, ohne deren Bedeutung mit zu übernehmen.

Der Bulle, der nun eigentlich weggetrieben werden soll, bleibt meist unbeachtet an der Stelle stehen, an der er angebunden ist. Auch hier hat die Abweichung vom idealen Verlauf praktische Gründe. Den Bullen, der das Übel wegtragen soll, kann man nicht wegführen, man müßte ihn wegtreiben, da er ja von den Menschen entfernt werden soll. Doch das wäre nicht zweckmäßig.

Auch das Reinigungsritual ist ein Überleitungsritual. Es markiert eine Grenzüberschreitung. Der Künstler verläßt vorübergehend die Gesellschaft, in der er lebt, um das Netrapratiṣṭhāpana zu vollziehen. Er wechselt aus dem profanen Bereich in den religiösen Bereich über[65]). Das Verlassen der Gesellschaft ist unproblematisch. Er geht in den Schrein und verschließt die Tür hinter sich. Damit ist er verschwunden. Schwieriger ist die Rückkehr, sie ist in zweifacher Hinsicht von Bedeutung: Die Person des Künstlers muß übergeleitet und die Grenze zwischen religiösem und profanem Bereich muß markiert werden.

Der Künstler, der hier ein Ritual durchführt, ist nicht gleichzeitig Priester, sondern er gehört einer niedrigen Kaste an und hat somit innerhalb der Gesellschaft einen fest umrissenen Aufgabenbereich. Im Ritual übernimmt er eine Rolle, die grundverschieden ist von derjenigen, die er im Alltagsleben innehat. Deshalb ist eine Überleitung notwendig. In dem Augenblick, in dem er aus dem Schrein heraustritt, verläßt er

---

[63]) In Yaṭihalagala (s. oben, S. 309).

[64]) So zerschlägt man z.B. eine Kokosnuß, wenn man den Bezirk des Haupttempels in Kataragama betritt.

[65]) Ich verwende hier die Bezeichnung religiös statt sakral, da hiermit nicht die Vorstellung des Heiligen impliziert sein soll.

nicht auch gleichzeitig den religiösen Bereich. Er wird sichtbar, doch er muß verschwunden bleiben, solange er sich im religiösen Bereich befindet. Deshalb wird er wegfingiert, indem sein Gesicht mit einem Tuch bedeckt wird. Es bleibt bedeckt, bis er die Grenze überschritten hat.

Der Blick des Künstlers ist gefährlich wie vorher der Blick der Statue. Das gemeinsame Merkmal des „gefährlichen Blicks" verbindet ihn mit der Statue. Er gehört damit zum religiösen Bereich. Diesen kann er nur verlassen, indem er den „gefährlichen Blick" aus seinen Augen entfernt. Bis dahin besteht Gefahr. Der Blick des Künstlers muß gemieden werden, d.h. Kontakt mit ihm darf nicht stattfinden. Ein solcher Kontakt mit dem Künstler, solange er sich im religiösen Bereich befindet, ist nicht geregelt. Die bestehenden Regeln betreffen seine Rolle im profanen Bereich. Sie dürfen hier nicht angewandt werden, denn damit würde die Grenze zwischen religiösem und profanem Bereich durchbrochen. Sie würde undeutlich werden und schließlich verschwinden, würde sie nicht bei solchen Übergängen stets deutlich markiert. Der religiöse Bereich würde mit dem profanen Bereich verschmelzen, und eine wichtige kulturelle Leistung der Gesellschaft würde rückgängig gemacht werden: die Differenzierung von religiösem und sozialem System.

Durch das Reinigungsritual wird die Grenzüberschreitung vollzogen und die Grenze markiert. Der Künstler wäscht den „gefährlichen Blick" aus seinen Augen und hebt damit die Verbindung mit dem religiösen Bereich auf. Damit ist er in die Gesellschaft zurückgekehrt und Kontakte mit den übrigen Mitgliedern der Gesellschaft können wieder nach den gewohnten Regeln aufgenommen werden. Der Übergang ist sowohl räumlich als auch zeitlich gedacht: Zeitlich, indem die Person des Künstlers aus einer Rolle in die andere übergeleitet wird, und räumlich dadurch, daß der Künstler aus einem Bereich in den anderen überwechselt.

Einige der beschriebenen Handlungen lassen sich aus dem dramaturgischen Konzept erklären, das dem Ritual zugrunde liegt. Dazu gehört das Vernichten des Baumes: Die Logik der Handlung, die ja die Situation verdeutlichen soll und deshalb verständlich sein muß, verlangt an dieser Stelle geradezu einen Zwischenfall. Der Künstler muß das Tuch von seinem Gesicht nehmen, um sich zu waschen. Dabei muß sein Blick irgendwohin fallen. Da dieser Blick gefährlich ist, muß an der Stelle, auf die er fällt, etwas geschehen: Der Blick fällt auf einen Baum, und der Baum wird vernichtet.

Ebenso verhält es sich mit dem Stier, dem Sündenbock, der das Übel davontragen muß: Nachdem der Künstler den „gefährlichen Blick" aus seinen Augen gewaschen hat, ist dieser damit noch nicht beseitigt. Er befindet sich vielmehr jetzt im Wasser bzw. in der Milch. Da der Blick aber gefährlich ist, muß er entfernt werden. Das geschieht, indem man den Bullen damit belädt, d.h. ihm das Wasser bzw. die Milch über die Hörner gießt. Er trägt es davon. Auch das erfordert die Logik der Dramaturgie. Der Blick wird als Substanz gedacht; denn er muß transportabel sein. Sein Weg — und damit auch die Handlung — muß ein befriedigendes Ende finden. Dieses Ende liegt irgendwo außerhalb des Bereiches, in dem der Blick Schaden anrichten kann.

Die Auffassung einzelner Informanten, nach der der Künstler zuerst auf den Bullen blicken soll, um dann erst den Baum zu vernichten, beruht offensichtlich auf einem Mißverständnis[66]). Diese Reihenfolge entspricht nicht der Logik der Handlung. Ebenso unzutreffend ist die Meinung Coomaraswamys, es fände eine „water cutting ceremony" statt[67]). Beide Mißverständnisse sind wohl darauf zurückzuführen, daß hier die Bedeutung des Schwertschlages nicht verstanden wurde.

4.7 Die Übergabe des Schlüssels

In dem einen von mir beobachteten Falle[68]) fand nach Beendigung des Reinigungsrituals eine feierliche Übergabe des Schlüssels statt. Der Künstler übergab nach den üblichen Ehrbezeigungen den Schlüssel des Schreins an das Klosteroberhaupt. Als „Gegengabe" überreichte ihm der Mönch ein Körbchen, das sein Entgelt für die getane Arbeit enthielt.

Der Künstler erklärte mir — allerdings scherzhaft — er würde den Schlüssel nicht aus der Hand geben ohne die geforderte Bezahlung erhalten zu haben.

5. Schluß

Die Schwierigkeiten bei der Aufbereitung des Materials zu dieser Untersuchung und die unbefriedigenden Ergebnisse bisheriger Untersuchungen desselben Gegenstandes machten deutlich, daß das äußere Erscheinungsbild eines Rituals nicht in jedem Falle mit dem übereinstimmt, was intendiert ist. Es mußten hier also Methoden gefunden bzw. in der praktischen Anwendung erprobt werden, die es ermöglichten, aus dem sichtbaren auf den intendierten, d.h. auf den idealen Verlauf zu schließen. Die Regeln, nach denen ein Ritual abläuft, entsprechen dem Sinn, der dem Ritual von den Beteiligten gegeben wird. Dieser Sinn ist im mythischen Begleittext formuliert, d.h. dort wird die Begründung für das Ritual gegeben. Begründet wird der ideale Verlauf. Das Ritual selbst soll darstellen und verdeutlichen, was innerhalb des sozialen System geschieht, der mythische Begleittext erklärt, warum es geschehen muß.

So sind die Zusammenhänge gleichzeitig auf drei Ebenen darstellbar: auf der Ebene des mythischen Begleittexts, auf der der rituellen Handlung und auf der Ebene des realen Geschehens innerhalb des sozialen Systems. Hier habe ich versucht, mythischen Begleittext, Beschreibung des idealen Verlaufs und Beschreibung des realen Geschehens innerhalb

---

[66]) Diese Reihenfolge schildert auch Gombrich, op. cit. (s. Anm. 1), S. 36.

[67]) Op. cit. (s. Anm. 1), S. 74.

[68]) In Nugegoḍa (s. oben, S. 309).

des sozialen Systems, die gleichzeitig die gesuchte Deutung des Rituals darstellt, so zu formulieren, daß in jeder Ebene für sich die gemeinsame Struktur sichtbar wird. Dabei sind Aufbereitung des Materials, Beschreibung des Verlaufs und Deutung des Rituals nicht zu trennen. Wir müssen dabei ständig von einer Ebene auf die andere überwechseln, um dort unsere Ergebnisse zu korrigieren, ohne — und das ist ebenso wichtig wie selbstverständlich — dem Material Gewalt anzutun. In einer Hinsicht bedeutet diese Methode allerdings einen Eingriff in den Bereich der „Tatsachen": Sie macht aus einer amorphen Masse von Material erst als solche erkennbare und verwertbare Tatsachen[69]).

6. Historischer Exkurs

Über den historischen Ursprung der Netrapratiṣṭhāpana-Zeremonie können nur Vermutungen geäußert werden. Der wohl älteste Hinweis auf die Zeremonie findet sich in Buddhaghosas Samantapāsādikā. Dort wird berichtet, König Aśoka habe ein Netrapratiṣṭhāpana (Pāli: Akkhipūjā) durchgeführt. Dasselbe wird im Mahāvaṃsa berichtet[70]). Damit wissen wir sicher, daß das Netrapratiṣṭhāpana mindestens seit dem 5. Jh. n. Chr. in Ceylon bekannt ist. Wahrscheinlich ist es älter. Weiherituale in irgendeiner Form dürften so alt sein wie die Buddhastatue selbst.

Das verhältnismäßig hohe Alter des Netrapratiṣṭhāpana in Ceylon spricht gegen einen hinduistischen Ursprung. Zwar gibt es eine Reihe hinduistischer Rituale, in deren Verlauf die Augen der Statue eingesetzt bzw. „geöffnet" werden (Netronmīlana, Akṣyunmeṣaṇa)[71]), doch diese Zeremonien können kaum als Vorläufer des Netrapratiṣṭhāpana gelten. Die Quellen, in denen sie beschrieben sind, sind alle jünger als die Samantapāsādikā[72]). Kernstück der hinduistischen Weiherituale ist das Zum-Leben-Erwecken der Statue, das nach dem Netronmīlana geschieht. Zwischen dem Öffnen der Augen und dem Zum-Leben-Erwecken der Statue findet eine Reihe anderer Rituale statt, zu denen u. a. eine Opferzeremonie (Kumbhastāpana), eine Abhiṣeka-Zeremonie (Kumbhābhi-

[69]) Eine ähnliche Methode wendet Panofsky in der Kunstgeschichte an. Siehe Erwin Panofsky, Iconography and Iconology: An Introduction to the Study of Renaissance Art, in: Erwin Panofsky, Meaning in Visual Arts, Harmondsworth (England) ²1970, S. 51–81.

[70]) Siehe Anm. 2.

[71]) Zu den entsprechenden Stellen in Vaikhānasāgama und Rauravāgama siehe oben, Anm. 1. Ferner: Agnipurāṇa (Ānandāśarama-Saṃskṛta-Granthāvaliḥ 41), Poona 1900, Kap. 62 und Kāśyapajñānakāṇḍaḥ, hg. v. R. B. Pārthasārathi Bhaṭṭācārya, Tirupati ²1960, Kap. 60.

[72]) T. Goudriaan, Kāśyapa's Book of Wisdom [Kāśyapajñānakāṇḍaḥ engl.], The Hague 1965, S. 10, datiert den Text ins 9.–10. Jh. n. Chr. Dieser Text diente als Vorlage für das Vaikhānasāgama. Das Rauravāgama dürfte nicht älter sein als diese beiden Texte. Die Stelle im Agnipurāṇa, die ein Pañcarātra-Ritual beschreibt, ist schwer zu datieren, doch sie gehört sicher nicht zu dem ältesten Bestand dieses Werkes.

ṣeka) und ein vedisches Homa-Ritual gehören. Die ganze Zeremonie ist also sehr stark durch theologische Spekulationen geformt. Dies ist bei dem singhalesischen Netrapratiṣṭhāpana nicht der Fall. Der deutliche soziale Bezug des singhalesischen Netrapratiṣṭhāpana weist auf die Ursprünglichkeit dieser Zeremonie hin. Im hinduistischen Netronmīlana fehlt das anschließende Reinigungsritual. Statt dessen wird der Statue zuerst eine Kuh mit einem Kalb und dann eine Gruppe von Menschen vor Augen geführt, bevor das Tuch, hinter dem sich das Ritual abspielt, entfernt wird. Hier können wir also nur einen gemeinsamen Ursprung beider Rituale vermuten, nicht aber einen hinduistischen Ursprung des singhalesischen Netrapratiṣṭhāpana.

Das Ṣaḍaṅga-Opfer, das dem singhalesischen Netrapratiṣṭhāpana vorausgeht, ähnelt sehr stark dem hinduistischen Kumbhastāpana. Doch letzteres folgt dort dem Netronmīlana. Das Ṣaḍaṅga-Opfer ist sicher hinduistischen Ursprungs, darauf weisen auch die Listen der Götter hin, denen geopfert wird. Es ist also später hinzugefügt worden. Wann dies allerdings geschehen ist, läßt sich nur vermuten. Möglicherweise geschah dies im 13. Jahrhundert, also zu der Zeit, in der auch die Rituale um die Zahnreliquie in Ceylon ihre feste Form erhielten. In den als Anhang zum Daḷadā sirita überlieferten Regeln König Parākrama Bāhu IV. (um 1300) ist eine Nānamura-Zeremonie erwähnt. Dabei handelt es sich um ein Abhiṣeka-Ritual, wie es auch im Verlauf der hinduistischen Weihe-Zeremonien durchgeführt wird.[73]). Möglicherweise ist auch die Durchführung des Ṣaḍaṅga-Opfers zu dieser Zeit vom König angeordnet worden.

Beide Zeremonien, Netrapratiṣṭhāpana und Ṣaḍaṅga-Opfer wurden durch die Rezitation der Kultätiologie, d.h. der Kosalabimbavaṇṇanā, miteinander verknüpft. Später hat dann das Ṣaḍaṅga-Opfer eine Umformung erfahren, die es den singhalesischen Bali- bzw. Śānti-Zeremonien anglich und die Kultätiologie entbehrlich machte.

Anhang: Das Ṣaḍaṅga vidhiya

Das Ṣaḍaṅga vidhiya enthält Vorschriften für die Durchführung der dem Netrapratiṣṭhāpana vorausgehenden Ṣaḍaṅga-Zeremonie, sowie die dabei zu rezitierenden Texte, d.h. die Kultätiologie, Mantras, Stotras etc.

Ich konnte für die vorliegende Beschreibung des Textes nur eine Handschrift benutzen. Sie ist beschrieben in W. A. de Silvas Catalogue of Palm Leaf Manuscripts in the Library of the Colombo Museum[74]) unter Nummer 2357 (Signatur: 7 H. 4).

[73]) Siehe dazu Hocart, op. cit. (s. Anm. 7), S. 35. Das Ritual in der Form, wie es in Ceylon durchgeführt wird, ist beschrieben bei Gombrich, Precept and Practice (s. Anm. 11), S. 134ff.

[74]) Colombo 1938.

Unsere Kenntnis der Ritualliteratur der singhalesischen Volksreligion reicht nicht aus, um den Text in irgendeiner Weise einzuordnen. Die Tatsache, daß nur wenige Handschriften dieses Werkes bekannt sind, kann zum Teil darauf zurückzuführen sein, daß sich Handschriften solcher Texte meist in Privatbesitz befinden und nicht in Klosterbibliotheken. Sie werden von ihren Eigentümern, den Ädurās, eifersüchtig gehütet und gelangen so selten in öffentliche Bibliotheken. Erst in jüngster Zeit werden in verstärktem Maße Ritualtexte der singhalesischen Volksreligion publiziert, doch dabei handelt es sich um unkritische Ausgaben, die häufig auch moderne Bearbeitungen darstellen. Ihr Quellenwert ist deshalb sehr schwierig zu beurteilen. Es besteht jedoch Grund zu der Annahme, daß diese gedruckten Texte immer häufiger bei Zeremonien benutzt werden, da Palmblatt-Handschriften nur noch sehr selten abgeschrieben werden und der Bestand deshalb immer mehr schwindet.

Die sehr unterschiedliche Form und die Art und Weise, in der diese Ritualtexte heute publiziert werden, zeigt deutlich, daß es sich dabei nicht um eine kanonisierte Ritualliteratur handelt, sondern um meist einmalige Niederschriften von Mantras, Stotras etc., die jederzeit wieder verändert werden können. Man kann also von der Ritualliteratur der singhalesischen Volksreligion nicht als von einer bestimmten Anzahl von Werken sprechen, sondern eher von einem — allerdings kaum übersehbaren — Bestand von Mantras, Stotras etc., die in einer — ebenfalls unbekannten — Anzahl von Texten in unterschiedlicher Zusammensetzung enthalten sind.

Unser Text kann also nicht als autoritativ gelten für die Ṣaḍaṅga-Zeremonie, sondern er gibt eher den Verlauf der Zeremonie so wieder, wie sie nach Ansicht des Verfassers — der möglicherweise ein gelehrter Ädurā war — durchgeführt werden sollte und von ihm wohl auch durchgeführt worden ist.

Es ist nicht möglich, den Text genau zu datieren. Die Herkunft einiger Verse läßt sich zwar nachweisen: Sie sind dem Vaijayantitantra entnommen[75]). Doch auch dieser Text läßt sich nicht genau datieren. Das Ṣaḍaṅga vidhiya dürfte zwischen dem 15. und dem 17. Jh. entstanden sein.

Im folgenden versuche ich eine kurze, auf einer ersten, allerdings noch sehr oberflächlichen Lektüre des Textes beruhende Inhaltsangabe zu geben. Ein genaues Verständnis des Textes ist ohne die Kenntnis der logischen Zusammenhänge der Ritualhandlung nicht möglich.

Unser Text ist am Anfang nicht vollständig. Er beginnt sehr unvermittelt ohne Segensformel und Einleitung:

---

[75]) Kap. 19, V. 43–66. Der Text ist nicht ediert. Benutzt wurden hier Abschriften von Handschriften aus der University of Pennsilvania Library. Siehe H. I. Poleman, A Census of Indic Manuscripts in the United States and Canada, New Haven (Mass.) 1938, Nr. 5357–5362.

1 V 1[76]):

sagge kāme ca rūpe girisikharatame cāntalikkhe vimāne
dīpe raṭṭhe ⟨ca⟩ gāme taruvanagahane gehavatthumhi khette |
bhūmyā cāyantu devā jalathalavisame yakkhagandhabbanāgā
niṭṭhantā santikedaṃ munivaravacanaṃ sādhavo 'me sunantu ||

— mantassavaṇakālo bhadantā[77]) namo tassa bhagavato arahato sammāsambuddhassa —

bhujagasuranarāṇam molimālābhipūjam
jahitacatuhi oghaṃ bhinnasabbārisenam |
gatasaraṇamuhuttaṃ vaṭṭadukkhappahānam
sucaraṇasaraṇatthaṃ taṃ namo buddhanāgam ||

Es folgt ein singhalesischer Kommentar zu dem ersten der hier zitierten Verse. Dieser Kommentar bricht ab, und es folgt unvermittelt ein Sanskrittext über Metrik mit Singhalesischer Übersetzung (2 R 3—3 V 3). Es ist möglich, daß dieser kurze metrische Text zum Ṣaḍaṅga vidhiya gehört und dazu dienen soll, den Ädurā über die richtige Rezitationsweise zu belehren. Doch er gehört mit Sicherheit nicht an diese Stelle; denn 3 V 3 folgt die singhalesische Übersetzung des zweiten oben zitierten Verses. Es ist schwer festzustellen, wie die richtige Reihenfolge der einzelnen Teile ursprünglich war. Offensichtlich sind die Blätter der Vorlage beim Abschreiben vertauscht worden und Teile des Textes — evtl. durch Beschädigung der Vorlage — verlorengegangen.

4 V 3 folgt ein weiterer Vers in Sanskrit:

indrātmabhūkṛṣṇamaheśvarāṇām
nāgānanaskandabṛhaspatīnām |
indrāgniyāmyādidiśādhipānām
kurve namaskṛtyavidhiṣaḍaṅgam ||[78])

Nach einer ausführlichen singhalesischen Übersetzung folgt (6 V 8):

pūrvadiśyādidevaś ca agnidiśyādidevatā |
yāmyāyām adhipādevo nairṛtyavaruṇādhipā ||
vāyavyottara īśāno diśo diśaḥ svake suraḥ |
apare sarvadevāś ca nandantu dhūmapūjaya ||

Die singhalesische Übersetzung dieser Verse fehlt. An sie schließt sich eine Beschreibung der 32 Mahāpuruṣalakṣaṇas und der 80 Anuvyañjanas in Pāli und Singhalesisch an. Diese Passage beginnt mit den Worten

---

[76]) Ich zitiere die Handschrift im folgenden jeweils mit Blattnummer, -seite und Zeile. 1 V 1 bedeutet also Blatt 1, verso, Zeile 1. R = recto. Offensichtliche Schreibfehler wurden in den Zitaten ohne Anmerkung verbessert. Ansonsten ist der Text jeweils unverändert wiedergegeben.

[77]) Diese Formel steht auch 25 V 3 (in Sanskrit).

[78]) Dieser Vers findet sich auch an anderer Stelle. Siehe Bōruggamuvē Girimānanda, Navanātha yantraya saha sāntiya (sic!), Nugegoḍa [2]1962, S. 29.

„yanu heyin…“ (7 R 1), was bedeutet, daß die kommentierten Verse fehlen.

Von hier wird nun übergeleitet zur Erzählung der Kosalabimbavaṇṇanā. Dieses Werk erzählt die Geschichte der Errichtung der ersten Buddhastatue durch König Prasenajit von Kośala. Im zweiten Teil behandelt es das religiöse Verdienst, das man erlangt, wenn man eine Buddhastatue errichtet, stiftet oder verehrt. Der erste Teil stellt also eine Kultätiologie der Verehrung der Buddhastatue dar. Die Geschichte, die hier erzählt wird, ist relativ alt. Sie wird bereits von dem chinesischen Pilger Fa-hsien (399–414) berichtet, und zwar im Zusammenhang mit der Schilderung seines Besuches in Śrāvastī. Die in unserem Text wiedergegebene Version des Textes besteht aus Pāliversen und singhalesischer Prosa. Der Text ist unvollständig. Anfang und Ende fehlen. Die vier vorhandenen Pāliverse stimmen mit den Versen der Pāli-Version überein. Die singhalesische Prosa folgt inhaltlich sehr eng der Pāli-Version.

An die Kosalabimbavaṇṇanā schließt sich die oben (S. 317) zitierte Überleitung zum Indrakīlapratiṣṭhāpana an. Von dieser Stelle an ist der Text vollständig.

Es folgen Mantras, die beim Setzen des Indrakīla rezitiert werden. Anschließend wird die Vorbereitung des Opferaltars beschrieben. Nach der Aufzählung der den neun Planetengöttern zugeteilten Farben, Opferblumen, Opferspeisen und Bäume steht folgender Vers:

> saptaviṃśatinakṣatraṃ dvādaśarāśisaṃyutam |
> navagrahasamāyuktaṃ kṛtaṃ ṣoḍaśamaṇḍalam ||
> mudgamāṣatilāśālīkaṃkinīśvetasarṣapam |
> saptabījāni dhānyāni buddhaiḥ kathitāni || (!) (11 R 3–4)

Der Altar wird also aus sieben Arten von Samenkörnern aufgeschichtet, aus zwei Arten von Bohnen, aus Senfkörnern, Hirse, Reis, Sesam und Kümmel. Die Oberfläche besteht aus einem Diagramm (*maṇḍala*), bestehend aus 16 Feldern (s. oben, S. 319 und Anm. 42).

Es folgen Vorschriften über das Mal bulat taṭuva puda für die Erdgöttin, das Aṣṭamaṅgala (s. oben, S. 321f.) über das zu verwendende Opfergras (*pavitra*) und ein Räucheropfer (11 V 2ff.).

Die anschließenden Verse behandeln die Zubereitung der Opfer. Sodann folgen Mantras, Stotras und ikonographische Verse, die bei der Aufstellung der Opfertöpfe (Kumbhasthāpana), der Einladung der Götter zur Annahme des Opfers (*diṣṭi*) und bei der Versöhnung mit den Göttern (*śānti*) rezitiert werden (12 V 2ff.).

Die ikonographischen Beschreibungen der neun Planetengötter stimmen weitgehend mit denen des 19. Kapitels des Vaijayantitantras, eines in Ceylon überlieferten Śilpaśāstras, überein[79]). Dieselben Verse sind auch zusammen mit den dazugehörigen Mantras und Stotras bei Sēdaraman[80]) wiedergegeben.

---

[79]) Loc. cit. (s. Anm. 75).

[80]) Op. cit. (s. Anm. 41), S. 186ff. Sēdaraman hat ganz offensichtlich unseren Text als Quelle benutzt. Es finden sich in seinem Buch noch andere Stellen, die

Die zu rezitierenden Verse stellen den Hauptteil des Textes dar. Der Text endet mit Blatt 25. Auf Blatt 26 beginnt ein neuer Text.

---

möglicherweise aus dem Ṣaḍaṅga vidhiya entnommen sind. Er gibt aber keine Quellen an. In Band I (s. Anm. 30), S. 105, merkt er allerdings an, daß er eine Palmblatthandschrift über das Kumbhasthāpana bearbeiten will.

The Buddha's Eye, the Evil Eye, and Dr. Ruelius

By RICHARD F. GOMBRICH

Since Dr. Ruelius has criticized both my description and my interpretation of the ritual in which Buddha images are completed and consecrated by painting in their eyes (*netrapratiṣṭhāpana*), Professor Bechert has kindly asked me to reply.

First the description. Dr. Ruelius questions my accuracy. On pp. 33–5 of my article[1]) I describe the ritual of placing pots (*kumbhasthāpana*), in which pots are arranged on a diagram and then ascribed to particular deities. I witnessed the ceremony myself and had the ascriptions from the officiant at the time, without even the intermediacy of an interpreter. Any reader can see that my account is coherent. Yet in his note 42 Dr. Ruelius says that my description of the pots' arrangement is inaccurate ("ungenau") and the ascriptions (which harmonize with the arrangement) are improbable ("unwahrscheinlich"). How does he know?

In the study of myth it is now a commonplace that there is no one "correct" version of a myth; on the contrary, understanding comes from the collection of variants and the perception of what they implicitly have in common. I would have thought that the same applied to rituals. Approaching Dr. Ruelius' paper, I hoped to read descriptions of further performances of the ritual, certain to deviate in some ways from the one I saw, which would enrich our understanding, and perhaps demonstrate how some external variables, such as an urban environment, affected the ceremony.

But no. Though a few new details can be gleaned by the careful reader, Dr. Ruelius' long article adds surprisingly little to our ethnographic knowledge, and he gives little detailed description of the two rituals which he himself witnessed. His attitude towards variants is intolerant; he argues (pp. 310f.) that from what actually happens in a ritual we must reconstruct its ideal form, that by comparison of different performances we may recognize and eliminate ("ausscheiden") variants.

But what are we trying to do? If to reconstruct a historically earlier stage of the ritual, as we might try to reconstruct a text, we may put aside demonstrable innovations—remembering always that the principles of textual criticism cannot be a sure guide through the complexities of social events. But historical reconstruction is not Dr. Ruelius' dominant concern; his "ideal" ritual is in the present.

Of course some parts of a ritual are more important than others. The participants can readily tell us what is essential, for they know whether

---

1) For this and other references see note 1 to Dr. Ruelius' article.

the ritual has been, or is likely to be, efficacious. Even if the parson was drunk, the wedding is still valid. But is the ethnographer to suppress the fact that the parson was drunk? Or is a colleague thousands of miles away to declare that the parson could not have been drunk, on no more authority than textual testimony that he ought to be sober?

In the two accounts of the ceremony, Coomaraswamy's and mine, the arrangement of the pots differs greatly. This merely tells us that their arrangement in one given way is not crucial to the efficacy of the ceremony. The fact that yet other arrangements are mentioned (or suggested) by two printed texts does not entitle Dr. Ruelius to reject our accounts. In the text (p. 319) to this note he seeks a finally valid clarification ("endgültige Klärung"). But this search is idle: there is no definitive version, no final validity. Worse, the search is misguided, for once we know the "ideal" ritual we can have nothing more to learn; the matter is closed, and new data can be "eliminated" *a priori*. There can be no change, only aberration.

Looked at another way, this can be seen as a question of authority: whose view is to weigh? Are we to defer to the participants or to Dr. Ruelius? Let us illustrate this from a part of the ritual more important than the precise arrangement of the pots. In the final purificatory rite, or sequence of rites (*śānti karaṇa*), the craftsman gets rid of the evil (*vas dos*) lingering in his own gaze (*bälma*) by procedures involving three adjuncts: a pot of milk or water, a tree with milky sap, and a bull. The painter transfers the evil from his gaze to the pot, and destroys that either by cutting it with a sword (Coomaraswamy's version), or by breaking it on the bull's horns (my version), or by just spilling the milk over the bull and breaking the pot separately (Ruelius' version); he cuts the tree with the milky sap; and he drives off the bull. All these actions occur in other Sinhalese rituals to get rid of *vas dos*, and as all symbolically achieve the same effect it is not surprising to find that the last can be omitted (Ruelius' version). Dr. Ruelius, however, has decided that there is just one ideal version, in which cutting the tree precedes driving off the bull, so those informants who reverse the order have "misunderstood" (p. 30). Coomaraswamy's report of the water-cutting is likewise declared wrong ("unzutreffend"). These *ex cathedra* pronouncements seem just as arbitrary as his statement (p. 325) that the use of a tree with milky sap is "certainly secondary". The point would seem to me to be that a milky exudation makes the tree more like an animal victim; be that as it may, what is the evidence for the "primary" use of other trees?

On p. 313 Dr. Ruelius says that I am "obviously wrong" to say that this purificatory ritual is "nicht typisch" of our ceremony. What I say is that it is "not specific to" a *nētra pinkama*. In his section 4.6 Dr. Ruelius says the same at some length, so is it obviously wrong? I suspect that, despite my attempt to clarify the point at the symposium, Dr. Ruelius has misunderstood: my words mean that the ritual occurs not only at a *nētra pinkama*, but on other occasions too. In this respect the final purification is like beginning the ceremony at an auspicious moment, a commonplace practice which Dr. Ruelius characterizes as "nicht . . . für diese Zeremonie typisch" (p. 323). His use of the word "typisch" seems to fluctuate.

We turn now to the interpretation of the core ritual, the painting of the eyes, concerning which the facts are not in dispute. The feature of the ceremony which particularly attracted my attention, and which Dr. Ruelius compares (p. 314) to a red thread leading through the action and its interpretation by the actors, is "the theme of the 'dangerous gaze'". The participants consider that the gaze emanating from a Buddha image while the eyes are being painted in is dangerous, and that this danger is to some extent transferred, despite his precautions, to the gaze of the painter. Dr. Ruelius himself dwells on this point several times. However, he severely criticizes my treatment of this matter (pp. 307f., 314), and the ostensible *raison d'être* of his article is to correct my interpretation.

Here I am under the grave difficulty that I cannot follow the logic of Dr. Ruelius' argument. The participants believe the Buddha's gaze to be dangerous, and act accordingly by keeping clear. The term "gaze" implies a living agent—the Sinhalese term, *bälma*, is even a verbal noun. Of course the Sinhalese do not "really" think that the statue is alive; they behave *as if* it were alive. I say this in the passage of my book which Dr. Ruelius singles out for criticism; I explain this "as if" on p. 5 of that book; and on p. 307 of his article Dr. Ruelius quotes with approval Professor Schlingloff saying that the Buddha is worshipped *as if* ("als ob") he were present. But Dr. Ruelius continues, "And should danger threaten from the Buddha's image?" It is here that I lose him. *He* may not think it dangerous, but—as he repeatedly tells us—the participants do; so what is the point of the question? And why does he go on to call reference to their beliefs "intuitive reconstruction" of their motives?

Here may lie a source of confusion. My account does not claim to provide a causal explanation of the ritual. Providing such an explanation I myself would consider to be a historical enterprise. But Dr. Ruelius is probing for an interpretation which will explain why the ceremony is what it is, and assumes that the question must be asked and answered in functionalist terms.

What, then, is his interpretation? He calls the ceremony a *rite de passage*; the statue passes from being a lump of material to a cult object. To this one might object, as Dr. Schalk did at the symposium, that it widens unacceptably the use of the term *rite de passage*, which is used in anthropology to refer to a *human* transition from one status to another. By applying the term to an object, Dr. Ruelius could thus be accused of doing just what he accuses me of: attributing life to the statue! Alternatively, if we agree with him (p. 316) in using the term for such events as unveiling monuments and housewarming parties, its application has become so broad that it is almost meaningless. If a *rite de passage* can centre on an inanimate object, it is hard to think of a public ceremony which could *not* be so called. The serious objection to Dr. Ruelius' interpretation, of course, is that it is banal: it is so general that it explains nothing. It tells us nothing about the ritual which we did not know before.

After this, it is comparatively trivial to object that this interpretation appears distorted in detail. Dr. Ruelius claims that the Buddha image (pp. 316, 324) and the painter (p. 327) are pretended not to be there ("wegfingiert") by the mirror and the blindfold respectively, despite the completely different explanations (dangerous gaze) given for both cases by the participants. If it were true that the painter was supposed to be entirely absent until he had purified himself (pp. 326f.), I cannot understand why he should not perform the purification, as he does the eye-painting, out of sight of the onlookers; that he comes out blindfold surely means that it is his eyes which are dangerous, not that they are *pars pro toto*. Moreover, Dr. Ruelius' argument at this point leads to an extraordinary conclusion: if the gaze of anyone undergoing a *rite de passage* is dangerous, why are people not blindfold at their weddings? No, it is an inadequate substitute for the particulars of this colourful ceremony to inform us (p. 323) that it "integrates the artefact into the existent cosmic order."

I am not so deluded as to think that my writings represent the last word on this subject. That would run counter to my central intellectual position. One cannot anticipate intellectual developments, but I would expect advances to come from more and better ethnography, and from intelligent historical research. I can give an example which illustrates both. In his doctoral dissertation[2]) Dr. Peter Schalk has not only properly illustrated that odd ritual implement, the *indrakīla*, which I feebly described as "roughly umbrella-shaped"; he has also shown that it is a symbol with a long history, which in this context must signify the superior position of the Buddha, to be remembered even in a rite directed to the gods.

Finally we must pick up our mirrors and face the question: why has Dr. Ruelius strayed, following neither logic nor his informants? From p. 314f. we may guess at an answer. At his request he was allowed to disturb the normal course of a ceremony; not indeed to witness the actual painting of an image's eyes, the most dangerous moment, but alone to receive—and photographically to record—the painter's unpurified gaze as he emerged from the temple and for a moment on the threshold removed his blindfold. The transferred gaze of the Omniscient One may have given Dr. Ruelius the retrospective clairvoyance to see the pots whose arrangement I ineptly recorded; or there may have been some *vas dos* left after all.

---

[2]) Peter Schalk, Der Paritta-Dienst in Ceylon, Lund 1972 (Akademisk Avhandling för Doktorsexamen).

Der Paritta-Dienst in Śrī Laṃkā

Von PETER SCHALK

(Zusammenfassung)

Der Paritta-Dienst ist in Śrī Laṃkā ein weit verbreiteter Kultus, der aus einem Komplex von verschiedenen Riten besteht, deren Zentrum die Rezitation kanonischer und nichtkanonischer Texte ist zum Zweck des Exorzismus, der Abwehr von Gefahren, der Behütung, der Versenkung, der Segnung und des Glückwunsches und schießlich des Erreichens von Wohlstand und Gesundheit[1]).

Die Anfänge des Paritta-Dienstes gehen auf den Pāli-Tipiṭaka selber zurück[2]). Die volle Entfaltung jedoch erreichte der Paritta-Dienst während der kommentariellen Periode in den ersten Jahrhunderten unserer Zeitrechnung[3]). Damals wurden die im heutigen Paritta-Dienst vorkommenden Elemente eingeführt: das Parittawasser, die Parittaschnur, das Maṇḍapa und wahrscheinlich auch der Indakhīla, der ein besonderes Problem darstellt[4]).

Das Rezitieren wird heute wie damals von Mönchen vorgenommen. Es gibt aber auch spezielle Paritta-Dienste, die von Laien ausgeführt werden, wobei sich zeigt, daß sie weit offener sind als die Mönche gegenüber der Aufnahme nichtkanonischer Texte. Anderswo habe ich versucht eine Typologie des Paritta-Dienstes in vier verschiedenen Typen zu zeichnen, die entsprechend den die verschiedenen Arten des Paritta-Dienstes durchführenden Personen (āraññavāsin, gāmavāsin, upāsaka, sonstiger Laien u.a.) eine unterschiedliche Zahl von kanonischen und nichtkanonischen Texten enthalten und dabei auch in der Funktion zwischen Versenkung und Exorzismus schwanken[5]).

In der Forschung ist bisher der Paritta-Dienst in den Bereich des Exorzismus verwiesen worden[6]). Diese Zuweisung ist zwar richtig, ist aber trotzdem nicht die ganze Wahrheit. Wie oben angedeutet, hat der Paritta-Dienst mehrere Funktionen, auch solche, die mehr mit der traditionellen Auffassung des Buddhismus als einer Religion der Versenkung und Liebe übereinstimmen, als die Funktion des Exorzismus.

---

[1]) P. Schalk, Der Paritta-Dienst in Ceylon, Lund 1972, S. 73.

[2]) A.a.O., S. 1–27.

[3]) A.a.O., S. 28–78.

[4]) A.a.O., S. 152–166.

[5]) P. Schalk, Der Buddhismus aus der Sicht eines buddhistischen Kultus in Śrī Laṃkā, in: Temenos 10 (1974), S. 79–113.

[6]) E. Waldschmidt, Das Paritta, Eine magische Zeremonie der buddhistischen Priester auf Ceylon, in: Von Ceylon bis Turfan, Göttingen 1967, S. 465–478.

Ferner hat uns unsere Analyse zu vier verschiedenen Typen des Paritta-Dienstes geführt. Man muß also vorsichtig sein, wenn man vom Paritta-Dienst redet und muß dabei klar machen, von welchem von ihnen die Rede ist. Besonders gilt das für jene Forscher, die „Strukturen" der Religionen in Śrī Laṃkā finden, die sich quer durch diese erstrecken. So z.B. stellt Yalman[7]) ohne weiteres den Bali und den Paritta-Dienst zusammen, und bei Wirz[8]) wird alles zum „Teufelstanz". Hierzu muß die Frage gestellt werden, welche Ausformung des Paritta-Dienstes sie meinen, den sie ohne weiteres in die „Struktur" eingliedern.

Auf dem damit gezeichneten Hintergrund möchten wir an Milford E. Spiro eine Frage richten. Dieser hat sorgfältig die verschiedenen Aspekte des Buddhismus überhaupt systematisch dargestellt und wird also der faktischen Mannigfaltigkeit des Buddhismus gerecht. So unterscheidet er zwischen einem „Nibbanic Buddhism", „Kammatic Buddhism" und „Apotropaic Buddhism" und einem „Esoteric Buddhism"[9]). Den Paritta-Dienst findet man unter dem „Apotropaic Buddhism" wieder[10]). Wir haben aber versucht zu zeigen, daß es mehrere Ausformungen des Paritta-Dienstes gibt. Wie aber steht es mit diesen? Sie scheinen selber eine Vermischung der verschiedenen Typen des Buddhismus zu sein. Sie enthalten sowohl Elemente des „Nibbanic Buddhism" wie auch solche des „Apotropaic Buddhism" und „Kammatic Buddhism". Auf den „Esoteric Buddhism" sind wir nicht eingegangen. Der Paritta-Dienst ist also eher ein Spiegelbild des Buddhism als nur ein Ausschnitt daraus.

Ein weiteres Ergebnis unserer Untersuchung ist, daß der Paritta-Dienst, so wie wir ihn geschildert haben, in keine der überlieferten Auffassung von der „Volksreligion" passen will. Was meint man denn eigentlich mit „Volksreligion"[11]) und wer ist denn eigentlich „das Volk"? Es gibt *wenigstens* acht Auffassungen davon, was „Volksreligion" ist und keine paßt auf den Paritta-Dienst.

Diese acht Auffassungen sind:

1. Volksreligion als ethnische Religion im Gegensatz zur Weltreligion.
2. Volksreligion als Nationalreligion im Gegensatz zur Menschheitsreligion.
3. Volksreligion als Massenreligiosität im Gegensatz zur Virtuosenreligiosität.

---

[7]) N. Yalman, The Structure of Sinhalese Healing Rituals, in: JAS 23 (1964), S. 137.

[8]) P. Wirz, Exorcism and the Art of Healing in Ceylon, Leiden 1954, S. 1.

[9]) M. E. Spiro, Buddhism and Society. A Great tradition and its Burmese Vicissitudes, London 1970.

[10]) A.a.O., VII, S. 263.

[11]) Siehe z.B. International Dictionary of Regional European Ethnology and Folklore, Copenhagen 1960, S. 126f., wo kein bestimmter Schluß gezogen wird.

4. Volksreligion als degenerierte Religion im Gegensatz zur ursprünglichen Idealreligion.
5. Volksreligion als die kleine Tradition, als ländliche Kultur im Gegensatz zur großen Tradition, der städtischen Kultur.
6. Volksreligion als Religion der tiefsten Gesellschaftsschichten im Gegensatz zur Religion der höchsten Gesellschaftsschichten.
7. Volksreligion als die Religion der Laxen, „der Stillen im Lande", „der schweigenden Mehrzahl" im Gegensatz zur Religion der Minderheit der religiösen Eiferer.
8. Volksreligion als existenzielle Erfahrung im Gegensatz zur existenzentfremdeten Spekulation.

Der Paritta-Dienst ist nicht ethnisch (1) oder national (2) verwurzelt. Er ist auch nicht an die sogenannten Massen gebunden (3). Er kann auch nicht als degeneriert betrachtet werden; denn er ist so alt wie der Buddhismus selber (4). Er ist auch nicht nur in der kleinen, sondern auch in der großen Tradition im Sinne Redfields verwurzelt (5). Die höchsten wie auch die tiefsten Gesellschaftsschichten widmen sich dem Paritta-Dienst (6), und es sind keineswegs nur die Laxen, die gewöhnlicherweise Paritta-Dienste besuchen (7). Der Paritta-Dienst vermittelt zweifelsohne eine existentielle Erfahrung (8), wo aber hört eine Erfahrung auf existentiell zu sein? Mit anderen Worten: Das Begriffspaar existentiell-unexistenziell ist aus wissenschaftlicher Sicht ein untaugliches Instrument um „die Volksreligion" von einer anderen Religionsform abzugrenzen.

Wir verhalten uns grundsätzlich offen gegenüber anderen Definitionen von „Volksreligion", um uns mit diesen dem Paritta-Dienst zu nähern. Wenn es aber nicht gelingen sollte, den Paritta-Dienst in eine solche hineinzuzwängen, wäre es dann nicht an der Zeit, den Begriff „Volksreligion" aufgrund seiner Mängel endgültig zu begraben, um statt dessen zu lernen, den Buddhismus in seiner Komplexität als organisches Ganzes zu sehen?

Schließlich soll noch bemerkt werden, daß der Buddhismus aus der Sicht des Paritta-Dienstes keineswegs als eine weltflüchtige Religion bezeichnet werden kann. Ganz im Gegenteil zeigt der Buddhismus in der Ausübung des Paritta-Dienstes, daß er die Bedürfnisse der Menschen anerkennt und er sie auch mit der akzeptierenden Erkenntnis der Vergänglichkeit des Daseins, von der Gier befreiend, zu Versöhnung mit der Umwelt führt. Der Buddhismus aus der Sicht des Paritta-Dienstes zeigt sich also ganz weltlich, und zwar ist diese hier gezeigte Weltlichkeit nicht „eine Umorientierung des an sich auf das übernatürliche Ziel des Nirvāṇa ausgerichteten Sangha"[12]), sondern diese Weltlichkeit ist so alt wie der Paritta-Dienst, wie der Buddhismus selber.

[12]) M. Bechert, Einige Fragen der Religionssoziologie und Struktur des südasiatischen Buddhismus, in: Beiträge zur religionssoziologischen Forschung 4 (1968), S. 275.

Sanskrit-Wörterbuch der buddhistischen Texte aus den Turfan-Funden

Begonnen von Ernst Waldschmidt. Im Auftrage der Akademie der Wissenschaften in Göttingen

herausgegeben von Heinz Bechert. Redakteur Georg von Simson.

Das Werk ist auf 20—25 Lieferungen (je 80 Seiten) berechnet und soll in 2—3 Bänden zusammengefaßt werden.

Lieferung 1: (a-, an-/antar-vāsa)
1973. XVIII, 80 Seiten, broschiert

Lieferung 2: (antar-hā/advadāta-varna)
1977. IV, 80 Seiten, broschiert

Dieses Wörterbuch ist ein Speziallexikon zu den buddhistischen Sanskrittexten, die im Verlauf der vier preußischen „Turfan-Expeditionen" in Zentralasien gefunden worden sind. Es erschließt die zahlreichen seither publizierten Werke aus dem buddhistischen Sanskrit-Kanon, und zwar vorwiegend dem der Sarvāstivādins, andere buddhistische Texte sowie zahlreiche Fragmente von Zauber- und Beschwörungsformeln.

Die Ausführlichkeit der Zitate sowie die vollständige Aufnahme des Wortschatzes und aller Belegstellen geben dem Wörterbuch den Charakter einer speziellen Konkordanz zu den Berliner Turfantexten. Gleichzeitig bietet es eine Phraseologie des buddhistischen Sanskrit der kanonischen Sarvāstivāda-Texte. Das Wörterbuch wird ein unentbehrliches Nachschlagewerk der Buddhismusforschung darstellen und gleichzeitig die Sanskrit-Lexikographie durch ein wesentliches Hilfsmittel bereichern, da es erstmals den Gesamtwortschatz einer bestimmten Gruppe buddhistischer Sanskritwerke erfaßt.

VANDENHOECK & RUPRECHT · GÖTTINGEN UND ZÜRICH

Bureaucracy and Democracy

Fourth Edition

To John O'Connor
—Steve

To Bert Rockman
—Bill

Sara Miller McCune founded SAGE Publishing in 1965 to support the dissemination of usable knowledge and educate a global community. SAGE publishes more than 1000 journals and over 800 new books each year, spanning a wide range of subject areas. Our growing selection of library products includes archives, data, case studies and video. SAGE remains majority owned by our founder and after her lifetime will become owned by a charitable trust that secures the company's continued independence.

Los Angeles | London | New Delhi | Singapore | Washington DC | Melbourne